# THE EIGHTEENTH CENTURY

## EUROPE IN THE
## AGE OF ENLIGHTENMENT

# THE EIGHTEEN

## EUROPE IN THE AGE OF

TEXTS BY

EDITED BY ALFRED COBBAN

*New York · St. Louis · San Francisco*

McGRAW-HILL BOOK COMPANY

# TH CENTURY

## ENLIGHTENMENT

ALFRED COBBAN

JOHN SUMMERSON

W. H. G. ARMYTAGE

D. C. COLEMAN

K. G. DAVIES

J. R. WESTERN

L. D. ETTLINGER

ROBERT SHACKLETON

OLWEN H. HUFTON

*589 illustrations,*

*173 in colour*

*416 photographs, engravings,*

*drawings and maps*

Designed and produced by THAMES AND HUDSON, London
MANAGING EDITOR: Ian Sutton BA
ART EDITOR: Ian Mackenzie Kerr ARCA, MSIA
EDITORIAL: Alice Hodgson BA
RESEARCH: Marian Berman BA, Fiona Cowell MA
MAP: Shalom Schotten
SPECIAL PHOTOGRAPHY: John Webb
BLOCKS: Klischeewerkstätten der Industriedienst GmbH und Co, Wiesbaden
PRINTED in Western Germany by Herder Druck GmbH, Freiburg i. Br.
PAPER: Woodfree white art paper supplied by Gerald Judd Ltd., London
Grey text Paper supplied by Mühlebach-AG, Brugg
BOUND by Van Rijmenam N. V., The Hague, Holland

© THAMES AND HUDSON 1969, LONDON

Library of Congress Catalog Card Number: 78-75160

11490

# CONTENTS

# CONTENTS

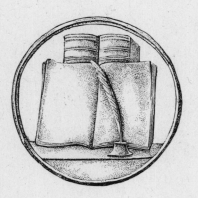

# CONTENTS

# FOREWORD

THE FASCINATION OF THE 18TH CENTURY first captured me when I studied what was called by the school examination authorities 'The Age of Johnson'. Soon after that I moved on to what might well have been described as the age of Voltaire in France. The supreme common sense which these two great men shared would have been less appealing if it had stood by itself, if the author of *Rasselas* had not also lived in the same century as the author of *The Prelude*, and if *Candide* had not been followed by Rousseau's *Confessions* and *Rêveries d'un Promeneur Solitaire*. The juxtaposition is enough to show that the 18th century is not to be summed up in any simple formula and it is not the object of this foreword to attempt to do so; but something needs to be said in these prefatory remarks of what is meant by the 18th century.

Clearly an age is not to be defined by merely chronological limits. *Le siècle des lumières* did not begin in 1700 and end in 1800, nor was its intellectual history synchronous throughout Europe, let alone the world. When it was dawn in Amsterdam or London it was still darkest night in Moscow. In a sense, indeed, the sense in which it was the Age of the Enlightenment, the 18th century was confined to certain countries of Western Europe, though its seeds sprouted, sometimes perhaps only temporarily, elsewhere in Europe, and took deeper root in the English colonies across the Atlantic. If we ask what it was, the answer is bound to be that primarily it was an attitude of mind. We can detect it already, in the 17th century, in the England of Pepys and the Royal Society and in the Dutch Republic of Spinoza, though rather less in the France of Louis XIV except in exile with Bayle. At the end, 1789 might seem its finest hour, but when the Revolutionary War and the Terror, preparatory to Napoleon, were dominating France, and England was swept by the panic of property and reaction, already the high days of the Enlightenment were over.

Something needs to be said to account for the attraction of the age to which this volume is devoted. It was above all, I believe, an age of rational optimism, when optimism itself was a reasonable deduction from the progress of the Western world. The 17th century had been a hard age, when life was lived—literally—in a cold climate. The weather improved in the next century, though there will be no attempt in this volume to present the 18th century, Enlightenment and all, *couleur de rose.* Whether we start from 1660 or from 1715, for most of the time wars were raging. Plagues had not ceased to devastate Europe. The horrors of torture still disfigured the face of the law in most countries. The slave trade reached monstrous proportions. The mass hanging of men, women and even children provided a popular diversion in Great Britain, as did breaking on the wheel in France and *autos da fé* in the Hispanic peninsula. Surgical operations had perforce to be done without anaesthetic. Hogarth has shown the brutalities of peace and Goya the horrors of war. In fact, life was nasty, brutish and short. Why then should we admire such an age?

This whole volume will, I hope, be an answer to the question, but immediately a brief and short justification may be attempted. It was an age in which classic and romantic met. The formalism of Georgian architecture or the little Trianon did not quarrel with the calculated disarray of the *jardin anglais*. Rococo may not be to everyone's taste but it suggests an interlude of lightness between the classical grandeur that went before and the Napoleonic pomp that followed. In England the Georgian age was aristocratic but vulgar, yet one in which good taste seemed natural, in which Rowlandson could transmute grossness into art and Gillray into stinging satire. In the countries where science and technology were making their influence felt, the everyday arts and crafts still survived, holding out as yet against the competition of mechanical progress. At the same time there was much material progress. Trade and industry were developing rapidly. At least until the exploding population began to catch up with increasing production towards the end of the century, the standard of living was rising in England and probably in France.

This was one ground for optimism, and there was an even more fundamental one. The inhumanities of the 18th century are not concealed in the illustrations to this volume, though the worst cannot be reproduced. Perhaps they will not surprise the reader who has known two World Wars, the destruction of cities and the atomic bomb, the terrorism and torture of colonial wars, the concentration camps of Soviet Russia and the mass extermination policy of Nazi Germany. But there is a difference. Tortures and executions in peace, massacres in war, slavery and the slave trade, go back as far as history reaches. Heretics, witches and the like had always been tortured and burnt. Base superstitions have always provided the rationale for baser actions. There was nothing new in all this. Gleams of rational humanity shine intermittently here and there in the pages of history; but what was new in the 18th century was that for the first time a great civilization, and one which was spreading throughout the world, seemed to be in the process of illumination by rays that shone steadily and over the whole range of human life. 'The Age of Reason' gives too narrow a picture of an age which went beyond the rationalism of the great minds of the 17th century and reached into a still continuing ethical revolution. I prefer the looser term *le siècle des lumières*. And its new ideas did not remain in the realm of theory but were passing rapidly into practice. A crusading spirit of humanitarian reform was at work, in greater or less degree, throughout the European world. What was accomplished was only a beginning but it was enough to justify the glow of rational optimism with which the men of the 18th century regarded their world.

ALFRED COBBAN

SHORTLY *after Professor Cobban undertook the editorship of this volume he learned that only a few months of life remained to him. He had already planned the form of the volume, chosen the contributors and embarked upon the chapters which were his special concern, but he did not think he would be able to do much more than set the work in motion. As events turned out he had time to go much further: before he died, in spite of immense suffering, he saw to it that each section was punctually delivered and he read and meticulously edited the whole. That he should thus busy himself whilst mortally ill with the minutiae of editorial detail was fully consonant with the whole tenor of his life and work. He was a perfectionist and at the last he derived satisfaction from the knowledge that he had left nothing undone. Textually he left this work, as all his other undertakings, complete, and my only assistance has been to see the volume through the press.*

*This then represents the last of his contributions towards an understanding of the 18th century and it is indeed apposite that it should be a volume concerned with the Age of Enlightenment. Alfred Cobban came to history by way of political thought and although, as his published work testifies, his historical range became greatly extended and in his later years he occupied himself much with the complications and controversies surrounding the socio-economic setting of the French Revolution, he was proud to assert that he could never totally sacrifice what went on in men's heads to what went on in their pockets. In the thought of the great Enlightenment figures he found a combination of idealism and realism which responded to something inherent in his own character.*

*The essential tolerance, the fight for justice, the optimism, honesty and freshness, the recognition of the intrinsic dignity of man and the search for rational humanity to which the 18th century at its best aspired were epitomized in Alfred Cobban and endowed his work on the period with particular sensitivity and insight even when he turned his attention, as here, to the more practical matters of government.*

*Those who knew him may well be struck by something of a physical resemblance to the bust of Voltaire illustrated in the volume: in the wise and kindly smile which his students remember so well. But be this as it may, in this the last of his undertakings, incorporating the work of a wide range of scholars, there remains a strong visual expression of the many facets of the 18th century to which Alfred Cobban was so keenly alive and in which he took so great a delight.*

OLWEN HUFTON

## Acknowledgements

The illustrations sections have been the responsibility of the publishers, who wish to thank all the authors for their patient advice on the wording of the captions. They are most grateful to Her Majesty the Queen for permission to reproduce a number of works in the Royal Collection. Generous help has been received from the many individuals and institutions credited in the picture-list, and in particular from:
Ulf Abel of the Nationalmuseum, Stockholm; Dr Lando Ambrosini of Radio-televisione Italiana; Colonel P. Arkwright; Professor I. R. C. Batchelor; Sir Alfred Beit, Bt.; Avv. Comm. Leonardo Bonzi; Miss S. F. Brown of the Agricultural Economics Research Institute, Oxford; The Marchioness of Cholmondeley; The Thomas Coram Foundation for Children, London; Richard B. Harrington of the Anne S. K. Brown Military Collection, Providence, R.I.; The Earl of Harrowby; Major P. Hope Johnstone; C. A. Jewell of the Museum of English Rural Life, Reading; Oscar and Peter Johnson Ltd; Mrs A. M. Keith; Lord Kings Norton; Dr Klemig of the Staatsbibliothek, Berlin; Leonard Koetser Gallery; The Earl of Leicester; Major J. U. Machell; Mr and Mrs D. Mainwaring Robertson; Dr Luigi Malle of the Museo Civico, Turin; Miss S. Mourot of the Mitchell Library, Sydney; The Paul Mellon Foundation for British Art; W. J. Miller and Son, Wooler; François Bergot of the Musée de Rennes; Denis Rouart of the Musée des Beaux-Arts, Nancy; Spink and Sons Ltd; Dr W. T. Stearn of the British Museum (National History), London; Miss Dorothy Stroud of Sir John Soane's Museum, London; Major and Mrs J. B. Warde.

# 1 THE PATTERN OF GOVERNMENT

*Kings, Courts and Parliaments from 1660 to the French Revolution*

ALFRED COBBAN

'It is in my person alone that the sovereign power resides . . .

and the rights and interests of the nation

are necessarily joined with mine and rest only

in my hands.'

LOUIS XV

## Autocracy was the lesson

that France had learned from a century of civil wars. When Louis XIV took up the reins of government in 1660 that lesson made him decide to keep absolute authority in his own hands; he used ministers who were ready to give him willing obedience; he obliged the aristocracy to surrender power for privilege; and he kept the people for long quiescent under a regime that promised stability even if it could not promise freedom.

Louis XIV had succeeded to the French throne at the age of four, and during the next sixteen years the government was controlled by Mazarin. Mazarin's death coincided with Louis' coming of age. He refused to appoint another first minister and for the rest of his life ruled personally, maintaining his position through a vast and unwieldy bureaucracy, a nobility serving only as courtiers and soldiers, and a palace – Versailles – that both expressed and reinforced his status as supreme monarch. In all these he was emulated by the other Courts of Europe, an emulation that provides a pattern for most of the 18th century. Other kings may have needed no teaching in despotism, but the style in which that despotism functioned was, through Louis' example, predominantly French.

The equestrian portrait by Pierre Mignard (opposite) is a typically Baroque expression of the young King's confidence and appetite for glory. Wearing vaguely classical armour, almost like a figure in a masque or pageant, he rides out to crush the foes of France while Victory hovers over him with the laurel crown. (1)

**Prussia** became a kingdom when the Elector Fredrick III of Brandenburg was given the royal dignity by the Emperor Leopold I. On January 18th, 1701, he crowned himself, at Königsberg, 'King in Prussia' (right). (5)

**In the Netherlands** the democracy established with such effort in the 17th century had become something like a constitutional monarchy by the 18th. The last of the Stadtholders was William V (1751–1806). During most of his long reign the effective ruler was his wife, Wilhelmina of Prussia (left), the strong-willed niece of Frederick the Great. (2)

**Tuscany,** on a miniature scale, enjoyed all the pageantry of a sovereign State. Here (above) the Archduke Leopold, later the Emperor Leo II, bestows the Order of the Golden Fleece on his sons. (3)

**Polish kings** were little more than puppets; elected by mass meetings of the Estates they were obliged to serve the interests of their most powerful backers. Left: the election of Augustus Stanislas II Poniatowski in 1764, by Bellotto. (4)

**Sweden** for most of the 18th century had a parliamentary government, but a more autocratic regime began with the accession of Gustavus III, seen (right) mustering citizens in 1790. (6)

**The despots themselves,** mostly men and women of no special distinction, inevitably occupy the attention of historians because of the immense political power that they were forced to exercise. A weak or stupid monarch was a crippling handicap to a country.

**Maria Theresa** (above) ruled the vast Austrian Empire from 1740 to 1780. Faced with a jealous and powerful nobility, she imitated Louis XIV by attracting them to Vienna and tying their interests to those of the house of Habsburg. (7)

**Charles III** of Spain (1758–88) also tried to follow the French pattern of centralized government and professional bureaucracy. The portrait (above right) is by Goya. (8)

**Peter the Great** (right) struggled to strengthen Russia against external threats and to transform her into a modern Western nation, aims which could not be accomplished without despotism of the most primitive kind. Under him the boyars were forced to give up their traditional independence and become servants of the State. (9)

**Frederick II** (1740–86) used the army that he had inherited from his father, 'the Sergeant King', to make Prussia one of the leading powers of Europe. He is seen here returning from man-oeuvres surrounded by his generals. His nephew, the future Frederick William II, is behind him on a black horse, and beyond him his great-nephew, Frederick William III. (10)

**Joseph II meets Catherine the Great** in 1787 (left). Joseph, succeeding to the Austrian throne on the death of his mother, Maria Theresa, in 1780, embarked on an ambitious programme of reform which roused heated op-position in many parts of his scattered Empire. Catherine, a German prin-cess who reached the throne of the Tsars by a devious route, maintained the despotic system of Peter. After the Seven Years' War, Russia and Austria dismembered Poland in alliance, but Austria was deeply suspicious of Rus-sian encroachment on the Ottoman Empire. (11)

Versailles was a world apart, cut off socially from the rest of France, though politically at its hub. As long as the King was as strong as Louis XIV and as gifted in choosing advisers, the system worked. Its inherent danger appeared when the King was weak, untalented or indifferent to public affairs. Then the Court became rent by rival factions and intrigue. Its theatrical splendour continued undimmed from Louis XIV to Louis XVI, but its irresponsibility and frivolity grew with the years and determined the constant and disastrous changes of ministers and policies which ultimately destroyed all semblance of effective government. Left: Louis XIV at the 'Grotto of Thetis', one of the earliest occasions when the sun symbol was used. Below left: Marie-Antoinette, Maria Theresa's daughter and Louis XVI's Queen, in her chamber at Versailles in 1775. Below: Versailles in 1772, when the Court returned to it after an interval following Louis XIV's death. In the foreground the royal family is arriving. The palace itself is seen as Louis XIV left it and before Louis XV began any of his alterations. (12, 13, 14)

**The magnet of honours** and pensions drew the higher nobility of France away from their country estates into the entourage of the King and the magnificence of Versailles. That, briefly, was the function of the Court, and Louis XIV operated it with unrivalled skill. He is seen here (left) initiating the Order of St Michael, a chivalric order whose members were intended to gather at Mont St Michel in Normandy. That spot seeming too desolate for most of them, a new chapel was built for them in Paris. (15)

**The 'lit de justice'** of the French kings was a special meeting of the *Parlement* of Paris at which the King presided to assert the royal will. The States General, a body representative of the whole country, was not called once between 1614 and 1789. (16)

**The British House of Commons** (right) was an institution to which the rest of Europe looked in envy. This painting shows it in 1793, during the animated debate preceding war with France. Among the identified members are William Pitt addressing the House, Speaker Addington in the chair, and Charles James Fox on the front Opposition bench, wearing a black hat. (17)

**Constitutional assemblies** existed in many European countries, sometimes exercising sovereign power, sometimes holding a precarious balance against despotism, sometimes merely creatures of the despot. The most unmitigated despotism was in Russia, where there was no legal check on the monarch's will. Great Britain was probably the least despotic nation. Although the franchise was limited to the propertied class, and in spite of the inevitable bribery and threats, the representative system was by Continental standards a model of political wisdom.

**The 'Tobacco Parliament'** (above) of Frederick I of Prussia, was merely an informal gathering of the King's advisers to discuss politics over a pipe. He and his Queen sit in the centre. (18)

**The Estates** of the Netherlands consisted of elected representatives forming a Parliament for each province, combining together in a sort of federation for purposes of foreign policy. Below: the Estates of West Friesland and Holland holding a joint meeting. (19)

The **18th-century popes** had a keen awareness of the spiritual obligations of their office but no great political acumen. Their influence on the great Catholic States, France, Spain, Austria, diminished with the mounting tide of anticlericalism. Clement XIV even sacrificed the Society of Jesus in an attempt to improve relationships with the Bourbon monarchies, but to little effect. The city of Rome, however, remained one of the great capitals of Europe. This painting (below) shows Benedict XIV (1740–58) arriving at Sta Maria Maggiore. The new façade, completed in 1743, was designed by Ferdinand Fuga. (20)

**Gustavus III of Sweden receives the crown** – a moment as ▶ solemn and significant in Protestant as in Catholic countries, though the theological sanctions behind it differed widely. Gustavus' reign (1773–1792) marked a return to absolutism after the so-called 'Age of Freedom'. But he was shrewd enough to know that his survival depended on good government and moderate reform. He tempered the forms of despotic government by creating a Council 'to advise but not to govern', and made concessions to the Enlightenment by encouraging music, literature and law reform. He was assassinated at a masked ball in March 1792. (22)

**Ecclesiastical power** was still a potent factor in political affairs for perhaps the last time in European history. But it was an ambiguous power. A Catholic king like Louis XIV, though consistently enforcing his own sovereignty in the Gallican tradition remained spiritually her faithful son and nominally respectful of the bulls that issued from the Vatican. Royalty was still a semi-divine status; it could be conferred only by the Church at the sacramental ceremony of coronation. Fold-out: the coronation procession of Louis XV in 1722. The setting is Reims Cathedral, as it had been all through the Middle Ages. (21)

**Fold out ▶**

**A private formality** matched the formality of public life, giving the pastimes and pleasures of the aristocracy something of the same air of pageantry that characterized Court ceremonial. Above: *thé à l'anglaise* at the Princesse de Conti's. An assembly of guests listens to a 7-year-old harpsichordist and composer: Mozart. Below, a performance of Gluck's opera *Il Parnasso Confuso*, given at Schönbrunn in 1765. Some of the Imperial family are acting, while the Archduke Leopold conducts from the harpsichord. (23, 24)

**'An exotic and irrational entertainment'** was how Dr Johnson defined opera. In spite of its strains on credulity, opera as an art form emerged clearly in the 18th century – from Handel, through Gluck to the mature works of Mozart. Music had an important place in private entertainment, from full scale operatics at Court to performances on the harp and piano in more modest homes. Opera was also available to the public at the theatre: here in the Teatro Regio in Turin an opera is in progress with sets by Giuseppe Bibiena. (25)

**'Routs',** public dances and masquerades gave the middle classes the opportunity to taste the delights of an aristocratic life. In London, Ranelagh and Vauxhall were the two most popular places, to be rivalled in 1772 when the splendid new 'Pantheon' (above), designed by James Wyatt, was opened in Oxford Street. Left: a fashionable Spanish lady chooses an ornament while her husband looks on. The shop also sells china, clocks, jewellery and various kinds of *objets d'art*. The 18th century was perhaps the first in which artistic 'good taste' became part of class consciousness. (26, 27)

**The demi-monde** of Paris: gentlemen, actresses and courtesans meet in the relaxed atmosphere of the Palais Royal (right) and the adjoining garden. The painting, by Debucourt, dates from 1787, but, surprisingly, he was able to portray a very similar scene in 1793. (30)

'**Saying grace**' by a Flemish painter who spent most of his life in England. The family belongs to the lower middle class: far from rich, but respectable and pious. The pattern was typical enough in England or Flanders, rarer in France or Spain, unknown in Russia. (28)

**Landlord and tenant** in the Netherlands. Patterns of land tenure and degrees of rural prosperity varied all over Europe. The substantial farmer was a far commoner figure in Britain and the Netherlands than in France or Spain or central Europe and might sometimes ape the style of living of his landlord. (29)

To be a country gentleman was an ambition that animated the hearts of the British middle classes no less than those of other Europeans. John Warde (above), gesturing complacently in the direction of his house, his son and daughter beside him and his well kept acres all around, was the son of a prosperous merchant tailor who became Lord Mayor of London. (31)

A family gathering in Paris listens to a reading from Molière. The quality of life lived by the 18th-century upper classes has been preserved for us in innumerable such paintings and in the furniture and decor with which they surrounded themselves. At no period were standards of artistry and craftsmanship more highly prized. Everything in this sumptuously decorated salon, from the brass clock to the parquet floor, proclaims the taste as well as the wealth of its owners. (32)

# Kings, Courts and Parliaments from 1660 to the French Revolution

ALFRED COBBAN

THAT THE *siècle des lumières*, the Age of Enlightenment, of toleration, increasing humanity and liberalism, should have been born in the second half of the 17th century, at the time of the absolutism of Louis XIV and the barbaric tyranny of Peter the Great, may seem a paradox. The correctness of the historical fact will be demonstrated later in this volume; but the paradox cannot be denied, nor can it be explained away by underestimating the importance of politics. The 18th century believed and, making all allowances for the extensive areas of life which were outside political control, rightly believed in the influence of government. When Arthur Young, on the first of his travels in France, in 1787, returned after a journey into Spain to Roussillon, he wrote:

> Here we take leave of Spain and re-enter France: the contrast is striking . . . From the natural and miserable roads of Catalonia you tread at once on a noble causeway, made with all the solidity and magnificence that distinguishes the highways of France. Instead of beds of torrents you have well built bridges; and from a country wild, desert and poor, we found ourselves in the midst of cultivation and improvement. Every other circumstance spoke the same language, and told us by signs not to be mistaken, and some great and operating cause worked an effect too clear to be misunderstood. The more one sees, the more I believe we shall be led to think, that there is but one all-powerful cause that instigates mankind, and that is GOVERNMENT!

Even if this is not true, the fact that the 18th century believed it to be true is important, and may provide a justification for beginning this volume with a chapter on the governmental system of the age.

## The age of Louis XIV

The paradox of Enlightenment and Absolutism runs throughout the 18th century. Its pattern of government was set by the absolute monarchy of France, whose language and culture dominated Europe. In 1660, when Louis XIV, young and yet untried, came to the throne, France for the first time in a hundred years—apart from the too brief reign of Henry IV—had a King who was capable of personal rule. This was what she needed, for it had been repeatedly demonstrated that the turbulent French nobility would not accept any other authority. Autocracy was the lesson that was drawn from a century of civil wars, and Louis inherited from the Cardinals the great officials, Lionne, Le Tellier, Colbert—founders of mighty bureaucratic dynasties—through whom he was able to put it into practice.

These were the ministers who laid the foundations of the first centralized bureaucratic régime in Europe. A necessary corollary was that the King should have his own agents throughout the country. The provinces being too closely bound up with the old aristocratic order, the newer administrative division of France into *généralités*, originally used for tax collecting, took the place of them. The royal agents were the *intendants, commissaires départis*, sent out from the Royal Council and returning in due course to it. Unlike the horde of venal *officiers*, they were appointed by, responsible to and dismissable by the King. The consequence of the new governmental system was that the local powers of provincial Estates and municipal councils were steadily undermined by *intendants* and

ministers, though the completeness of the process must not be overestimated. Even under Louis XIV the extent of autocracy and bureaucratic centralization was never as unqualified as critics like the Duc de Saint-Simon suggested or as historians have sometimes believed. The limitations on the power of the central government will have to be dealt with subsequently, but at the outset, it must be emphasized that Louis XIV, and his many imitators, had to manage, use and in a sense buy off the nobles, usually by increasing their social privileges, as the price of the diminution of their political power. Louis XIV set the pattern in the concessions he made to privilege as well as in his assertion of monarchical sovereignty.

The fusion of noble privilege with royal power was made possible because they both met in the most personal of Louis' achievements, his Court. This explains the importance of Versailles. The physical environment is an essential element in the functioning of all institutions. The absolutism of Louis XIV could never have developed in the Renaissance charm of the old Louvre, emerging like a surprising jewel from the confusion of medieval Paris. Its rooms and audience chambers were far too few and too small to hold all those whom duty or pleasure or the hope of gain brought to the Court of the *roi soleil*. It could provide no adequate accommodation for the swelling new bureaucracy. It was surrounded by narrow, winding streets and a teeming populace in which riot and revolution might be bred and a Coadjutor Gondi or a President of the *Parlement* might temporarily overawe the King's ministers. Louis did not forget the Fronde. The city was also the breeding place of an even more dangerous enemy, plague. Health and the royal pleasures of the hunt had to be sought in the countryside. These were some of the reasons why the Louvre was abandoned, and a new palace built at Versailles on a larger, grander scale. Here ministers and mistresses, high nobles and lackeys formed a world apart, yet one which through its daily Councils, and the regular reports of the royal emissaries and agents, kept the whole life of France and the policy of the Crown under constant review. This, at least, was the theory and, while Colbert and the other great ministers of the early years of Louis XIV's personal rule lived, it was an approximation of the facts.

At Versailles all aspects of national life and all possible centres of power were brought under royal control. Towns and provinces gradually lost most of the autonomy which they had once possessed. The *Parlements*, those venal and hereditary law courts which had so often played the game of the enemies of royal authority, even when they did not challenge it in their own right, were reduced to passivity. The Assemblies of the Clergy, controlled by the King's nominee, the Archbishop of Paris, performed only the royal will. The army became for the first time truly the King's army. The financiers and war contractors made greater fortunes than ever, but they were no longer practically a state within a state as they had been in the days of Fouquet. Royal manufactories were set up to promote industries; the crafts in the towns were compulsorily organized into guilds, which were created in far greater numbers than ever the Middle Ages had known. Overseas trade was regulated by royal companies. Academies were created to discipline the arts. And at the centre of the whole machine was *le roi soleil*, both the symbol of the unity of the State and—so far as

p 13 (1)

p 18–19

p 188 (20)

p 16 (9)

p 210
(10)

p 323
(24–26)

The Jesuit Order – the Society of Jesus – became progressively unpopular throughout the 18th century, not only in Protestant countries but in Catholic also, and even within the Church itself. Its theological and moral teachings were widely disputed (e.g. by the Jansenists); above all, its ultramontanism aroused the hostility of the French 'Parlements', anxious to find a pretext to assert their own power, and of other governments bent on controlling the Church within their own territories. In 1759 the Jesuits were expelled from Portugal, in 1764 from France, and in 1767 from Spain, Naples and Parma. Finally in 1773 Clement XIV was obliged to dissolve the Society altogether. A few of its members hung on in Russia and Prussia, where they were protected by the free-thinking sovereigns Frederick and Catherine. At the beginning of the 19th century, their existence was recognized by the Pope, and in 1814 the Society was legally reinstated. This satirical 'funeral' of the Jesuit Order appeared in 1773. Death leads the procession, which includes the breve of suppression, 'Dominus ac Redemptor' carried like a flag (VIII) and a host of real and allegorical figures, such as the foreign missions (XX) and the globe they sought to dominate. (1)

one man could be—its actual ruler, the first of a long series of despots who straddle what has been called, as well as the Age of Enlightenment, the Age of Absolutism.

It would be misleading, on the other hand, to suggest that Louis XIV, great as was the example he set, was the model from whom European monarchs learnt to be despots. Mostly they did not require teaching. In Louis' own day Peter the Great was struggling to civilize his backward empire by the methods of barbarism. Muscovy required no teaching in the ways of arbitrary despotism. Soon after, Frederick William I, the 'Sergeant King' was ruling the small but rising state of Prussia like a military camp. Habsburg Spain had set Europe lessons in civil and religious intolerance before France. The little Italian princes had long abandoned even the pretence of popular liberties. Yet, after all this has been said, it remains true that Louis XIV stands apart. When Montesquieu wanted to condemn despotism it was of the oriental despotism of the Ottoman Empire that he wrote, but the monarchy of Louis XIV that he had in mind. The image of the great King spread through Europe with the French tongue and French culture. Even the Huguenot refugees served as unwilling propagandists for the France that had persecuted and driven them into exile. It is true that what was copied was what was more superficial, the external appearances rather than the essence of society and government, and that as we penetrate deeper the differences from one country to another appear more clearly; but this must not lead us to refuse to see influences and similarities.

## Church and State

Most of these can be detected in an early form in the reign of Louis XIV. His persecution of the Huguenots and his firm religious orthodoxy, as he conceived orthodoxy, must not lead us to fail to observe one of the most important aspects of the new pattern of government. His reign opened an important new phase in the history of the relations of Church and State. Earlier rulers, such as Philip II of Spain, had certainly used religion in the interests

of their political ambitions and in this sense identified Church and State; but domestically the Churches had retained a measure of self-government through their own Assemblies; bodies like the religious orders extended across the boundaries of states and evaded in this way the more rigorous framework of the early modern State; and no Catholic king could afford to be quite indifferent to the bulls that issued from Rome. In Protestant countries religion was apt to prove an even more effective limitation on the power of the State. It is true that in these countries State churches, like the Anglican Church, had been established; but there were also Calvinist sects which, however oppressive they were capable of being where they dominated, mitigated the tyranny of the official religion where they were in a minority. It was no accident that associated so closely the progress of political liberty and the presence of Calvinist minorities in 17th-century states.

Nevertheless, potentially the Roman Catholic Church offered not merely a stouter barrier than the Protestant Churches to the power of the secular State, but a more formidable rival authority. Perhaps this was why the Catholic monarchs increasingly felt it necessary to try to reduce to subservience a Church which, while it was sometimes an ally could also be a dangerous enemy. Though he was the Most Christian King and a ruthless persecutor of those whom he saw as the enemies of orthodoxy, Louis XIV could not tolerate any restriction on his sovereignty by the claims of religion. For all his religious zeal, he began the policy, which was to be followed by the rulers of the next century, of taming the Church of Rome. The periodical Assemblies of the Clergy, which met to issue ecclesiastical regulations and vote the 'free gift' to the Crown which replaced normal taxation on clerical property, were brought securely under royal control. This was effected through Harlay, Archbishop of Paris, an immensely proud, wealthy and worldly prelate, who was the main agent of the King for the management of the Church. In return, the strictly orthodox party in the French Church could always count on the support of the King against any new and conceivably unorthodox movements.

The most notable victims of the King's determination to maintain uniformity within the Roman Catholic Church were the Jansenists who centred on the convent of Port-Royal. The success of the education provided by their schools, and the famous names associated with the movement—Antoine Arnauld, Nicole, Pascal, Racine—had already brought down on it, before Louis XIV's personal rule, the enmity of rival influences in the Church, especially the Jesuit Order. Under Jesuit influence the authority of the Crown was directed with increasing severity against Port-Royal, until the abolition of its pathetic remnants was decreed by the Pope in 1708 and the buildings themselves were razed to the ground in 1711. The Crown was thus taught by the Jesuits that it possessed a power which a half-century later they were to feel directed against themselves. Even the apparently innocuous mystical Quietism of Mme Guyon brought down on her supporter, Fénelon, the fulminations of Bossuet and the displeasure of the King, and on Mme Guyon herself imprisonment by royal command.

But though he might seem the servant of orthodoxy, Louis XIV knew what was due to Caesar, and there was little that was not. The King was much more effectively the head of the Church in France than the Pope. It was said that, in the royal chapel at Versailles, while the King bowed to the altar, the congregation bowed to the King. Where the interests of papacy and monarchy conflicted, there was no doubt which had to prevail. Louis XIV, like the Catholic rulers of the next century, did not hesitate to use all the weapons at his disposal against the Church. These were not weak. He could suspend the flow of papal revenues from France, and in particular he could annex, until the Pope yielded to the royal will, the papal enclaves of Avignon and Venaissin in France; and he could do this with the tacit or open support of the French clergy. There were only two qualifications to the success with which Louis XIV had reduced the French Church to subservience to the State. The first was that he had bought it off rather than subjected it. It remained in possession of its fiscal independence and though Louis XIV could extract contributions to his wars from the clergy, his weaker successors were to find the task of securing an adequate contribution to the royal revenue from the wealth of the Church a difficult one. Secondly, the clergy remained a privileged order and in so far as they were, largely independent of the authority of the royal bureaucracy. Moreover, the higher posts in the Church were a monopoly of the nobility. Potentially the basis existed for an alliance between the aristocracies of Church and State, which was capable of opposing royal authority, as it did successfully in the 18th century whenever a Controller General attempted to secure a fairer share of the royal revenue from either.

In all this a pattern was set for the rulers of the next century. Whatever the limitations that were to appear subsequently on the ultimate success of his policy towards the Church, in his assertion of the rights of the secular ruler Louis XIV was to be followed closely by the Catholic sovereigns of the 18th century. It was in the Habsburg dominions, and under that eminently religious Empress Maria Theresa, that the most vigorous struggle took place. The aim of the imperial Austrian government was simply to ensure that a more substantial share of the burden of taxation fell upon the vast estates of the Church and that newly acquired clerical possessions did not automatically gain all the exemptions from taxation of the existing ones. Earlier imperial measures directed to this end had remained largely unapplied in practice in the face of stubborn clerical resistance backed by all the influence of the papal Curia. A more stringent policy was initiated in the 1760s, but it was only after Joseph II became sole ruler, in 1780, that the State effectively asserted its authority over the Church. The decadence of the monastic orders, as well as their great wealth, made them the most vulnerable objectives of a policy of secularization. In France an ecclesiastical commission was at this time busy closing or amalgamating a host of petty, decayed religious houses. In the Habsburg Empire Joseph II went further. Many monasteries were suppressed and their property secularized, dioceses were reorganized, a patent of toleration was issued, the scope for clerical evasion of taxation was reduced; and all this was done with the passive acquiescence of the papacy.

Elsewhere a similar policy of extending royal control over the Roman Catholic Church was followed. The little Italian states in one way or another attacked the Church, seized church lands, imposed taxation on clerics, restricted the publication of papal bulls. Even in Spain a concordat in 1753 strengthened the already extensive powers of the State over the Church, and the reign of Charles III saw the process pushed much farther.

## The fall of the Jesuits

The most striking episode in the whole story, however, was the overthrow, in country after country, of the great Society of Jesus. *f 1* Founded to fight for the papacy and the Counter-Reformation, the Jesuits had concentrated their efforts on ruling élites and the princes. The support of absolutism having been their chosen route to religious success, it was ironic that it should have been by absolutism that they fell. Nevertheless it was quite logical. Of all the cosmopolitan organizations of the Roman Catholic Church the Society of Jesus was by far the greatest, the most powerful and the richest. Its power and wealth made it a source of envy to the aristocracies, and a centre of rival authority which absolute monarchs would not willingly tolerate. Where the Jesuits had achieved their most striking successes, found some of their greatest sources of wealth and power, and therefore aroused the greatest envy, was in their missions to America. In Brazil, from which the Portuguese monarchy drew an important part of its revenue, the Jesuit missions rivalled royal authority. Nearby Paraguay had become a Jesuit mission state, with an Indian population taught the simple crafts and agriculture and reduced by force of prayer to a spirit of total obedience such as the secular conquerors had never fully achieved by force of arms. Again, in the West Indies the French Jesuits had become a wealthy and prosperous trading company, until the Seven Years' War ruined them and their bankruptcy provided an opening for the attack of their bitterest enemies, the *Parlements*.

Since the time of Louis XIV the venal French law-courts had steadily regained their power. They claimed a supervisory authority over religion in the name of the monarchy, and had long waged war on the Jesuits in the alleged defence of a new Jansenism—now little more than a name for anti-Jesuitism. Louis XV and his successive ministers veered uneasily from side to side, in a struggle in which the interests of the Crown were necessarily neutral, for if the Society of Jesus was a rival of the royal power, the *Parlements* were its enemies.

However, it was not in France but in Portugal that the attack of the secular power on the Jesuits first came fully into the open. The Marquess of Pombal, who ruled Portugal for his *fainéant* sovereign, was a brutal despot, whose only aim was to eliminate all rival powers in the State. The Jesuits were charged with attempted regicide—an old accusation going back to the days when Henry IV of France was assassinated; their property was confiscated and in 1759 they were expelled from Portugal. In France, about the same time, the chief influence in government had fallen into the hands of Choiseul, whose object was to get France out of the Seven Years' War with no more loss than was inevitable and to prepare for a war of revenge against Great Britain. To free himself for the steps necessary to restore French power, he had to appease the *Parlements*. One way to do this, despite the reluctance of the King, was to throw them the Jesuits as victims. In 1764 the Society in France was dissolved and its members expelled.

The other Bourbon governments rapidly followed suit. The ministers of Charles III of Spain denounced the Society as a faction opposed to public interests and charged it with instigating popular riots. In 1767 the Jesuits were expelled from Spain and its empire and their property was confiscated. In the same year the governments of Parma and Naples took similar action. Many of the expelled Jesuits from other countries fled to the Papal States, where Clement XIII gave them refuge, but when the Pope died, in 1769, the Bourbon courts combined to secure the election of a more amenable successor. Austria having joined the other powers in expelling the Jesuits in 1773, Clement XIV finally yielded to the pressure of the powers and issued the bull *Dominus ac redemptor* dissolving the Society of Jesus. Louis XIV and his Jesuit confessor would have been very surprised if they had known whither their commitment to the assertion of secular rights over the Church was to lead.

## Courts and courtiers

Although only one, and perhaps at first sight not the most far-reaching example of the new absolutism, the subjection of the Catholic Church to secular authority needed to be dealt with first because it might be regarded as the most fundamental of all. The Catholic monarchs held their authority by divine right from God. They were consecrated by the Church and represented the secular arm whose first duty was its protection. For them to become the enemies of the Church was to undermine one of the foundations of their own sovereignty. Yet this was what they had done and their secularization was a sequel to, if not a consequence of, the policies pursued by Louis XIV.

A more obvious, if perhaps more superficial example of the influence exercised by the *roi soleil*, can still be seen scattered across the face of Europe, in the palaces that every ruler who could do so built in imitation of Versailles. These palaces were the centres of royal, imperial or ducal courts, for which they provided a setting far larger and grander than any that had been known before. Versailles and its copies must not be dismissed as mere manifestations of vainglory: they had a functional purpose and embody a specific phase in the history of government. Kings and Courts had been peripatetic throughout the Middle Ages and well into the 17th century. It was the only way of governing a country; but it also limited the amount of government that was possible, when the Court—or its more important members—had to travel round with the King, and ministers and secretaries did their work uncomfortably ensconced in corridors or scribbling on a chest in a corner of the King's temporary bedroom. The new royal palaces both provided accommodation for the new centralized administration and by concentrating so much more of the task of government at one spot made a greatly enlarged bureaucratic apparatus necessary.

P 45–49

This took different forms in different states and developed with different degrees of rapidity. Already in the 17th century, France had separate Secretaries of State dealing with specialized fields of government—Foreign Affairs, War, the Navy, the *Maison du Roi* (including much domestic administration), the *Garde des Sceaux* for justice and the Controller General for finance and most internal administration. On the other hand, England had two Secretaries of State, for the Northern and the Southern Departments, who shared the major functions of government, apart from finance, between them. Only in 1782, and then apparently by accident, were their duties divided on a more practical basis between Home and Foreign Affairs. Even after this, the Foreign Office of Great Britain consisted, in addition to the Secretary of State, of one Under-Secretary, ten clerks and a few miscellaneous and honorary officials such as the Secretary of the Latin language. The *Affaires étrangères*, on the contrary, had a total staff of at least 70.

France and England were similar in being governed by ministers. In other countries the central administration was in the control of official colleges or councils, though these were in course of time often doubled by ministers. In local administration there was an equally great variety. In both central and local government the new bureaucracies had normally been added to the old aristocracies without eliminating them.

This brings me to the second major function of the Courts. They provided a meeting-place of the old and the new. Such of the old nobility as by their own choice and the King's will entered into the active service of the royal government found their reward in the honorific posts and the more material perquisites and pensions distributed to the denizens of the Court. In respect of the higher nobles, who were too grand, too utterly incompetent, or for some reason unwanted in administration, the Court also served a purpose. It is sometimes said that Louis XIV gathered the *noblesse* of France at Versailles. If this had been done it would have needed to be a town larger than Paris. The size of the nobility in any European country prohibited such an attempt. Presence at Court was a privilege of the higher nobles, but these were the ones who mattered politically and whom it was important to draw by the magnet of honours and perquisites away from the provinces, where they could provide dangerous centres of opposition, into the entourage of the prince. This was the function of the Court.

Given the prevailing pattern of monarchical government, the development of the Court offered an obvious solution to the

problems of the early modern State. It also offered an irresistible temptation for the confusion of roles. Ministers almost inevitably had to be courtiers and courtiers aspired to become ministers. When Louis XIV began his personal rule, his ministers, though belonging to the order of *noblesse*, might practically be described as professional administrators; when Louis XVI was on the point of ending *his* rule, nearly every minister, apart from the Controllers General, belonged to the *noblesse de cour*. Court intrigues set up and overthrew ministers and to the influence of courtiers was added that of royal mistresses. Louis XIV did not exactly invent this function, though he turned it into something like an office of State. Those who were properly speaking his mistresses, such as Louise de la Vallière, 'that little violet' as Madame de Sévigné described her, and the Marquise de Montespan, proud, haughty, dazzling and a dabbler in the black arts, exercised little political influence. Of Louis XV's passing or more durable fancies, Madame du Barry has been credited with political influence, but unjustly. The Marquise de Pompadour exercised an appreciable influence over the choice of ministers but, except in this way, even she can hardly be said to have affected policy. Wives, indeed, were more dangerous to France than mistresses. Madame de Maintenon, almost certainly the secret wife to Louis XIV, imagined herself, according to Saint-Simon, the 'universal abbess' and in an insidious way exaggerated the King's religious intolerance; while the disastrous influence of Marie-Antoinette on French policy is too well known to need repetition. In Spain it was a Queen, Maria Luisa of Parma, wife of the feeble and stupid Charles IV, who was notorious for the flagrancy with which she gave herself to the young guardsman Manuel Godoy, almost as stupid as her husband but far more unscrupulous, and promoted him to the highest offices in the State. The consequences were to appear later in the miserable collapse of the Bourbon monarchy before Napoleon. Catherine the Great lived up even more effectively to the standards set by the masculine rulers of her age. Doubtless she used her succession of lovers more than they used her and probably apart from one of the last, the thirty-year-old guardsman, Platon Zubor, whom she took when she was 60 and whose intolerant and violent temper may have intensified the defects of her own character in her final years, none of them seriously influenced the policies of that formidable woman.

p 219 (1

Where the combination of Court and administration produced its most disastrous result was in the creation of heterogeneous governments, frequently composed of rival ministers, which normally possessed only such unity as the King himself could provide. Hence the dependence of the *ancien régime*, and not only in France, on the personality of the ruler. A Louis XIV, Peter, Catherine II or Frederick II could provide his State with a policy; under a Louis XV, a Louis XVI or a Frederick William II the State disintegrated internally and went down to defeat in its foreign policy. Perhaps no ruler could have permanently resuscitated Spain, but what could happen to Prussia under a weak King was shown by Jena.

## The French noblesse

So far I have stressed the absolutism of the age that extended from 1660 to 1789. This is the accepted picture, but taken by itself it is a misleading one. The role of aristocracy in European society had changed, but as has already been implied, the nobility still remained a potent factor. Here again France provides the model which other aristocracies tried to copy. The French *noble d'épée* anticipated the motto of Nietzsche that man is made for war and woman for the enjoyment of the warrior. He still imagined himself the representative of feudal chivalry—instead of, as he frequently was, the descendant only a few generations removed of an ennobled financier or lawyer who had bought his entry into the ranks of the nobility. His only expertise was in getting himself killed, bravely but often very incompetently, on the battlefield. Abstention from productive work of almost any kind was the one essential condition of preserving his status and privileges. His economic survival therefore depended primarily upon two sources of income—the exploitation of his estates, and this meant in the main the extraction of rents in kind or money, and similarly of seigneurial dues, from the peasants; and, with luck and assiduity, intriguing for sinecures and pensions from State and Church. Their legal status united the

This engraving, from a map dedicated to Marlborough in 1712, gives an idea of the multiplicity of states represented in the Empire. In schematic form, and with the usual allegorical trimmings, it shows a Diet in session, presided over by the Emperor. (2)

members of the order of *noblesse* in a single interest, though their possessions ranged in France, as in most other countries, from the vast riches of the princes of the blood to the poverty of the landless country gentleman whose standard of life might be below that of the struggling peasants, working their little farms on what might well have formerly been his own estates, who provided him with the pittance on which he lived. The social centre of the nobility had also changed. Either by the process of ennoblement of the patriciate of the towns, or by migration from uncomfortable châteaux to town houses, they were becoming urbanized. When a great minister like the Duc de Choiseul fell from power and was sent to his ancient château, this was banishment. On the other hand, lawyers and financiers, in the process of making themselves into gentlemen, were building houses in the country.

While its privileges remained as great as ever, and even increased, the French nobility was clearly a declining order in the 17th and 18th centuries. Its political power had gradually been whittled down to negligible proportions. Except for the greatest nobles, its wealth was being overtaken by the riches of merchants and lawyers. The ownership of land had gradually been passing into the hands of bourgeois and peasants. Even war, when it brought only a succession of defeats, was no longer as satisfactory an occupation as it had once been. To leave a nobility without occupation, said Sorel, was to render it *frondeuse*. Economic pressure, in the course of the 18th century, was producing a large body of discontented lesser nobility; while exclusion from the functions of government made the higher nobility restless to the point of rebellion. Put together, these two factors produced the aristocratic revolution which undermined the authority of the Crown and opened the door to the revolution of the Third Estate in 1789.

Such a development would not have been possible, however, if aristocratic institutions had not survived from the Middle Ages to provide centres of opposition to royal power and a constitutional justification for it. These were the Provincial Estates which still met in some of the provinces, and the *Parlement* of Paris, twelve provincial *Parlements* and four sovereign courts. In addition mention should be made of the horde of venal officers who, because they owned their offices, could not be dismissed by the Crown but were in constant rivalry with the *intendants* and could offer continual opposition to their policies. The Provincial Estates were mainly of influence in the way of obstruction, until the final stages of the *ancien régime*. The *Parlements*, when they had recovered from their long period of passivity under Louis XIV, after the excesses of the Fronde, throughout the 18th century increasingly became the main centre of resistance to royal policy. The *noblesse* of the robe and the sword, formerly rivals, were now united in defence of their privileges; and the *Parlements* not only provided a constitutional basis for aristocratic ambitions, but also stirred up popular agitation in the towns. It is now a platitude to say that the French monarchy fell not because of its despotism but because of its weakness. The aristocracy took advantage of this weakness to overthrow the absolute monarchy, and in doing so destroyed itself.

### Bourbon monarchies

In most other countries in Europe, monarchy and aristocracy were mixed in different proportions, and a regime compounded of the two survived into the 19th and even the 20th centuries. Spain, which became a Bourbon monarchy as a result of the War of the Spanish Succession, was the country in which one would have expected to see the French pattern of government most closely repeated; and so far as the Bourbon kings were able to do so, this was what they aimed at. The first Bourbon king, Philip V, introduced the system of government through ministers in place of the Habsburg conciliar system, though without robbing the councils of all their

p 320 (15)

p 20 (16)

functions. Under the ministers were *intendants*, also copied from France, who administered the provinces and struggled for power against the traditional *corregidores*. Provinces which had possessed local councils, such as Aragon, lost these. In fact the whole apparatus of bureaucratic absolutism appeared to be in process of creation. Charles III, who ruled from 1758 to 1788, continued the same trend, bringing into his service able professional administrators, under whom Spain seemed to be in the process of reversing the current of her national history and to offer the promise of returning to her greater days. It was an illusion. The success of all the European monarchies was bound up with the personality of the ruler. When Charles III, conscientious and capable of choosing able servants, was replaced by the weak-willed and stupid Charles IV, with his stronger but equally stupid consort, Maria Luisa and the unspeakable Godoy who held her in thrall, the whole achievement of Bourbon kingship in Spain collapsed, all the more easily because the fundamental social evils of the Spanish *ancien régime* remained, as they were long to remain, unremedied. Nothing had been done to remove the older forms of provincial privilege and noble exemptions from taxation and prohibition from productive work. The grandees of the Court and the hordes of poverty-stricken gentry in the country were equally useless to the State, but they preserved within the husk of monarchical absolutism the seeds of aristocratic anarchy.

There were also Bourbon rulers in Italy, in Naples and Parma, who achieved no more permanent results than they did in Spain. Italy was a collection of different types of government. There were Habsburgs in Lombardy and Tuscany; Sardinia was a kingdom, Venice and Genoa fossil republics and the Papal States a medieval relic. Sardinia had a comparatively modern centralized administration and the future Emperor Leopold III gave Tuscany a reforming government. But elsewhere the Italian states remained internally what Italy was as a whole, a mosaic of petty privileges in which the pattern of the modern State had hardly begun to appear. Power and privilege everywhere resided in the hands of the noble landowners and there was little effective challenge to them from above or below. Politically, a great part of Italy seems to have skipped the 18th century and remained in the 17th until circumstances flung it headlong into the 19th.

## The house of Habsburg

If in the Iberian and Italian peninsulas the past weighed so heavily on the present, the Austrian Empire might seem even more incapable of being adapted to 18th-century absolutism. It was an heterogeneous collection of provinces, united only by allegiance to the Austrian Crown. A description of them cannot be other than a catalogue. The lands of Austria proper stretched from the Alpine valleys to the Danubian plain and included the Tyrol, Breisgau and Burgen, Upper and Lower Austria, Carniola, Carinthia, Styria. These were mainly Catholic and German. The lands of the former Bohemian Crown, Bohemia, Moravia and Silesia, were Slav in race and language and in parts still retained memories of their Hussite past. Prince Eugene of Savoy had driven the Turks back to Belgrade in 1716 and by the Peace of Passerowitz in 1718 completed the emancipation of the Hungarian plain from the Turks; while about the same time the opposition of the Hungarian nobles to Austrian rule had been brought to an end by a compromise. But the Magyar nobles and the Slav peasants under them had nothing in common with the other peoples of the Empire. South of the Alps Austria had the purely Italian province of Lombardy; and finally she ruled the former Spanish and now Austrian Netherlands. To add to the complication, the Austrian Emperor was also Holy Roman Emperor, a position which brought with it no power but some potentially dangerous responsibilities. To bring all these varied territories into the kind of administrative centralization that the 18th-century monarchies admired more often than they could achieve it, was an impossible task.

To think of the government of the Habsburg Empire in terms of absolute monarchy is however something of an illusion. It should rather be seen as yet one more variation, or rather a series of variations, on the general theme of aristocracy and monarchy. The direct personal control of the sovereign was at its height in the

Austrian and Bohemian lands, where the Emperor ruling through his Privy Council and its Secretary was least restricted by aristocratic opposition. That imperial authority should be strongest in the hereditary Habsburg lands of Austria was natural; its strength in the lands of the Bohemian Crown is attributable to the passivity which had descended on them after the crushing defeat and reconquest at the battle of the White Mountain in 1620. A local official called the *Kreishauptmann*, originating in Bohemia as a representative of the Estate of Nobles, had gradually passed under royal control and been extended to the Austrian lands. He filled a role similar to that of the *intendant* in France. Nothing like this measure of centralization prevailed in the other lands, and the lack of unity in the government at Vienna was shown by the existence of five separate chancelleries, for Austria, Bohemia, Hungary, the Netherlands and Italy.

Under Charles VI, who ruled from 1705 to 1740, little progress in centralization was to be expected. The Emperor being primarily concerned to secure the inheritance of the whole of the imperial possessions for his daughter Maria Theresa, could not afford to antagonize the lands which still retained some of their local autonomy. In particular this meant Hungary. For their part, the Magyar nobles were still too conscious of the Turkish menace not to be willing to accept a compromise, especially if the terms were favourable to themselves. The result was that government in Hungary remained essentially aristocratic, in the hands of Estates dominated by the great nobles, who were prepared to recognize imperial authority on condition of retaining their own privileges. When, by virtue of the Pragmatic Sanction, Maria Theresa succeeded to the dominions of Charles VI and to an inheritance threatened with partition by the rapacious powers around her, she appealed to the Hungarian Estates for support. She obtained it, but again at a price, in the form of the preservation of the aristocratic Hungarian constitution and the continuance of noble exemption from taxation.

Extraordinarily, Maria Theresa emerged from the War of the Austrian Succession with only the major loss of Silesia. The lesson drawn from this war and the subsequent Seven Years' War was the need for reforms which would enable Austria to resist the Prussian threat and recover the lost province. After the conclusion of peace in 1748 a general reorganization of government, setting up specialized ministries, and of taxation, removing it largely from the control of the Estates, was undertaken in Austria and Bohemia, which now came to correspond much more closely to the ideal pattern of 18th-century autocracy, with rather fewer concessions to the noblesse than had been made in France. In Hungary, on the other hand, it might be said that the situation was reversed and it was the nobles who condescended to make some concessions to the Crown. The best that Maria Theresa could do with the great Hungarian magnates was to adopt the policy that Louis XIV had used with his greater nobles. By attracting them to the Court at Vienna, they were tied more closely to the Habsburg house, which in its turn was committed to the preservation of aristocratic privileges.

Under Maria Theresa's heir, Joseph II, a more intensive policy of centralization was attempted, combined with the promotion of Germanization through the educational system. Widespread unrest throughout the Austrian dominions, culminating in the revolt of the Austrian Netherlands, and the failure of the ambitious foreign policy which Joseph's internal measures had been intended to promote, proved that Maria Theresa had been correct in limiting her administrative changes to what she believed the different provinces of her Empire would accept peacefully.

## Prussian despotism

If the supposed absolutism, or enlightened despotism, of the Austrian Empire was so limited in its achievement and concealed so much variation within a single state, how much greater variety was to be expected in patterns of government throughout the whole of Europe. We have still not reached the heights of absolutism or the extremes of aristocracy. The kingdom of Prussia might seem to carry us a long way towards absolutism. In fact, what we discover is a simultaneous development towards a centralized absolutism and an increasingly privileged aristocracy. Branden-

*The execution of the strieltzy, 1699. The strieltzy, a sort of Praetorian Guard founded by Ivan the Terrible, formed an impassable barrier to Peter the Great's reforms. In 1698 they rose in revolt, were beaten in battle and about 2000 of them executed.* (3)

burg-Prussia was, like the Habsburg Empire though on a much smaller scale, a conglomeration of provinces; but unlike Austria its ruler in the 17th century, the Great Elector, was able to take the vital step which determined the whole future of his country—the provincial Estates gave up their rights of voting taxes in return for the confirmation of the exemptions of the nobles. With the revenue thus assured to the State a standing army, disproportionately large in relation to the size of the State, was built up. In other European countries the army was created to serve the State; in Prussia it might almost be said that the State was created in the service of the army. It has been pointed out that Frederick William I was the first European ruler habitually to be seen in uniform. If a centrally controlled bureaucracy developed early in Prussian history it was for the same reason. The local commissars who represented the King were primarily concerned with taxation and the army. They were responsible to a War Commissariat in Berlin. This was developed, early in the 18th century, into a General Directory controlling the whole administration. The basic organization of the State which was to make such a devastating impact on the p 17(10) international scene under Frederick II was the work of his father, Frederick William I, between 1713 and 1740. The son used the instruments created by his father but made no essential changes in them. Indeed, in the course of his reign inherent weaknesses appeared. These were most obvious at the top. They resulted in the first place from the survival of general, omnicompetent councils or officials alongside the growth of more specialized ministries. The consequent overlapping and confusion was perhaps not entirely uncalculated, for it left the final decision on all important matters in the hands of the ruler and provided the councils or ministers with no scope for the development of any independent policies which might be dangerous to his power. The whole success of the government therefore depended on the ability of the ruler. This was common to all the absolutisms but even the ablest and most hard-working of the 18th-century despots could only achieve a limited success. Frederick II governed from Potsdam on the basis of reports sent to him by ministers, who were no more than officials, from Berlin. The profound distrust with which he regarded them was met by the evasion and deceit which they employed towards him. Under a weak successor, after the death of Frederick, disaster struck the Prussian State.

If Prussia proved capable subsequently of a drastic reorganization of the administrative structure which did not change the traditional bias of the State, this was because the one major limitation which had remained on the autocracy in Prussia was also a major source of the strength and survival of the State. As almost everywhere, the ruler had purchased autocracy by guaranteeing and even increasing the social and economic privileges of the nobility. Also as elsewhere, the officer class in the army was recruited from the nobles. Where a marked difference is revealed is that in the absence of a middle class and given the comparative lack of wealth of even the higher nobility, the nobles and gentry were prepared, and needed, to play an active and not merely an honorific role in the higher ranks of the bureaucracy and at the head of local administrations, as well as in the army. When the central government collapsed, therefore, before the Napoleonic Empire, the aristocratic foundations remained intact for the reconstruction of a centralized military State.

The variations of government in the other German states are too great to be gone into here. For the most part they combined, in different proportions, most of the vices of aristocracy and monarchy with few of their virtues.

## Russia: absolutism supreme

To see absolutism at its height we must move east to Russia. Two powerful and ruthless aristocrats, Peter at the beginning and p 16-17 Catherine at the end, dominate the century. In between, women or (9, 11) children were set up as supreme rulers by Court factions and the Imperial Guard, or overthrown by palace revolutions. This was the despotism of the degenerate Roman Empire. Nevertheless what Peter and Catherine did, or tried to do, is not irrelevant to the general pattern of government, for it represents yet another variation on the theme of aristocracy and monarchy. Like Prussia, Russia in the 17th century was a military State, with an administration organized for defence or conquest. Under Peter the Great, and again under Catherine, extensive changes were made in both the central government and local administration. Their effectiveness is doubtful and their duration was limited. Essentially the government was and remained a pure despotism, exercised by the arbitrary will of the ruler. If there was one institution which was necessary to it this was the secret police, whose power was well established during the 18th century.

As in every other country, the basic problem of government in Russia was the relation between the sovereign and the nobility. Peter's solution had been to accelerate, sometimes by rather drastic means, the decline of the old class of boyars and replace it f 3 with a serving nobility. The theory was that after a compulsory education, from the age of 10 to 15, the young noble entered either the bureaucracy or the army, and continued in these for the rest of his active life, slowly working his way up through fourteen grades. The weaker successors to Peter found it impossible to maintain this system. In 1736 the term of service was limited to twenty-five years; and in 1762 compulsory service was abolished. In fact it still remained customary for many nobles to serve in the army or bureaucracy, largely for economic reasons. Their support for the tsardom was ensured not only by the reduction of their obligations but also by the increase in their privileges. This was particularly the work of the German princess, Catherine, who emerged as Empress in 1762 as the result of a military coup and the murder of her husband. Like her immediate predecessors, she multiplied the privileges of the nobles, though she kept political authority strictly in her own hands. The masses of the peasantry were consequently thrust into the depths of serfdom and the tyranny of the ruler was founded on the innumerable petty tyrannies of the class of landowners.

## Aristocracy in Sweden and Poland

While autocracy reached its height in Russia, in two of her neighbours, Sweden and Poland, the tide had been running in the opposite direction of aristocracy. What might be considered the arbitrary element in political history is illustrated by the opposite developments in the Scandinavian powers. In the dual Kingdom of Denmark–Norway a royal coup in 1660 established strong monarchical authority at the expense of a declining nobility. On the other hand, in Sweden aristocracy gained the upper hand. The long absence of Charles XII on his fantastic military adventures, and his death in 1718 without a direct heir, provided the Swedish Estates with an opportunity to introduce a constitution which gave them control of the Council of government. For the next fifty years Sweden had, like Great Britain, a parliamentary government, with the comparative strength of parties in the Swedish Diet reflected in the composition of the Council. In the absence of monarchical authority conflicts between the higher nobles and the gentry, and between the whole Estate of the nobility and the other Estates, provided one element in the political situation; but – again in contrast with almost every other country except Great Britain – the parties which developed, the 'Hats' and 'Caps', were something more than aristocratic factions. They were founded on disagreements about domestic and even more foreign policy. The term 'Hats', implying some sort of military uniform, was given to those who stood for a renewal of a forward foreign policy, and the 'Caps' to those who favoured a continuation of the peaceful, withdrawn policy that had followed the disasters of Charles XII's reign.

The parliamentary régime, largely though not exclusively aristocratic in nature, lasted from 1718 to 1772, when, with backing from France, a new and young King, Gustavus III, restored royal power in the government of Sweden. It was not to be a permanent

 p 25 (22)
p 15 (6)

restoration, but the way in which it was effected by foreign influence illustrates one of the great weaknesses of aristocracies in the 18th century. Even in an autocracy like Russia, or a monarchy like France, noble factions could be influenced, or bought, and the policy of their country perverted in the interests of foreign powers. The Dutch Republic was a battlefield for British, French and to some extent Prussian influences.

Foreign interference reached its height where aristocracy merged into anarchy, in the elective monarchy of Poland. The Polish kings were little better than puppets in the hands of foreign powers and aristocratic factions. The real rulers of Poland were the great noble families, owning vast estates and disposing of innumerable offices. They had the means of purchasing the support of – literally – armies of small landowners or landless gentry, the *szlachta*. The chief concern of the magnates was with their own bitter rivalries for power. This was the reality behind the constitutional devices which were not the cause but the result of Poland's governmental weakness.

The elections of monarchs by mass meetings of gentry were a mere method of registering the result of a particular struggle for power between rival factions of magnates backed by foreign money or troops. The *liberum veto*, by which a single deputy could nullify the decisions of a diet, served to prevent the development of any effective centralized government. The right of confederation merely sanctioned rebellion. Pride and poverty, and the pleasure of exploiting an increasingly depressed peasantry, kept the gentry loyal to the system of aristocratic anarchy. Poland inevitably sank into a state of dependence on its most powerful neighbour, Russia, until finally, at the price of allowing Prussia and Austria their smaller shares of what had once been the most extensive monarchy in Europe, Catherine cast away the *simulacrum* of independence that had been left to Poland and absorbed it into the Russian Empire.

p 14 (4)

f 4

Poland represents the aristocratic extreme in 18th-century Europe. Elsewhere on the Continent, however much it may have been tempered by aristocracy, the basic pattern of government was nearly everywhere monarchical. The exceptions were small, though not insignificant, states. The Venetian oligarchy can perhaps be dismissed as a mere relic of the past, of little European importance. The city-state of Geneva was another oligarchy. Apart from giving birth to Rousseau it only achieved political significance with the rise of the democratic movement when the century was drawing to its close. The same may be said of the Dutch Republic.

## The British solution

The Kingdom of Great Britain and Ireland remains as the one major power of the 18th century which broke away from the general pattern, for under a constitutional King it was undoubtedly an aristocracy, but a stable one. To trace the political contrast between England and all the major states of Europe simply to the English Civil War and the Commonwealth would be a superficial judgement. English political history began to diverge from that of the Continent early in the Middle Ages, when the centre of power and interest of the Norman and Angevin kings was on the Continent. This left the baronage in England very much to itself. A strong sense of loyalty to an absentee King never developed and the history of the English Middle Ages is punctuated with revolts of barons and the downfall of kings.

On the other hand, the administrative machinery of the State remained strong and periods of aristocratic anarchy were short and exceptional. This was perhaps because England also differed from France, as from most of the greater European countries, in size. The European monarchies in the Middle Ages were for the most part too large to be governed by a single authority. They were in effect federations of provinces, held together in peace when there was a strong ruler at the centre, breaking down in internecine war and anarchy every time there was a disputed succession, a minority or a weak ruler. The great nobles in their provinces were petty kings, strong enough to defy the central power and dominate their own vassals. Only by the development of autocracy could the State be held together and domestic peace maintained. In England, on the contrary, independent, or semi-independent, provincial powers rarely developed and never survived for long: the King was always

*The result of Poland's internal weakness was the first Partition of 1772. Here Catherine II, Joseph II and Frederick the Great prepare to carve up the 'Polish Plum Cake'. Louis XV is unjustly made a participant because, though he took no territory, he did not come to the defence of the Poles as had been expected. (4)*

The 'Glorious Revolution' of 1688, when William of Orange and his wife Mary (a daughter of James II) accepted the throne of England subject to far-reaching parliamentary sanctions, was a turning-point in European history. This Dutch broadside, 'The Wounded French Bear' celebrates the event. The bear is France; the honeypots that he has tried to plunder and whose bees are giving him such a painful time, are Britain, Holland and Portugal, symbolized by the unicorn, the lion and the tower. The same bear on the right, wearing a Jesuit's cap, dances to the command of a band from heaven. An eagle (Germany) is ready to pounce on it. (5)

near enough for the lesser lords and gentry to look to him against their immediate superiors. He, in his turn, increasingly used them as his agents and relied on their support, until, under the Tudors, the great barons of the Middle Ages disappeared, like the greater beasts of the forest, from the political scene. The lords and gentry who remained, already apprenticed to the task of government, were prepared to share power with the King, on condition that he respected their prejudices and interests. When, in turn, Charles I and James II failed to do this, they were rapidly shown who really ruled the country.

The Revolution of 1688 comes into our analysis not merely as an episode in the story of England. It was a major event in European history, both because of what it was and of when it occurred. The current of European polity had seemed to be sweeping irresistibly towards absolutism: Louis XIV was setting the trend towards centralized bureaucracy—the limitations on his achievement in respect of the government of France were not yet apparent. His religious persecution reversed the current, which had been moving in the direction of greater tolerance. His military successes threatened the independence of all western and even central Europe. Moreover his major rival, the Habsburg power of Austria, was in these matters little different from the France of Louis XIV. What difference did it make whether Europe was dominated by Austrian Habsburgs or French Bourbons? The little Dutch Republic, under its Stadtholder William of Orange, drained its strength in the struggle against French domination, but if it had been left as the solitary representative of a more liberal and tolerant system of government, the outlook would have been bleak indeed.

The England of William III and Marlborough was significant for the future of Europe because it was also the England of Locke and Sir Isaac Newton, of the Houses of Parliament and the Courts of Common Law. The ultimate frustration of Louis XIV's ambitions may be said to have dated from his failure to intervene effectively to prevent William of Orange from gaining the throne of Great Britain and Ireland. Military defeat meant much more than the beginning of the end of the French attempt to secure the hegemony of Europe. Autocracy and intolerance, in the person of the Sun King, had received a rebuff from which in their existing form they were never to recover. Success is the ultimate test—at least in the minds of contemporaries—of all political systems, and the moderate British and Dutch governments had defeated the absolutism of France. They had survived and even triumphed. Louis XIV in all his glory had been reduced to a desperate defensive war. The results could be traced on the map of Europe, but even more clearly in the minds of men. To the crisis of the European conscience, which Paul Hazard dates from 1680 to 1715, the international struggle of the same years is not irrelevant. In politics, at least in Western Europe, absolutism and divine right had suffered a severe blow.

The constitutional government of Great Britain now offered a rival model, and one if not to copy, at least to admire. But what was this government in actual fact? Montesquieu admired it because it was aristocratic and liberal and this is as good a brief summary as one could give. If it was a monarchy, even a constitutional one, the Hanoverian kings of Great Britain were as uninspiring a set as could have been found to embody the monarchical principle. It was generally recognized, in Great Britain and abroad, that real power lay in the hands of Parliament; and Parliament was an p 20 (17) aristocracy, partly hereditary partly elective, composed of a mixture of greater and lesser landowners, with some lawyers and bishops and a few merchants thrown in. At a lower level a corresponding mixture ruled the counties through Quarter Sessions. It was a government of amateurs, largely unpaid except in so far as they paid themselves by seeing that the laws were made in their own interest, and assisted by the most rudimentary and scanty bureaucratic apparatus. The problem is how such a government, of a country far smaller and less populous than its European rivals, should have become one of the great powers, victorious in war – except when she fought her own colonies and Europe in alliance – and prosperous in peace.

The first and most obvious answer is that Great Britain, except for a period in the reign of George III, possessed a reasonably united government. Even without a developed party system, Parliament seems to have provided a much sounder basis for a stable and united government than a Court. On occasions when the monarch attempted to play an active, everyday role in politics, as did Charles II and James II, and to a lesser extent George III, the result was p 332 (4) weak and divided governments. It may seem paradoxical that an absolute monarch, even a Louis XIV or a Catherine II, should have been unable to create and maintain a united government, but it was an inherent condition of absolutism to have a divided ministry, including bitter rivals such as Louvois and Colbert under Louis XIV, Machault and d'Argenson under Louis XV, Breteuil and Calonne under Louis XVI, in the same government. The presence at the head of the government of a *premier ministre*, like Walpole or the Younger Pitt, was incompatible with absolute monarchy, or only compatible when the King, like the young Louis XV, was prepared to efface himself behind a minister such as Fleury; and it was no accident that the ministry of Cardinal Fleury, from 1726 to 1743, was the one fully prosperous and successful period in the history of 18th-century France.

## The finances of absolutism

Eighteenth century painters were remarkably frank in their royal portraiture. The kings and their consorts, fat or skinny, goggle-eyed, pompous with vacuous expressions, stare out at us from their canvasses revealing the emptiness of the minds behind them. In Europe, as in France, the French Revolution triumphed over weakness not over strength, and the weakness which brought down the French monarchy was also the most deeply rooted and ineradicable disease of the *ancien régime* everywhere.

p 320–21 (16, 18) Where absolutism found its most insoluble problem was in finance. The survival of autocracy, in both domestic and foreign policy, depended on its ability to pay its way. The new bureaucracies required large revenues for their support in time of peace, but the real crisis came with war. The growth of large, professional armies, and the increased expense of armaments by land and sea far exceeded the normal financial resources of any monarchy of continental Europe. Every great war faced its major participants with financial exhaustion. The peasants, the main source of supply, had usually been milked dry. The financial demands resulting from the foreign policies of the great states were one of the sources of the deterioration in their conditions in the later years of the 18th century. As a last desperate resource an attempt would be made to extract a greater share of taxation from the privileged classes. This opened the door to constitutional conflicts with Estates, Diets and *Parlements*, and the struggle between monarchy and aristocracy which has already been described reached its highest pitch.

The final resource of the *ancien régime* was bankruptcy and inflation. Catherine paid for her Turkish wars, anticipating the French revolutionaries, by printing *assignats*. Financial collapse, caused primarily by the expenses of French participation in the American War of Independence, brought down the *ancien régime* in France. Only a primitive economy such as that of Russia, could survive it without serious hurt. Indeed a graph might almost be drawn up relating the survival of absolutism directly to the backwardness of the society, ranging on the continent of Europe from France at one extreme to Russia at the other.

## The wider world

Of course, strength and weakness in government are relative. The governments of the European monarchies may seem, by modern standards, inadequate. Under a close inspection we may be struck more by their weakness than their strength. It must be remembered, though, that from a medieval standpoint the perspective would be a very different one, and Leviathan was still only beginning to flex his muscles and exert his power. And if we extend our gaze to the whole world, the picture also becomes different. The progress of science and invention, industry and agriculture, and population in the more advanced countries of Europe, could not fail to produce a potential far greater than that existing in any other section of the globe. America had nothing to oppose to European occupation but wild tribes and dead civilizations. Africa was still unexplored and unknown, except on the fringes. Asia and the Middle East consisted almost wholly of decaying and disintegrating kingdoms and empires, from the Ottoman to the Chinese, with neither the military and economic strength, nor the governmental stability to offer serious resistance to the sea-borne empires of the West whenever and wherever they made their attack. The limitation of this study of government in the 18th century to Europe is therefore justifiable for elsewhere there was little but a void.

p 162–63
p 316–17 One exception must be made to this statement. Little need be said of the governments of French Canada and Spanish and Portuguese America, which were no more than extensions of those that prevailed at home. The English colonies, running down the Atlantic seaboard of North America, call for more attention, because they represent the beginning of something new. In the government of Great Britain, in the 18th century, the aristocracy

of the great landowners had been intensified. The great plantations of the Southern American colonies, run by slave labour, also produced an aristocratic society. They possessed representative assemblies but the pattern of society dictated the dominance of an élite of landowners.

The New England colonies were cast in a different mould socially, though politically the pattern may have seemed similar. They also had an elected legislative assembly, with a Governor and Council appointed by the Crown. The executive was nominally independent of the legislature, but since the latter controlled the revenue and paid the salaries, potentially it had the whip-hand. The situation, in fact, largely reproduced that in England in the early 17th century before the Civil War. Though there was no religious issue as then, the essential political bases for a conflict between the mother country and the colonies were all present. Crown patronage, often distributed to unworthy recipients, and attempts to extend the limited royal rights of taxation, became the centre of dispute in 18th-century America as they had been in 17th-century England.

Behind these conflicts there lay a difference of political theory which is not without its relevance to the theme of this whole chapter. The struggle in 17th-century England had been between the rising idea of sovereignty and the old ideas of common and natural law. With the growth of absolutism in the 18th century, sovereignty seemed to be winning all over Europe. Even in an aristocracy such as England, Parliament was asserting rights of sovereignty which emulated the powers of the continental despotisms. It was the attempt to assert these rights over the American colonies which, coming into violent collision with the colonists' inherited and older ideas of constitutional rights, led to p 314–15 the American Revolution. This was a different constitutional struggle from those taking place at the same time in Europe. There the aristocracies were fighting for the preservation and extension of their social and fiscal privileges against rulers who, at least in France and Austria and perhaps a few smaller states, might be regarded as attempting to introduce reforms in the interest of the unprivileged, even if these reforms were often also in the interest of the absolute monarchy. The New England colonies, on the other hand, although their franchises varied, could in no sense be described as aristocracies. In so far as their franchise was based on landowning, it was the landowning of small men. There was no exploited class of serfs or peasants, or subject class of slaves. Their revolution was based on political principles which, though they had been rooted in English soil, had failed to develop there in the 18th century and had even seemed to undergo a retrogression. If, at the beginning of the century, advocates of political liberty in Europe had found their model particularly in England, in the last years of Europe's *ancien régime* they found it – the fact of slavery forgotten – in the English colonies on the other side of the Atlantic.

With American Independence the *ancien régime* – though the absolute monarchs and their ministers whose armies and navies encompassed, or hastened, the defeat of Great Britain, or who applauded the fall of the proud island empire, of course did not know it – was entering its last days. But while the American Revolution opened the period which witnessed the decline of the pattern of government we have been studying, and the French Revolution carried it much farther, they did not at first seem to signify the end of the Age of Enlightenment, but rather its triumph. Neither interpretation would be entirely true, but where, in between, the truth lies, we must attempt to discover at the end of this book, when many other aspects of the century have first been explored.

# II THE ARCHITECTURAL SETTING

*Royalty, Religion and the Urban Background*

JOHN SUMMERSON

*'Architecture . . . applies itself, like music*

*(and I believe we may add poetry) directly to the imagination,*

*without the intervention of any kind of imitation . . .*

*In the hands of a man of genius it is capable of inspiring*

*sentiment, and of filling the mind with*

*great and sublime ideas.'*

SIR JOSHUA REYNOLDS, 13th Discourse, 1786

## Baroque art

is a kind of visual rhetoric, arrogantly re-assembling established grammar and familiar turns of phrase into new, sweeping, emphatic statements. The conventional frontiers are dissolved. The architect dissolves his rigid apparatus to admit the painter; the painter dissolves the surface offered, admitting a counterfeit sky; the sculptor dissolves the classic stances into momentary attitudes and poises of studied carelessness. Behind it all is still the rigorous discipline of the Renaissance but a discipline so well learnt, so perfectly transmitted, that the mood of a new age can sweep through it all – through architecture, painting, sculpture and every lesser art, with the crafts of the weaver, the silver-worker and the smith.

To enter such palaces and churches, or to walk through such cities, was in fact intended as a dramatic and enriching experience, like listening to music or reading poetry. In churches the experience was to be a spiritual one, made explicit, as will be shown later, by every device of imagery, symbolism and ritual. In secular buildings it was to be equally involving, but directed towards the glorification of the monarch or patron. In both, the appeal was through the mind to the emotions, and both depended on a new and highly inventive use of space. Baroque space – the deliberate creation of a total environment – was something without precedent. Its closest parallel was with German Late Gothic, but its forms were entirely classical. These forms (column, pilaster, entablature, etc.) had lost all connection with structure, and were used merely to suggest a fictitious structure. Sequences of levels, changes of scale, unexpected lighting, led the visitor onward through a calculated series of impressions, reinforced by dancing figure-sculpture and by skilful illusionist painting. It was in the churches of southern Germany and Austria that the art reached its climax, but a work such as the Residenz at Würzburg perhaps more fully represents its wider social aspects. It was built for the Prince-Bishop of Würzburg, a member of the Schönborn family, prolific in great building projects in Austria. His main architect was Balthasar Neumann, but many others in Germany and France were consulted and the result is therefore a combination of several ideas. The staircase (opposite) was begun in 1737. The visitor enters a rather low hall at the bottom, turns at a right angle and walks up the first flight of steps. Only when he reaches the landing can he appreciate the full width of the hall, with its balustraded galleries running above the stairs at either side. The chief plasterer was Antonio Bossi, and the ceiling – showing the Sun (Apollo), the Planets and the Continents against a background of billowing clouds – was painted in 1752, by Giambattista Tiepolo. (1)

**Three men** working in Rome in the mid-17th century gave Baroque architecture its form and impetus. One was Pietro da Cortona, whose tense interplay of concave and convex (above: Sta Maria della Pace) influenced works as distant as the transept ends of St Paul's, London. (2)

**The central genius** of the Baroque was Bernini, unrivalled as a sculptor and equally dominant as an architect. His Palazzo Chigi (above) articulates the façade by a giant order of pilasters supported on a massive ground storey (originally the porch was in the centre —the palace was doubled in length when the Odescalchi acquired

**The next generation** saw Borromini's experiments carried further by Guarini in northern Italy. The dome of S. Lorenzo, Turin (above), is an eight-pointed star of free-standing arches built in wood and plaster. (5)

**Leadership passed** at the end of the 17th century to France. Right: the east front of the Louvre as built. Perrault kept Bernini's fivefold division but crowned the centre with a pediment and recessed the two flanking wings behind a colonnade. (7)

it in 1745). Bernini's third design for the Louvre (below left) was a variant of the same idea. The long surface is broken into five sections, the lower part rusticated and the base 'natural' rock. The central section has columns, the end pavilions pilasters, and the top is crowned by a flat balustrade. (3, 6)

**The undulating façade** of Borromini's S. Carlo alle Quattro Fontane was to haunt the imagination of later architects in the north. Torturing the old classical vocabulary to express his complex geometrical conceptions, he opened up a new world of spatial possibilities. (4)

**The court of the Sun King** produced grandeur equivalent to that of the Roman Baroque but its leading architect, Jules-Hardouin Mansart, had not the originality of the Romans. His church of the Invalides represents the culmination of a long French tradition. His additions to Versailles (right) do not avoid monotony. Both the palace and gardens (laid out by Le Nôtre) were the envy of every European king and neurotically imitated from London to Naples and from Madrid to St Petersburg. (8, 9)

**Schönbrunn,** the Viennese Versailles, was begun in 1695, raising the Emperor Leopold to equality with Louis XIV. His architect was J. B. Fischer von Erlach, like Bernini a sculptor; and it was to Bernini that he turned for inspiration. The garden front, seen (above) in a painting by Bellotto of 1759, was extensively altered in 1744–49, but the long parade of pilasters is Fischer's. Left: the great gallery, based on the Galerie des Glaces, but interpreted in a lighter spirit. (10, 11)

**Fischer's successor** as Surveyor General at Vienna was Johann Lucas von Hildebrandt. His masterpiece is the Upper Belvedere of 1722 at Vienna (right), which in its slightly playful picturesqueness already looks forward to Rococo. Its broken skyline and four corner turrets owe little to French or Italian precedent. (12)

**Palace building,** the expression in architecture of despotic power, became a mania with the rulers of Europe. Typically, the English Louvre remained on paper—Wren's design for a new Whitehall Palace (above) with Inigo Jones's Banqueting House as its centrepiece. The three other palaces shown below all stem from the same ambition—Stockholm by Nicodemus Tessin (begun 1697), Berlin by Andreas Schlüter (1701) and Caserta, near Naples, by Luigi Vanvitelli (1751). (13–16)

**The only palace** actually built in England was not for the monarch but for a general: Vanbrugh's Blenheim for the Duke of Marlborough. (17)

**For an Elector-Archbishop:** Pommersfelden, by Johann Dientzenhofer. This is almost contemporary with Blenheim and although neither knew the other's work, they found similar solutions to their problems. (18)

**Grand staircases** gave Baroque architects many of their most splendid opportunities. That of Caserta (right) solidifies the dramatic conceptions of contemporary theatre design.

**England and Germany,** in spite of national styles, share the same aesthetic ideal. The Great Hall of Castle Howard (above) and the staircase of Pommersfelden (below) both form cages within the house. (19, 21)

**The Baroque-Rococo equation** was invented by Hildebrandt at the Upper Belvedere. Such features as the crouching giant holding up the roof of the lower hall introduce that element of fantasy that runs through all later German Baroque. (22)

**Russia had relied** on foreign architects ever since the 15th century, and with Peter the Great's ambition to westernize his empire, that reliance became even more absolute. His country palace of Peterhof (right) was designed by a Frenchman, Jean-Baptiste Leblond, tempted from Paris by a high salary in 1716. Peterhof, with its severe style (now softened by Rastrelli's alterations) and its formal gardens and fountains, was a successful attempt to translate Versailles into Russian. (23)

**Peter's daughter Elizabeth** who ruled Russia from 1741 to 1762, gave the new capital of St Petersburg a Rococo elegance that had been lacking in her father's time. Her favourite architect was the Italian Bartolomeo Rastrelli. He had come to Russia at the age of fifteen, studied in France, Austria and Italy and returned with a thorough mastery of contemporary idiom. His two largest works were the Winter Palace at St Petersburg (below) and Tsarskoe Selo (bottom) just outside the city. Both are characterized by enormous length, saved from monotony by inventive decoration. Part of Rastrelli's talent lay in his ability to combine various styles harmoniously. At the far end of Tsarskoe Selo old Russia peeps out in the five gilded domes of the chapel. (24, 25)

**Every court** in Europe strove as far as its resources allowed to emulate the great monarchies. The small state of Piedmont in north Italy had developed rapidly at the end of the 16th century and a series of energetic kings had turned its capital Turin into one of the greatest of Baroque cities. But Guarini, its leading architect, died in 1683 and it was not until 1714 that another appeared who approached him in genius: Filippo Juvarra. His most grandiose achievement, the royal hunting lodge of Stupinigi, completed in 1733, has a vast courtyard leading to a star-shaped block with a hall rising through three storeys (opposite), its shallow dome supported on four tall piers from which galleries spring. In its scale and its unashamed theatricality the Stupinigi comes within the orbit of German and Austrian architecture rather than that of any earlier models in Italy. (26)

**The dynastic dreams** of Augustus the Strong, Elector of Saxony (a State of even less international consequence than Piedmont) led to one of the most extravagant of all architectural fantasies, the Zwinger at Dresden. It was built as an open space for tournaments and court celebrations, and was originally intended as part of a much larger complex. The design was by Mathaes Daniel Pöppelmann, but the result owes at least as much to the sculpture of Balthasar Permoser; indeed the whole Zwinger is sculptural in conception. This view by Bellotto (below) shows it in 1758. In the centre is the Wall-pavilion, begun in 1716 and connected by low quadrant galleries to two high blocks, which form one side of a large rectangular court. On the right is the other showpiece of the Zwinger, the Kronentor of 1713. (27)

**Collaboration between architects** was the rule rather than the exception in central Europe. The Würzburg Residenz, as we have seen (pl. 1), contains contributory ideas from France, Italy, Germany and Austria. Neumann's original garden front (left) was modified by Hildebrandt, who added a third storey to the central pavilion and designed the graceful curved pediment above it. (28)

**Frederick the Great at home** required elegance and beauty that would remind him of England and Paris. Sans Souci (right) by Georg von Knobelsdorff was his personal summer palace, and combined suggestions from a wide variety of sources. The caryatids supporting the entablature recall the Zwinger but its other affinities—as the name suggests—are French. (29)

A religious division between Catholic architecture (shown on this page) and Protestant (shown opposite) is hard to define stylistically. As a general rule, Protestant countries tended towards classicism and restraint, Catholic ones towards Baroque and exuberance. Often, however, ideas were exchanged between one side and the other. One of the great Roman basilicas, S. Giovanni in Laterano, was given a new west front in 1732 (left). The architect was Alessandro Galilei, who had spent five years in England and been associated with Vanbrugh. (30)

Gothic translated into the classical vocabulary: the church of the Madeleine at Besançon (below) built by Nicolas Nicole, represents French ambition to be medievally bold and classically correct. (32)

In the same year as Galilei's façade to the Lateran (above) the French-Italian architect Servandoni designed the west front of St Sulpice in Paris (right). Here again the inspiration was English; his first version, subsequently modified, was based on the west front of St Paul's. (31)

The play of curves learned by German architects from Borromini and Guarini became one of the hallmarks of church façades north of the Alps. One of the earliest is Fischer von Erlach's Kollegienkirche at Salzburg (below), consecrated in 1707. Even more eclectic is his Karlskirche at Vienna (below right), where the Rome of Urban VIII meets that of Trajan. (33, 34)

**In Protestant England** the classical tradition of Inigo Jones and Wren went through periodic waves of Baroque influence. James Gibbs, a secret Catholic, had studied under Carlo Fontana in Rome. His early St Mary-le-Strand (right) reflects Roman prototypes; the later St Martin-in-the-Fields (far right) combined classical pediment and English spire in a way that proved popular all over the British Empire. (35, 36)

**The strongly personal style** of Nicholas Hawksmoor has been called English Baroque but his Christ Church, Spitalfields (below), and St Anne's, Limehouse (below centre) look equally to Rome, Wren and English Gothic. The only Englishman close to the spirit of Italian Baroque was Thomas Archer; the towers of St John's, Smith Square (below far right), are undeniably Borrominesque. (37, 38, 39)

**'A building that could vie** with those of the King'—that is, with Augustus' Zwinger—was demanded by the civic authorities of Dresden when they commissioned the Frauenkirche in 1722. It was designed by Georg Bähr, a self-taught artisan-architect who began as a carpenter. He produced a centrally planned church (right) with enormously tall windows and piers leading up to a huge dome and lantern; with its four corner turrets this dome dominated the skyline of Dresden. The interior (far right) was equally dramatic. The seats were arranged in tiers, like the circles of an opera-house, giving an uninterrupted view of the altar and pulpit. It was totally destroyed during the Dresden air-raid of 1945. (40, 41)

**The last flowering** of Baroque took contrasting forms in Italy and Spain. Italy, on the threshold of Neo-classicism, produced in Filippo Juvarra (the builder of Stupinigi, pl. 26) an architect who could match Neumann in spatial ingenuity. In his monastery church of the Superga (above) outside Turin, a simple diagram of cubes and cylinders is the basis for a majestic exposition of classical technique, to which the spreading balustraded platform adds immense dignity.

The interior of his Chiesa del Carmine (above right) again seems to sum up the experience of centuries of Italian building. Its basic plan goes back to Alberti's S. Andrea at Mantua, which Juvarra had in fact completed by adding a dome. But the Alberti formula dissolves into a new conception, with lighting above the side chapels, whose curving and projecting canopies rhythmically disconnect the rigid piers—a characteristically Baroque idea. (42, 43)

**A frenzy of ornament** gripped Spain towards the mid-18th century—the visual counterpart, perhaps, of its fanatical Counter-Revolutionary religion. It is a style associated with the Churriguera family, though its most extreme example is the sacristy of the Charterhouse at Granada by Luis de Arévalo, begun 1727 (right). Planning and colour scheme are relatively simple, but every architectural form—pilaster, capital, cornice, window-surround—is broken up into a mass of sharp edges and thick scrolls. (44)

**Light from heaven** seemed to pour down upon the *trasparente* of Toledo Cathedral (right)—an ingenious altar or *reredos* built behind the high altar in such a way that the Blessed Sacrament should be visible from both sides. It fills one bay of the old Gothic ambulatory, reaching from floor to ceiling in a blaze of marble and gold. It is the illumination, however, which provides the transcendant effect, for the vault above it has been removed and built up with coloured glass and sculpture, so that if the spectator turns and looks back he sees, high above him, a brightly lit opening surrounded by figures of angels, Christ and the prophets seated on clouds. The designer was Narciso Tomé and it was completed in 1732. (45)

**It was in central Europe** that the Baroque church style achieved its final and in many ways most rewarding development. Its greatest patrons were the monasteries. Both the older orders (Benedictines, Cistercians) and those of the Counter-Reformation (the Jesuits, the Theatines and others) initiated building programmes on a vast scale, intent on outshining the Protestant north. The Benedictine Abbey of Banz (above) was built between 1710 and 1718 by Johann Dientzenhofer, one of a family of working masons, who was later to design Pommersfelden.

Bohemia, then part of the Austrian Empire, contains some of the boldest experiments. At Brunau (right), near Prague, Christoph Dientzenhofer explored new possibilities in relating ceiling frescoes to architecture; while at Gabel (far right) Hildebrandt, the architect of the Belvedere, takes Guarini's 'three-dimensional arches' (see pl. 5) and weaves them into a fresh Rococo-like pattern. (46, 48, 49)

**High over the Danube** rises the Benedictine monastery of Melk, the work of another sculptor-mason, Jacob Prandtauer. The stroke of genius that makes Melk so outstanding is the idea of keeping the church enclosed within the monastic walls but opening up the west front by a low arched screen, through which the façade and towers become visible. (50)

**A sculptor's fantasia** on themes by Borromini: the little church of St Johannes Nepomuk in Munich. It was built between 1733 and 1746 by the brothers Cosmas Damian and Egid Quirin Asam, at the latter's expense. The façade (far right) with its concave-convex-concave rhythm and ecstatic sculpture leads into an interior (right) where all the arts combine to make a single effect. Above the cornice, mysteriously lit from behind, floats the Trinity—Father, Son and Dove of the Holy Ghost, wafted by angels. (51, 52)

**A magical revelation** of the divine was the effect aimed at by the Asam brothers in their two most spectacular works, the altars of Weltenburg and Rohr. At Weltenburg (left) St George, silhouetted against a blaze of light, rides triumphantly into the church, striking down the dragon at his horse's feet. At Rohr (right) the Virgin is raised to heaven by angels, while the amazed Apostles draw back in astonishment round her empty tomb. This was an art which, as the Asams realized, approached that of the theatre, but through its setting within the church and its association with the liturgy, the sense of wonder that it aroused was given a spiritual, even a mystical, character. (53, 55)

**The architecture of light** reached its **Fold** consummation in the work of another **out ▶** two brothers, Domenikus and Johann Baptist Zimmermann. The most brilliant of their works is the pilgrimage church of Die Wies (fold out). Here the oval nave, its vault supported on widely spaced coupled columns, opens into a chancel whose windows are set back behind a narrow ambulatory. The church was built as the setting for a miraculous statue, 'the Flagellated Saviour', and the whole interior is an expression of ecstatic faith. The Pelican and the Lamb, symbols of sacrifice, stand above the altar; in the ceiling fresco angels bear the instruments of the Passion to God the Father. The prevailing white and gold of the nave deepen here into red and blue — red for Christ's redeeming blood, blue for God's blessing and mercy. (54)

The living Gothic tradition exerted a compulsive influence on the Baroque architects of central Europe—far more, in fact, than the Renaissance to which Baroque is historically a sequel. The two vaults, shown left, are exactly 200 years apart, yet they are close in aesthetic feeling. The first (far left) is in the cathedral of Sta Barbara at Kutna Hora, Czechoslovakia, and was built by Benedikt Ried in 1512, the second is the vault of the Benedictine abbey church of Kladruby by Johann Santin, a Bohemian architect with an Italian grandfather; it dates from 1712. (56, 57)

**Oval plans,** one of the inventions of 16th-century Rome, were eagerly adopted in Germany and became ever more subtle and complex. A church might be laid out as several interlacing ovals, producing a restless yet ordered rhythm in the ceilings and walls. The interior of Banz (above) articulates the ovals by diagonal pilasters, above which the vault seems to open, revealing visionary Old Testament frescoes. (58)

**The church of the Fourteen Saints,** Vierzehnheiligen, was built over thirty years after Banz. Neumann's plan consists basically of five ovals of different sizes plus two circles. The largest oval (right) forms the nave, where, against all precedent, stood the altar. The stucco, woodwork, metalwork and painting, all of the highest quality, effortlessly echo the same sequence of spaces in their own terms. (59)

**Rococo** is the name given to a style of ornament that began in France in the early 18th century and spread to Germany in the 1730s. It was originally employed strictly for interior decoration, but towards the middle of the century was playing so large a part in the total architectural effect that it is possible to speak of it as the successor to Baroque. Its characteristic features are the arabesque line and the S-curve, pale colours including gold, elaborate use of mirrors and lighting, and naturalistic motifs such as clouds, foliage, birds, children, musical instruments, etc. woven together in a free and playful spirit. The genius of German Rococo was a Frenchman, François de Cuvilliès. His reputation was established by the Reichen Zimmer (1730–37) in the Residenz at Munich (left) and he gained European standing by the Amalienburg, a summer house in the grounds of the Nymphenburg Palace, just outside the same city (above). (60, 61)

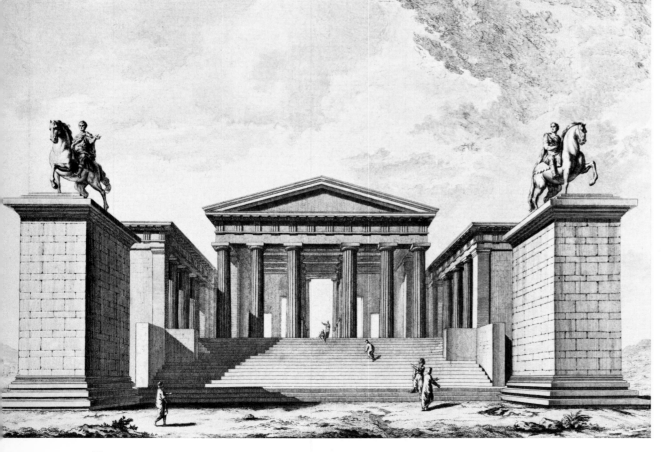

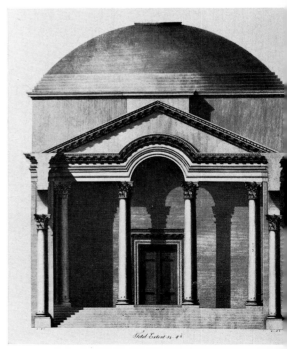

**The exploration of the past** by architects began seriously in the second half of the 18th century. Before that the only earlier style recognized as authoritative had been that of Rome, and even that was not copied with archaeological accuracy. Piranesi's etchings (left: the Arch of Constantine) revealed the picturesque possibilities of Roman grandeur. Others went farther afield. What they saw, and published in large volumes of detailed engravings, turned the course of architecture in new directions. (62)

**Baalbek** (centre left) was visited by the gentleman-amateur Robert Wood, later prominent as a politician, and sumptuously published in 1757. (63)

**Athens** had been shown in unreliable reconstructions by Leroy (below left: the Propylaea) in 1758; but in 1762 came the more scholarly survey (above: the Tower of the Winds) of Stuart and Revett, who went on to become the first architects of the Greek Revival. In 1764 Robert Adam published his volume on **Spalato** (below), a decisive influence on his own design for the Adelphi. (64–66)

An abstract style based on classical forms but dispensing with classical ornament appeared in the work of a few highly gifted architects at the end of the century. The interiors of John Soane's Bank of England (left) were classical in their basic disposition but completely original in most other respects—their smooth arches without pilasters or capitals, their shallow domes, segmental openings and sequence of intriguing spaces. (67)

Innovation and experiment marked the work of the two greatest French architects of the period—E. C. Boullée and C. N. Ledoux. Above: one of Ledoux's Paris *barrières* of 1784–89, too revolutionary for the Revolution. Left: Boullée's astonishing design for a cenotaph to Sir Isaac Newton, the patron saint of rationalism. (68, 69)

The revival of Gothic arose in England both as an attempt to harmonize with real medieval buildings, as in Hawksmoor's towers of Westminster Abbey (above), and as a romantic semi-serious essay in historicism. (70)

Two rich eccentrics built the best known examples of 'Gothick' during the 18th century: Horace Walpole's dainty Strawberry Hill (centre) and Beckford's huge and precarious Fonthill (right). (71, 72)

**England rejected Baroque.** As early as 1715 Colen Campbell, following Inigo Jones a century earlier, had looked to Vicenza, not to Rome, for guidance. Soon 'Palladianism' was the accepted alternative to Baroque in England and elsewhere.

**A Scotsman in Russia,** Charles Cameron, became leading architect to Catherine the Great and contributed his own notion of Englishness to some of her palaces. His gallery at Tsarskoe Selo (above) was added to Rastrelli's Baroque palace about 1780. For his interiors Cameron relied heavily on the mature style of the Adam brothers. (73)

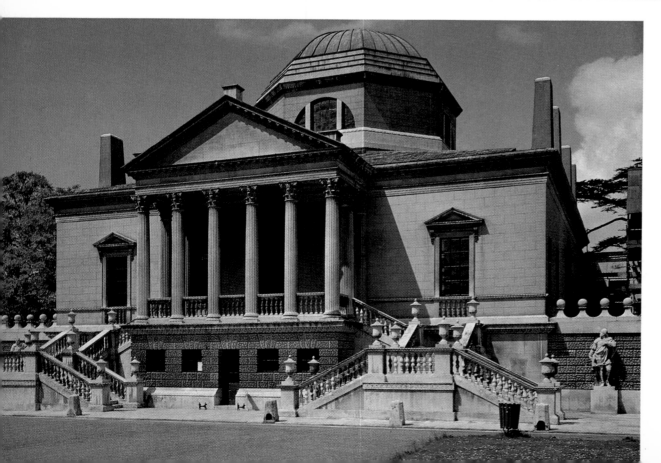

**The 'Adam style'** derived primarily from Robert Adam's archaeological interests. He went straight to ancient Rome for inspiration, by-passing the Baroque, by-passing Palladio, by-passing France, taking ideas from Spalato, Rome, Pompeii, Greek vases —as found in Italy—and combining them with consummate taste and fertile imagination. The result was essentially Neo-classical. The saloon of Syon House (above) shows his art at its richest. (74)

**The leader of the Palladians** was Lord Burlington, wealthy, talented and generous. In the grounds of his country home at Chiswick he built himself a miniature villa on the theme of Palladio's Villa Rotunda at Vicenza but with many variations. (75)

**In Paris,** the capital of Europe's most powerful monarchy, Neo-classicism assumed a more monumental aspect than in England. The great church of Ste Geneviève, now the Panthéon (right), marks the end of the French classical tradition. It was begun by J. G. Soufflot in 1757, though not finished until the Revolution. Its severity has been increased by the filling in of the original windows. (77)

**An elusive French quality** characterizes these buildings of the mid-18th century in spite of their strict Neoclassicism. In Jacques-Ange Gabriel's Ecole Militaire (above), it is chiefly the old-fashioned roof that betrays it. Bélanger's Bagatelle (below), though altered in 1860, reflects the aristocratic suburbia of Paris in the seventeen-seventies. Gabriel's Petit Trianon at Versailles (below right) captures some of the English Palladians' comfortable dignity but is still unmistakably French. (76, 78, 79)

Throughout Europe the vocabulary of Neo-classicism became standard for every sort of building. Colen Campbell's Wanstead (left), now demolished, had a Corinthian portico comparable in scale to a Roman temple. The Brandenburg Gate, Berlin (right) of 1789–93, magnifies the Athenian Propylaea (pl. 64) into a mighty Roman triumphal arch. Somerset House (below) by Sir William Chambers represents a union of Palladianism with the style of J.-A. Gabriel. (80, 81, 84)

For the State Capitol of the republic of Virginia (below) Thomas Jefferson adapted his favourite classical building, the Maison Carrée at Nîmes. (86)

Behind the plain exteriors of 18th-century London often lurked a surprising degree of luxury. Above: one of Robert Adam's interiors at No. 20 Portman Square. (82)

The 'Egyptian Hall' of Vitruvius and Palladio was realized in the purest classical style by Lord Burlington in the Assembly Rooms at York built between 1731 and 1732. (83)

**Extensions to Versailles** were carried out by Jacques-Ange Gabriel in a style that harmonizes with Mansart's. His two matching wings flank the entrance front (right); Mansart's chapel (one of his finest creations) can be seen behind it. Below: the Hotel de Salm of 1782–86. (87, 88)

**As the expression** of civic dignity Neo-classicism assumed a role which it retains in some quarters today. Above: the Ecole de Médecine, Paris, of 1769–76. (85)

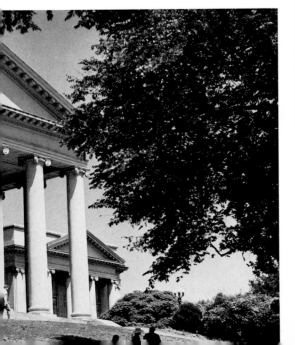

**The first modern theatre,** Victor Louis' theatre at Bordeaux (above) of 1770–80, set the pattern for the increasingly opulent opera-houses of the 19th century. Both the stone-built vestibule, with its staircase ascending in two flights, and monumental auditorium are in complete contrast to the Rococo frivolity that had been fashionable hitherto. (89, 90)

71

**The urban setting** of Neo-classicism became itself the expression of Neo-classical ideals. Baroque Rome had aimed at producing a series of exciting but isolated surprises; Versailles subordinated everything to the total scheme, worked out in terms of vast continuous vistas. In England the formality was relaxed. Beginning at Covent Garden, it became the practice to group well-to-do houses in squares, with more modest streets connecting them. The rapid expansion of Bath between 1725 and 1770 provided a striking innovation in the linked series comprising Queen Square, the Circus and the Royal Crescent. The town as a whole, seen here (above) in an easly 19th century vien, grew freely but retained formality in its elements. Above right: Hanover Square, London, laid out about 1718–20 and named after the new reigning dynasty. (91, 92)

**A Danish variation** of the *place royale* was planned for Frederick V (left) at Copenhagen. Here the corners are spanned by four identical palaces, formerly the residences of four Danish noblemen but acquired by the Crown in 1794. An equestrian statue of Frederick stands in the centre and the main axis is closed by the domed Fredericks-Kirke at one end and the harbour at the other. (94)

**The sequence of spaces** created at Nancy forms a uniquely fascinating piece of town-planning. In front of the ducal palace is an oval court; then a long open space, formerly a tilting yard; then a triumphal arch leading to the Place Stanislas (right), its corners closed by magnificent iron gates. (93)

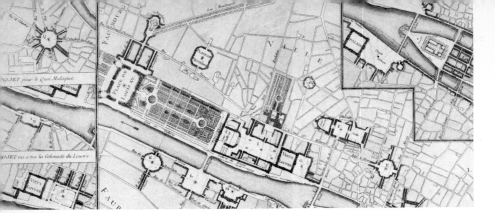

**The dramatic surprise:** Pierre Patte's plan of Paris (1765) incorporates over twenty projects for *places royales* to contain a statue of Louis XV. Each project is a Baroque explosion which virtually ignores the existing street plan. (95)

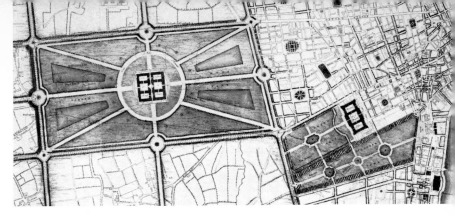

**The expected harmony:** John Gwynne's idea for the improvement of London (1766) represents a different ideal—the modification of the entire city to embody rational and continuous order, with a royal palace exactly in the centre of Hyde Park. (96)

**The Place Louis XV** as eventually built was designed by Gabriel and is now the Place de la Concorde. Two symmetrical palaces face the river. In the centre the King on horseback looked towards the Tuileries Gardens and the Louvre. (97)

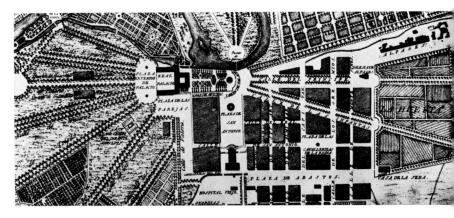

**To relate palace and city** was a task in which planners still followed the example of Versailles. Aranjuez, laid out for Philip V of Spain, again sets the palace between park and town, with streets radiating out into both. (98)

**Two riverside squares** integrating city and waterfront—the Praça de Comércio at Lisbon (top) and the Place de la Bourse at Bordeaux. (100, 101)

**The radial plan** of Versailles is carried to an extreme at Karlsruhe (left) where no fewer than thirty-two avenues converge on the royal palace. (99)

**When the new republic** of the United States of America decided to create a federal capital in 1783, the plan chosen (right) was curiously close to Versailles — the very symbol of absolutism. It is a combination of grid and radial lay-out, with the two main vistas, in front of the Capitol and the President's House, meeting on the banks of the Potomac river. (102)

**The pattern of the future** is foreseen most clearly in Ledoux's prophetic but largely ignored plan for the industrial town of Chaux, site of the state salt-mines (below). The centre, with the official buildings, conforms to a radial plan, but further out regularity is abandoned and streets are allowed to expand organically. French formality is here united with the looser more natural growth of such cities as Bath, but Ledoux was never able fully to test his ideas in practice. (103)

**The Picturesque** was England's contribution to 18th-century art—in literature and painting as well as in planning. The 'English gardens' that became a feature of continental cities during the 19th century had evolved in England during the 18th. Stourhead (left) was among the first and remains perhaps the finest. It was begun in the early 1740s by the owner, Sir Henry Hoare. 'Capability' Brown, the key figure in English landscape gardening, also worked there. The carefully contrived impression of wild nature is set off by 'architectural incidents'—grottoes, summer-houses, bridges, temples, artificial ruins and the like—designed to arouse pleasing romantic associations. Nearly all the leading architects gave their talents to these so-called 'follies', which often led to more serious historicist revivals. This view across the lake at Stourhead shows the 'Pantheon' by Henry Flitcroft. (104)

**The 'Chinese taste'**–*chinoiserie*–swept Europe in the mid-18th century, especially as a form of decoration for furniture and ceramics. The Chinese garden, too, played its part in the evolution of the Picturesque. In the royal garden at Kew, Sir William Chambers included a pagoda (above), as well as an 'Alhambra', a 'Mosque' and a 'Gothic Cathedral'. (105)

# Royalty, Religion and the Urban Background

JOHN SUMMERSON

APPROACHING 18th-century architecture as a continuous performance, abruptly curtained at 1700 and 1800, one seeks, in self-defence, some shaping generalizations. Here is one: the first half of the century was pervaded by the spirit and forms of the Baroque; the second was the age of Neo-classicism. With this goes another: the characteristic building types of the first half were palaces and churches; those of the second half private houses, institutional buildings and urban formations. These are useful generalizations and however much their pretensions are sheared away on closer examination, they are still not meaningless.

But what are we really talking about when we say 'Baroque' and 'Neo-classical'? Let us not pretend that either of these modern expressions can have a precise meaning. They evoke a certain emotional predisposition to what is being talked of and that is useful. Beyond that, the meaning must emerge in the course of exposition and in the comparison of the unfamiliar with the familiar. In the case of Baroque the familiar, for most people, belongs to the century preceding that with which we are concerned. What happened in Rome between Maderno's completion of the west front of St Peter's in 1613 and the death of Bernini in 1680 was of high importance to European architecture for at least two generations, though important in curiously different ways—sometimes in inspired acceptance, elsewhere in contemptuous rejection. These conspicuous happenings are connected with the careers of three men—Pietro da Cortona, Francesco Borromini and Gian Lorenzo Bernini himself. They, with Maderno, are the masters to whom posterity has learnt most especially to apply the word Baroque. Unlike as can be in their personal styles, they share a grandiloquence of statement, a mobility and sweep of invention which made them irresistible in their time and a challenge to every northerner who crossed the Alps thereafter. They summed up the whole past. They were the masters, not the slaves, of antiquity; they were the legatees of Michelangelo; they were the latest actors on the scene set by Bramante.

## Baroque: acceptance and rejection

When we cross the datum of 1700 the Roman Baroque scene must constantly be in our minds. Constantly, we shall be reminded in south German churches, of the plan-shapes devised by Borromini; often, in palaces, of the Roman façades of Bernini and the designs he made for the Louvre. An important point is that the Baroque masters were not looked back upon as academic models, to be imitated. They were liberators and the barriers they had broken were thrust down even further by the adventurous masters of central Europe—by Fischer von Erlach, the Dientzenhofers, Hildebrandt, Neumann, the Asams and Pöppelmann. In particular the originalities of Borromini, who tore apart the conventions of Bramantesque classicism and reassembled the fragments in results of shocking vitality, were the signals for these spatial adventures.

Now, the acceptance of Roman Baroque is scarcely less important in the history of 18th-century architecture than its total rejection. A significant instance is that of Colen Campbell, the Scotsman, who, writing in London in 1715, declared that the Italians had lost all taste for architecture in the pursuit of capricious novelties. Borromini was basest of all. He had 'endeavoured to debauch

p 82–83
p 44–45

Mankind with his odd and chimerical Beauties, where the Parts are without Proportion, Solids without their true Bearing, Heaps of Materials without Strength, excessive Ornaments without Grace, and the Whole without Symmetry'.

The Scotsman's rude intrusion brings us sharply to our next question—the meaning of Neo-classicism. In so forcibly condemning the Roman Baroque as wrong, what did Campbell recommend as right? The answer is simple. The foundations of architecture, he said, were in antiquity and the classic expositor of antiquity was Vitruvius; Vitruvius had found a modern interpreter of genius in Palladio; in England one architect and one only had understood this—Inigo Jones. So there was a triple loyalty—Vitruvius, Palladio, Jones—embodying (at least for the English) all architectural truth. Campbell supported his philosophy with the works (including his own) which he selected for his publication, *Vitruvius Britannicus*. He did not argue its merits at any length—merely stated, even rather naïvely, a view which he was confident would, in the England of 1715, be accepted. It was.

f 17

It would be wrong, of course, to assume either that Campbell's views are a precise reflection of the Neo-classical idea or that such views originated in Britain. What *is* Neo-classical in Campbell is his conviction that it was important, as he says, 'to judge truly of the Merit of Things by the Strength of Reason'. For Campbell, antiquity was rational and its revival was an abuse if its rationality was not respected. This view was not new. A literal acceptance of the antique as embodying all fundamental wisdom about building had been received in France and debated in French intellectual circles for a long time—at least since the foundation of Louis XIV's Académie Royale d'Architecture in 1672. Here the controversies between the 'Ancients' and the 'Moderns' had involved the head of the Académie, François Blondel, and the architect mainly credited with the east front of the Louvre, Claude Perrault. Perrault's annotated edition of Vitruvius on the one hand and Blondel's *Cours d'Architecture* on the other were texts which led to continuous debate and to the rapid propagation of the idea that there were vital distinctions to be made in the cultivation of classical architecture. The distinctions were, approximately, between a rational and a literal use of the antique—'rational' here implying a conception of the antique as having evolved out of building needs and being therefore capable of continued modification, and 'literal' implying an acceptance of antique forms as unalterable absolutes. Naturally, neither school of thought ever secured a real victory over the other; the important thing is that these arguments were sustained. The roots of Neo-classicism are intellectual, they grew in the asking of questions. As we enter the 18th century we shall find the questions being answered, and answered mainly where they were first asked—in France.

p 44 (7)

The part played by France in 18th-century architecture is not as obvious as is sometimes thought. Paris certainly enjoyed enormous authority throughout the century, but this was to a great extent carried on the momentum of Colbert's unparalleled triumphs under Louis XIV. The works of François Mansart and Le Vau—the Louvre and Versailles, Marly, the Collège Mazarin, the Invalides, the Place des Victoires, the Place Vendôme—had given Paris absolute architectural precedence in Europe. But all these belong to the 17th century, running a few years into the 18th. The

p 45
p 19 (14)

dominating architectural personality of the last phase—Jules-Hardouin Mansart—died in 1708. Then followed a period of thirty or forty years during which French architecture, in its general deportment, scarcely moved. The Académie and the Royal Works were in the hands of men who had been J.-H. Mansart's pupils or worked under him. Robert de Cotte was his immediate successor as *premier architecte*, Germain Boffrand the other most influential personality. These men embodied and preserved a tradition—the tradition which is perhaps best called French Classicism and which has its roots in de Brosse, the elder Mansart and Le Vau. They could, on occasion, be strikingly original. They did sometimes very nearly, but never quite, become Baroque. Their loyalty was to their antecedents and the test of loyalty was *le bon goût*. *Le bon goût* was an affair of combining common sense with acute sensibility, opposing mere fashion and proceeding (as Boffrand rather platitudinously put it) as far as possible from the good towards the excellent.

In this attitude was preserved the authority of the *grand siècle* with all its accomplishment but little of its ambition or invention, for which there were indeed, few opportunities. It was important, however, that the authority was there; French classicism remained a living force which was respected and frequently consulted throughout Europe. Only in England, wholly obsessed with the Vitruvius–Palladio–Jones equation was its authority ignored.

## Rococo and rationalism

Having said that French architecture of the decades following the death of Louis XIV moved very little, it must now be observed that in one particular direction it moved very briskly. This was in the invention of the Rococo. The style started quite distinctly as a grotesquely mannered version of Louis XIV interior decoration. This was disembodied and endowed with the aerial quality of antique arabesques. The heavy scrolls of the old style became snaky S-curves; the cumbrous panels dissolved into tenuous *boiseries*. Then came a phase of greater intensity. A brilliant young apprentice of J.-H. Mansart called Gilles Marie Oppenordt, was sent to the French Academy in Rome in 1692. There, instead of concentrating on the antique, he cultivated the marginal eccentricities of Borromini and returned to Paris with a singular knack of making the subsidiaries in a decorative scheme so energetic that the framework became redundant. Once this possibility had been disclosed there was no end to its development—no end, at least, until in the middle of the century, in the rising tide of Neo-classicism, it was laughed out of existence. For a time it was accepted in France even by men like de Cotte and Boffrand (for interiors and garden buildings only); the great exponents after Oppenordt were Meissonnier and Cuvilliès. Cuvilliès took the style to Munich, where it flourished into a school, distinctly different from what had been accepted in Paris and with a spectacular radiance. Every court in Europe had its Rococo phase. Even England was not totally immune; and there is some pretty Rococo in Ireland.

But apart from the grand manner of French Classicism and apart from the invention of Rococo there was something else going on in France in the early years of the century, barely noticed at the time but of far greater importance for the future. This was a new philosophical radicalism which emerged from the theoretical debating of what constituted a rational architecture. The first clear, totally radical, voice was that of the Abbé de Cordemoy who, in 1706, published his *Nouveau Traité de toute l' Architecture*. In this, he proposed a system of a revolutionary kind. The whole Renaissance tradition of architectural expression by the modelling of façades into *representations* of architecture (e.g. pilasters, half-columns, false pediments) was to be dethroned. More than that, arches were to be abandoned. Architecture was to return to what Cordemoy conceived to be the Greek mode—and the Greek limitations. It was to be column-and-lintel architecture, with rigorous articulation of all elements and little or no ornament.

A philosophy of this sort issuing in what was still the age of Jules-Hardouin Mansart could not be expected to have a very immediate impact on practical architecture. Cordemoy, however, had issued a challenge which was full of meaning. In a way it was like the challenge of the Rococo—but an opposite sort of challenge. The Rococo offered an immediate visual escape from tradition into

*The idea of the 'primitive hut' had been common to architectural theorists since Vitruvius, but Laugier was the first to illustrate it as a symbol of the idea that the classical orders should be used as functional, not merely plastic, elements. His emphasis on rational procedure in architecture was what less well publicized theorists had been advocating since early in the century. (1)*

a free world of linear romance; and Rococo was allowed to roam delightfully and safely in the salons and galleries. Cordemoy's theory offered no way of escape short of an undermining of the whole tradition of academic rules and *le bon goût*.

The eventual outcome of Cordemoy's thesis was the explosion of opinion in the middle of the century set off by another French cleric, the Abbé Laugier, whose *Essai sur l' Architecture* of 1752, borrowing extensively from Cordemoy became immediately popular, was translated into English and German, and was a textbook for those various lines of development which we now bracket together under the heading of Neo-classicism. Neo-classicism involves, as we shall see, far more than text-book theories. It involves archaeological investigation on the one hand and a release of imaginative invention on the other; it involves the puritanism of the English Palladians and the vertiginous romancing of Piranesi. But at the centre of it all is the Cordemoy-Laugier thesis of architecture as a totally rational system—as arguably functional as the wooden cabin which primitive man may be conceived to have built to keep himself dry. The germ of thought released by Cordemoy into the Renaissance-Baroque world of 1706 multiplied itself into a force which survived the extinction of that world and, in the long run, re-orientated architecture in a way which made the uneasy revolutions of the 19th century inevitable and the conclusions of the 20th possible.

## Three royal palaces

In 1700, three great royal palaces were being built—in Vienna, Stockholm and Berlin. If we glance at the incentives behind these, and consider the architectural results we shall understand something of the nature of palace-building in the 18th century. Take Vienna first. Under the Emperor Leopold I the city finally disposed of the Ottoman menace and after the relief of Vienna in 1683 there was a surge of optimism and national consciousness at once reflected in building activity. The two grand criteria for the builders were Paris and Rome and by 1691 a Viennese writer was

p 46–47
(10, 11)

boasting that the city surpassed the first and at least equalled the second. In 1695 the imperial palace of Schönbrunn was begun. It was outside the city—a Viennese Versailles—and the clear intention was to invest the imperial dignity with a symbol no less striking than Versailles. The architect was J. B. Fischer von Erlach, the son of a mason-sculptor and himself first a sculptor, who had spent twelve years in Italy. A clue to his attitude and to the atmosphere in which he worked is given by the remarkable book which he published towards the end of his life, the *Entwurf einer historischen Architektur* (1721). It is a pictorial history of the world's architecture containing besides reconstructions of the seven wonders of the world, all sorts of unexpected things, such as Stonehenge, Santa Sophia at Constantinople and the city of Peking. To these are added splendid engravings of Fischer's own works. It is obviously the composition of a man who saw himself at the very apex of all architectural performance up to his time.

*f 3*

Schönbrunn echoes Versailles in its plan, its great gallery and likewise in the lengthy (but not nearly so nauseatingly so) parade of pilasters on the garden front. It also seems to echo Fischer's idea,

*f 2*

as he gives it to us in his book, of what the Golden House of Nero looked like in antiquity. In other words, one might say that Schönbrunn is politically connected with Versailles and romantically with imperial Rome.

Rome and Paris, Paris and Rome—these were the foci of the architects' imaginations—though Rome meant Bernini more often than it meant the Caesars. This we see at Stockholm. Charles XI of Sweden had, in 1693, been explicitly recognized as holding supreme power and with a long series of military successes behind him an analogy with Louis XIV was not fatuous. Moreover, Charles had reduced the power of the Swedish aristocracy (as Louis had the French); his absolutism was of a kind which enforced the expediency of a powerfully representational setting. He was not a man of much culture but he had a remarkable architect—Nico-

demus Tessin II. Son of an earlier court architect, Tessin had studied in Rome under Bernini and had visited Paris in 1687. He was soon set to reorganize the old Royal Castle at Stockholm but in 1697 this was burnt down. In the same year Charles XI died and in the peaceful first three years of Charles XII a new royal palace began to rise. Being a town palace the model was the Louvre: the great court at Stockholm is about two thirds the size of that of the Louvre. The exterior architecture however is not French, but Roman Baroque, of a kind more loyal to its origins than any palace of central Europe. Bernini's Odescalchi and Labacco's Sciarra Palace are gravely quoted on its main façades. The interiors were delayed by Charles XII's wars but they are mostly French. Tessin brought in French decorators and craftsmen and after his death in 1728 his son continued the French ways. But it is as a Roman Baroque monument, a little out of time and far out of place, that the Royal Palace dominates, as massive and flat as the Quirinal, the city of Stockholm.

p 48 (14)

p 44–45
(3)

Berlin may well owe something to the Stockholm palace. Here, the incentive was the ambition of the Elector of Brandenburg, Frederick III, to acquire the style of King. He did so, in 1701, as Frederick I, King of Prussia. The building of a Louvre was a desirable preliminary. For this he employed Andreas Schlüter, a sculptor-architect of genius whose origins and early life in Warsaw are obscure. Schlüter planned a huge rectangle consisting of two courts, longer than the Louvre though not as wide (but exactly the width of Stockholm). He only succeeded in building one court before his dismissal as a result of the collapse of a too ambitious tower. The Berlin palace is no more; it was deliberately destroyed for political reasons (the reasons, in another context, for which it was built) in 1945.

p 15 (5)

p 48 (15)

With these three palaces—Vienna, Stockholm, Berlin—it is instructive to compare a palace that was never built. In 1698 the old Palace of Whitehall in London was (like the old Castle in

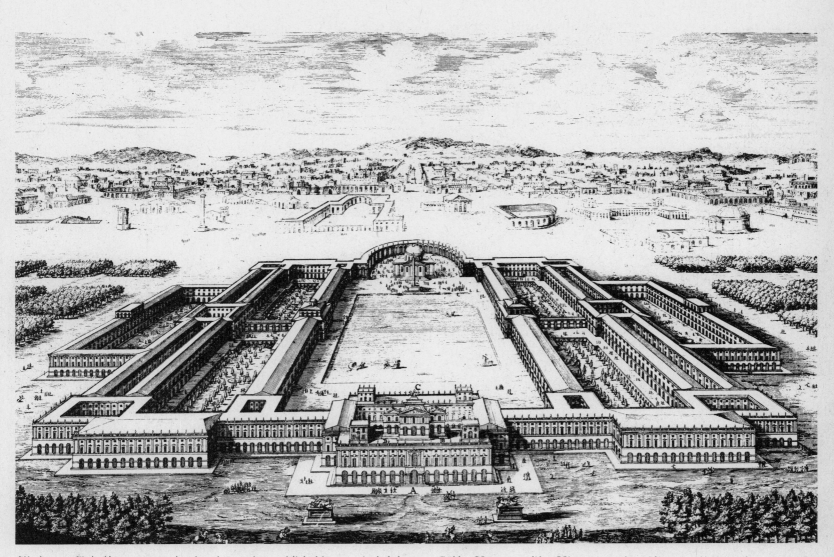

*Fischer von Erlach's monumental series of engravings published in 1721 included many reconstructions of historical buildings; this one shows his idea of what Nero's* Golden House was like. His purpose, he said, was to 'inspire the artist rather than inform the scholar.' (2)

Stockholm in the previous year) destroyed by fire. Immediately, the King's surveyor, Sir Christopher Wren, prepared plans for a new palace covering the whole site and incorporating the Banqueting House of Inigo Jones which had survived. That the palace was never built is not surprising: absolutism in England was extinct. But the plans remain as a project of extraordinary originality—less accomplished, to be sure, than Fischer or Tessin or Schlüter, but wonderfully expressive in their dramatic articulation. As at Stockholm, and to some extent at Berlin, the influence of Gian Lorenzo Bernini shines through.

p 48 (13)

## The flowering of German Baroque

These three—or, counting Whitehall, four—Royal palaces conceived at the turn of the century introduce an age of palace-building lasting for fifty years. Always it is Paris and Rome which supply the basic concepts (and sometimes, indeed, the architects) but in the German-speaking lands there emerged a few men of outstanding genius who conducted the Baroque idea into new and original paths. Three of these men were born within a few years of each other. Mathaeus Daniel Pöppelmann, a Westphalian who came to Dresden, was born in 1662. Johann Lukas von Hildebrandt of Vienna was born in 1663 and so was Johann Dientzenhofer, one of a family of architects in Prague who came to Bavaria and Franconia. If we seek names to set beside these outside central Europe we find in Italy nobody and in France only Germain Boffrand, born 1667, and he was almost wholly integrated in the Mansart tradition; but if we cast our net as wide as England there are Sir John Vanbrugh, born in 1664, and his collaborator, Nicholas Hawksmoor, born in 1661, who in spirit and even sometimes in form are singularly close to their German and Austrian contemporaries.

Of these names, Hildebrandt's becomes first the important one. He was an architect of a new type. The son of a German captain in the Genoese army he had no craft background but became a pupil of Carlo Fontana in Rome and studied military engineering. His great work is the Upper Belvedere built for Prince Eugene in 1721–22. Hildebrandt followed Fischer in many things but not in his romantic attachment to history. He was very much a contemporary designer, rarely using the conventional orders and achieving his effects by brilliant play with Baroque and Mannerist ornaments he had seen in Genoa and Turin. Then, Hildebrandt's Baroque dissolves swiftly into Rococo. His ornaments become the substance, as they do in the French Rococo of Oppenordt. The staircase at the Belvedere has no orders. The piers of the lower hall are crouching giants; the vault over the stair itself rises from 'terms' with human torsos; and the lines of the structure swim into a free play of plaster relief ornament. The exterior is necessarily more rigid but the glamorous modelling of every part exorcizes the rigidity of convention. Hildebrandt invented the Austrian Baroque-Rococo equation and it is seen in the Belvedere in full maturity.

p 47 (12)

p 49 (22)

Hildebrandt's work leads us easily to that of Pöppelmann and to his fantastic performance in the Zwinger at Dresden. Plans for a palace for Augustus the Strong, challenging Stockholm and Berlin, were made soon after he came to the electoral throne of Saxony in 1694. But wars delayed the project till 1709. By then Pöppelmann had taken over. He was sent on a study trip to Vienna and Rome in 1710 and the building of the Zwinger proceeded; the Kronentor was built in 1713 and the Wall-pavilion begun in 1716. The Zwinger is only part of a palace and a subsidiary part at that, its sole purpose being as a theatre for tournaments with a 'grandstand' (the Wall-pavilion) and a ceremonial gateway (the Kronentor). But there is probably no building in Europe since the Middle Ages where architecture and sculpture are combined with such immediacy. The architectural lines are remarkably rigid and in the proportions of the orders there is no serious distortion; but the architecture is deftly disintegrated to meet the flow of sculpture. The sculpture is the work of Balthasar Permoser but from the point of view of total effect it is difficult to judge where the architect stops and the sculptor begins. Virtually destroyed by bombs in 1944, the Zwinger has been successfully rebuilt.

p 52–53 (27)

The incentives to create a building of this kind are, in the case of the Zwinger, fairly obvious if we consider the almost ludicrous

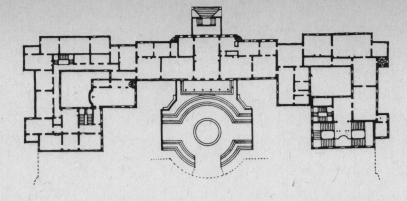

*Schönbrunn, by Fischer von Erlach. The immediate inspiration was Versailles, but Fischer economizes in length and introduces greater variety into his plan. (The view on p. 46 is seen from the garden, top of the page). The spaces in the middle of each wing are open courtyards; that on the right leads into the imposing 'Empress's staircase'. The palace was much altered later in the 18th century. (3)*

dynastic dreams of Augustus the Strong who, not content with Saxony, got himself elected King of Poland, losing and regaining that throne before his death in 1733. The patronage of personalities of this kind demanded nothing more profound than instant spectacle and spectacle of the utmost brilliance was what they got. Building was part of the power-game, which for an absolute ruler of psychotic energy like Augustus was the only game worth playing.

The mania for extravagant building we meet at every point in the age of palace-building. We meet it, for instance, at Pommersfelden, near Bamberg, where the Elector-Archbishop of Mainz—not, after all, a very consequential prince—confessed to an infatuation with architecture: 'building is a craze which costs much, but every fool likes his own hat'. Pommersfelden was designed by Johann Dientzenhofer, though not without the help of Hildebrandt who was responsible for the staircase. It was built in 1711–18.

p 48 (18)

p 49 (21)

It is in a house like this—not on the greatest royal scale—that one is drawn to consider the relationships of German Baroque with the two greatest houses of Sir John Vanbrugh—Castle Howard (begun 1699) and Blenheim Palace (begun 1705). There can be no question of derivation and yet the same spatial enterprise is there. Compare Dientzenhofer's immensely tall pairs of Corinthian columns, pushing up into the pediment and breaking it, with Vanbrugh's pairs of Corinthian piers at Blenheim pushing through the pediment to break even more violently the pediment of the hall. Compare, again, the way the Pommersfelden staircase is conceived as an independent cage, as is the hall at Castle Howard, though the one contains the stair while the other penetrates staircases on each side. One must suppose that architects of similar age (as Vanbrugh and Dientzenhofer and, indeed, Hildebrandt were) intuitively seek, in a given situation, similar emergences—even if they view that situation from opposite ends of Europe.

p 48 (17, 18)

p 49 (19, 21)

The whole question of Baroque forms as understood by German architects, comes most acutely to the fore when we reach the works of an architect more than twenty years younger than those we have been considering—Balthasar Neumann, who was born in 1687. Like Hildebrandt (and, for that matter, Vanbrugh) Neumann had some military experience before being taken into the service of the newly elected Prince-Bishop of Würzburg, who happened to be a Schönborn, one of the same family of prodigious builders to which the builder of Pommersfelden belonged. The Bishop had the same gargantuan passion for building and started the colossal Residenz at Würzburg in 1719. Neumann was his executant but the design passed through many hands, notably those of the great Boffrand in Paris and Hildebrandt in Vienna. Versailles, Schönbrunn and the Upper Belvedere are all reflected in this, the most majestic and accomplished of all German palaces. Neumann's own genius is especially conspicuous in the staircase which ascends in a single flight from a low, vaulted hall, dimly lit, then switches back in two narrower flights emerging in a hall over which floats one vast and fabulously brilliant painting by Tiepolo.

p 52 (28)
p 224 (12)

p 43 (1)

After Neumann, whose churches belong to a later section, the achievements of German Baroque—the counterparts in architecture of Bach and Handel in music—could hardly ascend further. Nevertheless, there is that ever-busy side-issue of the Baroque—the Rococo. This flourished supremely in Bavaria, thanks to the Elector Max Emanuel's discovery of genius in a French dwarf, Francois de Cuvilliès, who was born in 1695. He had him trained in Paris, then appointed him joint architect to his Court in Munich. The first purely Rococo pieces in Germany, distinct from the Baroque-Rococo of Hildebrandt, were the Reichen Zimmer in the Munich Residenz (1730–7). Then followed the summer pavilion known as the Amalienburg in the park at Nymphenburg. Here Cuvilliès brought Rococo decoration to a kind of naturalism which it never achieved in France; it was almost as if Rococo themes, artificially planted, had begun to grow of themselves. Here and in the Munich Residenz theater are the models of the finest German Rococo. Through his colleagues and imitators and through Cuvilliès' own engravings the style spread throughout Germany and beyond.

## Varieties of absolutism

In 1740, a monarch of equal celebrity as a political force, a military genius and a patron of the arts, succeeded to a German throne. Frederick II of Prussia had already revolted against the philistinism of his father's Court and taken as his architect the patrician Georg Wenzeslaus von Knobelsdorff. The King and his architect worked closely together, Frederick actually making sketch plans which Knobelsdorff interpreted in the light of his own talents which were considerable. He had been to Rome and, moreover, had mastered decorative art to the extent of being the author of the effective Rococo in the wing he added to Charlottenburg, one of his first works for the King. His next work, in 1741, was the Berlin Opera-House, a building which abruptly introduced into the Baroque scene an unexpected influence—English Palladianism. Frederick looked to England again when, years later, after Knobelsdorff's death, he built the Neues Palais at Potsdam—a rather sad derivative of Castle Howard. Meanwhile, the Stadtschloss at Potsdam showed an inclination towards Perrault's Louvre, while Sans Souci, the King's very personal summer residence at Potsdam, built in 1745–47, looked several ways at once. The entrance court with its Corinthian colonnades shows Knobelsdorff's tendency to a purer classicism. The garden front with its domed projecting centre is very evidently of Parisian derivation though the terms which support its entablature might, in their extreme Rococo animation, have come from the Zwinger at Dresden. The interiors of Sans Souci are similarly mixed. There is Knobelsdorff's severe Corinthian colonnade under the dome, but the music room is done in the perfectly accomplished Rococo of Johann Michael Hoppenhaupt. The stylistic varieties of Potsdam expose very clearly the restlessness of the 'forties—a restlessness beginning to be felt in all countries and which was only to be resolved in the renewed interest in theoretical principle in the next decade.

Palace-building, obviously, is part of the dynastic history of Europe and it follows that in countries where dynastic questions had been pretty well settled palaces were not built. Blenheim Palace is a freak which, in its very character as a gift to a national hero on the part of a Queen who built no palaces herself, underlines the truth of this for England. In France after Louis XIV palace-building was a meaningless proposition and the accumulated talent of French architecture sought outlets elsewhere. De Cotte and Boffrand were constantly in request at foreign courts. Boffrand, as we have seen, participated at Würzburg and his major works were the palaces for Leopold, Duke of Lorraine at Nancy and Lunéville, with the same Duke's country house called La Malgrange. The last two were never finished; neither was the palace he began for the Elector Max Emanuel of Bavaria near Brussels.

In Russia, under Peter I and his successors, the opportunities for immigrant architects were considerable. The first celebrity whom Peter drew to his new capital at St Petersburg was Schlüter, anxious for employment after the collapse of his Berlin tower. But Schlüter shortly died and Peter fared little better with the distinguished Frenchman, Leblond, who did, however, live long enough to provide the design for Peterhof and to train the first Russian-born

architect to practice in a full classical idiom, Zemtsov. But it was under Peter's daughter, Elizabeth Petrovna and her architect, Bartolommeo Francesco Rastrelli, that Russian Baroque architecture emerged as something with a character of its own. Rastrelli was the son of an Italian sculptor who had come to St Petersburg with Leblond and had thus been in Russia since the age of fifteen. He was sent to Paris to study under de Cotte, saw something of Germany and Italy and returned with a markedly Rococo taste. In the ten-year reign of Anna Joannovna he was set to reconstruct the Winter Palace as it then stood (the work of two obscure Italians) but his real opportunities came with the accession of Elizabeth in 1740. For her he completed the Summer Palace—a timber work, long since destroyed—proceeded to the Anichkov Palace (also destroyed), a gay, lofty building with a Baroque version of Russian domes on the pavilions, then reconstructed Leblond's Peterhof, doubling its length, and finally engaged on the total rebuilding both of the Great Palace at Tsarskoe Selo and of the Winter Palace at St Petersburg. In the last three of these Rastrelli had to cope with façades of preposterous length (that bitter legacy of Versailles). He divided them pavilion-wise and applied classical orders in quantity. At Tsarskoe Selo a lumpish Corinthian parades in three different heights; at the Winter Palace the Corinthian, fantastically elongated, balances over an Ionic and carries statues on pedestals at top, giving a sense of forced theatricality, a brutally literal Bibiena. Anywhere in Western Europe this would have been intolerable. In the tremendous water-girt flatness of St Petersburg it achieved what was needed, an effect of absolute, grim and careless dominion.

Rastrelli's palaces came later in the Baroque season; the Winter Palace was finished only in 1762. But, strangely, the last triumphant expression of the palace theme was in the country of so many of its sources—Italy. In the earlier part of the century there had been little occasion for palace-building. At Turin, indeed, the capital of the newly created Kingdom of Savoy, Filippo Juvarra brought French and Italian influences together in the Palazzo Madama and that tour-de-force in radial planning, the castle of Stupinigi, built in 1729–33. And from Turin, Juvarra gave the plans for the palaces of Mafra for John V of Portugal and of Madrid for Philip V of Spain. But the last episode in our story takes place at Naples.

Naples, after 230 years of delegated rule, obtained a dynasty of her own with the ascent to the throne in 1734 of the Bourbon Charles III. Twenty-five years of enlightened despotism followed with Charles entrenching his power on the classic model of his forbear, Louis XIV. The creation of a Neapolitan Versailles was predictable and it was for this that he called Luigi Vanvitelli from Rome in 1751. Between that year and 1774 the palace of Caserta was built. It is famous for its size. There are said to be 1,200 rooms

p 65 (61)
p 65 (60)

p 17 (10)

p 53 (29)

p 50 (23)
p 50 (25)
p 50 (24)

p 51 (26)

p 48 (16)

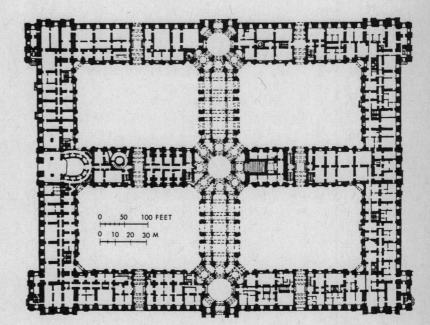

*Caserta, the royal palace outside Naples, by Vanvitelli, combines French grandeur with ideal Italian symmetry. Its huge rectangle is subdivided by four arms, two of them open colonnades. The staircase leads from the central octagon.* (4)

and the rigid lines of the lay-out stretch over the countryside as far as the eye can reach. But Caserta is not really on the Versailles model. Its plan—a cross within a rectangle providing four huge and identical inner courts—has something of the character of the Escorial and earlier 'ideal' plans of the Renaissance. In the architectural treatment, certainly, French Classicism is thoroughly reflected but in the monumental parts of the interior there is something different again—a contrivance (arising from the plan) of dramatic Baroque perspectives which remind one of Piranesi. Caserta is a splendid fusion, on Italian soil, of Italian and French skills, addressed to the palace problem in the last years when that problem could still be taken with immense seriousness and at unlimited expense.

f 4

p 49 (20)

## The expression of faith

The obvious division between the Catholic and Protestant worlds of the 18th century ought, one feels, to be reflected in obvious distinctions of plan and style in their respective religious buildings. It is, indeed, so reflected but with all sorts of subtle and intriguing distortions. As a wide generalization it is fair to say that high Baroque adventure belongs to the Catholic world and restrained classicism to the Protestant. Yet in London, under Anne, distinctly Baroque churches were being designed, while one of the first churches north of the Alps to have a classically Roman portico was the imperial Karlskirche in Vienna, begun by Fischer von Erlach in 1716. If, by a little special pleading one claims for the dome of St Paul's in London (finished 1709) a Protestant-classical sobriety, what Catholic element is discoverable in the still more restrained, more classical dome of Ste Geneviève, Paris (now the Panthéon), deriving from St Paul's fifty years later? The truth is, of course, that on the Protestant side, by 1700, the need for a distinctive architectural attitude had in most (though not all) parts of Europe somewhat faded. In England, both Inigo Jones and Wren had, long since, made their Protestant statements—Jones in his Tuscan temple at Covent garden (1630) and Wren in his galleried halls built after the London Fire of 1666. In Holland, Hendrick de Keyser had produced his Greek-cross model (the Noorderkerk, Amsterdam) by 1620. In France, where Protestant architecture was to have no future, Salomon de Brosse had in 1623 proposed a noble prototype in the form of a basilica. Some of these were departures of enduring importance but their lasting effect was in plan-form rather than style.

p 54 (34)
p 224 (10)
f 7

p 69 (77)

In the Catholic world there was no challenge to produce new types at a basic level. The challenge to Catholicism was of a different order—to reinforce and extend received traditions and to demonstrate with the utmost force the church's transcendental role. This was the sanction of the Baroque as it had flourished in Rome under Urban VIII and his three successors—the Baroque of Bernini, Borromini and Cortona. This Baroque was not the art of the Counter-Reformation but the art of the situation which it brought about. It was an art with a wholly new function: nothing less than the immediate conveyance through the senses and by the rhetoric of the combined arts, of religious illumination. By 1700 this new function had been fully demonstrated in Italy. In the next half century it was demonstrated again and again in central Europe in performances of the utmost brilliance.

It is in Austria and Bohemia that we see the first of the new Baroque episodes and in both countries the way had been prepared by immigrant Italians. We have already observed how the works of Bernini and Borromini inspired the palace builders. In church building they were no less a source of wonder and emulation. Bernini's oval church of S. Andrea al Quirinale in Rome is echoed time and again in transalpine plans. Borromini's little masterpiece, S. Carlo alle Quattro Fontane, with its sense of instantaneity, of dramatically arrested motion, was perhaps the most compelling influence of all. We see its effect at once in Fischer von Erlach's churches in Salzburg, built at the end of the 17th century. We see it again in churches in Prague with which the name of Christoph Dientzenhofer is associated. At Gabel in northern Bohemia, Lucas von Hildebrandt, the architect of the Belvedere, introduced the 'three-dimensional arch' (curved in plan as well as in elevation) which Guarini, Borromini's Piedmontese follower, had made famous at S. Lorenzo in Turin and which was to travel far through

f 5

p 45 (4)
f 6

p 54 (33)

p 58 (49)
f 8

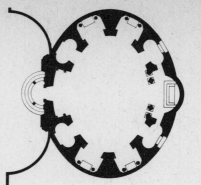

*S. Andrea al Quirinale, Rome, by Bernini: an oval 'Pantheon' whose porch and altar on the short axis dramatically oppose the thrust of the longer axis. (5)*

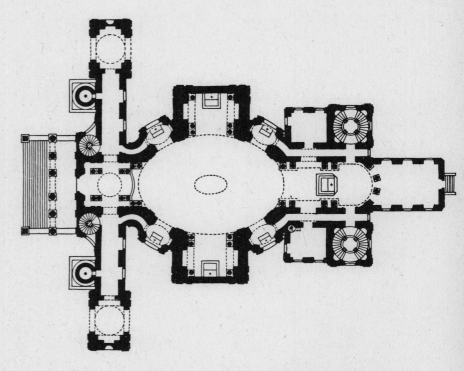

*S. Carlo alle Quattro Fontane, Rome, by Borromini: undulating walls, based on a diagram of triangles within circles, connect by subtle modulations with an oval dome. (6)*

*The Karlskirche, Vienna, by Fischer von Erlach: cumulative in its plan and theatrical in its style, the design forms a series of varying dramatic episodes. (7)*

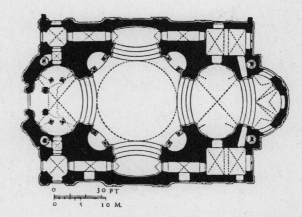

*St Laurence, Gabel, by Hildebrandt: a dome stands over 'three-dimensional' arches, curved on plan as well as in elevation. (8)*

central Europe. The originality and daring of these new interpretations of the Baroque is astonishing. Dientzenhofer especially, an illiterate mason of German origin, seized the Baroque ideas and handled them with all the authority of a Gothic master of two centuries earlier. Moreover, in his church of the Benedictines at Breunau, near Prague, he achieved that identity of architecture and fresco-painting which, deriving ultimately from S. Ignazio in Rome, runs through the whole of central European Baroque and is even more striking in church interiors than in the staircases and halls of the palaces.

From these beginnings in Austria and Bohemia the new church art spread into Franconia, Swabia, Switzerland, Bavaria and Saxony. Its carriers were the monastic orders. The monasteries of central Europe had, in the late 17th century, entered a period of considerable affluence. While their responsibilities, if anything, diminished their landed wealth increased and when ably administered they had much the same potential for building enterprise as the greater nobility. Countless Benedictine, Cistercian and Premonstratension houses rebuilt themselves in whole or in part, often on a scale and with a cumulative effect not inferior to great palaces. One conspicuous palace-monastery Europe already had in Philip II's Escorial. The greater monasteries of Austria and Germany are its later and far less dour equivalents.

Leonard Dientzenhofer, a brother of Christoph, rebuilt the hill-sited monastery of St Michael at Bamberg in 1696–1702 and that of Schönthal in Württemberg in 1700–13. Another brother, Johann, rebuilt in 1710–18 the monastery church at Banz, again on a spectacular hill top site over the Main. Here the Dientzenhofer genius struck a new note. The nave vault is a system of interlaced ovals with differential emphasis at succeeding levels, so contrived that the physical vault seems to gape apart to reveal a heavenly vault where events from the Old and New Testament are depicted. On the one hand, here is a brilliant variation on a Borrominesque idea; but on the other a revival of that plastic ingenuity which belongs to Bohemian Gothic, a style for which the Dientzenhofers must have had a deep respect.

The Dientzenhofers were a family of working masons and it is characteristic of much of the monastic building of the period that the designers came from this artisan class and were not of the courtly type like Hildebrandt, whose education was theoretical and connected with military affairs. Thus, at the great Benedictine monastery of Melk, towering over the Danube, the presiding architect was Jakob Prandtauer, a sculptor-mason, neither travelled nor deeply read. He replanned the whole monastery on its old site, placing the church on an axis between converging wings, with its towered west end standing over a court which grows bastion-like from the rock. In such a building it becomes evident that an ambitious abbot could have not only the same resources but the same addiction as any prince to the sheer lust for architectural performance.

In Bavaria, monastic patronage ran parallel with the Court patronage of the Elector, Max Emanuel, mentioned in a previous section. Max Emanuel's triumph was to bring Effner and Cuvilliès to Munich and foster the creation of Bavarian Rococo. In church architecture, patronage was in the hands of Benedictine abbots, the great artistic personalities being the brothers Cosmas Damian Asam and Egid Quirin Asam. Sons of a successful fresco painter, both had been sent under episcopal patronage to Rome. Cosmas Damian became a painter; Egid Quirin a sculptor. Both practised architecture. But the architecture of the Asams is of a kind which flows so immediately and equally into painting on the one hand and sculpture on the other as almost to be an art peculiar to itself. Cosmas Damian expressed the components of his art as *architectura: scenografia: decus. Scenografia* is the clue to much of it. His abbey church at Weltenburg, begun 1718, is on the lines of Bernini's S. Andrea al Quirinale but Bernini's swift motion is jerked to a halt, light is poured in from mysterious sources and in a blaze of light behind the high altar a figure of St George on horseback rides into the church—Egid Quirin being, of course, the sculptor. Egid Quirin was also the creator of the astounding *tableau vivant* at near-by Rohr, where the whole scene of the Assumption is as it were photographically caught and rendered into an awe-inspiring sculptural group. Egid Quirin, in later years (1733–46), built in

p58(48)
p223–
225

f9
p58(46)
p64(58)

p64(56)

p59(50)

p223
(8)

p60(53)

p63(55)

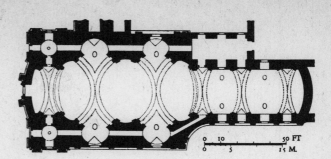
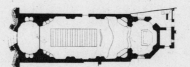

*The abbey church of Banz, by Johann Dientzenhofer: a plan in the Borromini tradition (see fig. 6) introducing an original play of ovals.* (9)

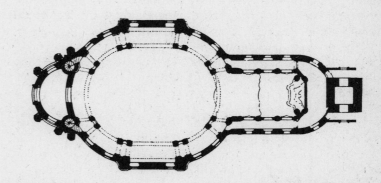

*St John of Nepomuk, Munich, by the brothers Asam: subtle scenographic effects compressed within a small area.* (10)

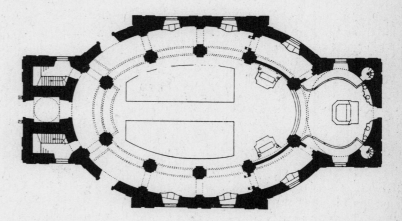

*Steinhausen pilgrimage church, by Domenikus Zimmermann: the use of the longitudinal oval may be compared with Bernini's use of the transverse oval.* (11)

*The pilgrimage church 'an die Wies' (in the meadow) by Domenikus Zimmermann: another version of the oval theme, in which a deep, narrow chancel emerges from a nave of conspicuous amplitude.* (12)

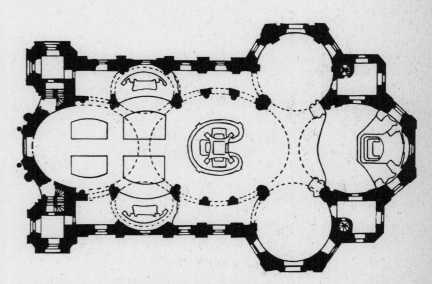

*The pilgrimage church of Vierzehnheiligen (Fourteen Saints), by Neumann: here, Barrominesque ingenuity in the handling of oval forms reaches a brilliantly harmonious conclusion.* (13)

Munich at his own cost and next to his own house a church dedicated to the then lately canonized St John of Nepomuk. Its narrow front is a sculptor's fantasia on themes by Borromini; its interior is again a fantasia this time with reference to Bernini as well. But these Romans are left standing, as the Bavarian sculptor dissolves their attributes into his own swift theatrical invention.

The brilliant Asams were in request far and wide, often installing their effects in the churches of other architects. Among their Bavarian contemporaries was another pair of brothers, a trifle older and remarkably different—Dominikus and Johann Baptist Zimmermann. Dominikus began as a working mason but rose to be an architect under Premonstratensian patronage. Johann Baptist was a painter and plasterer who acquired a reputation through his association with Cuvilliès at the Amalienburg. The two Zimmermanns together brought the Rococo of the Court into church architecture, converting it, in the process, into something far less sophisticated and, in fact, initiating the 'Bavarian style' echoed in so many hundreds of country churches. Their first important work was the oval pilgrimage church at Steinhausen, built in 1728–31, the very antithesis, with its quaint curly forms, of the Baroque sophistication of the Asams. But their triumph came fifteen years later in the pilgrimage church of Die Wies. Here, within a barn-like outer shell an oval dome rises from sturdy, angular pairs of shafts attached by arches to the walls. It is simple. But through the peasant simplicity blows a Rococo of fresh, almost naive invention, distributing its effects with unerring precision and lifting the peasant barn to a paradisiac level.

But the climax of monastic building in central Europe came when, under Cistercian patronage, Balthasar Neumann undertook the pilgrimage church of Vierzehnheiligen in 1743 and, under Benedictine patronage, the abbey church of Neresheim in 1747. Neumann was now, in his late 'fifties, the most brilliant figure in European architecture, with all the technical proficiency of the French school and a complete mastery of the innovations of the Bohemian and Austrian. Vierzehnheiligen stands superbly over the Main valley, with Banz, built by Johann Dientzenhofer thirty-three years earlier, on the opposite bank. The shape of Banz, we have seen, was based on a scheme of intersecting ovals. So is that of Vierzehnheiligen, but there the play of ovals is more elaborate and reaches a result which is not only more dramatic but, in its swaying continuity, exactly expressive of the church's double purpose—to embrace, centrally, a pilgrim shrine, while still culminating in a high altar. Neresheim, in the Swabian alps—a large straightforward abbey church—demanded a simpler solution and is therefore less complex, less mobile; it expresses with monumental felicity the conclusion of the Baroque story in central Europe.

## Return to classicism

During the first half of the century there is little else in Catholic Europe to approach the church-building achievements of the Dientzenhofers and Neumann. In Rome, the most sensational episode of the period was the competition held in 1732 for the façade of S. Giovanni in Laterano. Twenty-three architects took part and the winner was Alessandro Galilei. His design is related to Maderna's west front of St Peter's but the arrangement of the columns is in a more classical spirit and, in fact, much in the spirit of what was being done by Wren and his circle in England. As Galilei had spent five years in England and been associated with Vanbrugh it is difficult to avoid the conclusion that the new trend of English classicism was a factor in his success. Whether or not that is so, the façade of the Lateran church is a pointer to a change in Italian Baroque taste—a feeling for articulation as against generalization and a new objectivity towards the antique. Something of the sort is seen also in Fuga's new façade of Sta Maria Maggiore of 1741–43.

In Piedmont a short but really noble period of achievement opened with the reign of Vittorio Amedeo II of Savoy, who invited Filippo Juvarra, then at the height of his reputation, to enter his service. The result was a vast programme of palace-building, town-planning and church-building in and around Turin between 1714 and Juvarra's death in 1736. Two of the churches are among the most original of their time, for Juvarra, with all the experience and authority of the Italian tradition behind him, could still strike

84

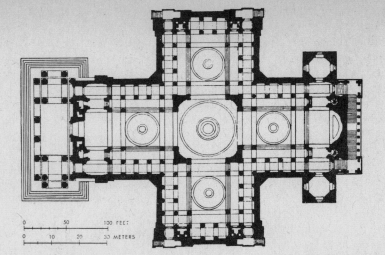

*The plan of the Panthéon, Paris, by Soufflot, represents an endeavour to rival the columnar audicity of the Gothic while using only the purest classical elements.* (14)

out inventions as daring as Neumann (his exact contemporary) on the other side of the Alps. At the Chiesa del Carmine in Turin (1732–35), for instance, he substituted for the traditional basilican section a section more nearly that of a northern 'hall' church with each aisle bay containing a chapel below and a gallery above, Gothic in essence but handled with faultless Baroque technique. High above the plain of Turin is Juvarra's masterpiece, the mountain sanctuary built by Vittorio Amedeo as a thank-offering to the Virgin—the Superga. This, built in 1717–31, consists of a rectangular monastery building from which projects a circular church carried upwards into a dome and forwards into a deep vaulted portico: no Gothic here but a wonderful new synthesis of Renaissance and Baroque experience.

Moving from Italy to France we again find that church-building is in no way comparable, either in patronage or performance, to that of central Europe. In France, as in Austria and Germany, there were indeed wealthy monasteries which employed their revenues in grandiose reconstructions by the best architects: the great Robert de Cotte, for instance, rebuilt the monastery of St Denis, as well as the episcopal palaces of Toulouse and Strasbourg (now used respectively as a town-hall and a museum). But France had moved too far from the Middle Ages to share that extraordinary union of spirituality and wilful extravagance which gave us churches like Ottobeuren, Vierzehnheiligen and Die Wies. The characteristic and significant product of 18th-century France is the new façade added to an existing church, a façade being a conspicuous and often costly gesture towards religion rather than a religious act. Such an attitude, in the age of Voltaire, is predictable. Most of these façades are based on Italian or Mansartian prototypes but it happens that one of them—that of St Sulpice, Paris—was a monument of considerable originality and influence. The architect here was J. N. Servandoni, a Florentine by birth with an anonymous French father, and he won the commission in a competition of 1732—the very year, as it happens, of the competition for the new façade of S. Giovanni Laterano in Rome. By a further coincidence, Servandoni's façade, like Galilei's, was affected by English influence and was in its first version, a paraphrase of the west front of St Paul's. In execution, however, it was greatly modified and its success has less to do with Wren than with Servandoni's concern to exhibit a grandiose and loyal interpretation of the Roman orders.

An intellectual thread of a different kind runs through some French church-building, arising from a lively but totally unromantic concern with Gothic. Louis XIV himself had dictated Gothic for the new west front of Ste Croix, Orléans, in 1709; but this was a grand irrelevance, for the new thought turned on the interpretation of Gothic ideas in classical language. There are, here and there, churches with immensely elongated classical columns supporting thin Roman vaults or domes. The most breathtaking of these is Nicolas Nicole's church of the Madeleine at Besançon where a soaring Gothic effect is obtained with the minimum of distortion in the classical elements. The integration of Classical and Gothic principles had become, by the middle of the century, an important

f 10
p 59
(51, 52)

f 11

f 12
p 61–62
(54)

p 64 (59)

f 9

f 13

p 54 (30)

p 22 (20)

p 56 (43)

p 56 (42)

p 54 (31)

p 54 (32)

f 14
p 69 (77)
aspect of emergent Neo-classicism. In the church of Ste Geneviève, Paris, later to become secularized as the Panthéon, it reaches a climax. The church was designed for Louis XV by Jacques Germain Soufflot in 1757–58, by which time the ideas of Cordemoy had been taken over and effectively propagated by Laugier. At Ste Geneviève, Soufflot attempted and very nearly achieved Laugier's ideal of a classical building of the utmost purity which nevertheless embodies the structural integrity of a vaulted Gothic cathedral. It is the first great church of the 18th century to stand completely outside the Baroque.

It is perhaps characteristic of 18th-century France that while in general there was no great incentive towards church-building, some of the churches built had a high philosophical, innovating importance. In Spain, on the other hand, the cultural bankruptcy reached under the last Habsburgs continued into the century of Bourbon rule. What distinguishes church architecture in Spain under Philip V is a violent intensification of some of the more neurotic aspects of Italian Mannerism, especially the destruction of conventional forms by a coruscation of ornamental detail. The naïve desire to produce amazement in the mind of the observer by leaving no surface, no edge undistorted is found in Germany but never with the same obsessional completeness as in the works associated with the Churriguera family in Spain. José de Churriguera, who died in 1725, was the most eminent but it was his brothers, his children and his followers who pushed the style to its most shocking extremes—in such works, for instance, as the sacristy of the Carthusian monastery at Granada begun by Luis de Arévalo in 1727. This kind of puzzle-work has a connection with Spain's own complicated 'Plateresque' of the 16th century. It has been suggested that its bizarre character may have been reinforced by acquaintance with the ancient art of Mexico but apart from the perpetual zig-zagging of cornices there is little to support this idea; and Arévalo's decomposed pilasters at Granada are not all that much stranger than those given in the etchings of Wendel Dietterlin published at Nuremberg in 1594–98 and very widely circulated. In short, the Churrigueresque is something of a throw-back, perhaps nostalgically to Spain's age of glory. More easily linked with contemporary practice elsewhere is the art of the *trasparente*, of which the greatest Spanish example, in Toledo Cathedral, is probably the most effective in the world, more surprising even than the Asams' performance in Bavaria. Designed to honour the Sacrament and as a protest against the Jansenist heresy it consists of a flood-lit altarpiece in high relief for which the source of light—a chamber over a dismembered and disguised Gothic vault—itself contains a heavenly vision. Completed by Narciso Tomé in 1732, it conveys, as so much of the architecture of Spain does convey, an intensity of feeling overriding any deep concern with architectural form.

p 56–57 (44)

p 57 (45)

## The Protestant world

It will be seen that the history of Catholic religious art in the 18th century flows in a great tide from Italy through central Europe, with eddies and pools in France and Spain—Italy herself, the source of it all, lapsing into relative calm. The Protestant world suggests a different image—local fountains of endeavour, rising and subsiding in circumstances of varied kinds. Protestant churches were not built for the glorification of God but for the accommodation of his worshipping servants and in most Protestant countries such accommodation was amply supplied by the thousands of churches standing over from pre-Reformation days—their architectural splendours reduced rather than amplified. There was no incentive to rebuild such churches—unless, indeed, they collapsed or were burnt down. Outside such (not infrequent) contingencies the only good reason for building a church was that a congregation required it. Typical circumstances in which this might happen were rapid urban expansion or the incursion of a tolerated Protestant population in a predominantly Catholic nation.

After 1700, England undoubtedly takes first place as a Protestant church-building nation. The Great Fire of London of 1666 had produced a crisis which involved not only the total rebuilding of a great metropolitan cathedral (St Paul's) but the construction of more than fifty new parish churches. By 1700 the work of reconstruction was virtually complete but in 1710 a change of ministers

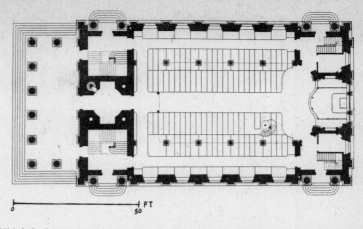

*Gibbs' St Martin-in-the-Fields, London, is a late comer to the School of Wren, strongly coloured by the Classicism of the Palladian movement. The portico is like that of a Roman temple but a Wren-like steeple, paraphrasing the Gothic, rises over the vestibule.* (15)

under Queen Anne brought about a state-patronized church-building movement, again in London but this time with the purpose of replenishing church accommodation in the rapidly expanding suburbs. In this new movement, the leading figure was Nicholas Hawksmoor and his six churches built under the Act of 1711 constitute an episode of singular originality and power. Much in Hawksmoor is taken from his master, Sir Christopher Wren, the genius of the post-fire reconstruction; but he had a strongly marked personal style, a feeling for the Roman Baroque, and an intense interest both in the more recondite areas of antiquity and in the architecture of the Middle Ages. He could combine, in Christ Church, Spitalfields, 1714–29, a Gothic broach spire with a Roman Doric portico. In another church, St Anne, Limehouse, the lantern on the tower can be read either as a paraphrase of the Gothic lantern of St Botolph's, Boston, Lincolnshire, or as a romantic reconstruction of the Athenian 'tower of the winds'.

p 55 (37)
p 55 (38)

Another English architect, whose ultimate influence in the whole English-speaking world can hardly be overestimated, was James Gibbs. He was almost the only one of his generation who had been to Rome and his first church, St Mary-le-Strand, London (built 1714–17 under the Act mentioned above) reflects his studies under Carlo Fontana. It looks like a Catholic church and we know, in fact, that Gibbs was a secret adherent to the old faith. The church was severely criticized and Gibbs' later masterpiece, the church of St Martin-in-the-Fields (1721–26) shows a very different approach. With its great Roman portico and its steeple in the style of Wren, it was accepted at once as a model church for Anglican worship. It was imitated throughout the British Isles, in the American Colonies, in India and eventually even in Australia.

p 55 (35)

p 55 (36)
f 15

p 162 (18)

It might be thought that so powerful and well established a school of church-building as the English would find imitators in Protestant countries on the Continent but apart from a few Wren-like steeples (that of the Sophienkirche in Berlin, 1729–35, is a good example) this was not the case. English churches tended to be built on the old nave-and-aisles model, often with a short chancel. Both Lutheran and Reformed congregations showed a marked preference for the central space idea as demonstrated in the 17th-century churches of Amsterdam and Haarlem and Johan de la Vallée's impressive derivative at Stockholm, the Katarina-kyrka of 1656. In Silesia, where, in 1707, the Protestant population was permitted to build churches, they are on the Greek cross plan of this Stockholm example, dictated by the patronage of Charles XII. The central space preoccupation led eventually to the one really powerful Protestant church, outside England, of the first half of the century—the Frauenkirche at Dresden. This was commissioned by the civic authorities of Dresden, designed by the city architect, George Bähr, and built in 1725–43 with the express intention of rivalling the splendours of the neighbouring Court of the Elector Augustus. It combined a bold handling of the central space idea with Baroque sensationalism of a high order. Out of a square body rose an immense and steep masonry dome, dangerously supported within on a ring of eight arches between whose

p 55 (40, 41)
f 16

*Though Protestant, the Frauenkirche at Dresden by George Bähr (destroyed 1945) was as daringly Baroque as any Catholic church. Eight piers supported the dome, round which seats and galleries were ranged as in a theatre.* (16)

piers galleries mounted like those of a theatre. From the corners of the square, delicate spirelets mounted against the dome. In the skyline of Dresden the church struck an attitude as fantastic in its way as the Zwinger. Its total loss in the war was tragic.

After the middle of the 18th century, the history of church-building in Europe, whether Catholic or Protestant, has no density or effective continuity. In every country, late 18th-century churches tend to be one of two things: either tired stragglers from an old and exhausted tradition or else surprising and even enthralling adventures undertaken in the larger context of the new architectural theories. What those theories were and the extent to which they established a norm by which all buildings, including churches, can be judged is the matter to which we must now turn.

## A choice of styles

Until fairly recently, the architecture of Europe after the middle of the 18th century was characterized as belonging to 'the age of revivals'. This prolonged the 19th-century notion that every age should have its *style* and that there was, somehow, something wrong with an age which had no style of its own but was obliged to borrow from another. It was not seen that the reproduction of an old style may be just as significant and 'historical' an act as the creation of a new one and may reflect a profound alteration of attitude to other things than styles. This was the case in the period with which we are concerned. The changes which became manifest in the arts about the year 1750 have less to do with style than with the complete reorientation of European man to his historic past.

Revivalism in architecture was hardly new. For three hundred years the architecture of the Roman world had been the basis of all legitimate endeavour. Roman values, in the way in which they were interpreted, were considered absolute. But this position was p 221 inherently unstable. Attachment to classical culture meant attach-<br>(6) ment to history and attachment to history meant the remorseless widening of horizons in every direction until the uniqueness of Rome began to dissolve in a more general and immensely more complex vision of the whole European past. By 1750, students of the antique had come to realize the priority and anticipate the artistic precedence of Greek art. With the extension of travel and the beginnings of practical archaeology the varieties of style within the Roman world itself stood revealed. Furthermore, students of medieval history were beginning to appreciate the seriousness of intention, if not yet the formal values, of Gothic.

At the heart of the new situation was the displacement of a belief in one authority—Rome—by the conviction that there were, or could be, a plurality of authorities—Roman, Greek, Gothic and, for that matter, Chinese and Indian. A plurality leads at once to the possibility of choice and, in this case, to stylistic eclecticism. This

or that style can be explored and exploited. This style can be combined with that style. And, most important of all, once the comparative study of historic styles is allowed to be legitimate, there is the irresistible analogue of a *new style*. This may be conceived as a personal style, a national style or simply as a rational abstraction from all styles. The way is clear for architectural revolution in a profound sense.

The word habitually employed for the architecture arising from this situation is 'Neo-classical'. This is misleading in so far as it seems to stress the archaeological and revivalist elements at the expense of the profounder philosophical and aesthetic character of the movement. Nevertheless, archaeology is of prime importance; indeed, the whole process of reorientation hinges upon it.

Systematic archaeological enquiry, as a development from the mere finding and collecting of antiquities, belongs to the mid-18th century. A landmark was the publication of the first volume of the Comte de Caylus' *Recueil des Antiquités* in 1752. Winckelmann's *Gedanken über die Nachahmung der griechischen Werke* came in 1755. Both Caylus and Winckelmann believed in the superiority of Greek art, with its 'noble simplicity', over Roman. This was not the view of Piranesi, the architect-etcher, who nevertheless did as much as anybody to uncover and display the wealth of the ancient world. Piranesi dedicated his genius to the pictorial reconstruction of Rome and the grandiose illustration of its ruins. His *Antichità Romane* belongs to 1748, his *Della Magnificenza*, championing the p 66 (62) grandeur and variety of Rome against the promotion of the Greek, came in 1761.

The collection of new material from the Greek and Roman worlds proceeded during the same years. Excavations at Pompeii, under Bourbon patronage, were begun in 1748. These, however, aimed at the recovery of objects and paintings and the architecture of Pompeii had long to wait for recognition. The monuments of Athens were more rapidly put in circulation. The Frenchman, J. D. Leroy, published *Les Ruines des plus beaux monuments de la* p 66 (65) *Grèce* in 1758, to be followed four years later by the first volume of Stuart and Revett's *Antiquities of Athens*. Meanwhile, Robert Wood p 66 (64) had led a party to Syria and published detailed records of Palmyra in 1753 and Balbec in 1757. In 1764 came Robert Adam's Survey p 66 (63) of the Palace of Diocletian at Spalato (Split).

In this greatly widening vista of the classical past there was a bewildering choice which, while it had the effect of reducing the authority of the time-honoured interpreters of Rome—Serlio, Palladio, Scamozzi and even Vitruvius himself—provided no new directive for the future of architecture. A new directive, however, was already there in the rational propositions of Cordemoy and his later popularizer, Laugier, mentioned earlier in this essay. Laugier, in his image of the primitive hut as the prototype of all architectural splendour was moving in the same direction as Winckelmann with his ideal of 'noble simplicity' in painting and sculpture. Both Laugier and Winckelmann acknowledged the supremacy of Greece although neither, in their crucial publications, possessed any detailed information concerning Greek buildings or, indeed, authentic Greek sculpture. And even when Leroy and Stuart and Revett had provided such information in their lavish folios it cannot be said that the impact on architecture was immediate. There was almost no literal imitation of Greek architecture on the Continent in the 18th century. There was a little more in England but the full 'Greek Revival' only commenced there after 1800.

## 'Noble simplicity'

The real nature of Neo-classicism in architecture is in a combination of the ideal of 'noble simplicity' with that of a rational application of the classical elements. With these ideals in their heads it was natural that architects should have continually before their eyes that ultimate image of nobility, simplicity and rationality which is the classical temple. To Laugier, the Maison Carrée at Nimes was the perfect building. Porticos, therefore, and colonnades of the strictest classical purity became essential attributes of churches and public buildings throughout Europe and it is these which have attracted such bored epithets as 'mere copyism' and 'cold imitation' to the Neo-classical movement. But in fact the spirit of the movement was far stronger than is evidenced by its specifically archaeologizing aspects. The very restriction to which architecture

*Mereworth, in Kent, is the Palladian circle's sincerest tribute to their hero. Designed by Colen Campbell in 1723, it is externally an almost exact copy of the Villa Rotonda at Vicenza. Only the dome is rather higher and more emphatic—its ribs cleverly utilized by Campbell to take the chimney flues. (17)*

submitted induced a new sensitivity to exact statement, unbroken surfaces, broad mass and clear-cut space. These were capable, as Boullée, Ledoux and Soane were to demonstrate, of emotional expression of a high order and of an extremely personal kind.

A striking fact about Neo-classicism is its international character. The reason for this is that it was not the stylistic product of a school of architects in one country but rather an ideological movement to which individuals in several countries contributed and whose principles were easily communicable. Laugier was French, Winckelmann German, Piranesi Italian and the reputation of each was, almost from the first, international. The doctrine of Neo-classicism, being abstract and general, ran against national traditions and in fact had almost extinguished them by the end of the century, when the architecture of Europe attained a uniformity which held until the coming of romantic national revivals in the mid-19th century. It is significant that Neo-classicism had very little to do with Italy. Piranesi apart, no Italians made any substantial contribution. Italy was persistently scoured by the grand tourists and its monuments, by now regarded as an international heritage, recorded again and again by students—students who also presented their designs at the Italian academies and frequently carried off the prizes. If we try to discover the roots of the Neo-classical movement we shall not find them in Italy, nor indeed in France. The first categorical revolt against the Baroque and the first architectural statements of the new attitude are to be observed in England.

Something has already been said of the movement towards a rational interpretation of antiquity led by Colen Campbell in England from 1715. Campbell's own buildings rely to a great extent on Palladio and one of them, Mereworth in Kent, is externally an almost exact reproduction of the Villa Rotonda at Vicenza. To another house, the demolished Wanstead, he gave a Corinthian portico of the full dimensions appropriate to a Roman temple. A disciple of Campbell's was Richard Boyle, third Earl of Burlington. Burlington was both a powerful patron of the arts and himself a fastidious designer. His own villa at Chiswick is a stylistic experiment introducing elements from Scamozzi, Palladio and the antique. A more daring experiment was the Assembly Rooms at York built in 1730 on the model of Palladio's reconstruction of the so-called 'Egyptian Hall'. Its classicism—which is to say its *Neo-classicism*—is totally uncompromising; it owes nothing to English tradition; it might have been built anywhere in Europe and at any time subsequent to its own and before, say, 1830.

Lord Burlington, with his friend and follower William Kent and a whole school of lesser men (James Gibbs being the only major architect not quite of their persuasion) succeeded in propagating his ideas to such an extent that English architecture up to 1760, at all levels from churches to farm-houses and common street-fronts,

*f 17*

p 70 (80)

p 68 (75)

p 70 (83)

presents an amazing consistency. The movement and its products are generally designated 'Palladian', but it must not be forgotten how many other influences it embodies—from Scamozzi, from Inigo Jones, from antiquity (through Palladio's eyes) and even sometimes from Wren and the Baroque.

The question of the extent to which English architecture of this time influenced the Continent is a difficult one. It may be a coincidence that in the two great west-front competitions of 1732—S. Giovanni Laterano, Rome and St Sulpice, Paris—the winning designs are more than suspect of containing English influence. In both cases, however, the influence would be from Wren and his school. Specific derivations from English Palladianism are rare. In France, the most obvious parallels are in the works of Jacques-Ange Gabriel. He was the son of Jacques Gabriel, whom he succeeded as *premier architecte* to Louis XV in 1742. In this office he built new wings flanking the entrance to Versailles, the Versailles Opéra, large additions to Compiègne and, in Paris, the Ecole Militaire and the two great palaces of the Place de la Concorde. Certainly, these designs move away from the exhausted style of J.-H. Mansart towards calm and precise statement such as one associates with Palladianism. On the other hand the modelling is always strongly in the French tradition and the calmness is that of Perrault's east front of the Louvre. Perhaps the only building of Gabriel's in which there is a germ of English thought is the Petit Trianon of Versailles. It is like a small Palladian country house, re-thought with all the expertise of French modelling and becoming in the end totally French.

p 71 (87)

p 69 (76)

p 69 (79)

p 320 (14)

## Beyond Neo-classicism

The really important French departures in the direction of Neo-classicism had nothing to do with English Palladianism and were made by a few original thinkers against the background of French tradition reaching back to Lescot, Ducerceau and Philibert Delorme. One of these thinkers was J. G. Soufflot who, as we saw in the last section, undertook to build, in the Church of Ste Geneviève (now the Panthéon), a perfectly articulated vaulted structure in terms of the purest classicism. It was an attempt, nearly successful, to realize an ideal set forth by Laugier. Nothing of this structural audacity was attempted again. Experiment took a different form in the work of a younger architect, E. L. Boullée, whose Hôtel Brunoy, built in 1772, opposed all tradition by having a façade in the form of a classical propylaeum with arches between the columns. But in imagination Boullée went much further than this. His executed works were few and his main contribution to Neo-classicism was in his theoretical writings and the astonishing series of designs made to accompany them. Boullée had been trained as a painter and conceived the idea that the full potentialities

*The rise of the Picturesque movement is illustrated by these two views of the same part of Stowe, Buckinghamshire, in 1739 and 1753. In the earlier one, straight paths lead away into the distance left and right, and trees and hedges are arranged in neatly ordered patterns.* (18)

of architectural form could only be realized, at least for the time being, in graphic representations of buildings. His designs begin with classical compositions of impossible size but in due course he begins to strip away the classical attributes and present us with naked geometrical masses in dramatic relationships. The most celebrated of these abstract creations is the proposed Cenotaph for p 67 (68) Isaac Newton, consisting of a sphere of something like 500 ft diameter, belted with cypress avenues and containing *space*, illuminated by stars, the latter contrived by minute penetrations in the surface. The tiny cenotaph itself rests at the bottom of the star-lit void.

Boullée might be dismissed as a superb freak if it were not for the fact that his influence counted for so much with the next generation. If we look through the published designs of those who carried off the Prix de Rome from their first publication in 1779 we find Boullée continually reflected and sometimes closely imitated. More important than this, Boullée was clearly the point of departure for one of the boldest innovators of the century—Claude Nicolas Ledoux.

Ledoux was born in 1736 and after a conventional training entered on a brilliant career as a designer of houses for the highest society, including one for Madame du Barry. Some of these houses have a rather English look but they are dramatically scaled and stress the hard edges of the volumes they contain. In 1771 he was appointed Inspector of the Royal Salt Works in the Franche-Comté and built the still partly surviving establishment at Arc-et-Senans. By this time he had developed an imaginative capacity as provocative and powerful as Piranesi's. Commissioned in 1784 to build the p 67 (69) *barrières* (customs barriers) of Paris he proceeded on lines of such p 326 extravagance that he was dismissed. He narrowly escaped the (34) guillotine and spent the rest of his life (he died in 1806) in following Boullée's example and expressing himself on paper.

Ledoux published his designs in a folio of 1804, sublimely entitled *L'Architecture Considérée sous le Rapport de l'Art, des Moeurs et de la Législation*. The book had been conceived long before and the designs probably belong mostly to the 'nineties. The import-

ance of the book is two-fold. First, in the absolute freedom which Ledoux claims for architecture and the calibre of his own performances within that freedom. Second, in his remarkable conception p 75 of an Utopian industrial city, fully elaborated and as fully expressed (103) in architectural projects. In Ledoux we see Neo-classicism transcending its archaeological terms and becoming the architectural equivalent of the thought of a Rousseau or a Condorcet.

Of Ledoux's generation no other architect attempted such startling innovations. French architecture still held to its long tradition and the *atelier* of Jacques François Blondel, where many of them (including Ledoux) received their training, inculcated moderation. Nevertheless, from about 1775, the general trend towards geometrical starkness, combined with an archaeologically-minded but sometimes bizarre use of classical ornaments is unmistakable. Patronage in these years was of a highly sophisticated and exacting kind with a strong predilection for brilliant novelties. Much talent was lavished on houses and villas in and around Paris, few of which have survived. Bélanger's Bagatelle, in the Bois de p 69 (78) Boulogne, is a notable exception. A sensational Paris building in its time was Jacques Gondoin's Ecole de Médecine of 1769–76 p 70–71 with its unmodulated Ionic colonnade towards the street, its im- (85) maculate portico and lecture-hall like a semi-Panthéon. Another was the Hôtel de Salm (now the Chancellery of the Legion of p 71 (88) Honour) of 1782–86. Among public buildings before 1789 some of the most prominent were theatres. Indeed, Victor Louis' theatre at Bordeaux, built in 1777–80, with its horse-shoe auditorium p 71 and magnificently ample lay-out of concert hall, administrative (89, 90) and reception areas is usually held to be the first great modern theatre.

### Art and nature

Paris can fairly be said to have been the centre of Neo-classical developments in the last quarter of the century. England, however, having established a sturdy architectural independence in the years of Palladianism proceeded towards Neo-classical interpretations p 28 (26)

*By 1753, although the rows of trees remain where they were, William Kent has softened the formality and the effect aimed at is one of sophisticated wildness. The little temple on the left, the so-called 'Rotondo', is by Vanbrugh, but altered. 'Capability' Brown worked at Stowe early in his career. (19)*

of her own. The most effective of these attitudes goes with the name of Robert Adam, the leading member of a family of Scottish architects who, after a period of four years in Italy, with Clérisseau as his tutor and Piranesi as a major influence, returned in 1758 to conquer London. This was at a time when the fashion for building enormous Palladian country seats was just past its peak. Interest in bleak and massive exteriors was giving way to a desire for new standards of interior elegance and it was in the re-planning and decoration of existing houses that Adam made his name. Adam's planning was an elaboration of Burlington's but the 'Adam style' meant a light and harmonious combination of themes from antique wall and vault decoration and from some of the 16th century Italian masters. It is seen at its idiosyncratic best in such princely mansions as Syon House, Middlesex, and Kedleston Hall, Derbyshire but nowhere better than some of his adroitly planned town houses of which No. 20 Portman Square (now the Courtauld Institute of Art) is the finest.

Adam was almost entirely independent of French influences. His chief contemporary and rival, Sir William Chambers, on the other hand, had studied under J. F. Blondel and modified the Palladian tradition a little way towards the style of J.-A. Gabriel. His principal work, Somerset House, London (a palace rebuilt to house government offices), is of considerable distinction but lacks the monumentality which English architecture had been able to achieve under Wren and his immediate successors. Indeed, neither Chambers nor Adam rank high as monumental architects and for this there is a significant reason. Political power had become vested in the landed nobility rather than the Crown and the English nobility preferred the country to the town. It was on their country seats that their money was spent and their interest in metropolitan public works was negligible. Furthermore, after 1760 it was the 'villa' rather than the commanding mansion which attracted interest and alongside this interest was a passionate interest in landscape. The landscape-gardening fashions of the English 18th century were, in fact, probably more significant in the whole European scene than anything achieved in English architecture,

with the possible exception of the English conception of Palladianism.

The English initiative in landscape-gardening was set off by the revolt of some of the literary figures of the early part of the century —Temple, Addison, Pope—against the rigid formality of lay-out inherited from the French and the Dutch. The result was the landscape-garden of William Kent, as seen at Rousham, Oxfordshire, and Stowe, Buckinghamshire. The principle of treating a natural landscape *as* a natural landscape but changing its character to intensify the effect was soon widely accepted. Between 1750 and 1780 nearly all the great English parks passed through the hands of Lancelot ('Capability') Brown who swept away the avenues and *parterres* and remodelled the grounds according to a vision of his own. This vision crystallized in a formula which embraced the new planting of clumps and belts of trees combined with the creation of new contours and artificial serpentine lakes. After Brown's death in 1783, a new leader arose in the person of Humphry Repton, whose theory of landscape-gardening is associated with the philosophy of the 'Picturesque' as expounded by Richard Payne Knight and Uvedale Price. Their approach was subtler than Brown's whom they criticized for failure to perceive the intrinsic character of each several landscape. To them this was the proper starting point, an 'improved' landscape being an original work of nature with blemishes and obstructions removed. It was from Brown and Repton that the phenomenon known as the *jardin anglais* spread throughout Europe. The Duke of Brunswick expressed an intention to lay out a park in the English taste as early as 1767. By the end of the century informal planting was a general practice.

Another factor which distinguishes the English scene from that of France and the Continent generally is the attitude towards Gothic. The French admired Gothic for its *hardiesse*, as a matter of structural accomplishment and were sometimes concerned, as was Soufflot at the Panthéon, to find equivalents in classical terms. When new stalls, pulpits or altars were required in ancient churches, they were in the prevailing classical fashion. This was not always

*68 (74)*

*70 (82)*

*70 (81)*

*f18, 19*

so in England, where a tradition of sophisticated 'modern Gothic' descended from Sir Christopher Wren. The west towers of Westminster Abbey were built in 1734–45; Kent designed a Gothic screen for Hereford Cathedral in 1742 and Gothic interiors for the Law Courts in Westminster Hall. This was a stylized Gothic with no pretensions to archaeological correctness. It was Horace Walpole who, in a long series of improvisations at his Thames-side house, Strawberry Hill, Twickenham (1748–77), introduced a Gothic revival based on historical sentiment and archaeological enquiry. Walpole's attitude was professionalized by James Wyatt who, in the last quarter of the century built quantities of Gothic country houses, 'abbeys' and 'castles', the most celebrated being the fabulous Fonthill Abbey, Wiltshire, for the millionaire romantic, William Beckford. It was begun in 1800–the harbinger of a century in which English attitudes to Gothic were to play a bizarre and conspicuous role.

Outside France and England, the history of Neo-classicism is almost everywhere dependant on what was happening in those two countries. In Russia, Catherine II was a patroness of architecture on a scale even more preposterous than that of her predecessor Elizabeth. The earlier buildings of her reign were either by French or Italian architects or by the two great Russians, V. I. Bazhenov and I. Y. Starov who had studied together in Paris and visited Italy. Later, in 1779, she took into her service Charles Cameron, a pupil of the minor English Palladian Isaac Ware; and about the same time the Italian Giacomo Quarenghi. The palaces and public buildings of these men were full-scale realizations of projects which in the West would have got no further than the paper sheets submitted in competition at the various academies. Bazhenov's Tauride Palace must, in its time, have been one of the noblest exemplifications of French Neo-classicism in Europe. Cameron's pavilion at Tsarskoe Selo—set, inevitably in a park landscaped *à l'anglaise*—is an ambitious but technically shoddy exercise in the Adam style. Quarenghi, in the English Palace at Peterhof, reverted to a severe Palladianism—less like Palladio, however, than like his English reviver, Colen Campbell.

What was true of Russia on a huge scale was true for Germany and even for Italy on a very small one. Everywhere there were Neo-classical stirrings but rarely the opportunities for their acceleration towards full expression. Everywhere, 'noble simplicity' was spoken of, everywhere parks in the English style were desired. But it was not till after 1800 that the full tide of Neo-classicism spent itself across the face of Europe. And by then the whole character of the movement had begun to change. Its inherent eclecticism had come to the surface, and if we look around Europe of the 1790s we can see it at work.

### Archaeology, abstraction and the exotic

Around 1800 there are three different characters in which Neo-classicism presents itself. First, there is the archaeological purism, which is the mainspring of the Napoleonic transformation of Paris—the work of Percier and Fontaine and, in England, of Thomas Hope and the Regency style—and which produced dramatic classical gestures such as the Brandenburg Gate at Berlin. Then, second, there is the quest of abstraction, dramatically exhibited in Ledoux's great work but more explicitly in some of the executed works of John Soane, whose first Bank of England halls belong to 1791, and most poignantly in the designs of Friedrich Gilly of Berlin who died in 1800 at the age of twenty-eight. Thirdly, there is the Neo-classicism which is not classical at all but which affects to be Gothic, Egyptian, Chinese, Turkish or Indian. If it seems absurd to apply the term Neo-classical to such extraneous products it would be even more absurd to pretend that they form an autonomous development. In all cases, wherever they are found, they are the work of Neo-classical masters, often, indeed, of the leading masters. It was Sir William Chambers, most prudent and academic of Neo-classicists, who designed the pagoda at Kew Gardens. At the other end of Europe it was Quarenghi who designed the 'Great Caprice' (a Roman arch surmounted by a Chinese tempietto) at Tsarskoe Selo. Most of these things we now regard as 'follies', but with questionable justice. Irrational experiments, undertaken for entertainment rather than use, they mostly were; but they were, equally, factors of disorientation, evidences of that sense of the

p 67 (70)

p 67 (71)

p 67 (72)

p 68 (73)

p 70–71 (84)

p 67 (67)

p 76 (105)

plurality of styles which eventually created the problem of 'style' which was to haunt the whole of the 19th century.

Of the three characters presented by 18th-century Neo-classicism, the archaeological is the most persistent, the most fundamental and, paradoxically, the one felt to be most rational. When Thomas Jefferson, after the American War of Independence, came to Europe and considered, in the course of his travels, the proper basis for the architecture of a new republic he found it, not in the contemporary architecture of England, but in that perfect exemplification of a Roman temple which was also Laugier's symbol of perfect rationality—the Maison Carrée at Nimes. Accordingly, when in 1785 designs were required for the State Capitol of Virginia at Richmond, Jefferson dictated a pro-style Ionic temple, divided into floors and with windows in its walls. It may not have been the most practical solution but it was the one nearest to the natural source of all architectural excellence. 'Noble simplicity' had crossed the seas.

p 70–71 (86)

### The urban image

At the beginning of this essay a rough generalization was proposed giving a 'Baroque' character to the architecture of the first half of the century and a 'Neo-classical' character to that of the second. More seriously considered, this clumsy division dissolved into a complex network of ideological and stylistic changes; but as a general shading it remains valid. If we now extend our view from individual buildings to groups of buildings and from groups to whole towns can we discern a parallel shading in what is today called 'town-planning'? Is there Baroque town-planning and Neo-classical town-planning? This is not an easy question. Towns of consequence, whatever the style of their dominating monuments, are in general much older than the 18th century and absolutely new towns are necessarily very rare. What we *can* discern is a change of attitude to the nature of towns—to the urban image. At the beginning of the century a town was regarded as an irreducible fact of nature—something which might be artificially limited or extended and into which new elements might be inserted but not as a totality capable of reorganization and improvement as such. By the middle of the century a more comprehensive attitude has emerged.

In 1765, Pierre Patte published a plan of Paris on which are marked a number of schemes by various architects for monumental *places* in honour of Louis XV. Each scheme is an individual, limited proposal but when distributed on the map they adumbrate something like a monumentalization of the whole city. Even more striking as evidence of the new comprehensive attitude is John Gwynn's plan for the reorganization of London in his *London and Westminster Improved* of 1766. This is, in a sense, Patte in reverse. Patte shows a number of separate monumental conceptions distributed on the existing map. Gwynn takes the existing map and by an elaborate system of street 'improvements' conducts the whole towards a certain degree of monumentality—what he calls 'Public Magnificence'. The differences between Patte and Gwynn demonstrate exactly the passage from one urban image to another —from the Baroque idea of dramatically planned features inserted into a town to the Neo-classical idea of a town considered as an organism capable of connected visual re-creation.

p 74 (95

f 20

p 74 (96

Baroque town-planning is necessarily related to the structures which figure most prominently in the Baroque age—the palace and the great church. But most conspicuously the palace. Among the palaces of the 17th century which served as models for the 18th, the Palace of Versailles takes absolute precedence. At Versailles, the successive labours of Le Vau, Le Nôtre and Jules-Hardouin Mansart had brought into existence not only a palace commanding the almost limitless vistas of a geometrically ordered park but, on the approach side of the palace, a town of corresponding regularity. Park on the west, town on the east, both converged upon the palace. Louis XIV died in 1715. In the same year Karl Wilhelm, Margrave of Baden-Durlach, began to lay out a Versailles of his own at Karlsruhe. It was designed for him by his military engineer, von Betzendorf. Here the wooded park is on the north, the town on the south of the palace. The radial ideal of Versailles is intensely exaggerated, no fewer than thirty-two avenues converging on the central octagonal tower of the palace, and the palace itself shooting

p 19 (14

p 74 (99

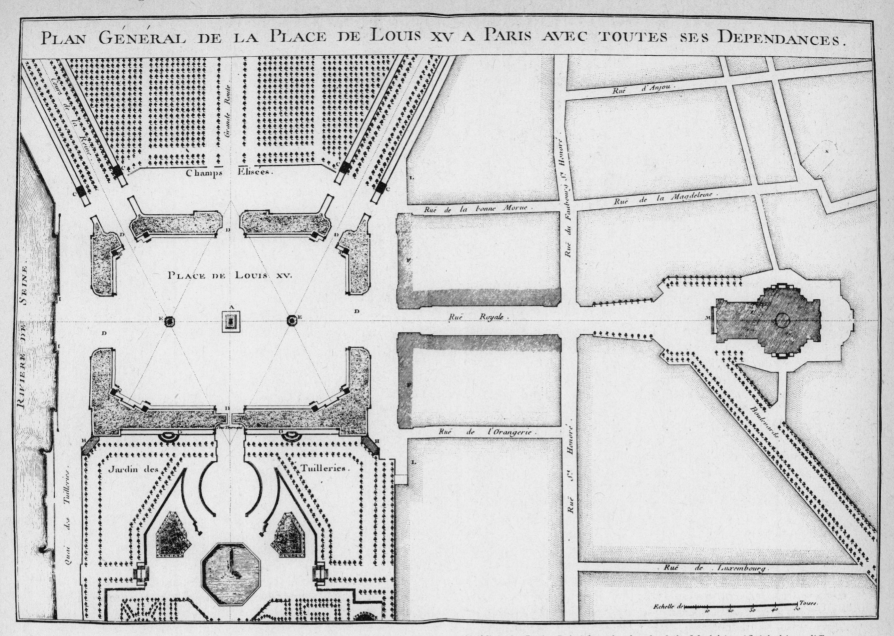

PLAN GÉNÉRAL DE LA PLACE DE LOUIS XV A PARIS AVEC TOUTES SES DEPENDANCES.

The *Place de la Concorde*, in Paris, originated in 1748 as a project for honouring Louis XV. It was built from 1753 onwards on the axis of the Tuileries and the Champs Elysées. It created a new axis, with new vistas—one between symmetrical buildings by J-A. Gabriel to the church of the Madeleine (finished in a different form under Napoleon) and the other to the bank of the Seine where the Pont de la Concorde was built in 1788–90. (20)

its wings into two of the urban radii. There is nothing here of the high sophistication of Versailles and Karlsruhe is a curiosity in which we may perhaps detect a survival of the 'ideal' city plans of the Italian renaissance.

Karlsruhe was never closely imitated, though the converging streets of Neustrelitz, laid out from 1733, and those of another Karlsruhe (Pokoj) in Upper Silesia are in much the same spirit and geometrically dependant on the princely palace. At Ludwigsburg, near Stuttgart, another *residenzstadt*, the new town built by Duke Eberhard Ludwig of Württemberg from 1709 is not subordinated to but laid out alongside the palace. In Spain the Aranjuez lay-out of 1748–78, for Philip V, stems directly from Versailles, with avenues radiating into the park on the west and into a newly planned town on the east. These radiating avenues appear again in St Petersburg (Leningrad) though here—in what used to be called the Nevsky, Admiralty and Ascension Prospects—they converge not on a royal palace but on the Admiralty building.

The emphatic visual dependence of a street plan on a building in which supreme authority is vested is a Baroque idea. Often the emphasis is of a purely symbolic kind and fades out quickly as we lose sight of the palace. Similar in spirit is another Baroque device —the *place royale*. This developed in France. The *place royale* is not normally dependant on a palace but is simply a formal area in a city, dedicated to the prestige of the monarchy and providing at its centre a site for a statue of the monarch. The first *place royale* was the one built in Paris under Henri IV and called Place Royale until it became Place des Vosges. Under Louis XIV came the circular

Place des Victoires and the octagonal Place Vendôme. Under Louis XV came a number of *places royales* in the French provinces —at Rennes, after a great fire in 1720, at Montpellier and at Bordeaux where the magnificent Place de la Bourse, designed in 1733 by J. J. Gabriel, makes a great spectacle on the bank of the Garonne.

Related in some respects to Bordeaux is the most famous *place royale* of all—the Place de la Concorde in Paris. Today, we are so accustomed to thinking of this space as a component—indeed, the central component—of the great formal framework on which the whole map of Paris hangs that we forget that in origin it was nothing of the kind. It started with a scheme of 1748 promoted by the civic authorities for a 'Place Louis XV' to honour the sovereign (this was the theme of Patte's plan already mentioned). The site was settled by Louis' gift of the ground westward of the Tuileries. A competition was then held (1753) for the lay-out but the final design was in large measure the work of Jacques-Ange Gabriel, son and successor of the Gabriel who designed the *place* at Bordeaux. His two magnificent palaces flanking the Rue Royale with the vista to the Madeleine originally commanded a space with a statue of Louis XV in the centre, bounded on all four sides by sunk gardens in relation to which the eight seated statues representing French towns were appropriately sited. It was only with the coming of the Pont de la Concorde in 1788–90 and the creation of the Rue de Rivoli under Napoleon that the Place de la Concorde lost its stately gardened isolation and became in due course the whirling centre of a planned Paris.

• 74 (98)

p 326
(35)
p 74
(101)
p 74 (97)

91

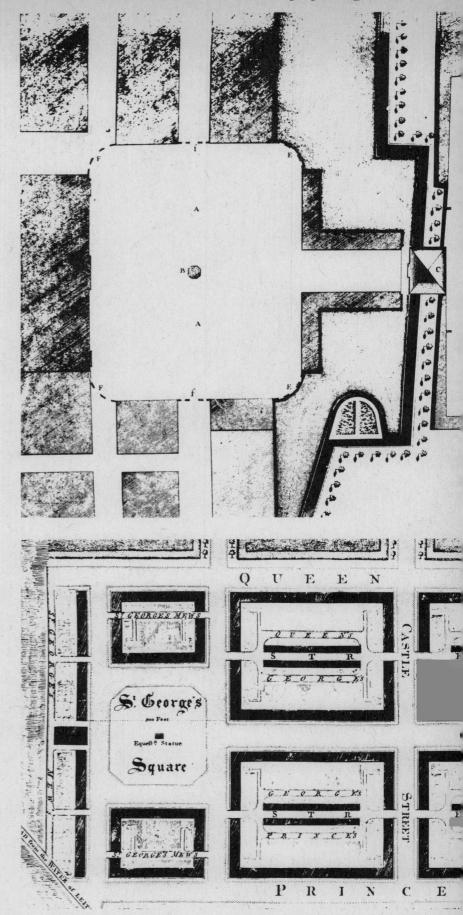

Contemporary with the Place de la Concorde is the Place Stanislas at Nancy, the capital of Lorraine. Here, Stanislas Leczinski, former King of Poland and by grace of his son-in-law, Louis XV, Duke of Lorraine, proposed the fitting tribute of a *place royale*. In this case, the *place* itself acquires special importance by its siting on the axis of an ancient tilting-ground at one end of which a palace was already proposed. Stanislas' architect, Héré de Corny, completed the palace (on reduced lines) gave it a forecourt with colonnaded hemicycles to left and right, designed uniform elevations for houses along the old tilting-ground (Place de la Carrière) and closed the far end of this with a triumphal arch, through which is entered the Place Royale (Place Stanislas). It is a wonderful sequence—perhaps the finest piece of formal town-planning produced in the 18th century. But the lay-out resulted from unique circumstances. Its character is still that of the traditional and limited *place royale* but its felicitous linkage with other emerging formal elements gives it the air of something more, while its architecture —delicately deriving from Versailles and the Louvre and enhanced by superb ironwork—is, in its own right, a minor masterpiece.

The *place royale* idea was not confined to France. We find it magnificently expressed in the Amalienborg at Copenhagen, begun under Frederick V in 1749. The architect was Nicolas Eigtved, a Dane, but the sources are French. Four palaces, much in the style of J.-H. Mansart, lie across the corners of the *place*. Built as family residences by four leading Danish noblemen they became the property of the Crown in 1794. In the middle of the square is Sally's equestrian statue of Frederick—one of the few statues designed expressly for a *place royale* to survive the rages of revolution. Of the four roads which lead out of the square one directly faces the Frederiks-Kirke with its portico and commanding dome (compare the Place de la Concorde and the Madeleine); another goes in a direct line to the harbour.

At Brussels, a *place royale* on the French model was begun by the Habsburg Governor of the Netherlands, Charles de Lorraine, in 1766. It proved to be only the beginning of a much grander project which matured ten years later when the Haute Ville was laid out as a formal residential area round the park of the former Ducal Palace. And in Lisbon we have the Praça do Comércio, created on the bank of the Tagus after the great earthquake of 1755. In both these—as, indeed, at Copenhagen—there is a greater awareness of the relationship of the *place royale* to the town as a whole.

## Formality dissolves

The theme of the *place royale* is, of course, something totally distinct from the theme of town *extension*. Most great towns of the 18th century tended to increase by the simple process of the sale of land and the building of streets of houses as a form of commercial enterprise. State control was more rigorous in some cases than in others. In Berlin, from 1721, large areas north and south of Unter den Linden were not only planned but to a great extent built by the State, sites being leased with half-built carcases (*immediatbauten*) already on them. In Paris, on the other hand, great private or corporate landowners like the Comte d'Artois, the banker Laborde and the Grand Priors of the Temple developed their lands for profit without very much regard to amenity; amenity in Paris being associated exclusively (apart from the Royal precincts) with the individual *hôtel*, its court and gardens. In London also it was the development of their properties by great families and institutions which created the extensive westward limb which in the course of the century altered the whole outline and balance of the capital.

London, however, developed in a way of its own. It lacked nearly all the great assets of Paris. Palaces were few and mean and lacked extensive formal lay-outs. Public buildings were not approached by lawns and tree-lined avenues. The great churches —even St Paul's—had not the courtesy of a *parvis*. Fountains there were none. And since fortifications had mostly disappeared with the Middle Ages, there could be no *boulevards* to replace them. London had, however, at the beginning of the century adopted a mode of development not without merit. This consisted in the development of streets round *squares*. The first 'square' in London was the arcaded oblong laid out by Inigo Jones at Covent Garden in 1630 and as this has some relationship to the Place Royale (des Vosges) of Henri IV we may perhaps connect, at that stage, the

idea of the London square with that of the *place royale*. But once that is admitted we must add that the ideas parted company at once. The London square became simply an element in the economics of estate development. The square, with its railed private garden, was the magnet with which to draw wealthy buyers. That achieved, the streets adjoining the square had, to the less rich, the prestige of proximity to the rich. Lesser streets followed in their grades. Easy access to a church or chapel-of-ease, as also to a market, was essential and both were often specially built. That was the London formula and it worked for a century and a half.

It worked mainly because the Court in London had never had the powerful attraction of that in Paris. Few of the English nobility aspired to great magnificence in their London houses; they were content with miniature splendour in a house in a row. In this they

P 73 (93)

f 21

P 72 (94)

p 74
(100)

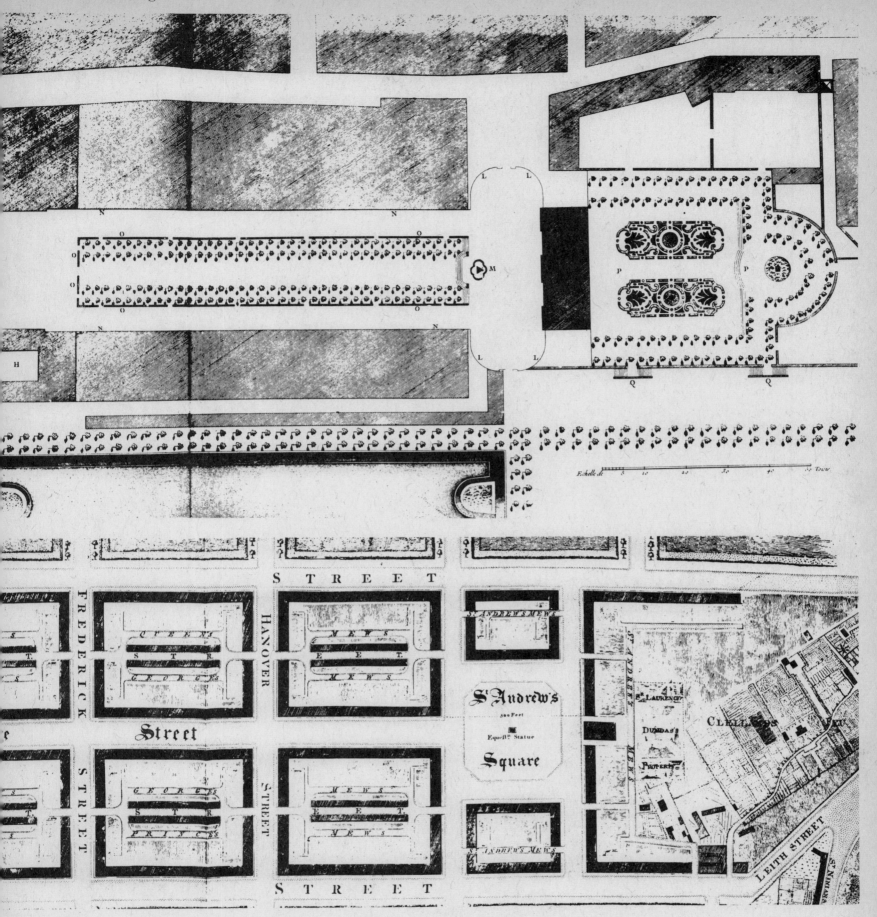

disappointed even their contemporaries. It was confidently supposed that St James's Square, formed soon after 1660, would consist entirely of a few palaces; and when Cavendish Square was laid out in 1717 the same hope prevailed. In each case one or two immense houses were built but no more. The three or four window frontage was enough—at least for those below the rank of duke.

The whole of that part of London, therefore, built between the reigns of Charles II and Victoria consists of a network of streets in which there is a frequency of squares—the squares mostly taking their names from the families to whom the ground belonged, as Bedford Square (Duke of Bedford), Grosvenor Square, Portman Square, Fitzroy Square (family names); or from names associated with the royal house, as Hanover Square, Brunswick Square, Mecklenburgh Square.

73 (92)

*Two examples of large-scale planning: the Place Royale at Nancy and the New Town of Edinburgh. Nancy (top) was developed in the 1750s for Stanislas Leczinski, Louis XV's father-in-law. On the right is the Governor's palace (the dark rectangle), with its symmetrical garden. The palace looks across a colonnaded forecourt to the long, tree-lined Place de la Carrière (an old tilting-ground, lined with identical new houses). On the left a triumphal arch (shown in a coloured engraving on p. 72) marks the entry to the Place Stanislas (formerly the Place Royale), an almost square space dominated by the Hôtel de Ville. (21)*

*Edinburgh New Town was laid out parallel with the old town during the latter part of the century. St George's Square and St Andrew's Square, each with a prominent building to close the vista, are linked by George Street. This detail is from James Craig's plan published in 1768. (22)*

Only rarely did the squares of 18th-century London submit to formal architectural control. Of those that did, Bedford Square is the only intact survivor. Nevertheless the idea of a row of houses treated as one palatial composition was present from early in the century and if it did not find much acceptance in London it did so elsewhere in England with dramatic results—namely in Bath.

p 72 (91) The extension of Bath from 1727 onwards was a truly extraordinary episode. It arose on the one hand from a sudden upsurge in the popularity of Bath as a centre of fashionable life when the London season closed and on the other from the practical ambition and naïve vision of a young mason-architect, John Wood. Bath was, in origin, a Roman city and it entered the head of John Wood that the exploitation of its new prosperity in building schemes could be matched with a restoration of its antique splendour in architecture. His earliest proposals included a 'forum', a 'circus' and a 'gymnasium'. These features would necessarily resolve themselves, in practice, into groups of ordinary town houses having, in bulk, the form of their nominal prototypes. No 'gymnasium' was ever attempted but a 'forum' was partly built (North and South Parades) and a 'circus' triumphantly completed (the Circus). A square of the London type (Queen Square) was added, with façades of greater architectural pretension than anything yet seen in the capital. After Wood's death in 1754, his son of the same name planned further extensions, incorporating in them an invention of his own—the *crescent* or curved terrace. Today, Queen Square, the Circus and Royal Crescent are the chief architectural features of the Georgian city. Highly original in themselves they are connected in a loose, informal way which admirably fits the hilly site. The elder Wood, though untravelled, seems to have been familiar with Le Nôtre's use of the *rond-point*; he may have known of Mansart's circular Place des Victoires in Paris. For the younger Wood's Crescent it is hard to think of any prototypes at all: even the rather curious designation 'crescent' seems to come from nowhere.

The achievements of the Woods and their followers at Bath influenced urban extension in Britain for the remainder of the century. Every major English town has its crescents and some have circuses. When James Craig made his plan for the New Town of f 22 Edinburgh in 1766 he did, indeed, adhere to conventional London practice; but the further development of the New Town after 1800 makes exhaustive use of the Bath elements. John Nash's great plan for Regent's Park and Regent Street of 1811 draws as heavily on the same source. In the United States, there was no planning on the Bath model until 1793, when Charles Bulfinch designed the Tontine Crescent in Franklin Street, Boston, destroyed in 1858. It was a building of Adam-like delicacy, remote from the robust Palladianism of the Bath original.

## Growing into the future

It is to America that we must, in conclusion, look to complete this brief survey. In America a wholly new town was necessarily a more realistic proposition than in Europe. William Penn's plan for p 162 (19) Philadelphia of 1682 and the plans of Baltimore, Savannah and Reading which followed it in the first half of the 18th century represent the making of new patterns on virgin soil; and the patterns are basically those of a vast military encampment. A slightly greater degree of sophistication comes with the plan of New Orleans made by a French engineer in 1721; an area divided into 66 square plots one of which—the Place d'Armes—provides for the emphatic grouping of church, arsenal and governor's

residence, the church being on the axis of a central street. Even more sophistication attaches to Annapolis whose radial plan, adopted shortly before 1700, anticipates Karlsruhe by fifteen years!

But the one great triumph of urban planning in 18th-century America was Washington, D.C. The decision to create a federal capital was taken in 1783. Major Pierre L'Enfant, son of a French painter of battle-pieces, offered his services in a theatrically phrased letter to President Washington in 1789. They were accepted and the site on the Potomac was chosen.

The most striking thing about L'Enfant's plan, seen in historical perspective, is the extent to which it depends on Versailles. Although the basic pattern is a monotonous criss-cross this is p 75 (102) overlaid by an arrogant counter-pattern of diagonals. These radiate from the Capitol and again from the White House. More diagonals cross them, meeting them and each other in squares and *ronds-points*, as Le Nôtre's avenues do at Versailles. The Mall before the Capitol echoes the great canal at Versailles and even the relation of Capitol to White House is approximately that of the Palace of Versailles and the Grand Trianon. It is curious, on the face of it, that the greatest symbol of absolutism ever constructed should provide so much and so immediately for the capital city of a nation opposed in every respect to the principles which Versailles embodied. But L'Enfant himself saw no objection. To him, the radiating avenues of Washington represented rays of enlightenment reaching out to all parts of the continent; and, at the same time, welcoming paths for all people, at all times, seeking the protection of the Union.

But the Washington plan remains distinctly a Baroque plan and an anomaly in the Neo-classical climate prevailing in America as well as in Europe at the time it was built. What, in other hands, might Washington have become? Perhaps the only architect of the time really equipped for the creation of a new capital city which should be at one and the same time a great symbol and an organism perfectly adapted to metropolitan life in a democracy was Claude Nicolas Ledoux. Ledoux never had the opportunity of planning anything on the scale of Washington but he did plan and even partly build, between Arc and Senans, south-west of Besançon, an industrial city of considerable pretension in connection with the state salt-mines. The ruins of its beginnings exist but for the whole conception, richly elaborated in Ledoux's imagination, we must turn to the aerial view in his treatise, already mentioned, of what is there called La Saline de Chaux. Here we see a town laid out, indeed, on a radial principle and with a formal though not overpowering centre. Outside the centre all formality is abandoned. Buildings and groups of buildings lie in the landscape, their forms suited to their varying functions; there is organization but no determination of the plan—it grows into the future as into the distance.

Ledoux's plan for Chaux is one of the great prophetic documents of the 18th century. Its influence was barely felt in his time (though John Nash's conception of Regent's Park must owe something to it) and it is only in our own day that its combination of the strictly formal with the functionally free has been recognized as a liberating gesture of high import. To compare it with L'Enfant's Washington is perhaps absurd, but in these two plans we have the two great urban images of the end of the century—the one rooted in that heritage of the 17th century which had, all along, so much enriched the 18th; the other a revolutionary flight of the imagination into a new world—a world based on industrial organization and democratic principle, a world in which Versailles at last, no longer exists.

# III THE TECHNOLOGICAL

# IMPERATIVE

*Scientific Discoveries in the Service of Man*

W. H. G. ARMYTAGE

*'The diffusion of a general knowledge, and of a taste for science,*

*over all classes of men, in every nation of Europe,*

*or of European origin, seems to be the characteristic feature*

*of the present age.'*

JAMES KEIR, 'Dictionary of Chemistry' (1789)

### Science, a gentleman's hobby

at the beginning of the 18th century, was to become steadily more and more dominant until by 1800 it had to be recognized as the great conditioning factor of the future. Few saw how rapid and complete the change would be, but all were aware of its seriousness.

This painting (opposite) is less of a fantasy than might be supposed. It shows part of the collection of a rich scientific dilettante, Bonnier de la Mosson, and all the objects are readily identifiable. On the floor, extreme left, is the diagram of a fortification, constructed on geometrical principles, as described in Chapter VI.

The first case contains optical instruments and lenses. At the bottom are models of crystals. The case on the right is devoted to mechanical models — cranes, water-wheels, a bridge, cannon and mortar. Typically for the period they are kept together as 'curiosities', mingled with sculpture and housed in an extravagantly Rococo setting. The whole collection seems to sum up the words of James Keir quoted above. For Keir himself owed much to French science, and his chemical works at Tipton manufactured alkali. Perhaps some of the crystals in the cabinet were of alum, for they were objects of *virtu* as well as of use. (1)

**Learned societies,** like certain other beneficient institutions, began in coffee houses. In early 18th-century England, particular coffee houses formed meeting places for men with particular interests, often combining business (such as insurance) with purely scientific pursuits. This gouache of about 1700 shows such a gathering. (2)

**Anatomy** as a scientific study only became accepted in the 18th century, though its founder, Vesalius, had lived in the 16th. New medical schools arose where it was taught like any other academic subject. William Hunter (seen, above, lecturing to the Royal College of Physicians) was a pioneer. (4)

**State patronage** of scientific research, then as now, was based on the idea that such research might, in the end, prove useful socially or militarily. Left: Louis XIV visits the Académie Royale des Sciences in 1671. As usual, every scientific pursuit is included — anatomical specimens on the walls, a telescope and an armillary sphere to represent astronomy, and in the frame being shown to the King, a plan of fortifications in the style of Vauban. (3)

**Universities adopted science** on their curricula sooner in Germany and Italy than in the rest of Europe. Right: the library of Göttingen University, founded in 1737. Among its eminent teachers were Albrecht von Haller and Georg Christoph Lichtenberg, famous equally as an aphorist and as a researcher into electricity. (5)

**The laboratory** of the University of Altdorf in 1720 (right) shows it to have been well equipped for experiments of many kinds. It was built originally by the first professor of chemistry, Johan Moritz Hoffmann, known in the republic of letters as 'Heliodorus II'. (6)

**Science fiction:** this engraving of an 'ideal natural history cabinet' of 1719 still belongs to the age when science meant a collection of curios, before it had taken the step (to adapt Marx's words) from describing the world to changing it. Specimens are displayed on the walls and tables exactly as if they were *objets d'art*. (7)

**The information explosion** is not peculiar to this century. Something like it happened in the 18th, especially in botany and zoology when Captain Cook's first voyage (1768-71) brought back a vast mass of new species to be recorded and classified. The naturalist of that expedition was Sir Joseph Banks, a learned amateur, later president of the Royal Society; and the artist responsible for drawing the new specimens was Sydney Parkinson. Parkinson died of malaria on the voyage home, but his detailed sketches (above) were of immense value to the botanical world. These two are the Australian plant *Banksia Serrata*, named after Banks, and *Bromelia Bracteata*, from Brazil. (8, 9)

**Banks as a butterfly,** hatched by the sun of royal favour — an unkind print by Gillray. (11)

**The thirty-six volumes** of Buffon's *Histoire Naturelle* formed the most complete record of 18th-century biological knowledge. It contained descriptions of every known animal and bird, and many hundreds of hand-coloured plates. This page (above) shows the South American vulture. Buffon himself was an indefatigable worker, the Superintendent of the Jardin des Plantes for many years, and a pioneer of evolutionary theory. His views on the origins of life brought him into conflict with the Church and he was obliged, like Galileo, to recant. (12)

**The scientific centre** of French studies was the Jardin des Plantes (left), founded as early as 1635. During the 18th century, not only botanists but zoologists, chemists and astronomers here received state aid and encouragement. (10)

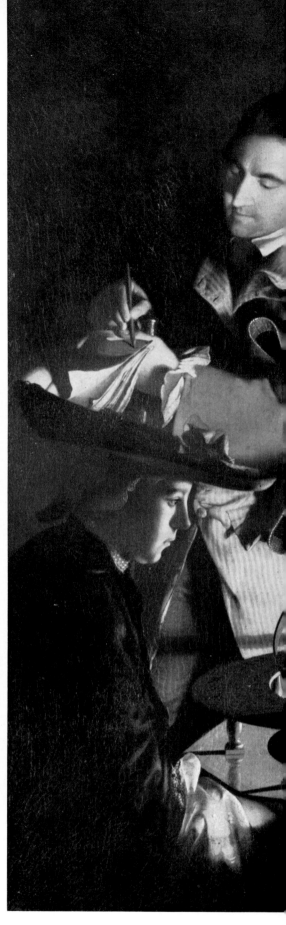

**The exploration of space** made momentous advances after Newton had explained its physical laws. Left: Herschel's telescope of 1789, the largest then in existence — 40 feet long and with an aperture of 4 feet. Herschel was self-taught (he began life as an organist) and at first had to make the telescopes he needed with his own hands. He discovered the revolution of the planets, the new planet of Uranus (the first since antiquity), two new satellites of Saturn, and the phenomenon of double stars. (13)

**National observatories** were soon being financed out of public funds. Above: the interior of the Royal Observatory at Greenwich, built by Charles II for Flamsteed, the first Astronomer Royal. Below: an even richer display of instruments at the Nuremberg observatory. They include sextants, quadrants and an armillary sphere. (14, 15)

**The sense of wonder** aroused by the revelations of science is nowhere better expressed than in some of the paintings of Joseph Wright of Derby. *The Orrery* (above) shows a large mechanical model of the solar system, lit by a bright 'sun' in the middle. (16)

**A moon-map** compiled from many sources by the Württemberg astronomer J. J. Mayer in the mid-18th century already shows many accurate features — the dark areas called 'seas', the craters and even the straight lines radiating from some of them. (17)

**Roads, bridges, aqueducts** combined to change the face of Europe more radically now than at any time during the past. The French government, the most progressive of all, had set up a special department to deal with such projects. Right: road- and bridge-building in France. Although cranes are in operation in the background, methods are still traditional and stone is still quarried at the roadside. (19)

**The second bridge** over the Thames was built by a Swiss engineer, Charles Labalye, at Westminster in 1750, using the new device of 'caissons' — water-tight timber boxes filled with stone and sunk in the required positions. (18)

**To raise water** for the reservoir of Marly near Versailles a famous *machine* was constructed (below). Fourteen huge wheels, turned by the river, worked 64 pumps at the lower level, 79 half way up, and 82 at the top. In this way the water was conveyed to the aqueduct, down which it flowed to the reservoir. (20)

**Iron for bridges** had been considered in France but was actually first used in England — at a place subsequently named 'Iron-bridge' (above) near Coalbrookdale. Designed by Abraham Darby and John Wilkinson in 1777, it rested on five semi-circular ribs, each composed of two 70-foot lengths pinned together at the top and supported by concentric rings with radial connecting bars. (21)

**Lavoisier's genius** dominates the chemistry and physics of the second half of the 18th century. Among his most famous experiments were those which demolished the phlogiston theory and demonstrated many of the properties of oxygen (which he named) — for instance, the way in which it acted with other substances in combustion and respiration. In a portrait by Jacques-Louis David (left) he is seen with his wife; on the table are some of the instruments he used to measure gases. The experiment shown below concerns the changes in the composition of air when breathed. Lavoisier is the figure towards the left, with arm raised. Madame Lavoisier sits at a desk keeping the records. On shelves all around are the bottles and jars containing chemicals. Lavoisier also secured uniformity of weights and measures throughout France. (22, 24)

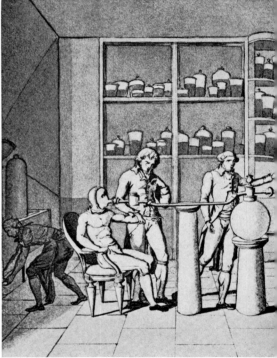

**Steam locomotion** was seriously discussed by the French government in the 1770s as a method of moving artillery. This model (above) had three wheels and a large boiler in front. (23)

**Gaslight** came to London in 1809, an event noted by Rowlandson (right). The idea of extracting gas from coal belongs to William Murdoch, an engineer employed by Watt. (25)

**Electricity's mysterious power** fascinated scientists. Before the invention of the Leyden jar in 1746, a weak current could be generated by rotating a glass globe against the hands. The apparatus shown (far right) was set up by the Abbé Nollet in 1749 to prove (surprisingly) that water flows more freely in the vicinity of electricity, that electrified animals lose weight, that electrified seeds germinate faster and that electrified leaves give off a faint breeze and luminosity. Electricity was also widely tried out in medicine. Right: a plate from J. G. Schäffer's *Electrical Medicine* of 1766. The current is conducted to the patient's ankle via three bowls of water at her feet. The doctor touches her with a wire in the same circuit, giving slight electric shocks as a cure for paralytic and rheumatic conditions. (26, 27)

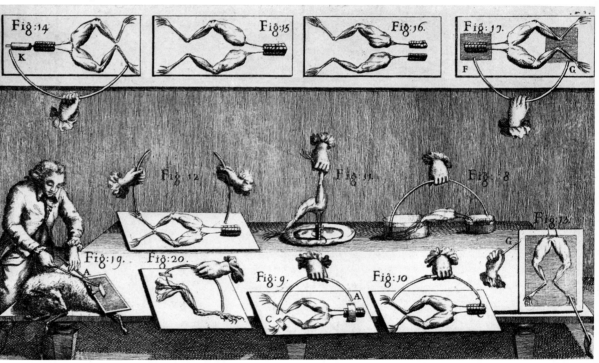

**Why do dead frogs' legs** contract violently when the nerve is touched by a brass or copper wire and the muscle by one of iron in contact with the first? Galvani, an Italian professor of anatomy, believed that the metals conducted 'animal electricity' already present in the frog. A plate from his book of 1791 (above right) shows various ways in which the experiment was tried. (28)

**Volta proved Galvani wrong.** The electrical charge had been produced by the contact of the two metals themselves. By using this discovery he was able to make a 'pile' battery consisting of a series of paired metal pieces in contact with each other, and connected by water or some other moist substance. In 1801 he was called to Paris (right) to demonstrate it to Napoleon. (29)

**'The balloon engages all mankind',** wrote Dr Johnson sarcastically. Other observers forecast the eventual importance of air-travel even if they did not always foresee its form very clearly. By 1794, at the Battle of Fleurus (above), observation balloons were used to assist the artillery (the picture comes from the lid of a snuff-box). Below: a fantasy that might have been taken seriously; it claims to be a record of a balloon that flew in Spain from 'Plazentia' to 'Coria' in May 1784. (30, 31)

# Scientific Discoveries in the Service of Man

W. H. G. ARMYTAGE

THOUGH MODERN SCIENCE has deep roots, its social and industrial implications are classically illustrated in the 18th century. Indeed that was the century that saw the coining of the word 'technology'. For though technology was in a real sense the contribution of the barbarian nations, with their windmills, stirrups and halters, their new weaving looms, chemical processes and gunpowder (which the ancient world, for all its glory and grandeur, had not known), it was not until the 18th century, with the rise of scientific societies, that technology 'took off'.

## An age of popularization

p 98–99 Behind this take-off were the numerous scientific societies and groups which diffused, by personal contact and through the medium of print, new knowledge at a faster rate than ever before. Following the Royal Society of London and the Académie Royale p 98 (3) des Sciences of Paris, founded in the 1660s, a number of others were founded not only in the capitals, but in many towns of Europe.

Aptly enough the Académie Royale des Sciences acquired a new constitution in 1700. This increased its membership from twenty to seventy and provided for its official organ the *Histoire et Mémoires*. In the same year the Societas Regis Scientiarum in Berlin, fruit of thirty years' effort on the part of Leibniz, began to take shape. In 1752 a similar institution was founded in Moscow. These four were terminals of a growing network of interlocking memberships, extensive correspondence and mutual preoccupations that, through more minuscule groups, extended to all the major towns not only of western Europe but to the eastern seaboard of America. It was a real community of thought and action; as Sir Gavin de Beer says, 'the sciences were never at war'.

By launching in 1695 a comprehensive scientific survey of technical appliances and manufacturing processes the Académie Royale des Sciences first channelled this technological interest. For the survey it obtained, in 1711, the services of the twenty-eight-year-old Réaumur, naturalist and physician. Fifty years later (and four years after he died) the first of the 121 parts of the survey, f 4 known as the *Description et Perfection des Arts et Métiers*, appeared. Unfortunately it had been virtually anticipated, to Réaumur's disgust, by the first volumes of another survey: the thirty-six-f 2 volume French *Encyclopédie* edited by Diderot and d'Alembert. This latter project (as we shall see in Chapter VIII) extended over the years from 1751 to 1780. Diderot was as avid a frequenter of factories and workshops as Réaumur, and, like him, spared no p 268 effort to make his *Encyclopédie* complete in technical references, including great volumes of plates. It stimulated amongst other things the establishment of the somewhat different *Encyclopaedia Britannica*. Issued in sixpenny pamphlets, beginning in 1768, the *Britannica* covered letters A and B in 697 pages, and the rest in less than 2,000. Thirty-three years later the two-volume supplement to the third edition, issued in 1801, and dedicated to George III, stated:

> The French *Encyclopédie* has been accused, and justly accused, of having disseminated far and wide, the seeds of Anarchy and Atheism. If the ENCYCLOPAEDIA BRITANNICA shall, in any degree, counteract the tendency of that pestiferous work, even these two volumes will not be wholly unworthy of Your Majesty's Patronage.

Germany—then divided into numerous principalities—also had its multiple academies. In one of these, the medical society known as the Imperial Leopoldine Academy, G. E. Stahl, 'a sour-faced metaphysician' and protagonist of the two great 'blind-alleys' of scientific thought in the 18th century, Phlogiston and Vitalism, f 3 was invested in 1700 with the title of 'Olympiodorus'. In this particular academy pseudonyms were *de rigueur*. One early member was known as 'Phosphorus I' (probably because his light shone before men), another, who served as physician to various German Electors as 'Hercules I', a third, a great traveller, as 'Apollo'. The Academy brought together various professors in the German universities. 'Thessalus I' (M. B. Valentini), who was also elected to the Royal Society of London in 1721, compiled a synoptic account of the papers of members. He did for physics at the University of Giessen, what 'Heliodorus II' (Johann Moritz Hoffmann) did for chemistry at the University of Altdorf, where he had become the first professor of the subject in 1682, and where p 99 (6) he built a laboratory. Amongst other members was 'Antenor II' (I. C. Lehmann), Keeper of the Natural History Museum in St Petersburg, and the first professor of chemistry, metallurgy, and pharmacy at Upsala in Sweden.

New universities, like Göttingen (founded in 1734) and Erlangen p 99 (5) (founded in 1743), incubated yet more societies. At Göttingen, the great systematizer Albrecht von Haller (1708–77) laboured from 1738 for seventeen years in a specially built theatre, founding the Königliche Gesellschaft der Wissenschaften, in 1751. Haller was a learned society in himself. Author of 13,000 scientific papers, physiologist, poet, botanist, novelist and experimentalist, he f 1 towered over his contemporaries.

## Science in the coffee houses

Ideas could only circulate in a society which provided informal meeting places for scientists, as well as the more formal academies. p 262 (2) In France the salons supplied such an environment; in England, the coffee houses. Here even lectures could take place. John Harris, p 98 (2) the author of one of the first technical encyclopaedias, the *Lexicon Technicum* (1704), and the Huguenot émigré Abraham de Moivre, author of the classic text on probability, the *Doctrine of Chance* (1716), both lectured at the Marine Coffee House in Birchin Lane, London. It was aptly named, but its clientele ranged from navigators (who needed mathematics) to insurance brokers (who needed some grounding in probability theory). In fact it housed the London Assurance Company until 1748.

The Marine Coffee House was but one of many in London. Others, proliferating after the Restoration, hatched insurance companies, news-letters, societies and clubs, provided opportunities for doctors to meet their patients, and for apothecaries to obtain advice from the specialists of the day. Above all, they facilitated such a diaspora of scientific ideas that, early in the new century, they could be regarded as having 'improved useful knowledge' as much as the universities.

These coffee houses also stimulated scientific societies. The botanists, an important service group of the country gentry of that day, used to meet at the Rainbow Coffee House in Watling Street, where in 1721 they formed the Botanical Society. At the Rainbow too, some fourteen years later, a Society for the Encouragement of

Learning was established 'with the general aim of promoting the Arts and Sciences'. An Aurelian Society similarly took shape in the Swan Tavern in Cornhill in 1745, till three years later it was destroyed by fire. In its resurrected form it used to meet at the York Coffee House in St James' Street, and then became the Linnaean Society in 1788. One of the Presidents of the Royal Society, Martin Folkes (1690–1754), haunted Rawthmell's in Henrietta Street, Covent Garden, so inveterately that, according to one Fellow, he chose the council and officers out of 'his junto of Sycophants', that used to meet him there every night.

The same coffee house gave birth to an ambitious venture on 22nd March, 1754, when a group of Fellows of the Royal Society listened to the proposals of a Northampton drawing-master to subsidize inventions by prizes, in much the same way as horse-breeding was fostered by competition at the Northampton horse fair. The drawing-master, Shipley, was anxious to find substitutes for cobalt and madder, both dyes used in the cloth trade, both imported, and both difficult to obtain. When they met again at Rawthmell's on March 29, they decided to make their meetings more formal, and arranged to foregather regularly at a circulating library in Crane Court, Fleet Street. From this grew the Society for the Encouragement of Arts, Manufactures and Commerce, perhaps better known today as the Royal Society of Arts.

Just as these coffee houses incubated societies, encyclopaedias, insurance companies and town libraries, so they provided also a forum and clearing-house for new discoveries in science. At 'Button's', in Russell Street, Covent Garden, of which Martin Folkes was also a member, there was a post-box where intelligence of all kinds was deposited for Addison's paper, *The Guardian*. Fashioned like a lion's head, it stood on the western side of the coffee house, 'holding its paws under the chin, on a box which contains everything that he swallows'. As Addison remarked, it was 'a proper emblem of knowledge and actions, being all head and paws'. This 'lion post-box' was later moved to the 'Bedford' which indeed became a virtual technological university. Here John Stirling FRS, and later J. T. Desaguliers FRS, a Huguenot émigré, lectured on experimental philosophy. Stirling, a friend of Nicholas Bernouilli and Isaac Newton, later went on to become a mine

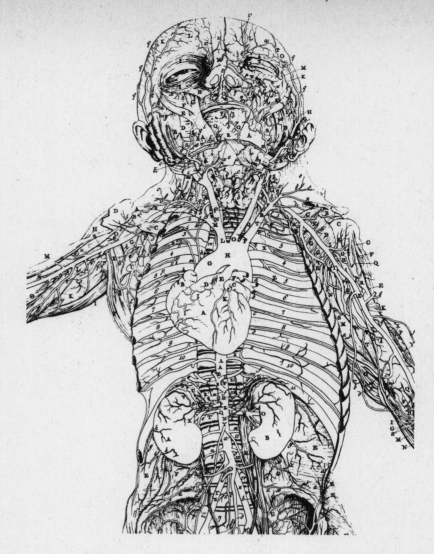

*Albrecht von Haller, one of the most learned men of his century, published a vast variety of books ranging from anatomy to poetry. This plate, from his 'Icones anatomicae' (1743–56), shows the human blood-vessels in unprecedented detail. (1)*

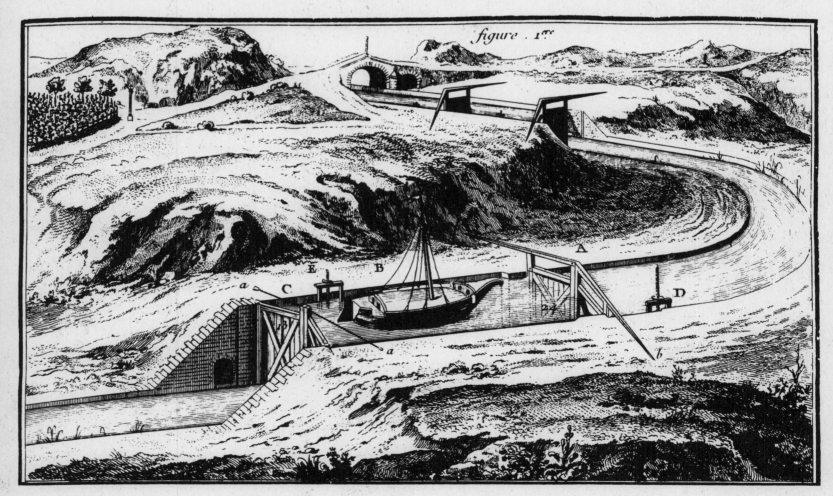

*The great thirty-six-volume French 'Encyclopédie', edited by Diderot and d'Alembert and with contributions from technical experts as well as writers, embodied many of the ambitions of the Enlightenment. The first volume was issued in 1751. Maintaining a strictly rational approach to all subjects, it contained articles often with explanatory diagrams, on a wide variety of topics. The engraving illustrates canal building and the principle of locks. (2)*

manager in Lanarkshire. Desaguliers, an authority on the steam engine, discoursed at large in a room over the Great Piazza at Covent Garden to anyone who came to listen.

Information acquired in such coffee houses enabled Joshua Ward to manufacture sulphuric acid at Twickenham by the bell process from 1736 onwards and to reduce the price of this valuable commodity some sixteenfold. The local inhabitants were so offended by the smell of burning brimstone and nitre that they forced him to remove his distillery to Richmond. By 1749 he had patented his process, and by 1758, when the French metallurgist and 'industrial spy' Gabriel Jars began visiting England, he noticed that Ward was employing Welsh women, probably so that the secret of his work would not be divulged. An 'elaboratory' at Robert's Coffee House in the Great Piazza, Covent Garden, enabled a number of crucibles to be tested in 1757. By 1782 a Chemical Society was meeting at the Chapter Coffee House in London.

These coffee houses offered, according to Professor Lewis Feuer, 'a rite of communion with the liberal spirit of the times' and he advances the theory that far from science stemming from the puritan spirit, it rose from the hedonistic spirit which enabled 'the senses to take a place at least the equal of intellect and intuition as a means of knowledge'.

## The politics of technology

The resources available from scientific academies were increasingly utilized by governments all over Europe, and governments in their turn granted privileges to academies. Thus in England in 1710 the

p 102
(14)

Royal Observatory was placed by Queen Anne in the sole charge of the Royal Society (the instruments, however, in spite of insistent demands, were retained by Flamsteed, the Astronomer Royal, and the Society did not actually gain possession of them until 1720, when Flamsteed was succeeded by Halley). Later, George III ordered the Astronomer Royal to obey the regulations drawn up by the Council of the Royal Society and stipulated that the Master General of Ordnance should provide such instruments as the Council thought necessary. The society was also empowered to publish the results of its researches at public expense and to set up other observatories in British possessions overseas.

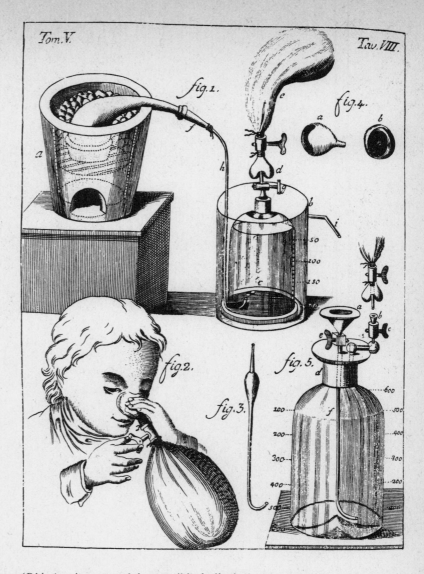

'Phlogiston' was one of the great 'blind-alleys' of 18th-century science. It was supposed to be an element given off in combustion and respiration – the 'stuff' of fire and of life. This page from an Italian collection of scientific papers of 1778, attempts to demonstrate the theory. (3)

The 'Description et Perfection des Arts et Métiers' rivalled the 'Encyclopédie', but although conceived as early as 1711 and placed in the hands of Réaumur did not begin to appear until 1761, after Réaumur had died. An engraving called 'Le

'Bain de Propreté' explains how hot and cold water can be made to flow from taps and the hot water taken to the bottom of the bath by means of a funelled pipe (E). (4)

Such favours were amply repaid by the Royal Society's learning being placed at the government's disposal. Its advice was solicited, for instance, on the problem of jail fever, which had been highlighted by the death of the Lord Mayor of London, two judges and an alderman, all as a result of being infected at the Old Bailey sessions. A committee was appointed to investigate the bad ventilation, and a ventilator was devised. In its erection seven of the eleven workmen caught the fever and died. But once erected the ventilator lowered the death rate in jails from eight a week to about two a month.

Another such committee of the Royal Society considered the question of how to protect buildings from being struck by lightning. Benjamin Franklin suggested pointed rods. His recommendation was rejected by the government with disastrous consequences, for an ammunitions dump blew up at Purfleet. An unkindly wit wrote:

> *While you great George for knowledge hunt*
> *And sharp conductors change for blunt*
> *Franklin a wiser course pursues*
> *And all your knowledge fruitless views*
> *By keeping to the point*

Franklin had put forward the theory that lightning was actually electricity in 1749. But hypothesis was easier than demonstration. The curate of Marly, using a forty-foot iron rod in a thunderstorm, escaped with an injured arm. In 1753 another experimenter, Rechman, was not so lucky and lost his life. Franklin himself succeeded in providing a safe and satisfactory proof in 1752.

Electricity in fact was in the air, in more senses than one. The first glass electrical machine had been made and described by Francis Hauksbie. His *Physico-Mechanical Experiments on Various Subjects* (1709) showed how electricity could be generated by rotating a glass globe against the hands or some material, the charge being taken off. A number of such generators were subsequently made and used by experimenters, until, thirty-seven years later, von Kleist of Pomerania and Musschenbrock of Leyden simultaneously discovered the Leyden jar. This attracted Benjamin Franklin, who worked with it from 1747 to 1755. To measure the new force, which became all the more necessary when it began to be used in medicine, Henley devised a kind of electroscope based on a scale behind suspended threads, the idea being to measure the angle of their separation.

p 107 (27)

p 107 (26)

But what in fact was being measured? Henry Cavendish compared the 'degree of electrification' to pressure in a fluid. Notions of resistance were also explained by him as well as by Joseph Priestley. When Galvani noticed that a frog's legs could be convulsed by bringing brass into contact with iron, to which they were attached, he thought he had yet another type of electricity. But Volta by further experiment indicated that it was the contact of the metals which produced the electricity, which the frogs merely registered. Described in 1797, this experiment ushered in the work of Ampère. Their three names were later honoured by the verb 'to galvanize' and the units 'volt' and 'ampere'.

p 107 (28)

p 107 (29)

The 18th century also saw a revolution in the teaching of medicine, which may be said to have deserted the lecture room for the bedside. Here Scotland took the lead. In 1729 a group of doctors who had received their training at Leyden persuaded the University of Edinburgh to establish a combined Hospital and Faculty of Medicine. Later another was added with provision for the insane. Edinburgh was at this date unique as the only provider of clinical instruction and university education in Britain, soon outstripping London. Englishmen began to flock there and outnumber the native Scots. Americans came too in large numbers and when the first medical school was established in Philadelphia in 1765 it carried an emblematical thistle above its main entrance.

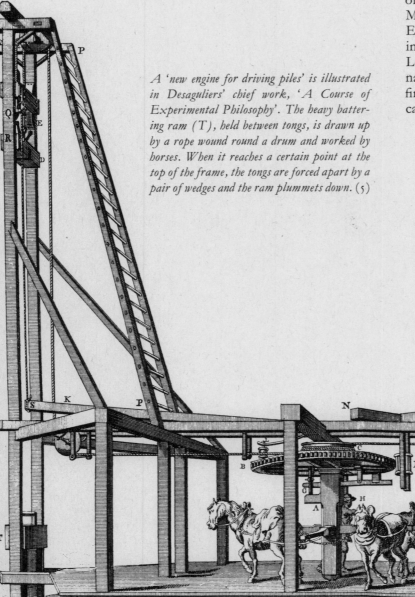

*A 'new engine for driving piles' is illustrated in Desaguliers' chief work, 'A Course of Experimental Philosophy'. The heavy battering ram (T), held between tongs, is drawn up by a rope wound round a drum and worked by horses. When it reaches a certain point at the top of the frame, the tongs are forced apart by a pair of wedges and the ram plummets down. (5)*

*Old Newgate Prison was a notorious breeding ground of disease until Stephen Hales provided a ventilator system which cut deaths from jail-fever by 90 per cent. This print shows the 'windmill' that carried air to the interior. The whole jail was rebuilt later in the 18th century. (6)*

Scotland also served as an inspiration to the English Quaker John Bellers who appealed to his countrymen in 1714 to build hospitals for the sick. His countrymen responded by founding Westminster Hospital (1720), St George's (1733), the London Hospital (1740) and the Middlesex (1744) in London and over thirty similar foundations in the provinces beginning with Winchester and Bristol (1736) and continuing with Dundee (1798).

One of the active promoters of the Westminster was Samuel Wesley. Four years after it was founded, his brother John wrote to their mother on November 1, 1724, from Christ Church, Oxford:

> Suppose you have seen the famous Dr Cheyne's 'Book of Health and Long Life' which is, as he says he expected, very much cried down by the physicians. He refers almost everything to temperance and exercise, and supports most things with physical reasons.

John Wesley's 'conversion' to Cheynian habits was to be handsomely acknowledged in his own *Primitive Physick,* published forty years later. The Cheyne to whom he referred had originally been known as 'Cheyne huge of size', or 'Three ells round huge Cheyne', for he weighed thirty-two stone. Cheyne brought his weight down considerably and described how he did it in *Observations Concerning the Nature and Due Method of Treating the Gout* (1720). Gout, like other English disorders, said Cheyne, was due to immoderate diet, lack of proper exercise, and an uncertain climate which closed the pores, making normal perspiration impossible. His book ran to eight editions in seventeen years, and was the subject of exegesis and comment throughout that time. He then conducted a four-year experiment with a vegetarian diet. The result was so successful that he published his *Essay on Health and Long Life* (1724). This ran to nine editions in thirty years, and was being published over a hundred years later. It contained nothing new, for an assault against beef-eating had been mounted by Thomas Tryon, the 17th-century vegetarian, and physical culture had been advocated by Francis Fuller in *Medicina Gymnastica* (1705), but it did publicize these ideas, since Cheyne was well-known to most of the distinguished neurotics of his day: Pope, Arbuthnot, Swift, Gay and Young. Consulted in 1734 by twenty-three-year-old David Hume, the philosopher and historian, who was suffering from scurvy and vapours, Cheyne's advice was that Hume's 'nervous paroxysms and paralytic tremours' arose 'chiefly from want of exercise, too much head work and great plenty of food'.

## The 'Common Market' of science

These advances in electrical and medical studies illustrate the way in which knowledge was exchanged not only within nations but also between them. Two Englishmen— John Martin and Ephraim Chambers translated and abridged the papers of the French Académie des Sciences and published them in 1742. So too, in 1784, the Council of the Royal Society of London petitioned for the establishment of a geodetical survey to enable the observatories of Greenwich and Paris to work together.

The most ambitious of such international enterprises was probably the arrangements made in 1761 and 1769 for the observation of the transit of Venus across the face of the sun (an event which would not occur again until 1874 and 1882). Several European governments made plans to send expeditions to various parts of the world, with the object of measuring the distance between the earth and the sun. Although the project, which in 1769 involved 151 observers at 77 different posts, failed in its chief aim, it did produce many valuable side-results—for instance the calculation of the exact position of some of the observation posts, and a series of detailed records of the flora where they were sited.

*f 7*   The part played by Americans in observing the transit of Venus in 1769 was a major factor in the recognition of American science, especially of the American Philosophical Society (which promoted the observations) and of David Rittenhouse in particular. Rittenhouse, a Pennsylvania clock-making genius, had provided it with its first scientific paper in 1768, the year in which the Society had merged with its great competitor, the American Society, to become the 'American Philosophical Society held at Philadelphia for Promoting Useful Knowledge'. When the strengthened Society issued its *Transactions* in 1771, the most important items were the descriptions, observations and calculations on the transit.

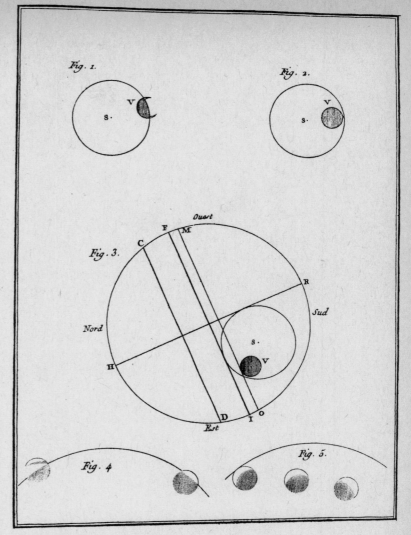

*The transit of Venus across the Sun in 1769 was the occasion for an international scientific enterprise; 151 observers at 77 different posts (including Captain Cook on Tahiti) made observations. This page is from the account by Jean Chappe d'Auteroches, who saw it from California.* (7)

The 'spin-off' from the activities concerned with the transit was important in other respects. The marking of boundaries and the laying out of large tracts of land were improved. Such work in turn gave opportunity for fresh observations and improving on boundaries like that drawn by Mason and Dixon between 1763 and 1768 between Pennsylvania and Maryland.

The 'Common Market' of Science in 18th-century England, is symbolized by Jean Deluc FRS, native of Geneva, who settled in England in 1773 in royal employ. He was also an honorary professor of physics at Göttingen and author of *Bacon tel qu'il est* (1800).

## The world of plants

America was the centre of a real 'plantocracy', and its leader was John Bartram, whom Linnaeus considered to be the world's greatest botanist. Bartram travelled all over America, collecting, labelling and packing examples for export to European gardens, while in his own grounds on the banks of the Schuylkill (which he bought in 1728) he carried out America's first experiments in hybridization. It was Bartram too who suggested to Franklin the idea of a great Western survey. Franklin passed it on to Jefferson who instructed Lewis and Clark when they actually carried out the survey.

One of Bartram's correspondents in Europe was the Englishman Peter Collinson (like Bartram, incidentally, a Quaker). What Bartram exported, Collinson imported: he conducted an extensive business in the American colonies, introduced over 100 new plants and shrubs to England (including the sweet chestnut and thirteen new species of oak), and built up a large collection of his own at Mill Hill, which later passed to Sir Hans Sloane, the founder of the British Museum. Collinson also enjoyed some prestige as a physicist, and has the credit of introducing Benjamin Franklin to the Leyden jar.

Botany's contribution in several fields—economics, medical and *f 8* educational—was largely made possible by the creation of botanical gardens. Here products from overseas were acclimatized, botanists and doctors were trained, materials from pharmacopoeias developed, new insights into nature obtained. They ranged from private gardens, like those of Stephen Hales at Teddington, of Fothergill at Upton, and of Clifford in Holland, to large public gardens, like the Jardin du Roi or Jardin des Plantes which were formidable state enterprises.

The last named, perhaps the greatest of them all, was known as 'le grand foyer scientifique de l'Europe'. Created in 1635, it had within six years rooms for the teaching of chemistry and astronomy as well as botany. From it went explorers like Guy-Crescent Fagon, nephew of the founder, and J. P. de Tournefort, whose *Elements of Botany* (1694) virtually set the stage for later developments.

When Tournefort was succeeded as director in 1708 by Antoine Jussieu (1686–1758), the heyday of the Jardin du Roi began. The Jussieu were a scientific dynasty active in the Jardin for the rest of the century. Antoine's brother Bernard (1699–1777) edited
*f 11* Tournefort's book, refined Linnaeus's sexual classification of plants, introduced the famous cedar of Lebanon into the Jardin, and explored the potentialities of the coffee bean. A third brother, Joseph (1704–1779), introduced heliotrope and added to his medical abilities those of an engineer. A nephew, Antoine-Laurent de Jussieu (1748–1836), also a professor at the Jardin, published *Genera Plantarum* in 1774, which carried the evolutionary idea perceptively forward. Antoine-Laurent's son André (1797–1853) carried this remarkable intellectual dynasty well into the 19th century.

*Botanical gardens were among the innovations of the 17th century, and throughout the 18th continued not only to provide botanists with the means of study, but to form meeting-places where scientists of all kinds could discuss their*

The Jardin grew with them. They built hot-houses, an amphitheatre and laboratories. Its titular connection with the office of the King's physician was severed. Perhaps its greatest superintendent, G. L. Leclerc de Buffon, took office in 1739. He was a great administrator, as well as a bold imaginative writer. The Jardin spread down to the Seine, and Buffon even vacated his apartments to make room for further collections. He himself did much to marry the knowledge of astronomers and mathematicians to the facts of the earlier history of the earth. His thirty-six-volume history made its story perceptibly clearer, and did much to forward the idea of modification of the species. The laboratory grew too. A chemical tradition was built up and its demonstrator, G. F. Rouelle (1703–70), was the first to recognize that salts were produced by the combination of acids and bases. He was also credited with the discovery of sulphuretted hydrogen and other compounds. A stimulating teacher, he attracted among others Lavoisier, while Diderot admired him and came to his lectures. His influence continued through his pupils. One of them, B. G. Sage, succeeded him in 1768 and established a chair of mineralogical chemistry at the mineralogical museum where Rome de l'Isle and F. A. Chaptal were trained. He also persuaded the government to establish the *Ecole des Mines*. Industries like dyeing and porcelain stimulated the creation of new chairs in the Jardin during the 18th century, for professors who also lectured to the public. Buffon died in 1788 and his successor La Billarderie, who took over just as the Revolution broke out, emigrated. His successor, Bernard de St Pierre, presided over the metamorphosis of the *Jardin* into a Museum of Natural History.

*work and pursue their researches. This engraving shows the medical garden (or 'Doctors garden') of Altdorf in Germany, of which the chemical laboratory has been shown in pl. 6. (8)*

*Hortus Medicus oder so genannte Doctors Garten zu Altdorf.*

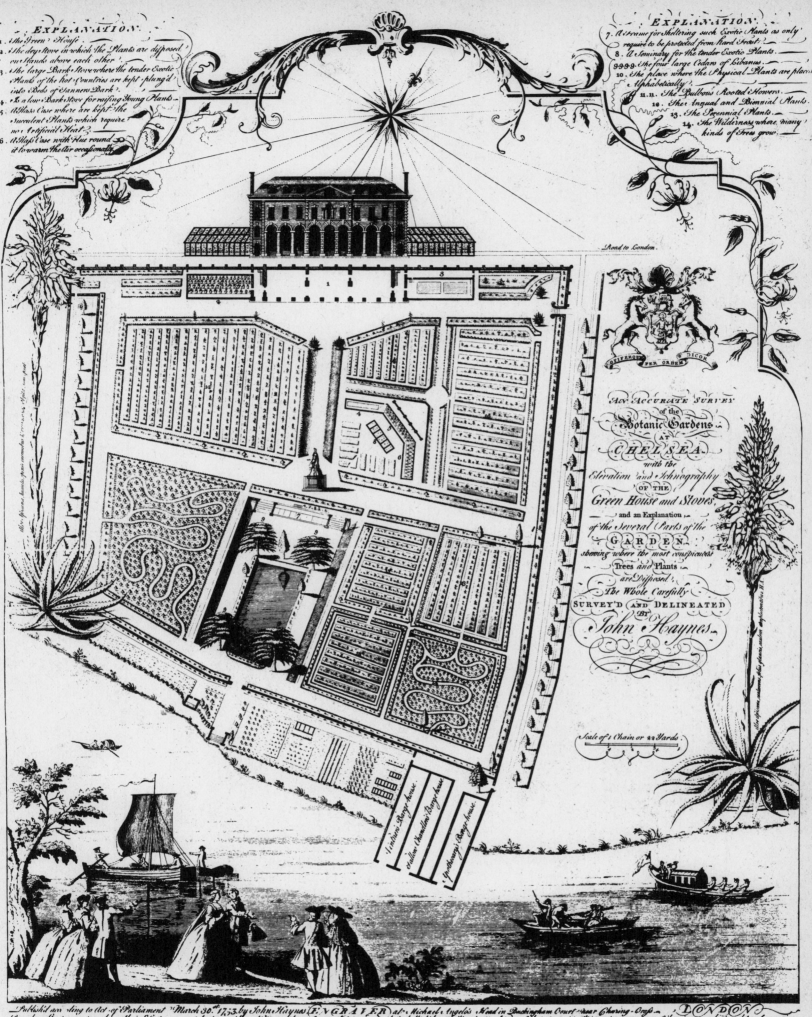

England's answer to the royal *Jardin des Plantes* was characteristically the creation of a private body. In 1676 the Society of Apothecaries began their 'Physic Garden in Chelsea', on land which later became the property of Sir Hans Sloane. He reduced their rent to a nominal £5 per annum, and energetically encouraged scientific research. This bird's-eye view of 1753, with its detailed 'Explanation', gives some idea of the scope of its activities. (9)

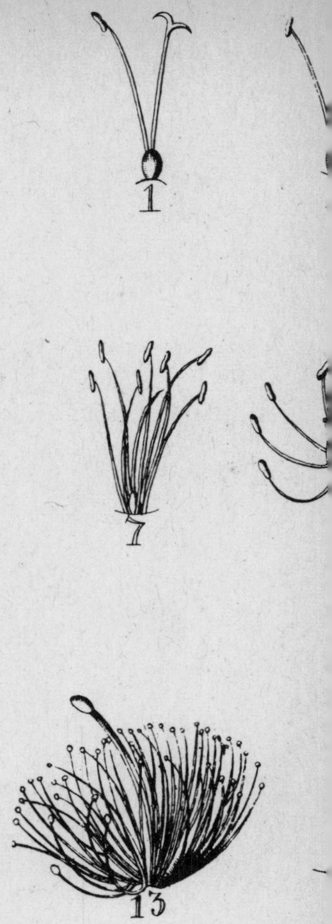


*The Swedish botanist Linnaeus stands out among 18th-century scientists. He was the first to recognize the sexuality of plants, announced in 1729 in his 'Preliminary to the Nuptials of Plants' (above, the hand-written titlepage). His most lasting work was the classification of plants based on the number of stamens in the flower. The total of 24 distinct classes are illustrated (above right) from his 'Systema Naturae' of 1735.* (10, 11)

The mere assurance that he would give a botanic garden to the university was apparently sufficient to secure the election of Richard Bradley to the chair of botany at Cambridge in 1724. His subsequent failure to do so led to an agitation to dismiss him, though he died (in 1732) before this had any effect. Nevertheless he was a voluminous writer. Farmers, doctors, even coffee-house keepers had good reason to thank his agile pen. His successor, John Martyn, so felt the lack of a garden that three years later he too ceased to lecture, preferring to live in London where he had access to the Chelsea Gardens. He subsequently withdrew to a farm on Streatham Common. On his resignation he was succeeded by his son, who held the chair for sixty-three years, during which time a garden was acquired. The father had been secretary of the botanical society that used to meet at the Rainbow Coffee House in Watling Street from 1721 to 1727, and had long contacts with the Chelsea Gardens; while the son became, in 1791, secretary of the Society of Naval Architecture: an indication of the increasing connection between the universities and such scientific and technological societies.

*f 9* The Chelsea Gardens, in fact (more precisely the Physic Garden at Chelsea), is worth looking at more closely. It was first rented by the Society of Apothecaries in 1676, and was a costly responsibility until a former student, Sir Hans Sloane, became their ground landlord. He ensured that it would be an active centre of research by giving them in 1722 a new lease in perpetuity at £5 per annum, on condition that every year for at least forty years, fifty different specimens of plants grown in the Garden, dried and mounted, were delivered to the Royal Society. Also in 1722 Sloane secured the appointment of the innovator, Philip Miller, as gardener—the first to germinate seeds by growing them in a tar pit, the first to grow bulbs in bottles of water, and to suggest the part played by insects in the fertilization of plants. Just as he continued the tradition of Sloane in having correspondents all over the world, so he communicated to Sloane's successor as patron, Sir Joseph Banks, the tradition of distributing new plants to other collections.

## Groping towards evolution

Following the division of flowering plants into monocotyledons and dicotyledons by John Ray in the second edition of his great *Historia generalis plantarum* (1681–1704), natural history became the passion of the century. Ray described some 18,600 plants in some 125 sections, and recognized their sexual character. This was denied by the great French botanist Tournefort, who concentrated on distinguishing genera. The climax of these researches came when the Swedish botanist Linnaeus published his *Systema Naturae* between 1735 and 1758. His students had foraged all over the world for new animals, plants, minerals (even diseases), which Linnaeus meticulously classified under Class, Order, Genus and Species. Much of his work, including many definitions and his divisions into Genus and Species, is still valid. It was he who coined the term *homo sapiens* for man and *homo troglodytes* for the orang-outang.

Linnaeus tended to concentrate on external characteristics. Others had been examining the working of the organism: the plant as factory, as it were. In his comfortable country living at Teddington, Middlesex, the Rev. Stephen Hales collected a series of plants to ascertain how plants breathe and how the sap rises. His *Vegetable Staticks* (1727) is not only a classic physiology of plants, but like *f 12*
his numerous other contributions (e.g. ventilation for prisons, and distillation plants for sea water) shows the rise of what one might call an engineering outlook. Indeed it was an engineer, Jan Ingenhousz, who showed how plants exposed to light, take in carbon dioxide and build themselves. His *Experiments upon Vegetables, discovering their great power of purifying the common air in the sunshine and of injuring it in the shade and at night* (1779) classically illustrates consequentiality of sciences, since his friend the chemist Joseph Priestley had, five years before, shown that plants immersed in water exhale 'dephlogisticated' air, whilst another chemist, Antoine Lavoisier, showed how this 'air' or 'oxygen' was an essential p 106
component in animal breathing. These discoveries connected with (23)
each other in a somewhat random way. As Priestley remarked to the Royal Society on March 23, 1775; 'more is owing to what we call chance . . . than to any proper design or preconceived theory in this business'.

Yet 'design' preoccupied scientists. Linnaeus at first believed that there could be no such thing as a new species—all species that existed had 'issued in pairs from the hands of the Creator'. Later he

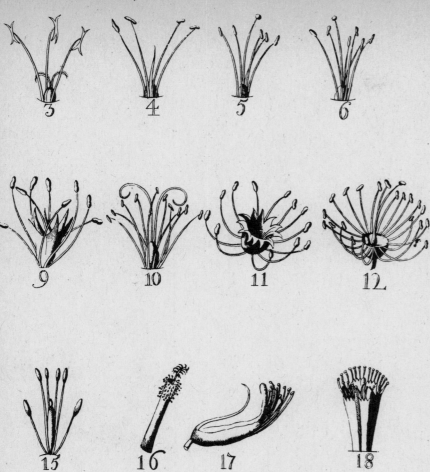

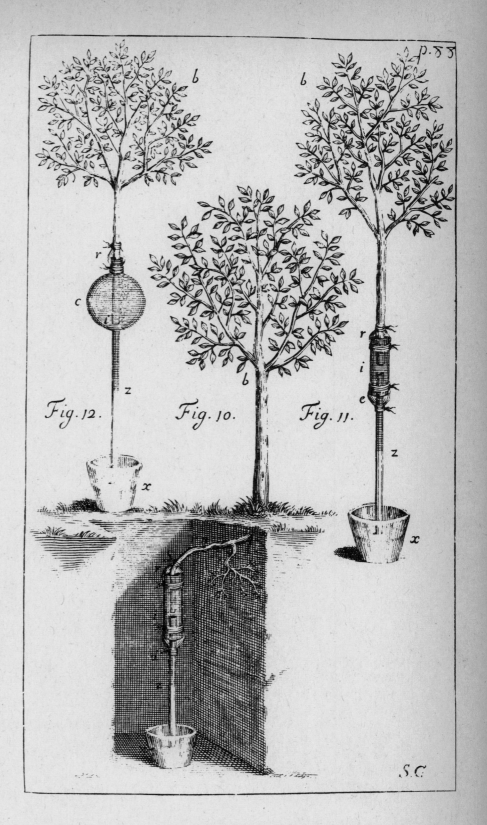

modified his ideas to the point of holding that only genera were original and that 'all the species of one genus constituted at first one species'. New species he explained as arising from cross-breeding. Vague intimations that species were not permanent were crystallized by the great industry of Buffon, whom we have already met as Director of the Jardin des Plantes. He translated Hales' *Vegetable Staticks* into French in 1735 and went on to publish his own thirty-six-volume *Histoire Naturelle* whose range transcended mere classification. He looked for likenesses not differences, seeing embryo or vestigial organs of one species in another which formed an offshoot of the first. His friend and associate in the Jardin, Lamarck, advanced the theory that such organs became vestigial owing to changes of environment. For example, a neck like that of a deer might have lengthened over the course of time in an environment where ground vegetation was scarce to one the length of a giraffe's, in order to feed on tree foliage. Lamarck's notions of studying organisms within their environment arose from his botanical and zoological interests and led him to coin the term 'biology' in 1802.

The most vivid and effective synthesis of the idea of evolution as produced by natural, artificial, environmental, or surgical means was articulated by Priestley's friend, Erasmus Darwin, the Lichfield physician whose statement of the influence of these external modifying factors and of their permanence is now known as 'the inheritance of acquired characters'.

Another adumbration of a fundamental biological concept was that of the cell. Here the German Lorenz Oken forecast modern doctrine and made considerable advances in embryology. His *Foundations of Naturphilosophie*, the theory of Linnaeus and the classification of animals based thereon (1802) also tried to construct an even more inner biology: that of the mind.

The great secular parable of the 18th century was that of a man in a natural garden, *The life and strange adventures of Robinson Crusoe* (1719). This embellished story of the endeavours of an ingenious Scotsman to keep alive in the unspoilt natural world of Juan Fernández from 1704 to 1709 was so universally popular that 'Robinsonaden' became a regular literary convention for airing ideas and concepts about society. As a kind of universal paradigm in discourses on man against nature, or man and society, it has retained its relevance to this day. Similar paradigms and models seemed to obsess 18th-century scientists as they struggled to reconcile science and religion.

*To measure how much water a tree imbibed, Stephen Hales cut the root of a pear-tree, and placed the end in a bucket of water. The drawing (above) comes from his 'Vegetable Staticks' of 1727. Below: insect studies by Charles Bonnet (1745). He showed that lice could be born from the female without fertilization. (12, 13)*

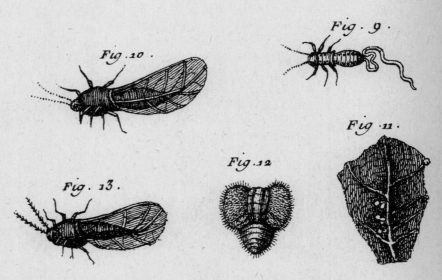

'To display before mankind a new Instance of the Amazing Power of the Creator,' Daniel Defoe's son-in-law, Henry Baker, published *A Natural History of the Polype* (1743) to show how these fresh water hydra daily progressed to becoming a perfect type of polype. The many attempts to square the apparently irrational jigsaw of discovery with the original design of the Creator led to a great deal of writing on subjects like *emboitement* (i.e. each female contained within herself the destiny of the entire species); parthenogenesis (i.e. *ex ovo* without fertilization = virgin birth) and spontaneous generation (i.e. *de novo*). Typical of the advocates of

f 13 the first and second was Charles Bonnet, a Genevan, whose *Traité d'Insectologie* (1745) was described by Charles Singer as 'very influential on the Christian side'. The third concept, that of spontaneous generation, is associated with the English Catholic priest, J. T.

f 14 Needham, accounts of whose experiments were published in 1748.

What is now called 'the philosophy of science' was then an integral part of philosophy. Thus even though the mathematical

p 264 physicist Kant held that 'man is the centre of things in nature and
(7) that he should act as if the principle by which he acted was about to be turned into a universal law of nature', his last book, *Religion within the Boundaries of Pure Reason* (1793), evoked official rebuke.

p 265 His fellow countryman Goethe insisted that *genera* expressed ideas,
(12) that there was a primordial animal and a primordial plant, each expressing an 'idea', and invented the word 'morphology' to cover the description, elucidation and comparison of everything.

Science was coming dangerously close to mysticism when a 'new Church' was organized in London in 1778 by the followers of the Swedish engineer Emanuel Swedenborg. His search for scientific explanation of the universe led him to conceive of God as Divine Man from whom emanate the two worlds of nature and spirit. Since the purpose of creation (the approximation of man to God) has been threatened, God descended to dispel the threat, leaving a set of rules (the Scriptures) to prevent that threat recurring. Swedenborg offered himself as the exegete of this 'rule-book'.

The 18th-century naturalist was no rationalist. As he looked down the ladder of nature, he saw man above mammal, mammal above cetacean, cetacean above reptile, bird, amphibian or fish. These in turn were above cephalopods, and cephalopods above crustaceans. Then, in descending order down to the humble sponge came the other anthropods, other molluscs, ascidians, and holothurians. These gradations were as fixed and immovable as the social system of his day. This ladder, which had been tentatively set up by Aristotle, was the basis of what Arthur O. Lovejoy has called 'the great chain of being' that stretched from the footsteps of God's throne to the lowest sponge (we may note, incidentally, as a sign of the growth of scientific knowledge, that the first use of 'to sponge', meaning 'to live parasitically on others' dates from 1693).

### 'The Great Ocean of Truth'

p 100 The search for plants, and the struggle for 'plantations' or colonies,
(8, 9) was a hazardous business, which carries us on to another theme: navigation. Between 1691 and 1721 England lost five naval squadrons because no one knew how to determine longitude at sea. Whereas latitude was increasingly easy to determine from the sun and the stars thanks to the introduction of the sextant by John Hadley early in the century, longitude, depending as it did on the difference between local time on the ship and standard time on a fixed meridian of reference, needed either accurate lunar measurements or an accurate chronometer. Lunar studies had led to the establishment of the Greenwich Observatory in 1675 and had been the starting point of Isaac Newton's *Principia* (1689). The former collected observations on 'the motion of the heavens and the places of fixed stars', the latter offered a theory of such motions. This theory, outlined in his *Method of Fluxions* (1704) was the culmination of thirty-five years' work on curves generated by the continuous motion of a point. It established the nomenclature of fluxions. Fluent was y, the fluxion of the fluent was ẏ; the fluxion of ẏ was ÿ. This nomenclature was adopted by English mathematics as opposed to the more convenient symbolism of Leibniz: differentiation, written dy/dz. Not until the early 19th century was the Analytical Society formed at Cambridge to advocate, as one of its members said 'the principles of pure *d*-ism as opposed to the

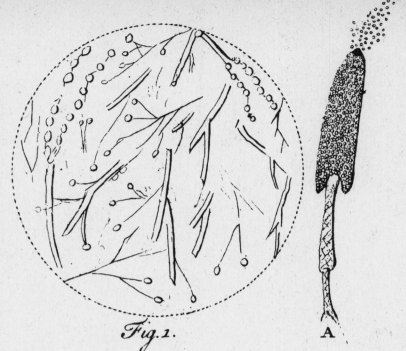

*Fig. 1.*  A

*J. T. Needham's 'Observations upon the Generation and Composition . . . of Animal and Vegetable Systems' was published in 1748. Needham was a believer in spontaneous generation and thought that he had proved his case by sealing wheat germs in sterilized flasks and observing the growth of minute organisms. This series of diagrams shows such a development.* (14)

*dot*-age of the university'. Leibniz himself generously acknowledged that 'taking mathematics from the beginning of the world to the time when Newton lived, what he did was much the better half.' Newton modestly compared himself to a boy playing on a seashore 'diverting myself in now and then finding a smoother pebble or a prettier shell than ordinary, whilst the great ocean of truth lay all undiscovered before me'.

But in actually calculating the position of the moon, the best methods of observation could not ensure a margin of error of less than two or three degrees—which for a ship at sea might mean anything up to 200 miles. In 1713, therefore, the British government offered substantial rewards for a satisfactory chronometer, and to assess the various proposals a Board of Longitude was formed. For twenty-three years no real progress was made. Then in 1736 the first of several chronometers was submitted by John Harrison. Not until he submitted his fifth in 1773 did he receive the full prize of £20,000 and then only by direct interposition of George III. In its ceaseless quest for solutions to the problem, the Board of Longitude evoked so many suggestions that Dean Swift was able to satirize them in his 'Ode for Music: On the Longitude'. Others who tried to improve lunar theory, like Butler and Mayer, were also rewarded. Mayer's tables, in fact, which reduced the margin of error to half a degree, were published by the Commissioners in 1766 as the first issue of the *Nautical Almanac*. — p 158–9 (11, 12)

The improvements in instrument-making meant, of course, enormous advances in the science of astronomy. In 1766 William Herschel began to construct telescopes with lenses of hitherto unattempted exactitude, with which eight years later he was able to identify a new planet, now called Uranus. As a compliment to George III he named it *Georgium Sidus* and was appropriately rewarded by being made Court astronomer in 1782. He could then afford to begin his great sweeps of the heavens which revealed, amongst other things, more than 2,000 nebulae. — p 102 (13)

Patient mapping of the positions of the sun and moon, and the computation of the orbits of stars and comets continued forward throughout Europe in observatories like those at Paris, Greenwich and Göttingen. Indeed, James Bradley's observations at Greenwich between 1750 and 1762 have been described as 'a magnificent series' which 'formed the most important contribution of the century to meridian astronomy'. — p 102 (15)

To provide equations to explain these and other phenomena, mathematicians came near to fulfilling Swift's ironic picture of the island of Laputa. The calculation of lunar and stellar movements gave Clairaut, Euler, d'Alembert, Lagrange and Laplace such an opportunity of improving the mathematical explanation of the solar system, that they virtually built a mathematical system around themselves; Lagrange's students formed what in fact became the Turin Academy of Science.

## The progress of the machine

The need for accurate marine chronometers elicited more sophisticated machine-tools. The first known treatise on the lathe, Charles Plumier's *L'Art du tourneur* (1701), contained an illustration of a watch-maker's screw-cutting lathe. This was further improved by the addition of a sliding rest perfected in 1778 by Jesse Ramsden (1735–1800) who produced screws of great accuracy. Such precision engineers also armed experimental scientists with the accurate measuring instruments that enabled, for instance, Joseph Black to establish his theory of latent heat and this in turn led to James Watt's improvements to the steam engine.

The age of power, in fact, was about to dawn, but its form was still uncertain. Jet power, understood in China for millennia, was first made known in Europe in 1687 by a Jesuit priest in China who claimed to have propelled a model by steam jet, blowing upon vanes fixed to the wheels. But an engine that transmitted power by pistons seemed more promising, and such a scheme had in fact been explored by Von Guericke in 1654. But what was to generate the power? Huyghens (in 1680) proposed gunpowder. Papin (in 1698) actually used steam.

Steam was used in a demonstration to the Royal Society in 1699 by Thomas Savery as a motive power for draining mines. And the wars of the 18th century needed metals—mines in Cornwall, Staffordshire and Northumberland began to use them. As early as 1724–27 Jacob Leupold proposed its use to push the piston against atmospheric pressure, but existing boilers could not produce nor existing cylinders contain it at that time.

Much high-grade basic science was applied to the improvement of these steam-pumping engines by men like J. T. Desaguliers FRS, Henry Beighton FRS, Martin Triewald FRS and John Smeaton FRS. Not only did they pump water out of the mines, but water into cities. In 1769–1770 a French army engineer, Nicholas Joseph Cugnot, actually made a model that ran nearly 1,000 yards in fifteen minutes (i.e. at about $2\frac{1}{4}$ m.p.h.) before it ran out of steam. Since this looked a possible gun-towing vehicle the French government set the resources of the Paris arsenal to improve it. From their work emerged a three-wheel vehicle, with the single front wheel driven by a pawl and ratchet. If the model in the Conservatoire des Arts et Métiers in Paris is anything to judge by, its practicability was questionable, for, apart from the unsprung chassis having to run on rough roads, the large kettle-shaped high pressure boiler housed above the front wheel would almost certainly have enveloped artillerymen in clouds of steam.

But the master application was to apply the new motive power to Matthew Boulton's factory at Soho in Birmingham. This was so successful that in 1775 Boulton signed an agreement with James Watt, who had designed and installed the engine, to exploit the patent for twenty-five years. Under legal protection they improved it, adding rotary motion, a throttle and a centrifugal governor.

An improved multi-tubular boiler engine is said to have been built by another Frenchman, Charles Dallery, in 1780. Yet another variant of the three-wheeled model, this time with the drive applied by a crank to the two rear wheels, was designed in 1784–86 by an assistant of Boulton and Watt's—William Murdoch, who at his employers' insistence discontinued the experiments. But others took them up, William Symington in Scotland, Robert Fourness and James Ashworth at Halifax. The latter patented and built a three-cylinder four-wheeled steam vehicle. In America Nathan Read and Oliver Evans built models that made it look as if Erasmus Darwin's hope would be fulfilled:

> '*Soon shall thy force* UNCONQUERED STEAM, *afar
> Drag the slow barge or urge the flying car.*'

The prime obstacle to all these attempts was the lack of a light small boiler which could raise steam quickly. This came only in 1801, when one was built at Camborne Redruth at the centre of

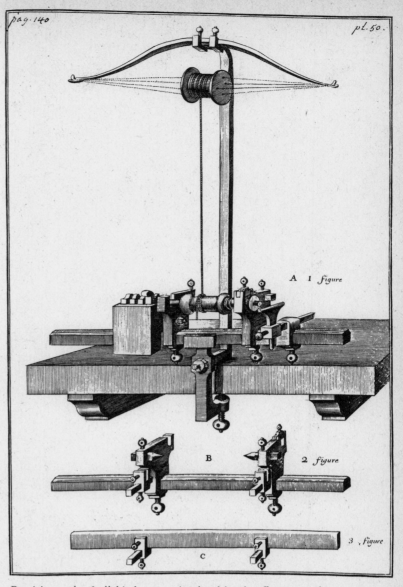

Precision tools of all kinds were stimulated by the effort to produce an accurate marine chronometer, and advances were made in many other fields of technology. Charles Plumier's 'L'Art du Tourneur' of 1701 contained this diagram of a watch-maker's screw-cutting lathe. Such sophisticated techniques were a necessity for further scientific advance. (15)

the mining engineering complex of Cornwall by Richard Trevithick, whose steam engine was the first to run on the roads. Patented the following year, it ran on the streets of London carrying passengers. Trevithick also appreciated, though he did not construct, the need for gears, to enable such vehicles to climb hills.

It is perhaps coincidental that, at the same time, as the heat engine was developing, rapid improvements were being made in the measurement of heat. The first 'thermometer' was devised by Galileo utilizing the expansion of air. By 1708 Römer was using thermometers filled with water or alcohol calibrated to the temperature of melting ice (which he called $7\frac{1}{2}°$) and normal human blood ($22\frac{1}{2}°$). Fahrenheit constructed a 'scale' between these two points, renumbering them 30 and 90. Later, to avoid fractions, he altered these to 32 and 96. By 1721 he was using mercury instead of alcohol in his thermometer. At about the same time Réaumur fixed a zero point at the freezing point of water and envisaged that the alcohol in his thermometer would expand from 1,000 to 1,080 units when submerged in boiling water. By 1742 a third scale appeared divided into a hundred equal parts with the freezing point of water as zero and its boiling point as 100. This scale was converted to our present 'centigrade' by Christian in 1743.

## Scientific dynasties

The name 'statistician' was first coined by Gottfried Achenwall (1719–72) to describe the increasing numbers of men who compiled tables of figures for use in insurance, manufacturing—or gambling. Mathematicians too were interested in problems posed by games of chance. By tabulation the Chevalier de Mere was encouraged to prophesy that a man would be safe in thinking that a 6 would occur at least once in 4 throws of the dice. Pascal was intrigued and with his friend Fermat worked out a mathematical theory of probability. This was seized upon by Jacob Bernouilli, one of the family of famous Swiss mathematicians, who postulated that 'it is practically certain that in a sufficiently long series of independent trials with constant probability, the relative frequency of an event will differ from that probability by less than any specified number however small'. Bernouilli's *Ars Conjectandi* (1713) appeared in the coffee houses at just the right time. Insurance companies were being launched, gambling was rife, and the fever of investment in joint stock companies was spreading. So what could be more natural than the appearance in a London coffee house of the Huguenot refugee, Abraham de Moivre, whose *Doctrine of Chances* (1718) paved the way for the huge actuarial empires of modern finance, no less than for the various efforts at planning made by firms and governments.

Bernouilli represents the beginning of a new phenomenon: the scientific dynasty. He was succeeded as Professor of Mathematics at Basle in 1705 by his son Johann, while his nephew Nikolaus held a similar chair at Padua before returning to Basle as professor of law and logic. Johann's three sons also held mathematical chairs, two of them at St Petersburg, as did one son of the third. The other son was an astronomer at Berlin.

The family of Jussieu of the Jardin have already been mentioned. Then there was the family of Cassini, astronomers all. Jean-Dominique, the first director of the Paris Observatory, was succeeded by his son Jacques in 1712, who was in turn succeeded by his son César in 1756, who was succeeded by his son Comte Jacques-Dominique in 1784. Jacques-Dominique's son gave up astronomy for biology.

Even more astonishing was the Monro dynasty in Edinburgh who held the chair of anatomy from its foundation in 1720 till well into the 19th century. Since they all had the same Christian name, they are differentiated as Alexander *primus, secundus* and *tertius*.

So too in the allied science of botany. Humphrey Sibthorp (who during his thirty-six years' tenure of the chair at Oxford is said to have only lectured once and then unsuccessfully) was succeeded by his son John in 1783. John gave the chair up to make a series of intensive study tours of Europe, and bequeathed his books and estate to endow a further chair, this time of rural economy, in 1796. All these cases show not so much hereditary talent as what later generations were to call the effects of home environment. Before either systematic scientific education or professional associations, each family became completely identified with its respective field.

Where the connection between scientists was not one of family it was often one of patronage. In England two great patrons

*The bridge of Pont Sainte-Maxence, near Paris, begun in 1774, made novel and daring use of flat elliptical arches. It was designed by Jean Perronet, director of the 'Ecole des Ponts et Chaussées'. Even more unusual was Forest de Belidor's* *proposed four-way bridge (below), a land cross-roads superimposed on a water one. The advantage, according to Belidor, was to bring together at one point all the principal communication routes of the province. (16, 17)*

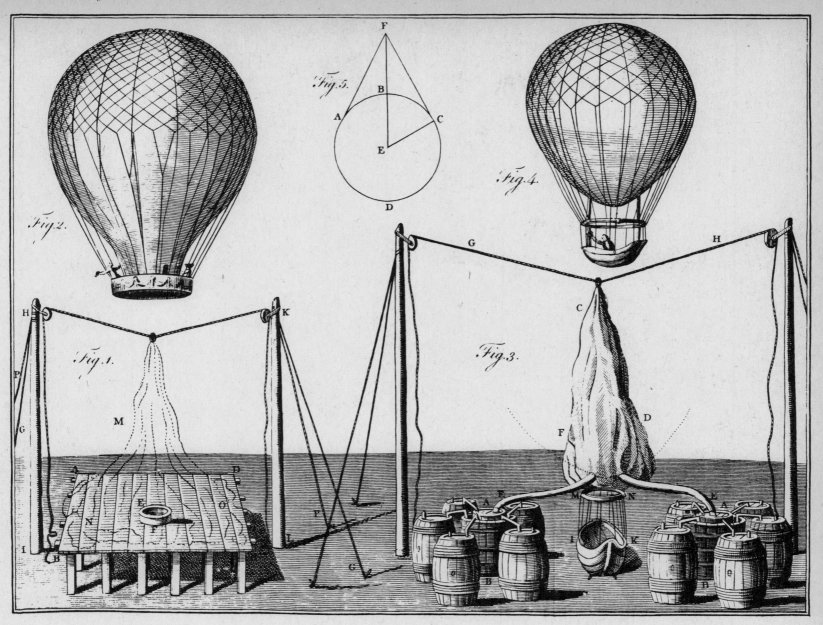

The two types of balloon in use during the late 18th century – the 'montgolfière' and the 'charlière' – are illustrated in this engraving from Tiberius Cavallo's 'History and Practice of Aerostation' (1785). On the left is the hot-air balloon, developed by the Montgolfier brothers; it was filled from a fire underneath the plat-form and could only be kept aloft by taking a brazier of coal up with it. The one on the right is a hydrogen- (or 'inflammable air') balloon, as made by the physicist J. A. C. Charles in 1783. This soon superseded the 'montgolfière', and balloon flights became commonplace in several countries of Europe. (18)

dominate the century: Sloane and Banks. Both left an indelible imprint on scientific life in Britain and Europe. Sloane, whose wealth came from the sale of quinine, became President of the Royal Society in 1727, having already revived the *Philosophical Transactions* thirty-four years earlier. He was a great collector of curiosities and manuscripts, later acquired by the nation and constituting the nucleus of the British Museum. Banks, on the other hand, inherited a private fortune, and had a pupil of Linnaeus as his personal librarian and companion. On becoming President of the Royal Society in 1778, he turned its interests towards natural history even at the risk of alienating the mathematicians. From his house in Soho Square he virtually decreed the survey of every continent for the enrichment of Kew Gardens, which he envisaged as a botanical entrepot for the British Empire.

p 101
(11)

## On the earth and in the sky

But governments could no longer rely on the accidents of heredity and the whims of patrons. In an increasingly technological society the technicians had to be trained and organized. Engineers, for instance, were needed for the wars which racked Europe; and the French here, as in other fields, set precedents by establishing the Corps des Ponts et Chaussées to approve the plans of all bridges, roads and canals in France. This momentous event marked the first stage of the professionalization of engineering. Since the Corps were a governmental department, its standards became prescriptive. To ensure their maintenance and to prepare its recruits more inten-

p 105
(20)

sively, the Ecole des Ponts et Chaussées was established in 1747. Its director, Jean Perronet, was one of the great engineers of the century, exploiting the thrust of flat masonary arches against each other, and devising ingenious water-wheels to pump water from the coffer-dams. The old Pont Sainte-Maxence, destroyed in 1870, and the Pont de la Concorde put France in the lead in this branch of engineering.

f 16

French-trained engineers also came to England. One of them, Charles Labalye, built a second bridge over the Thames at Westminster, introducing the great innovation of 'caissons'—great boxes of timber which were built on the bank, towed to the site, filled with the lower courses of masonry, and sunk on a previously dredged and levelled bed. The bridges at Westminster and Saumur were both built by this method.

p 104
(18)

Bridge builders took over ideas generated in the Military College at La Fère by B. F. de Bélidor. He synthesized all current techniques in his book *La Science des Ingénieurs* (1729) and *Architecture Hydraulique* (1737–1753), which were carefully studied by that great trinity of English civil engineers: John Smeaton, John Rennie and Thomas Telford. Indeed Telford learned French in order to read them, though he might, like George Semple, who built the Essex Bridge over the Liffey at Dublin in 1752, have done just as well by studying the excellent plates in Bélidor's *Architecture Hydraulique*. French ideas were further interpreted to Englishmen through the lectures of Professor John Robinson and the writings of Dr Thomas Young.

f 17

One result of the contact between French and British scientists was the development of the balloon. Two years after Cavendish discovered, in 1776, that hydrogen is lighter than air, Joseph Black suggested it should be released into a bladder. An Italian scientist Tiberius Cavallo, pursued the same line of research with soap bubbles, and on June 20, 1782, he described his experiments with a vessel so filled to an audience at the Royal Society of London.

It was not hydrogen, but another gas—which they called *air alkalin*—with which the brothers Montgolfier filled small *ballons* (oblong paper bags) at Annonay in France some five months later. They went on to fill larger *ballons* of silk or linen, and on June 5, 1783, released a balloon that rose to a height of 6,000 feet and travelled nearly 8,000 feet. The mysterious gas was investigated by the French Académie des Sciences, who found that it was just hot air emitted by the brazier which the brothers had slung underneath. Convinced that hydrogen was a far superior lifting agent, the Academy commissioned a geologist and a physicist, Faujas de Saint-Fond and J. A. C. Charles, to manufacture it for a 13-foot diameter rubber-impregnated lutestring balloon. This was successfully flown two and a half months later.

'This experiment,' wrote Benjamin Franklin to Sir Joseph Banks, 'is by no means a trifling one. It may be attended with important consequences that no one can foresee.' He foresaw it as a preparation 'for some discoveries in natural philosophy of which at present we have no conception.' It might enable ice to be obtained. It might even, by making armies and navies obsolete, help the cause of world peace.

*f 18*  Variants of these two contrasting types of aerial balloon, the hot air or *montgolfières* and the hydrogen or *charlières*, rose rapidly from now on. In a *montgolfière* a sheep, a cock and a duck were airborne for eight minutes on September 19, 1783, and the young scientist, J. F. Pilâtre de Rozier, followed them a month later, staying aloft for nearly five minutes at a height of 80 feet by frequent stoking of the brazier. A manned *charlière* travelled twenty-seven miles from the Tuileries to Nesle on December 1. As Benjamin Franklin told a friend in that month, 'We think of nothing here at present but of flying, the balloons engross all conversation.' The passion extended to dropping from the air, for in that month too Etienne Lenormand made the first parachute descent from the Montpellier observation tower. Every European capital caught the fever. An American, Dr Jeffries, travelled with Francois Blanchard's balloon which crossed the Channel from Dover to Calais on January 1, 1785. Trying to emulate them in the reverse direction, Pilâtre de Rozier used a *charlière* with a *montgolfière* suspended beneath it. The outcome was inevitable. The heat exploded the hydrogen just as the balloon was airborne, and Pilâtre became the first casualty in ballooning history.

p. 108 (31)

Persuaded by Guyton de Morveau, politicians became very interested, during the French Revolution, in the military possibilities of the *charlière* balloon which, like those of the steam truck, were obvious. To overcome their fears about the amount of iron and sulphuric acid which would be needed to produce the necessary

hydrogen, Lavoisier devised a process for obtaining it by passing water over red hot iron filings. Thereafter a Balloon Corps could take shape in 1793 under a former student of Charles, J. M. J. Coutelle, and a 30-foot diameter gummed silk balloon, the *Entreprenant* was built for observation. A ballooning school was also created at Meudon in 1795 under another scientist Jacques Conte and a second company of balloonists was raised. Twenty-two balloons were sent to the front. Taken to Egypt by Napoleon, the Balloon Corps lost their equipment when the British Fleet sank the *Patriot* at Aboukir Bay and their balloons when the *Orient* was captured at Alexandria.

p 108 (30)

## Illuminati

Major French cities had been lit by artificial light since the end of the 17th century, but the candle-lanterns were dim and unsatisfactory. In 1764 the Academie des Sciences offered a prize of 2,000 *livres* for an essay on the best way to light towns. From a strong field, which included ideas of Lavoisier, the reflecting oil lantern of Bourgeois de Chateaublanc was chosen. But simultaneously another inventor, Argand, had evolved an oil lamp which he preferred to patent in London. This caused various legal complications, and it was not until 1782 that Argand's lamp began to be manufactured in Paris. In 1800 it was improved by placing the wick above the oil reservoir and connecting the two by means of a pump. This was the famous Carcel lamp.

The future, however, lay with gas. Research in this direction had been initiated by a young army engineer, Lebon, who successfully extracted gas from wood, patented his process in 1799, but was murdered three years later while helping to organize the celebrations for Napoleon's coronation. The idea was taken up on the other side of the Channel. James Watt's son Gregory heard of Lebon's experiments and saw their relevance to those carried out by the firm's mechanic, William Murdoch, who was trying to extract gas from coal. James Watt took the hint; new machinery was installed in the works at Birmingham; and by 1809 the Gas Light and Coke Company was launched. Gas-light transformed the cities and the social habits of Europe and America, and may perhaps stand as a fitting symbol for the century of Enlightenment.

p 106 (25)

But already scientists were being forced to adopt public roles, and finding themselves burdened with political responsibilities not of their own choosing. The two greatest geniuses of the age illustrate the point with brutal clarity. Newton, who died in 1727, regarded his scientific work almost as a personal hobby. In 1794 Antoine Lavoisier, the father of modern chemistry and adviser to the French government on practically every scientific problem of the day, a man who combined pure science and practical technology in a way that has hardly any parallel, was guillotined as a Farmer General. If the scientist suffered, however, science itself was unchallenged. The same year which saw the execution of Lavoisier saw also the foundation of the Ecole Polytechnique in Paris, soon to be imitated in Germany and in Russia, and a potent indication of the world to come.

p 106 (22)

# IV COUNTRYSIDE AND INDUSTRY

*The Economics of an Age of Change*

D. C. COLEMAN

*'The greatest improvement in the productive powers of labour,*

*and the greater part of the skill, dexterity, and judgment*

*with which it is anywhere directed, or applied, seem to have been*

*the effects of the division of labour.'*

ADAM SMITH 'An Inquiry into the Nature and Causes of the Wealth of Nations' (1776)

## In the countryside,

where most people in the 18th century lived and worked, the amount and nature of change varied greatly from area to area. Old systems of land tenure and methods of cultivation were being superseded; traditional tools were being improved; scientific knowledge was being applied to crop-growing and cattle-breeding. But the process was slow. In some countries and regions the rural face of Europe remained much as it had been in the 16th century. Even the Industrial Revolution, which by 1800, in England at least, was already transforming the economy, had not so far done much to quicken the slow tempo of the agricultural year.

By poets and painters of the Picturesque or Romantic persuasion, however, the countryside was already being idealized as something more than a place where peasants worked and food was grown. The 'pastoral' – nature seen as the abode of innocence and peace – was part of the classical tradition but mostly had little connection with the realities of rural life. By the later 18th century this was changing. Town-dwelling artists and writers went to the countryside, looked with sympathy at its inhabitants, and portrayed it, within limits, realistically. Jean Baptiste Oudry, court painter to Louis XV, is typical of such an attitude. His *Farmyard Scene* (opposite) selects elements from an actual farm – the ploughman, the cows, sheep, goats and ducks, the rustic buildings – but shows that selection honestly: the perfect combination of document and idyll. (1)

**England took the lead** in agricultural progress in the 18th century, partly because its ruling class chose to remain on their estates and take a personal interest in managing them. This was not achieved without friction. The 'enclosure' of common land to promote more efficient farming was one of the bitterest issues in local politics. The watercolours below and on the right of the opposite page show surveyors mapping the land for enclosure in Bedfordshire. (2, 10)

**Several sorts** of rural activities and objects are illustrated in this fanciful and crowded engraving of 1727: grain growing, sheep and cattle raising; the vineyard and the dairy; the water-mill and the wind-mill. Note the 'great house' and its formal garden in the background. (3)

**Haymaking:** the well-known painting by Stubbs (below) is accurate enough in its details but omits the harsher aspects: it is labour without the fatigue and the sweat. (4)

**A dairy and a sheep farm;** engravings from a German work on farming published in 1705. Butter is made in the churn and packed on the tray in the centre. (5, 7)

**Flax and timber:** the flax-processing scene is German, like those on the left. The foresters come from an English treatise and show men measuring the volume of felled timber. (6, 8)

**Enclosure** is the term for a process which could be carried out in various ways with various results. Generally, it meant the extinction of common rights over fields cultivated by the old open-field system with its intermingled peasant holdings. The landlord replaced them by farms, enclosed by fences or hedges, which were then leased to tenants or farmed directly with hired labour. Sometimes, though not always, it led to improved farming; often, though not invariably, the English Enclosure Acts fell harshly upon the small man. (10)

**A pioneer** of agricultural theory was Arthur Young (above) – unsuccessful farmer but indefatigable observer, writer and traveller. His 'Annals of Agriculture' alone ran to 46 volumes. (9)

**Ploughing techniques** are illustrated in a plate from Diderot's *Encyclopédie* (above left). In the foreground the man is ploughing with a large-wheeled plough; the woman is sowing with a form of drill, but we can be sure that in reality much sowing was still broadcast by hand. Below: the light Rotherham plough, with triangular frame, introduced in 1730. Above right: one of the less successful inventions of the day, a Hertfordshire wheel-drill plough combined with seed and manure hopper. (11, 12, 13)

**Cattle and sheep-breeding** as a systematically controlled process begins in the 18th century. It became something of an obsession with some English gentlemen-farmers and the results, if we may judge from the animal portraits which they proudly commissioned, were sometimes fantastic. Thomas Coke, Earl of Leicester (above) of Holkham in Norfolk (the house is just visible in the distance), was a pioneer breeder who, by collecting all available information, was able to improve both cropping and livestock – cattle and pigs as well as sheep. His sheep were Southdowns, bred from the old Sussex type. Below left: the so-called 'Pangborn Hog' produced at Tidmarsh Farm in Berkshire – a prize beast whose size and colouring are equally difficult to credit. (14, 15)

**'The Lincolnshire Ox'** (above) is portrayed by George Stubbs, with his satisfied owner, John Gibbons standing beside him. The animal, which stood eleven hands high, was exhibited in London in 1790 at the Riding House, Hyde Park. (17)

**Robert Bakewell** (right), the son of a Leicestershire farmer, was probably the most successful breeder of 18th-century England. His farm at Dishley became famous and was visited as a model by his numerous rivals. Sheep-breeding was his speciality; he established the 'Dishley Society' to ensure purity of stock, hiring out his prize rams for as much as 100 guineas. The champion of them all was 'Two-Pounder' (left), so-called because of Bakewell's boast that England now 'had two pounds of mutton where there was only one before'. This sheep is said to have made 1200 guineas a year for his owner. (16, 18)

**Opportunities for the craftsmen** expanded with improved techniques of manufacture and with increased production of metals and other minerals. The 18th century attained a standard of elegance in pottery, silverware and furniture that has never been surpassed. Three of the most famous porcelain factories are represented on the right. 'Columbine' is from Nymphenburg (1755–60); the lady in the flowered dress comes from Meissen (c. 1745); and the actor in Turkish costume was made in Chelsea (c. 1765). (19, 20, 21)

**Silverware** could assume the most convoluted Rococo forms for the upper classes, or be plainly utilitarian for the less affluent. These two pieces, a sauce-boat and a coffee-pot, were both made by the Courtauld firm, the first in 1751, the second in 1730. (23, 24)

**Josiah Wedgwood** developed a type of pottery based, like the Adam style, on classical models, with graceful white decoration against coloured backgrounds. This coffee-pot is lilac jasperware. (26)

**New forms in furniture** reflected the precision of new tools and the qualities of the new woods that went to their making. Left: a side-table made for Louis XV, with marble top and gilt bronze mounts; the scroll-work – suggesting symmetry without being symmetrical – is typically Rococo. Above: a chair in the style of Louis XVI, with fluting, Ionic capitals and upholstery of Beauvais tapestry. Right: an English chair of West Indian mahogany (c. 1745). (22, 25, 27)

**Swedish iron** was exported all over Europe, especially to Britain, and at the beginning of the 18th century her own iron industry led the world both in quantity and quality. This painting shows part of the interior of a Swedish ironworks in 1781. Around the middle of the 18th century the Swedish government, fearful of the effects of wholesale deforestation, introduced restrictions on the output of iron. Meanwhile, new techniques were being applied in Britain, where the process of smelting with coal instead of charcoal was being pioneered at Coalbrookdale in Shropshire. By the end of the century the Swedish industry was falling behind. (28)

**Coal** was one of the keys to the Industrial Revolution. Above right: the pit-head of a Belgian colliery in the later 18th century. (29)

**Copper** came second to iron among Sweden's exports, but declined as the mines (of which one is shown right) became deeper, more expensive and less productive. (30)

**The Industrial Revolution** which transformed so many parts of the world in the 19th century had its origins in the large-scale application of technical discoveries made in the 18th. A combination of natural resources (chiefly coal and iron) with capitalist commercial enterprise helped to put Britain in the forefront of change.

Right: an early Newcomen engine for pumping water out of mines. It worked not by the expansive power of steam (too dangerous at that time) but by producing a vacuum in the steam-filled cylinder (C) through the injection of cold water from the tank (g) via a pipe (M). This drew down the right-hand end of the beam. (31)

**Direct steam power** was first harnessed by James Watt (far right), whose engines came to replace those of Newcomen. Urged on by his business partner, Matthew Boulton, he succeeded in 1788 in transferring piston-action to rotary-action; a typical Boulton and Watt engine is shown below. Pressure in the cylinder on the left pushes the beam upwards and by an arrangement of cogged wheels the descending other arm sets the large fly-wheel in continuous motion. Instead of being confined to pumping, steam could now be used to drive every sort of engine. (32, 33)

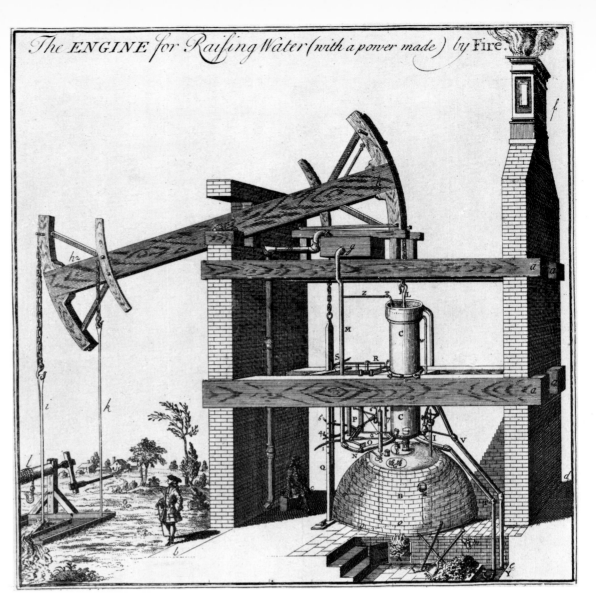

The ENGINE for Raising Water (with a power made) by Fire.

**New spinning machinery** made possible the mass-production of cotton yarn. Richard Arkwright (below), promotor of the 'water-frame', so called because it was designed to be driven by water power, organized some of the first textile factories. Powerlooms were later evolved to weave the yarn into cloth. Raw cotton was imported from America. (34)

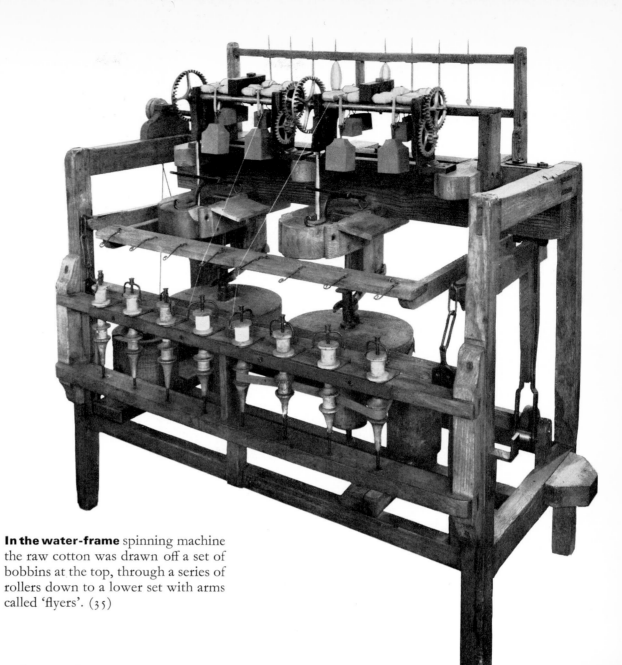

**In the water-frame** spinning machine the raw cotton was drawn off a set of bobbins at the top, through a series of rollers down to a lower set with arms called 'flyers'. (35)

**Ironworks** were in process of change; the earlier type, burning charcoal, is represented (below) by Backbarrow Furnace in Lancashire, in about 1740; molten metal is being carried in ladles from the furnace to the moulds. In the foreground are some typical products. (36)

**The industrial townscape** of the 19th century is prophetically portrayed in this watercolour of a Welsh ironworks in the 1780's. The exact location is uncertain, but may be Nant-y-glo. The group of buildings on the right with the tall chimneys is probably for converting pig-iron into malleable iron; those on the left seem to be blast-furnaces. (37)

**Industry had its own beauty** in the eyes of such painters as Joseph Wright of Derby, a man fascinated by the new world that science was opening up. He was a close friend of Arkwright the industrialist, and painted this view of Arkwright's cotton mill at Cromford, Derbyshire, its windows blazing with light, in the early 1780's. (38)

# The Economics of an Age of Change

D. C. COLEMAN

WHATEVER MAY HAVE HAPPENED in art and architecture, whatever the advances in commerce or industry, most people in the 18th century worked on the land, producing the food which gave sustenance to people, trade and towns alike. Moreover, many of them, perhaps the majority, worked with traditional tools, followed procedures that differed little from generation to generation, and operated within contractual or customary relationships which had been laid down in earlier centuries. The tenure and cultivation of land in strips according to the practices of the medieval manor; rights of common pasturage; the exaction of labour dues from serfs: all could be found in differing extents in different parts of Europe, just as could tiny peasant holdings, vast estates, and modern-seeming leasehold farms, consolidated and enclosed. Agriculture was changing, however, though it was generally a slow and piecemeal process. Innovations, whatever their importance, commonly took far longer than they do today to make their mark upon the national, let alone the international, scene. Their purely local or regional persistence makes generalization difficult if not simply misleading. Although, for instance, the potato had been introduced into Europe as far back as in the 16th century, its cultivation was still spreading slowly, and only in some parts of northern and western Europe, in the 18th century. It established itself firmly in Ireland, in a scattered fashion in England, France and, at the end of the century, in Germany. The use of 'artificial' grasses, i.e. lucerne, sainfoin and clover, together with such root crops as turnips, which had been adopted so successfully in the 17th century as a method of providing winter fodder for cattle in the densely populated Netherlands, was little copied in France and still less in Germany, but made significant and important progress in England. Everywhere, not only the obvious variations of climate but the less obvious variations of soil helped to determine the crops grown, the technical methods employed, the 'course of husbandry' followed. Upon those geographical, natural determinants, which man was then so little able to control or influence, there worked the varied forces of economic and social life: the pressure of population, the growth and change of market demand, the movement of prices, the attitudes of landowners or peasants, the fashioning forms of estate management.

## Tradition and improvement

By the end of the 18th century England had gained the reputation of having the most advanced agriculture in Europe. To explain how this came about historians have in the past often pointed to the great increase of land enclosure, sweeping away the old open fields by private Act of Parliament, especially after 1760; to the activities of a few well known innovators, improving landlords and propagandists— Jethro Tull (1674–1741) with his horse hoe and drill, Viscount 'Turnip' Townshend (1674–1738), Thomas Coke of Holkham (1752–1842), stockbreeders like Robert Bakewell (1725–95), and Arthur Young (1741–1820), tireless writer on farming matters and first secretary of the new, semi-official Board of Agriculture; to the introduction of a particular four-course rotation (wheat, turnips, barley, clover) especially associated with Norfolk; and to the growth of demand for foodstuffs arising from the increase in population. But the explanations which satisfy one generation stimulate the questions of another. Research over the

past two or three decades has shown what was once commonly described in textbooks as the 'English agricultural revolution of the 18th century' to be less peculiarly English, less revolutionary, and less 18th century. The technical changes in English agriculture which increased arable yields and, by the use of forage crops, allowed more stock to be fed and kept, are now seen to have been much influenced both by various methods already in use in parts of England and by the practices of the Low Countries introduced from about the middle of the 17th century, and to have spread thereafter at a time when total population was probably not rising, though both wealth and urban population were. They are seen as owing less to a few prominent innovators or popularizers and more to the prosaic activities of tenant farmers, seeking to reduce costs and reacting to a rise in livestock prices relative to those of cereals; and to numerous enterprising landlords willing to invest money in farming and keen for a good return on their capital. The process of enclosing arable land, which facilitated the use of improved techniques though it did not necessarily imply their adoption, is now seen as having been well under way during the preceding century, though by means less obvious than Act of Parliament. Much of the tripartite structure, so often regarded as characteristic of England in the 18th century—landlord, tenant farmer, and agricultural labourer, modified here and there by pockets of small owner-farmers—had been hammered out well before the great flood of Enclosure Acts began. Although Tull's seed-drill of 1701 was an important innovation, no less so was the light Rotherham plough of the 1730s which owed much to Dutch designs. The drill did not come into much general use before the end of the century though variations of the Rotherham plough were earlier at work on the lighter soils of eastern England.

As a result of such diverse and heterogeneous advances in agriculture in England in the later 17th and early 18th centuries, a better basis was being provided for increasing food supply when total population began to grow rapidly in the second half of the 18th century. Indeed, it may have facilitated that very growth. For it helped to remove the demographic crises which were the common inheritance of earlier centuries. In such crises, severe harvest failures and outbreaks of epidemic disease, themselves facilitated by food shortage, combined to cut back population growth by spreading disease and death across the land.

## Agriculture in Europe

Complex interactions of food supply, land tenure, and population growth can be detected by the historian in retrospect. To interested contemporaries, however, it was the doings of some exceptional aristocrat or squire, the flow of Enclosure Acts, the new agricultural shows, the popularizers and the pamphlets, which made the noise, attracted the attention and created the image of English agriculture transformed. The English example of the removal of common pasturage and the enclosure and consolidation of farms influenced the onset of similar developments in late 18th-century Denmark and Sweden, in part as a deliberate counter to the fragmentation of peasant holdings consequent upon population growth. It was certainly to England that the handful of French enthusiasts for agricultural reform looked for ideas and experience. Although there were great variations from area to area most of

*The open-field system, seen here in a village near Cambridge in 1688, had serious drawbacks. Sheep grazed the fields after harvest, so that it was not always easy to use individual plots to grow fodder crops, although in some areas this was done.*

*Herds too bred promiscuously and cattle and sheep diseases spread only too quickly. The farmer of enclosed land being more independent was better placed to introduce improvements, though not all such farmers did so.* (1)

French agriculture remained backward. Maize had been introduced in the south and had modified the ancient crop-and-fallow rotations of southern peasant agriculture; in the north, Normandy and Picardy had absorbed some of the Netherlands and English techniques in the use of fodder crops and cereals in mixed farming. But in general, despite some government efforts and the work of a few enterprising landlords, the attitudes of mind alike of the French nobility and of the French peasantry were inimical to practical agrarian change. With still more variations, be it in husbandry practice or tenurial relations, this was true over most of Europe. In Italy, some Tuscan landlords toyed with advanced methods; there were improvements in irrigation techniques and the use of fodder crops in Piedmont and Lombardy. But in Naples and Sicily large estates and primitive techniques coincided. Spanish agriculture, impoverished and stagnant in the first half of the century, showed little technical advance or organizational change despite half-hearted government instigated efforts at reform from the 1760s onwards. In Andalusia especially, as on the *latifundia* of the Italian south, vast estates were sustained by a poverty stricken rural proletariat and landlord indifference. In eastern Europe, over innumerable acres of the Habsburg domains

of Austria and Hungary, in Prussia as well as in Poland and Russia, the burdens of serfdom, earlier imposed, were little changed; the reforms, be they of Frederick the Great or of Joseph II, who formally abolished serfdom in the 1780s, little affected the privileges of the landowning classes; and agriculture remained barely changed in its methods and organization. Despite some alleviations in the peasants' position, the rule of the large estate, operating a commercial farming system on the basis of serf or semi-serf labour, remained much as it had been in the 17th century. Here again, however, a few enthusiasts paid increasing heed, during the second half of the century, to the newer techniques; and some formed societies to study English agrarian improvements. In the lands across the Atlantic, where Europeans battled for political and economic power, agriculture remained but little affected by the shifts of political authority. The communal practices of the English open field system disappeared from New England in the course of the century; and some of the new techniques found their way into such middle colonies as New Jersey and Pennsylvania. But, despite scattered western outposts, the transformation of American agriculture came, not with political independence, but with the great 19th-century move of the frontier westward. The

p 162–3

*This engraving from the 'Compleat Body of Husbandry' published in 1756 shows a very advanced system for the storage of manure. It incorporated a pit for*

*the disposal of dung so constructed that it also collected urine from the animal sheds by means of drains. We can be sure that it was not in general use.* (2)

p 168–9 slave-run tobacco and cotton plantations of the American South and the sugar plantations of the West Indies expanded to meet the increasing demands of trade whilst changing little in organization and techniques. The one really significant technical innovation was the cotton gin of Eli Whitney (1765–1825) patented in 1793, which facilitated the great increase in cotton output necessary to feed the spinning mills of the Industrial Revolution.

## Population and produce

All over 18th-century Europe population grew (see Chapter IX). It grew at different rates, at different times, in different places; but generally more rapidly after 1760 than before. No figures of the time are really reliable: French population perhaps rose from 22 million in the mid-century to 27 million around 1800; that of Italy from about 15.5 million in 1750 to 18.1 million around 1800; the population of England and Wales moved from about 5.4 million in 1690 to 6.1 million in the mid-century and then went to 9.2 million in 1801; and of Sweden from 1.8 million in 1750 to 2.3 million in 1800. As population grew so it posed the perennial problem of pressure upon food supply (and in this century also stimulated the first, classic, statement of this problem in Thomas Malthus' *Essay on Population* of 1798). The reasons for its growth have not been definitively established. Such limited advances as there were in medical knowledge and skills probably made little or no difference. Despite the apparent ubiquity of growth it would be unwise to assume that common causes were necessarily every-

p 282–3 where at work. The disappearance from western Europe after 1720 of the flea-carrying black rat, carrier of bubonic plague, may well have been one such cause but particular combinations of circumstances determined the patterns and provided the causes of national or local growth. In Ireland, a peasant population subsisting on fragmented holdings and prone to early marriage, was sustained by an intensive cultivation of the potato, thus creating conditions conducive to very rapid population growth in the early 19th century. In some areas, for instance in Finland and eastern Russia or, outside Europe, in North America, growth was apparently favoured by the ready availability of land for setting up new households. In others, especially England, it may have been aided by the growing range of opportunities in an expanding economy.

Whatever the particular mix of demographic causes—factors operating upon the death or birth rates, on age at marriage, or fertility within marriage—the growth itself appears in retrospect as the beginning of the great upsurge of population which is still with us today. This demographic phenomenon of the 18th century has consequently been labelled 'the vital revolution'. If the sources from which it originated remain imprecisely discovered, one fact at least is clear: it could not have been sustained unless agricultural output had increased at least sufficiently to prevent mass starvation. That this might occur was Malthus' nightmare. Ultimately, the reasons for the exorcizing of that spectre lie in the 19th century, in the opening up and exploitation of new lands, in substantial technological advances in food producing. Within the confines of the 18th century, however, European agriculture was able to maintain the increase but it is here that the effects of relative backwardness or advance reveal themselves. In the course of the century the extreme severity of recurrent famines and extra high mortality—such as, for example, attacked many parts of Europe in the late 1690s and reduced the population of parts of Finland by about one third in 1697—was everywhere mitigated. But England seems to have experienced these alleviations earlier and more generally than many countries. The widespread harvest failures, for example, of 1708–10 brought famine conditions and increased mortality rates to France but did not have nearly such serious effects in England. Improved agriculture and better communications enabled England to build up some defences to buttress the thin line of bare subsistence which elsewhere so soon cracked at a serious harvest failure: as it did, for example, in Sicily and Naples in 1763–64 and 1766 or in Saxony in 1770–72. From about 1680 to 1760 England was able to export substantial quantities of grain and yet to have relatively low domestic food prices. Although prices rose thereafter in the face of increasing demand, and although there was suffering amongst the poor in the war and scarcity ridden years of 1795–96, there was no return to the old

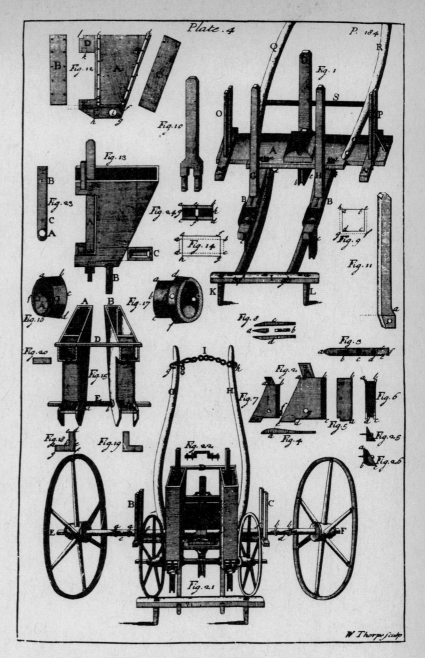

*Jethro Tull's seed-drill, invented in 1701, and made public in 1731, was not only the first practical drilling machine produced in England but a very important step in the reduction of manual labour in farm operations.* (3)

cycle of harvest failure and demographic crisis. To some extent this was true elsewhere, yet the clamour of a peasantry with holdings inadequate to feed themselves and their families, faced by rising prices and borne down by taxes, was to be heard far more loudly in France in the 1780s and 90s than in England. The price of inadequate agricultural change in later 18th-century Europe can perhaps best be measured by the extent to which the living standards of the mass of the people were maintained or fell, as their numbers rose.

From wherever agricultural produce came—from the leasehold tenants of English squires in their solid Georgian country houses or the farmsteads of Lombard peasants working on the system of *mezzadria* (share-cropping)—it flowed to meet a wide variety of needs. Some of the basic foodstuffs went, of course, to meet the subsistence requirements of big estates or tiny cottages in an age when grain was ground in the local mill and bread baked in the domestic oven. Beyond these immediate needs much grain flowed into the channels of trade, national and international: wheat from northern France to the granaries which supplied Paris or by coasting trade from Norfolk or Kent into London; rye, shipped along the rivers of eastern Europe to the ports of the Baltic, thence to move west and south. Hundreds of market towns were the receiving areas for foodstuffs—grains, meat, dairy products and fish— brought laboriously by heavy horse- or ox-wagon or more smoothly and cheaply by navigable rivers or coasting trade. Sheep

f 6

*Above: a large brew-house, illustrated in a work of the 1760s. Malt and water runs from the coppers at the back to the tuns, where it is stirred and strained before running out at the bottom. Below: part of a paper-mill. On the right the 'vatman' forms the sheet of paper made from pulped cotton and linen rags: it is then pressed between layers of felt, and on the left men take out the sheets and pile them. (4, 5)*

and cattle thus found their weary way to market; often they would have been brought down earlier in large droves to fattening areas, as Welsh or Scottish cattle were sent by the 'drove roads' to southern pastures before their ultimate despatch to Smithfield market. But the human needs for food were far from the only stimuli to agricultural activity in the 18th century. The improved techniques and new crop rotations in East Anglia, for instance, were nourished by the vigorous demand for barley by maltsters. They in turn supplied not only the local brewing industry—which grew rapidly to help assuage the thirst of 18th-century Englishmen—but also shipped malt from such ports as Kings Lynn and Yarmouth to the breweries of Holland. The hop fields of Sussex or of Flanders, the vineyards of France and Italy and Portugal, apples in Kent, olives in Sicily, oranges in Spain, market gardens in the environs of London: all were part of the varied agricultural sector in the economy of Europe.

Food and drink were by no means all of the output of that sector. Although the livestock breeders of 18th-century England were much engaged in trying to create fat beasts (at which they were sometimes only too successful) for meat, native wool remained the vital basis of the country's wool and textile industry. Merino sheep from Spain, the other great wool producing country of Europe, attracted the attention of stock breeders who at various times during the century introduced them into Prussia and Saxony,

*f 4*

p 128–9
(14–17)

*The salting of herring dates back to the twelfth century. In the Netherlands, where it formed an important item of export, the process depended on adherence to a precise specification formulated over the years and enforced by inspection and penalties. Herring, mostly caught off the British coast, were salted at sea aboard the herring-busses. They were then packed in barrels, topped up with brine, made air-tight and branded with the date of the catch. (6)*

Sweden, Austria and France—all in the hope of improving their native wool supply. Skins and hides from the cattle regions provided the raw material for the tanners and leather workers who turned a versatile commodity into uses varying from shoes to buckets. Cattle, too, provided the raw materials for other crafts of the day, for the makers of tallow candles or those soap-boilers p 126 (8) whose smelly task it was to turn tallow into soap. Forests continued to provide a vital building material. For all the Palladian stonework and the mounting piles of Georgian brickwork to testify to aristocratic enthusiasm for building or to the repatriated wealth of 'nabobs' and West Indian planters, timber was still the most important constructional material, in farms and barns, mills p 211 and warehouses, and in ships of every size. Oak, elm and chestnut; (11) spruce, fir and pine: all found their way into commerce. As they brought profit to landowners in Prussia or England, in Sweden or Russia so did they also provide the working material for village carpenters, for coopers or wheelwrights in market towns, for the p 199 shipwrights busy in shipyards building eastindiamen at Rother- (48) hithe or repairing French merchantmen at Nantes or Le Havre.

## Trades and Crafts

By thus providing raw materials as well as food and drink, agriculture lay at the base of much—though certainly not of all—industrial and commercial life in the 18th century. The processing of, or trading in, agrarian products provided jobs for many both in the countryside and in towns. The miller is merely the best known of a class of trades which included the butcher, the baker and the candlestick maker of the nursery rhyme as well as the tanner and the brewer, the innkeeper and the grocer, the fisherman and the fishmonger, and a great tribe of corn merchants.

After food and drink man's next requirement is clothing. In a way of economic life which was still far removed from the modern industrialized economy, it was the textile industries which took pride of place in manufacturing activity. During the first half of the century the European textile industries still drew their main raw materials almost entirely from within the frontiers of Europe though depending on more distant sources for dyestuffs, such as p 142–3 indigo. The homespun, peasant-woven, woollen cloth made for local consumption in many areas all over the Continent, from Sweden to Spain, drew entirely on local wool supplies. But European sources also served the complex and commercially

organized woollen or worsted industries of the English West Country, Yorkshire and East Anglia, or of Normandy, Languedoc and French Flanders, the products of which moved far afield in export markets. The same was true of linen and silk. European flax-growing areas supplied the linen and canvas industries of p 126 (6) Silesia, Brandenburg and Holland, of Normandy and Ireland. The silk-worm cultivators of Italy, France, and Spain—supplemented by the products of the Levant—supplied the European silk industry, with its greatest centre in Lyons. In the second half of the century, however, significant changes were wrought in these as in other aspects of industrial life. The great European trading expansion now began to have further effect. Just as, earlier in the century, European diets began to be affected by the growing import of tea from the East, or coffee and cheaper Caribbean sugar, so later came a rising inflow of cheap raw silk from Bengal and China and, most important, of cotton from the American South to feed the new, mechanized cotton mills of the Industrial Revolution.

Some crafts or industrial occupations, urban and rural, had, of course, no connection, or only a very indirect one, with agriculture. Certain urban trades were essentially providers of services: the apothecary, the goldsmith, or the scrivener. Others catered for the processes of commerce: the draper, the ship-chandler, the maker of navigational instruments. The paper mills of France or Germany f 5 or England, strung along fast flowing rivers, needed a supply of old rags, mainly linen, to turn into the paper ultimately marketed in London or Paris or Cologne. All sorts of non-agrarian jobs depended upon the extractive industries: potters, masons, and brickmakers depended upon the quarrying of clay, stone and brick-hearth; metal workers on the mining and smelting of iron, tin, lead, zinc, silver, copper and other minerals. The products of the craftsmen who worked with these materials catered for a wide range of incomes and diverse social positions. At one end of the scale the century saw the elegant porcelain products of the Meissen factory, near Dresden, or of the Sèvres works near Paris, at the f 10 other end, a growing volume of plain ware from unpretentious potteries testified to the rising incomes of artisans. Against the craftsmanship represented by cut glass or the elaborations of Venetian and German glassware, must be balanced the plate glass f 11 works at St Gobain in Picardy or at St Helens in Lancashire, the f 18 thousands of simple glass bottles shipped to London from works

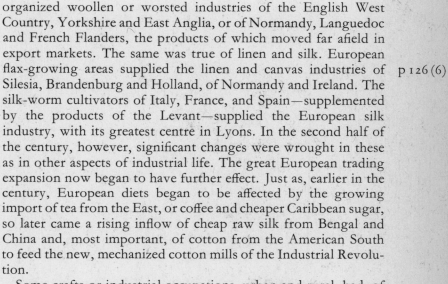

near Newcastle or the sheets of ordinary window glass which were improving domestic comfort. Neither the intricacies of French furniture nor the gleam of English silverware, both ornamenting the homes of the rich, should blind us to the work of humbler brass-founders, of joiners and furniture makers turning out products for the urban bourgeoisie, or of pewterers from whose wares most people still drank their ale. The French economy was sustained neither by the taste of Louis XV nor by the subsidized manufacture of *objets d'art*.

p 130–1

f 9
f 8

### The revolution in industry

The greatest theme of 18th-century industrial history is provided by the onset of the particular combination of changes which has come to be called the Industrial Revolution. It has no simply recognizable beginning and end; it can be defined in a variety of ways. Suffice, briefly, to concentrate on the bare essentials of a definition: the application to economic activity of new processes, some of them based on the scientific and technological advances described in Chapter III, in such a way as greatly to increase the output of certain goods and services, and the productivity of resources occupied in their production. In practice, this meant power-driven machinery, the advent of the steam engine, and revolutionary changes in some industries, notably iron and cotton textiles. The real importance of the Industrial Revolution lies not so much in its beginning as in its continuation. Starting in sundry corners of 18th-century Britain, it spread rapidly in the 19th century so that, between roughly 1760 and 1860, the British economy had been transformed to such a degree that there was no going back: the factory system had arrived and future changes had to build upon that fact. Here we are concerned simply with the beginnings of this transformation. Britain's was the pioneer industrial revolution and although the phrase was not coined until early in the 19th century, already in the later decades of the 18th the new British industrial techniques were attracting the admiring attentions of the

*Spinning, lace-making and knitting: an engraving by Chodowiecki.* (7)

outside world, even more than the country's agrarian improvement. There were still, it must be emphasized, large sections of the economy quite unaffected by these developments. The typical small enterprise, the artisan craftsman and his handful of assistants, time-absorbing manual processes unaided by power, tiny workshops in the metal industries, rural spinners and weavers in their cottages: all were still to be found in Britain, as elsewhere, in the 19th century as in the 18th. Nevertheless, in the industries which were being transformed, Britain was drawing ahead at a remarkable rate, and others could only seek to copy.

*Pewter-making. One man (1) pours the metal through a mould giving it its external form. Another (2) shapes the inside on a rotating shaft. The two on the left add spouts and handles by heating the inside and soldering (3), or (4) blowing a candle flame against the outside.* (8)

*A cabinet-maker covering the arm of a chair. Both the practice of upholstering furniture and the curving lines of this example are 18th-century innovations.* (9)

*Glass-blowing (top), pottery (above) and weaving (below). All the illustrations on this page are taken from a work published in Germany in 1774 with detailed engravings by Daniel Chodowiecki.* (11, 12, 13)

*Left: the last stage of porcelain manufacture – painting the surface. These men were artists in their own right and were adept at imitating exotic styles from abroad.* (10)

To consider why this should have been so it is necessary first to examine the British experience in isolation.

The beginning of the Industrial Revolution in Britain lay with steam and iron. Attempts to harness the expansive power of steam had occupied the attentions of a number of experimenters in the late 17th century. Practical results flowed from the efforts of two Englishmen, Thomas Savery (? 1650–1715) and Thomas Newcomen (1663–1729) both of whom developed what were essentially 'atmospheric' engines, i.e. dependent upon the twin forces of steam and atmospheric pressure. Savery, like Newcomen later, consciously directed his work to the solution of a practical problem: the invention of a powered device to replace existing methods of pumping water out of mines. He advertized his engine in 1702 as 'The Miner's Friend'. Newcomen, originally working quite independently of Savery, at about the same time and to the same end, developed a far more successful version of the atmospheric engine. The first practical 'fire engine', as contemporaries called it, with its big, prominent beam, was a Newcomen engine erected at a colliery in Staffordshire in 1712. The tin mines of Cornwall and the coal mines of the Midlands and north-eastern England were both areas of great potential demand for a device which would lower the costs and increase the efficiency of drainage—a problem becoming increasingly urgent as mines went deeper. In the course of the century, especially as coalmining expanded in England, Wales, and Scotland, more and more Newcomen engines were put into operation. In the later decades of the century the English engineer, John Smeaton (1724–92), made substantial improvements to the Newcomen engine, and his and other versions of it came into widespread use. By 1765 over 120 such atmospheric engines were in use in the Northumberland and Durham coalfield area alone.

Meanwhile, within the iron industry in Britain a momentous innovation had taken place. Iron manufacture had long been dependent upon charcoal for a smelting fuel; and the cost of charcoal formed a large element in the total cost both of smelting and forging iron. The comparatively cheap and plentiful supplies of coal presented an obvious challenge to anyone who could solve the technical problems which would enable it to be used to smelt iron. Others had been at work for some while before, in 1709 Abraham Darby (1677–1717), an ironmaster of Coalbrookdale, in Shropshire, succeeded in producing pig iron smelted with coke made with coal from the neighbouring coalfield. Although the new technique was not immediately disseminated across the country, the setting up of a big new coke-smelting ironworks, the famous Carron works, in Scotland in 1760 has often been presented as symbolizing the beginning of a new era. In the second half of the century a growing number of other big iron works prospered on the new process: those of John Wilkinson, for example at Broseley in Staffordshire, of the Walker Brothers in Yorkshire, or of successive generations of the Darby family, as well as others in South Wales. From this, the smelting and casting side of the industry, the trail of experiment and advance soon spread to the production of wrought iron. In 1783–84 Henry Cort (1740–1800) invented the so-called 'puddling' process of using coal in making wrought iron. In this process the iron, after coming out of a special type of furnace, was hammered under the forge hammer and then passed through rollers. These later stages of the process cried out for reliable power.

In the 1760s James Watt (1736–1819), maker of mathematical instruments for Glasgow University, was conducting systematic experiments with steam pressure and trying to improve the Newcomen type engine. Out of these endeavours he created the genuine steam engine, as opposed to the atmospheric engine. In the 1770s he went into partnership with a successful manufacturer of metal wares, Matthew Boulton; the famous firm of Boulton & Watt then set up in business near Birmingham; and, drawing upon the experience of local ironmasters, notably John Wilkinson, began to make and erect steam engines at collieries, tin mines, water- and iron-works. 'The people in London, Manchester and Birmingham,' wrote Boulton to Watt in June 1781, 'are steam-mill mad.' Between 1781 and 1788 Watt went on to solve the vital problem of using the steam engine not simply for pumping but to impart rotary motion. The link with the iron industry—already a very practical

one in the manufacture of parts for the engines—now became still closer, for steam power was available to drive the hammers and rolling mills necessary to produce wrought iron by the new puddling process. The charcoal based iron industry had long used water power at its furnaces and forges. But the hazards of summer drought or winter freezing limited the water-wheel's efficiency; the earliest uses of the Newcomen engines at ironworks were to pump water back over the dam so as to ensure a continuous feed to the wheel. Although industry generally continued to use much water power, in favourable locations, well into the 19th century, the advent of the true steam engine, and its ability to impart rotary motion, marked a tremendous step forward in man's control over natural forces.

By these innovations steam, iron, and coal were thus interconnected in a circle of demand and supply. Pig iron output in Britain rose from about 20,000 tons or so in 1720 to 250,000 tons in 1806; coal output rose from about two and a half million tons in 1700 and over ten million tons in 1800.

## The rise of the factory

Whilst these innovations were transforming the iron industry, introducing a new source of power and stimulating coal production, revolutionary changes of a different sort were being introduced into the textile industry. In the course of the 16th and 17th centuries the English woollen and worsted manufacture had grown into one of the major exporting industries of Europe. It was joined on a smaller scale in the early 18th century by a growing cotton-linen industry. Situated mainly in Lancashire and Lanark, it made small, all-cotton fabrics largely in imitation of the cotton cloths, imported from India with much success at the end of the 17th century, and rather more and larger cotton-linen mixtures or fustians. In common with the wool-using industries it was organized on the domestic or 'putting-out' system. The supply of raw materials and the marketing of the finished product were organized and financed by a merchant entrepreneur. He put out the raw materials to spinners and weavers who worked in their own homes; as necessary, he had the cloths finished and dyed; and he sold the final products to factors, drapers or exporters. This, in broad outline though subject to many variations in detail, was a method of industrial organization which had evolved to fit a particular mixture of economic and technical circumstances: processes which could be carried on in workers' cottages, and involved no expensive power-driven items of capital equipment; an adequate labour supply, chronically under-employed, and capable of being laid on or off according to fluctuations in demand; and no significant economies to be gained by concentrating workers under one roof. In the course of the 18th century, however, as the textile industry expanded its output to meet the demands of both the internal market and the rapidly growing markets overseas, especially across the Atlantic, difficulties within the existing structure became more and more acute. It took several spinners to keep one weaver at his loom; the bigger the labour force used the larger the area over which it was spread and therefore the longer the delays in transport of materials and semi-finished goods; and the harder it became to control the standard of the product. Economic pressures were thus being generated within the industry; conditions were propitious for mechanization, though conditions alone certainly did not bring it about.

After abortive attempts to make power-driven textile machinery, the first significant step away from the old spinning-wheel was made with the patenting by James Hargreaves in 1770 of the spinning 'jenny'. This simple machine was not, however, power-driven; it could be, and was, brought into use within the domestic system. The contemporaneous patenting by Richard Arkwright (1732–92) of the 'water-frame' brought the factory system in textiles a vital stage nearer. Operating on principles different from those of the jenny, it was designed to be driven by water power. It was first put into use in a large water-powered mill set up in 1771 by Arkwright with the financial assistance of a rich hosiery manufacturer, Jedediah Strutt, at Cromford, Derbyshire. Whether Arkwright was himself responsible for the invention is doubtful; what at least is clear is that he saw its economic possibilities and was prepared to back it with vigorous business enterprise. He

f 14

p 134 (31)

p 134 (33)

p 134 (32)

p 135 (34, 35)

p 136 (38)

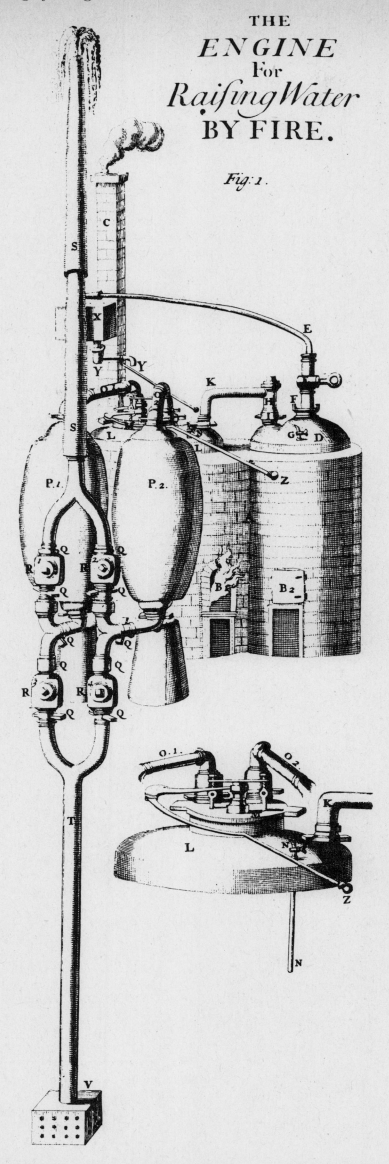

THE
ENGINE
For
*Raifing Water*
BY FIRE.

*Fig: 1.*

succeeded: Cromford became the first of a rapidly growing number of powered cotton spinning mills; Arkwright died as Sir Richard Arkwright and the owner of several factories and a substantial fortune; and the Strutt family moved up in time into the ranks of the English aristocracy. The industrial revolution in textiles had begun. It was pushed further forward by the development by Samuel Crompton (1753–1827) between 1774 and 1779 of an improved spinning machine, the 'mule', a compound in principle of the jenny and the water frame. These innovations on the spinning side of the industry rapidly brought pressure to bear on other processes in textile manufacture. The most important of these, weaving, was not however effectively mechanized until after 1800, though a power-loom was patented by Edmund Cartwright (1743–1823) in 1784. Partly for technical reasons, these striking changes mainly took place first in the cotton-using part of the textile industry rather than in the woollen branch. Yorkshire, by this time the most important area of the woollen industry, was slower in adopting the new methods than Lancashire. By 1800 a new, large-scale, cotton textile industry was rapidly being created in Britain. It was fed by an ever-increasing flow of raw cotton from America, imported through the flourishing port of Liverpool. British imports of raw cotton, less than two million lbs in 1700 and barely three million in the mid-century, had risen to over fifty million lbs in 1800.

Iron, steam power, cotton: here was the technical core of the Industrial Revolution in 18th-century Britain. Beyond this central core, comparable changes, in kind though not in degree, were scattered over sundry reaches of the economy. The invention in the 1740s by Benjamin Huntsman (1704–76) of the 'crucible' process of steel making both cheapened and improved the product, though this was not a development comparable in economic importance with those in iron making. In silk manufacture, the building of a big water-powered twisting mill in Derbyshire in 1717 signalled the arrival, though not until the 1760s and later, of a number of similar silk mills. The English pottery industry received an entirely new stimulus from the work of Josiah Wedgwood (1730–95). His new factory started operation in 1769 and made a fortune for its founder whose organizational ability was joined to a very keen eye for the nature of market demand for everyday ware. On the fringes of what was later to be called the chemical industry, important advances were made in the 1740s in the techniques of producing sulphuric acid; the discovery of chlorine in 1774 was followed by its use in textile bleaching, and this in turn led to the setting up near Glasgow in 1799 of a chemical works which soon became the biggest in Europe.

Outside manufacturing industry itself, the biggest single surge of new activity in the British economy came in the provision of improved transport facilities. Many roads had long been of poor quality: dusty and bumpy in the summer, muddy and half-flooded in the winter. The operation of Turnpike Trusts—private enterprises designed to maintain roads from statutorily authorized tolls—brought about some improvement in the course of the century. Many were far from efficient, but the best of them provided the framework of finance and organization within which the first real road engineers since the Romans left Britain, could get to work. More important, and also more spectacular, was a boom in canal building. Many miles of English rivers had already been rendered navigable when the 1750s and 60s saw the first of the new canals. The one which caught the public imagination was that constructed by James Brindley (1716–1772) for the Duke of Bridgewater in order to link the latter's coalmines to the Manchester market. Opened in 1761, the canal combined the merits of financial success, engineering achievement, and the halving of coal prices in Manchester. Many more canals were constructed in the next few decades, involving the investment of large sums of

p 131
(26)

f 15

*This diagram of the first practical steam-pump appeared in Thomas Savery's book 'The Miner's Friend' published in 1702, four years after he had taken out a master patent for the invention. He put it on display in London, and invited owners of mines and collieries to inspect it, assuring them they would be 'satisfied of the performance thereof, with less expense than any other force of Horse or hands, and less subject to repair'. (14)*

money, a process which reached a frenzy of speculative enthusiasm during the so-called 'canal mania' of 1792–93. Canals cut the cost of transport especially of such bulky goods as timber, stone, bricks, and grain, as well as of the coal and iron wares so vitally a part of the Industrial Revolution.

### European patterns

So much for this phenomenon in its British isolation. Put it in a wider context, and the existence of many similar signs elsewhere becomes apparent. Everywhere, however, these signs failed to develop in the 18th century in the manner that they did in Britain.

This pattern of similarity and yet of contrast is well exemplified in the development of steam power. Denis Papin (1647–1714) was working along lines similar to those followed by Savery and Newcomen, indeed in certain respects he anticipated their work; but no autonomous practical results followed in the shape of pumping engines installed at collieries. During the 1720s and 30s some Newcomen engines were erected on the continent of Europe, in France, Belgium and elsewhere. But by the end of the century the amount of steam power in use outside Britain was still trifling. There were no real counterparts to Smeaton or Watt even in France where theoretical science was the most advanced in Europe. Despite the invention of a steam carriage by N. J. Cugnot (1725–1804) and of the first workable steamboat which the Marquis de Jouffroy d'Abbans (1751–1832) demonstrated at Lyons in 1783, it was in Scotland and America that by the end of the century steamboats were coming into effective use. The only area of continental Europe to take up steam power with anything approaching the speed shown in Britain was Belgium. In the mining area of Liège, where a Newcomen engine had been installed as early as 1720–21, a number of atmospheric engines were at work in the later years of the century. Scattered examples of either atmospheric engines or true steam engines can be found: for example at Le Creusot, the one big ironworks in France, where

p 106
(24)

some Watt type engines came into use in the 1780s; in Saxony and Silesia where a few Newcomen or Watt type engines were in use by the end of the century. The close inter-relationship between steam power, coalmining and the iron industry which the Industrial Revolution was rapidly bringing to Britain had barely appeared elsewhere. Until the very end of the 18th century the largest iron producers in Europe were France, Sweden, Russia, and Germany, in that order. But, whether in the Nivernais or the Upper Marne valley, in the *bergslag* of central Sweden, the Siegerland of western Germany, in Silesia or in the Urals, the fuel for smelting was charcoal, and running water the source of power. For most of the 18th century Britain's iron industry had been far from able to meet the country's requirements which had necessitated substantial imports from Sweden and Russia. The rapid change of relative positions, so that by the beginning of the 19th century Britain was easily the biggest iron producer and still moving ahead fast, was entirely due to the British adoption of the new technology and, in contrast, the failure of other countries to take it up with comparable speed. In 18th-century France the new methods made virtually no progress despite attempts to introduce coke-smelting at Le Creusot in the 1770s; not until 1796 did the first coke-smelting furnace come into operation in Germany, in Upper Silesia; the Swedish industry—famous for the quality of its products and, at the beginning of the 18th century the largest producer in Europe—remained untouched by the new techniques. In textiles, the big and widening gap was only slightly less dramatic. The first German cotton-spinning mill, using Arkwright's water-frame, started up near Düsseldorf in 1794; power-spinning was just coming in to the textile industry of Saxony at the very end of the century. The domestic system, similar to that in Britain, remained widespread in the French textile industry—as in other countries—and the technical inventions that were made either achieved little practical success or did not involve the use of power. The pattern weaving loom invented in 1747 by Jacques Vaucanson (1709–82) did not make much

p 132–3

f 17

*Though slow to begin building canals, Britain rapidly extended her inland waterways in the second half of the 18th century. One of the first canals was the Duke of Bridgewater's built between 1760 and 1761 with the help of his engineer, James Brindley. In this print the Duke proudly points to the Barton aqueduct which carried the waterway across the River Irwell. 'Described in the Gentleman's Magazine' as a 'stupendous work' it was used primarily to carry coal from the Duke's colleries at Worsley to Manchester. (15)*

*Marten Triewald, the Swedish mechanic, spent ten years in England and gained expert knowledge of the new steam-pumps in operation there. In 1726, he returned to Sweden and it was under his supervision that the engine at Dannemora was built. This view of it is taken from Triewald's own description of the machine published in 1734, in which he acknowledged his debt to Newcomen and Savery. Nevertheless, his pump was the largest ever built at that time anywhere and he proudly claimed that it was 'capable of doing as much work in 24 hours and 528 horses'. (16)*

147

headway in the French silk industry, though it was the basis of the more famous draw loom of J. M. Jacquard (1752–1834), patented in 1801. Neither formed part of a line of development essentially based upon the use of water or steam power. Although some French inventors were working along lines similar to those of Hargreaves, it was in the main from England that the practical knowledge of the new textile techniques was derived. By about 1790 a few cotton spinning mills using the water-frame had started, especially in the cotton-linen industry of Normandy, centred on Rouen; and there were perhaps fewer than 1,000 jennies in use, compared with an estimated 200,000 in Britain. Probably the most rapid and striking advances in textiles outside Britain at this time were being made in a country otherwise little affected by the new industrial developments: Spain. The Catalonian cotton industry, centred on Barcelona, introduced English type machinery during the 1770s and in the 1780s became, for a brief time, the second largest European producer of cotton cloth.

The biggest questions in the economic history of the 18th century can be posed quite simply: why did the Industrial Revolution start in Britain and why did it start there and not elsewhere? As difficult to answer as they are easy to frame, such questions can be considered here only in broadest outline; and anyone who pretends to be certain of the answers is probably wrong. For they have to account for failure as well as success. Why, for instance, did so little come from the efforts by the government of Poland to support the establishment of ironworks and textile factories between the 1760s and 80s, and yet such success, albeit rather temporary, attend the protective tariffs designed by Charles III of Spain to stimulate the industries of Catalonia? Why, despite the efforts of Frederick the Great to stimulate textile manufactures and to improve internal communications, was Prussian industrial development still small compared with that of Britain? Why, again, were French canals—many of them built earlier than those in Britain—and French roads—many of them built better than those in Britain—both so relatively little used at a time when their British counterparts were busy with booming trade? And why, in general, did France, the richest and most powerful country of mid-18th century Europe so evidently fail to develop its potential at that time?

p 120 (17) p 105 (20)

The Industrial Revolution in Britain was essentially a product of

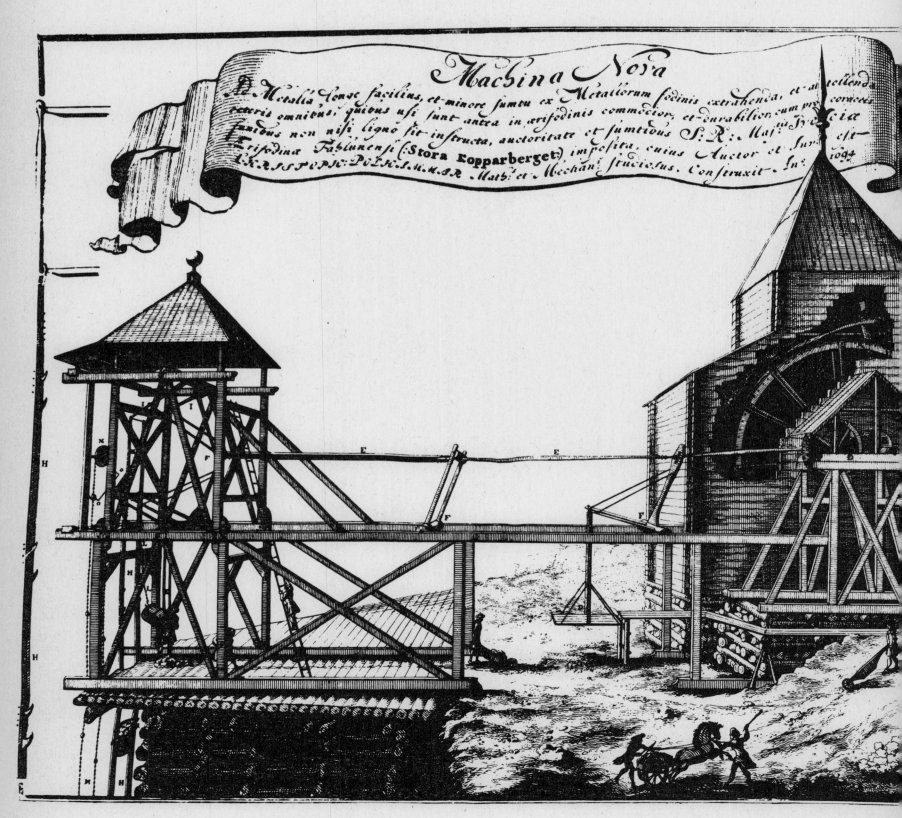

private enterprise operating within an economy in which the State, sometimes more by accident than intent, provided a measure of tariff protection for industry; and in which the social and legal systems sustained a tolerant admiration for the workings of the profit motive. This may or may not be the ideal recipe for inducing industrialization in other economies at other times but in the circumstances of 18th-century Europe, just as it worked in Britain so did it do little but offer contrasts elsewhere. In Britain, for example, the effective power of the guilds in economic life had been so whittled away in the course of the previous centuries that by the mid-18th, it was virtually non-existent. Where they survived, as they often did, their role was usually honorific rather than practical. In France, the elaborately centralized system developed by Colbert at the end of the 17th century sustained the power of the guilds and encouraged successive governments in policies of control and regulation which effectively hampered rather than helped the process of innovation. Whereas in Britain the State provided no direct support for industrial ventures—confining its role substantially to commerce and maritime power—in France it intervened directly through the setting up of *manufactures royales*.

Some of these indeed brought into being quite substantial works where large numbers of people were employed; many were concerned with the making of high class products designed for the luxury market, such as the tapestry, furniture and jewellery of the Gobelins. Similarly, in other parts of Europe, such rulers as Frederick William I of Prussia, the Empress Maria Theresa or Stanislas Augustus of Poland all tried their hands at sponsoring economic advance by the setting up of privileged industrial establishments. None of such enterprises depended for its capital upon the willingness of businessmen to take risks; nor for its size upon the economies of scale which could be secured by the use of power and the concentration of work under one roof. They provided incentives neither for the extension of technical innovation nor for cost reduction in industry. Only in the second half of the century were fashionable tendencies in politico-economic policy moving in different directions. In the 1780s Joseph II, as well as setting up protective tariffs to aid industry, took steps to curb the restrictive powers of the guilds; although in the territories of Prussia the guilds remained in unimaginative control over most of the craft industries, they were the object of some reforming

*Publications like Diderot's 'Encyclopédie' portrayed manufacturing processes on a misleadingly grandiose scale. This illustration of soap-boiling from a work published just after 1800 gives a humbler and more accurate picture. At the back, the 'ley' (a mixture of slaked lime and soda), is slowly boiled with tallow or some other fat and constantly stirred. Salt is then added and the soap separates into a layer at the top, leaving fluid underneath. It is then ladled out into frames and left to set. The man in the foreground cuts it into slices with a copper wire. (18)*

*Left: machine designed by the Swedish inventor and engineer Christopher Polhem (1661–1751) for raising metallic ore from mines (1694). Power is supplied by a 30-foot water-wheel (A); this turns two more cogged wheels (B and C) which move the long shaft (E) to and fro like a shuttle. At the other end, this horizontal motion is converted into vertical, moving the 200-foot arms (H) up and down. The baskets of ore are hooked onto these arms and go up in a series of hoists until they can be emptied at the top and the load taken away by men with barrows. The little platform (P) which is alternately raised and lowered by the movement of E, helps them up the steep bank. Empty buckets descend on a chain (M). (17)*

efforts by Frederick the Great. In France, movements towards economic freedom were making headway during the later decades of the *ancien régime*: after their suppression by Turgot in 1776 the guilds never recovered their power despite their formal restoration after his fall in the same year.

Outside Britain and the European continent, although the occasional seed of industrial or agrarian change had begun to germinate, old and well-tried techniques of production continued in operation. In Asia and Africa European commercial penetration neither met nor implanted many signs of significant industrial progress. Eastern civilization, once so far advanced compared with that of the West—and still, in some of its economic and technical aspects far from inferior—now seemed comparatively inert. In Japan, for example, though the century saw an extension of industry and commerce, the Tokugawa régime virtually sealed off the country from foreign influence. In America, despite the hostile legislation of the British, industry spread in the thirteen colonies but, neither before nor after independence, did it yet incorporate many of the technical changes which the British were pioneering. Water power was harnessed to sawmills and gristmills as well as to forges and furnaces; but charcoal remained the fuel of the iron industry. In textiles and the manufacture of small metal wares the domestic system developed in parts of New England. Only at the very end of the century, as a result of the enterprise of an English immigrant, Samuel Slater, was the new water-powered cotton spinning mill introduced.

## The key to economic growth

In Britain the substantial and rapid growth of overseas trade, above all the great expansion of transatlantic commerce, brought pressure to bear upon the industries, transport facilities and other services which supplied that trade. The value of British exports roughly doubled in the first half of the century and nearly quadrupled in the second half. The economy in which this happened was trammelled neither by industrial traditionalism nor by the limitations on mobility and incentive imposed by serfdom and a rigid social structure. Rapidly growing exports were not, however, by any means the only source of demand which stimulated industry and economic activity in Britain. Although the rate of growth of the export trade, and particularly of manufactures destined for the North American markets, was very high, especially in the later decades, the total volume of home demand was undoubtedly much greater. The falling food prices of the earlier part of the century brought increased real incomes; the British taxation system fell far less heavily upon the mass of the people than did that of France and other countries in Europe. Consequently the British economy was able to sustain a comparatively broadly based demand for the products of industry and overseas trade. In many other countries a heavy concentration of wealth, and therefore of effective demand, in the upper classes limited the scope of production for a large market and encouraged other tendencies towards the manufacture of luxury items. Very few industries in Europe were being thus presented with the challenge of a broad-based and rapidly growing demand for their products. An important source of demand in Britain was the large middle class of British (though not of Irish) society: the wide range stretched from the skilled urban artisans p 30(31) to the ranks of the rural gentry. The urban and mercantile sections of this society were growing particularly fast, not only in London but in the new towns and ports of the Midlands and North. Many of their members were Protestant Dissenters, excluded from participation in some of the political or official activities of society; from the more ambitious amongst them came many of the leading businessmen of the Industrial Revolution.

The very existence of such men—irrespective of their religious affiliations—provides a clue to one of the great distinguishing features of British economic endeavour in the 18th century.

All over Europe, as we shall see in more detail later, the idea of p 97(1) science was abroad, kindling an interest in inventions and tech- p 98(3) nology. In Paris the Académie des Sciences and in London the Royal Society and the Society for the Encouragement of Arts, Manufactures and Commerce (founded in 1754 and now known as the Royal Society of Arts) provided an intellectual stimulus. But more than this was needed, and it was in Britain far more than in France, that men could be found to invest money in the practical application of new ideas. The superb engravings in such French publica- f 4, 8 tions as the *Encyclopédie* and the *Descriptions des Arts et Métiers* have p 268 indeed certain misleading qualities: designed to illustrate a detailed description of an industrial process, they commonly placed that process in an idealized environment. Consequently, many of the illustrations tell the reader little of the economic reality of French industry but hint at a spurious grandeur of scale which it did not

have, any more than did most of English industry for most of the century. The small soap-boiler, for example, is a far more realistic f 18 and representative figure of the widespread, small-scale soap making industry than the big works shown in the more stylized illustrations. Moreover, the latter do not embody the practical results of autonomous economic change but rather the sort of stimulus to ordered, subsidized bigness typically given by the *manufactures royales*. Such illustrations embody too the characteristic attitude of the optimistic scientists of the Enlightenment: to impart information about the making of things, to present the processes as, so to speak, intellectual creations. But what mattered for practical effect was the felt pressure upon costs, a pressure which, moreover, could not adequately be met simply by adding more workers, as was perhaps easier in France and elsewhere than in Britain. What mattered, furthermore, was the existence of entrepreneurs disposed to try to reduce those costs by new techniques; the willingness of men to invest in them; the availability of factors of production to work them without impediment imposed by the force of traditional relationships. In time, as the Industrial Revolution got under way, the fracture of those traditional relationships helped to bring hardship to many just as the creation of new employment brought higher standards of living to others. The greater economic and social freedom in Britain than in most European countries in the 18th century can hardly have failed to permit a greater disposition to investment and innovation. Adam Smith's *The Wealth of Nations*, published in 1776, rapidly became the Bible of free enterprise economics. But freedom, of course, was not enough. The necessary inducements came in a variety of ways, not readily classifiable. The new ironmaking processes promised economies in fuel; those in textiles economized on time; steam power meant emancipation from the whims of nature and economized on labour. Some were less directly related to existing problems; coal-gas illumination or chlorine bleaching were simply new processes or products initially made possible by scientific discovery and inventive endeavour. None would have been of much use without the effective demand which came from the sustained expansion of trade, and from a growing population which an improved agriculture was able to feed and which possessed the purchasing power able to buy the goods of a more productive industry.

Suffice it thus to indicate something of what has to be taken into account in trying to answer the questions about industrial change in the 18th century. Over Europe as a whole, agricultural and industrial output, as well as the total number of the people, was increasing, especially in the latter half of the century. But much of this increased production was being achieved simply by the extension of old methods: more land brought under cultivation and tilled in the old way, more men and women put to work with familiar tools. Despite a prevalent enthusiasm for the new science and a dawning disposition to see greater economic freedom as a path to greater economic and political power, few countries achieved much in the way of significant economic growth. Only in Britain, indeed only in certain key sectors of the British economy, did economic, social and technical factors so coalesce as to induce spontaneous, rapid growth, greater productivity, and the beginnings of cumulative expansion. What is the key which exactly unlocks the particular historical combination of facts and forces that thus uniquely began the Industrial Revolution in 18th-century Britain? Nobody really knows; perhaps it does not exist. This will not stop many people continuing to search for it, however, because the vision beyond the door is of the industrialized world of today.

# V EUROPE OVERSEAS

*Slavery, Commerce and Empire*

K. G. DAVIES

*'The colony of a civilized nation*

*which takes possession either of a waste country,*

*or of one so thinly inhabited that the natives*

*easily give place to the new settlers, advances more rapidly*

*to wealth and greatness than any*

*other human society.'*

ADAM SMITH 'An Inquiry into the Nature and Causes of the Wealth of Nations' (1776)

## Europe's involvement

with the rest of the world was until the middle of the 18th century primarily commercial: America was a source of wealth in the form of precious metals, profits from slave-worked plantations, furs and fish; Africa was the source of slaves to extract America's wealth; the East was a rich trading area in which Europeans made most of the rules. But the Pacific, though it had been crossed by numerous explorers and adventurers, was still untouched — a few isolated landfalls, pinpoints of light in a map of darkness. No one knew whether Van Diemen's land stretched to the South Pole, or what vast opportunities there might be for business or for empire in that unknown continent.

The promotors of Cook's first voyage (1768–71), however, were not speculators: they were scientists. He was employed by the Royal Society (with assistance from the Admiralty) to observe the transit of Venus across the face of the Sun (an international enterprise already described in Chapter IV), to explore and chart the islands of the Pacific: and also to 'observe the Nature of the Soil and the Products thereof, the Beasts and fowls that inhabit or frequent it . . . You are likewise to observe the Genius, Temper, Disposition and Number of the Natives . . .' His ship was a floating laboratory and museum. Besides the astronomical equipment which Cook himself was skilled in using, she carried the English naturalist Joseph Banks, the Swede D. C. Solander with

an assistant, and two artists who were to record the voyage and the discoveries in pictures.

They entered the Pacific via Cape Horn, visited Tahiti (where the observation of Venus was made) and other Polynesian islands, circumnavigated New Zealand, charting it accurately for the first time; sailed along the east and north coasts of Australia; and returned home via Java and the Cape of Good Hope.

Cook's career up to this time had been relatively undistinguished. A Yorkshireman, without formal education, he was 39 when he was recognized as the Navy's best map-maker and chosen to command the *Endeavour*. He proved to be the ideal choice — practical, systematic, devoted, and with an unerring gift for command. On his second voyage, which again lasted three years (1772–75), he sailed further south than any man had been before — 71° 10'. His third voyage (1776–79) took him to the North Pacific, where he explored the coasts of Siberia and Alaska before being killed in a skirmish with natives on Hawaii.

In eleven years he had dispelled the mystery of the Pacific. He had enriched botany and zoology with hundreds of new specimens and masses of detailed research. He had proved beyond question that the Southern Continent was a myth. This portrait (opposite) was painted in 1776, when he was at the height of his fame, and about to leave England for the last time. (1)

**Buying a crayfish:** one of the *Endeavour*'s crew barters with a Maori in New Zealand during the second voyage. (3)

**Tahitian war canoes** — 320 boats and nearly 800 men — were seen by Cook's men on their second visit, one of the last demonstrations of the old culture ever to be held on Tahiti. (4)

**'I can be bold to say',** wrote Cook, 'that no man will ever venture further than I have done and that the lands that may lie to the south will never be explored.' The boast remained true until steam power enabled ships to push further through the ice. The painting (below) by Hodges shows the *Adventure* taking on ice for drinking-water; the *Resolution* is further away on the left. (5)

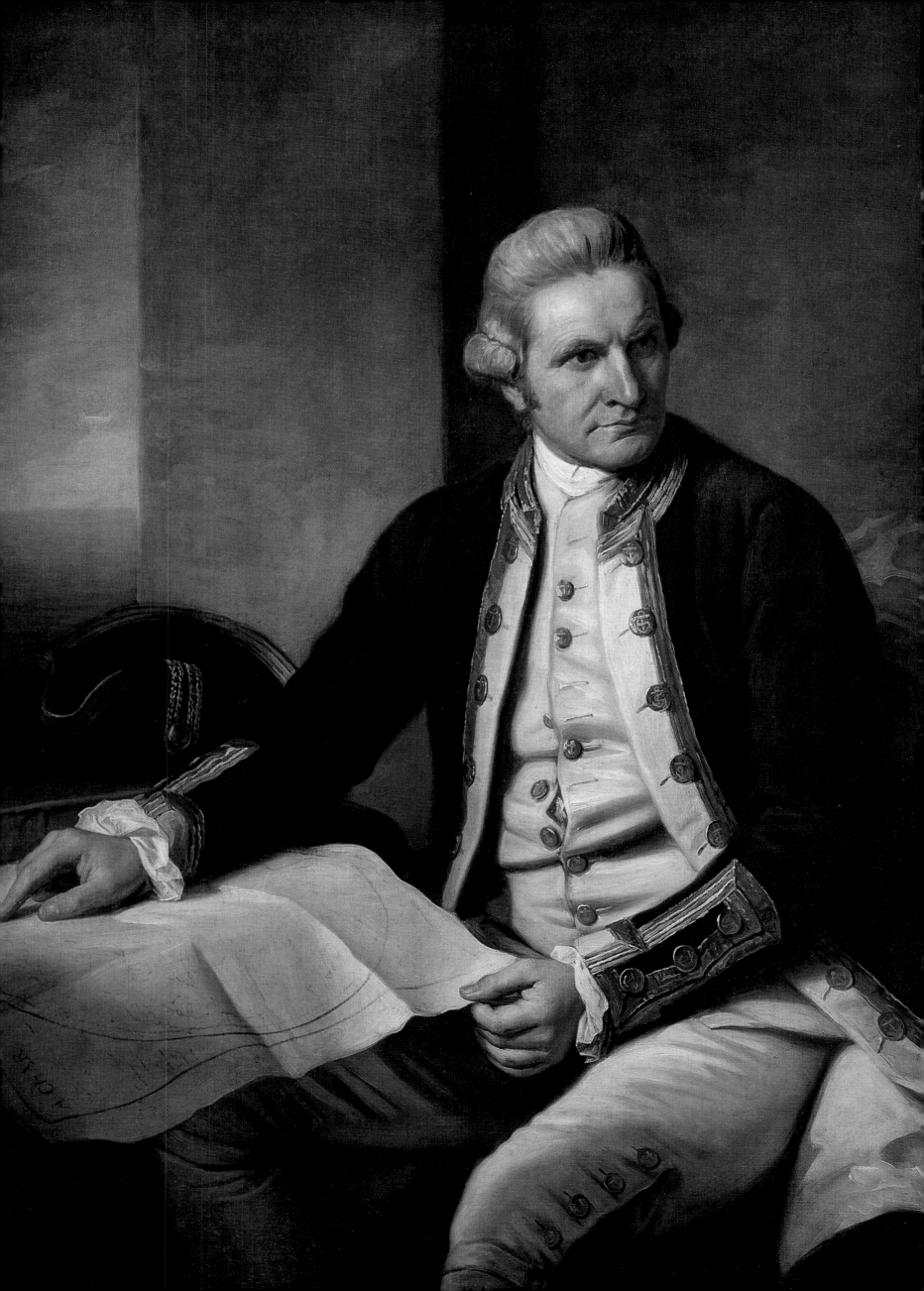

**Cook's ships** were all around 400 tons with crews of about 100. This painting (left) by Hodges, the artist of the second voyage, shows the *Resolution* and the *Adventure* lying in Matavai Bay, Tahiti. The accounts of Tahiti, especially that of Banks, made a profound impression on Europe. It became the prototype of the island paradise, peopled with innocent children of nature. (2)

**The kangaroo** was a discovery of Cook's first voyage, along with a host of Australian animals previously undreamed of in Europe. Banks brought back a kangaroo-skin, and from that and a few rough sketches George Stubbs was able to create this life-like portrait. (7)

**Cook died** unnecessarily in a trivial quarrel with islanders on Hawaii. He had gone ashore to investigate the theft of a cutter; a fierce argument developed and as he retreated to the boat he was clubbed and stabbed from behind. The scene (below) was sketched by a carpenter of the *Resolution*, James Clevely, and made into a finished aquatint by his brother John, a well-known marine artist. (6)

**Travellers before Cook** had brought back wonderful stories, some of which proved true. John Byron, in 1764, visited Patagonia (above) and reported that the inhabitants were giants, a fact not confirmed by Cook.

Tahiti had been visited by Captain Wallis in 1767 (below), the year before Cook, and had stayed five weeks; one of Cook's officers had sailed with Wallis and his acquaintance with the Tahitians proved useful. (8, 10)

**Time-keeping at sea** was one of the crucial factors of navigation, since it was only by comparing local sun-time with some standard time on a fixed meridian of reference that longitude could be calculated. In 1713 the British government offered a prize for an accurate chronometer, which was won by a series of instruments made by John Harrison. Right: his first model of 1735 and (above) his fourth, of 1759, in the form of a watch only five inches in diameter. Cook took one of the latter on his second voyage and called it his 'never-failing guide'. (9, 13)

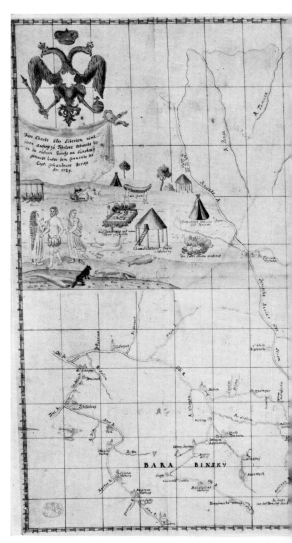

**In Cook's wake** other European nations attempted to claim an empire or exploit the Pacific's wealth. La Pérouse, the French admiral (seen here with Louis XVI, who commis-

sioned his voyage), explored the east coast of Asia and investigated the possibilities of whaling, but vanished with his ships in 1788, wrecked off the New Hebrides. (11)

**Map-making,** Cook's primary task in all his voyages, depended absolutely on instrumental precision. This theodolite, to measure horizontal angles, dates from 1765. (14)

**Whether Asia was joined** to America was still an open question in 1724, when Peter the Great appointed the Danish navigator Vitus Bering to lead an expedition across Siberia to the Kamchatka peninsula. Here Bering built a boat and sailed north, passing through what is now the Bering Strait. This map (below), published soon after his return in 1730, shows East Asia from Tobolsk to the tip of Siberia. The drawings show inhabitants of Yakutsk, the central region. (12)

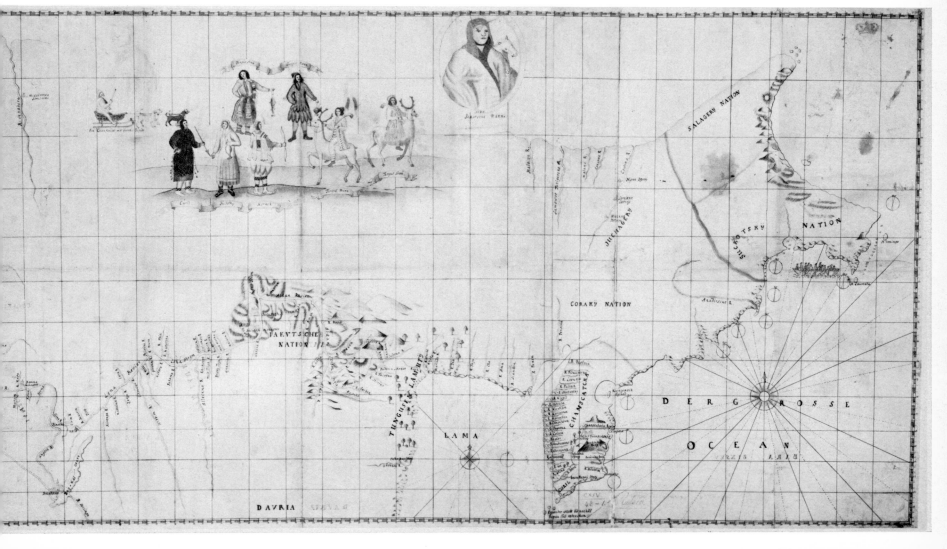

**The port of Dieppe** was typical of several along the French coast — Nantes, Bordeaux, Brest, St Malo — from which a busy trade was carried on with the French settlements in Quebec, New Orleans and Martinique. Cheap cloth, guns and beads were exported to West Africa, where they were exchanged for slaves.

These were taken across the Atlantic and the ships returned home laden with rich American cargoes such as sugar and tobacco. Dieppe, seen here, was a fine modern town in the 18th century, having been rebuilt after bombardment during the War of the League of Augsburg in 1694. (15)

**London and Bristol** (right, above and below) were, with Liverpool, the leading English ports. European penetration into the rest of the world created a boom in shipping. (16, 17)

In the New World of America, Europeans virtually recreated their old culture, without reference to the previous inhabitants. Charleston, founded in 1670 and named after Charles II, had by the mid-18th century grown into a substantial town, closely modelled on towns of the home country. The church of St Michael (left) is a provincial version of the style of Gibbs, which had been made popular by his books of engraved designs. (18)

Baltimore (right) grew more slowly. This drawing shows it as it was in 1752, when there were less than fifty houses and 200 inhabitants. The church stands on top of the hill. Baltimore's importance was chiefly that it exported Maryland's tobacco and wheat. (21)

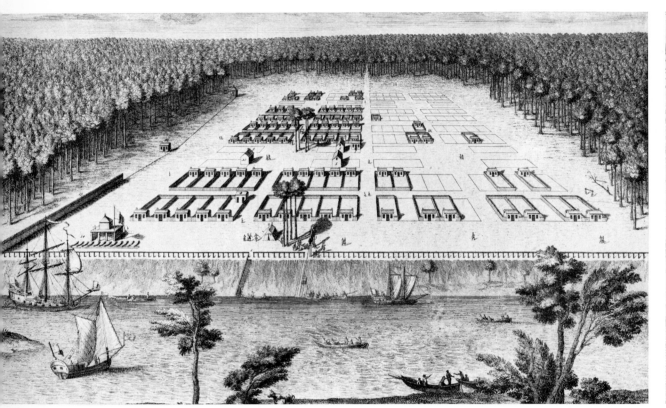

Religious conflict in Europe peopled America with dissenters. Protestants from Salzburg (above right) settled in the new British colony of Georgia. Savannah, the capital, was laid out on ambitious lines. An engraving of 1734 (above) shows it when about 100 plots had been taken. (19, 22)

South American Baroque stands in marked contrast to northern Neoclassicism, developing even more exuberance than that of Spain and Portugal. Left: the church of São Francisco, at Ouro Preto, Brazil. (20)

A new migration of colonists still wishing to maintain their ties with the mother-country was caused by the American Revolution. They moved north, into Canada. Here (right) a group of loyalists pitch their camp at Johnston on the St Lawrence. (23)

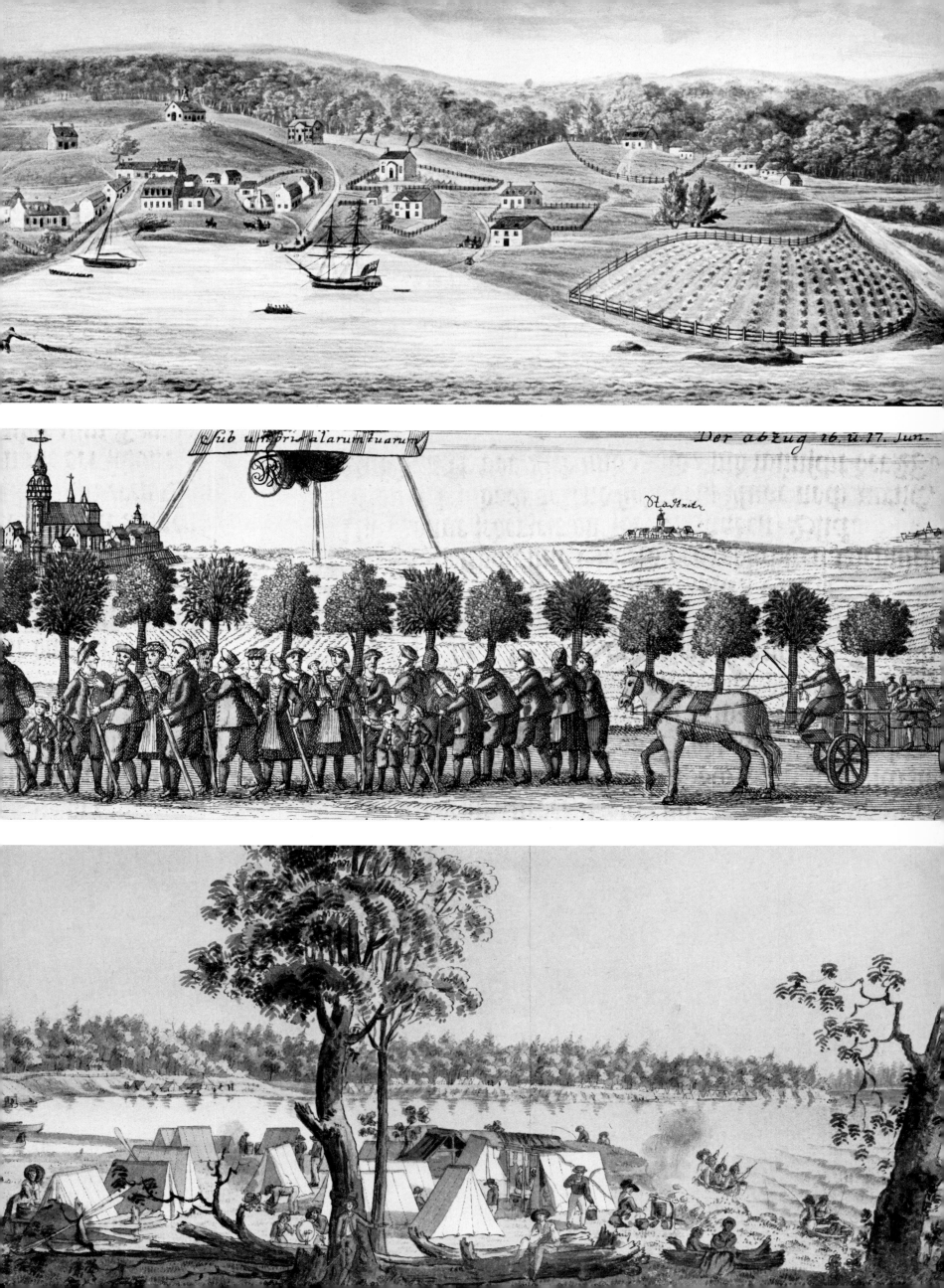

Sub umbra alarum tuarum                                    Der abzug 16. u. 17. Jun.

**Africa and the Far East** exemplified the *ancien régime colonial*. The maritime nations of Europe — Portugal, the Netherlands, Britain, France — had taken bites out of the African coast. The earliest European settlement on the Gold Coast was Elmina, now in Ghana, founded by the Portuguese and captured in 1637 by the Dutch. Throughout the 18th century it was the chief port of the region, exporting gold and slaves. By 1750 about 10,000 negroes were being sent annually from the Gold Coast to America. The Dutch governor, Adrianus Swalmius, is seen here (left) with slave in attendance and the fort of Elmina visible through the window. (24)

**Calcutta** (right), the centre of Britain's mercantile empire in Bengal, was founded in the 17th century by the East India Company, and grew rapidly. This view of 1795 shows the 'Manufactury and Bazaar', a classical building near the river. (26)

**Japan** had been closed to Europeans since the middle of the 17th century, the only exception being the Dutch trading post at Nagasaki, on the island of Deshima. Apart from busy periods when the ships from Batavia were in port, it was a luxurious but boring life, the officials being (in the words of one of them in 1775) 'dead and buried in an obsure corner of the globe'. In this section of a Japanese illustration of 1690 we see the main street, and in the upper rooms the rich merchants with their servants and slaves. (25)

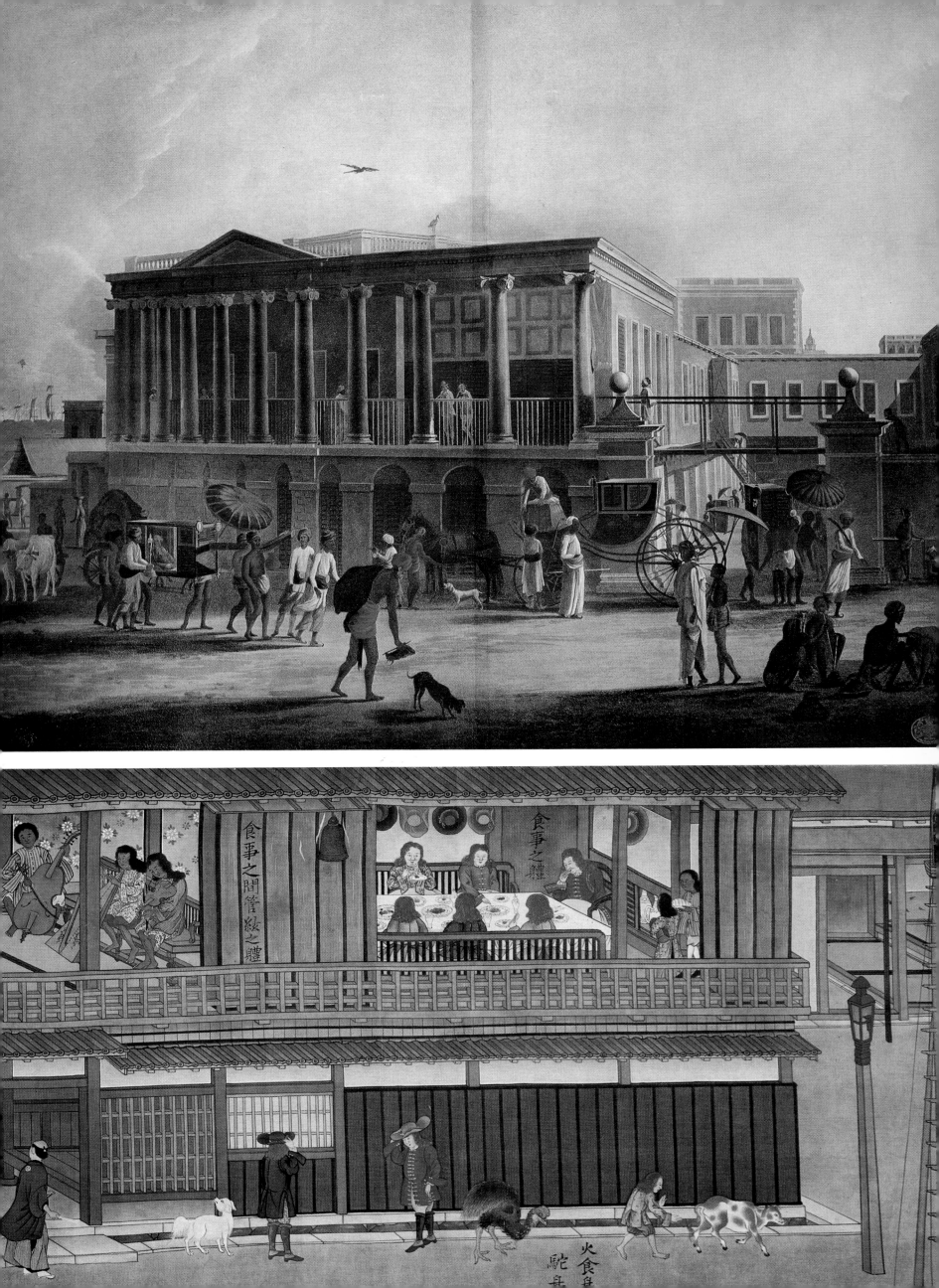

**Slavery was the foundation** of 18th-century imperial wealth, and of much of what is most admired in 18th-century culture (e. g. the Adam drawing-room on p. 70 was built for the widow of a sugar magnate.) The fact that it involved misery and suffering almost without precedent in world history troubled only the sensitive few. Josiah Wedgwood, the potter, was one; his medallion (left) was adopted as the seal of the Slave Emancipation Society. (27)

**Diamonds from Brazil,** sugar from the West Indies, tobacco from the southern states of what is now the U.S.A. — all depended absolutely on slave labour. Right: negro slaves washing for diamonds under the eyes of white overseers. (28).

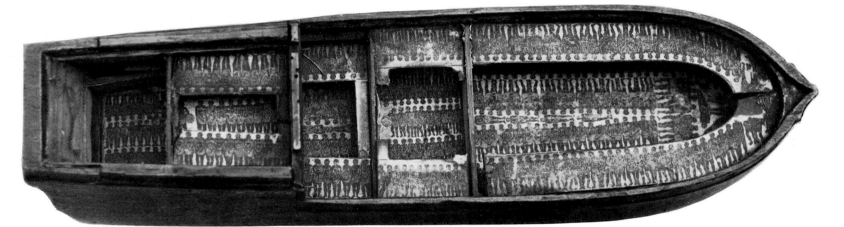

**The slave-ships** stacked their cargo between decks; each slave had a space about five feet by two, was taken out once a day for exercise and fed twice. This model (above) was made by Wilber-force in an attempt to force Members of Parliament to realize the truth. On a good trip five in a hundred died, on a bad one thirty or forty. The slaves were often bought from African rulers (below left: the King of Dahomey in 1793, receiving European visitors). Below right: slaves being sold in Martinique. (29, 30, 31)

**Abolition came** throughout the British Empire in 1807, when Charles James Fox introduced a bill prohibiting participation in the slave trade. A negro kneeling in gratitude (right) was included in Fox's memorial in Westminster Abbey, but the man most responsible was William Wilberforce (below), whose whole life had been dedicated to the struggle. Abolishing traffic in slaves did not mean emancipation, nor did all other nations follow Britain's example. In 1840, it has been calculated, twice the number of slaves were landed in America (North and South) than the annual average fifty years earlier. (32, 34)

**The only slave revolt** to succeed was in St Domingue. Led by the heroic Toussaint Louverture, the slaves of France's richest colony rebelled in 1791, defeated all opposition, including a professional army, and founded the negro state of Haiti. In 1794 three deputies from the island attended the Convention in Paris. One was Jean-Baptiste Bellay, seen here with a bust of Raynal, the author of the *Histoire philosophique des Indes* (1770) and Toussaint's inspiration in his fight for freedom. (33)

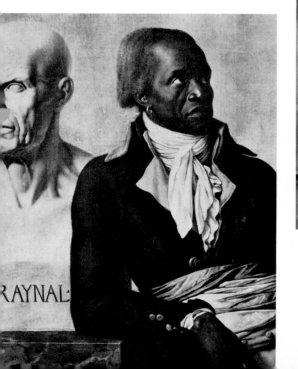

167

**Sugar** was, with tobacco, the commodity in which European fortunes were amassed and which made the greatest demands on slave labour. The plantation shown here (above) is at Pernambuco, in Brazil. The cane was brought in from the fields, crushed in a roller-mill, boiled, mixed with lime and egg-white and left to crystallize. (35)

**Tobacco** (upper right) proved in some areas even more profitable than sugar, as the habit grew both in the colonies and Europe; taking it as snuff, chewing it and smoking it in a pipe were equally common. (37)

**Tea** reached Europe from China (left) chiefly in Dutch vessels, to be auctioned at London or Amsterdam. The 18th century was a great age of tea-drinking, especially in England. It was in an attempt to compete with the Dutch that tea-growing in India was undertaken. (36)

**Chinese porcelain** became one of the most valuable items of Eastern trade; European factories were quick to imitate oriental styles but could not match their technical quality. Right: ceramics being packed for transport. (38)

**The idea of the noble savage** had a twofold origin: in the writing of moralists like Rousseau, who blamed civilization for most of mankind's vices and therefore idealized the state of nature; and in the accounts of travellers who were inclined to dwell more on what was attractive in primitive societies than on what was barbarous. The traditional religious picture of Adam before the Fall was no doubt also a factor. It comes out very clearly in art, where savages are habitually represented on the model of classical nudes: one can see this in West's *Death of Wolfe* (p. 242) and Westmacott's Fox Memorial (pl. 34), as well as in Hodges' Tahitian landscapes (pl. 2). *William Penn's Treaty with the Indians* (above), also by West, shows the same tendency, as indeed did the event that it commemorates. William Penn, the Quaker, had landed in America in 1677 as a trustee of Quaker property in New Jersey, the early constitution of which, a model of social justice, was largely his work. In 1681 he began the 'Holy Experiment' of Pennsylvania (actually named after his father, Admiral Penn). He made several treaties with the Indian inhabitants, traditionally 'under the elm tree of Shackamaxon'. These agreements protected the rights of Indians and were faithfully kept by both sides. Voltaire called it 'the only treaty between these peoples and the Christians that was not ratified by an oath, and that was never infringed'. (39)

**Negroes in Europe** normally suffered little hardship. France in particular had a good record. The myth of the noble savage, confined as it was mostly to non-colonists and non-travellers, no doubt helped to cause this discrepancy. This sensitive portrait (left) by Maurice-Quentin de Latour of a negro servant buttoning his collar dates from 1741. (40)

# Slavery, Commerce and Empire

## K. G. DAVIES

THE 250 years from the first discoveries by Columbus and Vasco da Gama to the mid-18th century form a fairly coherent period in the history of European expansion. By about 1750 it is possible to speak of an *ancien régime colonial* paralleling the *ancien régime* in Europe, and likewise to be transformed beyond recognition in the next two generations. Under this *régime* Europe's interest in the rest of the world was effectively confined to half the globe; for the Pacific Ocean, though crossed by a few Spanish ships sailing from Manila to Acapulco and by rare interlopers of other nations, was uncharted and virtually unknown. Sea routes across the Atlantic and Indian oceans were familiar enough, but with few exceptions the Europeans eschewed inland penetration and stuck to islands and coasts. The sea was their element and they could get most of what they wanted without straying far from it. The *ancien régime colonial* was in the first place maritime, and Europe's interest in America, Africa and Asia was principally commercial. Colonies, trading-stations and spheres of influence were valued in commercial terms, or more precisely for the contributions they made to the flow of agricultural and other products to Europe. As markets for Europe's own goods these distant lands were not negligible, but they were less important than they were to become in the 19th and 20th centuries, and for obvious reasons. Africa was too primitive to want and too poor to pay for our relatively high-priced goods. The same was true of the indigenous peoples of North and South America, while settlement by Europeans in those regions had not before the 18th century proceeded far enough to provide a mass market. In the East, which was populous and sophisticated, such a market existed but could not yet be tapped. European workmanship, with one or two important exceptions such as ship-building, was either inferior or not markedly superior to that of the East itself; and until the Industrial Revolution, European methods of production were neither more efficient nor cheaper. So great was Europe's demand for exotic products by about 1700, and so restricted the demand of the rest of the world for Europe's manufactures, that there was some difficulty in balancing trade between the two, especially trade with the East in which exiguous shipments of European goods had to be supplemented by large consignments of precious metal. This difficulty disappeared with the Industrial Revolution when Britain began to export cheap cotton goods to the East instead of, as before, importing them from India.

Gold and silver had played a big part in first drawing European adventurers across the oceans. That lure still worked: at the close of the 17th century gold was found in Brazil, and at about the same time the production of silver in South America, which had dwindled to very little, picked up and reached about 1740 a higher level than ever before. But whereas in the 16th century gold and silver were virtually all Europe got or hoped to get from America, by the 18th century they were, relative to other products, of far less importance. Exotic foods and beverages had worked major changes in the pattern of European consumption. Some items, rare and expensive in the Middle Ages, became cheap and available: such were spices and sugar. Others, like tobacco, tea and coffee, formerly quite unknown in Europe, became common articles of consumption. They had not, by 1700, reached down to the daily diet of the European peasant but they were certainly within the reach of *bourgeois* families. Other products indigenous to distant lands proved capable of naturalization: potatoes notably in Ireland, artichokes in France, maize in Spain and the Balkans, and pineapples in the greenhouses of the rich. More than anything else, the colonies meant to Europe an improved and diversified diet.

## The ocean routes

These products of agriculture lead us to the grand ocean routes of the 18th century over which passed most of the trade between Europe and the rest of the world. First and most spectacular were the routes between Europe and the East, linking Lisbon to Goa and Macao, Amsterdam to Batavia, Malacca, Ceylon and Nagasaki, and London to Surat, Madras and Calcutta. Outward cargoes of suitable European goods, as already stated, were not easily furnished, and it is clear that, without the Spanish and Portuguese discoveries of gold and silver in America, Dutch and English trade with the East would have been crippled. Europe, for much of America's silver, was no more than a staging-post. Between 1721 and 1726, for example, the export of precious metal from Amsterdam to the Orient averaged 3 million florins a year.

The round-trip to the East and back to Europe usually occupied at least two years. In India or Indonesia ships might engage in local commerce before returning with cargoes of Indian textiles, China tea, Japanese copper, pepper from Malaysia, cinnamon from Ceylon, nutmegs from the Moluccas and cloves from Amboyna. At great public auction sales in London and Amsterdam these goods were sold for distribution throughout Europe, with small quantities re-exported to Africa and America. Takings at the Amsterdam sales between 1778 and 1780 averaged nearly 30 million florins a year, spices accounting for about one quarter, textiles nearly one third, pepper one tenth and coffee and tea one fifth between them. The decline of pepper from a position of greater consequence and the rise of coffee and tea date from about 1660.

Far less glamorous, but an important contribution to the European diet, was the trade from western Europe to the cod fishing grounds off Nova Scotia and Newfoundland. Dartmouth was Britain's leading port for this trade, with Exeter, Poole, Bristol and other western towns as well as London taking a share; La Rochelle, Nantes, St Malo and Dieppe led the French competition. This trade was highly valued by politicians and economists, partly because it employed and trained seamen who were useful for service in the navy, and partly because the catch was paid for, not by visible exports, but by labour. Nothing went out from Europe but salt for preserving the fish, provisions for the crews, and tackle, while the returns were not merely fish but also the products of Spain, Portugal and Italy. For this trade was conducted partly on a triangular footing, cod caught and cured off Newfoundland being sold in Lisbon or the Mediterranean and thus financing, amongst other things, British purchases of port. In the first half of the 18th century the annual catch by the British rose from less than 100,000 quintals to more than 500,000, while the French (whose rights were reserved despite the loss of Nova Scotia in 1713 and Canada in 1763) were not far behind; at times they did better, having an advantage in their plentiful supplies of salt from Ré, Oléron and elsewhere on the Atlantic coast.

p 211 (12)

f 2 26 (23)

f 3

p 161–2

*Gold and silver had first drawn Europeans to the Americas. Top: treasure being taken away in crates. Later, other products, including some previously unknown in Europe, were found to be highly profitable. An engraving of 1775 (bottom) shows a tobacco merchant supervising his cargo. (1, 2)*

The transatlantic sea routes joining Europe to the settled parts of America carried diverse cargoes to and from many ports but they may be considered as a single group, performing a common economic function, and comparable to one another in their demands on ships and seamen. From London and Bristol to Boston, New York, Charleston and Kingston; from Lisbon to Recife and Bahia; from Seville and Cadiz to Vera Cruz, Portobello, Cartagena and Havana; from Rouen, St Malo, Dieppe and Nantes to Quebec, New Orleans and Martinique: hundreds of ships crossed the Atlantic each year, carrying provisions, wine, clothes, furniture, books, weapons and all other things needed to make life tolerable in the seaboard communities of America. In return, the tropical colonies shipped sugar, rice, tobacco, and dyewood for Europe's textile industry; Spanish America, still under-exploited economically in 1700, produced silver and hides; Brazil sugar and gold; Canada and the British northern colonies furs. Given average conditions the Atlantic could be crossed in between one and two months, but unlucky ships might be windbound in the English Channel for weeks. Winter sailings were avoided if possible, and a ship could not normally be expected to complete more than one round-trip a year.

## Slave trade

Distinct from the transatlantic trades between Europe and America, and distinctive too in the place it has been given in history, was the slave trade, carried on by ships from Amsterdam, London, Bristol, Liverpool and Nantes. Their cargoes of cloth (mostly of the cheaper sort), guns, liquor and glass-beads were either landed at depots on the Gold Coast—similar to the forts and factories of the East but smaller—or sold ashore in the estuaries of the Calabar and Niger rivers to African merchants or kings. Then, loaded with 200 to 600 men, women and children, jammed between the decks, the slave ships cleared for the Middle Passage. With a good wind, as few as five in a hundred slaves would die; becalmed, one third or more might be dead on arrival in Brazil or the Caribbean. Such were the risks of trade. In this lottery the

*f 4*

p 166
(29)

slaves themselves could only lose; either they died on voyage or they survived to labour in regimented gangs on tropical plantations. A few were lucky enough to become flunkeys in a planter's household.

Nothing done by Europeans in the 18th century, neither wars nor persecutions nor the exploitation of the weak, has left behind so great a bitterness or so much guilt as the slave trade. Yet till 1750 few voices were raised against it, except perhaps to deplore the risks to the pockets of traders. All leading European countries engaged in it. Catholic priests baptized slaves in Angola as they queued to be branded and shipped; John Locke put money into the English Royal African Company, of which King James II was governor. In Europe itself, in 1700, slavery was legal; there were many slaves in Lisbon and some in other big cities. In the East the Europeans had met slavery everywhere and had adopted it. But it was in America that Europeans made their biggest mark by introducing slavery in its most objectionable form, plantation slavery. On the sugar estates of the Caribbean and Brazil, on the tobacco and rice plantations of Virginia and Carolina, and in the silver mines of New Spain, slavery was at the bottom of the great edifice of Atlantic commerce reared for Europe's benefit. The institution, the trade itself, were Europe's most baneful gifts to the New World, and they were vital parts of the *ancien régime colonial*.

p 168–
(35, 37)

## Europe's commercial supremacy

Over the grand ocean routes went Europe's *direct* trade with distant continents. But by the early 18th century Europe's commercial empire was already too sophisticated to be measured simply by the number of ships going in and out of her principal ports. There were also *indirect* trades, from country to country and from continent to continent, which Europeans had either created or taken over. In the East, first the Portuguese, then the Dutch, then the English, participated in the port-to-port shipment of goods which Europe never saw but which made profits to Europe's benefit. This was another way in which the balance of payments problem could be eased: silver exports primed the pump of what

p 168–9
(36, 38)

was called the 'country trade'. Much could be made by licensing and taxing Asiatic traders; more still by participation. Persian silks were wanted in India; Indian textiles, China tea and porcelain in Indonesia; Japanese copper on the Coromandel coast. Europeans supplied them.

This 'country trade' in the East antedated the arrival of the Europeans; in the Atlantic they had to build up their own network, though national rivalries and protection policies interfered with, if they did not altogether prevent, a free flow of goods. The Spanish colonies in particular were seldom adequately supplied with either slaves or manufactures, and it was the great object of French, Dutch and English smugglers to make good these shortages. The British colonists of North America were forbidden to trade with French and Dutch, but Rhode Islanders were often at Martinique and St Eustatius. Not all port-to-port trade in the Atlantic was illegal: from New York and New England to the British Caribbean came dried fish for slaves, provisions and barrel staves for transporting sugar, with molasses as the return cargo. In 1713 the British obtained by treaty the right to supply slaves to the Spaniards and to send a ship a year with manufactures for Portobello. And from the early 18th century, West Indians were freighting cargoes of rum to Africa to buy slaves for themselves. Legally or illegally these trades increased, though unlike the country trade of the East, they contributed more to the prosperity of the colonies than to the wealth of Europe.

Europe's supremacy over the rest of the 18th century world is nowhere more marked than in the efficiency with which Europeans supplied their own needs and those of others. China, certainly not Europe's cultural inferior and probably not inferior industrially or technologically, was uninterested in foreign goods and foreign trade; that removed one potential rival. India and Indonesia, other possible competitors, were extremely interested in trade and had in the widespread Islamic community an advantage which might have secured them control over the commerce of at least some parts of Asia. That they were subdued by Europe proceeded partly from their own internal divisions but also from the superiority of European ships; a superiority which, if anything, became more marked in the 18th century with growing efficiency and lower costs, faster sailing and closer to the wind, and improved charts and map making. This commercial hegemony was won and kept by Europeans at the expense of the rest of the world, but there were incidental advantages on the other side. An important achievement under the *ancien régime colonial* was the dissemination throughout the world of crops and livestock hitherto confined to certain continents. Europe was the principal beneficiary, but in the long run America gained from the new staples and livestock including the horse, Africa from cassava, maize and sweet potatoes, and Java from coffee. The incentives for furthering these migrations were of course selfish, but the result was a matching of crops to climates and soils which over centuries increased the world's food supply.

## Settlers in the New World

Trade on the scale attained by the early 18th century necessitated European settlement in selected parts of the world, though trade was seldom the sole direct reason for emigration to America. Before and after 1700, Europeans crossed the Atlantic to escape persecution, to live by farming, to manage plantations, to convert heathens, and to govern the natives and each other. A common impulse to emigration is and always has been the hope that in the new land life may be lived of a kind and quality which the migrant believes himself to be entitled to enjoy in the old world, but which for some reason (economic accident, disinheritance, personal misfortune) he is unable to obtain. The aim in the first place is to reproduce the familiar patterns of living but in an ideal form. Spanish *hidalgos*, too poor to live on shrunken estates in Spain, too proud to labour, too honourable to trade, sought positions of authority in America or at least an Indian village to live off. New England's land and climate were apt to receive Englishmen who aimed to become the independent yeoman farmers who were disappearing from the mother country in the 18th century. Further

*The discovery of rich fishing grounds off Nova Scotia and Newfoundland opened up new opportunities to the European fishing industry. In this engraving of 1720, A is the fisherman, B the baited line, C 'the manner of fishing', D, E and F the gutting and salting of cod, G and H the cleaning, I a press to extract the oil from cods' livers into the barrel (L) and M the fish laid out to dry. The ships then returned to such ports as Dartmouth and La Rochelle. (3)*

south, in Virginia, St Domingue or Jamaica, the life of the planters resembled that of country gentlemen in England and France. Their 'great houses' (though some were quite small) were inspired by

p 136
(7)

European models, and happily the Georgian style was easily transplanted and adapted to the needs of the tropics and North America. George Washington's home at Mount Vernon, his life before the American Revolution, his tastes, pursuits and reading, took after those of English gentry: the main differences were that his servants were black slaves and his view over the Potomac more beautiful than most Englishmen enjoyed. If a distinctive colonial way of life can be said to have emerged by the middle of the 18th century, it had been formed more by the American environment than by the conscious purpose of the settlers.

One of Europe's exports to North America—though Central and South America already had them—was towns. Even in colonies, where agriculture was the livelihood of the great majority, a strong tide of urbanization was making in the 18th century. As ports, seats of law-courts and centres of administration, dock-yards and barracks, towns were essential. Jefferson's ideal of a North American nation of farmers was obsolete when first formulated. By mid-18th century the Atlantic seaboard of the Americas was studded with towns which, if they did not match European capitals, compared well in size and sometimes in amenities with provincial cities in England and France. Such were Boston, New

p 317
(8, 9)

York, Philadelphia, Kingston, Havana, Vera Cruz and Bahia; Mexico City and Lima were the only big towns in the Americas not closely linked to the Atlantic. Better planned and cleaner than the medieval cities of Europe, the best American towns were pleasant places to live in. Philadelphia, founded in 1682, had a population of about 35,000 by 1776. It was laid out on a grid, with a college founded in 1751 which had attracted 300 students seven years later, a fine hospital (1754), a theatre (1766), many public buildings of which Carpenters' Hall (1770–74) is a good example, and dozens of excellent town-houses. The Americas by mid-18th century were producing painters and sculptors of their own but, as we have seen in Chapter II, it is broadly true to say that architecture was the first and greatest of the colonial arts.

Despite these amenities—not by any means found everywhere—the European population of the Spanish colonies, Brazil and the Caribbean, grew quite slowly in the 18th century. Only in British North America was there a population explosion antedating Europe's own: here the increase was from half a million to a million and a half in the first 50 years of the century. In 1738, for example, the governor of New York reported that the population of his province had increased in seven years from 50,289 to 60,437. Five-sixths of this population being white, it follows that the increase owed little to imported slaves. Partly it was natural growth (one third of the whites in New York in 1738 were under 10 years of age); partly it resulted from a conscious and fairly liberal encouragement of immigration by the British and colonial governments. Settlers came from Switzerland and Germany to occupy cheap land in Pennsylvania and the Carolinas. Scotland too provided colonists, but the Protestant religion being a condition of approval, Ireland was not a favoured recruiting ground. For the Scots poverty at home was the spur; for some Germans,

p 162–3
(19, 22)

the Palatines for instance, it was a revival of Roman Catholic persecution.

A new American colony, Georgia, came into being in the 1730s as a refuge for victims of bigotry and an attempt to give a new and healthier life to London's poor. Georgia, had the hopes of the founders been fulfilled, might have transformed the British southern colonies and in time the southern states of U.S.A., for it was meant to be a colony of small proprietors, with no slaves, no lawyers and no hard liquor. Despite subsidies from the British Parliament, these ideals were lost in the early years of struggle and disappointment.

Nothing but good, it seemed, could come from these schemes for promoting settlement. They quickened the pace of economic growth, furthered trade, and furnished a militia to oppose the French and Spaniards. Few foresaw, in the early 18th century, that the rising prosperity and increasing population of the British North American colonies would furnish men and money to oppose the mother country.

In the Caribbean and in South America there was no comparable growth of European population; on the contrary, in the West Indies the proportion of whites to negroes went down alarmingly. The most important demographic developments here were the growth of a black slave population in plantation-colonies and a rise in the number of coloured people. The *gens de couleur* of St Domingue and the mulattos, quadroons and octaroons of the British West Indies, were the offspring of unions between whites and negroes, that is to say, between white men and negro or coloured women. In the Caribbean islands the pre-Columbian inhabitants had virtually disappeared—the Arawaks worked to death, the Caribs hunted to death because too fierce to be put to work. In South America, on the other hand, the pre-Columbian Indians had survived; much reduced in the 17th century, their numbers appear to have risen in the 18th. Here, though whites copulated with negroes as in the Caribbean, a commoner element in the population was the offspring of Spaniards and Indians. These *mestizos*, like the French *gens de couleur* and the mulattos of the British tropical colonies, were a potentially disruptive force in the colonial *ancien régime*. Steadily increasing in number, aspiring to self-improvement and resentful of white supremacy, the coloureds played a leading part in the complicated rebellion and long drawn out war of independence in St Domingue, and might in time have done the same elsewhere had not the Spanish American *creoles* themselves taken up the cause of national freedom.

## Traders in Africa and the East

In Africa there was no European settlement comparable to that in the Americas; the Portuguese island of São Thomé and the small Dutch colony at the Cape were the only possible exceptions. Luanda in Portuguese Angola was just recognizable as a European town; elsewhere, at El Mina for example (Dutch), or Cape Coast (British),

p 164
(24)

the Europeans lived in forts around which grew up African townships without amenities or public buildings. Only a few European eccentrics tried to live in the country, and none (except the Dutch farmers of South Africa) by agriculture.

In the East, European life was lived almost entirely in towns which had begun as trading stations and acquired a predominantly Asian population, though Europeans held all official posts of importance. Macao in 1745 had 13,000 inhabitants (only one third of the population of a century earlier), of whom 8,000 were Chinese, many of the rest of mixed blood, and only a handful of European birth or wholly European descent. Batavia, the head-quarters of the Dutch East India Company, was bigger, perhaps 30,000 within and without the walls in the early 18th century. The Company's officers, the men who ran Dutch trade in Java and throughout the East, were few; they and the 'free citizens' of Batavia have been computed at between five and ten thousand. The 'free citizens' were not Company employees, but were of European descent though not necessarily on both sides; they married Indonesians or women of Indo-Portuguese origin because of the shortage, here and elsewhere in the East, of European women.

Perhaps the most remarkable city created by Europeans in the East or anywhere else during the *ancien régime* was Goa, noted in the late 16th century for its magnificence and its vice. In the 18th century, like Macao, Goa was a place of decay but as late as 1675 it had impressed an English traveller, Dr John Fryer:

The City if a *Rome* in India, both for Absoluteness and Fabricks, the chiefest consisting of Churches, and Convents, or Religious Houses; though the Laity have sumptuous ones all of Stone; their Streets are paved, and cleaner than the tops of their Houses, where they do all occasions, leaving their Excrements there. They live with a splendid Outside, vaunting in their number of Slaves, walking under a Street of their own Umbrelloes, bare-headed, to avoid giving Distaste in not removing their Hats: they being jealous of their Honour, pardon no Affront; where-fore to ogle a Lady in a Balcony (if a Person of Quality) it is to be revenged with a *Bocca Mortis* [blunderbuss], or to pass by a *Fidalgo* without due Reverence, is severely chastised.

To rule settlements like these and the colonies in America, and to safeguard the interests of the nation against others, political

*A European commercial settlement on the Guinea coast of Africa in the early 18th century. The four compounds belong to Portugal (left), France (centre),* *England (right) and Holland (right foreground). In the left foreground the French director (numbered 14) returns with his train of servants. (4)*

connexions had been created and institutions of government set up which to some extent mirror the traditions of each European country. Obvious national exports include the elected houses of representatives in British colonies in America and the West Indies; the *gouverneurs* and *intendants* of New France, Martinique and Guadeloupe; the *camaras* (town-councils) of Portugal's overseas territories which resembled, where they were not modelled on, those of the mother country; and the viceroys, *audiencias* (appeal-courts), *cabildos* (town-councils) and *corregidores* (residents) of Mexico and Peru. But these diverse institutions did not necessarily work in just the same way in the New World as at home, and the differences between the administration of one European empire and another were sometimes more apparent than real.

In the East, at the start of the 18th century, Europe can scarcely be said to have ruled at all, save over quite small territories such as Goa and Batavia. Elsewhere they were nearer to being tenants than landlords, though tenants it would have been difficult to evict. The Portuguese in Albuquerque's time may have thought of direct rule over subject people: in the 18th century Portuguese enclaves continued to be administered by the Crown. But their competitors had no such ambitions: Dutch and English confided their national interests to chartered companies which saw no profit in assuming the burdens of direct rule. They preferred to work by influence, through treaties, informal agreements, bribes and an occasional show of force. By means of their officials, soldiers and fleets, the Dutch were able to control the output of spices (in order to keep up prices in Europe) and to safeguard their own monopoly in Indonesia: these were their two principal objectives and no further commitment seemed necessary. The British in India were in a less strong position about 1700, but their ambitions were of the same order as the Dutch. The Moghul Empire still formed the largest and strongest political unit in India; not till its disintegration were

the British at once tempted and obliged to assume a greater measure of responsibility. In short, the East about 1700 presented no acute political problem to the governments of Britain and the Netherlands: their national interests were safe in the hands of profit-making companies with a century of experience behind them. It was enough for the purpose of supervision that these companies had charters periodically coming up for scrutiny and renewal.

## Government at a distance

In the Americas Europe had ruled from the start, over indigenous people and over settlers; after some experiments in other directions, most of the government in force at the beginning of the 18th century was royal government. A few British colonies (Pennsylvania, Maryland and Rhode Island) were still proprietary, i.e. ruled by private owners with only light control exercised from London; the remainder were Crown colonies, as were French and Spanish possessions. All these European empires had autocratic pretensions, and all the autocracies were mitigated by inefficiency. In theory the colonies had little independence. All laws made by British colonial legislatures required the royal assent, and there were no conventions against withholding it. Both before and after the American Revolution, the British Parliament at Westminster passed laws which were quite opposed to the declared wishes of the colonists. The Navigation Acts of the 17th century are one example, though by the 18th some colonists had become supporters of a commercial system which largely guaranteed them the British market. The Molasses Act of 1733, designed to stop trade between the North American colonies and the French and Dutch West Indies, is another example; and the abolition of the slave trade in 1807 a third and greater. In like manner the Spanish government tried to regulate trade to America for the benefit of Old Spain by making it unlawful to import except from Seville or to buy slaves except from the *asientists*. In these and other ways the nations of Europe asserted their own interests at the expense of those of their colonies. In only two instances, under the *ancien régime*, were colonists given seats in a European legislature: these were, rather surprisingly, in the Portuguese *cortes* in which Bahia was granted representation in 1653 and Goa in 1674, but the principle was nullified from 1698 when the metropolitan *cortes* ceased to meet. French colonial representatives were admitted to the National Assembly only after the Revolution; the British never. Nor was interference by the mother country only a matter of legislation without representation: the chief officers of the British, French and Spanish empires were appointed by the respective Crowns and in most cases were natives of Europe, not of America. Crown nominees in turn appointed some of the inferior officers, with many of the best jobs going to expatriates, a matter of more concern in Spanish America than in the British colonies where trade offered better prospects of wealth than office.

Such were the aspirations of metropolitan government; the effects were different. The British colonists had no members of Parliament of their own at Westminster but influenced other people's. Till late in the 18th century when the slavery issue emerged, the West Indian interest in Parliament was a strong and respected pressure group. All colonies had agents in London to look after their interests by frequent appearances at boards of government. But a still better safeguard of colonial self-rule than lobbying, and one common to all empires, was the three to five thousand miles of water between Europe and America, the length of time taken for decisions to be made and dispatched, the delay before infractions of those decisions could be detected and reported, the postponements and adjournments of trial of those infractions, and indeed a whole armoury of prevarication to frustrate the actions of the metropolitan government. Amongst the colonists, and amongst the royal officials themselves, the ocean bred a mental climate of independence. An illustration of colonial *insouciance* is smuggling, common enough in Europe but a matter of survival in America. The Rhode Islanders smuggled the meaning out of the Molasses Act by trade with French and Dutch West Indies, while the Spanish settlers were for long periods entirely dependent on slaves and manufactures illegally supplied by foreigners. With so much coastline and so many harbours, illicit trade could not be smothered: to impose a new restraint on colonial commerce was to create a new branch of the smuggling industry.

The impressive edifice of Spanish autocracy and the prerogatives of British governors were not what they seemed. True a British governor alone could summon and dissolve an assembly; but so could George II a British Parliament, yet it did not bring him much real power. And in Massachusetts or New York a governor wielded little of the patronage which George II and his ministers used to help parliamentary business along. Some governors depended for their salaries on the pleasure of a House of Representatives, quite ready to exploit that weapon to win concessions. Spanish viceroys did not have to face assemblies, but had problems of their own. Till well into the 18th century many public offices in Spanish America were saleable, putting power into the hands of persons not necessarily willing instruments of government. *Peninsulares* (Spaniards from Spain) were generally loyal to the mother country but *creoles* (Spaniards born in America), though respectful to the King, tended to put colonial interests first, and those of Old Spain second. In the course of the 18th century the Bourbon Kings of Spain brought French-inspired reforms into their colonial government: *intendencias* and *subdelegados* arrived, non-venal and staffed at key-points by *peninsulares*. But the price of greater efficiency was a widening rift between *peninsulares* and *creoles* and ultimately the separation of Spain from her colonies.

Yet after all the colonies in America were dependencies in the first half of the 18th century. The greater the matter at issue, the more likely the mother country was to exert herself. Independence in practice covered a multitude of small things; it did not include foreign relations. When in 1736 the Spanish governor of Florida signed a treaty on his own initiative with James Oglethorpe regulating the Georgia-Florida boundary, Spanish reaction was swift and terrible: the governor was recalled and hanged. Defence was the strongest card in the metropolitan hand: almost all British

and French colonies felt in danger from rival powers. From New England to Georgia, the British feared French encirclement from the line of the Mississippi, while the Caribbean colonies were almost helpless victims of whichever nation had the strongest navy. All the major French islands except St Domingue were in British hands at one time or another in the 18th century; even the Spanish stronghold at Havana fell to a British force in 1762. For warships, regular troops, arms, ammunition and fortifications, and for protection of their trade, the colonies were compelled to look to Europe. They were not yet separately rich enough, nor sufficiently capable of collective action, to undertake their own preservation. This enforced submission, or at least reluctant acknowledgment of imperial leadership, was steadily eroded in the 18th century. North Americans worried less about France after Britain won Canada in 1763. Equally important, and common to all empires, increasing wealth gave to the colonists the means of self-defence, even against their own mother country.

p 197
(41, 43)

## Christianity overseas

Europe's mission to spread Christianity round the world, sometimes tarnished and often relaxed, was still at work in the 18th century. Christianity was certainly one element, though not the only one, in the superiority which Europeans assumed over other races. But that superiority was not such as to preclude sharing the good news with less fortunate people. In the first two centuries of European presence in the East, tremendous efforts were made by Roman Catholic missionaries to win converts. In places where Portuguese influence was paramount there were some successes, but by the 18th century Christianity's impact on the East was still negligible by comparison with the millions of adherents of competing religions. Highly effective against the inchoate superstitions of primitive people, Christianity proved almost powerless against organized alternatives. There is much of interest and something heroic in the work of Jesuits, Franciscans and Dominicans from India to China, but it is only of secondary importance in the 18th century. The missionaries did little to influence European government, partly because there was so little in the East to influence; and they certainly did not bring about a displacement of the civilizations and manners of Asia. The Dutch and English Company officers, when they took Indians, Indonesians or Chinese as wives, mistresses or servants, did probably as much as the missionaries to spread European values in the East.

*f 6*

In the western hemisphere the story is different, though the British showed little interest in converting the Indians of North America. The French in Canada tried harder, and so did the Spaniards in California: some of their 18th century mission-churches, like that of Santa Barbara, still stand. Effective conversion of the Amerindians depended on their being either brought into colonial society or protected in reservations, and these were not the purposes of the British settlers who brushed the natives aside the moment they wanted Indian land more than they wanted Indian trade. In Central and South America, on the other hand, the Spaniards had come to live off the labour of others; they needed the Indians. For this reason, and because Spanish traditions were strongly religious, Spanish America became the shop-window of Christianity overseas.

It cannot be said that the goods in the window in the 18th century were particularly attractive. The Church was rich, too rich in some respects to do its job properly. It condoned and practised slavery. If converts were numerous, as they were, the quality of belief was imperfect. The number of Indian and *mestizo* priests was small, though it is fair to say that distaste for celibacy was a deterrent to those who might have aspired to ordination. From early days the Church had played an important part in government, and if at certain points it succeeded in humanizing Spanish rule, at others the connexion was unhealthy. Nevertheless if any trace of a collective European sense of responsibility for non-Europeans is to be detected under the *ancien régime*, it must be sought in the Spanish Church in America. All round the world, it is true, individual Europeans can be discovered who pitied, sentimentalized, admired or even understood non-Europeans; but there is little indication that they influenced policy at home or abroad. They did not halt the dispossession of the Mohicans by the colony of Connecticut;

*Religion was a powerful motive in European expansion, and missions were undertaken by almost every Christian denomination. Above: negro slaves being baptised by a Moravian minister in North America. Below: the frontispiece of a collection of Jesuit missionary letters. A sort of Jesuit Mercury, with the slogan 'I bring you tidings of great joy', has the present world in tow, while the Jesuit ship brings the four continents (symbolized by animals) to the 'New World' of salvation. (5, 6)*

they did not stop the slave trade or the savage treatment of slaves in St Domingue; they did not prevent the Dutch patrols destroying the spice harvests of the Moluccas because they were surplus to the needs of the European market. But in South America, some influence of the Church on policy can be found. A moral purpose existed and was recognized to exist, though there were many departures from it. The most spectacular example of this purpose in the 18th century, one which illustrates the vices as well as the virtues of clerical influence, is provided by the 'State' in Paraguay where 100,000 Guarani Indians formed an enclosed community ruled by Jesuit priests, from which Spanish colonists were excluded. This 'State', more enlightened than the enlightened despotisms of Europe, and for that matter more despotic, was a caricature of good intentions. The Indians were protected from exploitation, and that was a tremendous benefit; they were employed to the profit of the community and not worked beyond their capacity; and they were treated as second class people unfit to run their own lives or even to be taught how to do so.

Ironically it was the Enlightenment in Europe, with its suggestion of a better deal for subject people, which weakened the Church in Spanish America, the institution with the best record of work on behalf of Indians. A series of anti-clerical moves began in 1717. In 1759 the Jesuits were expelled by Pombal from Brazil, and in 1767 they were expelled from Spanish America. As well as leaving the Paraguay reserve to run down, the departure of the Jesuits was a setback to the intellectual life of South America, and it is possible that the Spanish imperial government was weakened by its own action. In the later 18th century it relied more on the army than on the Church, and of the two the army was more adaptable to aspirations of independence.

A new feature of Christianity overseas in the 18th century was an awakening interest in missionary work on the part of Protestants, after a long period of virtual abstention. The net effects were not great, but at least an effort was made. Conspicuous amongst those who took the field were the Moravian Brethren, with whom John Wesley was briefly associated in Georgia. Animated by Count Zinzendorf, and operating from headquarters at Herrnhut in Saxony, the Moravian missions were anything but flamboyant. In Greenland and at posts in the north of Labrador they preached to Eskimos with no fear of competition; in Georgia they tried to convert Indians and left when war with Spain offended their pacifist consciences. The West Indies, Danish and British, were their special field. They worked in Surinam, one of the least pleasant places in the 18th century, and they preached to slaves in Jamaica and the Leewards. By 1798 they claimed a congregation of 11,000 in Antigua alone. Moravian principles were against slavery, as well as war, but in the Leewards these had to be compromised: the planters for the most part welcomed the missionaries as allies who would teach submission to the negroes. They were allowed to work as long as they behaved themselves, and towards the end of the century the British started missions of their own. The Anglicans had founded the Society for the Propagation of Christian Knowledge in 1698 and the Society for the Propagation of the Gospel in 1701, but they worked chiefly with white settlers. Only in the last decade of the 18th century were new missions founded to work with non-Europeans, the Baptist Missionary Society (1792), the London Missionary Society (1795) and the Church Missionary Society (1799).

Labour and dedication by individuals were always to be found. But Christianity overseas in the 18th century must be regarded as a failure in two respects. First, no native ministry was trained; the exceptions are too few to matter. What could one make of a religion with universal pretensions in which all the officers were white Europeans? And, secondly, with the partial exception of the Church in Spanish America, the missionaries scarcely ever till the late 18th century succeeded in influencing the policies of governments at home or abroad, let alone the policies of the chartered companies; in many cases they did not even try.

Such in brief was the *ancien régime colonial* which reached its apogee in the first half of the 18th century. A dependent America, a subservient East and an unknown Pacific; trade, and wars to defend and extend trade; slavery; and largely unrequited Christian effort: these were the main characteristics of Europe overseas. From

*ff*

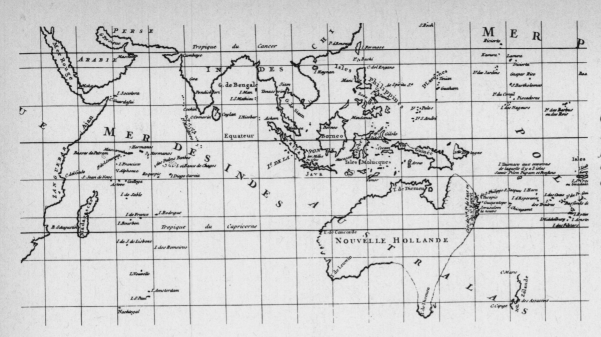

*On the eve of Cook's voyages the coasts of Africa, Asia and the Indonesian Islands were fairly well established, but uncertainty reigned over large areas of the Pacific. The French map of which this is a detail was published in 1756. Australia's eastern half was still unknown; Tasmania was assumed to be part of it; and New Zealand was a mere fragment of coast-line.* (7)

about 1750 this *régime* began to crumble and crack until by the early 19th century it had either been torn down by its victims or dismantled by Europeans who no longer had faith in it. Like the ending of the *ancien régime* in Europe, the changes in overseas territories were political but much more than political; as in Europe, they were accompanied by violence and revolution in some places, while in others the end came peacefully and through constitutional means. When the process of destruction and transformation was over, a new imperialism, to last till the mid-20th century, had begun to take shape.

## Voyages east

In the first place, the world of the *ancien régime* was greatly enlarged, and in the course of this enlargement fresh European attitudes were stimulated. Until the 18th century the two arms of Europe's advance, across the Atlantic to America and round the Cape of Good Hope to the east, never effectively met: it would have made little difference to Europe if the world had proved to be flat. The western shores of the Pacific were known, though imperfectly, and the Dutch had reached out to touch (but no more) the north-western coast of Australia. Maps and charts, if honest, left most of the ocean blank; others filled out scanty certainties with legend. A southern continent, of great size and imputed wealth, was widely believed to exist, and plausible reasons were devised as late as 1769 why this had to be. All was changed by a series of voyages of which Cook's were the greatest. Because the exploration of the Pacific was so long deferred, it had when finally undertaken a more purposeful appearance than earlier voyages of discovery. Sponsorship by the governments of France or Britain became a matter of course, with scientists accompanying some of the expeditions. Dampier (1699) was followed by Anson (1740), Byron (1764), Bougainville (1764 and 1766), Wallis and Carteret (1766). Most of them did some good work, but none can be said to have come to grips with the South Pacific as a whole. That was the achievement of James Cook in voyages which brought the greatest addition to Europe's stock of geographical knowledge since Columbus. On the first (1768–71) Cook circumnavigated New Zealand and sailed along the dangerous reefs of eastern Australia (New South Wales and Queensland); on the second (1772–75) he sailed far to the south to dispose of the myth of the southern continent; and on the third (1776–79) he explored the northern ocean and answered beyond reasonable doubt the old question whether navigable water joined North Pacific to North Atlantic. On all these voyages Cook found, named and charted, islands and groups of islands which Europeans either had never seen before or had imperfectly observed.

Cook was a genius. As explorer he was resolute where his predecessors had faltered. As captain he followed rules of health which were known but seldom enforced, and so conquered scurvy amongst his crews. And, most important of all, his journals and charts were of a precision beyond anything formerly achieved. If he could not single-handed close the gap between what mathematicians and astronomers knew and what seamen could learn and practise, at least he narrowed it. For navigation to be safe and sure, navigators required mathematics; from Cook's time the need was recognized if not yet generally met. They needed better instruments, too, above all a means of fixing longitudinal positions at sea. Latitude could be determined by observations of the sun but longitude required either difficult calculations based on sights of the moon (which Cook could make but most seamen could not) or an accurate chronometer for finding the difference between local time and G.M.T. In 1714 an Act of the British Parliament offered a prize of £20,000 for the discovery of longitude at sea, and after many experiments and false hopes the prize was given in 1765 to John Harrison (see Chapter III). Cook carried a duplicate of one of Harrison's models on his second voyage and reported that 'it had performed its part well'.

Cook recorded his discoveries and impressions in a simple, effective prose. The following extract from the journal of his second voyage reports the decision on January 29, 1774, to turn northwards after failing to find the southern continent:

I will not say it was impossible anywhere to get farther to the south; but the attempting it would have been a dangerous and rash enterprise; and what, I believe, no man in my situation could have thought of. It was, indeed, *my* opinion, as well as the opinion of most on board, that this ice extended quite to the pole, or, perhaps joined to some land, to which it had been fixed from the earliest time; and that it is here, that is to the south of this parallel, where all the ice we find scattered up and down to the north, is first formed, and afterwards broken off by gales of wind, or other causes, and brought to the north by the currents, which we always found to set in that direction in the high latitudes. As we drew near this ice, some penguins were heard, but none seen; and but few other birds, or any other thing, that could induce us to think any land was near. And yet I think there must be some to the south behind this ice; but if there is, it can afford no better retreat for birds, or any other animals, than the ice itself, with which it must be wholly covered. I, who had ambition not only to go farther than anyone had been before, but as far as it was possible for men to go, was not sorry at meeting with this interruption; as it, in some measure, relieved us; at least shortened the dangers and hardships inseparable from the navigation of the southern polar regions. Since, therefore, we could not proceed one inch farther to the south, no other reason need be assigned for my tacking, and standing back to the north; being at this time in the latitude of 71° 10′ S., longitude 106° 54′ W.

The exploration of the Pacific was one of the 18th century's great achievements. Of less immediate effect, but in the long run even more important in shaping 19th-century imperialism, was the beginning of penetration into the African interior. In 1788 an association was formed in London to promote discovery in the

*f* 7

p 158 (8, 9)
p 187 (17)

p 154–7

p 153 (1)

p 158 (11)

inland parts of Africa, and in 1795 Mungo Park was dispatched from the Gambia to discover the upper and middle Niger. It is wholly characteristic of the ignorance of Europeans that after three centuries on the west coast of Africa they were uncertain in which direction that river flowed. Park's journal was partly ghost-written and is much inferior to Cook's. The climax of the march is described as follows:

> looking forwards, I saw with infinite pleasure the great object of my mission—the long sought for majestic Niger, glittering in the morning sun, as broad as the Thames at Westminster, and flowing slowly *to the eastward*. I hastened to the brink, and having drank of the water, lifted up my fervent thanks to the Great Ruler of all things, for having thus far crowned my endeavours with success.

Park's second expedition ended in his death below Timbuktu, but part of his journal was brought home and is all the better for having been published without polish.

While Park was beginning the exploration of Africa, two other land journeys went some way to rounding off knowledge of North America. Alexander Mackenzie was the first white man to travel by land from the Atlantic to the Pacific over what is now Canada (1792–93), and a few years later Meriwether Lewis and William Clark did the same over what is now the U.S.A. (1804–05). Both journeys were the culmination of advances made in the previous hundred years or more; they do not have the glamour of Cook's work or Park's because Europeans had sailed round the Horn to the Pacific coast of North America a long time before.

Towards the enlarged world opened by the explorers, Europeans were taking a more scientific attitude. Guess-work gave way to observation and record, travellers' tales to the foundations of anthropological study. Cook himself exemplifies these trends, but working scientists also made notable contributions especially at two points where science touched the world of discovery and colonies. The first was navigation. It is true that the longitude prizes went to clockmakers, not scientists, in France as well as Britain, but distinguished men—Hooke, Halley and Huygens for example—worked on the problem and evolved a method that was sound if not convenient. The first task given by Louis XIV to the *Académie des Sciences* (founded in 1666) was to measure the length of a degree, and in 1735 a party of French Academicians travelled to Peru to measure the arc of the meridian at the equator. Edmund Halley's isometric map, showing magnetic variations in different parts of the globe, was published in 1701 and many times reprinted in the 18th century. He also studied tides and currents. John Hadley FRS, produced an octant in 1732 with which more accurate sights of the sun could be taken. Astronomers accompanied Bougainville's voyage of circumnavigation in 1766 and Phipps's North Polar expedition in 1772. And, as has been noted in Chapter III, the immediate reason for Cook's first voyage to the Pacific was to observe the Transit of Venus, the Royal Society having proposed that observers be sent to the South Seas, Hudson's Bay and North Cape, with the object of calculating the sun's distance from the earth.

p 113 (6)

p 100–01 (8–12)

The other main point of contact between science and the non-European world was in botany. Naturalists began the classification of exotic plants and contributed to the dispersal of crops already mentioned. By the end of the 18th century there were botanic gardens at Capetown, Mauritius, St Vincent, Jamaica, Calcutta and Penang as well as in mainland America. In the career of Sir Joseph Banks (1743–1820), exploration, colonization and botany were closely associated. Banks was a man of independent means who devoted his life to science. This aspect of his work is described more fully in Chapter III. If, as President of the Royal Society for 42 years, he sometimes behaved like a senior scientist of the 20th century—on every committee and jealous of power—he nevertheless fully earned his European reputation. At 20 he went to Newfoundland to botanize, and at 25 (already FRS) he sailed with Cook to the South Seas. With him, on the *Endeavour*, he took Solander, a Swedish naturalist, three artists and a draughtsman. Their work is recorded in Cook's journal and in Banks's own, though perhaps the best known reminder of it is Botany Bay, which Cook named for 'the great quantity of plants Mr Banks and Dr Solander found

in this place'. Less than twenty years after their visit, convicts began to arrive in New South Wales, to be followed by free settlers; a second British Empire was taking shape.

After Banks became President of the Royal Society he did no more world travelling. But he sent plant collectors to various parts of the globe, corresponded with naturalists in Europe and beyond, and helped to develop Kew as a garden for the plants of the world. It was Banks who drafted Bligh's instructions in 1787 for the voyage to the South Seas beginning 'The sole object of Government in chartering this vessel in our service at a very considerable expense is to furnish the West Indian Islands with the Breadfruit and other valuable productions of the East'. This expedition, like Cook's, had commercial and imperial implications, but it had a scientific purpose too.

In zoology, too, the non-European world became an important field of study. Finely illustrated books on birds and animals began to appear, of which the *Arctic Zoology* (1784–87) of Thomas Pennant, the Welsh naturalist, is an example. Pennant's paper on penguins to the Royal Society in 1768 furnishes one instance amongst many of the application of common sense to myth:

p 157 (6)

> The proper name of these birds is Pinguin (*propter pinguedinem*), on account of their fatness. It has been corrupted to Penguin; so that some, imagining it to have been a Welsh word signifying a white head, entertained some hopes of tracing the British Colony, said to have migrated into America, under the auspices of Madoc Gwineth, son of Owen Gwineth, AD 1170. But as the two species of birds that frequent that coast have black heads, we must resign every hope founded on that hypothesis of retrieving the Cambrian race in the new world.

## Transformations of empire

New discoveries, and new attitudes towards them, made it easier for Europe to adjust to the ending of the *ancien régime colonial*. Between about 1750 and about 1820 the political ties joining Europe to the rest of the world underwent profound changes: France, Britain and Spain lost land empires in America, while in India the indirect influence of the East India Company began to be replaced by rule under the supervision of the British government. Where there had been colonial status there was independence, and where there had been only influence there was the basis of colonial rule. These momentous events are often-told tales and will not be rehearsed here. They proceeded in the first place from events in America and India themselves, which lend to them a certain suggestion of inevitability. The American colonies in the 18th century, Spanish as well as British, were getting richer; riches begat impatience with metropolitan restrictions on acquiring still more riches, and at the same time supplied the sinews of self-assertion. In India, on the other hand, the British stumbled into an imperial role from 1750 onwards, partly for fear that if they did not the French would, and partly because the disintegrating Moghul Empire made it necessary to uphold law and order simply to protect trade. The capture of Delhi in 1803 and the taking into custody of the emperor were represented, not as aggressions but as the liberation of the Moghul ruler 'from the hands of a desperate band of French adventurers'. The entry of the British into the city was described as follows:

> The crowd in the city was extraordinary; and it was with some difficulty that the cavalcade could make its way to the palace. The courts of the palace were full of people; anxious to witness the deliverance of their sovereign from a state of degradation and bondage. At length the commander-in-chief was ushered into the royal presence: and found the unfortunate and venerable Emperor; oppressed by the accumulated calamities of old age, degraded authority, extreme poverty, and loss of sight; seated under a small tattered canopy, the remnant of his royal state, with every external appearance of the misery of his condition.

In these political developments, in America and the East, the governments of Europe often appear more forced than forceful. But events in Europe also contributed to the liquidation of the *ancien régime*. Would the Thirteen Colonies have won their freedom when they did if France had not been set on revenge for defeats in the Seven Years' War and formed with Spain and the Dutch a coalition which British seapower could not resist? Would the *gens de couleur* and the slaves of St Domingue have been able to create the independent republic of Haiti without the confusion and equivocation caused by the French Revolution? Would South America have become independent in the early 19th century without Napoleon's invasion of Spain in 1808, the abdication of King Charles IV and the political turmoil that followed? These questions are, to say the least, arguable. Certainly there were independence pressures and independence movements before the revolutions in both North and South America, nurtured by a thousand grievances. But in so far as these grievances were generalized into ideologies of revolt, they were directed against European governments not against European ideas. The idioms of self-determination were European idioms, Locke's in the American Revolution, those of Rousseau and the *philosophes* in Latin America.

If the Enlightenment exposed the unreasonableness of European empires in America, the Industrial Revolution began, in Britain, a profound and prolonged revaluation of colonies which would have taken place even without the War of Independence. Adam Smith's *Wealth of Nations*, which questioned the assumptions of the Old Colonial System, was published in the same year as the Declaration of Independence. In the two next generations, there were some in Europe who revolted from the burdens and disappointments of empire as whole-heartedly as the colonists revolted from the mother country. There were others, more moderate, who came to believe that colonies like children grew up and left home just when their earnings began to make a difference to the family budget. Everywhere there was growing recognition of the need for more liberal economic laws; even Spain by the end of the 18th century was aware of this, and the British could not help seeing that their trade with America survived the War of Independence. Former articles of faith were called in question. The staple colonial products of the *ancien régime*, once a major component in Britain's re-export business, were diminished in value by the rising output of cheap manufactures and the cultivation of sugar beet in Europe. Ancient jewels like Jamaica and Martinique became in the 19th century something of an embarrassment to their European owners. India, once a feared competitor in textiles, became a passive market for Lancashire's cotton mills.

## Moral purposes and noble savages

Contemporary with this changing evaluation of empire, and owing something to it, there appeared in Europe a sharpened sense of responsibility for the rest of the world. Moral purpose, as we have seen, had burned low in the 17th and early 18th centuries, and it was not to be exactly a devouring flame in the 19th. It was incomplete, easily compromised, apt to run to hypocrisy. It did not stop famines in India and it did not mitigate Belgian exploitation of the Congo. But it is also true that when such abuses came to light there were Europeans who strongly condemned them in moral terms. A sense of responsibility, begun by the trial of Warren Hastings, expedited the transfer of British India from a virtually autonomous profit-making company to a government responsible to Parliament. And, above all, moral purpose contributed to the abolition of the slave trade and the ending of slavery, the foundation stones of the *ancien régime*. In 1787 a Society for Effecting the Abolition of the Slave Trade was formed, and in the following year the French Société des Amis des Noirs. In 1789 a far reaching enquiry into the trade was conducted by the British Privy Council, which supplied material for a series of propaganda campaigns. War held up the work, though it brought equivocal emancipation to slaves in the French West Indies. Finally in 1807 Britain abolished the slave trade, and other nations followed suit. With great care the

Caribbean planters might have kept slavery in being for some time even without the slave trade (as the Americans did), but they failed to furnish that care to Parliament's satisfaction. Emancipation came in 1834.

Behind the humanitarian movement, it has been argued, lies a new and cynical attitude to the West Indian colonies, and hence to plantation slavery. Britain needed those colonies less, and could afford to make a moral gesture. And this is true. But to see abolition and emancipation as nothing more than contemptuous disregard is to carry cynicism to the point of credulity. It is to ignore the parliamentary debates, to misconstrue the activities of British evangelical Christians, and to overlook that powerful 18th-century myth of the noble savage. Wilberforce and the evangelicals were at the heart of the Parliamentary campaign against slavery; at the very lowest valuation of their work, they hastened the passing of the Acts of 1807 and 1834. Nor were they unaware of the need for constructive alternatives to slavery and the slave trade; they were active in founding Sierra Leone for free negroes in 1787, and they supported the exploration of Africa in search of commodities for legitimate trade. p 167 (32)

France had no evangelicals, but she had the Rights of Man; the cult of the noble savage at least raised the question of extending those rights to coloured and slaves. Rousseau was not the first to use the myth, nor did he give it its most radical expression. Montaigne had given currency to it long ago, followed by Aphra Behn in England. Most often it was used in furtherance of self-criticism, European vices and effeteness being contrasted with the robust virtues supposedly found in savages. But it had an obvious application to the ways in which Europeans treated South Sea Islanders and Amerindians, and to the destruction of an innocence which had reigned, according to Dryden,

> *Ere the base laws of servitude began*
> *When wild in woods the noble savage ran.*

Tahiti, visited and described by Bougainville and Cook, particularly caught Europe's imagination as a paradise on earth, though here as elsewhere there was a division of opinion about the nobility of the savages. The sexual freedom of the Tahitians is a case in point. Some Europeans credited the natives with enough intelligence to be educable in Christian doctrine and enough nobility to renounce this particular freedom. Others, impatient with Europe's conventions, used Tahitian evidence to raise awkward questions about just what kind of behaviour was natural. Hawkesworth, glossator of Cook's journals, rounded off a description of copulation in public with the enquiry 'Whether the shame attending certain actions, which are allowed on all sides to be themselves innocent, is implanted in Nature, or superinduced by custom?' p 154 (2)

Several noble savages came to London and Paris in the 18th century, and did more good than harm to the myth. Aotouru, brought back from the Pacific by Bougainville, and Omai, who came with Cook, were the most famous 'South Sea Islanders'. Omai made a considerable stir in London society, impressing Fanny Burney and Dr Johnson, not in general a believer in the nobility of savages. Omai was presented to George III, taken on a tour of Yorkshire by Banks, and painted by Reynolds. He was finally returned to the Society Islands on Cook's last voyage, where, it was said, he went to the bad. p 170 (40)

There is more than a hint of patronage in the idea of the noble savage, as well as a long streak of romance. Sophisticates who admire primitives generally prefer to do so at a distance. There was far to travel before Europeans could regard non-European races as neither more nor less noble than themselves. But Europe's most pressing moral problem at the end of the 18th century was to get rid of slavery; and to that the myth of the noble savage made a contribution.

# VI WAR ON A NEW SCALE

*Professionalism in Armies, Navies and Diplomacy*

J. R. WESTERN

*'For war is quite changed from what it was in the time of our*

*forefathers, when in a hasty expedition and a pitched*

*field the matter was decided by courage; but now the whole art*

*of war is in a manner reduced to money; and now-a-days,*

*that prince who can best find money to feed, clothe and pay his army,*

*not he that has the most valiant troops,*

*is surest of success and conquest.'*

CHARLES D'AVENANT 'An Essay upon Ways and Means of supplying the War' (1695)

### The profession of arms

took on a new and more modern meaning during the 18th century. The European states had become rich enough to keep substantial naval and military forces permanently on foot. For an increasing proportion of the officers – and for some even of the common soldiers and sailors – military service had become a settled career. Instead of casual employment in times of trouble, there was life-long service with some provision for retirement at the close. This made possible higher standards both of discipline and of technical proficiency. Battle formations also became increasingly complicated and there was a growing demand for the services of administrators and scientifically trained gunners and engineers.

The new regular armies were an important factor in the growth of monarchical absolutism and European monarchs identified themselves closely with their armies – even the constitutional British monarchs. The office of Commander in Chief of the British army was held whenever possible by a prince of the blood: the Dukes of Cumberland and York were followed under Queen Victoria by the Duke of Cambridge. But the last British king to lead his troops in battle was George II at Dettingen in 1743 (opposite), and he was only nominally in command. Dettingen was an indecisive battle typical of the 18th century. The British and Hanoverian troops supporting Maria Theresa during the War of the Austrian Succession had to fight it to prevent the French cutting them off from their base and they achieved nothing beyond this by their victory. But it won the King much popularity at home. Handel wrote a Te Deum in his honour. This picture by John Wootton shows him with the Duke of Cumberland, his second son, who is holding a broken rein. (1)

**The cavalry charge** remained important; even Frederick the Great relied on it to complete an assault begun by the other arms. 'Light cavalry' (above) were indispensable for scouting, and the tactics and costume of the Hungarian-Turkish frontier spread all over Europe. (3)

**The real execution** on the 18th-century battlefield was done by artillery; its mobility and rate of fire were greatly increased during this period. This in turn caused a revolution in the tactics of defence. Above: the British Artillery Train at Hellenraad, in the Low Countries, in 1748. Above right: assembling a field gun by means of chains and pulley. Below left: a town under siege being bombarded by cannon and a mortar, which fired explosive shells from behind temporary breastworks. Cannon could fire a single solid ball or a number of small ones which could (below right) be made red hot. (2, 4, 5, 6)

**Old and new armies** in confrontation are seen in this skirmish between Scots and English troops during the Forty-Five Rebellion. The English, in uniform, have probably fired once or twice before charging with the bayonet. Plug-bayonets, which filled the musket-muzzle, were used in the 17th century. The ring-bayonet, fitting over the muzzle without interfering with fire, became universal in the 18th (below left: drill for fixing the bayonet) when infantry normally fired in three ranks (below right), the first kneeling, the second standing, and the third firing over the shoulders of the second. (7, 8, 9)

**Military costume** became increasingly unlike civilian dress as a professional spirit developed: compare the Dutch infantry of about 1680 (below left) with the Irish regiment in the service of Louis XV (below right). Officers tended to put appearances first and wanted tall handsome soldiers like the Giant Grenadiers of King Frederick William I of Prussia (right). The grenadiers' mitre cap can be seen in several of the illustrations: it enabled them to throw grenades unimpeded by a wide brim. (10, 11, 15)

Regiment d'Infanterie.
Bulkeley. Irlandois.

**Frederick the Great's infantry** reached the acme of military stiffness with their tight uniforms and heels-together position, to facilitate close packing in the line. Prussia was copied everywhere. Above are a Hessian officer, NCO, grenadier, private and drummer. Note the retention of useless pikes and swords. But there was also a vogue for the irregular troops found on the frontiers of the European world. Below left: Prussian Hussars – copied, uniform and all, from Hungary. Below right: American riflemen (normally they had no bayonets.) (12, 13, 14)

**Senior officers** were distinguished by the increasingly magnificent ornamentation of their uniform rather than by badges of rank. Uniforms began to be worn off duty. This is Lord Clive, embodiment of the new European military superiority over Asians. (16)

**The first British naval uniform** dates from 1748; the officers asked for it in order to keep up with the army. Ordinary sailors had to wait another century. Admiral Lord Anson wears full-dress uniform for his portrait (right) by Reynolds. (17)

**A captain and his son** (right) show that by 1775 the original uniforms had changed considerably. For a short period from 1767 dress uniform had been abolished, but in 1774 what had been the undress uniform was upgraded into full dress, and a new 'frock' introduced. Thus the uniform worn by Captain Bentinck as full dress is an only slightly modified form of the original frock. The boy is probably wearing the uniform of the Naval Academy. (18)

*--- Pugnæque cient simulacra sub armis.* *Virg. V. Æneid.*

*Cum Pr. S. C. Maj.*

**Persuasion and force** were needed to raise the large new armies and navies. Voluntary enlistment brought in a certain number of men, mostly social misfits, but compulsion was always needed in wartime. Officially inspired representations of army life (such as this German print called 'Military Exercises' of c. 1720, left) painted a rosy and optimistic picture of the soldier's prospects. (19)

**Raising the militia:** in France (above), conscripts were chosen by lot and a civilian official, not a recruiting sergeant, was in charge of enlistment. Below right: the 'King's shilling' was a way of escaping prosecution for many petty crimes. Below left: a press gang seizes a young man for service at sea. This arbitrary way of obtaining seamen remained in force in England throughout the century. (20, 21, 22)

**Military academies** arose in most European countries during this period in order to train officers in the increasingly difficult science of waging war. This engraving (right) shows a German academy in 1726, with boys receiving instruction in the theory of fortification. A commander needed a good grounding in engineering, mathematics and geography. Experts like Vauban owed as much fame to their theoretical writings as to their practical achievements. (23)

**Drill** was the basis of 18th-century tactics: parade-ground movements were meant to be actually executed on the battlefield. Saxon troops (right) stand in the early 'attention' position, with legs apart. The wooden horse on the left is for punishment, not exercise. (24)

**The firing-squad,** a relatively novel mode of execution, awaited the most serious offenders. Public punishment was held to increase the deterrent effect. Here three highlanders are shot in the Tower of London in 1743. Punishments for more ordinary offences were ruthlessly harsh, even for that harsh age. (25)

190

**The two faces of military life** find expression in contemporary paintings. Above: the Horse Grenadier Guards being inspected by General Onslow in Hyde Park – the army as fashionable society saw it. Left: the footguards setting off to fight the Young Pretender, as Hogarth saw them. At Tottenham Court Road Turnpike they bid farewell to the ladies of a brothel. George II refused the dedication of the engraved version of this painting, so Hogarth dedicated it to Frederick the Great of Prussia. (26, 27)

**Troops camped** in formation – each company's tents in lines, arms, colours and sentries in front, officers' tents behind. Below left: sutlers and camp followers lived in less order in the rear. Below, the French army before Tournai. (28, 29)

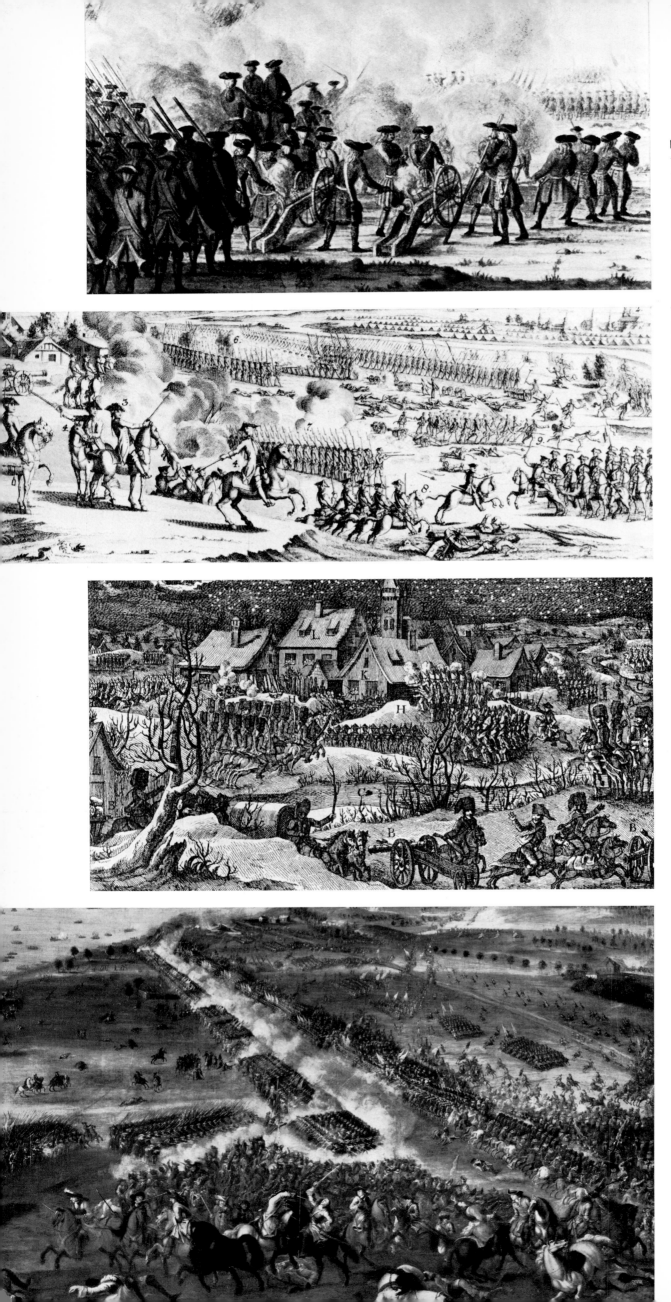

**Infantry and artillery** combined were the decisive factor in most 18th-century battles. Gustavus Adolphus had developed the use of small, mobile guns and the Swedish system of giving each battalion two small cannon (as in Charles XII's army, left) was copied everywhere. But eventually more emphasis was placed on larger batteries of heavier guns. (30)

**The 'oblique order'** was evolved by Frederick the Great for attacking the flank of an army already drawn up in line of battle. Liegnitz in 1760 (left) was one of his many battles decided by action on a flank. (31)

**Winter campaigns** remained the exception because bad roads made movement and supplies difficult, and because the health of the troops deteriorated. But they might be unavoidable. Below left: an action near Görlitz on New Year's Day 1757. (32)

**The Swedes** attack the Saxons outside Riga, 1701 (left). This was how a battle in linear formation was supposed to look – the reality was generally more confused. At that date the lines were thicker than they later became. (33)

**Combined operations:** the Siege of Gibraltar from 1779 to 1783 was one of the most prolonged and hard-fought sieges of the whole century. The Spaniards raised elaborate siegeworks on the landward side, but the climax came on September 13th, 1782 with an assault by ten strongly armoured ships, all eventually set on fire and exploded by red-hot shot. (35)

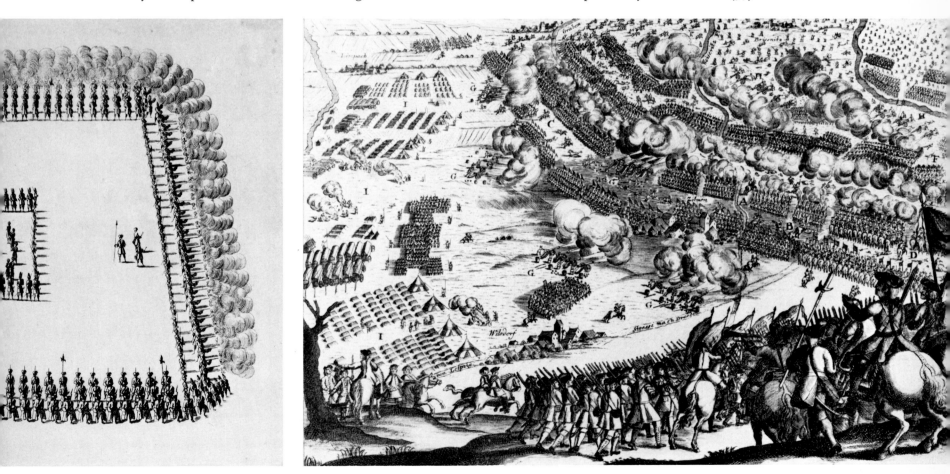

**The hollow square** was the formation in which infantry commonly resisted the attacks of cavalry, since it could not be outflanked. The square's capacity to do this was a decisive new feature of 18th-century warfare. (34)

**The capture** of the enemy's artillery was a decisive stroke. At Kesseldorf in 1745 (above) the Prussians, in the foreground, turned the Saxon left flank and overran their cannon. The Prussians concentrated their own guns in batteries. (36)

**The field of Fontenoy,** May 11th, 1745, displays the topographical aspect of 18th-century tactics. It was an attempt by the Allies (English, Hanoverians, Scots and Dutch), under the Duke of Cumberland, to raise the Siege of Tournai, which was surrounded by the French under Marshal Saxe. In this panoramic view by van Blarenberghe, the viewpoint is that of the French high command. On the right is the river Scheldt and the town of Antoing, held by the French; towards the centre, the village of Fontenoy, with its church, also held by the French; and on the left, Bary Wood, in front of which the French had built two redoubts. Antoing and Fontenoy were fortified and three more redoubts built between them can be picked out by their puffs of smoke. Saxe was a strong believer in redoubts as a means of breaking up the attacking force.

He here created a semi-circular defensive position. The Dutch half of the allied army attacked half-heartedly on the Fontenoy-Antoing sector and were easily repulsed. They are scarcely visible in the picture, though the French are seen firing at them. The Anglo-Hanoverians, however, penetrated the gap between Bary Wood and Fontenoy and slowly advanced in square formation into the centre of the French position. But they were under heavy fire from three sides, unable to break through and subjected to fierce cavalry attacks. After four hours they broke and fled. It is this moment that is represented in the painting, the disordered infantry scattering to the left. In the bottom right-hand corner an officer brings the news to Louis XV and Saxe, whose fame as a commander was established by this battle. (37)

**The first skirmish** of the American War of Independence. In 1775 British redcoats dispersed a force of rebels at Lexington with a volley of musket fire (right). The Americans at first had only local militias but they soon formed a 'Continental' army basically like those of Europe. (38)

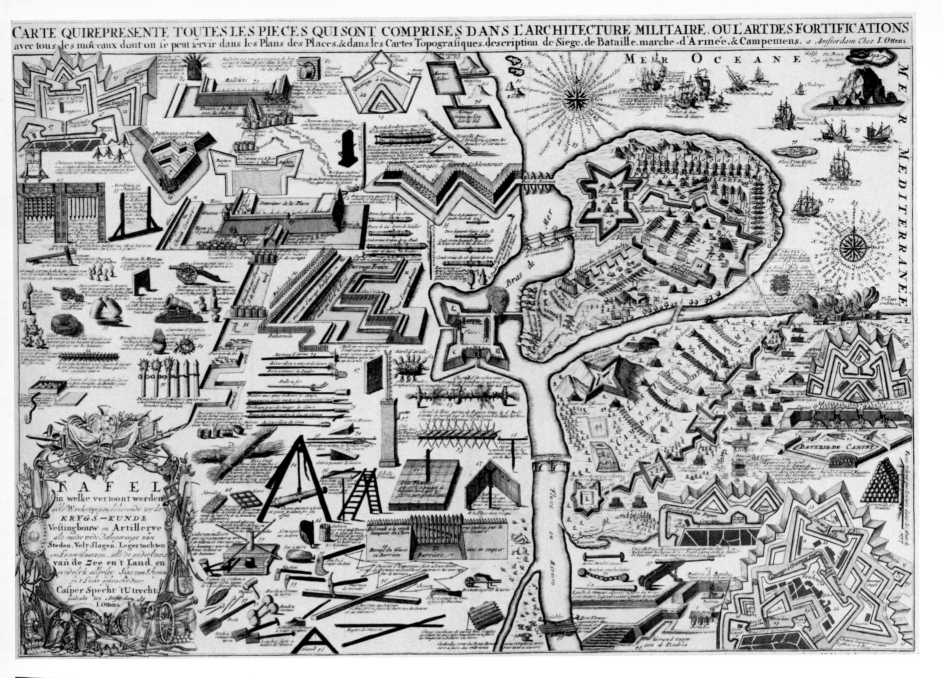

CARTE QUI REPRESENTE TOUTES LES PIECES QUI SONT COMPRISES DANS L'ARCHITECTURE MILITAIRE, OU L'ART DES FORTIFICATIONS
avec tous les morceaux dont on se peut servir dans les Plans des Places, & dans les Cartes Topografiques, description de Siege, de Bataille, marche d'Armée, & Campemens. a Amsterdam Chez I. Ottens

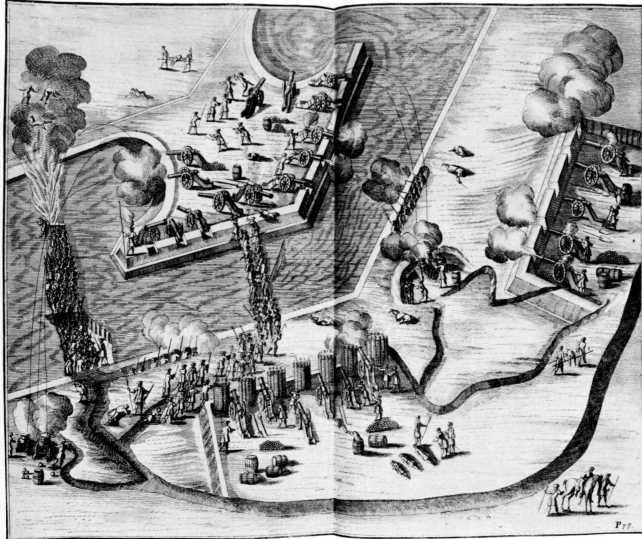

**How professional** the art of war had become is made clear by diagrammatic charts such as this of about 1700, cataloguing some of the items involved in fortification. The fort between island and mainland is laid out according to earlier Italian principles; that on the lower right-hand corner shows how these principles had developed by Vauban's time so that several lines of defence gave mutual support. In the centre are shown various tools needed for making ramparts and, towards the left, guns and different kinds of shot. (39)

**The assault** on a well defended position required thorough preparation for success. Another schematized drawing (left) shows how guns concentrated on a bastion fired both forwards and sideways, to defeat attacks made across the dry ditch under cover of trenches. Mortars on the attacking side drop missiles behind the rampart. (40)

**A well placed mine** could shatter the defences of the strongest stone-built castle. In August 1762 a British force successfully stormed Moro Castle, Havana, after demolishing one of the seaward bastions in this way (above). The attacking batteries (right) were placed on timber platforms behind a parapet of fascines. (41, 43)

**The approach to a fortress** was made by digging zigzag trenches. Vauban shows (above) how the diggers could provide the necessary cover from fire by using the excavated earth. During the siege of Barcelona (below) in 1714, troops can be seen beginning a network of trenches while transports bring up fascines. (42, 44)

**Powerful national fleets** became a feature of the maritime countries and shipbuilding was increasingly organized as a government responsibility. The chief French naval base was Toulon (right) on the Mediterranean coast. It was an ancient port, newly fortified by Vauban. In 1707 it was unsuccessfully besieged by Austrians and Sardinians. (46)

**The Baltic Powers** had substantial fleets. Here Christian VI of Denmark-Norway (1730–46) inspects the plans of a new dockyard at Copenhagen. (45)

**The British Navy,** christened 'Royal' by Charles II, was the strongest in the world in the 18th century and growing stronger. Right centre: George III reviews the fleet at Spithead. Right: the dockyards at Chatham, on the Thames Estuary – founded in the 16th century, greatly enlarged in the 17th, and further extended in the 18th until they occupied a river frontage of over a mile. (47, 48)

**Weapons dictated tactics** at sea as on land. A ship of the line (above) had two or three gun-decks and displaced between one and two thousand tons. The greatest concentration of fire, was achieved by all the ships sailing in line so that they did not mask each others' broadsides. Almost all guns fired sideways, so ships normally could not fire while approaching the enemy. (49)

**Use of fireships** and boarding were the favourite Dutch tactics. The English increasingly relied on close-range bombardment. Right: the Battle of Texel, 1673, in which Cornelius Tromp defeated the English by the skilful use of fireships. (51)

**Line formation** exchanging broadside salvoes: the Battle of Negapatam, fought between British and French fleets off India in 1782. (52)

**Galleys,** incapable of carrying heavy guns, still had an advantage in coastal waters. Right: Russians and Swedes fighting in 1714 at Hangöudd. (53)

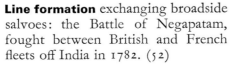

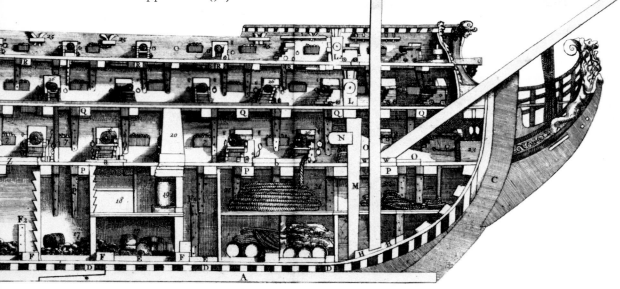

**A three-decker** (below) could carry 100 guns or more, usually 32-pounders on the lowest gun-deck, with smaller calibre on the upper two. (50)

**Frigates** in the later 18th century (above) were smaller than ships of the line, though bigger than most merchantmen. They had only one gun-deck, carried up to 36 guns, and were used for actions that did not involve the enemy's main fleet. (55)

**Raking** (left) was a manoeuvre whereby a ship crossed the path of another and so could bombard it almost without retaliation, the balls passing right through the enemy ship from end to end. (54)

**Breaking the line** was dramatically achieved by Rodney at the Battle of the Saints in 1784 (above). Penetrating the French line, he raked some of their ships and cut off their retreat by seizing the lee position. The British henceforth adopted more dynamic and flexible tactics. (56)

**The Four Days' Battle** of 1666, when English and Dutch fleets, by close-range cannonades, fireships and boarding parties, fought each other to exhaustion, was typical of the costly chaotic style of 17th-century naval warfare. This resulted in elaborate Fighting Instructions which preserved order in battle but cramped initiative and prevented decisive victories. Here the ship in the foreground is De Ruyter's *Zeven Provinzien*. Note how the ships are keeling before the wind; this often hindered the attacker (normally to windward) from using his lowest tier of guns, while the defender could the more easily disable him by hitting his rigging. (57)

# Professionalism in Armies, Navies and Diplomacy

J. R. WESTERN

THE STRENGTHENING of the European states described in the first chapter was closely bound up with improvements in their military organization and greatly altered the character of international relations. It was during the reign of Louis XIV that standing armies became the rule rather than the exception in Europe. Almost everywhere there was a great increase in the size of armies and there was a particularly big increase in the number of troops kept on foot in the intervals between wars. Expansion promoted efficiency. The governments now had a substantial body of men who were permanently in their service and it was easier to maintain standards of discipline and training with them than among the casually hired mercenaries and other temporary levies that had hitherto predominated. The European navies were transformed in much the same way as the armies and something similar happened in the diplomatic service. There was an increase in the number of permanently resident ambassadors and in the effectiveness of the foreign offices directing their work. Changes on the military and naval side were very closely associated with important new developments in the art of war in the late 17th century—notably the introduction of the flintlock and bayonet and the growing predominance of linear formations in both land and sea tactics. More generally, the military, naval and diplomatic developments were made possible by the general growth of bureaucratic centralization and government revenues—things which, in turn, were greatly promoted by the strengthening of the armed forces.

War and diplomacy now afforded better prospects of a regular and settled career: this gave officers and diplomats an incentive to become expert specialists. More than before, the practitioners of each art came to have the character of professionals, distinguished by the mastery of certain techniques and the acceptance of a code of conduct and a body of theoretical principles. This made for more rational efficiency in the safeguarding of State interests—in the choice of objectives, the selection of appropriate military or diplomatic means to achieve them, the conduct of campaigns and negotiations. But the experts did not work in ideal conditions. Sovereigns were only just beginning to be something more than glorified landlords; their states were heterogeneous, often lacking a sense of national identity. Foreign policy was no longer purely dynastic but it often bore little apparent relation to the general needs of the community. The swollen armed forces did not yet have adequate human and economic foundations. Wars petered out through financial exhaustion. Armies composed of social outcasts and commanded by aristocratic loafers too often fought without intelligence or determination. But much was achieved with the imperfect means available. Built up by military and diplomatic effort, the great powers which emerged in the 18th century were to dominate Europe until the world wars, and the military institutions founded in the era of Louis XIV provided the framework and traditions within which all significant military development took place down to 1945.

## Were foreign policies 'national'?

In the choice of international objectives, the states paid heed to something a little wider than the interests of the rulers. Governments were conscious as never before of the need to promote economic prosperity in order to increase their own revenues and so their power. Overseas expansion and the conquest of lucrative territories in Europe were means to this end. The economic theorists of the time encouraged the belief that the amount of trade in the world was more or less fixed and that a nation could only build up its commerce and industry at the expense of its competitors. The exclusion of foreign goods from the home market might therefore bring prosperity and so might the military conquest of markets and sources of supply abroad. These ideas were never universally accepted and there was a strong reaction against them in the 18th century; but for most of the period under discussion there is no reason to suppose that they were unpopular. British opinion readily sanctioned economic and military measures against the country's main commercial rivals—Holland and France successively—and the republicans and high tories, the groups usually least in sympathy with the government, were ardent for colonial conquests. It may fairly be claimed that when continental autocrats adopted policies of aggression for economic reasons, they were conforming to the notion then most widely current of the national interest.

Commercial rivalry led to three wars between the British and Dutch in the mid-17th century. Colbert meanwhile harassed the Dutch—and to a lesser extent the British—in their trade with France and excluded foreigners from French colonies. For economic reasons he urged the French King to go to war with the Dutch and thereby played his part in inaugurating forty years of conflict. It is not surprising to find the British and Dutch replying in kind, the former opposing the French beyond the seas throughout the 18th century. Colbert indeed had imitators everywhere. In 1684 Philip von Hörnigk in a pamphlet entitled *Oesterreich über alles wann es nur will* exhorted the Emperor to use the economic weapon in his struggle against France, protecting native industry against her in his Austrian dominions and so building in Germany a power to rival hers. The territorial rivalries of eastern and central Europe often centred on economic prizes. When he undertook the conquest of Silesia, Frederick the Great was seizing from Austria her main industrial area, whose textile industries were an important source of revenue for the State. When he joined in the first partition of Poland his main tangible gain was control of the lower reaches of the Vistula, and so of much of Poland's external trade—especially the extensive grain exports to the west via Danzig. By seizing much of the Baltic coast and control of the principal German estuaries, Sweden in the 17th century was able to levy profitable tolls on much of the trade of northern Europe. With the defeat of Charles XII (from 1709) Sweden lost most of her conquests, Prussia and Hanover being the beneficiaries in Germany while Russia took what is now Estonia and eastern Latvia. Peter the Great had already *f 1* achieved the impossible by endowing his nearly landlocked empire with a navy; Russian trade was now able to flow freely through the Baltic. He had also attempted to reach the Black Sea and this was accomplished by Catherine the Great, who drove the Turks from the Ukraine and the Crimea. Thereby she won both rich corn lands and the ports through which to export the grain: in the next century this was to be Russia's principal trade route.

Strategic as well as economic motives prompted territorial expansion. The immediate purpose of the Russian drive south was defensive: the Crimean Tartars constantly ravaged Russian

203

territory and levied ransom. Developments in the science of fortification brought a general desire for more readily defensible frontiers. Vauban tried to protect all the approaches to France by fortresses systematically arranged in mutual support. He was helped in this by the advance of the northern French frontier under Louis XIV and his advice guided the government in deciding what territory to take. Here again the constitutional states were at one in their aims with the autocrat. The Dutch worked for a line of barrier fortresses across southern Belgium to protect them against France; they did not seek to annex the territory between themselves and their barrier, content if it was in friendly hands. The British appreciated the value of fortified points in naval warfare: it was in deference to public opinion that George I's government clung to Gibraltar. The search for strategic frontiers was followed in due course by more ambitious schemes for rationalizing the territorial holdings of the powers. Each of them tended to acquire a sphere of influence in the areas between them occupied by weaker states. It was sometimes convenient and possible to substitute effective control for this more informal power. Arrangements come to in the 1730s enabled France to complete her territorial consolidation by the eventual occupation of Lorraine: Maria Theresa's husband who gave it up, was compensated by being allowed to seize Tuscany. A consolidation scheme that was never carried through was Joseph II's plan to gain Bavaria by giving its Elector the Austrian Netherlands—the present Belgium—which lay at a distance from Joseph's other dominions and which British and Dutch jealousy prevented the Austrians from fully developing economically. Prussian hostility and the indifference of his French allies frustrated him.

A vaguer defensive idea which underlay some of the territorial aims of the great states was the old notion of the balance of power. This became increasingly fashionable in the late 17th century, both because of the dangerous preponderance of Louis XIV and because the new physics made it more natural to think in terms of an equilibrium between several bodies, deriving from their sizes relative to each other. When Louis XIV accepted the bequest of the Spanish throne to his grandson (1700), a great coalition was formed to prevent this further extension of French power. After a decade of fighting they managed to secure a partition of the Spanish Empire and undertakings that the French and Spanish Crowns should never be united in the same person. The treaties of Utrecht specifically invoked the balance of power in justification of this arrangement and of the war. An even more famous instance of partition in the interests of the balance of power was the carving up of Poland, begun in 1772 and completed in 1793 and 1795. Of course it was also another instance of territorial consolidation. Foreign powers had long dominated the political life of this ramshackle aristocratic republic and now outright annexation was substituted—not least because the Poles were beginning at last to offer effective resistance to foreign domination. But in 1772 especially, it was the prospect of Catherine the Great's gains from Turkey which hastened partition. Austria and Prussia thought that Russian aggrandizement might be dangerous for them if they did not receive some territory too.

Even in the 18th century there were those who disliked the doctrine of the balance of power and denounced the arbitrary sharing out of territories among the European autocrats. But once again the policies of the despots were reasonably in line with the opinions of the educated class in general. Nowhere was the balance of power a more popular theme than in England. The partition of the Spanish empire—and partition was as odious to the Spaniards as to the Poles—was Britain's work as much as anybody's. The preamble to the Mutiny Act long named the maintenance of the balance of power as a reason for a standing army.

## Dynastic and religious factors

Policies of territorial aggrandizement and consolidation in the interests of security and economic development pointed forward to the Europe of nation-states. The idea of the balance of power was a pointer of sorts towards how such states could coexist. But there continued to be factors of the greatest importance in international affairs which had nothing to do with the national interest. Some of these were dynastic or personal to the princes, others were religious,

the relics either of the medieval unity of Christendom or of the disruption of that unity at the Reformation. Some monarchs—Louis XIV in particular—regarded their prestige and their ranking among the sovereigns of Europe as of supreme importance. In the endless disputes over precedence that envenomed all diplomatic proceedings there may perhaps be seen some lingering sense of the unity of Christendom: it was natural to think of princes, not as quite separate and equal, but as filling the top ranks of a European aristocracy. Some princes again were governed by their personal whims in State affairs—as with Tsarina Elizabeth's dislike of Frederick the Great or when Abigail Masham replaced the Duchess of Marlborough in the affections of Queen Anne. Princes might embark on war in order to provide for their relatives: Elizabeth Farnese, Queen of Spain, caused endless turmoil in the 1720s and 1730s by her efforts to win principalities in Italy for her sons. The simple fact that most European states were still hereditary monarchies was a potent source of discord. Disputed successions were legion and an ever-ready pretext for aggression: Frederick the Great made use in this way of claims which his family had to parts of Silesia. Sometimes a disputed succession served as a cover for a conflict of far deeper significance. When Louis XIV tried to win the Spanish empire for his grandson, he was serving the colonial and strategic interests of France. But Elizabeth Farnese's assertion of Spanish claims in Italy served no useful national purpose—though it may have appealed to national pride—and sometimes succession questions arose independently of the wider plans of statesmen and made other rivalries more intractable. Emperor Charles VI had only a daughter, Maria Theresa, to succeed him in the Austrian dominions. As his different territories had different rules of succession, the division of the inheritance could only be avoided by special legislation—the Pragmatic Sanction—to which the Emperor felt that he needed the concurrence of all the European powers. The concessions required to gain this weakened Austria and failed in their purpose, since they encouraged attacks on her. Frederick the Great would probably have attacked in any case, but the same cannot be said of Bavaria and France.

Because of the respect shown for the hereditary principle even in changing the dynasty, the English revolution of 1688 increased the country's international problems. The royal power passed to relatives of the fallen line—William of Orange and eventually the house of Hanover. William was the greatest foe of Louis XIV and this exacerbated, though it did not cause, Anglo–French hostility. The Hanoverian kings were forbidden by law to use British resources for the aggrandizement of the Electorate. But this did not prevent Britain's enemies from attacking Hanover and when this happened the British felt obliged to come to its defence. Britain's international operations were frequently impeded by this commitment.

Along with dynastic interests and rivalries, religious warfare survived into the 18th century. The Ottoman Empire was still at its greatest extent in 1660, with millions of Christians both Latin and Greek among its subjects. In 1664 even Louis XIV felt obliged to give his Austrian rival military aid against the Turkish infidels. The wars which from the 1680s pushed back Turkish rule were for Austria a matter of regaining the lost provinces of Hungary; for Poland and Russia they concerned the rich territory of the Ukraine and for Venice they were a last attempt to rebuild her Mediterranean empire. But for a time a Holy League united these powers, whose existence and strength owed much to the diplomacy of Pope Innocent XI. Religious motives combined with secular ones in Russia's age-long drive to the south, and the Treaty of Kutchuk Kainardji (1774) acknowledged the right of the Tsar to be the protector of the Ottoman Christians. France, in particular, tried to counter this religious imperialism by protecting the Latin Church in Palestine against both the Turks and the Orthodox. In France itself, the renewed persecution of the Huguenots led not only to a civil war in the Cévennes and the flight of business men and skilled artisans but also to an emigration more directly political in character. The enemies of Louis XIV gained the services of skilled officials, able soldiers and above all of intellectuals and propagandists who sought to arouse European opinion against the French tyrant and the menace to Protestantism. British persecution of the Catholics, especially the Irish, meant an important movement

p 193
(35)

p 38
(4)

*Part of the Russian fleet, observed by the Austrian envoy to Russia in 1699. Peter the Great created his navy from scratch, at first officering it mainly with* *foreigners. Note the galleys in the background, still useful for fighting in land-locked waters.* (1)

p 322–3

in the reverse direction. Religious conflicts could thus both transcend national differences and cut across national loyalties. Of course, like dynastic rivalries, they could also at times reinforce a trend towards nationalism in a country's foreign relations. Religious faith was almost the only thing then capable of arousing popular passion in the manner of a modern secular political creed. When a Christian state fought the Moslems (Russia) or a Protestant state fought a Catholic one (Britain), there was more chance than at other times of mobilizing popular enthusiasm behind State policy. This had important consequences in war as we shall see.

In retrospect, therefore, the aims of the powers in the century before 1789 were in some respects modern—pointing towards the world of nation-states—but in many important ways there appears to have been little change since the Middle Ages. Another chapter will describe the protests of thoughtful men against the waste of life and treasure in quarrels of no concern to the people.

## Weapons and tactics on land

States used both war and diplomacy to achieve their aims but what a diplomat could accomplish depended in the last resort on his master's strength in the field. The military situation is therefore the main subject of this chapter—the methods of fighting by land and sea, the forces that could be made available, the strategic result that it was possible to attain.

Tactics on land in the 18th century were dominated by two things—the growing superiority of infantry and the fact that this

was something new and precarious. In the earlier Middle Ages the mounted man at arms had been supreme and though his position had been repeatedly challenged since the 14th century, he had not hitherto been dethroned. In the Thirty Years' War half or even two thirds of an army engaged in battle might consists of cavalry. A great change came towards the end of the 17th century with the adoption of the firelock and the bayonet. The firelock was dis-charged by sparks from a flint and steel, activated by a trigger and igniting a small pinch of powder. Previously the soldier had had to carry a match—a long length of slow-burning fuse—with which to ignite the charge each time he fired. The new mechanism enabled him to fire faster and was more reliable in wet weather. Another aid to faster firing was the iron ramrod, first used by the Prussians in 1698. The bayonet enabled each infantryman to combine the roles of musketeer and pikeman. The pike had long been con-sidered a clumsy and ineffective weapon, but pikemen had been necessary to protect the musketeers while they reloaded—especially against cavalry attacks. Early in the 18th century they disappeared; abolished in France in 1703, they lingered in Russia till 1721. Uniformly armed with a dual-purpose weapon of enhanced fire-power, the infantry moved into the ascendant. At Ramillies (1706) it was still the cavalry action that decided the day. At Mollwitz (1741) the Prussian cavalry was routed by the Austrians and King Frederick hastened from the field, thinking that the battle was lost. But times had changed: the Prussian infantry stood firm and the Austrians were beaten.

f 3
f 2
p 185 (7, 8)

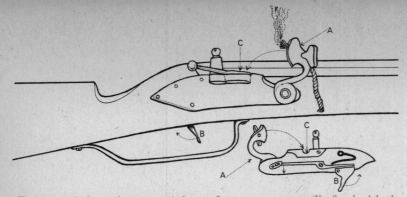

For most of the 17th century, infantry firearms were normally fitted with the matchlock (above). The soldier held a length of slow-burning match between his fingers and when he wished to fire he fixed the end of it to the weapon by means of the 'serpentine' (A). When the trigger (B) was pulled, this was pushed downwards into the pan (C), igniting the powder. The firelock (below) used similar mechanical principles but instead of a match the serpentine (D) held a flint. Pressing the trigger released a cog (E) under pressure from a spring, causing the flint to snap downwards against the steel (F) which also covered the powder in the pan (G). As flint met steel, the steel was knocked backwards and a spark fell into the pan. A second spring then returned the steel to its original position. (2, 3)

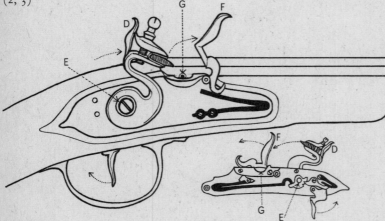

*Drill exercises from a Saxon military manual of 1726. At this date soldiers were still wearing loose and full-skirted coats, later changed after the Prussian model to tight-fitting but less comfortable uniform.* (4)

Serious deficiencies remained however in the armament and consequently in the tactics of the infantry. The firelock was a smooth-bore muzzle-loader firing round bullets about half an inch in diameter. It had a ferocious recoil and emitted clouds of smoke on discharge. There was no backsight adjustable according to the range. Well trained men could be confident of hitting a large target at 100 yards and had to be rather lucky to hit anything further than 300 yards away. If aiming was dispensed with, it was possible to fire up to three shots a minute. To make the best of this dubious weapon, it was necessary to bring as many of them as possible into action simultaneously and this was done by forming the men in line. Around 1700 the line was commonly five ranks deep, but then the rear ranks could not join in the firing. Three ranks eventually became the rule, the front rank kneeling and the rear rank firing over the shoulders of the second. It was usual to have a second line of several ranks in reserve some way behind the first and to post the cavalry on the wings. The men were trained to fire together in salvoes and, to make the firing more continuous, the different battalions, platoons or some other subdivision of the line would be ordered to fire alternately.

p 185 (9)

This was a formation with serious weaknesses. The long, thin line was helpless if the enemy could pierce it and still more so if he could attack its end instead of in front. In attack, the line was clumsy. It was a complicated business to form a line since the troops approached the battlefield in a quite different formation, the column. It was even harder for the line to advance at anything more than a snail's pace for it had to be kept straight and the men evenly spaced. In defence, sections of the line could be drawn up at an angle to each other and this enabled them to take advantage of irregularities in the ground and to protect their flanks. They could also be formed into hollow squares for defence against cavalry and they could strengthen their position by building field fortifications in front. There was no similar flexibility in the attack and any break in the ground was an embarrassment to the ponderously advancing line. Moreover the enhanced firepower which was supposed to be the advantage gained through forming in line was itself of very limited effectiveness. There was little faith in the killing power of the weapon and it was valued mainly for the moral effect of the quick succession of noisy salvoes. In order to fire, an attacking line had to halt and troops who had fired were at a great disadvantage until they could reload. At Fontenoy (1745) the British and French both tried to gain an advantage by provoking the other side with taunts into firing first. Frederick the Great regarded the bayonet as the offensive weapon, the function of the musket being defensive:

p 193 (34)

p 194 (37)

*A swiss field-gun of 1717. The engraving includes instructions for loading and firing, and boasts that it demonstrates the cannon's strength and the horror which it can inspire in the enemy. Note the three rods strapped to the barrel; one with a spoon-like end for inserting the powder; one to ram it down; and a brush to sponge the barrel after firing.* (5)

*A foundry for bronze cannon, from 'Memoires d'Artillerie', Paris 1697. At this time, even though much standardisation had taken place, there was still a great variety of types and sizes: 24-, 16-, 12-, 8-, and 4-pounders were the commonest. In France gun foundries were highly developed and state-owned, but there was no standard recipe for the bronze, which might contain varying amounts of copper, tin and brass. (6)*

p 184

at one time he ordered his troops not to fire at all when they attacked. He concentrated on increasing the rate of fire and to this end forbade his men to aim their weapons properly. The design of Prussian muskets henceforth reflected these ideas: the 1782 model was very difficult to hold steady for aiming.

*f 5, 6*

The real execution on an 18th-century battlefield was done by the artillery. Smooth-bored, muzzle-loading weapons were again the rule; those in use on land were mostly made of brass, which was stronger in proportions to its weight than cast iron. The commonest sizes of gun were in the range between four-pounders and twelve-pounders. With solid iron shot they could be expected to hit targets 500 yards away. Sometimes their effective range was considerably more and their effectiveness against troops was further increased by ricochet fire—invented by Vauban—in which the balls were made to bounce along the ground. For ranges up to 300 yards the various kinds of case or grape shot—a bag or tin of bullets in place of a ball—were used. There were also mortars and howitzers which could fire an explosive shell detonated by a lighted fuse. It became usual to allot two small guns to each battalion in the line. The heavier weapons would be placed in batteries at advantageous positions, the best of all being on a prolongation of the enemy's line so that you could fire along it and not just across it. The amount of artillery in service was always tending to increase, which enabled the armies to hit much harder but made their movements even slower.

p 184 (5)

p 192 (30)

Linear tactics had drawbacks both in attack and in defence but it will be seen that it was to the defence that they were best suited.

A line was very vulnerable if superior force could be concentrated against one of its flanks but it was hard to do this with another line equally strung out. It was Frederick the Great who came nearest to solving this problem. The Prussian army which he inherited was unusually well drilled and the featureless and seemingly defenceless lowlands over which he ruled were ideal for linear tactics. He devised a whole series of expedients for strengthening one end of his line and attacking with it while 'refusing' the other, weaker end. Sometimes the strengthening consisted of short extra lines posted in front of or behind the two main ones; sometimes the extra men would be deployed against the side or rear of the enemy's position. With his 'oblique order' Frederick could sometimes defeat an army bigger than his own. Superior speed in complex evolutions was essential to its success—in particular, rapid deployment from marching order into line, which made it possible to conceal until the last moment where the main attack was to fall. At Leuthen (December, 1757) Frederick waited until the Austrians had formed their line before marching his army across their front and deploying against their left. Frederick had himself been attacked in a comparable way at Rossbach (November, 1757) but on that occasion it was the defence that was too quick for the assailants—they were routed while still on the march.

*f 8*

p 192 (31)

Frederick relied on superior drill for the weight as well as the speed and precision of his attacks. He packed his men more densely in the line, making them stand with their heels together instead of apart. He used his cavalry to develop the attack launched by infantry or artillery and he made them charge knee to knee at top

p 186 (12, 15)

p 184 (3)

speed. This had long been the ideal in cavalry tactics but other armies had not practised the movement sufficiently because it wore out the horses and so threatened the officers, whose property they were, with financial loss. Cavalry tactics bespoke the same lack of confidence in weapons as those of the infantry. With both arms, Frederick counted on rapid movement and close packing to overwhelm the enemy, the weapons being scarcely used.

Frederick's achievement was remarkable. His rather small country held its own against several much bigger ones and Prussia replaced France as the pace-setter among European armies. But his victories were always limited in their effects and his successes diminished as his enemies grew in defensive skill. His tactical ideas helped to inspire a more potent and flexible approach to war. But in the short run it was the instrument of those ideas, the mechanical perfection of Prussian drill, that was thought to be the secret of his success and, accordingly, was everywhere copied with stultifying effect. Symbolic of its suppression of initiative and even proficiency in the individual soldier in favour of uniformity were the tight-fitting uniforms on the Prussian model which spread to all the European states in the mid-18th century. The wearing of

p 186   uniforms was a characteristic feature of the new standing armies. Armour went steadily out of use in the later 17th century and gave place to long and fairly loose military coats. To facilitate the dense packing of men in line, the Prussians replaced these with close-fitting tail coats and breeches, which were smarter but less weatherproof and uncomfortably constricting.

## Weapons and tactics at sea

At sea no less than on land, linear tactics predominated by the end of the 17th century—with the same eventual result that the defence was favoured against the assailant. This development owed something to direct army influence. The professionalization of the naval service was assisted at the outset by the transfer to it of a number of experienced army officers. The cases of Blake and Monk in England were matched by Opdam in Holland, and d'Estrées (a

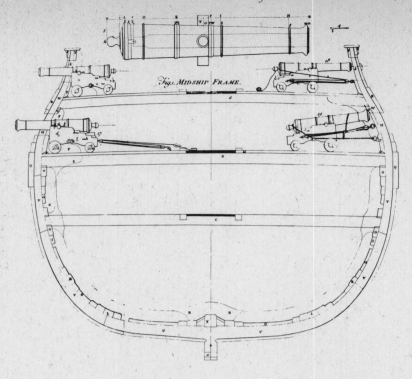

failure) and Château-Renault in France. But in the main it was, as on land, the weapons that dictated the tactics. It had been firmly established in the 16th century that in sailing ships, maximum firepower was achieved by mounting heavy guns in the hull, firing broadsides. From this it followed that a fleet would achieve maximum firepower if it engaged in line ahead, so that no ship masked the broadside of another. This conclusion was not immediately drawn, probably because the naval linear formation was a rather unnatural one—the assailant moved parallel to the enemy instead of towards him—and because it took time to discover how

*f 7, 9*

p 200
(52)

*Frederick the Great of Prussia taking a review. His father had built up his army from 45,000 on his accession in 1713 to 83,000 at his death. Austria, whose*   *population was nearly ten times that of Prussia, had only 100,000 troops when attacked by him in 1740. (8)*

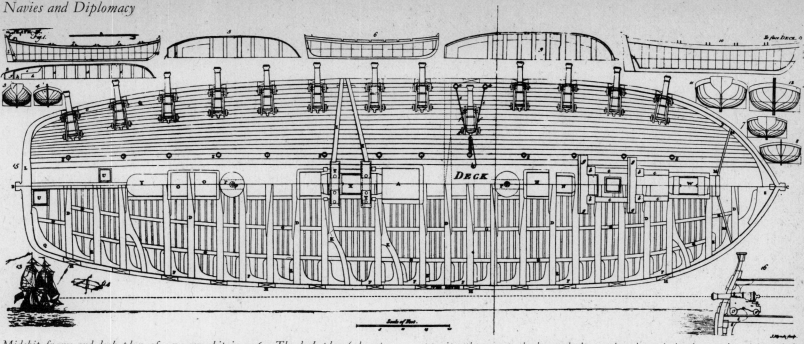

*Midship frame and deck-plan, of a 74-gun ship in 1769. The deck-plan (above) shows on one side the timbers by which it was supported. One of the guns is drawn in by its breeching, a rope to prevent it from recoiling too much. In the section opposite, the gun on the lower deck, numbered 19, is in the usual position of the lower-deck guns when not in use, with the muzzle wedged against the upper edge of the gunport. (7, 9)*

to make the broadsides rapid and lethal. In the Anglo-Dutch wars, the Dutch still relied for victory on boarding and the use of fire-ships as much as on their guns. It was the British who took the lead in introducing the line of battle and in seeking to crush the enemy by a cannonade at the closest possible range.

p 200
(51)

These tactics had in turn an effect on the design of the weapon. Originally ships varying greatly in size were placed in the line; standardization was needed to give it uniform strength. In Britain it was not until Anson's tenure of the Admiralty in the 1750s that a firm rule was laid down as to the size of ship 'fit to stand in the line'. The bulk of them were 64- or 74-gun ships (two gun decks), reinforced by some 'three-deckers' with 90 or 100 guns. Some smaller battleships were retained for lighter duties but a distinct type of vessel now emerged for these, intermediate between the battleship and light craft. This was the frigate, with up to 36 guns on a single deck. The biggest ships of the line exceeded 2000 tons and were the largest vessels afloat by far. Frigates were of up to 1000 tons and as large as the biggest merchantmen—the eastindia-men (few merchant ships then exceeded 500 tons and most were under 200). Fleets could carry a much greater weight of artillery in proportion to their manpower than armies. Their guns were more numerous, bigger and usually made of iron (heavier but cheaper than brass). Battleships commonly had 32-pounders on their lowest decks and 12-, 18- or 24-pounders higher up. A frigate's main armament would be 18-, 12- or 9-pounders.

p 200
(49)

p 201
(55)

When linear tactics first emerged at sea, they were not unduly rigid, attempts being made to pierce the opposing line or to concentrate superior force against one end of it—as the abler generals did on land. But such incidents as the defeat of the British and Dutch at Beachy Head (1690) or the defeat of the French off Barfleur (1692) seemed to show that at sea these manoeuvres were too difficult to be safe. British Fighting Instructions hence-forth gave first priority to the defensive need of keeping the line unbroken and coterminous with the enemy fleet. The only method of attack which this allowed was for all the ships in line to turn together towards the enemy, come close alongside their opposite numbers and simultaneously overwhelm them with their broad-sides. This never really worked. A fleet could only attack at all if it could get the 'weather gauge'—i.e. get to windward of its opponent. It was impossible in practice for the ships to reach the enemy's line simultaneously and so the shock effect was lost. While they were moving towards the enemy, the attacking ships were exposed to 'raking'—that is, the enemy's broadsides could pass through them from stem to stern and they could make almost no reply. When the attacking fleet reached its firing position, a strong wind might make the ships heel over and so prevent them using their lowest tier of guns; the opposing fleet, also heeling over, would meanwhile tend to fire into their assailant's rigging, blunting

p 201
(54)

their attack by lessening their mobility (the British regarded this as an unsporting French trick to escape defeat but it probably happened by accident as well as by design). To make things worse, the British Admiralty required its commanders to conform to the official Fighting Instructions and the official code of flag signals comprised only orders for the movements therein prescribed. Fortunately there were no rigid rules governing the pursuit that was supposed to follow a collapse of the enemy's formation and enterprising admirals who caught the enemy unawares were able to pretend that this was a pursuit and not a battle. In this way looser and more aggressive tactics were developed, sometimes with official encouragement, and some important successes were won. But for a century after Barfleur, the British navy did not win a proper pitched battle at sea and some of those in command of it seem to have believed that such a victory was impossible. During the American War of Independence, when the British fleet was numerically inferior to the forces of France and Spain, Lord Mulgrave and Admiral Pye consoled themselves with the doctrine that a fleet of thirty sail of the line was indestructible: an enemy fleet strong enough to destroy it would be too unwieldy to fight.

## Problems of expansion: officers

The trend towards powerful standing armies and navies was complementary to the new developments in tactics. The weapons and mode of fighting of the infantry were getting simpler, their strength increasingly came from numbers and discipline rather than individual prowess. Specialist knowledge was essential in the artillery and even in the cavalry; the latter never quite lost their chivalric associations and the troopers might be men of some substance. But the infantry were semi-skilled labourers at best. Quality mattered little: a state could increase its military power if it could simply amass large numbers and keep them together for a long time, so that the habit of total, unquestioning obedience could be thoroughly instilled. Now it was about this time that the European powers acquired the administrative and financial resources needed to maintain large forces constantly on foot and sought thereby to give military expression to their growing internal strength. Standing armies further promoted that strength: not only did they crush rebellions, enforce the law and compel the payment of taxes, but they were themselves less liable to rebel than the more casually organized forces of the past. Of the great captains of the Thirty Years' War, Wallenstein had died a traitor's death and Condé had joined an aristocratic rebellion against his sovereign.

p 321
(16)

Monarchs who had long maintained a small permanent force of guards now expanded them into true armies. The pace was set by Louis XIV who, starting his personal rule in 1661 with an empty treasury and a few ragged regiments, had 280,000 men under arms

f 10

*The royal bodyguard swearing loyalty to the new King of Prussia, Frederick William I in 1713. It was under this King that the Prussian army was to be developed into the magnificent machine inherited by Frederick the Great.* (10)

by 1689. In England, Charles II's guards were 3,500 strong in 1663; during King William's war there were up to 90,000 men in pay. The Austrian army was the fruit of the wars with the Turks in the 1660s and 1680s: it eventually rivalled the French in size. The armies of the northern powers were created mainly in response to the challenge of Charles X and Charles XII of Sweden. In Brandenburg-Prussia the Great Elector had under 3000 soldiers on his accession in 1640, and 29,000 on his death in 1686. Remarkable efforts in the next century increased this eventually to 200,000, equal to some $3\frac{1}{2}\%$ of the population. The new Russian army had already reached this number by the death of Peter the Great in 1725. Sweden, which had been a great power in the days of smallish armies, sank into the second rank in the 18th century, as did the Dutch. The two great eastern empires—Russia and Turkey—faced a special difficulty in building up standing armies on the western model in that they could not use their old-established corps of

guards—the strieltzy and the janissaries respectively—as a nucleus. Opposed to all western ways, these formations were on the contrary an obstacle to reform both military and civil. Peter the Great surmounted the problem by the massacre of the strieltzy (1698). The janissaries were not massacred till 1826 and Turkey failed to keep pace militarily with her neighbours. Spain on the other hand revived somewhat and with Denmark and Piedmont-Sardinia completed the second rank of military powers. p 37 (f 3)

Navies, unlike the armies, continued to rely mainly on skilled manpower, but they too required men in great numbers. To manoeuvre and attack in concert, in accordance with the new and complex tactical rules, called for many more men to handle the sails and guns than were required just to sail the ship. A large battleship had a complement of nearly 1000 and even a frigate might have over 200 men aboard. It was the growing power of the State which increased the supply of seamen, by measures like the English Navigation Acts which artificially accelerated the growth of the mercantile marine. This strengthened the navy, which in turn protected the trade which supplied its sailors—just as the army ensured the collection of taxes for its pay. The Dutch already possessed an abundant sea trade and England too was a well established sea power; a more direct and impressive result of the growing power of the State was the entirely artificial creation of several navies in response to mercantilist beliefs about the importance of maritime trade. Colbert in 1661 took over a French navy with only 18 sailing warships, mostly unseaworthy. In 1689 France's larger naval vessels totalled 93, against 69 Dutch and 100 English. Besides the fostering of merchant shipping, Colbert's most significant naval measures were the building up of a well trained corps of professional officers, the virtual foundation of France's naval dockyards and arsenals and the improvement of ship design by the collection of experts from all over Europe. In the science of shipbuilding and in the whole theoretical side of naval warfare, the French were henceforth superior to the British —though the British trust in mere practical experience was not of course in vain. Peter the Great, as already observed, created a navy from scratch; it long relied heavily on the help of foreign officers, often British. Peter had the advantage of working in the landlocked Baltic with its island-studded coasts. Rowing galleys were still important in the fighting here and a land power could create a force of these fairly readily, manning them with soldiers. Peter made Russia the leading naval power in the Baltic, though Sweden and Denmark long kept pace with her. Spanish power revived somewhat on sea as on land. p 198 (45) p 198 (46) f 11 f 1 p 200 (53)

The officers were the linchpin of the new standing forces since on their maintenance of discipline and understanding of the new system of tactics all else depended. In recruiting them, the govern-

*Naval architects at work. In the design of a war ship, it was of vital importance that the elevation of the battery was correct, and this depended on working out in advance how deep in the water the loaded ship would sit. The men here are conducting an experiment to this end, with inch cubes of cork and copper and a lead weight.* (11)

*A plate from a Dutch manual of 1719 showing ships under construction and being launched. The method of launching in Holland was different from that in the rest of Europe: the scaffolds (numbered 7 in the picture) were placed parallel under the ship both to support her while she was under construction and to act as sliding-rails as she was pushed into the water. The French used two wooden buttresses which entered the water with the ship.* (12)

ments were in something of a dilemma. It was the nobility who regarded war as their calling and were the traditional first servants of the State. On the other hand they were turbulent and lazy and not always intelligent: the new mode of warfare based on discipline and science did not come naturally to them. Nor were they always numerous enough now that armies were getting larger. The claims of wealth had also to be considered. We shall see later that the governments could only just manage to pay and organize their new forces and they were willing to grant advantages to those who would advance funds and undertake the trouble of raising and clothing men. The sale of commissions was common, captains usually had some sort of proprietary interest in their companies and colonels sometimes had the same in their regiments. They ran them to make a profit even if they were not allowed to sell them. Systems of appointment and promotion were a compromise between the claims of birth, wealth and military experience and ability. The 'scientific' arms as they were called—the artillery and engineers—needed ability and thorough professional training. Talented men of modest rank and fortune were the rule here; sometimes with radical political sympathies like Carnot or Bonaparte. The navy also required sound professional training but there the lower ranks consisted largely of skilled men, with a strong body of warrant officers (mates, boatswains, gunners, etc.) who could make the ships go and teach their aristocratic superiors. Promotion in the British navy was more dominated by aristocratic jobbery than promotion in the army. Colbert thought the best way to officer a ship was to have three gentlemen seconded by three seamen: to ensure good fellowship, all should come from the same province. There was no skilled plebeian element in the ranks of the fast-growing infantry but this too made for upper-class predominance in command: not many privates had education enough to be sergeants, let alone commissioned officers.

The period of general military expansion after 1660 made the forces quite an important channel of social advancement for newcomers with capital or military talent. Afterwards something of an aristocratic reaction set in. In Britain, royal disapproval did not prevent the system of buying and selling commissions establishing itself for all ranks up to lieutenant-colonel. This was held to ensure the loyalty of the army to the constitution by placing most military commissions in the hands of men from the upper classes that held political power. In France and Prussia, sections of the nobility were

at first politically suspect. Louvois, the main creator of the new French army under Louis XIV, gave the chief commands to lesser nobles at the expense of traditionally powerful families. But in the late 18th century, the higher ranks of the French army were increasingly reserved for the greater nobility and it became increasingly hard for a non-noble to get a commission at all. In the Prussian army there was a purge of non-noble officers on the reduction of strength after the peace settlements of 1713 and 1763. In these states the monarch bound the nobility to him by giving them employment in the army. In Russia though, there was almost a reverse trend. Peter the Great made service either in the forces or the administration compulsory for all noblemen; commoners who served were ennobled on promotion. The Russian nobility regarded compulsory service as a grievance: it was abolished in 1762.

Though the aristocracy did not make ideal officers, the better element among them succeeded in creating an impressive military tradition. Writing in the mid-18th century, the Chevalier d'Arc extolled the poorer nobility as the great repository of military virtue. The combination of frugality with a knightly code of honour produced officers who were thrifty and enterprising and yet brave and honourable. D'Arc despised the soft-living rich whatever their lineage, but he thought that common soldiers who displayed valour deserved to rank as nobles and become officers. Plutocratic and courtly influence prevented the triumph of his ideal in pre-revolutionary France. But in Prussia it was indeed the poorer nobility who officered the army and were the foundation of its triumphs both in the 18th and succeeding centuries. Whether they were nobles, bourgeois or ex-rankers, it was largely the hardworking poorer officers, often under the command of wealthy drones, who caused war to be taken seriously as a profession. Tradition hitherto had made it the nobleman's privilege and duty to serve the prince in both military and civil affaires—but with no special training being thought necessary for either. Now it gradually came to be thought that a man should not be given military command unless he had qualified himself by technical training and probation. An outward sign of this new professional consciousness was that officers (like priests) began to wear their professional costume even when off duty. Even monarchs came to identify themselves with the military profession in this way: Charles XII of Sweden is an early example.

p 189 (23)

p 17 (10)

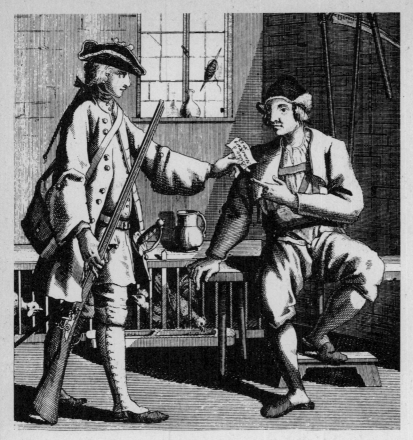

*A French officer demands a billet in the house of a lamenting German peasant, who (in the original caption) foresees that he and his wife will have to give him their bed, food, drink, and even money.* (13)

## Problems of expansion: manpower

The common soldiers of an 18th-century army were, as far as possible, long-service professionals like their officers. The necessary iron discipline could not, it was thought, be maintained otherwise. But there was a limit to the number of men willing to make war their life's work, as there was to the number that the State could afford to employ permanently. Conscription and short service were therefore important to the professional forces of the 18th century, although they seem to belong to a later age when the army was intended to be the whole nation in arms. The combination of opposites appears more logical in the navies. The work and training of the sailors in peacetime fitted them for war service and the demand for their services in peace was deliberately stimulated for military reasons. When war came it was therefore natural to conscript as many as were required for the navy, returning them to civil employment in due course until next needed. In Britain the arbitrary pressing of seamen by royal command was hallowed by tradition: no parliamentary sanction was required for this infringement of the subject's liberty. Colbert created a less arbitrary system for France—the registration of all seamen and fishermen in an *inscription maritime*, with the rudiments of a social security system for those liable to serve.

p 188
(21)

For the armies, it was not easy to get either the type or the number of men required. In many countries it seems to have been mainly the townsmen who were willing to enlist. Living out their lives in isolated villages, peasants were frightened to leave home: those who did often became ill through exposure to infections not hitherto encountered or even through homesickness. Townsmen had often made an initial move from the countryside and were at any rate more accustomed to novelty. They were also more likely to be driven to enlist by unemployment. In France the disruption of trade by Britain's command of the sea did much to solve the recruiting problem in wartime. But townsmen's physique was poorer than countrymen's and they were supposed to be less docile and less well behaved. The skills of the craftsmen were moreover a valuable economic asset, which recruiting might destroy: even if the men survived the war, the expectation was that in the army they would lose both their skills and the will to work. Idleness and dissipation were considered to be essential characteristics of soldiers.

Voluntary enlistment brought under arms a host of men who had lost their roots in society and were happy to find a place in the vagabond community of soldiers. In addition, noblemen serving as officers could often induce some peasants from their estates to follow them. Lastly, some poor, mountainous areas produced a surplus of men who developed the custom of going to serve as soldiers for their richer neighbours—Switzerland, Scotland, Hesse. The supply of volunteers was spread more evenly by the continuing custom of enlisting foreigners. No state was fussy about the nationality of its troops and some preferred to conserve their native manpower for industry—the source of war funds. Up to a half or more of the Prussian army consisted of foreigners in the 18th century, though most of them came from other German states. The Dutch army included Scottish, Swiss and German regiments, the French had Swiss, Germans and Irish. The richer countries hired large contingents from indigent princes who thus acquired the means of figuring as military powers. In 1700 Britain and Holland promoted peace between Sweden and Denmark so that they could hire the Danish troops for use against France. But no expedient short of conscription proved able to fill the ranks of the armies in time of war. Peter the Great built his army by ordering the nobles to furnish contingents of serfs—most of whom were never heard of in their villages again. In Britain, acts of Parliament required the magistrates to press the unemployed. Louvois created a militia in France which was originally intended to relieve the army of the burden of home defence but increasingly was used as a simple source of recruits. It was raised by drawing lots among the men fit to bear arms. King Frederick William I of Prussia built up his army in part by obliging the men of his territories to undergo training in it; but both in France and in Prussia it was possible to buy exemption from service and large classes of people, notably members of the professions and skilled trades, were exempt automatically.

p 188
(22)

p 186
(11)

p 188
(20)

The professional character of the armies was diluted not only by the inclusion of large numbers of more or less unwilling conscripts but by various approaches to a short service system. No state could afford to keep permanently in arms the full number of men required in wartime. Large numbers of soldiers and sailors were discharged when peace was made; the governments tried to keep the maximum number of regiments in being and officers in pay so that re-expansion would be easy. Prussian conscription was a development of this system: in peacetime the conscripts were normally called up for two months' service and training with their regiments each year. Even when men were actually serving, there was a desire to diminish the burden which their idleness represented for the national economy. Troops even in wartime were frequently unoccupied: winter campaigning, though by no means unknown, was not usual. Peacetime training, since it was largely confined to routine drill, occupied only a limited time. Soldiers were therefore allowed to work. Prussian barracks were converted into spinning mills. Everywhere soldiers helped with harvesting and threshing: this was sometimes indispensable. Men were given lengthy furloughs in winter and returned to their homes; others might be allowed to take temporary jobs in their garrison town and worked at the trades in which they had been employed before enlistment. At least one such man served as a university tutor. The officers too were not fully occupied in military service; save when there was actual fighting, leave was very generously given. The new professional armies thus did not make a clean break with their more casually organized predecessors and they were much less cut off from civil life than was to be the case in the 19th century.

p 192
(32)

It will be seen that behind many features of military organization lay financial stringency. The states could now afford standing forces but they could only just do so and shortage of money caused endless trouble. Soldiers' pay was miserably low and deductions were made from it towards the cost of food, clothing and other essentials. Even so, payments to the forces were constantly in arrears and officers of all ranks were driven into debt by the need to meet necessary expenses before the government could make the money available. Sailors were traditionally paid off at the end of each voyage but in wartime they were kept endlessly at sea or sent back afresh without pay and sometimes saw no money for years. The poor food and unhealthiness on the overcrowded ships need

*Prussian military discipline: one man is flogged while another has to walk between files of soldiers who beat him with canes. Severer discipline meant fewer outrages by the troops but was quite compatible with extortion organized from above. Violence in any case was commonplace and not confined to soldiers or to wartime: below, a German village being plundered in 1771. (14, 15)*

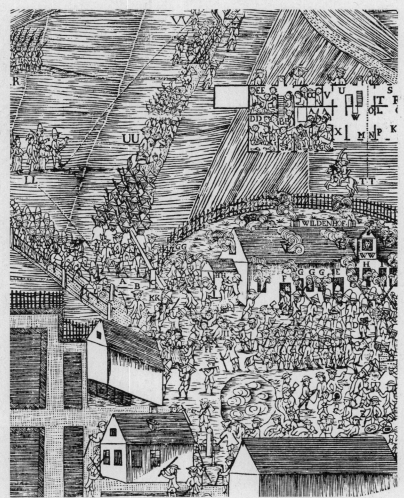

no stressing: the Franco-Spanish fleet that sailed against Britain in 1779 was crippled by disease and the sea was so full of corpses that the people of Devon, it was said, refused to eat fish for a month. This was partly unavoidable but conditions in barracks were much the same: French soldiers had to sleep two to a bed. Britain had not even a proper number of barracks: they were shunned as expensive and as endangering liberty by separating the army from

the people. British troops lived a vagabond, uncomfortable existence in inns. Provision of clothing was inadequate. Sailors had no uniforms. Louvois did not wish to have uniforms in the French army. When uniforms were introduced, not only was comfort sacrificed to display but the clothes had to last too long and such items as shoes, underwear and greatcoats tended to be short. Army and navy surgeons were probably about as good as could be expected but hospital organization tended to be perfunctory, as did the religious life of the forces. Soldiers could not really afford to marry and it was not encouraged. But soldiers' wives were invaluable as washerwomen, nurses and so forth, in filling the gaps in the official domestic arrangements and a certain number were commonly allowed to accompany the troops.

Poor conditions of service help to account for the low quality of many of the recruits. The two things together largely explain the massive rate of desertion characteristic of 18th-century armies and which only the periodic offer of an amnesty kept within limits. p 190 (28) It was almost a way of life—men repeatedly deserting in order to re-enlist with a new bounty. Harsh punishments were needed to keep order among men who had so little to gain by behaving well. The French army detested the terrible and constant floggings f 14 characteristic of German—and British—armies and would not imitate them; but French discipline was poor in the 18th century. The good side of the harsh discipline was the decline in military lawlessness. The mercenaries of old had plundered and massacred p 189 (28) f 15 without stint. This could still happen when troops were long unpaid or in some way provoked. But pay was less irregular than it had been and bureaucratic centralization meant the better enforcement of military law by courts martial. The civil population had less to fear from the troops.

## A strategy of limited objectives

The prevailing system of tactics made it hard to win a decisive victory in battle. This fact, along with the shortcomings of the armed forces and the primitive state of communications, meant that there was little hope of any campaign ending with the annihilation of the enemy. Armies moved so slowly that they could not properly exploit even such victories as they won. The most obvious reason for this was their dependence for supplies on depots painfully built up in their rear by slow-moving waggons and barges, often in the hands of dilatory civilian contractors. Contrary to the common belief, armies never ceased to try to live off the produce of the land through which they passed. In particular, the fodder required for the great host of cavalry and draught horses was so bulky that local supplies were almost indispensable to supplement what could be carried. But armies were now too big for most localities to feed. By carrying bread or biscuit with them, they could be independent of their depots for a few days but no more. Yet the slowness of armies should not too readily be put down to the supply factor, since it was no less apparent in short-range movements. There was too little done in the way of pursuit when a beaten enemy was flying in disorder from the battlefield: the defeated army could almost always regroup and recover at leisure. Slowness was aggravated by the practice of keeping armies concentrated. The prevailing tactical idea was that an army should fight as one unit and only a limited use was made of detachments. Armies were not so organized that they could readily fan out across a wide expanse of country, and it was correspondingly harder for them either to live off local supplies or to track down an elusive enemy. The real reason for much of this slowness and rigidity was the widespread lack of ardour and enterprise among both officers and men. They might fight well enough in battle under the general's eye, but when continuous hard marching or active vigilance in detachments were called for, they tired readily and took full advantage of the increased opportunity to desert. Frederick the Great advised his generals against several types of operation because they increased the risk of desertion.

The object of a campaign was therefore the limited one of discomfiting the enemy and gaining ground. The attacker manoeuvred so as to threaten the enemy's line of communication or one of his fortresses. The enemy gave battle or withdrew, choosing the alternative that seemed least dangerous. The reward of victory was territory, the resources of which made it easier for the victor to maintain his army and carry on the war, while for the vanquished these things became more difficult. Winter brought bad roads and shortage of fodder and normally put an end to the fighting. The next campaign would be fought in the same way and perhaps reverse the result just attained.

p 196–7 Fortresses had an essential part to play in this strategic system. The 17th century saw a great advance in the science of fortification —a very effective answer to the challenge of gunpowder. The new fortresses were huge and costly, yet more testimony to the growing wealth and power of the states whose strongholds they were. Mere barons could not afford to build them and the mass of lesser castles and fortifications were swept away, leaving only those of value to the central government. Fortresses were useful firstly as secure places where enormous quantities of supplies could be assembled. Armies could manoeuvre more freely if they had copious supplies within easy reach and did not have to worry about the safety thereof. A well stocked fortress in a forward position could even spearhead an attack on neighbouring territory. Secondly, fortresses barred the route of an advancing enemy and threatened his supply lines if passed. A siege tied up a force superior in number to the garrison and aggravated the assailants' supply problems. The art of attacking fortifications was perfected by Vauban simultaneously

f 17 with the art of building them and successful resistance to a siege became increasingly difficult. But a siege wasted so much time that it could make a whole campaign abortive. Sieges often ended in an honourable capitulation, the assailant buying a little time by allowing the garrison to escape. The science of fortification was yet another ramification of linear tactics: lines of ramparts were so juxtaposed as to give each other covering fire, just as were lines of infantry in a defensive position. As noted already, an army on the defensive in the field could strengthen itself with temporary fortifications: at his last gasp in 1761, Frederick the Great took refuge in an entrenched camp at Bunzelwitz and held off his enemies till the end of the campaign.

At sea too, it was hard to annihilate the enemy by superior strength. If he took refuge in harbour, not only did he escape destruction but unless he was very weak it was difficult to bottle him up. To maintain a blockading squadron of adequate strength in the face of storms and pestilence was a superhuman task. Once an inferior force was on the move, the size of the ocean and the vagaries of the wind made it even harder to catch than was the case with armies. In the worldwide conflicts of Britain and France, the French were globally inferior but often achieved local superiority and conquests because the British could not accurately tell where their ships would be sent. At sea as on land, what might be accomplished was to reduce the resources available to the enemy for the support of the war and to augment one's own. This meant in the

first place an attack on commerce. Seaborne trade was of relatively greater importance then because of the poorness of land communications. The swift, small vessels that preyed upon it were hard to catch and the prospect of booty made it easy to finance a war on trade. The privateers to whom it was largely left were the most important survival of the days before standing forces. Defence of trade by convoy was difficult and expensive, given the multitude of tiny ships that carried it. Nor was a thorough blockade needed to disrupt commerce: as losses rose, so did insurance premiums until the profit vanished and the merchants ceased to sail. The French sometimes laid up their battleships and relied on commerce raiding alone. But a navy enjoying superiority at sea could attack commerce more systematically than unsupported cruisers and privateers and it might also capture the places traded with and so augment its own country's trade and revenue. This was how the elder Pitt made war pay for itself.

Relative advantage was thus all that was to be gained by fighting, either by sea or land, and war was in many ways like a continuation of peacetime mercantile rivalry—a fight for sources of revenue which ended when one side became financially exhausted. It was all the easier to combine it with the haggling of diplomacy into a single process of international competition for piecemeal gains in territory and influence. Frederick the Great was perhaps the greatest exponent of this combination. In the 1740s he won Silesia by a clever alternation of peace and war, first winning a victory, then selling his neutrality to the hard-pressed Austrians, then re-entering the war when they seemed to be doing rather too well against their other opponents and finally repurchasing peace on better terms. International relations had many points in common with a modern 'cold war'. Great powers increasingly shrank from the crushing burden on their resources represented by open war among themselves but continued the fight by devious means. The colonies of the different powers fought each other in private wars. Powers fought as auxiliaries of other powers without declaring war themselves; Britain and France opposed each other in this way in 1740–44. Finance came to the assistance of diplomacy in the form of subsidies to princes and bribes to their courtiers—not then miscalled international aid. Military missions to backward countries were also just beginning: French influence in Turkey was enhanced under Louis XV by the presence of an adventurer named Count Bonneval as military adviser to the Sultan.

## Diplomacy and neutrality

For the diplomatic services which carried on the bloodless side of the international struggle, the era of Louis XIV was once more a great formative period. Permanently resident ambassadors had appeared somewhat earlier but it was Richelieu who drew from this the logical inference that the main business of diplomacy was not the making of specific agreements but continuous negotiation —to gain information about the designs of other governments, build up good will and respect, and so be able to exercise a useful influence on the policy-making of other states. At the end of Louis XIV's reign a high French official, François de Callières, gave classic expression to these ideas in his treatise *On the Manner of Negotiating with Princes*. They were reflected in the increasing number of ambassadors, in the emergence of foreign ministries as centres for the collection and dissemination of information, and in the voluminous instructions now given to ambassadors—detailed briefings in the local political situation which they would be expected to influence. In all this, France was the model for Europe. It is not surprising that in the 18th century French replaced Latin as the language of diplomacy.

Respect for neutrals was an important new feature of the military and diplomatic system of the 18th century, with its emphasis on limited ambitions and the building up of influence. Neutrality achieved a new moral respectability with the decline of the idea that it was possible to tell which party in a war had right on his side. Grotius (1583–1645) still believed this and to some extent he thought that every state was bound to help the injured party. Bynkershoek, a later Dutch writer on the 'law of nations' (1673–1743) did not believe it and held that states might properly remain neutral, with equal rights and duties in respect of all belligerents. There was a general campaign to secure neutral rights, especially

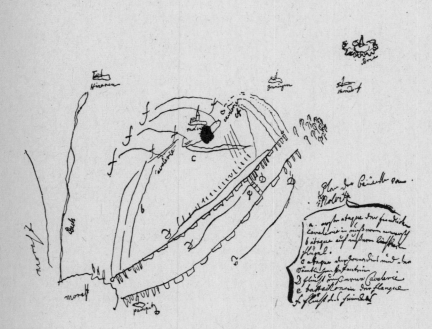

*A sketch by Frederick the Great in a letter to Leopold of Anhalt-Dessau, one of his generals, showing the disposition of the army at the battle of Mollwitz in 1741. Mollwitz was one of the first battles in which infantry proved decisive.* (16)

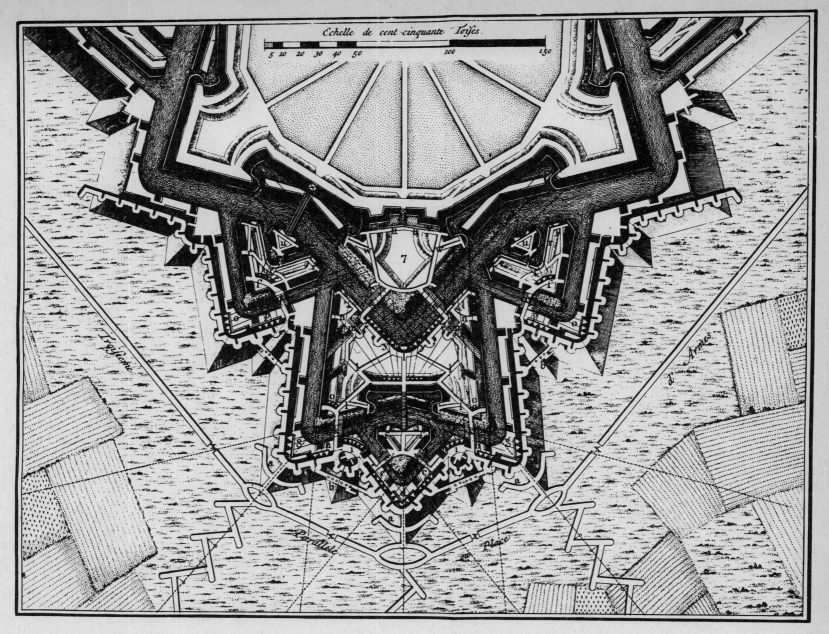

*Detailed plan of an attack from Vauban's great work, 'De l'attaque et de la defense des places'. Methods of attack and defence improved simultaneously: sieges therefore remained lengthy though probably no fortress was now impreg-*

*nable. Here the hornwork projecting in front of the bastion (7) and the demilunes (u) at the side have to be taken before the main assault. Note the separate batteries for making breaches and for stopping the defenders' fire. (17)*

apparent in the treaties of commerce which multiplied at this time —a natural counterpart and moderator of mercantilism. Besides regulating tariffs and so forth, they laid down how the parties were to treat each other's trade in the event of one being at war and the other neutral. When belligerents proved recalcitrant, neutrals sometimes banded together to defend their rights. Denmark and Sweden had a system of joint convoys during the Anglo-French war of the 1690s. From 1756, attempts at a neutral front were encouraged by France in the hope of uniting Europe against British preponderance at sea, as it had once been united against French preponderance on land. Catherine the Great's 'League of Armed Neutrality' (1780) was the most notable of these attempts. None was very successful.

Moderation was found in the behaviour of belligerents towards each other as well as in their treatment of neutrals. Prisoners were a nuisance to keep and so they were exchanged. A treaty between the belligerents assigned a money value to each rank and if one side captured prisoners to a greater value than the other, a ransom payment made up the difference. Protection of commerce was considered so vital to the strength of the State that there was a reluctance to forbid anything that business men considered necessary for profit making. Trading with the enemy was usually forbidden but sometimes it was sanctioned and frequently it was tolerated. When the Dutch island of St Eustatius was captured by the British navy in 1780, a great quantity of merchandise belonging to British smugglers was taken; they did not hesitate to press in the courts for its recovery and received much parliamentary

backing. Armies usually tried to protect civilian life and property in conquered territory: they could levy taxes in return for protection, whereas if they frightened the farmers off the land there would be no forage for them on the next campaign. The system of immunity for diplomats was fully developed and ordinary travellers often passed without difficulty through countries with which their own was at war. It is often said that this moderation represents the enlightenment of the 18th century and its freedom from the religious frenzy of earlier and the ideological fury of later times. There is some truth in this but the practical considerations noted above were more important. When reasons of State required it, there was plenty of brutality. Louis XIV's armies twice devastated the Palatinate and when Frederick the Great seized Saxony in 1756 he pressed its unfortunate soldiers into his army. There was still plenty of scope for denunciation by haters of war like Voltaire.

## Towards Napoleonic warfare

The system of war and diplomacy described here represented a particular phase in the development of the military art and of national organization. Men had not learned how to do better and mostly they lacked the incentive to try harder. But when extreme danger or a specially glittering prize appeared, 18th-century armies regularly surpassed themselves. Marlborough's long march across Germany to the rescue of the Austrians before Blenheim was an example of this; so on a smaller scale was Villars' flank march in pitch darkness before Denain (1712) when France was at her last gasp. Frederick the Great was orthodox in condemning winter fighting as destructive to the troops but he conquered Silesia in winter and his disciple Ferdinand of Brunswick saved Hanover from the French by the winter campaign of 1757–58. At sea, Hawke ended the French invasion threat of 1759 by chasing their fleet into the rocks and shoals of Quiberon Bay at the height of a December gale. On the frontiers of the European world, the needs of local defence obliged the population to join in the fighting in a way that it had ceased to do elsewhere. The Croats, Hungarians and Cossacks defended themselves against the Turks; some of the British settlers in America had to fight the Indians and the French. Irregular forces emerged which were relatively weak in discipline but strong in the personal qualities of the soldiers: initiative, marksmanship, scouting, the use of cover. Austria brought them from her Turkish frontier to the German battlefields, with great effect. There had long been an interest in 'light infantry' and 'light cavalry' (such as the hussars of Hungary) and in the later 18th century it became a vogue, threatening the supremacy of Prussian ideas.

To make the peaks of achievement the rule rather than the exception needed both new techniques and a general sense of urgency. The 18th century produced the techniques, though not without much wasted effort in the exploring of dead ends. Despairing of the line and the firelock as instruments of attack, French theorists like Saxe and Folard proposed a return to assaults by dense columns of infantry. Columns had not firepower enough to be the sole or even the main attack formation. But they did prove to be the means by which superior force could be concentrated at a key point and this made them vitally important in the Napoleonic era. Columns also appeared in naval warfare, the attacking fleet breaking through the enemy line, raking the ships between which the columns passed and seizing the leeward position so that the broken line could not retreat. The British first did this at the Battle

p 201
(56)

of the Saints in 1782, and this success reinstated tactical boldness as the orthodox British naval doctrine. In strategic thinking, a dead end not finally escaped from until the 19th century was the attempt of learned staff officers (mainly German) to deduce war-winning principles from mathematics and topography. The occupation of dominant physical features or the preserving of certain geometrical relationships in the positioning of the army were held capable of bringing victory almost without fighting. Far more fruitful was the work of the Frenchman Bourcet, who in the 1760s and 1770s was discovering how an army could be reshaped into divisions, each comprising contingents of all arms, and how these divisions could operate separately but in concert. A system of divisions, enabling the army to fan out and corner an inferior enemy, was the strategic key to Napoleonic victories, as the column was one of the tactical keys. Military primacy was about to pass back from Germany to France.

Technological and economic advance contributed much to improved military methods. At sea there were improved systems of signalling, the copper-bottoming of ships and the use of lime-juice against scurvy. Ships and men could better withstand the rigours of blockading an inferior enemy. Artillery both by sea and land was more scientifically built and was made easier to move and handle; the foundation for this was the ballistic researches of

p 105
(20)

Benjamin Robins (1707–51). Over much of Europe, roads im-

proved and production of food and fodder grew: this meant that armies could move faster.

But the new discoveries were useless without a willingness for great exertions and this only came with the French Revolution and the passionate desire of its adherents to defend it and of its opponents to crush it. The American Revolution foreshadowed this to some extent. It was defended by a militia of armed civilians as well as by a small army of enlisted men. This last was not a standing army since it was disbanded at the peace and almost disbanded several times before that: patriotic enthusiasm alone held it together when pay and all else were lacking. But its organization and mode of fighting were orthodox and the War of Independence was typical of its century. The British won several victories but could not destroy the American army. As they had to remain concentrated in face of it, they could not destroy the militia either, and so the Americans remained in effective control of their territory. When the British were exhausted, the war ended. France was not protected by the Atlantic as America was and from 1792 the revolutionaries there faced a military threat of correspondingly greater seriousness. They had to swell their armies by thorough-going conscription and adopt the latest military methods. A new military system emerged, formed like the one we have been describing by the interaction of military inventions with changes in political conditions.

p 195
(38)
p 315
(6)

Great changes in the balance of power, due partly to military effort, partly to deeper causes, took place in the period surveyed in this volume. Europe established military superiority over Asia. In 1683 the Turks nearly took Vienna and in 1711 they routed Peter the Great, newly triumphant over the Swedes at Poltava. By the 1790s the Ottoman Empire was at the mercy of the Europeans, while the British were achieving supremacy in India. Due in part to Turkish and Moghul decadence, this transformation also reflected a growing European superiority in tactics. Within Europe, Louis XIV's ascendancy rested ultimately on his having twice as many subjects as any other Western monarch. The aggressiveness of Turkey and Sweden also helped him: they were usually friendly with France, and even when they were not their activities distracted France's neighbours from resisting her. Despite the coalitions against Louis XIV, Spain and her colonies passed to the Bourbons: France and Spain were usually, though not always, allies in the 18th century and they were very strong in Italy and the Mediterranean. But simultaneously France's European position was weakened by the eclipse of her eastern friends, Turkey, Sweden and Poland. Austria, Russia and Prussia supplanted them, thanks to a growing military power which reflected both rising populations and increasing administrative efficiency. Britain's ascendancy overseas owed much to the internal decay of her rivals—Spain, Portugal and later Holland—and to France's difficulty in paying for a navy as well as a great army. British demographic ascendancy probably doomed the French to eclipse in North America; in India they did not always try hard enough. Portugal, with Brazil, became almost a British colony.

Thus we may sum up the 18th century as a great formative period in power politics. Its great powers—Austria, Russia, Prussia (later expanded into Germany), Britain and France—were dominant until 1914. And it is only now that military methods are emerging which owe nothing to Frederick the Great.

# VII TASTE AND PATRONAGE

*The Role of the Artist in Society*

L. D. ETTLINGER

> *'There is no other way of making a reasonable being out of sensuous man than by making him aesthetic first.'*

FRIEDRICH SCHILLER

## The central decade

of the 18th century represents the high-water mark of one style of art and the beginning of an ebb in the opposite direction. And not only a style of art – a whole intellectual climate and way of thought. Indeed the change is noticeable first of all in philosophical writings; these in turn affected patronage, and patrons began to employ artists who could express the new values. Briefly summarized, it was a movement away from a view of art as a means of pleasurable sensation towards one of art as a medium for moral improvement. The change can be detected in many aspects of 18th-century life (we have seen it already in Chapter II, in the swing from Rococo to Neo-classicism in architecture) and was to work itself out explicitly in the pages of history. The paintings which begin and end this chapter are almost sufficient to make the point in themselves. The symbol of the first half of the century is the court of Louis XV, led by the elegant and sophisticated Madame de Pompadour; that of the last half the murdered Marat.

The portrait of Madame de Pompadour (opposite) is by François Boucher and was painted in 1758. She was at the height of her influence over the King, an influence which she exercised for twenty years with tact, intelligence and charm, and which was largely responsible for making Versailles the civilized and civilizing centre that it was. Musical, witty and discriminating, she was the friend of writers like Montesquieu and Voltaire, took an active interest in the theatre and above all had a flair for the visual arts that few great patrons have equalled. She was concerned in the founding of the royal porcelain factory at Sèvres and in the running of the tapestry workshops of the Gobelins. She collected pictures, sculpture, furniture, jewellery and ceramics. She created an environment where art was a necessity and where it could flourish – within the wide limits of her Rococo taste – to perfection.

Boucher was her favourite painter and it is easy to see why. He stood at the end of a tradition which, beginning in 16th-century Venice, had been given superb panache by Tiepolo and poetic delicacy by Watteau. If Boucher was a lesser artist than either, he is still more completely representative of his age. No one was better able to combine flattery with truth, to present real people and real passions under the soft disguise of prettiness, to make pleasure supreme and to lull the harsh promptings of morality. (1)

**To see, to enjoy and to buy** works of art on the scale to which the 18th century aspired involved the creation of new institutions: the public gallery, the professional art-dealer, and the academy. In England the Royal Academy grew out of earlier private societies for the exhibition of paintings. George III signed its *Instrument of Foundation* in 1768 and exhibitions of works by 'artists of distinguished merit' were held annually thereafter. That of 1771 is shown here (right). (2)

**Private collections** became part of aristocratic life and valuable prestige assets. In Pannini's meticulous portrayal of Cardinal Gonzaga's gallery (detail below) almost every painting can be identified, but not all of them were actually owned by the cardinal. (3)

**The academies** which were founded in most European capitals during the 18th century included schools as well as facilities for exhibiting. A class at the Madrid Academy is shown above. It was institutions such as this which eventually superseded teaching by individual masters, and so substituted academic for studio training. (4)

**The Medici collection,** begun in the 15th century, was the choicest and most famous in Europe. It had long been semi-public and was visited by all connoisseurs on the Grand Tour. During the 18th century the most admired items were kept in the Tribuna of the Uffizi, where they are depicted here by Zoffany. In the centre of the room stand various pieces of classical sculpture, together with the Etruscan *Chimaera* and Titian's *Venus of Urbino*. On the walls are works by Raphael, Annibale Caracci, Rubens, Van Dyck and others. (5)

**Connoisseurs gather** in the library of the English collector Charles Towneley (right). This painting neatly illustrates the change in taste that took place in the latter half of the century. The emphasis is now all on classical sculpture, of which Towneley had one of the best private collections in the world. After his death in 1805 it was purchased by the British Museum. (6)

**All that Baroque painting had learnt** was displayed with apparently effortless accomplishment by Luca Giordano. Born in Naples, he knew Flemish, German and Spanish art as well as Italian. For the ceiling of the Capella del Tesoro in the Certosa at Naples in 1704, he painted the *Triumph of Judith* (above). Judith stands with the head of Holofernes in her outstretched hand. On all sides the Israelites, aided by angels seen in dramatic airborne foreshortening, struggle with their enemies in fierce battle. (7)

**Total drama,** the ambition of the Italian Baroque, was fulfilled most completely in southern Germany by artists like the Asam brothers. The altar of their church at Weltenburg has been illustrated in Chapter II (p. 60). Above it is a complicated dome (right) lit by concealed windows, the lower part stuccoed, the upper painted. The illusion is of another dome, supported on a ring of columns, ending in the centre in a yet higher cupola. In the pictorial space thus created St George is received into heaven amid rejoicing angels, patriarchs and saints. (8)

**In their setting** Baroque paintings gain a new dimension, surrounding and involving the spectator. Above: two Austrian dome-paintings – *the Glorification of the Trinity* at Dreieichen, of 1752, by Troger and Rottmayr's *S. Carlo Borromeo interceding* in the Karlskirche at Vienna, 1727–30. (9, 10)

**The miraculous,** the supernatural, the ecstatic – these were always the effects which Baroque ceiling painters could achieve most dramatically. Above: a detail from Maulpertsch's *Baptism of Christ* at the Old University, Vienna. (11)

**When Tiepolo came to Germany** in 1750, he found for the first time architecture wholly in tune with his own genius as a decorator. His first commission was to paint Neumann's Kaisersaal (right). Its subject is a light-hearted mixture of Greek mythology and the history of Franconia; the central part shows the arrival of the Emperor Barbarossa's bride in Apollo's chariot. (12)

224

**Painters and architects** were used to working closely together, and when both were men of genius the result was something greater than either could have imagined alone. This remains true even when they were separated in time, as Neumann and Tiepolo were at Würzburg. In Vienna the Hofbibliothek (Royal Library) designed by Fischer von Erlach in 1722, was decorated by Daniel Gran between 1726 and 1730. Its main room with bookshelves rising to a domed ceiling, is seen below. The ceiling fresco (right) is treated as a continuation of the architecture, a painted gallery with spectators weaving its way round the windows above the real galleries. The subject of the exuberant central composition is the *Apotheosis of the Emperor Charles VI and the Humanities*. (13, 14)

**The end of Baroque painting** came when Neo-classical taste, led by Winckelmann, demanded a return to sobriety and high moral purpose. One of the key figures in this change was Winckelmann's friend Anton Raphael Mengs, a German painter who spent most of his life in Italy. His *Parnassus* (right), painted for the Villa Albani in 1761, renounces both Baroque energy and Baroque freedom to overflow the frame. Painting and architecture are segregated once more, essential perhaps for the monumentality, dignity and truth which was to characterize the new age. (15)

**Venice preserved** the feeling for colour and light that had characterized its golden age during the High Renaissance, and the fact that it was politically in decline only gave it an added nostalgic charm. By the beginning of the 18th century Venice was already living on its past, both economically and culturally. It had become a show-place and a pleasure-city, and Venetian art, losing its earlier gravity, began deliberately to exploit that vein of make-believe which lay at the heart of Rococo. Opera flourished with the most elaborate scenery in Europe; Tiepolo and his studio transformed palaces and churches into visions of delight, asking only the same 'willing suspension of disbelief' as did the composers; while the unique city itself was displayed like a vast stage-set where visitors could lose themselves in a world of exotic imagination.

Venetian painters had been attached to their native place at least since the days of Jacopo Bellini, and no city is so well recorded in art. But the purely topographical picture, the *veduta* as a genre, seems to have begun only about 1700. These works were chiefly for export; they were sold to rich travellers who wanted souvenirs of their visit. Luca Carlevaris' painting of the *Arrival of the Duke of Manchester* (right) is an early example. The familiar scene is set, to remain unchanged until today – the Ducal Palace on the right, Sansovino's Library in the centre, with the two columns of S. Teodoro and the Lion; the Salute in the distance and Palladio's Redentore away on the far left.

The most famous of these topographical painters was Canaletto, who owed his immense popularity to his combination of accuracy, brilliance and industry. Many hundreds of his works gave the aristocracy of Europe, and especially of England, an enduring image of Venice at its most attractive. The view (below) of the Salute across the Grand Canal is typical.

Francesco Guardi was a subtler and more imaginative painter, and perhaps for that reason failed to match Canaletto's professional success. Below right: a seascape of the inner lagoon, the *Torre di Mestre*. In these extraordinarily atmospheric paintings, Guardi seems to be on the threshold of Impressionism. (16, 17, 18)

**Venice conquered Europe** through her art. Tiepolo's stay in Germany has already been noted. Canaletto went to England and showed Londoners Wren's splendid new city more clearly than they could see it for themselves. Sebastiano Ricci, part of the same tradition, had earlier been invited to Vienna and to London. Here he failed to get the commission to paint the dome of St Paul's, but he stayed for five years and contributed a *Resurrection* (right) to the chapel of Wren's Chelsea Hospital. Another such visitor was Gian Antonio Pellegrini, who worked in France and Germany and was brought to England by the Earl of Manchester in 1708 to decorate the interior of his house, Kimbolton Castle, Huntingdonshire, newly built for him by Vanbrugh. This detail of musicians (below) is from the grand staircase, completed in 1719. (19, 20)

**The master** of Rococo bravura, and the acknowledged leader of large scale decorative painting, was Tiepolo. His panel pictures are few. What he preferred was the spatial, illusionistic effects that integration with the architectural setting could give. His works at Würzburg are the most complex, but Venice and the neighbouring towns and villas abound in equally splendid examples. The decoration of the Palazzo Labia (right) dates from before his German visit. As always, the figures are life-size, the architecture of the painting merges with the architecture of the actual room and the dramatis personae, no matter what their historical period, are dressed in the opulent fashions of the 16th century. This scene shows Cleopatra dropping a pearl into her wine during a banquet with Antony. (21)

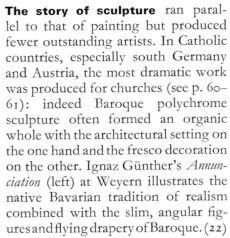

The story of sculpture ran parallel to that of painting but produced fewer outstanding artists. In Catholic countries, especially south Germany and Austria, the most dramatic work was produced for churches (see p. 60–61): indeed Baroque polychrome sculpture often formed an organic whole with the architectural setting on the one hand and the fresco decoration on the other. Ignaz Günther's *Annunciation* (left) at Weyern illustrates the native Bavarian tradition of realism combined with the slim, angular figures and flying drapery of Baroque. (22)

One of the images of power was the equestrian statue of king or emperor, the horse rearing up proudly and the whole group supported (with considerable technical expertise) on the two hind legs. *Peter the Great*, 'the Bronze Horseman', at St Petersburg (right) by the French sculptor Falconet is the most dramatic of all. (23)

The drama of death fascinated Baroque sculptors and often brought their work close in feeling to the later Middle Ages. Above: *Death* in the Library of the Abbey of Admont, in Austria. Right: the Nightingale Tomb in Westminster Abbey by Roubiliac. (24, 25)

The Neo-classical revolution is perfectly illustrated by the work of its greatest exponent, Antonio Canova, who may in many ways be compared to Jacques-Louis David (see pl. 51–53). In 1820, at the end of his long life, he made the statue of Charles III of Naples (right) in bronze. Horse and rider have both frozen into an attitude of implacable dignity. (26)

Garden and fountain gave scope for imaginative compositions that equalled stage-sets in ingenuity. Top left: *Pegasus* by Ferdinand Dietz at Veitshöchheim; the lower slopes of the island represent Parnassus. Left: a single figure *(Providence)* from Donner's dismantled fountain in the Mehl- markt, Vienna; the material is lead. Right: a group of statuary in the grounds of the palace at Caserta, by several artists. Actaeon, transformed into a stag, is torn to pieces by dogs, amid the rocks and rushing waters of a vast cascade. On the other side are Diana and her nymphs. (27, 28, 29)

A vein of lyric poetry runs through 18th-century art – suspended, as it were, between Rococo frivolity and Neo-classical earnestness. Its supreme exponent was Watteau, a native of Flanders who came to Paris in 1702 and created a style that was personal in feeling, revolutionary in technique and yet strangely in tune with the spirit of the age. He is often compared to Mozart, for his combination of profundity with artifice, and the quiet melancholy that seems to suffuse his scenes of happiness. Like Mozart too he constantly repeats the same simple motifs, using formal elements – nature, music, masquerade – to suggest infinities of meaning. His *Embarkation from the Island of Cythera* (above) is something like an allegory of love. Venus' shrine is on the right. The four main couples (the first two totally absorbed, the third preparing to leave, the fourth looking longingly back) are making their way to the boat, waiting inevitably to take them away, back to the ordinary world. The sad pierrot figure of *Gilles* (right) brings out another side of Watteau's nature – his insight into the psychology of isolation. Gilles, like his creator, stands aside from the boisterous scene around him. Silent, serious, lonely, he is an actor who has stopped playing a part, invested with a strange dignity at odds with his grotesque appearance. (30, 35)

Watteau had no heirs and few later artists can have understood him fully. One of these, however, was Gainsborough, whose so-called 'fancy-pictures' are conscious echoes of Watteau's *fêtes galantes*. Even his large-scale professional works show Watteau's influence. In the *Morning Walk*, thoroughly English as it is, the feeling for atmosphere, the use of natural landscape as the expression of mood, and the subtlety of the painting of costume are all close to Watteau. (31)

**Watteau's imitators** could take up the themes that he had invented, but could not give them their master's poetry. In the hands of Lancret and Pater the conversation-piece tended to become merely charming, the *fête galante* merely pretty. Both, however, were painters of high quality with distinct artistic personalities. Left: Lancret's *Youth* — springtime untouched by any thought of winter. Right: *Fête Galante* by Pater, a very close imitation of Watteau, down to the water-nymph reclining in the background. (33, 34)

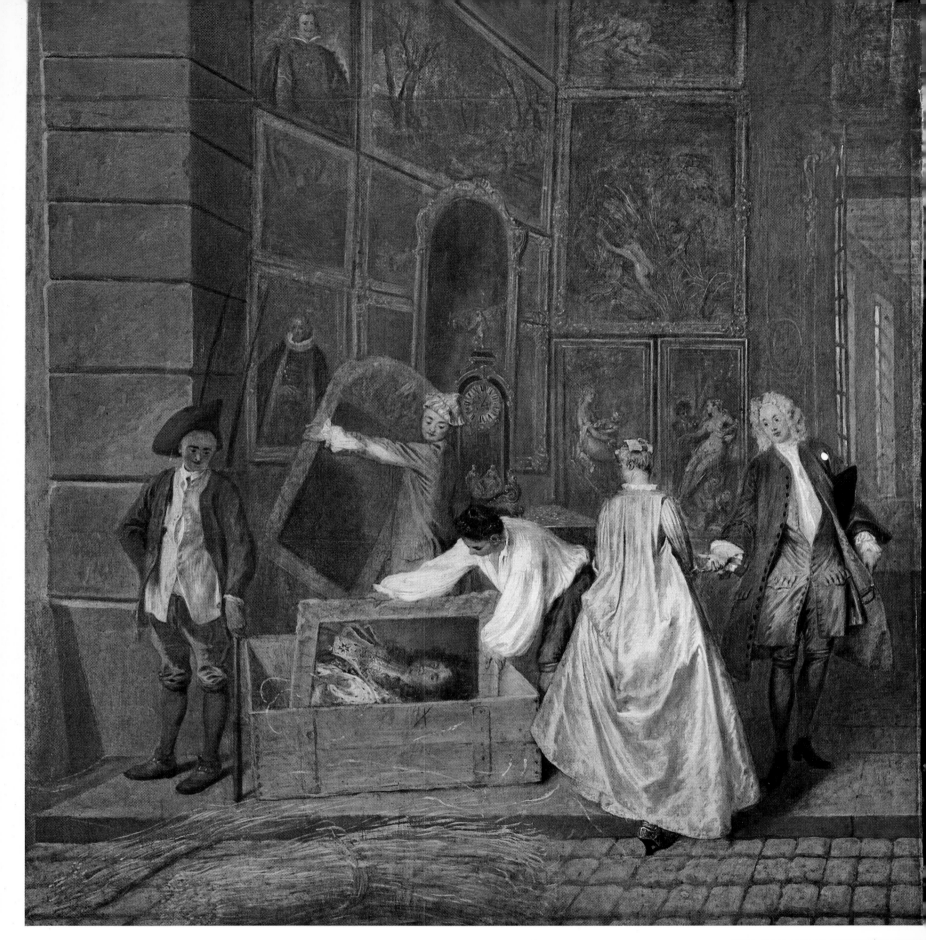

**In the last year of his life** Watteau painted for his friend the art dealer Gersaint a work which is as much of an enigma as any of the others. Ostensibly, it shows Gersaint's shop, full of assistants and customers. But our knowledge of Watteau's other works inevitably prompts further questions. The very pictures on the walls surround the figures with seductive images. The couple in the foreground seem to be more than casual acquaintances; they stand isolated and self-absorbed, as so many couples in Watteau do, like an unanswered question. The man and woman to their right (older than the others, we feel, although their backs are turned) are gazing with wrapt longing at a picture suggesting the pleasures of love. And the group on the right by the counter: is it perhaps a mirror that the girl holds, in which the woman sadly sees her own face? And are the men looking at it or at the girl holding it? (32)

**The world of fashion** found its perfect apologist in François Boucher. His *Modiste* (right) is more than an observation of aristocratic life; it conveys clearly in its caressing textures and warm colours the pleasures which made that life irresistible. An elegant lady has just had her hair done and is trying to decide what ribbon to wear. Boucher's values were those of his sitters, and neither he nor they wished to look deeper. (36)

**Boucher's eroticism** is more substantial than Tiepolo's and has none of the wistfulness of Watteau's. It consists simply in the frank enjoyment of the senses and avoids pornography by its very frankness. The *Girl on a Couch* (left) is Louise O'Murphy, an Irish girl who was for some years the mistress (though not *en titre*) of Louis XV. She had several children by him but lost his favour by asking innocently one day: 'What terms are you on now with the old lady?' meaning Madame de Pompadour. (37)

**On a humbler social level** Chardin too was painting scenes closely observed from real life, but his concern is more thoughtful than Boucher's and shows itself not only in his choice of subject matter but in the very quality of his paint. He was fascinated by 'the light of common day', by everyday objects in themselves and the way they were used. His *Toilette du Matin* may be contrasted with the Boucher opposite. It is in keeping with Chardin's sympathies that his characters should be plain, serious and middle class. (38)

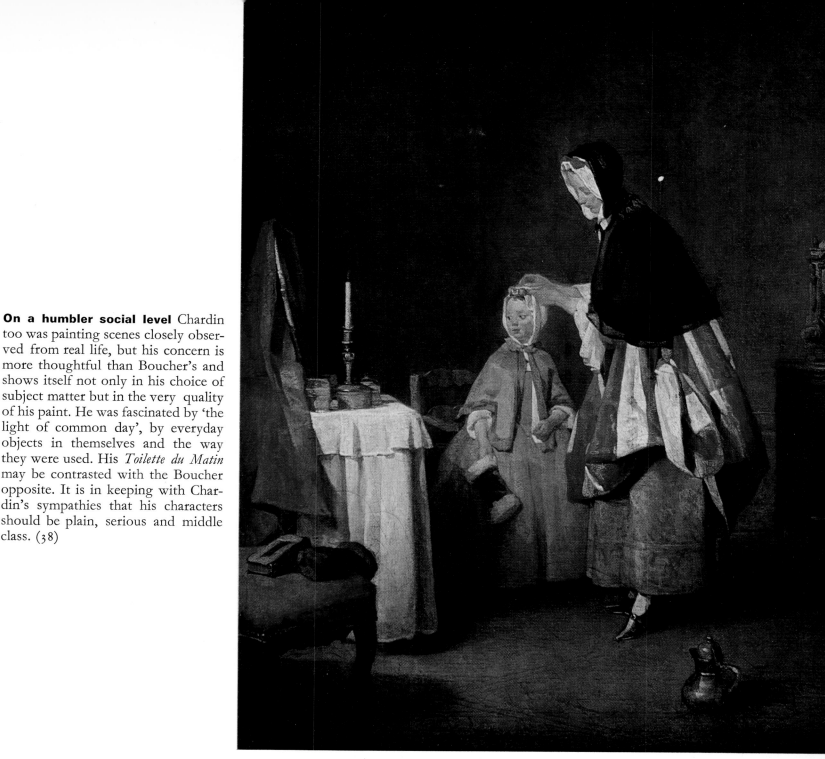

**Those who followed Boucher** could only develop still further the sensuousness and eroticism that he had exploited so successfully. Jean-Honoré Fragonard had a lighter touch than Boucher; his play of light is more subtle, and in such paintings as *Bathers* (left) he even has something of Tiepolo's vibrant energy. But he lived too long. Wedded to the frivolous, the Rococo and the aristocratic, he could not survive the twin blows of Neo-classicism and the Revolution, and he died in 1806 outmoded and barely tolerated. (39)

**'Modern moral subjects'** which would 'entertain and improve the mind' made up Hogarth's artistic programme. In series such as the *Harlot's Progress* (above), he spells out the moral as explicitly as Diderot could have wished. The six original oil paintings have been destroyed but the engravings survive. Four are shown here: the country-girl is welcomed to London by a bawd; she entertains her Jewish protector while a lover escapes behind; arrested for being a prostitute, she is imprisoned in Bridewell and made to beat hemp; and finally dies and is buried with rowdy funeral celebrations. (40–43)

**'The Quack'** by Pietro Longhi may be taken to represent the Italian version of a 'modern moral subject'. The quack-doctor selling his cure-alls to a credulous public is portrayed with (for a Venetian) unusual matter-of-factness, but without the bite of a Hogarth. (44)

**Sentimentality** was the inevitable outcome of the confusion between art and anecdote. Greuze fulfilled Diderot's requirements: simple people in affecting scenes, registering appropriate emotions. His *Accordée de Village* (right) of 1761, a rustic betrothal, has all his merits and defects. (45)

**The mirror of art** could now reflect every detail of the real world. Subjects which had been ignored by previous painters, or which had figured only incidentally as parts of larger works, were now being enjoyed for their own sakes. This new type of picture, the 'still-life', had begun in Holland in the 17th century, but was given its widest range by French artists of the 18th. Jean-Baptiste Oudry, who died in 1755, attained an almost miraculous *trompe-l'oeil* realism in his paintings of dead animals and birds (left). Such a technique, with its precise observation and meticulous fidelity to appearances, can no doubt be connected with growing scientific interests, but in fact it is aesthetic considerations – balanced composition and subtle colour harmonies – that are usually uppermost. In this painting the shadow of the glass on the white wall is a typical Oudry tour-de-force. (46)

**Chardin's vision** went deeper. His genre scenes avoid explicit anecdote; they are neither satirical, like Hogarth's, nor sentimental, like Greuze's. Yet he manages to express a very definite moral meaning: a sense of dignity, of human worth, of the values of ordinary life. Right: *Saying Grace*, one of two Chardins owned by Louis XV. (48)

**'It is Nature iself'** exclaimed Diderot in front of a Chardin still-life. No paintings are more difficult to define than these. *Pipe and Jug* (below) is characteristic: its power comes partly through the texture of the paint, which conveys the texture of reality not with photographic exactitude but with a sort of intuitive *rapport* unequalled until Cézanne; and partly from his feeling for the whole context of the objects represented, which seem to be part of an ordered world, known, used and cared for by human beings. Where the components of an Oudry have obviously been carefully chosen and placed in position, those of a Chardin seem to be where they belong. (47)

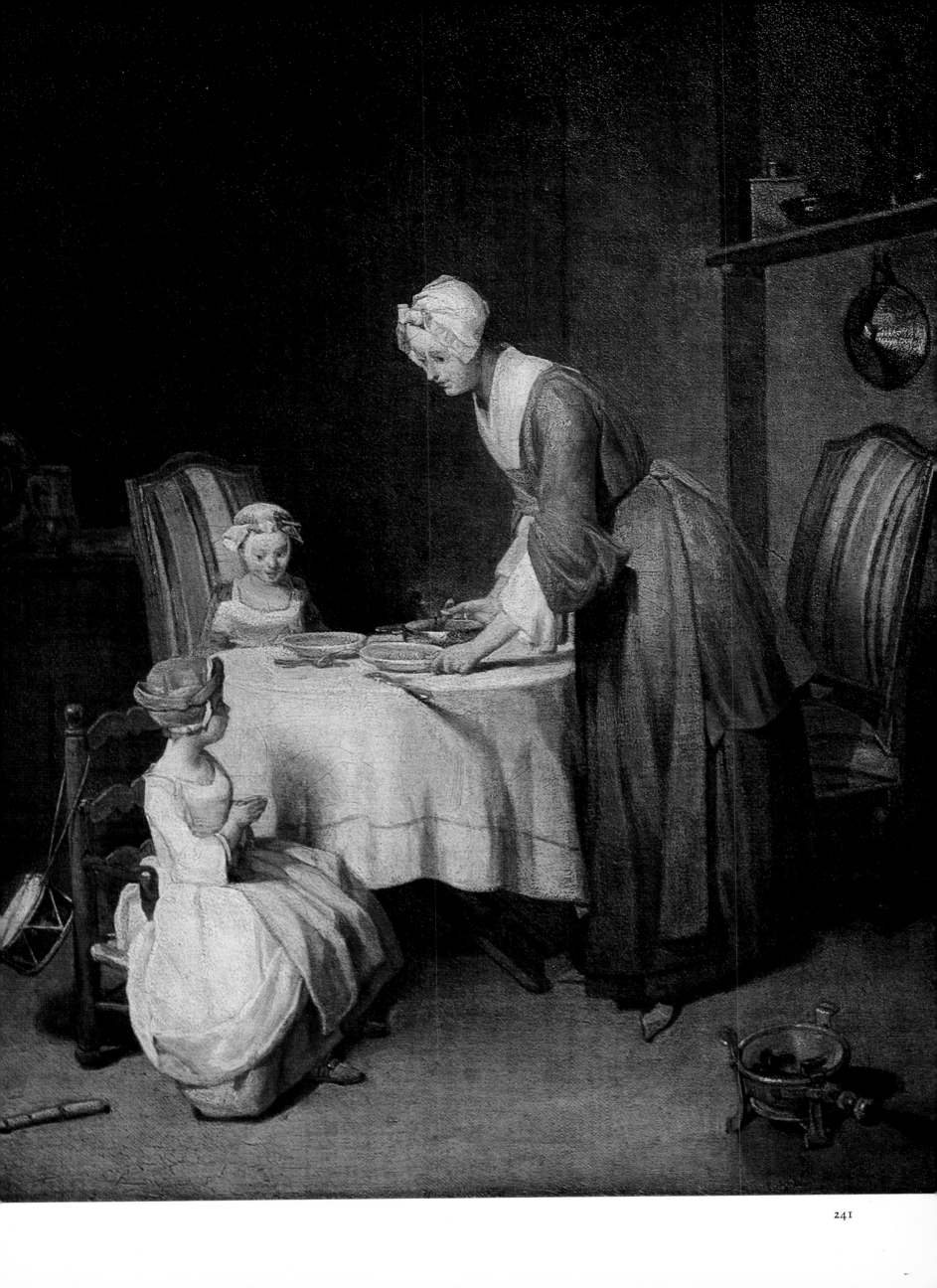

**Heroic virtue** expressed in 'Roman style' was what Diderot ideally wanted, and as the temper of the century became graver, this was increasingly what was achieved. The subjects are no longer mythological but historical, and with an urgent reality. Classical history offered most scope for examples of stoicism, fortitude and courage, but beginning with Benjamin West's *Death of Wolfe* (above) in 1771, more recent events could be made to convey the same message. Right: Gavin Hamilton's *Achilles mourning over Patroclus* of 1763. Hamilton and West, together with Anton Raphael Mengs (pl. 15) succeeded in making Neoclassicism the accepted style for serious works after about 1765. (49, 50)

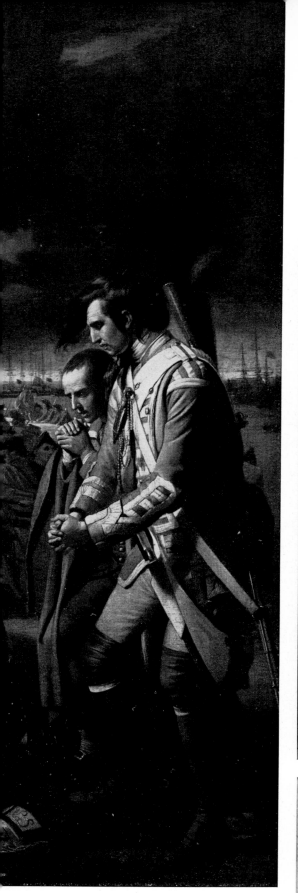

**'It was alongside heroic deeds'** that the arts flourished in Antiquity', said the greatest of the Neo-classical painters, Jacques-Louis David. The feeling that life and art should go together, that the way to restore great art was to revolutionize society, had been implicit in the aesthetic theories of the *philosophes*. David's work is its living demonstration. His pre-1789 pictures take up the task of West and Hamilton, of extolling civic virtue and self-sacrifice. The *Oath of the Horatii* (below) was painted in 1785. The three brothers swear on their swords 'to win or die for liberty', a tale of fanatical patriotism. (51)

**The Bastille fell** on July 14th, 1789. A few weeks later David exhibited his *Lictors bringing Brutus the bodies of his sons* (right). Politics had caught up with art. The story in Livy is of Brutus the Consul who, with inflexible justice, condemned his own sons to death for fighting against Rome. Brutus, silent in the shadows before a statue of Roma, contrasts with the brightly lit group of anguished mother and daughters. The political implications of these works, with their settings of cold, archaeological accuracy, were more apparent later than at the time they were painted. (52)

# The Role of the Artist in Society

L. D. ETTLINGER

To THE ART HISTORIAN centuries rarely are neat and tidy units, which can be filed away under one simple heading. This is particularly true of the 18th century. The first half, even if we call it Rococo, is a continuation of the Baroque; the second—if we must use labels—saw the birth of Neo-classicism and Romanticism, two closely linked movements.

## The two faces of 18th-century art

Until about 1750 the arts stood in the service of architecture. Painters and sculptors did their most spectacular work in the decoration of churches and palaces. Their chief patrons were the Church, kings, princes and nobles. Elaborately frescoed ceilings, large altarpieces, figures in marble, bronze or wood—often polychrome—glorified God and were meant to give visual expression to the eternal truths of Christianity. This festive religious art had its exact counterpart in a secular art which gave grace and splendour to palaces and stately homes, often celebrating the apotheosis of the ruler and his house. The inspiration for this art, both religious and secular, came from Italy, and its best practitioners, with few exceptions, were Italians.

After the middle of the century both architecture and Italy lost their leading position. In different ways and different fields France, Germany and Britain came to the fore. But the shift in emphasis was not only geographical. Boisterous and exuberant Baroque made way for a more austere kind of art, which became subject to moral and aesthetic theories to a degree it had been hardly ever before. Diderot, Winckelmann and Reynolds have no counterparts during the early decades of the 18th century, for their artistic theories are part only of a much wider complex of an essentially moral philosophy. Moreover their outlook, without in the least being anti-religious, was purely secular, informed by the Enlightenment, to which Diderot himself in particular contributed materially.

---

◀ **Marat assassinated:** When the Revolution came David had no need to look to ancient Rome for his heroes, though he continues to portray them with classic dignity and restraint. Marat, one of the Revolutionary leaders, was murdered on July 13th, 1793, by a young girl from the provinces, Charlotte Corday, who believed him an unscrupulous tyrant. She gained admission to his room (where he worked sitting in a bath of warm water to relieve a painful skin disease) by pretending to bring news from Normandy and then stabbed him with a dinner-knife. David, who knew and admired Marat and had visited him a few days earlier, spares none of the realistic details – the knife, the bloodstained bath water, the letter from Charlotte Corday. At the same time the scene has a static Roman *gravitas* like a tomb monument, an effect enhanced by the inscription on the table in the foreground. This is David's greatest work, and certainly the strength and sincerity of its political involvement are among the secrets of its tragic power. It seems to symbolize the ordeal of the 18th century itself, passing from ardour and idealism to violence and disillusion. (53)

These wider implications need stressing lest we think of change only in formal terms. The obvious differences between, say, Tiepolo and Mengs or Boucher and Greuze are not just the result of a swing of the pendulum of fashion in art. The distaste for everything Baroque or Rococo, generally felt by about 1760, was by no means only due to satiety, to a surfeit of rich colours and ample forms. The critics, while deriding the forms of Rococo, never tired of pointing out the utter immorality of treating art as nothing more than a plaything for the senses.

But changes in outlook must be seen in conjunction with changes in patronage, which in their turn imply changes in the function of art. In the late 1720s Daniel Gran decorated the dome of the Hofbibliothek in Vienna (now Nationalbibliothek), built by Fischer von Erlach for Charles VI. These illusionistic paintings, in the Baroque manner, show the apotheosis of the Emperor, allegories of his rule, personifications of the arts he had fostered. By the time Anton Raphael Mengs thirty years later painted the ceiling of the *salone* in the Villa Albani (Rome), public art had become private. For his patron, a cardinal who used the Villa to house his fine collection of antiques, Mengs furnished a general allegory of the arts—the *Parnassus*—and he eschewed illusionism. But the change could be even more drastic. Canvasses, usually of moderate size, take the place of huge frescoes as the private wishes of humbler patrons replace large scale commissions. Small easel pictures, painted for their own sake, are seen instead of elaborate decorations once modest houses rather than stately mansions offer artists their tasks.

p 225 (13, 14)

p 225 (15)

Another preoccupation of late 18th-century art also makes for a significant difference: the concern with moral education. The Marquise du Châtelet, who died in 1749, is credited with saying: 'We have nothing else to do in this world but seek pleasant sensations and feelings.' Such a sentiment well characterizes the attitude of the first half of the century. No one would have dared to utter these sentences a generation later. English writers, almost invariably puritan in their views about art, had in fact protested a good deal earlier about such flippancy, when Shaftesbury insisted that 'the knowledge and practice of the social virtues, the familiarity and fervour of the moral graces are essential to the character of a deserving artist and just favourite of the Muses'. Sir Joshua Reynolds, in the third *Discourse*, delivered in 1770, referred to the course of a young artist's training and added: 'The wish of the genuine painter must be more extensive: instead of endeavouring to amuse mankind with the minute neatness of his imitations, he must endeavour to improve them by the grandeur of his ideas . . .'. In France Diderot demanded: '*Rendre la vertu aimable, le vice odieux, le ridicule saillant, voilà le projet de tout honnête homme qui prend la plume, le pinceau ou le ciseau.*' (To show virtue as pleasing, vice as odious, to expose what is ridiculous, that is the aim of every honest man who takes up the pen, the brush or the chisel.) But these ideas were given their most profound formulation only during the last decade of the century, when the German poet Friedrich Schiller published his *Letters on Aesthetic Education*. By writing 'There is no other way of making a reasonable being out of sensuous man than by making him aesthetic first', he was not advocating some hazy 'education through art'. Schiller knew that art, unlike reason, does not uncover any truth which can fit man to perform his tasks

245

better, but he maintained that an aesthetic education can give him a development of personality, which in turn may allow him to make better use of all his faculties. He accords to art in the last resort both a moral and social function, but these come into being only indirectly.

## Italy: from Baroque to Rococo

When a notable English collector, Lord Exeter, visited Italy during the 1680s, buying paintings wherever he went, he ordered in Florence no less than fifteen from Luca Giordano (1632–1705). As the pictures from many hands still at Burghley show, Lord Exeter may not have been the most discerning of connoisseurs, but his predilection for this Neapolitan master—at the time engaged on his frescoes in the Palazzo Medici-Riccardi—shows clearly that he was aware of the supreme international standing of an artist, whose somewhat later ceiling of the Sacristy of the Certosa near Naples (1704) has been called 'a model for the decorative undertakings of the 18th century in Northern Europe'. This widely felt impact is hardly surprising for Luca brought several advantages to the tasks awaiting the prominent painter of stylish decorations. He was a prolific and fast worker—his nickname, not without good reasons, was *Luca fa presto*—and his manner derives from the great Venetians, particularly from Veronese, as much as from the outstanding master of Baroque splendour, Pietro da Cortona. Yet his art lacks depth and sharp characterization. It is ideally suited to entertain, since his brilliance is purely technical. Mr Michael Levey has recently summarized Giordano's achievement in a way which explains well his enormous influence over the early 18th century: 'He took the Baroque and painlessly squeezed profundity out of it, twisting the style to make effects by economical means, astonishing and delighting but never imposing, and himself always producing a *virtuoso* solution. Part of his success undoubtedly lay in the fact that he was moving in the direction that taste was already going . . . His paintings express a wish above all to please—whatever their

p 222
(7)

destination.' As so often in the history of art, it was an efficient but minor master who was best suited to hand on the vocabulary of a style.

Giordano worked in many Italian towns and spent ten years in Spain. But his influence spread farther. The Austrian architect Fischer von Erlach was deeply impressed by his work and the apparently transparent ceiling paintings, which Fischer regarded as an integral part of his buildings—take for example the Hofbibliothek in Vienna, already mentioned—owe their very existence to this source of inspiration. To give another example: an Austrian painter falling most strongly under the spell of Giordano was Paul Troger (1698–1762). As a young man he spent several years in Italy, staying in Venice, Rome and Bologna. Soon after his return to Austria he settled in Vienna, where he was particularly influential when, after 1754, he headed the Academy.

p 224
(9)

It should be noted that Giordano fascinated patrons and artists in northern Europe long after his death; in fact it can be said that there was a time lag of considerable length before the full effects of Italian Baroque were felt. The reasons for this are to be found in the unhappy political history of the 17th century. The Empire, cleft by the religious differences of its Catholic and Protestant members, was embroiled in the Thirty Years' War with its aftermath of poverty, misery and foreign invasions. The Peace of Münster (1648) was not followed by a period of quiet and prosperity since the Turks threatened central Europe before they were driven back through the relief of Vienna (1683). Louis XIV's expansionism added further to the general insecurity. But a number of events helped to create greater security for the 18th century and with it a climate more propitious for the arts. The Peace of Ryswyck (1697) curbed the ambitions of France and the final defeat of the Turks by Prince Eugene of Savoy (1717) finished a nightmare which had lasted for decades.

The gay exuberance of German and Austrian Baroque certainly owes a great deal to the feeling of relief which was felt everywhere.

*The Palazzo Labia, in Venice, an etching from Luca Carlevaris' collection of Venetian views published in 1703. Carlevaris also did large-scale paintings (see pl. 16) that anticipate Canaletto, but his graphic work, bought in quantity by foreign visitors, gave him, and 18th-century Venice, a far wider popularity. It was in the Palazzo Labia, some forty years later, that Tiepolo painted the famous frescoes illustrated in pl. 21. (1)*

Above all others, Venetian painters became leading and influential exponents of that late version of the Baroque which somewhat loosely has been called Rococo.

Strangely enough, during the first half of the 18th century Venice rose to artistic pre-eminence while the political and economic power of the Republic declined. In 1686 Morosini had still been feasted as the conqueror of Greece, but thirty years later Venice lost again all her Greek possessions, and with them vanished her political role in European affairs. Only the inherited great wealth of the State and its leading families postponed the economic collapse until almost the end of the 18th century, when Napoleon gave the Republic the *coup de grâce*.

Yet the arts, painting particularly, thrived, and two factors were responsible for the extraordinary enthusiasm for Venetian art. The town with its many churches, palaces and collections—to say nothing of its nostalgic charm as a city—attracted visitors. Professor Haskell, in his book, *Patrons and Painters* (1963), has said in this respect: 'The city was one of the greatest cosmopolitan centres of Europe, an acknowledged resort of international tourism which the government did everything possible to promote.' In fact, the demand of English tourists in particular, who wished to take home souvenirs, was responsible for the birth of a new genre in painting: the town view. With the possible exception of Rome (where in any case the classical ruins were the chief topic of the view painters and draughtsmen) no other town has been so frequently painted as Venice during the 18th century. Luca Carlevaris (1663–1730) began a fashion whose most celebrated contributor became Antonio Canaletto (1697–1768). It is significant that Carlevaris not only painted *vedute* but that he also etched them for cheaper and wider distribution, and published them in book form (1703). Canaletto, some forty years later, followed this precedent, though his many painted views are his chief claim to fame. He was particularly popular with English tourists and as early as 1730 Joseph Smith—who was the leading figure among the foreign connoisseurs and later became British Consul in Venice—had arranged to buy up Canaletto's choice pictures. The *camera obscura*, which Canaletto frequently used, not only guaranteed him strict topographic accuracy but also speedy working—surely an important consideration in view of his vast output. That buyers required exactness from their view painters is clear from the at first baffling fact, that Canaletto's objective descriptions of Venice were preferred to the much more imaginative evocations of the town and its surroundings by Francesco Guardi (1712–1793), whose popularity is only of comparatively recent date.

But the tourists did not come only in order to admire the charm of fading Venice and muse over its past glories. There were many

p 226
(16)
f 1

p 226
(17)

p 227
(18)

contemporary painters who proved popular. Sebastiano Ricci (1655–1734), his nephew Marco (1676–1730), Gian Antonio Pellegrini (1675–1741), Giovanni Battista Piazetta (1683–1754), and most of all Giambattista Tiepolo (1696–1770) added lustre to a tradition which proudly harked back to the great days of the 16th century and their supreme decorator, Veronese. Besides all these there were many lesser but highly successful painters. Characteristically many of them had their start in their native town only to become 'cultural exports', thanks to the prestige of everything Venetian.

Sebastiano Ricci's life is a typical case history. He was familiar with the whole of Italian tradition, having learned his trade in Venice, Bologna, Parma and Rome, yet Veronese and Luca Giordano were really his guiding lights. *The Virgin enthroned with Saints* (Venice, S. Giorgio Maggiore, 1708) is perhaps best described as 'a Veronese' seen through 18th-century eyes and treated in an 18th-century technique. There are other examples of his work, showing that he must also have tried to outdo the airy illusionism of Giordano. Technical brilliance and the obvious ability to give pleasure through painting made Sebastiano enormously popular. He was invited to Vienna, where he worked in the Schönbrunn Palace and painted an altarpiece for the Karlskirche, where Johann Michael Rottmayr (1654–1730)—who had been in Venice as a young man—had already painted the dome with the *Glorification of San Carlo Borromeo* and another altarpiece had been done by Daniel Gran. These are excellent companions. In England Sebastiano Ricci failed to get a commission to paint the dome of St Paul's, and his main work remains the fresco of the *Resurrection* in the apse of Chelsea Hospital chapel. With its airy lightness and Rococo sense of movement the fresco adds grace to a more sombre and classical building.

p 224
(10)

p 228
(19)

Pellegrini was another of the itinerant Venetians who helped to spread the fashion for brilliant and colourful decorative painting. He took this style to France, when in 1719 he painted an allegorical ceiling for the Banque de France in Paris. Earlier Vanbrugh had brought him to England and set him to work at Kimbolton and Castle Howard. Of his *virtuoso* style Vertue remarked that 'he painted prodigious quick'. Finally Pellegrini worked also in Germany.

p 228
(20)

The genius among these talented artists, however, was beyond doubt Giambattista Tiepolo. His originality and imagination were far greater than theirs, and his treatment, even of familiar themes, was more spontaneous. In a century which saw architecture, painting and sculpture still as one, that is to say believed in their interaction under the dome of a church or in the hall of some palace, Tiepolo had a heightened sense of what one might call

f 2

'appropriateness'. His wall and ceiling frescoes fit their place as a well-cut glove fits a hand. Small wonder that he preferred grandiose decorative schemes in rich architectural settings to cabinet pictures, which he painted rarely, and probably just in order to keep up with the rising fashion for them.

A brief summary of Tiepolo's life is relevant, since the subjects he treated and the patrons for whom he worked tell their own tale about the social and intellectual setting of his art and of 18th-century taste.

The *Sacrifice of Abraham*, painted for the Ospedaletto in Venice when he was barely nineteen, made Tiepolo famous at once. But from the beginning his career had a double aspect. The old established rich Venetian families, who were his chief patrons, used his talents to the full, when they commissioned not only religious pictures but also sumptuous secular decorations for their palaces and country houses, allowing him to perfect his technique both in oil and fresco painting. The Dolphin family are a typical case in point. For Daniele he painted during the 1720s ten large canvasses with scenes from Roman history—chosen of course in such a way that they could be compared with equally glorious exploits from Venetian history—and for another member of the family, who as Patriarch of Aquileia resided in Udine like a worldly prince, he painted frescoes of Old Testament stories in the Cathedral and in the Archiepiscopal Palace (1725–28). It was incidentally while working in Udine that Tiepolo acquired that light, airy and colourful style, so eminently fitted for his tasks.

## The flowering in Germany and Spain

The Udine frescoes were Tiepolo's first major commission outside his native town, and they helped to spread his fame afar. Commissions from the Venetian nobility, from Milan, Bergamo and other places in north Italy followed in rapid succession, and in 1750 came an important invitation from abroad: the Prince-Bishop Karl Philip von Greifenklau asked him to Würzburg to decorate the Kaisersaal of the sumptuous Residenz, which Johann Balthasar Neumann had completed barely ten years earlier. Tiepolo's standing may be judged from the fact that the Prince-Bishop offered him the unheard of sum of 10,000 Rhenish florins for painting the Kaisersaal alone, and that the fresco over the great staircase—ordered on completion of the former—was paid for separately.

p 224 (12)

Tiepolo's power of imagination can be judged in Würzburg perhaps better than anywhere else. The Rococo grace of Neumann's Kaisersaal must have been as unfamiliar to the Venetian as were the subjects he was asked to paint on its vault and walls: incidents from the life of a medieval German Emperor, Frederick Barbarossa, chosen because he had celebrated his marriage in Würzburg and had endowed the Bishop with the title of Duke of Franconia. A generation or two later historical exactitude in costumes and setting might have been demanded. But in 1750 the fancy dress could still be 16th-century Venetian and on the central fresco a painter could show the *Arrival of the Emperor's Bride in Apollo's Sun-chariot*.

p 43 (1)

The fresco over the staircase presented Tiepolo with a challenge of a different kind. Only a painter deeply in sympathy with the architect's aims could have perfected Neumann's magnificent spatial planning. A central flight of stairs emerges from a comparatively low and dark hall, leading up to a half-landing, next turns through 180 degrees and returns to a brightly lit first floor by two still stately flights of steps. Tiepolo extended, as it were, the light upper hall upwards, painting against a background of sky and white billowing clouds the *Four Continents paying Homage to Karl Philip von Greifenklau*, a fantasy as meaningless and as delightful as any he was asked to paint for the houses of decaying Venetian nobles, or in the Ducal Palace where only a few years earlier he had painted an equally out-of-date fancy: *Neptune Paying Homage to Venice*.

Tiepolo's brush created a perfectly real world of unreality for the grandiose dreams of his patrons. Even before Würzburg, where he was from 1750 to 1753, he had painted the *Banquet of Cleopatra* in the *salone* of the Palazzo Labia. A rich family, notorious for its extravagance, must have been flattered by such a historical allusion. Just before he finally left Venice for Madrid in 1762 he painted the most exorbitant of these glorifications, that of the

p 229 (21)

Pisani on the ceiling of their palace at Stra. *Fama* spreads their renown through the whole world while the Virgin herself looks admiringly on the living members of the family, who are portrayed before her.

Tiepolo's genius was singularly suited to the taste of his patrons, and the continued success of his inventions must have increased the appetite for them, since they granted at least temporary release from an increasingly harsh political and economic reality. It seems that he was aware of this. Nor was he above flattering his employers, saying quite plainly: 'Painters must try and succeed in large scale works capable of pleasing the noble and the rich, because it is they who make the fortune of artists . . . Hence a painter's mind must always be aiming at the sublime, the heroic and the perfect.'

The stay in Madrid, where he spent the last eight years of his life (1762–70), was both a climax and an anti-climax to Tiepolo's long career. Charles III charged him with the decoration of the Throne Room in the Royal Palace, where he painted fittingly yet another of those illusory visions of non-existent grandeur: the *Apotheosis of Spain*. More commissions followed, but it was oddly enough in Spain that history caught up with him. His altarpieces for the chapel at Aranjuez were removed shortly after their completion, because a powerful party at Court preferred the manner of another and younger royal painter: Anton Raphael Mengs, surely an infinitely lesser artist. But to Tiepolo's misfortune Mengs—a close friend and collaborator of Winckelmann—was a vociferous exponent of the new Neo-classical and puritan creed, which condemned the alleged frivolity of all Baroque and Rococo art. It is tragic irony that at the end of his days the greatest painter of the century was not faced by a worthier opponent in this symbolic clash of styles.

The craving for a pleasant world of dreams and the love of colourful splendour are to be found all over Europe during the earlier part of the 18th century, and in this respect there is little difference between religious and secular art, at least in the Catholic countries.

The outstanding patrons in Germany were to be found among the many art loving rulers of the principalities (frequently men of limited means) and even more among the educated and wealthy princes of the Church, those prince-bishops who, through the quirks of the history of the Empire, had not only the spiritual care of their diocese but also the administration of their often considerable territories. The Schönborn family are the most noteworthy among them. Its members held at various times the bishoprics of Würzburg—where Johann Philip Franz Schönborn built Neumann's immense Residenz, called by Emperor Joseph II 'Germany's prettiest vicarage'—Bamberg, Trier, Mainz and Speyer. Another Schönborn became Imperial Chancellor. They all were men of discerning taste, whose ancestors had already been collectors of Italian Baroque art. The example they set was widely followed, by the religious orders for example, but even small village churches in Franconia, Bavaria and Austria often enough display some faint yet charming echo of greater Rococo art.

p 52 (28)

The best and still most pleasing Austrian and German painting of the period was decorative—frescoes on walls or ceilings, huge altarpieces dominating a church choir—and can hardly be considered apart from the buildings it adorns. When the Elector Lothar Franz Schönborn, Bishop of Bamberg, had a new palace built, the walls of the main salon were large and plain so as to be free for painting. Whether erecting churches or palaces, both patrons and their architects were after some resplendent *Gesamtkunstwerk*, that is a 'total' work of art in which architecture, sculpture, ornament and paintings combine to give the fullest possible effect. And in this respect the patron usually knew exactly what he wanted. Another Schönborn, Cardinal Damian Hugo, stipulated for his chapel: 'As regards colours, agreement must be reached with the painter who does the fresco, and sweet colours are always best.' The last remark is revealing; pleasure was to be given by art, even in a religious setting. Again the choice of an outstanding painter for Würzburg—Tiepolo—is typical; only a man of stature could be the equal of the architect Johann Balthasar Neumann and would be able to realize his intentions.

Tiepolo's presence in Würzburg highlights yet another facet of German 18th-century art: its Italianate orientation. This tendency can be traced back to the beginning of the century, when Leopold I summoned the past master of Baroque illusionism, Padre Pozzo, to Vienna, where he painted frescoes in the Jesuitenkirche (he himself was a lay member of that order) and the Liechtenstein Palace.

The most enchanting and perhaps most perfect of these 'total' works of art were created by two Bavarian brothers Cosmas Damian Asam (1686–1739) and Egid Quirin Asam (1692–1750), who had been trained in Rome and were thoroughly familiar with the aims and tricks of Roman High Baroque. Cosmas Damian really was a painter, Egid Quirin a sculptor, but they worked together as architects and decorators. One characteristic work of theirs is the church of the Benedictine Abbey of Weltenburg (near Ratisbon), begun in 1718 and built over an elliptical plan with shallow chapels, thereby betraying Roman influence. Cosmas Damian painted the illusionistic fresco with the story of St George under the dome, and Egid Quirin made for the high altar the equestrian statue of the Saint: riding out of a dark recess on to a brilliantly lit stage, appearing like a heavenly apparition before the congregation, since the source of the lighting is concealed. Thus light and colour are put into the service of uniting architecture, painting and sculpture. It is impossible to explain the result in rational terms, but its highly charged emotional impact is immediate.

The vibrant dynamism of this Rococo art was continued well into the second half of the century by the Austrian painter Franz Anton Maulpertsch (1724–96). Two factors made him still successful at a moment when Rococo was under attack from all quarters: the extraordinary quality of his brushwork and the fact that this painter of miracles worked in an intensely religious country. His whole work seems to be a constant protest against the rising tide of rationalism. Saints wafted aloft, angels floating through a serene sky, mysterious orientals silently watching the *Baptism of Christ* (Vienna, Old University), draperies disobeying the laws of gravity—these are the enticing means of an art which has been carried to its extreme frontiers. It never thrived in the colder climate of northern Protestantism and it could not survive in the Age of Reason.

## 'Fêtes Galantes'

French art of the 18th century is often described as if it had been in the main a sharp reaction against the regal splendours of the Baroque. Louis XIV and Louis XV, Le Vau and Gabriel, Lebrun and Watteau are contrasted. But all this is an oversimplification which distorts history. The seeds of 18th-century art and architecture were sown well before the advent of the Regency in 1715. In particular the last two decades of the *roi soleil* were very different from his earlier years, and that is true not only of politics, but also of literature and the arts.

Many factors contributed to this, and among them not the least was the ageing monarch's change of taste. The greater intimacy of Marly and Meudon—all due to remodelling at the end of the 'nineties—is in sharp contrast to the grandiloquence of the State Apartments at Versailles. It is an open question how much the restraining influence of Mme de Maintenon had to do with this greater austerity.

But personal taste apart, there was a widespread and fundamental change in outlook well before the turn of the century. The long *Querelle des Anciens et des Modernes* came to a climax with the writings of Charles Perrault, notably his *Parallèle des Anciens et des Modernes* (1688–97), in which modern authors were declared to be superior to their classical forebears. In 1700, Boileau, writing to Perrault, implicitly conceded defeat when he admitted that recent authors at their best could be equals of the ancients.

This literary quarrel had its close parallel in the contest between 'Poussenists' and 'Rubenists'. The former were the representative of a classical style in painting, the defenders of line and design, of rules and restraint in expression. The latter, led by the critic Roger de Piles, whose *Dialogue sur le Coloris* (1673) and *Abrégé de la Vie des Peintres* (1699) were the principal manifestoes of the new movement, were colourists allowing at the same time genius to make its own rules. They were prepared to give Poussin his due, but really admired Rubens and the Venetians. De Piles' advocacy paved the way for the success of Antoine Coypel, Charles de la

Fosse and, of course, Antoine Watteau, all of whom gained recognition and royal acclaim before the death of Louis XIV. Watteau, supported by de la Fosse, became an *agréé* of the Académie in 1712.

Under the Regency the new movement in art gathered momentum and circumstances favoured this development. Louis XV was in 1715 only five years old. The Regent, Philippe d'Orléans, moved the Court from Versailles to Paris, where he himself lived in the Palais-Royal. The courtiers, bankers and businessmen connected with the Court now built their houses in Paris and had them decorated in the latest fashion.

The Regent himself, though given to gross debauchery, was a man of taste and a connoisseur. During the eight years of his rule he collected a large number of well chosen paintings, mainly by Italian masters, but he did not altogether neglect the French and commissioned at least one picture from Watteau. It is significant also that he himself was an amateur artist of above average ability. Fiske Kimball, the American historian of the Rococo, well summed up Philippe d'Orléans' attitude to art, when he wrote of him: 'He exemplified the characteristic advantages of aristocracy at its best for the patronage of art: eagerness to accept the latest in creative invention, superiority to philistine and bourgeois timidity and reaction.' One might modify the last part of this assessment somewhat, remembering that in his entourage there were a number of bourgeois sharing his taste in art. But it should be noted that it was a combination of changing historical circumstances and personal predilections which brought about the birth of French 18th-century art. It can also be seen that given the different social and intellectual context, this art had to be different from that of Italy and Germany.

Charles Lebrun, Colbert's chosen tool in giving the fine arts an important place in his political-cum-cultural programme of making France great, died in 1690 after directing the affairs of French painting for some forty years from his commanding position in the *Académie*. Antoine Watteau was born in Valenciennes in 1684, became a painter in Paris, and delivered his *morceau de réception* in 1717, five years after his admission to the Academy. One may well ask what Lebrun would have thought on seeing *The Embarkation from Cythera*.

Too much has been made of Watteau's origin, although his friend Julienne called him 'Vato, peintre flamand'. His interest in (and undoubted indebtedness to) Rubens was nothing strange at the moment when he arrived in Paris; in fact, it simply made him one of the *modernes*. Rubens apart, there are no other antecedents to his art in his homeland, nor was there any contemporary in Flanders who shared his interests. Watteau's art is intensely personal—he is one of the great innovators of the early 18th century—but its formulation is French, to be precise Parisian. It is the most perfect response to the claims of taste during the declining years of Louis XIV and the Regency. As always, success in satisfying the appetite of his patrons increased the demand for more.

Soon after Watteau, then aged about eighteen, first came to Paris, he worked for a while with Claude Gillot (1673–1722), a theatre painter and designer of ornament, *l'un des plus grands artistes en ce genre*, as a contemporary critic said. Later he associated with another painter and ornamentalist, Claude Audran (1658–1734), who as Keeper of the Palais du Luxembourg could give Watteau opportunities to study Rubens' Marie de Medici cycle. The close association with the chief inventors of Rococo decoration was as decisive for his development as was acquaintance with one of Rubens' major works.

From Gillot Watteau must have taken his interest in the characters from comedy and ballet who so often appear in his later paintings. From Audran he learned the skilful intertwining of figures and ornaments to form those arabesques and decorative panels embellishing the small rooms in the houses of patrons. But the difference between Watteau and his masters is significant, for it is not a difference in manner or technique, but one of human content. The clowns and musicians of the *commedia dell' arte* become under his hands real human beings. The tragi-comic figure of a clown in his white costume—*Gilles* (Louvre)—stands gauche and almost helpless before us. A guitarist in a striped comedian's dress

p 223
(8)
p 60 (53)

p 224
(11)

*f 3*

p 235
(35)

strums his guitar with a desperate expression on his face (New York, Metropolitan Museum).

The same human quality also appears in Watteau's decorative paintings. Audran had used classical deities in his arabesques, but they lack the kind of reality Watteau imparted to them when he painted for the dining-room of his friend Crozat *Zephyr and Flora*, a pair of charming young lovers rather than remote figures from mythology. It is this quality of unabashed eroticism which gives pictures like this one their human truth. Again, when he painted a room in the house of M. de Chauvelin with a *Bacchic Feast*, the grotesques still hark back to Audran, but the central scene only Watteau himself could have painted.

Chauvelin and Crozat are typical of the patrons for whom Watteau worked. The former became Keeper of the Seals and for a time together with Cardinal Fleury was responsible for foreign policy under Louis XV. The latter was a rich financier—some of his wealth sprang from his monopoly of the trade with Louisiana —and one of the most noted collectors of his day, in whose house Watteau lived for a time. The Comte de Caylus, an outstanding connoisseur and another close friend of Watteau, wrote in his biography of the painter: 'M. Crozat, who was fond of artists, offered Watteau board and lodging at his house. The offer was accepted. This fine establishment, which at that time housed a greater number of valuable paintings and curios than perhaps any private owner had hitherto brought together, provided the artist with a thousand new incentives. Of these the most exciting to his taste was the large and admirable collection of drawings by the great masters.'

This account of the young artist as a member of the household of the rich collector is important in throwing light on Watteau's standing. The wide circle of his friends also bears witness to it. Among them were the critic and collector Mariette, the owner of the *Mercure de France,* Antoine de la Roque, the collector Jean de Julienne, who acquired many of Watteau's paintings, and the picture dealer Gersaint, for whom Watteau painted just before his death in 1721 the famous *Enseigne de Gersaint*. Thus the range of friends and patrons stretches from the Regent through the aristocracy and the government officials into the merchant class. This wide and active interest in contemporary art is characteristic of the Regency and the age of Louis XV.

p 233 (32)

When Watteau was admitted to the Academy the subject of the customary admission piece was left to himself. Such a decision would have been unthinkable in the days of Lebrun; it was to be unthinkable again after Watteau's time. But such freedom was less a personal tribute than a sign that authoritative direction of the arts was abandoned, at least for the time being. In an age which used painting not to instruct but to delight no such direction was needed. Hence the subject which Watteau finally chose—the *Embarkation from the Island of Cythera*—was acceptable, though his treatment of a mythological theme was highly unorthodox. In fact, Watteau created an entirely new genre of painting, and this was recognized when the picture was listed in the records of the Academy as: *une fête galante*.

p 232 (30)

It used to be thought that the picture represents a pilgrimage of lovers to Cythera, the island of Venus, but Mr Michael Levey has shown recently that it rather represents their departure from the island, and he has admirably summed up Watteau's theme: 'In its own way, the *Departure from Cythera* is a history picture, but a modern one. Its mythology is of Watteau's creation but it manages to tell a completely comprehensible story—unlearned yet universal —and there need be little doubt that Watteau constructed this elaborate scene because of its final destination, the Académie. By his standards, it is unusually full of narrative content. His subject is more 'natural' than visions of gods and goddesses or scenes from classical history. It is concerned not with heroism but with passion.'

All this is perfectly true, but we must be careful not to overstress the word 'natural' (wisely put in inverted commas by Mr Levey); we are not yet in the age of Rousseau. Heroism, a public virtue, had furnished the great exemplary themes of official 17th-century painting. Passion, a private emotion, can introduce a whole range of new themes into painting. But we must note that Watteau's statements about passion, so to speak, are not direct. He borrows

from the world of ballet and theatre; his lovers wear costume, some that of fashionable society, others that of the peasantry. Seriousness thus is made unserious, and the contemporary title given to the picture—*une fête galante*—makes this abundantly clear. To say that Watteau depicted all classes of society as being subject to the passion of love would be an anachronism. He never was a rebel, neither in art nor over questions of social order. Yet he knew how to use the conventions of his age in order to tell a human truth which transcends their limitations. This is the personal quality of his art and one has only to compare one of Watteau's *fêtes* with similar pictures by Pater (1695–1736) or Lancret (1690–1743) in order to become aware of this.

p 233–34 (33, 34)

If any European painter can claim to have grasped the whole range of Watteau's genius, it surely was Gainsborough (1727–88), even if we allow for his different subjects. Those of his works which Reynolds called 'fancy-pictures' are more than echoes of the *fêtes galantes*; they are transformations into another social climate. Yet the very fact that an English painter could take up this genre only as a kind of 'hobby' once he had established himself as a portrait painter, reminds us of the different demands made on French and British artists by their clients.

p 232 (31)

## 'C'est un vice si agréable'

The brothers Goncourt—to this day the most perceptive critics of French 18th-century art—accorded Boucher (1703–70) a central place. 'Boucher,' they write, opening their essay on him, 'was one of those men who indicate the taste of a century, express, personify, embody it. In him French 18th-century taste was manifest in all the peculiarity of its character. Boucher was not only its painter but its chief witness, its chief representative, its very type.'

Boucher's sensuous imagination ideally suited the court of Louis XV with its mind always upon grace and charm. To quote again the Goncourts: 'Prettiness, in the best sense of the word, is the symbol and seduction of France at this airy moment of history.' Boucher's art could never have flourished under the sterner rules of Louis XIV's reign. But it required not only a different society; it is also unthinkable without the precedent of Watteau, who had been dead for just over a decade when in 1734 Boucher was admitted to the Academy after his return from a prolonged stay in Italy.

At the height of Louis XIV's glory Colbert had determined the scope and function of the arts. In the days of Louis XV not the first Minister of State but Mme de Pompadour became the most influential arbiter of taste. This signifies not only a change from a male to a female sensibility, but also a transfer of the arts from the public to the private sphere. Boucher, her favourite painter, greatly benefited from this.

p 219 (1)

The part played by this clever and highly cultured woman should be considered for a moment. Today it is hardly necessary to stress that her personality shared nothing with the stock image of the seductive and frivolous concubine, blushingly hinted at in historical fiction. She was the King's mistress only for a brief period but remained his truest friend and confidential adviser in all affairs, political and private, for more than twenty years. She was the determined and level-headed daughter of an influential banker, and thus belonged to Parisian bourgeois society. Her house was open to all sorts of people, and among her friends were Crébillon, Montesquieu and Voltaire. Her interest in the fine arts was genuine and her exquisite taste infected the King and his circle. In this respect her influence grew strongest when in 1746 her brother, the Marquis de Marigny, became *Directeur Général des Bâtiments du Roi*, a position which gave him practically dictatorship over the arts in France. Mme de Pompadour had a hand in founding the Sèvres porcelain manufactory, she took an interest in the various royal tapestry workshops and suggested the appointment of Boucher as director of the Gobelins. She collected not only pictures and sculpture, but also examples of applied art and particularly jewellery. After her death in 1764 it took several weeks to compile an inventory of her possessions.

p 261 (1)

But Mme de Pompadour was no ordinary collector: The works of art with which she surrounded herself were quite literally the indispensable framework of her life. We ought to realize this in order to appreciate the essentially decorative nature of Boucher's art—whether destined for her, or for one of those who shared her aesthetic ideals. Boucher's paintings were rarely meant to be seen alone. Many of those today displayed on the walls of museums were only made to serve as designs for tapestries; others, once set in a wall within rich ornamented gold and stucco surrounds, formed part of the decor of elegant rooms together with *objets d'art*, mirrors, tapestries and so forth.

The nature of Boucher's art was determined by the style of a self-consciously artistic society. For example, the cartoons he made for tapestries destined to be hung in Mme de Pompadour's Château de Bellevue and depicting *Sunrise* and *Sunset* (London, Wallace Collection) are neither lyrical landscapes bathed in soft morning and evening light, nor are they traditional mythological allegories, although the sun-god Apollo is the central figure in both. Here, as elsewhere in Boucher's art, classical motifs are only a kind of dressing-up, or rather undressing, for the nude is the final object of his brush. But unlike Titian or Rubens, both artists who certainly influenced him, Boucher does not give us a new corporeal vision of the ancient gods. His effeminate Apollo is less conspicuous than the galaxy of naiads whose shimmering naked bodies are conjured up by him. A *Triumph of Venus* (Stockholm) becomes a dazzling ballet performed by beautiful nude girls.

Yet it would be wrong to talk of pornography in front of Boucher's pictures (as some 19th-century authors did). He never meant to corrupt, even when he painted with all the brilliance at his command the bewitching body of the famous *Girl on a Couch*. He frankly depicted the erotic charm of a young woman—the King's favourite at the time—whose beauty delighted everybody at Court, as Casanova tells us in his autobiography. The sensuality of this art must not be taken for decadence or immorality. It is in tune with the standards of a society which was far from condemning the pleasures of the senses.

Even so, Boucher's unabashed eroticism never becomes vulgar or coarse. He seems to conform to some stylish etiquette, some decorum which applies even in games of love. After all, his patrons were members of a sophisticated ruling class. This may help to explain the apparent paradox pervading his art. Individual figures, their appearance, expressions and gestures are carefully observed and seem quite natural. Yet settings and contexts are highly artificial and contrived; often they are reminiscent of the contemporary theatrical stage for which Boucher also did some designing. There is a quality of unreality—whether in the pseudo-mythologies, the pastorals or the few pure landscapes he painted—the conjuring up of a world not as it is, but as it might be in some golden careless dream. Boucher's universe is a figment of the imagination no less than Tiepolo's, but it is conceived within the style of that French society for which he supplied these agreeable pleasures. It was a society which increasingly came under attack for its lack of realism and deficiency in a sense of responsibility. It is therefore to be expected that those who wished for higher moral standards also in the arts would strongly object to Boucher. But even these critics could not help being beguiled by his spell. Diderot had to confess: '*c'est un vice si agréable*'.

## Art and morality

Diderot was too sensitive a critic not to appreciate the painterly qualities of Boucher, but the very fact of the seductiveness of his art made attacks on its moral emptiness all the more pressing. Some of the most trenchant passages in the *Salons*—the reviews of the official exhibitions which Diderot wrote for Grimm and a small circle of friends from 1759 onwards—were dedicated to this task. An incident from the closing years of Boucher's career can show the power of Diderot's influence, and the beginnings of a significant change in taste, which is all the more remarkable since the *Salons* had not appeared in print by then. They were published for the first time, after the Revolution, in 1798 when the morality in art demanded by Diderot had won the day.

In 1764 it was decided to redecorate the royal Château de Choisy, and Marigny in his capacity as *Directeur Général des Bâtiments du Roi* approached Charles-Nicolas Cochin, the secretary of the Académie, with a request for a suitable programme of pictures. Cochin, it should be noted, was friendly with Diderot and engraved for him a year later the celebrated titlepage of the *Encyclopédie*. It is therefore

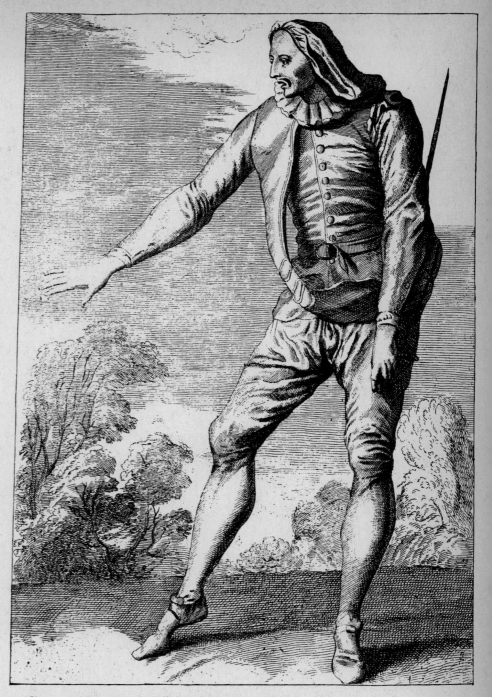

*'Scaramouche' by Claude Gillot. Gillot, a theatre painter and decorative artist, was Watteau's teacher and did much to influence his style. It must surely have been from him that Watteau acquired his interest in actors, masques, dance and make-believe.* (3)

not astonishing that he decided against the usual erotic mythologies in Boucher's manner, and suggested decorations of a kind which must have pleased Diderot: incidents from Roman history illustrating a ruler's love for peace, as for example *Augustus closing the Gates of the Temple of Janus*, *Titus freeing Prisoners taken at Jerusalem*, and so forth.

Quite apart from any didactic and moral purpose this choice must have been prompted by a deliberate return to the ideals and the practice of the 17th century, when Lebrun had treated similar subjects in praise of Louis XIV. Furthermore, in 1764 there was probably also a more immediate cause for this choice, for the recent end of the Seven Years' War would have inspired Cochin to honour the King—without much justification—as a prince of peace. Whatever the reason, the small incident is portentous, since art was linked not only to moral teaching but also to contemporary history —even if only by flattering allusion. One thing only is rather unexpected: Cochin wanted Boucher to paint one of these historical allegories, and the painter, in order not to lose favour, was prepared to undertake this uncongenial task. Ironically enough, in the end Louis XV himself rejected the series. Moral sermons, even in noble Roman disguise, were not to his taste. He wanted something more light-hearted and Cochin reported to Marigny: 'In order to replace these pictures through others I have commissioned Boucher, whose brush, guided by the Graces, seems the most suitable for the embellishment of so pleasant an abode.' But this triumph of Rococo

p 236
(37)

p 268
(22, 23)

*One of the first writers to expound the theory of art as a medium of moral improvement was Lord Shaftesbury. His 'Inquiry concerning Virtue or Merit' was translated by Diderot, with this allegorical engraving as its frontispiece. (4)*

art because it illustrated the great themes of ancient literature. Lord Shaftesbury, in whose writings the most expanded and influential account of these views is to be found, voiced the same Whig thinking when he stressed that nothing is 'so congenial to all arts . . . as that reigning liberty and high spirit of a people, which from the habit of judging in the highest matters for themselves, makes them freely judge of other subjects.' And again most succinctly: 'Thus are the Arts and Virtues mutually friends; and thus the science of *virtuosi* and that of virtue itself, becomes, in a manner, one and the same.' The pun *virtuosi*-virtue is more than an elegant rhetorical device: for Shaftesbury it enshrines a revealing truth. Somewhat naïvely he expected these lofty ideals to become political and artistic realities after the War of the Spanish Succession, when free and victorious England should be capable of becoming 'the principal seat of the arts.'

The platonic background of Shaftesbury's thought needs no stressing. More important in our context is his claim that the *virtuoso*—the knowledgeable critic of the arts—must play a decisive part in leading artists and art. Shortly before his death in 1713 he told an Italian painter how to paint his allegorical portrait as a *virtuoso*: he wished to be shown deep in thought, surrounded by examples of classical art, a copy of his own treatise *The Choice of Hercules* in his hand, for from this 'one recognizes the subject which he is at present contemplating'. The subject of Prodikos' fable, it will be remembered, had been the choice between Virtue and Pleasure. To Shaftesbury's mind both this and the classical setting of his picture were inseparable.

Diderot's debt to Shaftesbury is part only of that greater debt the French Enlightenment owes to English thought. The empirical approach of the *philosophes*, their preoccupation with ethics, the practical ends of the *Encyclopédie* (anyhow an enterprise modelled on an English prototype), they all and much else remind us of this fact. It is therefore wrong to speak of Diderot (as has been done) as if he had been nothing more than a gifted spokesman for the rising bourgeoisie. The fact that he was the son of a humble artisan has little to do with his outlook, and among his friends and collaborators on the *Encyclopédie* were members of the aristocracy as well as of his own class. We therefore should not credit him with some kind of post-Marxian class consciousness, but must try to understand the intricate social and intellectual pattern which helped his development as a writer and critic.

In the age of Louis XIV Versailles had been the virtual centre of France, in politics as well as in art. But this changed, as has been said already, with the Regency and the reign of Louis XV when Paris assumed her traditional leading role once again. For the arts this meant that the King and his Court lost their monopoly of patronage. The aristocracy, the rich middle class, the merchants and financiers, all became collectors and patrons, so that we may find one and the same painter working both for the King and perhaps one of his bankers.

The new pattern of society was also responsible for the revival of the *salons*, the regular social gatherings in some cultured private home of a group of friends, usually presided over by the lady of the house. They flourished during the 18th century more than at any other time, precisely because Versailles no longer was the sole magnet for talent and wit. While there did exist some exclusive aristocratic circles, the intellectual *salons*, such as those of Mme d'Epinay, Mme Necker (the wife of the banker) or Baron d'Holbach, cut across social distinctions and were a meeting ground for like-minded men and women of all classes. Diderot's presence in several of these *salons* is known, and his art criticism, a *correspondance littéraire* addressed to Baron Melchior Grimm, is in a manner of speaking an extension of these assemblies and a substitute for conversational exchanges of the kind we might hear in a *salon*.

Art and its criticism benefited in yet another and perhaps more lasting way from the political and social changes. In 1667 Louis XIV, at the suggestion of Colbert, ordered the *Académie Royale de Peinture et de Sculpture* to hold a public exhibition, another followed in 1673, when for the first time a *livret*—a catalogue—was published, two more were held in 1699 and 1704. They took place in the *Salon Carré* of the Louvre, whence the name *Salon*. But only after 1737 did these exhibitions become a regular event, normally taking place every second year. The date is of importance for it coincides

p 262–63
(2)

p 265
(16)

charm over the sterner virtues was no more than a temporary respite. Ten years later—and only four years after the painter's death—Louis XVI ordered the removal of Boucher's *Mars and Venus* cycle from the former home of Mme de Pompadour. The new monarch regarded these paintings as indecent. The appeal of Diderot and his associates was winning the day, even at Court.

But Diderot, certainly a brilliant propagator, was not really the begetter of this radical philosophy of art. One of his earliest publications had been a free rendering into French of Shaftesbury's *Inquiry concerning Virtue or Merit*, and it is to Shaftesbury and England in the early 18th century that we have to turn if we wish to find the roots of the ideas on art and morality, which were debated all over Europe during the second half of the century.

English writers did two important things, which however are closely related: they linked good taste and good morals; they also turned to Greece and Rome for their exemplars in art and morality. The Whig element in this becomes apparent as early as 1701 when Joseph Addison compared the ancient Romans and the modern English in their heroic defence of liberty. He also praised ancient

f 4

not only with the arrival of new and more numerous patrons of art, but also approximately with an easing of censorship which made possible the publication of the writings of Voltaire, Condillac, Montesquieu and others. As far as the arts are concerned the *Salons*, though controlled by the *Académie*, let in a wider public and broadened taste. Their significance is best characterized by a French author who wrote in 1745: '*Le public est l'arbitre souverain du mérite des talents.*' (The public is the supreme judge of talents.)

## Nature and truth

The ideology of the *philosophes*, the interests of the new Paris intelligentsia, the art exhibitions and their large public drawn from many strata of society—all these belong to the context in which we must set Diderot's art criticism. His attacks on Boucher and others were not a veiled political attack on the ruling class and its aesthetic or moral standards. '*Cet homme a tout excepté la vérité*' (This man has everything except truth), his crushing dismissal of Boucher when he became *Premier Peintre du Roi* in 1765, makes it clear that the attack was launched in the name of a higher principle. 'I do not know what to say about this man,' he writes in the same year at the beginning of his *Salon* note on the painter, 'the degradation of taste, of composition, of characters, of expressions are in keeping with the depravation of morals.' By contrast, he praises Chardin for one particular quality of his paintings: '*Le genre de la peinture de Chardin est la vérité.*' (Chardin's genre is truth.) And this is expanded when he adds in another place '*C'est la nature même; les objets sont hors de la toile et d'une vérité à tromper les yeux.*' (It is Nature itself; the objects stand out of the canvas with a truth that deceives the eye.) The repetition of the word *vérité* is the most telling part of Diderot's comments. It is a concept which has nothing to do with 'class', but rather reveals the deeper social conscience underlying his appraisal of all art. Mme du Châtelet's pleasure principle is now found wanting. Those who are in the habit of calling the new aesthetics simply '*bourgeois*' would do well to consider that they were first proposed by an English lord.

p 240 (47)

The popularity of Chardin (1699–1779) was by no means confined to the rising bourgeoisie. A few years older than Boucher he joined the Académie as a painter of genre in 1728. '*Le gros public*', as a contemporary noticed, certainly liked his meticulous renderings of daily life, but it should be emphasized that the admirers of Boucher's delicious nudes had also a taste for the harder art of Chardin. Louis XV acquired some of his pictures, and so did (among others) the Swedish collector Count Tessin.

Tessin, in fact, bought pictures from both painters which allow us a particularly interesting comparison. Chardin's *La Toilette du Matin* was painted in 1741. A young mother dresses her little daughter, before going out with her. The child, with just the slightest hint of coquetterie, is looking into a mirror. It is no more than a hint, for the tone of the picture is restrained and serious, quite in keeping with good education. Boucher's *Modiste* was painted four years later. Tessin's secretary tells us that the picture formed part of a series illustrating the *Times of Day*, this one being *Morning*: 'A lady has just had her hair done. She is still in her dressing gown and is amusing herself by looking through the trifles displayed to her by a milliner.'

p 237 (38)

p 236 (36)

Superficially both pictures depict scenes from daily life and belong to the category of genre. But there are telling differences. Chardin dresses mother and daughter in their Sunday best; they must be getting ready for church. Thus, there is just a hint of some didactic element. Boucher, by contrast, shows a young woman leisurely choosing ornaments to improve her appearance. Tessin's secretary records that the *Evening* of this series depicted the same lady with her maid, who has just brought a letter inviting her to an amorous rendez-vous. Had there been a corresponding *Evening* by Chardin, it might have shown the little girl saying her prayers, something like his *Bénédicité* (Louvre).

p 241 (48)

When Boucher's *Modiste* was engraved, the print was published with a little poem addressing the lady:

> *Quittez-vous donc toujours, Philis, votre toilette.*
> *Montrez-vous dans l'état de la simple Nature.*
> (Give up your adornments, Phyllis,
> Show yourself in the simple state of nature)

But Nature—a term constantly on lips in the 18th century, in different contexts and with different meanings—meant for Boucher the frank erotic charm of a naked young girl on a Rococo sofa, for Chardin and Diderot, however, it had to do with truth and the whole of human life. Boucher never was wholly serious, and we cannot say in front of his pictures whether we are witnessing real life, or a scene in some play or ballet. No such doubts are possible when looking at Chardin's intensely serious art, where *truth* is certainly to be found.

But the artist whom Diderot admired even above Chardin was Jean-Baptiste Greuze (1725–1805). The *Salon* of 1765 which dealt so savagely with Boucher's moral depravity praised Greuze, because he appeared as the first artist to '*donner des mœurs à l'art*'. With this the critic observed that Greuze painted subjects equally fit to be treated by a novelist. One can easily see what attracted Diderot to pictures with such sentimental titles as, *L'Accordée de Village, Le Père expliquant la Bible à ses Enfants,* or *La Mère bien Aimée,* for these alone tell their own story. Greuze seemingly dealt with human emotions in simple, often rustic, settings. This was 'nature' in more than one sense of the word. But in the end even Diderot had reservations, since he could not fail to be struck by the false note in Greuze, whose rural world, after all, is one of theatrical disguise and make-believe, just as that of Boucher's pastorals and idylls.

p 239 (45)

Diderot had to be satisfied with genre painters in his search for truth and morality. He looked in vain for classical grandeur in the works of the history painters of his day, although La Font de Saint-Yenne as early as 1754 had expressed the hope that history painting would become again what it had been in the days of Poussin and Lebrun: '*Une école des mœurs,*' depicting the virtuous and heroic deeds of great men from the past. It is true, by 1769 the examples of Greek and Roman virtue did become more numerous among the entries for the Salon exhibitions, but as Diderot remarked in one case which can stand for all: 'This is not in the Roman style; it is small and mean.' In other words, while artists may have picked the right subjects, as yet they still lacked a proper style in which to clothe them.

Among the painters whom he discussed in his last *Salon* of 1781, there was only one who seemed to Diderot to possess all the qualities required of the true history painter: Jacques Louis David, then aged thirty-three and just back from Rome, whose *Blind Belisarius Begging* was on show that year. Diderot at once recognized David's genius: '*Il a de l'Ame . . .*'. This is praise which nobody would have applied to Boucher, not even to Greuze. The word *âme* had a precise meaning for 18th-century critics, implying that a heroic and moral subject had been treated in a fitting manner, that content and form were in full accord. Four years later, in the *Salon* of 1785 appeared a picture which was the perfect answer to all the demands made on art by the moral critics since Shaftesbury, David's *Oath of the Horatii*, but Diderot, who had fervently waited for just such a painting, had died the year before.

p 243 (51)

## Art's social responsibility

None of the English monarchs of the 18th century shared the taste of Louis XV, and Britain never had that kind of purposeful Court patronage which gave France a 'style'. The Hanoverians, in fact, took scant interest in fostering the arts, and patronage was in the hands of the aristocracy and a middle class steadily gaining in importance. Among Reynolds' sitters were three of the Georges, members of the royal house, the great nobles of the realm and their wives, country squires, and the wealthy bourgeois families of London. George Vertue, whose diaries give a lively insight into the art world of the period, records as early as 1730 Hogarth's favour with the general public: 'The daily success of Mr Hogarth is painting small family pieces and conversations with so much air and agreeableness that causes him to be much followed and esteemed, whereby he has much employment . . .' One can easily understand that group portraits on a small scale—the family and conversation pieces—found ready takers, particularly among the middle class. But the immense popularity of Hogarth rested even more on his moral satires, and after the publication of the *Harlot's Progress* in 1732 Vertue explicitly drew attention to the nation-wide appeal which knew no class distinctions: 'The most remarkable

p 187 (17)

p 238–9 (40–43)

subject . . . that captivated the minds of most people, persons of all ranks and conditions from the greatest quality to the meanest . . .'.

p 190
(26)

William Hogarth (1697–1764) was less a chronicler of 18th-century society than its critic and satirist, and the social set-up in England, where more freedom of expression was granted than elsewhere in Europe, favoured the development of his art. Originally he had wanted to become a serious history painter, but to his chagrin he found out that his countrymen would only buy large decorative pictures by an 'old master', or by a foreigner, and preferably by somebody who was both.

Early in his career, he became a nationalist, attacking with crotchety malevolence those who propagated the introduction of a classical and Italian taste. One of his principal targets was the circle of Lord Burlington, but through them he aimed at the much travelled cultured members of the aristocracy who built themselves houses in the Palladian manner and filled them with Italian paintings. His engraving *The Man of Taste* is a satire, answering Pope's *Epistle on Taste* (1731) addressed to Lord Burlington. Burlington Gate, built in 1718 by Colen Campbell as the entrance to Burlington's house in Piccadilly, laden with Italian details and inscribed with the word TASTE, dominates Hogarth's print. On top of it stands not some classical hero or deity but the architect and painter William Kent, triumphantly brandishing brush and palette. Raphael and Michelangelo, reclining on the pediment look up to him in admiration. Pope, standing on a scaffold, is whitewashing the gate, and Lord Burlington in the humble role of a builder's mate is going up a ladder carrying a trowel. It is all quite witty, but we must admit also a little childish, since Hogarth made no attempt to come to terms with Burlington's ideals.

f 5

The print, however, is more than a statement in a battle of styles and different tastes. It is also social criticism since Hogarth blames members of the ruling class, with sufficient money and education to be patrons, for stifling a truly native art. Yet his strength, and with it his greatest appeal, rested on very different works, which were understood at once also by those not familiar with the feuds among connoisseurs and critics. The *Harlot's Progress*, the *Marriage à la Mode*, the *Rake's Progress* were bound to fascinate the readers of Richardson, Fielding and Smollett, since they too took their material from the English scene of the day.

Hogarth himself, in his autobiographical notes, has told how he hit upon these subjects. 'I therefore turned my thoughts to a still more novel mode, viz. painting modern moral subjects, a field not broken up in any country or in any age . . . I wished to compose pictures on canvas, similar to representations on the stage; and further hope that they will be tried by the same test and criticized by the same criterion . . . In these compositions, those subjects which will both entertain and improve the mind, bid fair to be of the greatest utility, and must therefore be entitled to rank in the highest class.'

These proud claims are telling and merit to be seen in their proper historical context. The bold assertion that 'modern moral subjects' were his own invention has been shown to be exaggerated, since his models for the *Harlot* and the *Rake* were series of older Italian engravings telling the same sad and didactic tale. Nevertheless there are significant differences, and part at least of the boast is true. The earlier examples are rather in the manner of broadsheets, combining a kind of street ballad with illustrations; they invariably operate with standard types rather than with individuals. Hogarth dispenses with the text and lets the pictures alone do all the work. But in order to be effective without explanatory words he has to characterize his figures sharply and make them individuals. They become character players who enact a morality for our benefit. Since he wishes both to 'entertain and to improve' he is, quite logically, entitled to argue that his pictures belong to the highest class, that is to say, that they rank with tragedy and its pictorial equivalent, history painting. If we look through his pictorial cycles, we notice indeed Hogarth's talent as a dramatist, selecting for each picture some climatic or turning point, raising a folk genre to the level of art. Yet his great success was not only due to his genius. He invariably treated themes of social actuality, obvious to his contemporaries regardless of class.

The *Harlot's Progress* is a particularly clear example. The six paintings, acquired by William Beckford and lost when Fonthill

burned down in 1755, were an immediate success, and of the engravings, which Hogarth made after them, he sold well over a thousand sets. On looking at this sordid pictorial chronicle it is obvious that the artist was not in the least interested in any erotic, or worse salacious, entertainment, to which so delicate a topic might have lent itself. On the contrary, he describes with unsparing accuracy the physical and moral decay of an innocent country girl, corrupted by the turpitude of immoral Londoners. Yet all individual touches notwithstanding (some of Hogarth's figures are supposed to be recognizable portraits of notorious characters), this is not a journalist's case history, nor is it the personal tragedy of one girl, but a deeply felt and powerfully rendered accusation against a society permitting such evils. The rich seducer, the quack, the shady members of the underworld—they all belong to 18th-century London. They are symbols of corruption. The *Rake's Progress* and the *Marriage à la Mode*, though less savage, aim in the same direction.

p 284
(8)

On occasion Hogarth put his art into the service of direct political intervention. Laws passed early in the century encouraged the consumption of cheap gin through making licensing easy and by putting a very low tax on spirits. For distilling, as Defoe pointed out, put to use corn, thereby filling the pockets of the landed interests so well represented among members of Parliament. The effects upon social and physical health, particularly among the poor, were disastrous, and the rise of the death rate during the 'thirties and 'forties may in part at least be attributed to excessive gin drinking. Hogarth and his friend Henry Fielding, who as a magistrate experienced at close quarters the consequences of alcoholism, were among the most active protagonists demanding legal reform, and in 1751 Hogarth published two complementary prints as part of this campaign: *Gin Lane* and *Beer Street*. These vividly described scenes with their wealth of descriptive detail point an obvious moral. Gin is bad for you; the results are poverty, decay and illness. Only the pawnbroker and the undertaker do good business. Beer, on the other hand, is a healthy and harmless national beverage. The pawnbroker has had to close his shop; well-to-do businessmen and artisans are enjoying their drink, a new house is going up, and the tile-layers are celebrating with a glass of beer. Incidentally, even on this occasion Hogarth manages to include a dig at his countrymen for their alleged neglect of the arts. Only the painter, busy with nothing grander than an inn sign, is dressed in rags in the midst of an affluent society.

p 307
(14)

Hogarth liked to refer to himself as 'a comic history painter' and in doing so he clearly used the word 'history' in its precise 18th-century sense, that is as a story pointing a moral. His choice of topics from everyday life and the injection of humour into them gave him at the outset a wider audience and an advantage over the history painter proper with his learned subjects from classical mythology or the ancient authors. It also adds to his sermonizing actuality and bite, things hardly to be found in Greuze's sentimental anecdotes. Yet his high purpose, in spite of being allied to issues of the day, stems in the last resort from the doctrines of Shaftesbury. Hogarth tried to make art and its benefits, as he saw them, accessible to all classes, for in his own way he practised didactic art just as much as those who wished to teach ethics through the high examples of classical heroes. But there is also an important difference. Hogarth essentially remained a satirist, holding up to society a distorting mirror. Rarely did he use art to depict the values in which he believed. Hence his true successors are to be found not among painters but among the great English caricaturists, such as Gillray and Rowlandson.

p 292
(31)

## Education through art

The three men whose writings exercised the greatest influence on artists and art lovers during the second half of the 18th century—Diderot, Reynolds and Winckelmann—were all fervent educators aiming well beyond a reform of taste. Their roles, however, were different, and were in part at least determined by the society to which they addressed themselves.

Diderot's activities as a critic and as the author of the *Essai sur la Peinture* should be read as a contribution to the far reaching intellectual and ethical reforms propagated by the so-called *philosophes*, of whom he was one. The *Salons*, though addressed to

*Hogarth's engraving 'Taste' satirized Lord Burlington and his circle. Alexander Pope, the dwarfish figure on the ladder 'white-washing and bespattering anybody that comes his way' rather surprisingly never replied in print, fearful perhaps of provoking Hogarth to an even more biting rejoinder. The figure at the top (E) is William Kent, receiving the homage of Raphael and Michelangelo. Hogarth objected to Palladianism mainly because it was Italian and therefore foreign. (5)*

a small circle, belong with the *Encyclopédie*, for as Diderot told Catherine II of Russia: '*Instruire une nation, c'est la civiliser.*' It is understandable why the *Salons* and the *Essai* were published soon after the Revolution.

Reynolds, through upbringing and perhaps on account of those for whom he worked, was more concerned with an educated élite. Nevertheless, in his first *Discourse* (1769), delivered at the opening of the Royal Academy, paying his respects to George III for promoting the enterprise, he voices in fact his own convictions when he says: '. . . we are patronized by a monarch, who, knowing the value of science and of elegance, thinks every art worthy of his notice, that tends to soften and humanize the mind.'

Winckelmann's case is different again. A scholar, moving among scholars and connoisseurs, he wrote for his friends and—as he himself repeatedly insisted—for young artists. He was concerned with teaching the teachers a new approach to art, and through art to education. Goethe, deeply sympathetic to him and steeped in his writings, said with true insight: 'One does not learn anything by reading him, but one becomes something.'

Reynolds' paintings are less relevant in our present context than is his role in establishing and running the Royal Academy, whose first President he became at its foundation in 1768. His history paintings, which should furnish visible proof that he practised

what he taught his students, are comparatively few, and most of his innumerable portraits are a shrewd compromise. He had to reckon with the prejudices of a public still convinced that nothing but portraits could possibly be good from the hands of an English painter. As one collector put it: 'You surely would not have me hang up a modern English picture in my house, unless it were a portrait.'

Reynolds himself became aware that there was dissension between him and a large and influential section of society over the true function of art. When in 1773 he and Benjamin West proposed a series of paintings for St Paul's, the Bishop of London prevented their execution. Reynolds fully understood the deeper reasons for the failure of his plan and commented: 'It is a circumstance to be regretted, by painters at least, that the Protestant countries have thought proper to exclude pictures from their churches: how far this circumstance may be the cause that no Protestant country has ever produced a history painter may be worthy of consideration.' With perhaps better sense than certain modern historians Reynolds recognized that predilection for portraiture had little to do with the desire of a wealthy ruling class to see itself immortalized, but sprang from more profound ideological roots.

But Reynolds also knew his own limitations as a painter and he realized where his talent lay. The historical portraits which he painted—*Miss Morris as 'Hope nursing Love'*, the *Duchess of Manchester as Diana taking the Bow from Cupid* and many others—are likenesses and allegories designed to flatter the patron. While introducing a didactic and moral element into portraiture, they exploit to the full his gift for rendering character and dignity.

But for all Reynolds' determination and the King's support it would still not have been possible to make the Academy a success if the English public had not been slowly becoming ready for it. There had been tentative starts before. The Society of Arts, founded in 1754 (and now called the Royal Society of Arts), had encouraged taste by giving prizes for paintings, sculpture, drawings and architectural designs. In 1759 a Society of Artists was formed with the avowed purpose of arranging exhibitions, and the first held in 1760 attracted literally thousands of visitors—the catalogue sold some 6,500 copies in two weeks. Other shows followed, and with them the usual squabbles among rival factions, until finally in 1768 George III signed the *Instrument of Foundation* for a Royal Academy, setting up an organization more comprehensive than any of its predecessors.

At the outset the Academy was given three clearly defined and closely related functions. Its members were to be 'painters, sculptors or architects, men of fair moral character, of high reputation in their several professions.' Yet membership was not an empty honour, for the Academy's schools were put 'under the direction of the ablest artists . . . elected annually from amongst the Academicians . . .; painters of history, able sculptors, or other persons properly qualified; their business shall be . . . to examine the performances of the students, to advise and instruct them, to endeavour to form their taste . . .' Lastly, 'an annual exhibition of paintings, sculpture and designs . . . open to all artists of distinguished merit' was made an integral part of the new Academy's task. Since the works exhibited were for sale, and the proceeds in part were 'employed in the support of the institution' both artists and the public were to benefit in more than one way.

p 220 (2)

It has rightly been remarked that public criticism of the exhibitions was slow in developing—slower certainly than in France, where in any case discussions about art were part of the routine business of the *Académie*—but the first President's fifteen *Discourses*, delivered at the annual prize-giving between 1769 and 1790, are a unique guide to the high aims and standards set by him. They have been called 'the most vital contribution of the 18th century to the literature of criticism, and they are also a monument of Reynolds' ability as a writer, just as the successful establishment of the Royal Academy is the monument to his practical sagacity' (Ellis Waterhouse). In speaking of Reynolds as a writer and critic, it should be mentioned that his house in Leicester Square was a meeting place for intellectuals, and that Dr Johnson, Burke, Goldsmith and Gibbon were among his friends. He was, unlike his French contemporaries, a 'learned painter' and in this respect he can be compared only with Anton Raphael Mengs, who, however, was of lesser intellectual calibre.

The hub of Reynolds' philosophy is his definition of the ennobling quality of art. He was aware that his ideas in this respect were not new, but the very fact of their classical ancestry proved to him their validity. An often quoted passage in the third *Discourse* gives his own formulation of the identity of the beautiful and the good. After referring to Plato and Cicero, who had stated that great artists do not copy objects presented to their sight but images conceived in their mind, he continues: 'The Moderns are no less convinced than the Ancients of this superior power existing in the art; nor less sensible to its effects. Every language has adopted terms expressive of this excellence. The *gusto grande* of the Italians, the *beau idéal* of the French, and the *great style*, *genius*, *taste* among the English, are but different appellations of the same thing. It is this intellectual dignity, they say, that ennobles the painter's art; that lays the line between him and the mere mechanic; and produces those great effects in an instant, which eloquence and poetry, by slow and repeated efforts, are scarcely able to attain.'

William Blake, who in the paranoiac marginalia scribbled into his copy of the *Discourses* was less than fair to Reynolds, fully recognized the social implications of Neo-classical aesthetics, when he observed: 'The Arts and Sciences are the Destruction of Tyrannies or Bad Governments. Why should a Good Government endeavour

to Depress what is its Chief and only support? . . . The Foundation of Empire is Art and Science. Remove them or Degrade them, and the Empire is No More. Empire follows Art and Not Vice Versa as Englishmen suppose.' This furious outburst is less over the stylistic principles of Reynolds' *great style* than over the supposed social consequences of a kind of art which Blake hated, because in his view it stultified the creative, free genius. Yet Blake's reaction is only the most extreme form of the Romantics' objection to the strict discipline of a classical education and the particular ethics it implied.

Reynolds, his impressive literary output notwithstanding, was first and foremost a practising teacher of painting, and this fact determined his other activities. It is too easily overlooked that the *Discourses*, though an excellent means of telling the English what art might do for them, were in the first place addressed to the students of the Royal Academy, and were at least in the eyes of the President, an integral part of their intellectual training. The annual Academy exhibitions also had a very real purpose. By introducing a wide and new public to contemporary art, they propounded *taste*, and made the buying of pictures fashionable among a middle class emulating the older collecting habits of the aristocracy. Common sense and a cool, businesslike approach in all matters concerning art are perhaps the most remarkable traits of Reynolds' personality. Thus he belongs to that empirical tradition which is typical of the 18th century in England.

## 'Imitation of the Ancients'

Johann Joachim Winckelmann (1717–1768) also regarded himself as a teacher, but he was a passionate and emotional mentor, instructing a public rather different from the one for which Reynolds worked. Moreover he never held any public office which allowed him to play an active part in the shaping of the art of his time. It is true, he tried to make Mengs the executant of his ideas, but was unfortunate in his choice of this volatile second-rate painter who always reflected the strongest influence from his surroundings.

A man of humble origins—the son of a poor cobbler—Winckelmann went to university with the help of scholarships and had to work in a number of menial posts before settling in Dresden, where he made friends among scholars and artists. His final goal from earliest days, however, was Rome, where he wished to devote himself to the study of classical art. Yet it was not disinterested scholarship, which drew him to the fountainhead of the classical tradition, but something he hoped to reach through and beyond the acquaintance with the monuments of antiquity. To him a study of art was the most effective instrument of education, a better one even than thorough familiarity with the classical authors, which as a true humanist he took for granted. He was obsessed by the desire to open the eyes of young men to the beauties of Greek art —of sculpture in particular—and to show them the spiritual truth and ultimate goodness revealed through the physical beauty of perfect form. Greek art represented for Winckelmann absolute values. Goethe understood this perfectly and suggested that he became such a tremendous influence because he was consumed by a fire stronger than a burning quest for knowledge.

It is well known that Winckelmann, who never visited Greece, knew Greek art almost exclusively from Roman copies. However, he was willing to grant that Raphael, Michelangelo and Poussin, perhaps also Annibale Carracci and Guido Reni, could provide substitutes for the lost originals of the ancients. But this was hardly a new idea; it had formed one of the tenets of 17th-century academic art theory. In any case, it is not the originality of Winckelmann's mind which still commands attention but the eloquence and fire with which he preached his gospel of education through art.

Moreover, Winckelmann's fervent advocacy of Greek art did not stem from any profound visual experience in his youth, and it is truer to say that he came to an appreciation of art only after an unusually extensive reading in Greek literature. To this must be added his familiarity with the writings of Shaftesbury—he filled many pages of his notebooks with verbatim extracts from the *Characteristicks*—where he found a doctrine which, reformulated, became the battle-cry with which he opened his own first essay: 'Taste, which is increasingly spreading through the world, was first formed under Greek skies.'

**Johann Winckelmanns,**
Präsidentens der Alterthümer zu Rom, und Scrittore der Vaticanischen Bibliothek,
Mitglieds der Königl. Englischen Societät der Alterthümer zu London, der Maleracademie
von St. Luca zu Rom, und der Hetrurischen zu Cortona,

# Geschichte der Kunst
## des Alterthums.

### Erster Theil.

Mit Königl. Pohlnisch- und Churfürstl. Sächs. allergnädigsten Privilegio.

Dresden, 1764.
In der Waltherischen Hof-Buchhandlung.

*Winckelmann's writings constituted the theoretical manifesto of the Neo-classical movement. His first essay, published in 1755, before he left Germany, advised artists to 'imitate' (but not to copy) the works of the Greeks, and his major book, the 'History of Art in Antiquity', published in 1764, was a sustained analysis of classical values in art and the necessity of applying them to contemporary painting and sculpture. Dedicated to his greatest disciple, Anton Raphael Mengs, the titlepage (right) featured an early Greek engraved gem, showing five of the Seven against Thebes. The works that Winckelmann most admired seem now (especially in the engravings in which he published them) to be somewhat tame and sentimental, and in fact he knew Greek art only through Roman replicas. But it was his view of art as a moral and spiritual education that made him so dominant an influence. (6)*

This essay, *Gedanken über die Nachahmung der griechischen Werke in der Malerei und Bildhauerkunst*, was published in 1755 just before he left Dresden for Rome. The title clearly implies that these 'Reflections on the imitation of Greek works in Painting and Sculpture' were written for the enlightenment of artists. In fact, Winckelmann often regretted that he himself was not born to be an artist, but insisted that he was writing for their benefit. Characteristically he dedicated his principal work, the *History of Art in Antiquity*, to his friend Anton Raphael Mengs, and his very last publication, *Versuch einer Allegorie,* in an entreaty to painters and sculptors to use images by which they can express an eternal truth.

Winckelmann's most frequently quoted maxim sets out, with the utmost brevity, a programme for the future of art: 'The only way for us to become great and, if possible, even inimitable is through imitation of the ancients.' But this apparent paradox is not a recommendation to copy Greek art. In fact, Winckelmann took pains to point out that there was a world of difference between 'copying' and 'imitation', the latter being concerned with principles rather than external forms of art.

For him, steeped in Greek culture, there was a compelling reason in preaching *imitation*. It was, in his view, the only way to the essence and ultimate purpose of art. Already in his first essay, and again in later writings, he adduced climate, landscape, race, and social institutions in order to explain why he thought that the Greeks had perfect physical beauty, which in turn gave rise to perfect art. For those living under less favourable conditions the process had to be reversed and the creation of perfect art had to bring about perfection of life.

Another famous claim of Winckelmann's must be understood in the same context. 'The general and predominant mark of Greek masterpieces is noble simplicity and calm grandeur . . .' These qualities as characteristics of ancient art had already been discussed by other 18th-century critics, but Winckelmann, obsessed with education through art, gave them a particular meaning. He argued: as the perfect manly beauty of the Greeks results from the physical conditions under which the nation lived, so the serene expression in works of art is the outward sign of a noble soul. This highly personal formulation of a belief in the identity of the beautiful and the good explains why he held that a proper appreciation of Greek art will give the moderns not only good art but something more important, a sense of nobility.

In spite of much common ground the differences between Winckelmann on the one side, and Reynolds and Diderot on the other, are obvious. Winckelmann, strictly speaking, concerns himself only with the individual and his education, while they were anxious to give society the right kind of art. Hence his impact was rather different from theirs. As far as painting and sculpture are concerned it was disastrous, since artists following him misread 'copying' for 'imitation', so that whole regiments of deadly white marble statues were carved in the name of Winckelmann. But his impact on classical education, particularly in Germany, was profound, and his apollonic interpretation of Greek art went unchallenged until it was overthrown by Nietzsche. Diderot, as early as 1765, gave a historically valid assessment of Winckelmann's role when he pointed out that this *enthousiaste charmant* was an excellent guide to a truer understanding of past art, but a will o' the wisp when addressing himself to practising artists.

## Art and politics

'*C'est à côté des actions mémorables que dans l'antiquité brillait le génie des arts. Ces vertus reparaissent . . .*' (It was alongside heroic deeds that the arts flourished in Antiquity. These virtues are again to be seen . . .) These words, addressed by Jacques Louis David to the Convention, could have been spoken nowhere but in France, for they presuppose a belief in the social function of art lacking in the country of Winckelmann, while in England the virtues upheld by artists and critics tended to be more down to earth.

David (1748–1825) practised what Caylus, La Font de Saint-Yenne and Diderot had preached, and he went further still when

p 266 (21)

he willingly made his art into an instrument of political propaganda, either by designing the new Festivals of the Revolution or by painting the memorials of its martyrs. Yet before accusing him of having been a time-server who sold his genius to the politicians, one should ask whether such a development was not the logical outcome of the doctrines of his mentors. It is true, the leaders of the Revolution had an awareness of the persuasive power of visual images and therefore used them for purposes of which a Colbert, who after all had used Lebrun to enhance the glory of Louis XIV, surely would have disapproved. But this is a difference of degree rather than of kind. Any Frenchman, who had had the classical education which David enjoyed first at the Collège des Quatre Nations and later as an *élève protégé* of the Académie, must have felt during the 1790s that the Revolution was at last reviving all ancient virtues and bringing them up to date. Marat and Lepelletier—to take the two revolutionary heroes whom David immortalized—had become the true successors to a Socrates, Brutus or Seneca, and could be celebrated as such. Seen from within the Revolution there was, therefore, every reason to paint now a *Death of Marat* instead of a *Death of Socrates*.

p 243 (51)

The *Oath of the Horatii*, shown in the Salon of 1785 four years before the Revolution, and the *Brutus*, exhibited in the Salon which opened a few weeks after the Fall of the Bastille, are not political, let alone revolutionary, manifestos. They would not have been accepted for show otherwise, nor could they have been bought by the Crown. They belong firmly into the revived tradition of moral history painting which looks back to Poussin both in content and in form. Their Stoicism is yet another example of a philosophy which had nurtured literature and art for years before the actual Revolution. The *Oath of the Horatii* is a veritable paradigm of moral history painting, extolling civic virtue and personal sacrifice. There is no allusion, over or hidden, to any of the political issues of the day. The *Brutus*, though portraying Rome's first consul, deals with a theme which, as a perfect example of stoic morality, had already fascinated Diderot, who had vainly tried to persuade Greuze to use it for his *morceau de réception*: Brutus has condemned his sons

p 243 (52)

to death for siding with the enemy and is waiting for their bodies to be brought home. David himself told a friend that his picture deals with 'Brutus as a man and father', which means that he had executed not a political, but a moral rendering of a well-known Roman theme. In this he followed Voltaire, who in his tragedy *Brutus* of 1730 had done the same. But neither David nor Voltaire can be held responsible for the fact that their works were used for propaganda purposes when, after the autumn of 1791, the Revolution turned to a more violent and republican line.

But when David painted the *Death of Marat* he did produce intentionally a political image of the utmost actuality. Yet even in

p 244 (53)

this case, the restraints of the classical tradition imposed the dignified form of the martyr's memorial. The painter had visited the sick deputy, who was a personal friend, shortly before he was murdered by Charlotte Corday, and like her had found him working even in his bath. Although it was David's plan to show the people how Marat had died, he did not paint a narrative picture, as others in fact did. There is no domestic setting, and he shows the dead man alone before a plain background as on a sepulchral monument, reminding us of some marble relief. The improvised side-table inscribed A MARAT DAVID recalls a tombstone. The conscious choice of the undramatic moment when all is over, makes the dead deputy into a timeless hero.

David, in fact, was not the first painter to treat contemporary history as if it were the exemplary past. Benjamin West (1731–1820) with his *Death of General Wolfe* (1771) had preceded him. But he

p 242 (49)

was nonetheless the first artist who became an active politician, not only because he had himself elected to the Convention, but more so, because he put art into the service of a political movement. With this step the artist had moved as far as he possibly could from the position held by a Watteau or Boucher.

# VIII THE ENLIGHTENMENT

*Free Inquiry and the World of Ideas*

ROBERT SHACKLETON

*'We live in curious times and amid astonishing contrasts:*

*reason on the one hand, the most absurd fanaticism on the other . . .*

*sauve qui peut.'*

VOLTAIRE

### Intellectual force

is notoriously difficult to pin down and dissect; nor is it easy to chart the course of ideas as they flow through the various strata of society or from one country to the next. One can say that the philosophers, moralists, historians and political thinkers of 18th-century France, England and Germany shared a common attitude of mind – an optimistic faith in reason and a confidence in empirical research – and that they saw themselves as fighting what was essentially a common battle against tyranny in politics, dogma in religion, prejudice and hypocrisy in morals. The advance of science and the increasing awareness that Europe, or even Christendom, did not make up the whole world, had led to a general dissatisfaction with things as they were and a new urge to ask questions. But the answers that men found, and the degrees of their dissatisfaction, differed profoundly. There was no manifesto of Enlightenment (not even the *Encyclopédie* was that). Apart from the more superficial quarrels, there were figures who fitted into no scheme, like Samuel Johnson with his morbid fear of damnation, or Jean-Jacques Rousseau, for whom feeling was a better guide than logic. Even Voltaire, the poet-laureate of the Enlightenment, had no consistent respect for scientists.

Voltaire, indeed, who in so many ways epitomizes what was most typical of his age, is an apt illustration of how it refuses to be categorized. His first success as a young man was that of a poet and a dramatist, producing works which at their worst are hopelessly stilted and conventional, though he was already a foe of churches and tyrants. A three-year visit to England, 1724–27, confirmed his thoughts in this direction. The intellectual freedom that he found there opened his eyes to the lack of such a blessing in his own country. The first fruits of his new vision were the *Lettres philosophiques* but many years of other activities intervened (including an experiment in enlightened despotism when he stayed at Potsdam as the adviser of Frederick the Great) before he assumed the role with which he was to be identified. He lived to be 83, and all his greatest achievements belong to the last thirty of those years: the pamphlets and stories, the anticlerical satires, the passionate indictments of injustice, the irresistible cynicism whose finest flower is *Candide*. Voltaire's wit made the Ancien Régime ridiculous; his moral fervour made it hateful. Something of both is conveyed by Houdon's bust (opposite). 'He was always active with an insatiable activity', in the words of Lytton Strachey. 'His long gaunt body, frantically gesticulating, his skull-like face, with its mobile features twisted into an eternal grin, his piercing eyes sparkling and darting – all this suggested the appearance of a corpse galvanized into an incredible animation.' (1)

**'The Antiquarian Monkey'** or *Singe Antiquaire* by Chardin (left), painted in 1740, indicates popular disrespect for erudition. The monkey is examining a medal through a magnifying glass. A similar spirit informs the *Lever de Voltaire* (right), showing the sage of Ferney dictating to his secretary even while putting on his trousers in the morning. (3, 4)

**The meeting-place** of intellects was the salon. Several salons became internationally famous, and they account in great part both for the rapid dissemination of ideas and for the elegance with which they were commonly expressed. The salon of Madame Geoffrin (above) brought together almost every notable talent in Paris. A typical evening in 1755 is recreated here by Lemonnier. At the table, under a bust of Voltaire, the actor Le Kain reads *L'Orphelin de la Chine*. In the left foreground, leaning back, is Buffon, with Réaumur behind him; to the right of the table d'Alembert and (in blue) Helvetius. Madame Geoffrin (in a pale blue dress) sits towards the right with the Prince de Conti on one side and Fontenelle (then 98 years old and apparently sleepy) on the other. A complete key to all the figures is given on p. 277. (2)

**D'Alembert,** the illegitimate son of an officer (he was actually exposed as a baby near a church in Paris), made himself the leading mathematician of Europe, doing original work on the calculus, the motion of fluids, vibrations and (in astronomy) the precession of the equinoxes. His contributions to the *Encyclopédie* brought him more popular fame, though (having less appetite for battle than Diderot) he withdrew from the fray after the first few volumes. (5)

How far the Enlightenment was a cause of political change is a question that can be endlessly debated. What the *philosophes* did was, firstly, to create a climate of opinion which saw change as something necessary and good; and, secondly, to supply a new ideology once the old one had been destroyed. In this context, one of the most influential of all books was Montesquieu's *L'Esprit des Lois*, in which he traced the history of civilization through its laws. In this frontispiece (right), Montesquieu is surrounded by allegorical figures, including Justice, and – in the left-hand corner – copies of his works, *Le Temple de Gnide*, *Lettres Persanes* and *L'Esprit des Lois*. (8)

**Hume** (below left) and **Kant** (below right) represent opposite philosophical poles: the empirical and the metaphysical. Hume – fluent, popular, persuasive – dismissed as meaningless any assertion not based on observation and experiment. Kant, in tortuous, technical German, showed how our knowledge of the world must rest upon logical concepts. (6, 7)

**Fontenelle** (above left), who was Corneille's nephew and lived into his 100th year, published his *Histoire des Oracles* as early as 1687. In it, under the pretence of ridiculing classical religion, he mocked the absurdities of excessive Christian credulity too. **Helvetius** (above right), in his best-known work, *De l'Esprit* reduced mind to sensation, morals to self-interest and intelligence to education. Attempting to give a completely empirical account of human conduct, he was naturally attacked for undermining religious sanctions. (9, 10)

**Algarotti** (above left), 'the swan of Padua', as Voltaire called him, came to Paris at the age of twenty and travelled in Russia, Poland and Germany, winning admiration on all sides, before returning to Italy in 1754. His best-known work was a popularization of Newton's optics, called *Neutonianismo per le dame*. Like many of the *philosophes* he combined scientific knowledge with an interest in art and music. **Buffon** (above right), the prolific author, botanist and zoologist of the Jardin des Plantes, we have already met in Chapter III. (11, 12)

In Benjamin Franklin the worlds of Enlightenment and Revolution do overlap. The student of electricity, of marine currents, of meteorology, of light and of diet was the same man who stood firm for the rights of the American colonists, and who helped to draft the Declaration of Independence – including in it the characteristically Euclidean phrase: 'We hold these truths to be self-evident.' This allegorical sketch by Fragonard (right), in which the *génie* of Franklin casts down tyranny, bears witness to his reputation in France in 1778. (15)

Dr Johnson (below left) hated the Enlightenment. A deeply convinced Anglican, he regarded religious scepticism as a sin, and political radicalism as little better. Yet his intellectual integrity, his impatience with cant and his restless curiosity make him supremely representative of the 'age of common sense'. Gibbon (below right), surpassing all previous historians in knowledge and method, also extolled moderation but turned upon Christianity the weapon of his superb irony. (13, 14)

Herder (above centre) and Goethe (right) typify two generations of intellectual life in Germany. Herder, a pupil of Kant, soon abandoned Classicism for the more turbulent literature of the North. Goethe, one of the masters of Romanticism, tried to combine both worlds in the second part of *Faust*, and retained a lifelong interest in science. The Frenchman Baron d' Holbach (left) was bold enough to make explicit the determinism and atheism that lurked unexpressed in the writings of men such as Helvetius. (16, 17, 18)

**The Revolution claimed Rousseau** (left) after 1793 as its spiritual father, even though his major work, *Le Contrat Social*, had been little read by the men of 1789. An allegorical painting of about 1793 (above left) shows him presiding over the eye of Truth and the tricolour, an obelisk to Equality, a monument to the revolutionary virtues (rods and axes topped by a red cap), the tree of liberty and two half-built columns of 'regeneration'. (19, 20)

**The Fête of the Supreme Being,** held on June 8th, 1794, was an attempt by Robespierre, at a rather crude level, to put Rousseau's religious ideas into practice. Rousseau, a deist, had rejected churches and priests, but believed in a Supreme Being who manifested himself in Nature. After the abolition of Christianity, Robespierre felt that society needed a secular religion, and its inauguration was stage-managed with great effect by the painter David. Around a statue of Wisdom, enthroned in a chariot, allegorical characters enacted a ritual of dedication. Rousseau, in fact, after early attempts at collaboration on the *Encyclopédie*, had been rejected by the Enlightenment, both because of his impossible temperament and because of his hostility to many of its 'civilized' values. But his emphasis on individual freedom and on equal human rights was to be crucial for later social thought. (21)

**The name of Diderot** (above) has become synonymous with the most sustained intellectual achievement of the century – the *Encyclopédie*. It occupied fifteen years of his life, during many of which he had to struggle alone against clerical and political opposition. The frontispiece (left) picturesquely summarizes its aims: Truth, in the centre, radiates light which disperses the clouds; at her side Reason and Philosophy pull away her veil; at her feet Theology receives light from on high. To the right are the sciences, to the left the arts, led by Imagination, preparing to crown Truth with a garland. The *Encyclopédie* was outstanding not only for the avant-garde tone of its articles on religion, etc., but also for the wealth of technical information which it assembled for the first time. Practically all its eleven volumes of plates are technical. This one (below) shows a chemical laboratory with a furnace (note the bellows upper right), rows of vessels, apparatus for heating and condensing and several assistants preparing experiments. (22, 23, 24)

# Free Inquiry and the World of Ideas

ROBERT SHACKLETON

ENLIGHTENMENT is defined by Kant in a celebrated essay as man's intellectual coming of age: the shaking off of external control in the use of his mind, this external control having to a large extent been self-imposed, or at least quietly accepted. In this sense more than one age in human history could be fairly described as an Age of Enlightenment, the Age of the Renaissance having in particular a strong claim to that title. The 18th century above all, however, is marked by that spirit of free and untrammelled inquiry which is the essential spirit of enlightenment, and though the Enlightenment of the 18th century is a phenomenon which marks the whole of Western civilization, it is in France that the focus of its development is found.

## The Prelude

The France of the last years of the 17th century seemed a remarkably unpropitious ground for the development of new ideas in a spirit of freedom. The polish and the glory of French civilization under Louis XIV represented in the public mind the highest achievement of mankind, and to question them seemed a fruitless occupation. The principle of religious uniformity, summed up in the phrase *cuius regio eius religio*, had its analogue in most spheres of human thought. The government was intolerant not only of criticism but even of silent dissent, and vigorous persecution was the fate of all forms of heterodoxy.

But even when Louis' renown was at its height there were signs of the intellectual revolution which was to follow. Among these was a stream of translations of independent and unconventional Italian works which poured into France. Fra Paolo Sarpi's history of the Council of Trent, inspired by a spirit of anticurialism, appeared in French translation in 1683. In the same year *The Prince* of Machiavelli was translated, to be followed eight years later by the *Discourses*. Meanwhile from the vigorous and unresting pen of the Protestant convert Gregorio Leti came first a famous work on the nepotism of the Roman Court (translated into French as early as 1669), another on the conclaves of the Roman pontiffs, and a work with the menacing title *La Monarchie de Louis avec les Moyens de la Détruire*. The most widely read and most influential of the Italian writers then becoming known in France was Gian Paolo Marana, a Genoese. His *Esploratore turco* (1684) enjoyed great vogue both in France and in England where, under the title *Letters writ by a Turkish Spy who liv'd five-and-forty years undiscover'd at Paris*, it was expanded to many volumes. It consists of a satirical account of French life and manners as seen by an imaginary Turkish traveller: a work designed above all to shake national prejudice.

Within the frontiers of France the two major forms of religious dissent during the reign of Louis XIV were Jansenism and Protestantism, against both of which his long arm was directed. Jansenism proved to be the more intractable victim of the two. It was driven underground but did not diminish in strength and during the next reign was one of the strongest forces turned against the Court. Calvinism met a different fate. The system of toleration set up by Henry IV was ended by the Revocation of the Edict of Nantes in 1685 and French Protestants in large numbers went into exile. They found refuge in England, in the Low Countries, and in Prussia. They created in London a lively community of writers and

*Pope's 'Dunciad', first published in 1728, was re-issued the following year as 'The Dunciad Variorum', with copious mock-scholarly notes on the authors satirized in the poem. The ass shown here appeared on the titlepage; he carries a load of boring literature surmounted by an owl.* (1)

Newton's criticisms of Descartes' physics were in the nature of things less understood, but they were scarcely less talked of, although an attempt was made by Fontenelle to stifle discussion of them in the French Academy of Sciences. Popularizers of Newton were numerous in the first half of the 18th century: Pemberton in England, Algarotti in Italy, Maupertuis and Voltaire in France. Anecdotes about Newton abounded. It was Voltaire who first reported the story of Sir Isaac being inspired to frame the theory of gravity by the sight of an apple falling to the ground. But what Newton above all signified to the 18th century was that which he had in common with Locke, the experimental or inductive method, and Pemberton, in the introduction to his *View of Sir Isaac Newton's Philosophy* (1728), was stressing an essential aspect of Newton in emphasizing his 'method of arguing by induction, without which no progress could be made in natural philosophy'.

The deist movement was another important part of English thought at the turn of the century. Deism was defined by Dr Johnson in 1755 as 'the opinion of those that only acknowledge one God, without the reception of any revealed religion'. Although both the word and thing had been known previously, and in other countries, it flourished particularly in England in the late 17th century. Locke's celebrated essay *Of the Reasonableness of Christianity* (1695)—though Locke is not to be ranked as a deist—and Toland's *Christianity not Mysterious* (1696) indicate by their very titles the line of thought. Toland was the first of the outspoken English deists. He proclaims with clarity:

p 265
(13)

> To believe the divinity of Scripture, or the sense of any passage thereof, without rational proofs and an evident consistency, is a blamable credulity and a temerarious opinion.

The main tenets of the deists were a belief in the rational accessibility of a simple monotheism, the rejection of revelation, the disparagement of ceremonial, a belief in toleration, and the laying of a greater stress on morality than on faith.

From this questioning mentality which grew in both France and England sprang the Enlightenment. Its exponents differed in outlook and emphasis as much as they differed in education and in class. Those who agreed in religious matters often disagreed in politics. Some wrote or tried to write poetry: others were accused of *lèse-poésie*. Some—and these were not the least interesting—were solitaries and worked out their ideas in loneliness; others belonged to social groupings and framed their philosophies in the salon or the academy. These last provide a fruitful approach to the study of the Enlightenment and enable its organic life and structure to appear clearly.

## The attack on prejudice

The first phase of the Enlightenment began about 1715. The Peace of Utrecht, the condemnation of the Jansenists in Clement XI's Bull *Unigenitus*, the Hanoverian Succession, and the death of Louis XIV, were all events which marked the threshold of a new era. All of them occurred within the three years 1713–15. The two decades which follow have a clear unity. The intellectual activity which distinguishes them is based on three centres, London, Paris, and (on a more modest scale) Naples.

In London the Royal Society was flourishing. It united in its ranks the country's men of letters and men of science and, under the presidency of the now aged Newton, had a uniquely central and all-embracing role in cultural life. Pope in his *Dunciad* explained how it brought together the élite of the nation:     f 1

> *Her children first of more distinguished sort,*
> *Who study Shakespeare at the Inns of Court,*
> *Impale a glow-worm or Vertù profess,*
> *Shine in the dignity of* FRS.

The Charter Book of the Society in which Fellows write their names on admission lists many illustrious foreign visitors as well as English members, Montesquieu and Maupertuis being among them; and the proud device *Nullius in verba* insists that nothing is to be taken on trust, on the mere authority of any individual.

In 1714 there was established in London a club which enjoyed great literary renown. This was the Scriblerus Club, of which Pope and Swift were the most illustrious figures, and which included also Lord Oxford, Gay, Parnell, and Dr Arbuthnot. Its actual life was not long, but its aims and spirits lived on and inspired much subsequent literature. The *Memoirs of Martinus Scriblerus* are a diminishing mirror of the thought of the age, whether the writers agree with it or satirize it. A brief essay, *The Origin of Sciences*, treats facetiously a theme which philosophers of the day were treating seriously, and the authors, in tracing back the sciences to the pygmies of Ethiopia, are perhaps thinking of Bishop Huet who claimed that fictional literature was born in India, where the sun inflamed men's imagination. Martinus Scriblerus travelled to this land of the pygmies, thereafter to the land of the giants, and later discovered 'a whole kingdom of *Philosophers*, who govern by the *Mathematics*'. There can be little doubt that from this sprang Swift's masterpiece *Gulliver's Travels*, inspired also by the fantastic     f 2
tales written in the previous century by Cyrano de Bergerac. The imaginary voyage, in which the writer takes licence to speak to his friend about the conventions and presuppositions of his age, is the literary genre in which the Enlightenment most excelled. It was fostered by the discussions of the Scriblerus Club.

There is some criticism in the *Memoirs of Martinus Scriblerus* of the freethinkers or deists; but Pope, the leading member of the Club, gave in his *Essay on Man* (1734) the most famous and memorable expression of the ideas of many of the deists. Translated into the various languages of Europe, reprinted in the course of the 18th century not less than seventy-one times in France alone, the *Essay on Man* ranks with Locke's *Human Understanding* as one of the great seminal works of the Enlightenment. Its ideas may sometimes be shallow and usually are second-hand; its optimism may after such a disaster as the Lisbon earthquake of 1755 seem naïve and unreal; its notion of the great chain of being may be fanciful and archaic. But in its brilliant couplets Pope gave lasting form to widely held ideas: the ordered system of the universe, the nice balance of reason and passion in human psychology, the union in nature of self-love and altruism. He teaches the disparagement of earthly grandeur, and gives an account of the rise of political oppression which is a foretaste of Rousseau and Holbach:

*Force first made Conquest, and that conquest, Law;*
*'Till superstition taught the Tyrant awe,*
*Then shar'd the Tyranny, then lent it aid,*
*And Gods of Conqu'rors, Slaves of Subjects made.*

p 98 (3)

In France meanwhile the Academy of Sciences and the Academy of Inscriptions formed centres of discussion. The youthful Montesquieu, coming to Paris in the last years of the reign of Louis XIV, found interest in the papers read in these bodies, and formed a friendship with Fréret, learned to the point of knowing 264 (9) Chinese, and with Fontenelle, already an old man but destined to die only as a centenarian in 1757. Fontenelle's greatest literary activity had been in the 1680s when he attacked literary obscurantism in his *Histoire des Oracles*, popularized the Copernican system in his exceedingly successful *Entretiens sur la Pluralité des Mondes*, and produced a simple but incisive critique of Descartes in his *Digression sur les Anciens et les Modernes*. As perpetual secretary of the Academy of Sciences, which he remained until 1740, he was able to give full scope to his belief in the importance of spreading knowledge, while in the salons of Paris he was able to display the gentle cynicism with which that belief was tempered, and which is illustrated in his much quoted *mot*, that if his hand were full of truths, he would take good care not to open it.

When Montesquieu returned to Paris in the 1720s, he attached himself to two influential literary groupings. The first of these was the salon of Madame de Lambert. In her drawing-room in the Rue de Richelieu nobility and middle classes met to discuss topics of general moral and philosophical interest. Fontenelle was prominent among the guests, along with his friend the poet La Motte. Papers on philosophical topics, especially of a relatively uncontroversial moral character, were read; but one of the main activities of the salon was the selection of possible candidates for the French Academy and the organization of campaigns for their election.

Overlapping with Madame de Lambert's salon in membership but different in activity was the Club de l'Entresol. This was a body of men (nobles and bourgeois being linked again) who met to discuss political topics. The Chevalier Ramsay (a link through his Jacobite connection between France and Scotland), the Abbé de Saint-Pierre, the idealistic advocate of perpetual peace, the Marquis d'Argenson, author of memoirs which were to become famous, Gallican in ecclesiastical leanings, and known to his contemporaries, on account of his advocacy of royal democracy, as Secretary of State of the Republic of Plato: these were the principal members of the Entresol, along with the loosely attached Montesquieu and the occasional visitor Bolingbroke. Here for the first time political ideas of an advanced kind were discussed in an organized body.

### 'The footsteps of human reason'

f 4

Two French writers were beginning to emerge in these years: Montesquieu and Voltaire. The first published in 1721 his *Lettres Persanes*, one of the century's most brilliant and successful works. It is the imaginary correspondence of two travellers, Usbek and Rica, who leave Persia to inspect the civilization of Europe. They are in France at the time of the death of Louis XIV. They witness the struggles of Jesuits and Jansenists, the financial experiments of p 321 (16) John Law, and the circulation of new philosophical ideas. Drawing abundantly on the *Turkish Spy* of Marana, Montesquieu took delight in infusing the atmosphere of the East into his travellers' letters. The ideas they encountered and expressed were inspired by the inquiring and doubting method of Descartes rather than by that of Locke. Usbek writes from Paris to a dervish left behind in Persia:

> There are Philosophers here who indeed have not attained to the summit of the Oriental wisdom; they have never been caught up to the Throne of Light . . ., nor felt the raptures of a Divine Fury: but left to themselves, deprived of holy aid, they follow in silence the footsteps of human reason.

Montesquieu's name was made by the *Lettres Persanes*, but he sought a more serious reputation. After travelling in Italy and England, he wrote and in 1734 published a robust work on the history of Rome, the *Considérations sur les Causes de la Grandeur des*

*Romains et de leur Décadence*. Here, though he has not developed an irreproachable historical method, he shows himself to have a reflective and inquisitive mind and in his analysis of historical causes he is preparing the way for a greater historian than he, Edward Gibbon.

Voltaire meanwhile had become a celebrated figure. In 1718 he p 261 (1) had introduced violent anticlerical propaganda into a tragedy on the Oedipus theme. Four years later, in a poem *Le Pour et le Contre*, which enjoyed a wide clandestine circulation, he announced himself as a non-Christian. He came into conflict with authority and twice saw the inside of the Bastille before going into temporary and fruitful exile in England. After his return he published what was perhaps the 18th century's best-known work, the *Lettres Philosophiques* (1734), in which almost every aspect of English life p 323 (24, 26) was gaily analyzed. The multiplicity of religions and prevalence of religious toleration, the balances of constitutional monarchy, the science of Newton, the epistemology of Locke whom he saw as p 20 (17) vastly superior to Descartes, all these were expounded in brilliant and seductive language to the French reader, who was also told almost for the first time of the existence of the dramatic works of Shakespeare.

France and England were the two main centres of new thought at this stage in the 18th century, and to a point were interdependent. Voltaire and Montesquieu had visited England and drew largely on this experience. In Naples also there was significant intellectual activity. Gravina was well known as a poetical theorist and as an originally minded student of Roman law. Celestino Galiani, best known now as the uncle of the famous *abbé* who enlivened

'Gulliver's Travels', ostensibly a satire on travel books, was in reality the 18th century's most scathing indictment of human meanness and greed. In its four books, the Lilliputians (shown in this engraving from a 1797 French edition) are petty, the Brobdigagians gross, the Laputans deranged, the Yohoos obscene. (2)

Parisian society in the 1760s, was celebrated as an educationist who became involved in trouble for introducing the study of Locke into the Neapolitan schools. Paolo Mattia Doria was a prolific polymath with influential friends. More important was Giannone, whose *Istoria Civile del Regno di Napoli* (1723), as well as being a pioneering work in the field of social history, was so radically anti-papal in its attitudes that the author was held by the populace to be personally responsible when the traditional miracle of the liquefaction of Saint Januarius's blood failed in 1723. Giannone was famous throughout Europe, but in Naples he was outlawed and ended his days in miserable exile. He was praised by Voltaire, Montesquieu, and Gibbon. The greatest of the Neapolitan writers of this time, though not the best known in his day, was Vico. A new and individualistic approach to human history is found in his *Scienza nuova* (1728 and 1730), which develops a cyclical theory of civilizations on a basis of philosophy and philology. Vico lived a modest and withdrawn life in the heart of Naples, but after his death, his fame was to spread far and wide. He is not in any ordinary sense a man of the Enlightenment, but he must rank as one of the 18th century's greatest figures.

## Forming a party

The year 1734 was a year of great events in the development of thought: the *Essay on Man*, the *Lettres Philosophiques*, and the *Considérations sur les Romains* all saw the light of day. The *Lettres Philosophiques* provoked a furious reaction on the part of public authority. Denounced to the police, condemned by the *Parlement* of Paris, the work was burnt by the public hangman. Montesquieu encountered less trouble, but found it necessary to have cancels inserted in his text and to withdraw a Paris edition; he abandoned for the moment his intention of writing on the English constitution. Nor did Pope escape censure. The Genevan Crousaz produced a polemical critique of the *Essay on Man*, which Johnson translated into English; a French ecclesiastic called Gautier published a work with the forthright title *Essai sur l'Homme Convaincu d'Impiété* (1746). In this he declared that Pope's poem should be held in execration by every Christian. Louis Racine, son of the great dramatist, drew attention to traces of deism or of the philosophy of Spinoza in the *Essay*; he received from Pope a complete profession of Catholic orthodoxy.

The ten years following the appearance of these controversial works are marked by few significant new contributions to the Enlightenment. They constitute a period of assimilation of ideas already in circulation. Voltaire's *Eléments de la Philosophie de Newton* (1738) popularized in France the optics of the English scientist.
p 264
(11) The Venetian Francesco Algarotti had the same aim for Italy in his elegant *Newtonianismo per le Dame* (1737). The ideas of Pope inspired Voltaire's *Discours en Vers sur l'Homme* (1734–37), while Mandeville's economics underlay the more controversial *Le Mondain* (1736). The Marquis d'Argens appealed to a wide public in works of which the ablest was *La Philosophie du Bon Sens* (1737), where the philosophy of Locke was lucidly simplified. Meanwhile the ideas of France and England were beginning to spread to Germany. Frederick II of Prussia did not await his succession to the throne in 1740 to interest himself in men of letters, but when he became king his patronage was more widespread and more decisive. His Court, where French was the normal language, and the Academy of Berlin were cosmopolitan centres where Maupertuis, d'Argens, Voltaire, and Algarotti were welcomed.

If in Prussia the new ideas were encouraged by the monarch, in France they were driven underground. Many works which it was dangerous to publish, circulated clandestinely in manuscript, being passed from one reader to another, often being recopied. Sometimes the works of which they were copies had been printed, more often they remained manuscript. Many of these secret documents have survived and have their place in libraries today. More than a hundred titles have been identified. Some of them are, or are claimed to be, extracts or abridgements of works of Boulainvilliers, of Spinoza, of Collins, Bolingbroke, Pope, Fréret, Saint-Evremond, Toland and many others. One, particularly widely spread and much discussed, professed to be the recanting testament of the priest Meslier who, dying in 1729, allowed the world to know that he had been an atheist throughout the later part of his life. Others were

*Atheism is implicit in several writers of the Enlightenment, but it was still dangerous to profess it openly. 'De Tribus Impostoribus' (above), ridiculing Judaism, Christianity and Islam, was presented as an ancient heretical work.* (3)

presented as the ancient heretical diatribe *De tribus impostoribus*, in which Moses, Christ, and Mahomet were pronounced deceivers *f 3* who had sought to exploit the gullibility of the human race.

Meanwhile in Paris public attention was focused on the allegedly miraculous cures of diseases effected in the churchyard of Saint-Médard at the bottom of the Rue Mouffetard. Persons crippled or incurably ill were taken to the tomb of the Jansenist François de Pàris and there, passing through convulsive tremors, they were often restored to good health. Pàris having been a Jansenist, these cures were deemed to attest divine disapproval of the Bull *Unigenitus* which proscribed Jansenist doctrines. The government was alarmed by the threat to civil peace; the men of the Enlightenment had no sympathy for the miracles. But common opposition to the convulsionaries, as they quickly came to be known, did not reconcile the government and the advocates of the new ideas. Instead, the government became more and more sensitive to all forms of dissent and intensified its persecution of independent thought.

The middle 1740s saw a new development in France which had its echoes throughout the civilized world. This was heralded by one of the clandestine manuscripts, attributed to an unbelieving *abbé* called Dumarsais, and entitled *Le Philosophe*. The author asks who the real philosopher is, and gives the answer: the real philosopher is the man who has freed himself from the prejudices imposed by a religious education, who recognizes that religion is no more than a human passion, born of wonder, fear, and hope; who is given to the study of causes; who is governed by reason as the Christian is governed by grace. He bases his principles on observations; he realizes that all ideas come from the senses; he studies the universe but without believing that he will succeed in discovering all its secrets; he lives in society and owns his overriding duty to society; he achieves probity because he follows reason.

This picture of the philosopher or of *le philosophe* is characteristic of the 18th century. The treatise was published in 1743, along with other essays of which two were by Fontenelle, in a tiny volume with the suggestive title *Nouvelles Libertés de Penser*. It is from this moment that we begin to be able to talk of the *philosophes* as forming almost a party in the social and political life of France, and from 1746 to 1759 we see a richness of output of literary works with a philosophical content such as few countries had seen before. The conflict between writers and public bodies, Church or State, became more bitter. The eyes of the whole Western world were on France, and the battles which were fought in Paris were the battles of mankind.

## Paris, the intellectual battlefield

In 1746 there appeared a small book, not having more than the dimensions of a pamphlet, with the title *Pensées Philosophiques*. It had been hastily written between Good Friday and Easter Day. Its title caused its readers to think of the *Pensées* of Pascal, but its contents had a very different character. Vigorous scepticism with a deistic bias was the spirit of the work, not the careful, allusive, allegorical writings of earlier deists. Echoes of Montaigne, of Shaftesbury, of Bayle, are found in these short paragraphs, but the expressions are clear and undisguised. The titlepage quaintly warns the reader that the work is not destined to appeal to every-one: *Piscis hic non est omnium*, but it discloses no author's name. But it was soon discovered that the work was from the pen of a little known hack writer with a dubious police record. This was Denis Diderot. He had already published some translations from English, but no one in 1746 could divine the rich literary career which lay ahead of him. The *Parlement* of Paris rapidly ordered the work to be burnt.

p 268 (23)

Two years later another hack writer, Toussaint, met the same fate. *Les Moeurs* shocked contemporary opinion; had it appeared ten or fifteen years later, it would have been regarded as innocuous, for it was a deistic work, written at a time when the most advanced thinkers were about to turn to atheism. This new trend is fore-shadowed by La Mettrie's *L'Homme Machine* (1748). The 17th century had debated with vigour Descartes's distinction between man who had an immaterial soul characterized by the power of thought, and animals which were no more than machines, and this discussion had continued into the 18th century. Dissent from Descartes's view usually took the form of an assertion that animals did in fact possess some power of thought. But the unpopular Breton doctor, exiled because of previous works, who was the author of *L'Homme Machine*, argued differently. Descartes was wrong, not for denying a soul to animals, but for allowing one to man. Beasts certainly, he said, were machines, but so was man. Bolder than any before him in France he declared that the soul was only an empty term representing no idea. La Mettrie—known to his contemporaries as 'Monsieur Machine'—was the most auda-cious writer in France in the first half of the century.

In the same year, 1748, there appeared at Geneva the two pon-derous volumes of what posterity was to regard as the greatest work of political theory since Aristotle. This was Montesquieu's *L'Esprit des Lois*. After publishing the *Considérations sur les Romains* in 1734, Montesquieu withdrew to his estate at La Brède near Bordeaux. Here, with the occasional interruption of a visit to Paris, he devoted himself relentlessly, despite failing eyesight, to the reading and documentation which he saw as the necessary prelude to the composition of a major political work. The *Lettres Persanes*, though brilliant, were light and needed no great toil. The work on the Romans involved much more study, but on a relatively restricted subject compared with the all-embracing scope of the major work. The greatest labours in preparation came at the last stage, when the sequence of the work brought the author to the study through their sources of feudal customs and laws. 'All these documents,' he writes, 'cold, dry, insipid, harsh, I must read them all, and devour them all, as Saturn is said to have devoured stones.' The scope of *L'Esprit des Lois* is astonishing. The first books are concerned with the classification of different forms of government, and Montesquieu, not content with the traditional division into monarchy, aristocracy, and democracy, produces a division of his own and assigns to each form of government its distinctive activating principle: the republic is inspired by virtue, monarchy by honour, and despotism by fear. Not interested in theorizing on the origin of governments or the state of nature, Montesquieu is intensely concerned with the relations between morals and politics, and considers States not at one moment in time but in a historical perspective. Though he has new things to say both on the classification of governments and on their evolution through the centuries, and though his attitude to feudalism is original and has won the commendation of modern experts, the two main topics on which his thought is significantly new are those of the British constitution and of the influence of climate. Basing his remarks on first-hand observations and on contemporary periodical literature such as Bolingbroke's *Craftsman*, he discerns in the constitution of

*Portraits of Montesquieu are rare, and perhaps the liveliest is this caricature by Pier Leone Ghezzi. Short of stature (he was only 5 feet 2 inches tall), near-sighted, large-nosed and absent-minded, he did not always shine at social gatherings.* (4)

England a carefully contrived system of balances in which every abuse of power is carefully guarded against by the segregation of the legislative, executive, and judicial parts of government. And if he does not go so far as to draw up clear normative principles valid for other States on the basis of his interpretation of England, he at least leaves no doubt about his personal views. On the theory of climate he had much to say. Having at the back of his mind the medieval notion of the horoscope of religions, he works out, on the basis of experiments which, if sometimes naïve, are nevertheless original, a theory about the mode of influence by which climate moulds human societies. If his enemies accused him of introducing fatalism into politics and of seeking to govern by means of the thermometer, nevertheless he was moving thoughtfully towards the study of historical causation: a path in which both the *Lettres Persanes* and the *Considérations sur les Romains* show him to be already engaged. *L'Esprit des Lois* appeared twenty-seven years after the *Lettres Persanes*, but the same preoccupations, the same general principles, and even, from time to time, the same phrase-ology mark the two works.

Montesquieu was a parliamentary magistrate and the outlook of that profession is evident in *L'Esprit des Lois*. The *Parlement* of Paris took no action against his work, nor did the government; but ecclesiastical opposition was vocal. The theology faculty of the University of Paris, the General Assembly of the French Clergy, and the Holy See, all turned against him. The Sorbonne's opposition became a spent force, and the Assembly of the Clergy found that it had other enemies to crush; but the papal Court was relentless, although the Pontiff, Benedict XIV, was personally in his favour. *L'Esprit des Lois* was in due course placed on the Index of Prohibited Books, a condemnation which moved Montesquieu far more than he in a calmer moment thought it ought to have done. His masterpiece is nevertheless a landmark in the history of liberal thought: religious toleration, political liberty, and the rule of law remain for ever associated with it.

## The beginnings of the Encyclopédie

Happiness, for most Enlightenment figures, is a direct result of knowledge. The more effectively knowledge can be recorded and placed in circulation, therefore, the more happiness can be attained. Nor, in the recording of knowledge, should its humbler forms be disdained. The work of the craftsman and the artisan is not less worthy of being studied, described, and handed down to posterity than the refinements of the liberal arts and of philosophy.

Two historical and biographical dictionaries which enjoyed great success were first published in the 17th century: the *Grand Dictionnaire Historique* of Louis Morery, and the *Lexicon Universale* of Johann Jacob Hoffmann, published respectively in 1674 and 1677. Morery's dictionary enjoyed very great success and its final edition (1759) retains usefulness to the present day. At the end of the 17th century increasing interest was taken in manual arts and crafts, even the French Academy being sufficiently concerned to publish, under the direction of Thomas Corneille, a supplement to its dictionary of the French language under the title *Dictionnaire des Arts et des Sciences* (1694). Ten years later an English FRS, John Harris, published his *Lexicon technicum*, with similar aspirations and marked success. In 1728 appeared a work of greater renown: the *Cyclopaedia* of Ephraim Chambers. In his two folio volumes, well illustrated with plates as well as with small engravings, Chambers sought not only to record knowledge but to show the inter-connections of its various branches. The classification of knowledge under its various heads had been the concern of other writers in the past, notably of Francis Bacon. To this Chambers alludes in his preface, itself an important document of the early Enlightenment. It emphasizes the distinction between knowledge and judgement:

> The ultimate view of a work of this or any other kind should be the forming a sound Mind. . . . The end of Learning and Study is not the filling of our heads with other men's ideas; that is an enrichment which may prove for the worse, if it carry any ill quality with it.

He continues with a comparison that must be held original, for few authors liken their works to dung:

> There are many manures which the Husbandman dares not use, by reason they would corrupt the Land at the same time they enriched it. . . . A little pure Logic, or Theology, or Chymistry, in some people's heads, what mischief have they not produced?

But he largely dismisses these dangers, and offers his book to the reader with confidence that it will bring him to live in harmony with nature.

The *Cyclopaedia* was one of the great successes of the age. By the middle of the century five editions had appeared in England, and Italian translations had been started both at Venice and at Naples. A leading Paris bookseller, Le Breton, decided that a French translation was needed, and after two false starts with inadequate staff signed a contract for the preparation of the work with two collaborators of higher quality. These were Diderot, the hack writer whom we have already encountered, and d'Alembert, a recognized scientist who was already a member of the Academy of Sciences, the illegitimate son of the celebrated Madame de Tencin, and a man whose involvement made the enterprise respectable. The two editors moved in different circles. They shared the task of finding other collaborators. Diderot, well acquainted with the semi-underworld of letters, brought along other hack writers and translators, while d'Alembert was able to introduce other members of the Academy of Sciences and university professors. But what Diderot brought above all was a sense of mission, conviction of the importance of the enterprise, and a capacity (which d'Alembert proved to lack) for triumphing over all obstacles. The obstacles were going to be many and grave.

p 263 (5)

p 268 (22)

The first volume appeared in 1751, with a preface by d'Alembert which was a survey of the sciences. First he gives a philosophical account of the sciences, relating them to the experience of primitive man and explaining how, from a gradual awareness of himself first, and then of the external world, man built up a complete corpus of knowledge on the basis of sensation as it was envisaged by Locke. This is followed by a psychological discussion, in which the different branches of knowledge are related to the faculties of the human mind. Finally there comes a historical account, in which modern sciences are shown in historical relation to the ancient world, and in which the roles of the Renaissance, of Descartes, and of Locke are set in a sequence of historical evolution. This *Discours Préliminaire* of d'Alembert is one of the great texts in 18th-century history. It shows how the *Encyclopédie* fits into the story of human history; how its protagonists and its enemies fall into a clear

274

alignment; how a theory of progress can be tested against the cultural history of the modern world.

The actual content of the *Encyclopédie*, as of any work of reference, contains much material of a routine and wholly unexciting character. Not every page—far from that—contains incendiary ideas never previously openly expressed. The impartial order of the alphabet nevertheless brought into the first volume such controversial topics as *Ame* and *Athées*. Both topics were assigned to a young contributor of independent outlook, the Abbé Yvon. His article on the soul is characteristic of many writings of the *philosophes* when treating a dangerous topic. He pursues a rationalist and philosophical method, setting forth the doctrines of Spinoza and writing mockingly of some of the Fathers of the Church; but his conclusion, however unorthodoxly reached, is an orthodox one. The article on atheists shows increased audacity in method. The arguments for the existence of God can perfectly easily be inverted to prove his non-existence. Looking at the bitter controversies which have opposed Catholics and Protestants, he declares it not surprising that atheism should have arisen. Seeking to refute what Bayle has written on atheism, his exposition of Bayle's ideas is nevertheless at least as clear and persuasive as his refutation. Another article in the first volume is that of d'Alembert on *Aveugles,* which is still more daring. For in 1749 Diderot had again been in trouble with legal authority as a result of his *Lettre sur les Aveugles à l'Usage de Ceux qui Voient*. Here, studying the reaction of a blind man to whom, by means of an operation, the power of sight was given, he produced cogent arguments in favour of the Lockean doctrine that all ideas come from the senses. Partly on account of the ideas themselves, partly on account of the mode of expression which gave offence to a powerful lady at Court, Diderot was ordered to prison, and spent over three months imprisoned in the Château of Vincennes. D'Alembert's article consisted almost entirely of extracts from Diderot's *Lettre*, fully acknowledged and accompanied by glowing praise of the original.

The *Encyclopédie*, then, starting ostensibly as a wholly innocuous project for the translation of Chambers, is clearly shown, even by the first volume, to be closely linked to the philosophical movement. This link was very soon shown to be even closer than the text had suggested.

Towards the end of 1751 a young ecclesiastic, who happened to be a close friend of Yvon, submitted to the Sorbonne a thesis for the degree of doctor of divinity. Written in Latin, the thesis was not a long one. In accordance with the usage of the time its entire text was printed on one sheet of paper in very small type, with the title *Jerusalem Caelesti*. His examiners (their chairman being the Abbé Hooke, whose father had been a friend of Pope and who himself was to have amiable relations with Johnson) read his thesis no more than perfunctorily, and it was after it had been approved for the doctorate that other members of the faculty scrutinized it more closely, and found it to contain many ideas not normally expressed in theological theses (for example, that Christianity was too boastful of its miracles, and that the miracles wrought by Christ were equivocal) as well as some sentences textually borrowed from d'Alembert's *Discours Préliminaire*. While the *affaire* was at its most heated—and excitement in Paris reached unprecedented levels—the second volume of the *Encyclopédie* appeared and was discovered to include a very suspect article on '*Certitude*' written and signed by the Abbé de Prades himself. At this stage the Abbé took flight from France and sought refuge in Prussia, where Frederick the Great promptly appointed him to the office of royal chaplain. Official resentment, which was violent, rebounded on to the *Encyclopédie*, and leave to publish it was withdrawn.

## The Encyclopédie concluded

The Government, however, was oddly sympathetic to the enterprise, and in the following year the *Encyclopédie* was allowed to resume publication. Its pages continued to contain daring articles as well as commonplace assemblies of facts. The field of contributors was extended. Much can be learnt of the structure of the Enlightenment from a study of their backgrounds and personalities. The scientists were numerous: Malouin, a professor at the Collège de France, was a relative of Fontenelle; La Chapelle was an *abbé* who wrote on mathematics; three members of the Daubenton family contributed their quota, though an article promised by Buffon failed to materialize. In addition to unbelieving *abbés* like Yvon and Prades, there was a sincere priest called Mallet, professor at the Collège de Navarre. Dumarsais, reputed author of *Le Philosophe*, wrote on grammar and philology. Hack writers previously associated with Diderot included Toussaint and Eidous. Among these prominent in social and intellectual life was Duclos, Marmontel, Montesquieu, Voltaire, and (paradoxically because of the opinions he was simultaneously expressing) Rousseau, whose articles, with the important exception of *Economie Politique*, were on music. True to his intention of dealing thoroughly with manual arts and crafts, Diderot called on workmen and artisans to write. A tin-worker called Mallet was a relative of the Abbé Mallet, and gave information about his craft; two silk-workers, Laurent and Bonnet, a hosier called Barrat, a tanner called Germain, were among those who either wrote or sent in information, and Le Breton's devil, Brullé, wrote and signed the article *Prote*.

The contributors to the *Encyclopédie* did not hold physical assemblies. It is true that some of them met in the salons of Paris, where Madame Geoffrin was almost a patroness of the work; but the uniting force was the planning, co-ordination, inspiration, and example, to some extent of d'Alembert, but much more and for a longer period, of the resolute and self-sacrificing Diderot.

p 264 (10)

Not all the leading literary figures, and not even all the more prominent of the philosophes, contributed to the *Encyclopédie*, but its fortunes were linked to theirs; and when Helvétius, the most active of the *philosophes* who did not contribute, fell into serious trouble in 1758, the repercussions on the *Encyclopédie* were grave. In the summer of that year, openly and with the approval of a censor, Helvétius published *De l'Esprit*. This engagingly and persuasively written book, advocating publicly the doctrines of Locke and by allusion but not less clearly those of materialism and atheism, slipped by a readily influenced censor and was read by an astonished public. *De l'Esprit* itself was inevitably condemned by the *Parlement* and sentenced to be burnt, and dragged with it other works. Some of these, like Voltaire's deistic *Poème sur la Loi Naturelle*, ought, in the climate of 1758, to have been held harmless. The *Encyclopédie*, of which seven volumes had now been published, did not escape condemnation, though on account of the great sums which had been sunk in the enterprise it succeeded in avoiding the flames. Church and government were now united in their desire to extirpate the conspiracy which they believed they detected, and when in 1759 the Roman Congregation of the Index placed the *Encyclopédie* under its ban, and pronounced excommunication *ipso facto* on those who read or possessed it, the fortunes of the Enlightenment seemed to have sunk to their lowest point. The grimness of the situation was reflected in the gently cynical pessimism of Voltaire's *Candide*, published in the same year.

This moment of blackness was not, however, destined to last. The work of preparation of what remained unfinished in the *Encyclopédie* continued. D'Alembert severed his connection with the work, but Diderot continued with a team of writers of whom some were new, and among whom the most industrious was the Chevalier de Jaucourt, a friend of Montesquieu and a man of a wide range of culture who regarded no task as too humble and no subject as too rebarbative, and who is credited with no fewer than 60,000 articles. In spite of an unpleasant act of treachery on the part of Le Breton, who without telling Diderot mutilated some of his articles at the proof stage in the interests of tranquillity, Diderot was able to complete his task, and the remaining ten volumes of text appeared simultaneously in 1765, with titlepages bearing no authors' names and a false place of publication. The task which had seemed at times impossible was now complete, and Diderot, in the preface to the first of these ten volumes, begged his compatriots to remember that it had been seen through to its end by a small number of men isolated, frustrated, calumniated, and outraged; but, he says, they will be adequately rewarded if posterity says of them that they have not lived wholly uselessly.

The *Encyclopédie* represents the climax of the French Enlightenment and its most characteristic achievement. It was also a European phenomenon. During the period of suppression, a group of scholars at Lucca in Tuscany decided to reprint the work in the original French, notwithstanding the interdict of the papal Court and the fact that most of them were ecclesiastics. In 1769 a publisher at Leghorn sought leave to produce another edition, in French likewise, and promised to prune the text of all the theological errors of Diderot. The Archduke of Tuscany, when giving leave to publish, said that he would prefer the text of Diderot to be printed as it stood. At Yverdon in Switzerland, an Italian exile called Felice began in 1770 to publish a new *Encyclopédie* which consisted of a wide selection from the original text with a large number of new articles. Simultaneously with this a supplement to Diderot's *Encyclopédie* was being prepared by a minor *philosophe* called Robinet, who was established in the tiny autonomous duchy of Bouillon. The four volumes of the *Supplément* appeared with Paris and Amsterdam imprints in 1776 and 1777. Soon after this the Paris bookseller Panckoucke undertook the publication, under the title *Encyclopédie Méthodique*, of an edition in which the articles would be arranged by subject order, not according to the alphabet. This vast publication, in which much new material was introduced, reached eventually 196 quarto volumes, without however being completed. A reprint was started at Padua on the press of the Seminary. The *Encyclopédie Méthodique* was partially translated into Spanish, while extracts from the original works were translated into English. The most important consequence in Great Britain was the publication in 1771 of the first edition of the *Encyclopaedia Britannica*. Other encyclopaedias proliferated on a scale which, in the 19th century, was to become enormous: a far-reaching change from 1701, when the dictionary of Furetière had recorded that *encyclopédie* was merely a facetious term.

The importance of the *Encyclopédie* in the Enlightenment is twofold. In the first place it was a vehicle for the most advanced ideas of the 18th century. The attack on revealed religion is prominent in its pages. There are assaults on despotism and intolerance. The Lockean principle that all knowledge is based on experience and that all ideas come from the senses; the critique of orthodox doctrines on the nature and immortality of the soul; the assertion of materialism; the economic and scientific thought of the age; to some extent, though less, its historiography: all these find expression in the *Encyclopédie*. But as well as being a vehicle, the work had its intrinsic importance. Its stress on the manual arts and crafts, shown both in the articles and in the volumes of excellent plates, illustrates a socially progressive aspect of its outlook, and finds its echo in many quarters. Not least interestingly is it found in the *Rambler* where, very shortly after the publication of the first volume of the *Encyclopédie* in 1751, Dr Johnson writes with enthusiasm of 'the productions of mechanick art' and talks of entering the shops of artificers to study their trades.

p 268 (24)

In a more general sense it can be said that implicit in the conception of the *Encyclopédie* is the theory of intellectual progress, the belief that knowledge itself is a liberating force, and that its diffusion necessarily promotes the well-being and happiness of the human race. Some of the *philosophes* were destructive. The encyclopaedists (for the term is not synonymous) were essentially constructive because they sought to build, and what they sought to build, if not a heavenly city, was an idealized city of men, whose door was opened by the key of knowledge.

## Knowledge from the senses

One of the paradoxes of the 18th century is the co-existence of the idealistic belief in progress which underlay the whole conception of the *Encyclopédie*, with the common sense doctrines of empiricism. Locke's *Essay on Human Understanding*, as has been seen, was translated into French in 1700, but his ideas were unknown to the general public when Voltaire published the *Lettres Philosophiques* in 1734, and there was much official resistance to them. By 1760 the situation had changed. Empiricism had received its philosophical consecration in the works of the Abbé de Condillac, whose *Traité des Sensations* (1754) was a systematic, as opposed to a polemical, exposition of sensationalism. He begins by imagining a statue of human form, but possessing only one of the five senses, that of smell. He traces out the growth in the statue, from that hypothetical starting-point, of mental capacities and activities: the power of distinguishing between pleasure and pain, and between past and present; memory and habit; hope, fear, and other passions.

Condillac continues this by assigning to his statue the other senses in turn: hearing, taste, sight, and touch, and relates the whole mental equipment of man to his sense-perceptions.

p 264 (6)

The greatest 18th-century philosopher of empiricism, however, was not Condillac or any other Frenchman, but a Scot: David Hume. Educated at Edinburgh University, which was more intellectually alive than English universities of the age, Hume travelled in France at an early age. The reading of Locke and Clarke, according to his own account, destroyed in him all religious belief, and life in Paris at the time of the convulsionaries convinced him of the extent of human gullibility. Soon after returning from France he published the *Treatise of Human Nature* (1739–40), his most important work but one not fully appreciated until after his death. He starts in the *Treatise* from the principles of Locke; but while Locke insisted on induction as the only valid method of philosophical investigation, and rejected all others as arbitrary, Hume sees induction also as being arbitrary. All our faculties for him, are fallible. Knowledge may indeed be derived from the senses, but their evidence is unreliable. All logical deductions, all assertions of causal relationships, all processes of argument, are invalid:

> All our reasonings concerning causes and effects are derived from nothing but custom . . .; belief is more properly an act of the sensitive, than of the cogitative part of our nature.

Hume vividly described his reaction to the negative conclusion of his speculations:

> I am first affrighted and confounded with that forlorn solitude in which I am placed in my philosophy, and fancy myself some strange uncouth monster, who not being able to mingle and unite in society, has been expelled all human commerce, and left utterly abandoned and disconsolate.

Many other works came from his pen after the *Treatise*. In his *History of Great Britain* (1754–62) Hume showed himself to have ambitions as a historian, but he was little more than a partisan opponent of the Whigs. In his *Natural History of Religion* (1757), however, he shows a more marked historical talent. Rather than writing to deplore or to defend religion, he aims at explaining how religious sentiment has grown in human society: not by revelation, not by rational speculation, but through fear and wonder:

> Convulsions in nature, disorders, prodigies, miracles, though the most opposite to the plan of a wise superintendent, impress mankind with the strongest sentiments of religion. . . . Madness, fury, rage, and an inflamed imagination, though they sink man nearest to the level of beasts, are . . . often supposed to be the only dispositions, in which we can have any immediate communication with the Deity.

This psychological approach to religion is different from that of those writers who see an imposture in all religions, and illustrates one of the minor though most interesting aspects of the Enlightenment. Fontenelle and Montesquieu had preceded Hume in this approach, and two later works are strongly marked by it: *Du Culte des Dieux Fétiches* (1760), based on the study of primitive tribes, by the Président de Brosses, who was known to Hume, and the *Recherches sur l'Origine du Despotisme Oriental* (1762, posthumously), by Nicolas-Antoine Boulanger, a friend of many friends of Hume, notably of d'Holbach. Boulanger ascribes the rise of religions to early terrestrial catastrophes, such as the flood, which filled men's minds with the fear of superior powers, and turned them to the worship of gods. The *Natural History of Religion*, showing a more original historical sense in Hume than do his ostensibly historical writings, has its own place in the development of this approach

p 265 (17)

which culminates in 1784 in Herder's *Ideen zur Philosophie der Geschichte der Menschheit*. Here the history of beliefs, whether superstitions or not, is used to illuminate the general history of humanity.

### Atheists in the drawing-room

When Hume, in the passage from the *Treatise* quoted above, feared that he might be unable 'to mingle and unite in society', the danger was imaginary. In Scotland and in England he was a social, con-

vivial figure. In October, 1763, the Seven Years' War having ended, he accompanied to Paris Lord Hertford, the newly appointed British ambassador, in order to serve as secretary of embassy. He remained there until the beginning of 1766. It was not as an unknown figure that he came to France, for he had already been there three times, and his reputation in Paris was high. He threw himself at once, with alacrity and success, into the social life of literary circles. He knew all the leading figures: Diderot, d'Alembert, Duclos, Marmontel, Buffon, Helvétius, Turgot, Raynal, Morellet, and d'Holbach, the benevolent host, all of whom can be described as *philosophes*. Diderot tells us of Hume's assertion, in d'Holbach's drawing-room, that he had not met a single atheist in Paris. D'Holbach retorted, glancing at the eighteen other guests, that there were eighteen atheists in that very room. This was the decade of the great hostesses: Madame du Deffand and Madame Geoffrin are those best known to history, Madame de Boufflers was the one closest to Hume. Their salons were cosmopolitan: Grimm and d'Holbach came from Germany, Galiani from Naples, Beccaria from Milan. Seldom have intellectual and social life been so intertwined.

p 264 (12)

p 262–3 (3)

The anecdote of the atheists in d'Holbach's drawing-room may or may not be veracious. It is certainly indicative of currents of opinion. The empiricism of Locke was too undogmatic, too well-balanced, indeed, to remain a satisfying philosophy for the intellectually unsophisticated. This fact is both illustrated and exploited by Helvétius in *De l'Esprit*. He argues that if all ideas come from the senses (which he maintains far more rigorously than Locke ever did), then our ideas, including our opinions, are dependent on the sensory equipment of the body. This sensory equipment is not ours to create or to modify. It is a datum outside our control. Our thoughts then are not free, and all our intellectual activity is predetermined. Helvétius nevertheless retreats from a position of absolute determinism. This is partly no doubt from prudence, since (in his own figure of speech) if the face of the earth is covered with prejudices it is wise to send out from time to time a few isolated truths, like doves from the ark, to see before finally emerging oneself if the flood is subsiding. But partly also the explanation is that Helvétius is much more interested in moral philosophy than in metaphysics, and the moral philosopher is always incommoded by determinism. The influence of Helvétius is greatest in three respects: the heavy stress laid on education, the positive value discerned in strength of passion, and above all, the social conception of virtue. The just man, he declares, is the man whose actions tend to the public good.

Where in 1758 Helvétius had been content to hint, d'Holbach in 1770 was bold enough to speak outright, and added new audacities of his own. On the second page of the *Système de la Nature* he denies the existence of moral man. He asserts that man is purely a machine, subjected in everything to the forces of nature; the errors of metaphysics are simply hypotheses invented by puzzled man to explain the working of his machine. Mankind is governed in all its actions and at all times by necessity. Free will is non-existent. Education—highly important in society—is simply the explanation of necessity to children. A consequence of the reduction of everything to the physical is the denial of the existence of God. Until 1770 dogmatic atheism had found its expression in France in clandestine manuscripts and in the solitary work *L'Homme Machine* of La Mettrie. Now it was open and avowed. God as the theologians depict him says d'Holbach, is wholly impossible, and belief in such a being does not even procure any social advantages. Man can hope for an improvement in his lot only if he eradicates from his mind all idea of God. D'Holbach falls not infrequently into inconsistency. When he conjures men to submit themselves to necessity he does not explain with what resources they might do otherwise. But above all, writing with an eloquence so great that many of his pages have been ascribed to Diderot, he took the ideas which were circulating by word of mouth in drawing-rooms and in secret manuscripts handed from friend to friend, and published them for all to read in their clearest form.

p 265 (16)

This was also their most frightening form. 'May God (if there is one) have mercy on my soul (if I have one)', wrote Voltaire after the publication of the *Système de la Nature*; and Goethe describes his reaction to its appearance: 'It came before us so grey, so

p 265 (18)

cimmerian, so corpse-like, that we could hardly endure its presence, and shuddered before it as before a ghost.' D'Holbach, by drawing to their extreme conclusions some of the Enlightenment's doctrines, did not consolidate the unity of the movement but dealt it a serious blow. Those whose overriding concern was to flout God and priest could accept allegiance to the *Système de la Nature*, and many remained loyal. D'Holbach's work provided for them not only propagandist slogans but sometimes a genuine and heart-felt inspiration. This is the case with the youthful Shelley, who was well-read in d'Holbach, and who in his *Queen Mab* eloquently exclaims:

> *Spirit of Nature! all-sufficing Power,*
> *Necessity! thou mother of the world!*
> *Unlike the God of human error, thou*
> *Requir'st no prayers or praises.*

Those thinkers, however, in whom philosophical scepticism was lined with some degree of confidence in humanity, found the new dogmatism of d'Holbach no less objectionable than the old dogmatisms which they had for years fought against. For Voltaire, the leading figure of the Enlightenment, who was to live for eight active years after the appearance of the *Système de la Nature*, the book's intolerant atheism was repulsive. From the days of the Regency he had attacked error and tyranny wherever he found them. He had been a deist then and was a deist now. If he appeared to have changed from radicalism to conservatism, it was because others had moved around him. He, however, volatile and unstable in his enemies' eyes, had remained constant in the essentials of his philosophy.

## Rational politics

If in its theory of knowledge the 18th century shows a move from the *a priori* theories of the Cartesian to Lockean and post-Lockean empiricism, a similar evolution is shown in the political thought of the age. The principal legacy of the 17th century in the field of political theory had been the doctrine of natural law: the belief that there are in politics certain initial given principles to which States should adhere and against which they can be tested. These principles were held to be rationally discoverable and of universal application. This doctrine, whose great exponents were Grotius and Pufendorf, though challenged in the 18th century, continued to have many adherents. Burlamaqui, a Swiss writer of Italian Protestant origin, gave a restatement of natural law doctrines in his *Principes du Droit Naturel* (1747), which became an accepted text-book. Most political writers of the 18th century have a debt to the natural law school, but most of them are also moving away from it to empirical attitudes. The co-existence of the two schools of thought gives the political thought of the Enlightenment its special character and interest.

Montesquieu shows an oscillation between the two points of view. He is empirical in his study of the different States about which, from personal observation or from travellers' tales, he can document himself, he is empirical in arguing about what ought to be on the basis of what is. He has nevertheless certain firm *a priori* beliefs to which he constantly returns: that no one should do harm to himself, that freedom of conscience is good, that freedom itself is a good. Most revealingly, when discussing slavery he argues at one moment that slavery, if it exists, should be organized in a particular way, at another that it is evil and ought not to exist at all.

A similar and yet more complicated alternation of views marks the most influential political philosopher of the Enlightenment, Jean-Jacques Rousseau, whose varying attitudes but unvarying candour have perplexed the scholars of two centuries. In his earliest political works, the *Discours sur les Sciences et les Arts* (1750) and the *Discours sur l'Inégalité* (1755) he is destructive. In the first he writes to deplore intellectual progress which he sees as the concomitant and indeed the cause of moral regression (though he is simultaneously contributing articles to the *Encyclopédie* and is thus committed to its progressive aim). In the second *discours* he writes to deplore the modern State and the circumstances in which man emerged from his innocent pre-social condition to call it into existence. The elements and the phraseology of insurrectionism appear here in Rousseau's writing and were fully exploited by the

p 266 (20)

*Madame Geoffrin's salon: a complete key to the painting reproduced on p. 262–3.* *1, Buffon. 2, Mlle Lespinasse. 3, Mlle Clairon. 4, Le Kain. 5, D'Alembert. 6, Carl Vanloo. 7, Helvétius. 8, Duclos. 9, Piron. 10, Crébillon. 11, Bernis. 12, Duc de Nivernais. 13, Duchesse d'Anville. 14, Le Prince de Conti. 15, Mme Geoffrin. 16, Fontenelle. 17, Joseph Vernet. 18, Comtesse d'Houdetot. 19, Montesquieu. 20, Clairault. 21, D'Aguesseau. 22, Mairan. 23, Maupertuis. 24, Maréchal de Richelieu. 25, Malesherbes. 26, Turgot. 27, Diderot. 28, Quesnay. 29, Barthélemy. 30, Caylus. 31, Danville. 32, Soufflot. 33, Bouchardon. 34, St Lambert. 35, D'Argental. 36, Bust of Voltaire. 37, Duc de Choiseul. 38, Hénault. 39, Rameau. 40, Rousseau. 41, Raynal. 42, La Condamine. 43, Thomas. 44, Vien. 45, Marmontel. 46, Marivaux. 47, Gresset. 48, Bernard de Jussieu. 49, Daubenton. 50, Abbé de Condillac. 51, Madame de Graffigny. 52, Réaumur. 53, Madame du Bocage. (5)*

Jacobins of the Revolution. In *Du Contrat Social* (1762), which is a sustained treatise, not a concise essay, Rousseau describes the natural condition of mankind in Hobbesian terms as a lawless state of war. He explains how man emerges from that state by the signing of a freely negotiated rational contract. The terms of the contract are fixed and uniform; they result in the surrender of the unrestricted natural liberty of the individual into a common pool of sovereignty vested in the entire people. So far, Rousseau is enunciating general rules which tolerate no exceptions and which are conceived in the tradition of the theorists of natural law. When his account of the setting-up of the State is ended, however, expediency comes into its own. Expediency, not fixed rules, determines the composition of the *prince* or executive authority in the State, expediency—or even its extreme form, *raison d'Etat*—establishes an obligatory religion within the State.

Insurrectionists and revolutionaries could certainly find slogans in the pages of Rousseau. They could find them also in *Le Code de la Nature* (1755) of Morelly, one of the founders of socialism. In his book property is roundly denounced as the cause of all unhappiness, *fons et origo malorum*, and the communist principle, 'to each according to his need', is picturesquely expressed when the author says that the world is a well-stocked table on which the food belongs now to all, because all are hungry, now only to some, because the others are satisfied. Progressive ideas of a different type appear in the *Considérations sur le Gouvernement Ancien et Présent de la France* of the Marquis d'Argenson, written in the 1730s and after enjoying a prolonged manuscript circulation, published finally in 1764. D'Argenson's family had long held important offices in the French State, and his political thought is influenced by his experience. He envisaged, and described in considerable detail, a State in which the role of the *Parlements* and the *noblesse de robe* was reduced to the minimum, and which can be described as royal democracy. The power of the Crown was to remain undiminished, and the wishes of the people were to be directly articulate. Deploring the concentration of power in the hands of functionaries who have acquired their offices by purchase, he recommends the establishment in each locality of popular magistrates charged with local government and finance (though not the levying of taxes as then understood, for taxes would be abolished in favour of free gifts to the Crown). D'Argenson's proposals, visionary and naïve as they are, provide another example of social idealism developing within the framework of the *ancien régime*.

More significant because more fruitful, and involving an alliance between idealism and empiricism, is the famous work of Cesare Beccaria, *Dei Delitti e delle Pene*, 1764 (see also Chapter X). A Milanese nobleman who at the age of twenty-three was won over to the cause of the *philosophes* by reading the *Lettres Persanes* and *De l'Esprit*, he was only twenty-eight when he produced the work of which it was said that never did so small a book have so great an effect. Its influence was great indeed. The utilitarian school of philosophy was the next and normal development from the ideas

p 266 (19)

of Helvétius and Hume, and received expression before Bentham in d'Holbach's able and much neglected *Système Social* (1773). This movement owes much to Beccaria. It is in his preface that we find the celebrated phrase, previously indited by Hutcheson, 'the greatest happiness of the greatest number'. Attempting throughout his work (as d'Holbach was later to do) to explain the moral world in physical or mathematical terms, Beccaria continually provides echoes of Montesquieu. He insists on the rule of law: penalties should be determined by laws and not by magistrates, and the laws should be written for all to read. His underlying doctrine is that a legal penalty should be proportionate to the gravity of the offence. The gravity of the offence depends, not on the motive of the offender, nor on the dignity of the person offended, nor on the element of sin contained in the offence, but on the harm done to the State. This is his essential principle, rigorous, fair, and enlightened. Towards the end of the book he writes: 'Would you prevent crimes? Let liberty be attended with knowledge.' This is the characteristic wish of the Enlightenment.

## Diffusion: Germany, Russia, America

Though London and Paris have each been held the birthplace of the Enlightenment, its real cradle is to be seen in the dialogue between the two, in the interaction of the two cultures in the period 1680–1734. From this double centre the new ideas spread in varied directions, often finding and being fertilized by indigenous intellectual developments in other places. This geographical radiation is one aspect of the diffusion of the Enlightenment. Another is the gradual permeation of the new ideas into different fields of human activity, culminating in their conquest of the seats of political power.

If the relationship of the Enlightenment to scientific activity was always a close one, from the earliest works of Fontenelle to the limitless curiosity of Franklin and Jefferson, the same cannot be said of its relationship to the world of scholarship. In spite of the undoubted learning of Bayle and Fréret, the *philosophes* often mocked the erudite, and the contempt in which scholars were often held in France is engagingly represented by Chardin's p 262 (3) satirical painting, *Le Singe Antiquaire*. In England, Prussia, and Italy the opposition was less marked. In France, scepticism about historical studies had found its extreme expression in the Jesuit Hardouin who claimed that all (or almost all) the literary texts of the ancient world were forgeries. An important exception to the separation of *philosophes* and scholars is afforded at the middle of the century by Montesquieu, less in his work on the Romans than in the last books of *L'Esprit des Lois*, which show a remarkable mastery of a difficult and obscure historical period. It is, however, not until 1776 that the spirit of the *philosophes* becomes clothed in p 265 (14) sustained, peerless scholarship, in Edward Gibbon's *Decline and Fall of the Roman Empire*. Though Gibbon's *Memoirs* disclose his disapproval of 'the intolerant zeal of the philosophers and Encyclopaedists, the friends of d'Holbach and Helvétius' his complaint is of the 'bigotry of dogmatists' with which they preached their tenets, and that October day of 1764, when, sitting musing amidst the ruins of the Capitol, while the bare-footed friars were singing vespers in the Temple of Jupiter, he first formed the notion of writing the decline and fall of Rome, is one of the great and decisive moments in the history of the Enlightenment.

It might seem unlikely that between the Enlightenment and the Churches there could be any other relationship than one of complete opposition. This was not so. The belief in freedom of conscience which was one of the *philosphes*' firmest principles is often expressed by Protestant divines. In Switzerland and in Prussia the attitude of Protestants to the new ideas was often open-minded, and in England the dividing line between non-conformity and deism is not always easy to draw. But even in the Roman Catholic Church the new philosophy was not always at once rebutted and still less were its exponents always ostracized. An amiable correspondence was possible between Voltaire and Benedict XIV, and between Montesquieu and Cardinal Passionei. In many Catholic countries the 18th century is marked by the growth of anti-curialist parties within the Church. These, often nationalist in inspiration, sought

to resist any extension within their own country of the power of the papal Court. They were inspired by a deep dislike of the Jesuits, as the most prominent and faithful instruments of the policies of the Holy See, and in this respect were the heirs to the Jansenists of the previous century. Anti-curialism was indeed the principal form which Jansenism assumed in the 18th century; and since anti-curialism had much in common with some of the ideas of the philosophers, there developed a *de facto* alliance, in many respects surprising, between Jansenism and the Enlightenment. This alliance was less evident in France than elsewhere. From the days of the convulsionaries onwards, the Jansenists' journal, *Nouvelles Ecclésiastiques*, was the leading scourge of the philosophical movement. But even in France a common hostility to the Jesuits brought some elements on each side closer together.

In Italy the Jansenists represented liberal opinion, with the paradoxical result that French writers, persecuted at home by Jansenists, turned to the Jansenists of Rome for protection against attacks by the Holy Office. It was in Spain, however, that the role of Jansenism—or regalism, as it was there called—was greatest in relation to the Enlightenment. The new ideas had penetrated but little into Spain in the first half of the century. Feijóo, a monk whose *Teatro Crítico Universal* (1726–39) shows the influence of the inductive philosophy of Bacon and of the scepticism of Bayle, and a contempt for scholasticism, is the prime figure in the early Spanish Enlightenment. He was followed by Cadalso, whose *Cartas Marruecas* (1789, posthumously) are an imitation of the *Lettres Persanes*. On the accession of Charles III in 1759, regalism became a dominant force at the Spanish Court, where the ideas of the *philosophes* also began to make themselves heard. A similar development in Portugal, where the chief minister Pombal showed himself to be a vigorous reforming figure, led to the expulsion of the p 32 (f 1) Jesuits in 1759.

The ideas of the Enlightenment are thus seen to have become active in courts and ministries. The process had in fact started earlier. In small Italian states, such as the Archduchy of Tuscany and the Republic of Lucca where the *Encyclopédie* had found a second home, enlightened and independent rulers were often found. Frederick the Great was ready to welcome the *philosophes* to his court at Potsdam. Catherine of Russia welcomed them to Saint Petersburg. That the ideas of the political philosophers of the age found a hearing at many courts is to the credit of the monarchs. In Austria, Russia, Sweden, and Tuscany reforms in criminal law were inspired by the doctrines of Beccaria. The portrait of the Emperor Leopold II, painted by Pompeo Batoni, which hangs in the Kunsthistorisches Museum at Vienna, shows him with a copy of *l'Esprit des Lois* in his hand.

The most important geographical extension of the Enlightenment, however, was across the Atlantic. Fontenelle, in 1688, anxious to destroy complacency, had advanced as a wild hypothesis that the *beaux-esprits* of future ages might be Americans. When the Abbé Raynal almost a century later treated American history in his extremely successful *Histoire Politique et Philosophique des Deux Indes* (1770) he was answering a widespread demand. America, in the interval, had become well known in France, and the advanced ideas circulating in Europe had penetrated into the American continent. If the effect of the Enlightenment in South America was not to reach its peak until the 19th century, though General Miranda had already been a travelling intermediary, assimilation in the British colonies was more rapid. At the age of sixteen Benjamin Franklin had, through the reading of Shaftesbury and Collins, become 'a real doubter in many points of our religious doctrine' and at eighteen, influenced by Woolaston's *Religion of Nature Delineated* for which he was setting up the type, he published *A Dissertation on Liberty and Necessity* (1725) which shows him already well acquainted with the ideas of the deists and the controversies of the day. Reading, experiment, and travel made him a characteristic example of the Enlightenment, surpassed in this, in his own country, only by Thomas Jefferson, by whose hand the political ideas of the day received consummate and fruitful expression in the Declaration of Independence. This was the culmination of the Enlightenment.

# IX THE RISE OF THE PEOPLE

*Life and Death among the Very Poor*

OLWYN HUFTON

*'Patience, labour, sobriety, frugality and religion*
*should be recommended to them; all the rest*
*is downright fraud.'*

EDMUND BURKE, in 1795

**Those who worked the land**

could expect little but hardship, undernourishment and toil. The 'peasant population' is a convenient phrase, and one is inclined to forget that in fact it covered most of the men and women alive in Europe. This book, like most history books, has so far ignored them, concentrating on the privileged few who made up 'civilization'.

The lives of these anonymous millions had always been hard, but during the latter half of the 17th century and the first decade of the 18th, conditions rapidly deteriorated with the tragic regularity of widespread harvest failure. Lack of food left the people a prey to disease. Epidemics of typhus and enteric fevers were common, and every few years came the killer of killers, the plague. Those who survived were often ruined and had sold what land they possessed to buy food. The sick and destitute sought refuge in the towns where they perished in garrets, cellars or on the streets.

Such a picture of the early 18th-century countryside is not often reflected in art, which was produced for patrons who preferred comfort, prettiness and charm. One of the exceptions is the Italian painter Giacomo Ceruti, called 'Il Pitochetto' – the Beggar. He came from Brescia; the dates of his birth and death are unknown, but he was active between 1720 and 1750.

Ceruti is a man of outstanding interest, not only for his quality as an artist, but also for the range of his curiosity and sympathy. Trained in the decorative style of Tiepolo and Piazzetta, he completely abandoned the frivolity of Rococo and turned for his subjects to the life of the very poor – labourers, beggars and outcasts. This old man leaning on his spade is typical: precise in its observation, compassionate without being sentimental. (1)

**Against the plague** Europe had no effective remedy. The disease was attributed to a variety of causes, most commonly to poisonous vapours. The real carriers were fleas which preyed on rats and men. Above: a doctor dressed in protective clothing. The 'beak' contained strong-smelling medicament thought to be prophylactic against contagion. (2)

**The plague struck Naples** in 1656. One who witnessed it was the painter Micco Spadaro, who left a vivid record of what he saw (below). Galley slaves with hooks are dragging corpses to the carts taking them to the burial pits. The sedan chairs, on the right and against the wall on the left, were used to carry the sick to plague hospitals. (4)

The last great outbreaks were those of Marseilles in 1721 and Messina in 1743, both strictly localized. At Marseilles (above) many tried to escape by taking to boats, but the whole quayside soon became heaped with dead bodies. The black clouds represent the plague-polluted atmosphere. (3)

The end of the plague is symbolized (below) in the *Pestsäule* at Vienna, erected to celebrate the city's recovery from the epidemic of 1679. (6)

Victims of disease were treated in such hospitals as these, often crowded, together into a single large room. This hospital of 1746 is at Hamburg. In the foreground an amputation is carried out by a neatly bewigged doctor and, on the left, a priest administers the last rites to a dying man. (5)

'Bedlam' – the Bethlehem Hospital in London, originally a nunnery – was presented to the city by Henry VIII as a lunatic asylum. The palatial new buildings erected for it at Moorfields in 1678 (right) are evidence of public concern but not of the conditions inside. It was not until 1792 that Pinel, in Paris, released lunatics from their chains, and this example was for long not followed in the rest of Europe. Hogarth's portrayal of Bedlam as the last scene of the Rake's Progress (below) is certainly not far from the truth, with its overcrowding, barred windows and groups of elegant visitors who have come to gape at the madmen. (7, 8)

The barber-surgeon (top right) still exercised what skill he possessed on the poor, though surgery, as described in Chapter III, was making progress in the medical schools of Paris, Edinburgh and London. (9)

Prisoners in the 18th century, often debtors rather than criminals, were at the mercy of their gaolers until they could pay for their delivery. Filth, brutality and lack of food characterized prison life for the poor. John Howard (below right) made it his mission to reform the system in England, and as a result those found not guilty or held on spurious charges were released and conditions inside the gaols made healthier. (10)

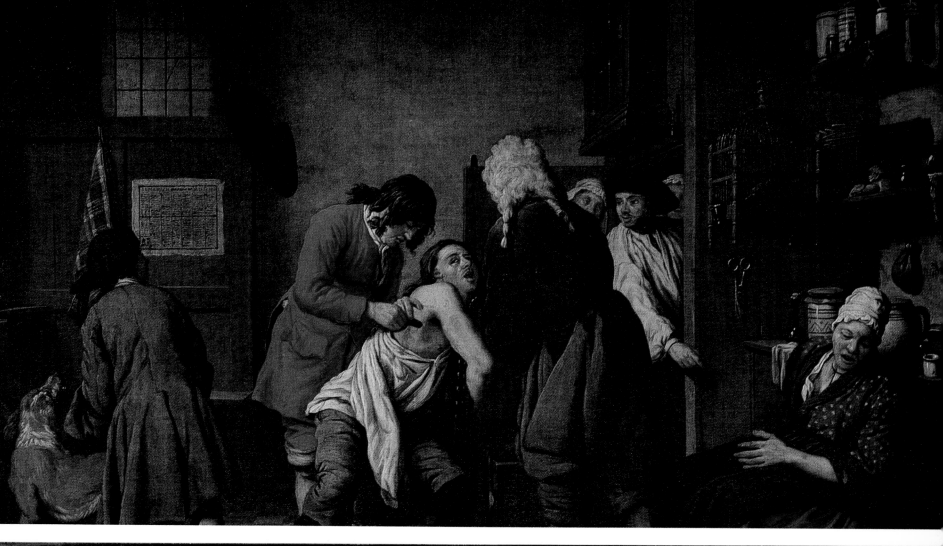

**The duties of charity** were acknowledged by the public, though in France St Vincent de Paul's success in reminding Christians of their moral obligation to help the weak was made an excuse for official parsimony. An 18th-century painting (left) shows the saint – who had died in 1660 – in an orphanage with a group of his Dames de Charité. Reformers had to struggle against much self-interest and bigotry. Abandoned children were seen as the fruits of sin (as in the engraving above) and it was held that to protect one was to encourage the other. (11, 12)

**A new foundling hospital** was opened in 1740 by the philanthropic ex-sailor, Captain Thomas Coram (above). Left: a contemporary engraving of babies being brought to its gates. In 1756 the hospital was given a parliamentary grant. (13, 14)

**The children of the poor** were lucky if they survived infancy. Yet in spite of the mortality rate, population grew during the 18th century. The number of mouths kept steadily ahead of the food supply, and to a family living at the limit of its resources an extra baby could spell disaster. Children, sent out to work as soon as they had the strength, were expected to be self-supporting from infancy. Right: a mother begging for her children, by Ceruti. (16)

**The midwife** (above: a satirical print by Rowlandson) was often the oldest woman in a village. The crudeness of the methods used for delivering babies made cripples of many of them. (15)

**'Make me dutiful** and obedient to my benefactors' ran a *Poor Girl's Primer* of 1789. Charity schools alleviated suffering, but inculcated ideas of subservience thought appropriate to the deserving poor. Left: the chapel of the Foundling Hospital in London, and (above) Louis XVI and his family visiting a similar institution in Paris. (17, 18)

**The streets teemed with life,** constituting a new force which, as the century advanced, grew more and more dangerous – the urban proletariat, 'the mob'. These three town views in different countries show the crowded but on the whole peaceful face of European cities. Above: Dublin, Capel Street; a poor man tries to beg from the horseman on the left. Right: Turin, a market in the Piazza San Carlo, about 1752. Below: Paris, part of Les Halles during a celebration for the birth of the Dauphin in 1782. (19, 20, 21)

**Those without work begged.** Those who could beg no longer, died. Children were trained to beg from infancy, and every European city had its hordes of beggars, turning easily to pilfering and crime when the opportunity offered. Ceruti's beggar with his little daughter (right) has by sunset done well enough to be able to eat for one more day. (23)

**'Thus do the useful** end their days'– Goya's grim comment on the old age that awaited the labourer. (22)

**Close to death** another aged beggar stretches out his hand for a last crumb of comfort. Ceruti here preserves a sight that must have been common enough in the poorer streets of most 18th-century cities. (24)

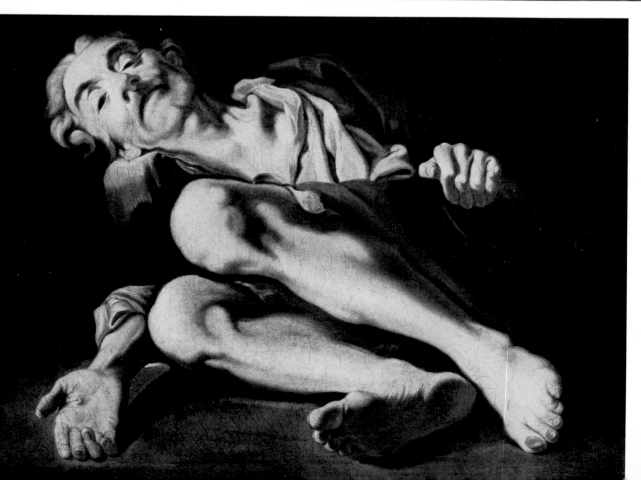

**A family of beggars:** it was to cure such situations as this that schemes for child-labour were hailed as philanthropic improvements. (25)

**Poverty bred crime** and crime brought savage punishments from a society that feared for its own safety. The depravity of the poor was a myth which the propertied classes took comfort in believing, but their belief helped to make it a reality. Girls from the country were forced into prostitution in the towns, to end their lives in disease and degradation. Right: prostitutes in Vienna being made to sweep the streets. (27)

**Torture and death** were meted out with horrifying readiness. Above: breaking on the wheel, an agonizing death practised in France and Germany in which the victim's bones were broken with an iron bar. Right: branding on the hand and (far right) the ordeal of the pillory. Below: Hogarth's Idle Apprentice, whose story typifies middle class attitudes, on his way to hanging. (26, 28, 29, 30)

**Winter in London:** in the vegetable market of Covent Garden, which was also the pleasure-quarter of the town, women from the country warm themselves at an early morning fire, while two of the girls attract the attentions of some returning revellers. In the centre a spinster on the way to church, with a servant boy carrying her prayer-book, looks at them with disapproval. Tom King's Coffee House, shown here, was among the most notorious haunts of London. (31)

# Life and Death among the Very Poor

OLWEN HUFTON

THE ECONOMIST MALTHUS, concerned in the 19th century with the problem of maintaining the precarious balance between population and supply, saw as the only answer the two natural checks, famine and disease, which rising at intervals applied a ruthless shears to a growing populace whose demands were rapidly outstripping food production. He might well have chosen the latter half of the 17th century and the first decade of the 18th as classic crises of the type he delineated. Indeed, so general was harvest failure in almost all the countries of Europe that historians have conjectured a change in climate, have noted the growth of glaciers—a little ice age—and attributed the hardship to a meteorological upheaval. The debate remains undecided but certainly the closing years of the century did see an extraordinary run of disasters for European food supplies from Castile and Sicily in the south to Finland in the north; striking alike Alpine villages, the cornlands of Poland and even the chestnut crop of the Tarn. In the north the enemy was damp—rain which caused the corn to rot in the fields before it reached fruition or which brought the grain weevil, the *hanneton* of Normandy, to consume the crop; in the Mediterranean lands the enemy was drought, which—ironically—produced a bumper wine harvest but which reduced corn production to one of the lowest recorded levels and brought with it to Spain and France plagues of grasshoppers which descended like locusts and stripped the fields. In the train of famine came disease. It is almost a truism to point out the enhanced susceptibility of an undernourished population to epidemics, to typhus, enteric fevers, influenza and so on; but as well as these, the food crisis of the late 17th century was accom-

p 282-3

panied by the killer of all killers, the bubonic plague, a disease which could strike the nourished as well as the undernourished and which had a devastating effect upon town populations in particular. The coincidence of serious plague outbreaks with protracted harvest failure leaves no doubt that these two events were in some way associated. But whether this was because at such times the rat hosts of the fleas which carried the plague migrated to towns and granaries in search of food, or whether the plague fleas multiplied most rapidly in the same climatic conditions which caused harvest failure is still not known. Great Britain was last struck by plague in 1665 and though the years immediately after 1693 were known as the 'seven ill years' because of the heavy death toll from typhus, France and Spain suffered far more from plague in the 'nineties. Then in 1708 came the outbreak in Poland which spread through Silesia, Brandenburg, the Baltic countries and Scandinavia, halving the population of Danzig, fractionalizing those of Copenhagen, Königsberg, Prague, Cracow, Stockholm and Helsinki, leaving 11,000 vacant farms in East Prussia alone and

f 2

pressing west through north-west Germany in 1712, to Austria, Bohemia and Bavaria in 1713 and there petering out mysteriously before making its route southwards to Italy.

The combined effects of dearth and disease arrested population growth and in some areas led to decline. The impact was nowhere quite the same. Most probably the population of Europe was slightly higher at the end of the 17th century than it was at the beginning though it was differently distributed. By 1700 Spain had 932 *despoblados*—deserted villages—mostly gathered in the arid interior whilst the littoral, healthier and better watered, bore a relatively prosperous air. After 1640 the population of England

either remained static or experienced an increase, slight in comparison to the estimated growth of the previous century, and the same could be said of Italy and France though that tentatively in the light of very defective figures. But beyond doubt, the food shortage and the great epidemics both checked population growth and caused a severe dislocation in the economic life of Europe.

## A century of suffering

One can do scant justice in a few sentences to the effects of famine and epidemic upon the lives of the European populace. The small landowner was forced to consume seed needed for the next sowing and to borrow in order to plant the next crop; his mounting indebtedness to the large landowner from whom he had to borrow corn at interest until repayment of the debt might even force him to part with his land. This is only one aspect. Women rendered infertile by starvation, an increase in the number of still births, and family units cut down by quite minor diseases in face of lowered resistance are others. Nor did the countryside alone suffer, for local industries were seriously affected by the shrinkage of rural markets in times of dearth when the small peasants, forced to spend their entire income on food, simply ceased to buy other goods. Small towns in affected areas found themselves flooded with the starving and destitute from the surrounding countryside who came hoping to draw attention to their plight. The towns of the plain of Languedoc, for example, became the burial ground of the mountain dwellers of the Massif Central who, disease ridden and weak from lack of food, swarmed out of the barren hills and perished, mere names and a date in a death register.

The effects of plague or virulent epidemic were no less terrifying —indeed perhaps they were more so for no one knew where and who they would strike, the flea being no respecter of persons—and if the rat-ridden hovels of the poor rendered them the most susceptible, the rich were not guaranteed immunity. The best account of the psychological aspects of an outbreak remains Defoe's imaginative *Journal of the Plague Year*. It depicts the rich fleeing, panic stricken, from the scene of the outbreak, the suspension of trade, the inadequacy of the attempts to seal off the victims, the carelessness of the poor who did not hesitate to invade abandoned houses for loot and deal in old clothes and objects which may well have been contaminated. He also touches on another point of relevance—the revival of religious intensity in face of impending death. One of the strange ironies about the late 17th century is that at a time when intellectuals were taking their first tentative steps along a road that was to lead them to disbelief, the larger part of the populace was moving in the opposite direction. Processions of penitent sinners, barefoot and sometimes indulging in self-flagellation, led by bishops and clerics, were designed to wring mercy from the deity; and when the plague had passed, splendid ceremonies brought together dignitaries of the Church, town officials and magistrates in flowing robes, with *Te Deums* and orations to offer humble thanks for delivery.

p 322 (23)

It is certainly not surprising that every country in Europe between 1660 and 1685 found it necessary to reconstitute its methods of according poor relief—a fact we shall examine more closely later—and that it is from this period that date the foundation of many of the great European *hospices*, for example of Dijon and

Lyons, whilst in Spain the Hospital de la Caridad in Seville serves as a good instance, decorated by Murillo with scenes to recall the love of God for the destitute, his infinite mercy towards the poor and afflicted and the shelter offered by the Church to those in need. Splendid buildings, founded on private philanthropy yet insufficient to cope with the extent of the misery with which they were designed to contend, remain as the expression of yet another paradox—that for all its magnificence, at root *le grand siècle* was a century of poverty, human suffering and squalor.

## The plague relents

The 18th century proper presents a different picture. The hardship of the late 17th century and the first decade of the 18th is without parallel thereafter in western Europe. There were, it is true, occasional years of shortage scattered at intervals through the period but the cumulative effect of year after year of scanty harvests had vanished for ever. This factor provides the single most cogent explanation of the sudden upward movement of population in the 18th century. Throughout Europe the mortality rates declined rapidly not in normal years but because of the abatement of the great crises: 'the peaks rather than the plateau of mortality were lowered'. Secondly, with the mysterious dying out of the plague —the last outbreaks were in Marseilles and Provence in 1721–22 and Messina in 1743 and both were strictly localized—the greatest killer of adults and children alike had vanished. Other epidemics struck with less virulence and were predominantly infantile often leaving the family unit reduced but essentially capable of repairing the breach.

p 283
(3)

One would wish to create the impression of a population that breathed more easily for its liberation from famine and plague without overstressing the extent of that liberation. The population of Europe and especially the poorest sections remained a prey to

f 1

typhus, enteric fevers (typhoid in particular), smallpox, measles and diphtheria; the first two reigned perennially in all large European cities—indeed in London they killed a minimum of 1,000 people a year and perhaps only a small proportion of those afflicted died: and in Sweden 10 to 12,000 people of a population of under two million perished annually from typhus and smallpox. Known as putrid, malignant or intermittent fever, depending on the severity of the outbreak, typhus, transmitted by the bite of a body louse, was predominantly the disease of the poor and associated with the depths of human misery, undernourishment and infestation with body lice. Gracious as doubtless were the

*Vienna fell victim to a series of dreadful plagues for many years. Here a service of thanksgiving is being held after the epidemic of 1679. (2)*

public buildings of the great European cities, the streets remained filthy with refuse, and drainage was totally inadequate. Berlin could be smelt six miles away: Linnaeus compared the stench of Hamburg to an open sewer. In Stockholm, Amsterdam and Venice stagnant water and damp dwelling houses offered an open invitation to typhoid and malaria. Every city had its share of ramshackle dwellings, cramped together in medieval confusion, sometimes spilling over the still present medieval town walls. In continental Europe all except the rich let out the upper parts and the cellars of their houses to the poor. Whole families lived within the confines of one room, sleeping on straw, their only possessions a few blankets and battered cooking pots. Hygiene in rural areas was if anything even less apparent. Dwelling in one-roomed cottages where light and air were secondary considerations to warmth, and huddled together often with their animals for the heat their bodies afforded, the labouring poor lived in habitations that were an abnegation of all standards of cleanliness. To read Bishop Berkeley on the cabin of the Irish peasant filled with pigs, stinking children and animal excrement, or Doctor Bagot on the odours that issued from the Breton farm labourer's cottage, is to understand why if the winters were in any way prolonged and the family longer confined than usual the death toll was heavy, for these tiny dwellings were breeding grounds for disease. But though perhaps more perished from typhus than ever before, and though mortality rates in many large cities exceeded the birth rate, in no way did they

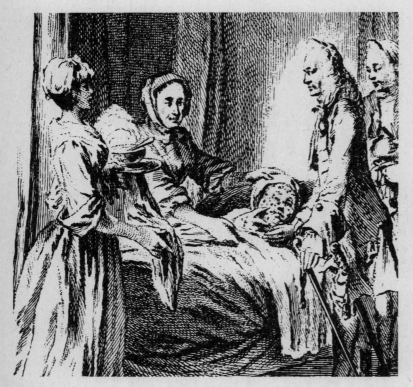

*In 1721 three convicts lying in Newgate were used as guinea-pigs for the inoculation against small-pox. It succeeded, though it was not until 1746 that an inoculation dispensary was set up in London for 'relieving poor People afflicted with the SMALL-POX'. This print shows a patient being tended. (1)*

approach the numbers annihilated in the previous century. Only one French province, Brittany, suffered a demographic setback from *la maladie de Brest*, typhus, which originated in the ports and spread rapidly through the hinterland of chronically underfed beings, whilst in England only the great towns were seriously affected.

## A demographic push

Indeed, to explore the conditions of extreme misery in which the population expansion of the 18th century took place is to render yet more horrible the demographic stagnation of the late 17th. Every child that was born jeopardized the life of its mother, and the female relatives or the village wise woman who assisted at the labour, were powerless to save her if the presentation of the foetus was in any way abnormal. The entry for 'accouchement' in the *Encyclopédie Méthodique de la Jurisprudence* gives at least one explanation for the larger number of crippled and deformed who counted among the poor in the 18th century:

> One sees men who are blind, crippled or physically handicapped from birth owing to the ignorance of the midwife who pulled or pressed too hard bones still soft and membraneous with the result that many are mentally or physically damaged for life.

French doctors, given the opportunity in the 1770s, inveighed against midwives who were in fact well-meaning murderesses of mother and child, their only knowledge based on observations, their only implements farm tools. Small wonder that the hazards of birth and infantile proneness to disease caused the young baby

to be regarded with a singularly dispassionate eye by its parents who reserved affection for the older children who had survived the rigours of infancy.

If disease and conditions of reproduction make the phenomenon of expansion remarkable, the quality of the diet in the 18th century makes it more so. In spite of the improvements in agriculture the Lancashire cotton worker and the Yorkshire woollen worker lived largely on a monotonous diet of potatoes and oatcake, and could count themselves amongst the best fed in Europe. Even if meat and protein foods were conspicuously lacking from their food they lived substantially better than the peasant farmer of central France who lived largely on boiled chestnuts or the Breton with his *bouillie*—a form of gruel made largely from buckwheat, a cereal now reserved for feeding poultry—or the Spaniard on his grease-soaked rye bread. In any country meat appeared only on the table of the relatively wealthy.

Yet in spite of the circumstances, the population growth of the 18th century was unprecedented not so much because of the rate of increase as for the fact that the upward movement started from a higher level and that this was *maintained*. It was also markedly uneven. To point out that Europe as a whole sustained a growth of 20% between 1700 and 1750 and of 30% between 1750 and the end of the century is to overlook a variety of regional changes. Broadly speaking the demographic push showed itself first in southern not northern Europe, in Spain, Italy and the Mediterranean littoral of France, west of Marseilles—Catalonia, for example, doubled its population between 1718 and 1788—but the growth had slackened by the 1780s when that of northern Europe

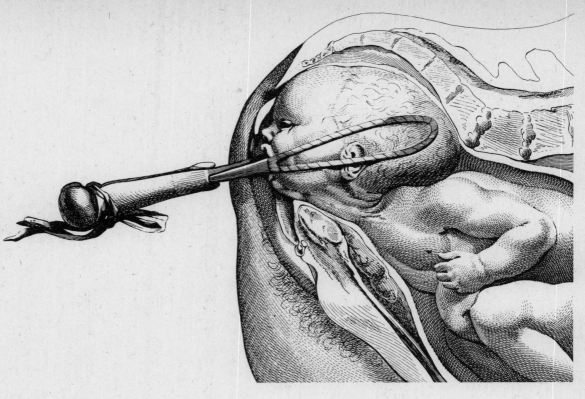

*Dr William Smellie's 'Sett of Anatomical Tables', published in 1754, were the result of fourteen years of practising and teaching midwifery in London. His techniques were so successful that they soon displaced the old haphazard methods of the midwives. On a visit to Paris he benefited from the teaching experience of the leading doctor in the field, Grégoire, and later developed the use of mechanical models of the mother and child for his lectures on midwifery. He also gave skilled professional care to poor women in their houses in return for permission to bring pupils with him and it was his work, together with others, which led to the foundation of lying-in hospitals in increasing numbers. Though by no means the first to use forceps he greatly improved the design of the instrument so that its use became less of a hazard in delivering a child. (3)*

was accelerating and indeed was very rapidly to overtake it. From 1750 to 1800 Scandinavia, the Low Countries, Russia, England and Wales, Ireland and Germany underwent an annual growth of about 1% (higher in Russia and Ireland) whilst Spain, Italy and France sustained one of less than 0.5% per annum. By the end of the century the population of Britain had risen from about 5,500,000 in 1700 to 9,200,000, and that of France from 18,000,000 in 1715 to over 26,000,000, to quote only two examples. But population figures alone are meaningless; the significant question to ask is how European society responded to this protracted growth.

## The demand for food

Very evidently the fate of Europe hinged upon the two basic factors of feeding and employing this rapidly growing population. For unless the supply of food could be increased sufficiently then the periodic devastation caused by famine would eventually be replaced by long term malnutrition and even before that stage had been reached the price of food would have risen in view of the greater demand. If potentialities of employment were not enlarged, either by bringing under cultivation new land or by developing new industrial resources, then the result would be underemployment, a ridiculous subdivision of existing holdings, and a surplus labour force whose wages would not rise to counteract the rise in prices. Put another way, the population explosion made more efficient and intensive farming essential everywhere and, in many cases, industrialization crucial to the well-being of the state concerned.

Both the nature and limitations of agrarian change and industrial progress have previously been analyzed in this volume, and the striking contrast between Britain and to a less extent northern Europe on the one hand, and the rest on the other, made plain. The former group was able to increase both its food production and its industrial resources and except in highly abnormal years such as 1794, was able to cope with an enlarged population: the latter by the last three decades of the 18th century was entering upon an extremely difficult phase. In France and Spain in particular, but also in parts of Germany, Italy and the Habsburg lands the demand for food had outstripped production, with a resultant increase in the cost of living unparalleled by a rise in wages, and industrial enterprise had not broadened sufficiently to absorb all the surplus manpower.

Moreover, though one should perhaps not overstress this, even in those countries which were developing most rapidly and which could provide a solution to the problems presented by population growth, economic gains were often secured at the expense of those displaced in the course of change—the artisan in an industry rend-

ered uncompetitive or redundant in a world of larger scale industries and the rural worker, both male and female, when domestic industry dried up, or those turned off the land by enclosure in the pursuit of agrarian progress. In Great Britain especially, this period might be regarded simply as one of painful adjustment to changing circumstances: the gradual transition, for example from the family as the basic unit of production to larger scale manufacturing which took production out of the home and hence disrupted the whole pattern of the family economy. Moreover each country had special problem areas: those which were chronically overpopulated in relation to their resources and disgorged their excess into adjoining areas—often with the effect of universalizing poverty. The Irish, for example, refugees from misery, were already beginning to pour into London and the larger English cities to infest the cellars and attics with their tubercular lice-covered bodies, creating their own ghettos of poverty where the rich never set foot.

France had the problem nearer to hand. The north and northeast, the wealthy cornlands of the Beauce, the great areas of viticulture of which Bordeaux and Marseilles were the ports must be balanced against the infertile Massif Central, the Alps and the Pyrenees all of them reservoirs of men and human suffering where available land was only too readily saturated by increased demand. Something under a fifth of the destitute of the Mediterranean littoral were actually indigenous: the rest were drawn from the desolate hills to the north. In Marseilles it has been estimated that a settled population of 106,000 supported a floating population of 30,000 who reserved the profits of their efforts to buttress a minute holding more likely than not in the barren Dauphiné.

## 'The common sort'

Such circumstances make more readily understandable an apparent contradiction: that it was fully possible for progress and relative emancipation from famine and plague to produce a greater number of poor than ever before. A starving population generally speaking cannot reproduce itself, an undernourished one has no difficulty in so doing. In the hierarchy of wretchedness there is a world of difference between the man who is literally starving—even for a short period—and he who is merely undernourished all the year round. To understand this particular subtlety of the problem of poverty is to understand something of the difference in many European countries between the early 18th century and the end. For if by the end of the period the number of those fitting into the first category had almost vanished, the other had multiplied beyond all proportion. Indeed, the most significant consequence of the population explosion was the broadening of the base of the social pyramid more widely than ever before and this was to endow the 18th century with its most distinctive feature: proliferation of those whom contemporaries referred to in a vocabulary of distaste as 'the meaner kind', 'the common sort', the 'mob', 'rabble' or *canaille*. They were in reality the labouring poor but with a crucial difference for not only were they now scattered throughout the countryside, docile peasants whose occasional *jacqueries* burnt themselves out beyond the pale of civilization, but increasingly they were gathered in towns. All European societies, both at the beginning and end of this period, were predominantly agrarian and moreover in every country the population expansion, as far as it has been analyzed, appears to have been a rural phenomenon. Certainly in the large cities, and often in the less considerable towns, mortality rates continued to be higher than the birth rates but if urban growth was not self-generated it occurred notwithstanding because of the heavy rural influx. London perhaps provides an extreme case: there the number of deaths seems to have surpassed that of births annually until 1790, yet the population rose from about 674,500 in 1700 to 900,000 in 1801. Nevertheless smaller cities like Strasbourg, Montpellier, Nottingham or Leghorn would provide equally good examples. Flooded by immigrants from the surrounding rural area and often almost totally without the means to employ them, they were impotent to arrest the process. Driven thither in a search for employment, attention, relief or because of the enhanced possibilities of criminal pursuits, the intensely mobile poor swarmed into the cities and small towns; teeming humanity gathered together, depressed, emotionally unstable, volatile, potentially dangerous, something for governments to fear or repress. Between the peasant risings of distress in the wake of the great famine of the later 17th century and the vicious vindictiveness of the Gordon Riots lies something of the difference. It is expressed eloquently in the works of the Le Nain brothers on the one hand and Hogarth on the other. The first, in the 1640s, saw the poverty of the small French peasant and painted exactly what they saw, without pausing to moralize: they saw suffering and patient resignation, acceptance of starvation, pain and deprivation. The other, unparalleled as the painter of the urban poor, caught an element of the times. He depicted the poor as vicious, cruel and immoral: his subjects were alive struggling beings responding vigorously to the hardship of their surroundings, anaesthetizing themselves to the ugliness of their lives with cheap alcohol or eking out a pitiful income with prostitution or pilfering or both. Often what he saw as the causes of poverty were perhaps the results, but no one conveyed better than he the conglomeration of human misery that made up the back streets of London, 'the great wen'. That in Europe in the 18th century the working classes became the dangerous classes is

p 322
(21)

p 292
(31)

p 326–7

a meaningful juxtaposition, and 1848, when urban revolutions shook Europe and brought down governments, is perhaps the most natural corollary of events started in our period. Nor is it insignificant that Hogarth's harlot like Cleland's Fanny or Restif's *La Paysanne Pervertie* is a country girl corrupted by the evil influences of the city—a common enough literary device but one which became increasingly frequent in works of this period—for to begin to discuss the condition of the people in the 18th century one must inevitably begin with the victims of changing conditions in the countryside: with the subsistence farmer, those of whom Arthur Young remarked in his 'Travels in France' they 'marry on the *idea* of an inheritance,' a tiny unit fractionalized by each generation; and with the even commoner figure, the day labourer looking for work in an overcrowded market; and with their wives and sons and daughters and perhaps even their grandchildren. However else one sees the problems of the 18th century one must see them as family problems and begin with the recognition that the family economy of the working classes was their natural economy—the family needed the work of each of its component members to support the whole. Hence, broadly speaking, the man who had sufficient land to provide for the wants of his family had sufficient to employ that family. In the event of his not having enough, he or his family or both must seek an alternative source of income. In the case of the day labourer or the wage earner this was doubly true for nowhere in Europe could the wage earner expect to earn more than he needed for his own personal maintenance. Indeed, at the beginning of our period this factor was an integral part of current economic theory, an aspect of mercantilism in which the wage was allied with the costs of production and hence must be kept low if goods were to remain competitive. But laying theory aside, one does not need to look any further than the state of the labour market, overcrowded to an unprecedented extent, to appreciate that one did not need to pay the labourer more than a minimal personal subsistence rate and that he was lucky if he could command even that. To do so he had perhaps uprooted himself, travelled vast distances, possibly leaving his family behind to fend for themselves and his situation became less and less tenable as more and more joined his ranks.

p 238
(40–43)

p 127
(9)

Indeed, one can almost make the generalization that nowhere in Europe did any section of the working class stand a chance of bettering their condition in their lifetime and in southern Europe at least an actual deterioration in living standards took place between 1750 and the end of the century. The remark must be qualified, however, because in certain industries at certain times—good instances would be the English weavers in the period immediately following improvements which accelerated spinning output, and the building workers of expanding Barcelona who could command the best salaries of their kind in Spain—temporary demand made an exception to this rule.

## Women and children

If one takes as a point of departure the limited earning capacity of the working man, one must then consider not only his potentialities for employment but also those of his wife and children. In most societies the young unmarried man was not a real problem for poor law administrators, he could make out—perhaps not with ease—but he was one of the most mobile sections of the population in his search for work, and he was the one for whom uprooting caused the least trouble and who had the least to restrain him. The same could not be said of the married man or of the wives and daughters of labouring men. Marriage and procreation brought a whole series of new problems; there was certainly no spirit of academic dispassion behind the demand, reiterated throughout the French *cahiers* of grievances of 1789, that extra taxes should be placed on bachelors for the support of the children of large families.

In any society in the 18th century, women of the working classes were expected to work to support themselves both when single and married: 'Consider, my dear girl,' runs *A Present for a Serving Maid* (1743) 'that you have no portions and endeavour to supply the deficiencies of fortune by mind. You cannot expect to marry in such a manner as neither of you shall have occasion to work and none but a fool will take a wife whose bread must be earned solely by his labour and who will contribute nothing towards it herself.'

*By the time it was six years old, a child was already expected to contribute towards its own maintenance. This print shows a family of chimney sweeps. Very young children were particularly open to exploitation in this trade, since only they could climb up the narrow constricted chimneys.* (4)

In fact they had no option but to do so. Generally speaking female employment fitted into three main categories. The first, restricted to the unmarried, was domestic service, perhaps the most highly sought after employment by the unmarried girl because it made her independent of the family and she needed little skill or tuition— though Irish women in London and the Savoyardes in Paris were considered too barbaric to perform even the most menial tasks in the home.

Secondly, domestic industry of several kinds which could be carried out either by the unmarried or the married but which, in the latter case especially, was of crucial significance to the family economy. The commonest forms of this were, of course, spinning wool or cotton and the manufacture of lace. The first might or might not form part of an integrated family manufacture—the children helping in the initial stages of washing and carding the raw material, the women in spinning, the men in weaving. In this case the woman was not paid a wage as such: rather was the whole family awarded a single sum for the completed cloth and the family, it should be remembered, was up to the end of the period the commonest unit of production.

Elsewhere domestic industry formed a useful supplement to work in the fields for the women of the household. To textile spinning should be added the production of lace which in northern France, Belgium, Holland and parts of southern England came a very close second to spinning in the numbers it occupied. The value of the lace lay almost entirely in the handiwork, for the quantity of linen or silk thread involved was slight. Sometimes this was a skill taught by religious orders with the express purpose of making the wives and daughters of the poor self-supporting, and in France and Belgium often the profits from the sale of the work went in large part to the religious who used it to train more workers whilst the lacemaker herself earned a pittance for her labours. Domestic industry was essentially for women *at home* and herein lay much of its value. The baby could lie in the cradle and the smallest children play on the floor whilst the mother kept to her wheel or attended to her lace bobbins. If she fell behind in her tasks they could be completed late into the night, whilst the children slept. But changes were taking place which were to threaten the continuance of this situation—at least as far as spinning was concerned. For the distribution of the raw material and collection of the finished product an elaborate network of travelling merchants was involved, a lengthy and irregular process. Little wonder that spinning was the first process to be subject to industrial change, an important point for no changes were to disrupt more the family economy. They were to take the spinner out of the house and destroy the family as a unit of production and hence to render

p 142
(7)

employment in some cases very difficult for married women. Early town factories in England in fact accorded preference to the unmarried.

By far the commonest kind of female labour throughout the world at this time was simply the lowest kind of heavy and distasteful tasks such as load carrying. Nothing in fact was too menial. They carried soil, heavy vegetables to market, water, coal—anything. The terraces cut into the steep mountain hillsides of Spain, France and Italy were kept watered by thousands of women who daily made the steep ascent with buckets—in the Auvergne it was estimated that the climb could take anything up to three hours and often they performed as many as three a day. The Scottish miners employed their wives as 'fremd bearers' to carry coal from the face. The mines at this period had no winding gear and the women had to climb with their burden up a spiral staircase winding around the walls of the shaft. Sometimes the return journey could take up to four hours. The man was of course paid a single wage and if unmarried, had to find a girl to act as his beast of burden to whom he paid a part of his earnings. Irish women, unable to sew or clean who found their way to London acted as load carriers or helped their husbands work as navvies. Elsewhere women found employment as rag sorters, cinder sifters, refuse collectors, assistants to masons and bricklayers and so on.

f 6

f 5

Easily the most mobile section of the population in their search for work, women, especially unmarried ones, would travel many miles in the hope of finding employment. Annually women from North Wales left their homes to work on the fruit harvest in Middlesex; carrying a load on their backs into the London markets and sometimes walking anything up to fifteen miles a day during the fruit season. Moreover they had walked from Wales. One must imagine the wives and daughters of the poor condemned to a lifetime of drudgery in an attempt to keep themselves and their offspring fed. Women enclosed in tiny airless rooms, pouring over lace bobbins, working late into the night by the light of candles until their eyes would serve them no more. Blindness was the likeliest fate of the lacemaker. Even those who worked at home and delivered the fruit of their labours to a wandering merchant could not afford to be irregular in their production of work. Washing and mending, cooking and cleaning had to be done afterwards and childbirth had to be accomplished with the minimum of disruption. It is not surprising that they were old women by their late twenties.

The question of child labour was perhaps of even greater importance than that of female labour. The wage of the average working man was enough for his personal upkeep and perhaps, if his wife was employed, for that of two young children. Keen social observers were quick to point out that real trouble started for families with the advent of the third child. This consideration alone entitled the silk and diamond workers of Antwerp to some slight relief, but the situation was too common for the funds of public assistance to allow help to every man in this state.

The advent of child labour has often been depicted as the outstanding evil of the factory system and of the tragic plight of many children in the early factories there can be no doubt. But to approach the question from this angle is to view it with 20th century eyes, for life was hard for the children of labouring men in all European countries in the 18th century. They were expected to become self-supporting *as soon as possible* so as to relieve the strain on the family budget. Indeed, the children of the poor were committed as soon as they left the cradle to an unremitting struggle for survival in a hostile world. It is possible that children in areas of domestic industry were singularly privileged. The tasks they performed were unskilled and demanded little physical strength. In manufacturing areas of England and Belgium and Normandy children of seven and upwards were relatively self-supporting. Even four-year-olds were capable of certain jobs. Samuel Crompton's eldest son, George, has left a telling account of the kind of work performed by weavers' children:

f 4

> I recollect that soon after I was able to walk I was employed in the cotton manufacture. My mother used to bat the cotton wool on a wire riddle. It was then put into a deep brown mug with a strong ley of soap suds. My mother then tucked up my petticoats about my waist and put me into the tub to tread upon the cotton

*Women miners were common enough in certain mining regions. This engraving, from a French work of 1768–79, ostensibly illustrating the geological strata, shows women at the pit-head of a primitive coal-mine.* (5)

*'Brooms, brooms' – a plate from a volume on the 'Cries of Paris'. This woman is a specialized trader; most women of the poorer classes were forced to do random manual work of the most exhausting kind.* (6)

at the bottom. When a second riddleful was batted I was lifted out, it was placed in the mug and I again trod it down. This process was continued until the mug became so full that I could no longer safely stand in it when a chair was placed besides it and I held on by the back.

The cotton was then dried and carded by the grandmother and mother.

In Belgium children earned enough to support themselves after the age of seven by emptying silk cocoons. But in most communities and especially heavily agrarian communities child employment was almost totally lacking. Bishop Berkeley might fulminate against the Irish peasant who left his eight-year-old child idle in his nakedness and poverty and point out the glowing example of the Protestant Dutch who were held to make a child self-supporting at the age of five, but unless rural industry was in any way developed or the family holding large, there was little to employ women and children apart from a few days' work at hay-making and harvest. When such circumstances prevailed the question of how the family eked out a living assumes complex proportions, unanswerable in simple terms and demanding recourse to hosts of specific examples.

## Migrant labour

The poor did not sit back and let starvation overtake them: amongst the labouring poor there had always been a tradition of mobility, of temporary or seasonal migration into areas offering short-term work prospects and during the period under review they were to assume important proportions. The most extensive migrations doubtless took place from the most mountainous regions of Europe: the Pyrenees, the Alps, the Massif Central, the Ardennes, Dolomites, Snowdonia and parts of Ireland, for several reasons of which the most cogent was that climatic conditions made all-the-year-round work impossible and secondly a limit was sooner reached on the amount of land that could be brought under cultivation. The mountain dweller was a traditional migrant though a temporary one; what was new was the extent of these migrations and what was striking was the extent to which they served to buttress an uneconomic unit which on the surface would not have appeared to afford the owner or exploiter enough to live. But if the adult males could earn something extra during the dead season, or for a part of the year, then the family income could be stretched a little further. Hence the small peasant of the Campine or the Ardennes, in Belgium or Luxembourg was prepared to make a weary biennial walk to Hungary or a shorter but less lucrative one to serve as a navvy in Amsterdam: the Pyrenees emptied annually in the winter of men who went into Spain or to Bordeaux offering themselves as rough labourers. The Irish wended a rowdy way into London or the large English cities: men and women worked as navvies or—more commonly in the case of women—as load carriers of water or coal or groceries. These people embarked with none of Dick Whittington's illusions that the streets of the capital were paved with gold. The step was one of distress, a recognition that they could not earn a living at home. A perfect example of how initiative and ingenuity could together keep families alive under the most adverse circumstances is afforded by the Massif Central. Every year thousands of men left the villages leaving their wives behind to care for the holding which often meant merely picking up chestnuts as they fell, one by one from the trees. Some walked to Spain; others to the Midi to work on the grape harvest; some to Portugal as woodcutters, a winter occupation; some to Normandy and Brittany as pedlars of pins and needles; some to Paris and indeed almost every part of France as chimney sweeps. Some stayed away for a few years—the levellers of hills (*terrassiers*) and tinkers who made the long trek to Spain. Wages were perhaps lower in Spain than France but the high metallic content of the Spanish currency gave it a peculiarly high value in France where there was an acute shortage of *specie*. Others only stayed away a few months. Each village had a traditional destination, traditional employments, traditional times for departure and return and traditional routes and stops which were closely followed. The degree of organization involved was impressive. Those who returned from a four or five year stay in Spain perhaps hoped never to leave again and to use the capital they had amassed to eke out a miserable living. Those who merely spent five months in Normandy or Paris perhaps hoped to do no more than keep themselves and pay their taxes and spend the rest of the year on their meagre land. In whole villages in the Auvergne taxes were paid in *pesos* and significantly this was one of the first areas to be depopulated in the 19th century.

## The brink of ruin

The family economy was very obviously a frail edifice from which no one stone could be removed without jeopardizing the continuing existence of the whole. Again, this is best illustrated by example: Davies (*The Case of the Labourers in Husbandry*) cites the case of a family of seven persons whose yearly income was £39 17s. 4d. and whose yearly expenditure on basic necessaries was £39 14s. 4d. Although the mother of the family earned only 4½d. a day, without that meagre sum the family would have lacked basic essentials. In her own words 'the earnings of her husband and boys maintained the family in food and that what she herself and the girls (aged respectively 7 and 5 years) earned by spinning and at harvest, found them in clothes, linen and other necessaries'.

However convincing figures may be, they remain strangely inadequate to convey the full human consequences attendant upon economic change: nor do the annals of the poor, though numerous, often throw much light on how economic questions conditioned the attitude of a man and wife to each other and their children or how the family coped with the failure of the wage of the working man or woman to keep pace with rising costs, a problem felt most nearly in the home and in one's immediate relationships. It meant that one lived daily from hand to mouth without provision for old age, sickness, incapacity to work, or disasters such as harvest failure or even the arrival of a baby. It affected one's attitude toward one's aged parents and made one's own advancing years something to fear; it presented the working man with the demoralizing experience of toiling all day only to return home with a pittance inadequate for the decent maintenance of his family; it made theft and violence, drunkenness, vagabondage and prostitution constant features of this society and understandably so, for it was only too easy to cross the narrow boundary between poverty and destitution. It needed only some everyday occurrence, a sickness of the main earner, his death, the drying up of domestic industry, the birth of a third or fourth child, to plunge the family into difficulties from which recovery was almost impossible. The ease with which the boundary between poverty and destitution could be crossed provided the century with its most cogent social problems. The sick or crippled who could earn nothing and the aged who were enfeebled might form a relatively small part of the population but the same could not be said of the family that could not manage because of its restricted earning capacity. In France probably something like a third of the population teetered on the fringes of destitution whilst something like a tenth had already crossed that boundary, and an extensive survey made by the French government in 1791 revealed that young children spelt disaster for the family economy. The corollary of this was that in many areas begging children plagued the street crying for alms, begging bread, serving as decoys for pickpockets or as little tinkers peddling pins and ribbons. 'Babies' a sub-delegate of the Auvergne moaned, 'have scarcely left the cradle before they are taught how to beg so

as not to be a burden to their families.' In Paris groups of children made a poor living by selling bundles of firewood or working for rag and bone merchants. Elsewhere they acted as water carriers, sellers of flowers or melons or anything that they could gather together by their own labour and sell for a few pence.

## Beggars

The 'mudlarks' of London, scavenger children making a living from tidal refuse, Anderson's little match girl who died frozen in the streets are as much 18th- as 19th-century figures and there is nothing picturesque about them. Far more often in non-industrial societies they made out by begging and semi-criminal practices. Any visitor to a European city in the 18th century would expect to be besieged by hordes of children, forming packs and loitering on street corners to plague the passer-by for alms, tugging at his coat sleeves, dogging his footsteps in tireless pursuit until they received a coin for their exertions. Long before adolescence they had learnt the tricks of the begging trade to perfection and had nothing to learn from the Brechtian-type beggar. They knew how to hang around the doors of churches, the largest houses, the market stalls, the best bread shops where their demands might arouse some pity; how to tote their smaller brothers and sisters from door to door with long and pathetic tales of misfortunes and parental cruelty. Their parents aided them and encouraged them in deceit. They hired them out for the day to women who wanted to elicit pity and charity by the appearance of a large family or to tinkers who could thus urge unwanted wares upon the public in the name of charity. Thousands of children hovered on the fringe of criminality. The most appealing waif with the largest eyes and hungriest look might well be decoy for an accomplished pickpocket or engage one's attention whilst his brother nipped the hair off one's horse's tail—horse hair fetched a good price from mattress makers. In the salt court of Laval alone in 1773–74 over 12,000 children were arrested for smuggling salt between Brittany—an area of untaxed salt—and the Maine. They had their stories ready in the face of capture, a litany of woes designed to melt the heart of any judge: they had no shoes, no shirt, a sick mother or a drunken father, tales perhaps true or perhaps learnt parrot-fashion from each other. They were also excellent distributors of illicit tobacco. It was all too easy for a little girl to make a slow and steady progression from petty beggar to petty thief to part-time prostitute. Deformed by rickets and vitamin deficiency diseases, the begging children became the great fear of administrators. Would they ever take to a steady job or would they become so demoralized that living on their wits would become an ingrained habit? Small wonder that anyone who created work for children was regarded not with horror as an exploiter of the weak, but as a benefactor whose reward in heaven would be great, or that this was the great age of the charity school.

For poor children there was no age of innocence, only one of

*f 7*

*Poverty was the root-cause of prostitution, as of most of the so-called 'vices' of the poor. Here prostitutes in Germany are being led away to prison. (7)*

*Business in the criminal courts was always brisk. In May 1750, at the famous Black Sessions at the Old Bailey in London, about 100 prisoners were brought for trial from Newgate. If they were fortunate enough to survive the scourge of jail fever while in prison, their sentences usually led them to the gallows. This scaffold erected at the Old Bailey speeded up the process of execution by dealing with 10 prisoners at a time. (8)*

learning to make one's way in the world of the economically under-privileged, and there was no escape route: nothing by which one could guarantee that one's children would ever do any better. Hogarth's contrast between the idle apprentice who ended on the gallows and the industrious one who became lord mayor of London was a myth of the comfortable classes who saw, and hence believed in, the depravity of the poor.

Every year, Arthur Young noted with alarm, young girls flocked to the capital hoping to secure work as servants and ended, inevitably, on the streets. Adam Smith went further and analyzed the pressure-areas from which they were drawn—in the case of London largely from Irish girls who arrived penniless and for whom there was no employment. Many of those convicted in the courts as prostitutes used lack of work as their main excuse and as rigid a magistrate as Henry Fielding was forced to believe them. The same stories were told in French courts and many of the women who told them were in full time work and used prostitution as an ancillary income because their wages were insufficient to support them. The picturesque pedlars and street vendors of lavender and oranges, caught in over-romantic light by Beechey, were commonly part-time whores—for the 'Cries of London' and every European capital were cries of anguish. The prostitute duly became a disease ridden old woman, like those of Amsterdam who hurled obscenities at respectable citizens if refused alms, accusing them of having enjoyed and used them in their youth only to leave them to die in old age. The eternal dilemma of the poor was that virtue and their continued subsistence were incompatible.

## Brutality, violence and crime

No other period of history has produced so many criminals who have passed into popular legend and have been condoned by popular morality. Highwaymen and smugglers, forgers and confidence tricksters are thickly woven into literature and popular song and their attempts to evade a broadly despised justice are shrouded in myth. Turpin and Mandrin of the Dauphiné or women like the Breton Marion de Faouet constituted no threat to the landless and poor but they were the terror of the isolated farmstead upon which they would descend *en masse*, burning hayricks and barns if the family money was refused. Looked at closely they are not pretty figures. Marion, for example, a child of a beggar, spent her short life continuously in and out of prison dragging her illegitimate children with her and perishing ultimately on the gallows, after being broken on the wheel, for theft and murder. Whole villages in France depended on salt smuggling by obscure routes, the secrets of which were jealously passed on from father to son; the coast of Devon and Cornwall was the stronghold of wreckers and smugglers of silk and alcohol. Some of them perhaps robbed only the revenue but others went further, because the corollary of rock bottom poverty was brutalization, violence and ultimate indifference to the fact that if caught the likelihood was the death penalty or the living death of the galleys or the hulks.

Mandeville, the doctor and economist, commented on this defiant acceptance of even the worst punishments amongst the prisoners of Newgate:

> When the day of execution is come, among extraordinary sinners and persons condemned for their crimes who have but that morning to live, one would expect a deep sense of sorrow with all the signs of a thorough contrition . . . But the very reverse is true . . . the substantial breakfasts that are made . . . the seas of beer that are swilled: the never ceasing outcries for more . . . But what is most shocking to a thinking man is, the Behaviour of the condemned whom, (for the most part) you'll find, either drinking madly or uttering the vilest ribaldry . . . At last out they set and with them a Torrent of Mob bursts through the gate. Amongst the lower Rank and working people, the idlest and such as are most fond of making holidays, with prentices and journeymen to the meanest trades, are the most honorable part of these floating multitudes . . . All the way from Newgate to Tyburn is one continued fair for whores and rogues of the meaner sort. Here the most abandoned of rakehells may light on women as shameless; here trollops all in rags, may pick up sweethearts of the same politeness . . .

The great proportion of those who languished in Newgate had committed crimes against property and it appears that throughout Europe during the period, offences against property as opposed to crimes of pure violence for its own sake, were on the increase and were those with which legislators and administrators were more concerned than ever before. In England between 1660 and 1820,

*Prisoners: a manacled man pushes a barrow, three others are led off to the galleys, while two more are kept bound in a dungeon. (9)*

301

*It is impossible to know how many children were killed at birth. This German engraving tells the story of one infanticide that was discovered. Top left: the child is found smothered under a mattress. Bottom left: the mother repents in prison,* *and is taken away to execution. Right: she is decapitated sitting on a chair, amid a vast crowd of spectators. Note the wheels in the distance for 'breaking' prisoners.* (10)

190 new crimes against property were introduced into the statute book, though many judges would not apply them. In parts of northern France the numbers of those convicted for theft rose sharply; so did they in Venice where on average ten people a day made their way to the hulks. Perhaps middle-class society cared less or did not seek to know too much about offences which were regularly committed in the back streets of every town and even in isolated hamlets, like child abandonment or infanticide—and if the latter was difficult to discover the same could not be said of the former. Every year in Paris towards the end of the old régime 6,000 babies were placed into the hands of charity, almost twice as many as a century before. In Brussels over 2,000 and in quite modest-sized towns, like Bayeux in Normandy, fifty new-born babies were annually left nameless to charity. Abandoned in the porches of churches, at city gates, or on the steps of public buildings, little ragged bundles with perhaps a christian name scrawled on a piece of paper or a few grains of salt to denote they had not been baptized, the abandoned child was by the end of the period perhaps the commonest social problem. Their anonymity was their greatest handicap, for at the beginning of the period they were almost universally regarded as the shameful product of some illicit union, paying dearly for the sins of their parents. The marked increase in their numbers as the century progressed began to suggest to administrators that very probably they were the product not of sin but of poverty, children of parents too poor to support them and who preferred to sacrifice them in order to preserve the rest. Infanticide was perhaps harder to perceive but when, for example, Rennes was rebuilt after the fire of the 1720s, a disused drain which was cleared away was found to contain over eighty small skeletons of children suppressed in the first hours of life. The *lieutenant-amman* of Brussels claimed in 1771 that he came daily in his work across reports of the bodies of new-born children found in drains, rivers, cellars and occasionally public places but he would only speculate upon whether they were the product of shame or the product of poverty. Elsewhere, organized rackets existed for the

disposal of new-born children from isolated villages. The foundling hospital in Paris, one of the few institutions that catered for children throughout the period under review, found itself swamped with basket-loads of babies who had made the journey from Lorraine, Normandy or Brittany and even Belgium, piled upright into paniers strapped to donkeys, many of them only a few days or weeks old, only a fraction of whom survived even the journey.

Indeed the hardships entailed in keeping a family together often proved too much for parents—especially for fathers—and the last recourse was to opt out entirely. To leave one's obligations behind and to hit the open road might be the coward's way out but many took it. The Curé d'Athis in a letter to the Bishop of Bayeux analyzed the type of man who reverted to this solution:

> Day labourers, artisans are those who produce beggars. As young men they work and are able to put aside sufficient to marry. They produce one child, they have much difficulty in supporting two and if a third should come along their income is no longer sufficient. At such a time they do not hesitate to take up the beggar's staff and to take to the road and they do this the more readily if their fathers did this before them.

Every vagrant was a potential criminal, likely to resort to violence if his needs were not satisfied, but he had one solace, that he could not sink any lower. He was totally demoralized. Observers were quick to note that however destitute the poor, they did not cease to frequent hostelries, gin palaces, *cabarets* but what they did not so readily concede was how much cheaper it was to get drunk than to satisfy one's hunger and that perhaps it made the squalor of home and hungry children somewhat easier to face. Living for the day, because there was nothing to put away for the morrow, undernourished, lice-ridden, drunken, their honesty and virtue with good reason suspect, and many of them indulging in almost every crime in the calendar, swelling in numbers in spite of dwelling in foetid cellars where typhus was a constant threat, the poor could not fail to provoke a response in other sections of the population.

f 10

p 287 (18)

But the nature of that response was perforce confused: it was too easy to confuse the results of poverty with the cause. The thief, the prostitute, the vagrant, the begging children, the abandoned baby, the day labourer drunken in the streets were on view and it was all too simple to equate their vices with the ruin of the labouring poor: to see them as the product of poverty needed a far greater degree of insight and compassion: it needed perhaps a Vincent de Paul—and he would have been the first to admit that although the poor were infinitely deserving they were equally infinitely unvirtuous.

## The 'ideal' poor

p 29
(28)

One might say that there existed amongst administrators everywhere a concept of a personage whom we might call the 'ideal' poor person. Such an individual was remarkable for his industry, thrift, and patient resignation in the face of hardship. He did not frequent gin palaces or *cabarets*; his response to deprivation was to pull in his belt a couple of notches and to pretend that nothing was happening. His clothes were cleaned and darned; his children washed and tidy. He kept up appearances and confided his troubles only to the *curé* or the pastor. He was emphatically not a migrant: he did not abandon his cottage at the first sign of difficulty leaving wife and child to the care and cost of the parish. He was immensely grateful to those of his elders and betters who deigned to help him or even to employ him; touching his forelock or bowing low or kissing a hand or whatever social convention demanded should be a token of respect towards the munificence of his benefactor. And his solace in his earthly miseries was God and the promise of a heavenly reward for his tribulations. Even if administrators did not believe in the value of religion for themselves they certainly believed in it for the poor and could cite chapter and verse to reinforce their position: Dives and Lazarus; blessed are the poor, the meek, the weak, the poor in heart, the hungry and oppressed —and all this whilst they themselves were fed to satiation.

To reconcile this ideal with the way in which the poor actually lived was not easy and the difficulties involved in effecting that reconciliation became peculiarly apparent when the poor man ceased to be self-sufficient and sought to make a claim on the public purse—when he became, in fact, a pauper, or, to use the more specific French terms, passed from being merely *pauvre* to being *indigent*. Deep-rooted amongst administrators was a great, and in part reasonable, fear of being tricked by those who sought to make a claim on the resources of charity. This caused them to concentrate their energies upon the attempt to discover where an effective dividing line could be drawn between the deserving and undeserving poor, rather than upon the essential questions, who are the poor and why are they there? All were ready enough to concede the needs of the widowed and the sick, orphaned or aged,

by tradition the socially acceptable poor, but less prompt to consider what proportion these constituted of the totally destitute. Indeed, not until the extensive inquest made in France by the *Comité de Mendicité* in 1791 was any statistical approach adopted towards the poor and when this did happen disquieting facts were revealed before which the French government simply recoiled: not least the fact that a third, and more often a half, of those in need of assistance *in any community in France* were children whose parents earned insufficient to support them. The registers of English or Dutch poor houses could, had they been used for this purpose, have thrown another aspect of the question into relief—that is, the preponderance of women amongst those seeking assistance. In short, the problem could be interpreted in two ways: either as the inadequacy of the labourer's wage to support wife and child or, and this was a much more acceptable approach to contemporaries, as the insufficiency of employment for women and children. In the main this second point was one which was clear enough to anyone directly concerned with the problem of poverty though many fought shy of the implications that recognition of it involved. Moreover there was no approach to the question of poor relief uncoloured by religious, social, political or simply economic factors which endowed every aspect of the topic with complex overtones.

## Poor relief: the Protestant North

The history of European poor relief is at least as old as European Christianity and is one of change from a religiously based, voluntary charity, as expounded by the evangelists, to the complete assumption by the State of responsibility for the weakest members of society. In that history there is no more seminal period than the late 17th and the 18th centuries. During that time, under the pressure of rapidly changing economic circumstances, principles were hammered out and experiments tried, and both equally often abandoned.

In 1660 the fundamental belief that the poor should be succoured by the Church and the faithful still lay at the root of almost every provision for poor relief in Europe, though already there were differences distinguishing Catholic from Protestant countries and even within the Protestant ones between Lutheran and Calvinist; for the Reformation, in secularizing Church land, had destroyed the principle, hallowed in canon law, that ecclesiastical revenues were intended to be divided into two parts, *necessitas* and *superfluas*, the one for the upkeep of the clerics, the other for the sustenance of the poor. It had not, however, destroyed the notion that voluntary charity, the alms of the faithful, should be the means out of which the poor should be succoured. On the other hand, in altering the relationship between Church and State, a step, though one which was far from obvious to reformers, had been taken towards such a change. The new national Churches were State directed and the State assumed functions hitherto a Church monopoly; it might well still use the vocabulary of Christian charity and pronounce the blessedness of almsgiving but the presence of paupers ultimately redounded not to the discredit of the Church but of the State, and if voluntary almsgiving proved defective the State had to take action. This in the course of our period was to push the Protestant countries, without exception, into the evolution of far more sophisticated forms of poor relief than those practised in Catholic Europe.

The change was most strikingly apparent in England and the Lutheran countries, where the head of the Church was a political figure and religious issues were also political issues, though it was effected neither smoothly nor overnight. In England the inadequacy of voluntary charity was formally admitted by the enactment of 1601 which empowered magistrates to levy a parish rate, if the need arose, for the deserving poor; but it was not until the 1660s, the height of the economic crisis in northern Europe, that the parish rate was made an obligatory tax. Twenty-three years later, the Scandinavian countries took a similar step but with much greater forethought as to the nature of the relief and its administration. The Danes in particular elaborated a plan which marked them out as the most socially advanced country of their day. The Danish government proclaimed that every pauper had a *legal* right to relief and in the category of pauper was included the unemployed

*The disabled could do nothing but beg. Crowds of beggars were part of every urban scene, and it was only in Protestant countries that relief was made a public rather than a private duty.* (11)

and those who could not, upon examination, afford to support a family. In exchange, the pauper lost his freedom and could be made to work far from his home on roads, draining marshes, or digging canals. The Danes also created a salaried bureaucracy for the administration of poor relief—a respect in which the English remained sadly deficient throughout the period, and the whole scheme was financed out of the proceeds of government sanctioned indirect taxation. Yet even in these countries, the ideal of Christian charity was not totally abandoned. The English almshouse and the Danish *fattighus* were alike the result of individual religious initiative and there lingered a curious residual conviction amongst Christian men that the treatment of the deserving poor must be the ultimate criterion by which a Christian State should be tested.

*f 12*   In Calvinist countries, and here the Dutch case is worthy of examination, the alliance between the Church and the poor remained much closer. The elders of the Church were also the judges of the needs of the poor of the parish; but to sustain them they were empowered by the State to levy an obligatory tax upon the congregation and failure to pay this incurred penalties. This factor is perhaps the most significant to our theme for it is here that the contrast is greatest between Protestant and Catholic Europe.

## Catholic charity

In the latter the spirit of poor relief was that given fresh expression at the Council of Trent. The Catholic Church regarded the pauper as the linchpin in the salvation of the rich; for only by charity, the giving of their substance to the poor and the weak, could the wealthy elicit divine mercy. The question was not merely a consideration of what was materially good for the pauper in this world, but far more what was of crucial significance for the rest of society, and particularly the rich, in the next. The Tridentine Councils admitted the failure of the medieval Church to cope with the problem of poverty and underlined the need for a radical reappraisal of the situation. At the same time they insisted that the bishop assume complete control over diocesan charity and reiterated the obligations of the Church to society in the traditions of the medieval schoolmen.

The exhortations of Trent did not fall on stony ground, for immediately the Jesuits in Spain, Portugal, France and later Italy took up the message and in the mid-17th century, and more thoroughly than the Jesuits, St Vincent de Paul provided the Catholic Church with a new and seemingly comprehensive scheme of poor relief of which echoes at least were found in every Catholic country—except Ireland—by the end of the century.

St Vincent's starting point was that society need have no horror of 'decent poverty' or of the laboriousness of the average countryman's life. But that the sick should be totally uncared for, the old man past work left destitute and the children of the poor to run wild was a different matter. To St Vincent such a state of affairs was not a matter for legislation, what was needed was a rechristianizing of the people to make them realize their social obligations and to inspire them with compassion for their poorer brethren. He visualized the setting up of *bureaux de charité* in every parish, that is a parish fund of voluntary alms and the income from legacies, to be distributed to the deserving poor by the parish priest, an idea which the Jesuits and the Priests of the Mission propagated, with varying degrees of success, throughout Catholic Europe.
*p 286*   Secondly he gave his encouragement to associations known
*(11)*   alternatively as the *Dames de la Charité* or by the poor as the *Marmite des Pauvres*, which were formed by ladies of quality who took it upon themselves to distribute food to needy families. The example of the de Gondi household, the patrons of St Vincent, served to give a certain social *cachet* to the practice but St Vincent himself found he could expect little from these women for they were too far removed from the truly poor. He came to place his trust in a new religious order, of which Louise de Marillac at his instigation was the founder, the Sisters of Charity recruited from good village girls, who were to visit the sick, comfort the needy and teach the children of the poor to say their prayers. Lastly, and as it turned out most significantly—though this was very far from being St Vincent's intention—he evolved the idea of the *hôpital général*, an institution in which the aged, sick, crippled or orphaned poor could take refuge and which would be financed by donations from the

wealthy and run by the Sisters of Charity. The essence of the *hôpital général* to St Vincent was its voluntary nature. The poor would come, without coercion, because they would see in the institution an asylum from their wretchedness, a place provided by an all-merciful God to succour them; and the rich would freely donate towards its maintenance because they would be aware that this was what God expected of them. What better expression could there be of the brotherhood of rich and poor in Christ?

The beauty, simplicity, even nobility, of St Vincent's ideals were indisputable and the subsequent distortion of them by the French government has been severely criticized. The Crown saw in the *hôpital général* an attractively easy solution to the problem of poor relief without recourse to a new tax and one which threw the onus of creation and administration not upon the government but upon the Church, the faithful and local initiative. Hence an edict of 1662 urged the creation of *hôpitaux* throughout the country. But, and here the government and St Vincent parted company, the former intended, once they had been created, to intern coercively all the poor within them and to clear the streets of beggars; it was to be nothing short of *un grand projet du renfermement des pauvres*. Historians have seized upon this act as an aspect of developing French absolutism, an example of the desire for uniformity at the expense of St Vincent's idealism, but this criticism is unfair because, like England in the 1660s, France was faced with difficult economic circumstances. To leave the creation of modes of relief within the very hazy, if immensely beautiful, framework of St Vincent's ideas would have been even more inadequate than in fact the scheme proved to be. As it was bishops, spurred on by royal edicts and vying with one another in the generosity of their action, invariably

*In the Netherlands poor-relief was organized by the churches, and taxes were levied on the congregations. It is evident from illustrations like this, however, that the problem was not completely solved. (12)*

*Charity was a part of piety in both Protestant and Catholic countries. Here, as part of the propaganda of alms-giving, a prosperous middle-class family is shown giving food and drink to a beggar, who is actually given a faintly Christ-like appearance.* (13)

established an *hôpital général* in all diocesan centres and municipal councils or important clerics did the same in all sizeable towns. By the end of the old régime there were about 2,185 of these establishments in France though some had as few as six internees. The idea spread rapidly throughout Catholic Europe. In the Austrian Netherlands, Spain, Portugal, Savoy, Italy and even parts of Poland, the *hôpital général* under the administration of the Sisters of Charity and similar orders seemed an ideal solution because it combined Christian charity with an institutional form. It was an institutional form, however, intended to embrace only a fraction of the poor, in spite of the French government's grandiose pretensions—the aged, the sick and the orphaned. The rest—the bulk of those in need—were left to the charity of their fellow men. It is an extraordinary realization that 18th-century Catholic Europe was left to cope with the victims of an unprecedented population expansion and a rapidly changing economy with an insubstantial, inflexible, 'coin in the plate' charity in which the able-bodied poor were utterly dependent upon the caprice of voluntary charity.

In fairness it should be pointed out that the work of St Vincent was accomplished within the context of a stagnant population, many of whose difficulties were due to runs of bad harvests followed by plague or virulent epidemics, where there was no real problem of unemployment. Under such circumstances, the Sister of Charity with her bowl of soup and words of encouragement to the dying, and the philanthropic bishop encouraging donations to the *hospices* might have had some meaning. They were helpless against the rising tide of impoverished labouring men with families riddled with disease in the next century. The fact that the Church had reassumed responsibility for the poor simply enabled governments to sit back and blame the Church for its failure to cope with the swelling numbers of indigent whilst human lives were dragged out in misery.

There was a worse position than this, however. In Russia and parts of East Prussia the lord of the manor was theoretically responsible for the serfs under his control and the premium placed on human life was nil. In Russian towns a curious custom prevailed whose origins are almost impossible to trace. Society was divided into five parts, nobles, clerics, merchants, artisans and the rest; each category was responsible for the upkeep of its own poor but obviously since the latter almost all fell into the last category the burden of the poor was borne by the relatively poor and hence nothing could be done. Catholic charity, though piecemeal, was certainly more adequate than this. Indeed, in prosperous areas it worked well enough. A *curé* of the diocese of Tours has left a description of how the families of the poor of his parish managed by a cooperative effort. He himself cut up a loaf every morning after mass and distributed the pieces to those who attended the service, significantly enough, always women and children. Later in the morning, the children of the poor would call at the more prosperous farms and be given a drink of milk and towards the end of the day poor women would call at the same doors and be given a hunk of bread dipped in gravy or vegetable stew left from the main meal of the day. But if the system worked in rich parishes, elsewhere the inhabitants were powerless to help each other. Nevertheless, even here, something was shared. The poorest Irish cabin, for example, was at the disposal of the poor migrant if he wanted shelter for the night and a share of whatever the meagre cooking pot held. Ireland, after Russia, was perhaps the least fortunate part of Europe: a predominantly Catholic country but with a poor native clergy who were unable to give their flock anything and at the same time not falling subject to English schemes of poor relief. The Irish poor had no recourse but to depend on each other, if not for alms, at least for shelter and a crust as they roamed the country in search of work. Indeed, the crust of bread, the bowl of milk, the meat bone, the ladle of vegetable stew given here and there constituted the bulk of private charity in Catholic Europe. The Belgian and French rural clergy, when questioned, were adamant that money was very rarely given to the domiciled poor and that one of the ways in which a distinction could be drawn between the *indigent* and the *vagabonds* or vagrant poor was that the latter were only interested in money whilst the former did not expect it.

These, however, were the practises of a small, relatively closely knit, rural society which catered as far as in it lay for its own familiar poor, not for outsiders. When the resources of the parish were inadequate and the pauper moved out into the towns his position was delicate. True, he there belonged to a large and assertive community which was prepared to intimidate in order to gain its ends but he was forced to clutter the pavements and the porches of churches to elicit the pity of the passer-by and the worshipper in the name of Christian charity. *Misereri nostri*, the cry of the medieval leper, was still the common plaint of the 18th-century beggar. 'There is no section of the population,' commented de la Mare, in his famous *Traité de la Police*, 'which has God so constantly on its lips and so patently absent from its heart'. But given the state of provisions for relief in Catholic Europe, they had no alternative; no other grounds on which to stake their claims than an appeal to Christian ethics. It is possible that many of them had, like the English poor, ceased to attend religious worship. Certainly those interned in the *dépôt de mendicité* of Carcassonne were reported ignorant of the most common prayers and responses and a *curé* of the diocese of Rodez, doubtless one of the many clerics embarrassed by the dilemma of the deserving but unvirtuous poor, announced to his bishop that his flock was too wretched to obey any injunctions to attend divine service.

## The English poor

Yet though unquestionably less adequate than English poor relief, one does not find in Catholic countries the most distasteful aspects of the English system. In England the unit of relief was the parish and the parish demanded a rigorous residence qualification. After 1723, the English themselves experimented with a '*projet du grand renfermement des pauvres*' by making relief dependent upon entry into a workhouse which banded together old and young, the lazy, the vicious and the merely unfortunate—it was the least discriminating institution of its type in Europe. English poor law registers abound in records of sums paid to local ruffians to chase from the parish maidservants born outside the boundaries but made pregnant within and likely to discharge their offspring on the parish. An examination of the Hereford quarter sessions books revealed many cases of women being moved from one parish to another when they were so near their confinement that the removal was responsible for their death. And if the woman lived to give birth, parishes wrangled with each other as to who should accept responsibility for the child—a debate usually brought to a speedy termination by the high mortality rate of children within the workhouse. A House of Commons' committee in 1767 stated that for every hundred children born in the workhouse seven survived infancy. Indeed, the English treatment of poor children was scandalous even by 18th-century standards. French émigré priests who took refuge in St Pancras during the Revolution were astonished at the lack of concern demonstrated by the English for the very young and made attempts to form a small orphanage. Moll Flanders' conviction that, as the child of a criminal, orphaned early, she would have enjoyed better treatment in France was fully justified: and far more compassionate than those in France were the practises of the humane Dutch *weehuis*.

## The Enlightenment looks at poverty

Everywhere the mere number of those begging a part of their livelihood, migrating in search of work or living without fixed abode was sufficient to demonstrate the inadequacy of social provisions for the poor and the necessity for change. The question was how change should be effected, a problem at its most acute in Catholic countries where to alter existing provisions needed a radical change in Catholic social philosophy. The anti-clerical Enlightenment decried Catholic charity from every aspect; in part

because of its allegedly pernicious effects on the human character (*pauperes semper habeamus*, assumed poverty was an eternal feature of society and hence made the pauper accept that his only recourse was to live, parasite like, on the alms of others), in part because of its inadequacy (it did not accord help where it was most needed); and in part because it was held to be over-generous. '*Malheur à l'état qui a tant d'hospices,*' Montesquieu moaned, for there the poor had no incentive to save for old age—he did not consider out of what—but they accepted resignedly that an *hôpital général* would shelter them. In fact, philosophers and economists of the Enlightenment, with a few rare exceptions, predominant amongst whom was Turgot, were totally blinkered in their approach to the problem of poverty. Working upon scanty data, inbued with fervent anticlerical attitudes, they took as their point of departure the immediate need to abolish all existing provisions of relief. This done, the evil would already be in some part cured, for at least the truly poor would be separated from those who had merely acquired an ingrained habit of living on the community. Who were the truly poor? The children of large families, the widow, the orphaned, the old man crippled by a lifetime of labour—the Enlightenment did not move one inch away from the traditional religious concept of the deserving poor. And what was their social due? Support as long as they were too frail to support themselves. Society had an obligation to provide sustenance to each of its component members and to expect, in return, their labour.

How then did the *philosophes* and the physiocrats contend with the next obvious question: supposing that there was no work? To this, their answer was unanimous and deceptive in its simplicity: let it be created. Whatever else they believed in, they believed in the work project: the giving of work to the unemployed which would enhance their dignity as human beings rather than diminish them by according them graciously, but with condescension, alms. By work they did not mean industry, for many were insistent that this was inconsistent with the natural capacities of the rural worker, but the rough navvying involved in the building of roads and canals or the draining of marshes. Few European systems of poor relief, whether in Catholic or Protestant countries, did not find themselves, by the 1770s, permeated by these assumptions, though none until France during the Revolution was prepared to abolish existing provisions.

p 105
(20)

This volume began with the assertion that the 17th and 18th centuries believed in good government; it followed that the poor could be legislated away by the enactment of the right laws. Cervantes in *Don Quixote* (1615) described how Sancho Panza, finding himself the governor of an island, declared that his first official act would be

> to clear this island of all manner of filth and rubbish, especially vagabonds, idlers and sharpers; for I would have you know friends that your idle and lazy people in a commonwealth are like drones in a beehive, which devour the honey that the labouring bees gather . . . He laid severe penalties upon those who should sing lewd and immoral songs either by day or night; and prohibited the vagrant blind from going about singing their miracles in rhyme unless they could produce unquestionable evidence of their truth; . . . He appointed an overseer of the poor not to persecute them, but to examine their true claim; for under the disguise of pretended lameness and counterfeit sores, are often found sturdy thieves and hale drunkards.

Sancho-Panza-like, the so-called enlightened despots threw themselves energetically into the task of abolishing poverty eternally. Severe penalties were enacted against professional beggars: branding and imprisonment in France; expulsion from the province in Holland; the knout and exile to Siberia in Russia; but they were accompanied by sincere efforts to provide public works for the unemployed. The ground of the question, however, shifted from the desirability of creating work to how this work was to be financed, especially as it was in great demand and every country in Europe hesitated before the implications entailed in the imposition of a new tax for the poor. Hence in the Habsburg lands and Portugal the confiscated property of the Jesuits was partially used for the extra financing of poor relief; in some areas of France, the *corvée*, commuted into a money tax, contributed towards the

'Beer Street' was published together with its companion 'Gin Lane' in 1750, when in Hogarth's words 'the dreadful consequences of gin-drinking appeared in every street', and to promote beer-drinking seemed the best solution. While gin brings with it only idleness, poverty and distress, beer-drinking radiates mirth and thriving industry. Here, it is only the pawnbroker's house that is going to rack and ruin; other tradesmen wax fat and prosperous. (A note in the advertisement ran 'As the subjects of these Prints are calculated to reform some reigning Vices peculiar to the lower Class of People in hopes to render them of more extensive Use, the Author has published them in the cheapest Manner possible.' Nevertheless, the engravings sold at one shilling each.) (14)

payment of paupers in *ateliers de charité*: State lotteries, taxes on drinks and other commodities were other expedients used, and still there was not enough. The work project was no more able to cope with the problem of poverty than Catholic charity based on almsgiving. Except in very rare cases, the work project only catered for the adult male beggar, a small fraction of the total number, and not only were funds lacking to pay the poor, but State work had obviously to be remunerated at a lower level than current wage rates lest State work be demanded by those who could find work elsewhere. The work project in fact foundered in the mire of the living wage.

Nevertheless, work for the poor became the slogan of 18th-century social philosophy and was absorbed by progressive thinkers in the Catholic Church. In parts of France the Church went so far as to reward those who created work for the poor with Church land. Spinning schools were opened by the Church for women and girls but most had only a short existence before bankruptcy.

The 18th century work project has left its mark on the face of Europe. A period which used the words 'medieval' and 'gothic' as terms of abuse was not overawed by historic remains: innumerable ancient town walls and fortifications were razed by men, women and children carrying away buckets of dirt and gravel. Here and there canals were begun, and sometimes abandoned, like the one at Port-en-Bessin designed to link the River Aure with the sea. At Leixlip in County Dublin stands the 'wonderful barn' built by the local unemployed in the hard winter of 1742 when such was the cold that the fish froze in the rivers and the shrimps disappeared from the strand of Iristown never to return.

By the end of the old régime, then, two separate, and mutually hostile approaches existed towards the problem of poverty: that of St Vincent de Paul, backed by the Catholic tradition, and that of the work project, backed by the new philosophy. Even together, however, they were still impotent to contend with the swelling numbers of poor.

## Charity schools

As well as these expedients for dealing with the present poor, existed a further set of plans designed with the future in mind. One of the aims, dear to St Vincent, was that of rescuing children from a life of begging and petty felony and this was to become, in the course of one period, the commonest object of philanthropy throughout Europe. From London to St Petersburg, from Stockholm to Marseilles, charity schools sprang into being, the product of donations and legacies from those with a social conscience. In France a new religious order, St Jean-Baptiste de la Salle's *Frères des Écoles Chrétiennes* was of paramount importance in the plan to rescue the children of the poor from the follies of ignorance. By 1729 there were about 1,420 charity schools in England catering for some 22,503 pupils, and Wales, where the institutions developed slightly differently but more rapidly, had some thirty years later nearly 3,500 schools with more than 150,000 pupils. Even Catherine the Great, ruling a country which had no provisions for the poor, felt it necessary, in order to preserve her reputation as an enlightened despot, to open a charity school for girls. But whilst no one questioned the need for establishments to inculcate the love of industry and the fear of God in the young, attempts merely to foster literacy in the poor were universally condemned: in England because they educated the poor beyond their station:

> The charity school is another universal nursery of idleness: nor is it easy to conceive or invent anything more destructive to the interests and very foundation principles of a nation entirely dependent on its trade and manufactures than the giving of an education to the children of the lowest class of her people that will make them contemn those drudgeries for which they were born. (*Anon. Considerations of the fatal effects to a trading nation of the excess of public charity*, 1763)

In France they were condemned because, as Richeprey, Necker's emissary in the Rouergue put it, a literate idler is one thousand times more to be feared than an illiterate one.

Girls in England were taught needlework and to read, the more intelligent to write and cast accounts. After training they were apprenticed to such trades as mantua-making. The boys were apprenticed or made to enter the navy. In Holland, little girls were taught to spin: in France and Belgium to make lace: in *bien pensant* households everywhere they were given preference for posts as servants. In all these establishments religious instruction was accorded priority: religious instruction to teach the children their rightful position in life, to urge upon them the wisdom of thrift, industry, frugality and the virtues of cleanliness and respect for one's elders and betters. One cannot but detect in the curricula of

CHARITY SCHOOL.

CLOATHED AND EDUCATED
80 BOYS

MAINTAINED CLOATHED AND EDUCATED
40 GIRLS

*R. Clark fecit, Rupert Street Soho.*

Received of Mr Booth May 17th 1792 the Sum of One Guinea being his Annual Subscription for the Benefit of the Charity School in the Parish of St Martin in the Fields for the Year 1792

£1. 1. 0

*W. Bayley*

*St Martin-in-the-Fields Charity School, which issued this receipt, was opened in 1699, a year when parishes in London were vying with each other in setting up schools for the children of the poor and the supporting of them was a favourite form of practical piety.* (15)

*This detail from an engraving shows the London charity children in the Strand on 7th July 1713, a day appointed by Queen Anne for public thanksgiving for the Peace of Utrecht. As the procession made its way to St Paul's Cathedral, pupils dressed in clothes made specially for the occasion, sang hymns to God and the Queen – 'A Nursing Mother to thy FOLD, Long, long may She remain'. (16)*

the charity schools a reflection of that element of fear which ran through affluent society that the poor were passing beyond their control and must in some way be brought back:

> Make me dutiful and obedient to my benefactors . . . Make me temperate and chaste, meek and patient, true in all my dealings and industrious in my station

ran the *Poor Girls' Primer* (Sheffield Girls' Charity School, 1789). They did not add 'so that I might more adequately conform to my superior's conception of the ideal poor person'. Charity schools founded by the English in Ireland hoped not only to make the Irish industrious, but much more important, Protestant, and the whole project in the British Isles became ensnared in the High and Low Church controversy. This is not to diminish the major element of genuine philanthropy involved in the creation of the charity school but rather to demonstrate more fully the extent to which even philanthropy was cluttered by pre-determined religious, social and political attitudes.

## The young and the old

Indeed, if one wishes to find philanthropy relatively unadulterated by lesser motives in the treatment of the poor in the 18th century, perhaps the greatest breakthrough was in public attitudes towards foundling children. When St Vincent de Paul approached the *Dames de la Charité* with a baby he had found abandoned in a church porch, they refused to touch it. Even Louise de Marillac drew back. That the very foundress of the Sisters of Charity should recoil before something she had learned to regard as the product of sin and illicit pleasure is indicative of public revulsion for these unfortunate creatures; yet within fifty years, aided no doubt by their swelling numbers and the high premium put by social and economic thinkers on the virtues of a growing population, attitudes were changing. A minority were asking how one could be sure that the children were illegitimate and from that question they moved on to ask did it matter whether they were or not? Interestingly enough, this attitude was prompted not so much by the conviction that the sins of parents should not be visited upon the children as a realization that to neglect them meant a loss to society of their labour. Paris had a foundling hospital by the end of the 17th century, Tours by 1740, Rennes and many other French provincial centres by 1780; the building of a foundling hospital was dear to Maria Theresa, though in fact accomplished by her son. Even Catherine the Great as one of her random meretricious philanthropic experiments erected a small hospital to this end in St Petersburg. Thomas Coram, a retired sea captain, dedicated his life after 1739 to the building of the London Foundling Hospital, the most impressive monument that English 18th-century philanthropy produced. Coram saw the foundling children of his institution as the future artisans of extended English colonies and was prepared to withstand any amount of hardship to achieve his ends.

p 286
(14)
p 286
(13)

Allied to the theme of social waste was that of social gratitude and the aged poor were here the beneficiaries. Joseph II's concern, for example, that each commune should pay for the support of the old labourer and retired soldier who had usefully served the community; the Abbé de Montlinot's addresses to the *Comité de Mendicité* on this theme; and the compassionate treatment of the aged artisan in contemporary literature and art, the subject for example, of Goya's drawing, '*Thus do the useful end their days*', are indicative of this awareness. But to be worthy of assistance the aged had also to be deserving; for those old in the ways of vice little was done. Perhaps the Dutch alone—they have been called pioneers of penology—tried anything savouring of correctional training. The *tuchthuis*, a 16th-century foundation established in all large cities, was aimed at teaching the idle poor the habits of industry. The cellar of the Amsterdam *rasphuis*, with the waterwheel which the ingrained idler was made to tread if he wished to save himself from drowning, was allegedly obligatory sightseeing for the socially concerned traveller—though the more intelligent, including John Howard, questioned its efficacy. In the main, however, correctional training was not an end which attracted philanthropic effort.

p 290
(22)

p 285
(10)

In the last analysis, though some are impressive, it must be admitted that the monuments of philanthropy were a puny response to a problem which daily grew more and more out of hand. Our story stops short of the period when men would look towards the dynamic of a rapidly industrializing economy as a way of solving old social problems but it comprehends two developments, both in the last decade of the century, important in the history of European poor relief. The one, the French Revolution, constitutes the most curious episode in that history for it attempted to put into practice the ideas of the *philosophes*, to destroy traditional Catholic charity overnight and to substitute the work project. The attempt was accompanied by total failure. Only a fraction of the poor could be employed in public works and the funds to pay even that insignificant number simply evaporated in the midst of inflation and food shortage. Abandoning their theories, the French scurried back to shelter in the skirts of Catholic almsgiving and the whole experiment was to be used mercilessly and effectively, as late as the early 20th century, by the French Right whenever socialism demanded a State based assistance.

The other, the food crisis of 1795–97, felt with particular severity in northern Europe, brought an honest response from a group of Berkshire magistrates at Speenhamland who used the funds of public relief to supplement the labourer's wage so that he could, in face of mounting costs, feed himself and his family. It was a real admission that the wage was not a living wage though, tragically for the poor, it was but a topical response to immediate pressure, an easy interlude before the Act of 1834.

The lesson of the 18th century was that there was no quick or simple solution to the problem of poverty; that appeals to 'submission' and 'contentment' were of little avail and that pity and *noblesse oblige* were outworn attitudes. But the poor remained stranded somewhere between two concepts: as the children of God and the test of a Christian State on the one hand and as the enemies of society on the other. They were left an amorphous, ill-defined mass of men, women and children, old and young, able-bodied and sick and as such they were destined to remain until, caught up in the momentum of a rapidly industrializing economy, economic progress carried sufficient of them above the most precarious subsistence level. That achieved, the problem of poverty was reduced to such manageable dimensions that gradually an 18th-century ideal could be realized and the poor indeed legislated away.

But this is to look far into the future. The student of social history is drawn to the 18th century in part at least because of its infinite variety. The elegant town houses and public buildings caught in the earlier pages of this volume bear witness to the refined tastes and new wealth of substantial sections of the community but they are only one side of the coin. It is hoped that these pages have shown something of the other. Whilst the merchants of Liverpool grew rich on an amalgam of slaves and cotton, Irish immigrants perished in the cellars of the city; whilst the profits of the wine trade built a new and beautiful Bordeaux, the garrets of the old town were crammed with the influx from the Pyrenees.

Our period is *par excellence* one of contrasts in which, to an unprecedented extent, European society was sharply divided into rich and poor, a dichotomy which became more and more apparent as urbanization intensified and the two dwelt closer together—indeed we are not far from the day when Disraeli would speak of the 'two nations' between whom there was no contact and even less understanding. The road from the conquest of plague to the welfare State and social security was long, circuitous, uncharted and if by 1800 a way-stage had already been passed, for the most part the journey was still only beginning.

# X EPILOGUE:

# REFORM AND REVOLUTION

*The End of the Ancien Régime*

ALFRED COBBAN

*'We hold these truths to be self-evident,*

*that all men are created equal, that they are endowed by*

*their Creator with certain unalienable Rights,*

*that among these are Life, Liberty and*

*the pursuit of Happiness.'*

THE DECLARATION OF INDEPENDENCE

### Legitimate, justified rebellion

offered, in an age of absolutism, the only means of radical change. Its impetus came not from the lowest, most exploited sections of the community, but normally from the upper classes — the aristocracy, prosperous bourgeoisie and intelligentsia — chafing against unreasonable restraints and lack of political responsibility. The revolts that broke out and were suppressed in Geneva and the Low Countries were of this kind; so was the American War of Independence, and so was the first stage of the French Revolution. None of these was a 'democratic' uprising in the modern sense, though they all attempted to distribute power on a broader basis. Their aims were moderate, conservative, sober and honest — qualities embodied for the later 18th century in the almost archetypal figure of George Washington.

Washington was a man of many virtues and no vices. Before the rebellion he had been a successful soldier in the British army, serving against the French and the Indians; an ambitious land-owner who married a rich widow and accumulated a fortune in stock certificates and rents; and a conscientious representative of Frederick county in the House of Burgesses. During the War of

Independence, it was his integrity and gifts of leadership rather than any brilliance as a strategist that pushed him to the top; and the same assets caused him to be elected first president of the new republic and to hold office for two terms. This portrait (opposite) was painted in 1777, when he was 45 and had been commander-in-chief for two years, and when the War had another five years to run. Impressive in bearing (he was 6 feet 2 inches tall), straight-forward in character, practical and serious in intellect, he was a perfect father figure for his country, though something more was needed in the shape of posthumous myth-making to turn him into an inspiration and a hero. For him, as for most of his countrymen, liberty was not a moral abstraction, still less a slogan of social upheaval; it was simply the best means of ensuring America's continued prosperity. But ideology was thrust upon him. If the British stood for tyranny, the rebellion must stand for freedom. The result, enshrined in the Declaration of Independence (a document in which the Enlightenment proclaims itself in every line), was the formulation of an ideal — the manifesto of every later democratic movement throughout the West. (1)

'We, the ladies of Edenton, do solemnly engage not to conform to the pernicious custom of drinking tea . . .' A crucial step towards a break with England came over the collection of a tax on tea. The 'Boston Tea Party', when in 1773 £ 18,000-worth of British tea was thrown into Boston harbour, was an overt act of defiance. (2)

Revolutionary congresses were held in 1774, 1775 and 1776, each time moving closer to the conclusion that complete independence was the only way out. After hostilities had already begun, on July 4th 1776, the famous Declaration was signed. The painting (right) shows the drafting committee, led by Thomas Jefferson, with Franklin on his left, presenting the document to Congress. (3)

War escalated during the early 1770s. Below left: the 'Bloody Massacre' at Boston in 1770, when British troops, acting against orders, fired on civilian rioters. Below centre: the Battle of Breed's Hill, June 1775. Breed's Hill, part of the Charlestown peninsula opposite Boston, had been fortified by the revolutionaries. Although it was eventually retaken by the British, the raw American soldiers inflicted ruinous losses – over 1000 dead and 3,000 wounded. Far right: Washington reviews his army. A few years were sufficient for the training of a disciplined force comparable to any in Europe. (4, 5, 6)

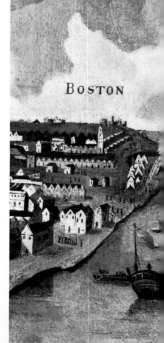

**The new society** that victory created made few radical breaks with traditional values. Common law, for instance, was based on English precedent, though the way the regional judiciary was organized was allowed to vary from state to state. The second Chief Justice of the Supreme Court was Oliver Ellsworth, seen here in 1792 with his wife Abigail in their home at Windsor, Conn., which by an artistic licence is also visible through the window. (7)

Boston (above), one of the centres of rebellion, survived the War largely unscathed. The 'Massacre' took place in front of the Old State House in the centre. As the capital of an independent Massachusetts, it had many qualities of an English country town. (8)

New York (left) had already grown into a major city in 1757, when this view was painted. In the centre is Trinity Church, on the left wharves and a fort. An English fleet lies at anchor with a captured French vessel. New York's population rose from about 12,000 in the mid-century to 33,000 in 1790. For five years, 1785–90, it was the capital of the whole country. (9)

**The blessings of democracy,** admired by the rest of the world, were viewed more cynically by those Englishmen who saw it at close quarters. The population was eight million, the electorate a quarter of a million – a better proportion than other countries. But the system was corrupt. Below: Robert Dighton's impression of the Westminster election of 1788. In the foreground is the beautiful Duchess of Devonshire and Lord John Townsend, gathering votes for the Whigs. Fox's mascot is held aloft. Wilkes has his pocket picked. (12)

**Buying votes** was the accepted way of fighting an election. Far left: a detail from Hogarth's 'Election' series, showing an agent slipping coins into the hands of a couple of supporters. Left: an idiot brought to the polls and induced to register his choice. Right: the hustings of the 1796 election, also held at Covent Garden and also painted by Dighton. There are three candidates, one of them (in the centre, his coat buttoned over an ample stomach) Charles James Fox. The boards show the state of the poll on probably the last day. (10, 11, 13)

**The ineffectiveness of absolutism** became increasingly apparent in France as the financial position grew more and more hopeless and the privileged orders steadily refused to make the necessary concessions. Lavish spending by the court and nobility was not a primary cause, though popular opinion naturally saw it so. Spectacles such as the illumination of the Trianon gardens (above) or the *alfresco* banquet given by the Prince de Conti in 1766 (below) were remembered and resented later during the Terror. (14, 15)

**Desperate remedies** had been tried as early as 1716, when John Law, a Scots banker, set up a state bank issuing its own paper money. At first confidence was high, but in 1720 it collapsed and in spite of an attempt to make gold and silver illegal tender, no one wanted Law's notes. This scene (above) shows the Mint at Rennes where – at the grille under the porch in the centre – a lucky few were able to exchange their notes for silver. (16)

**To save the situation,** Louis XVI called in Necker (left), a Swiss banker who had grown rich largely at the expense of the French treasury. His failures were concealed by a masterly *compte rendu* which shifted the discovery of the extent of the deficit on to the shoulders of his successors. By 1788 'Le Défécit' had become a subject for English humour; Louis and Necker stand astonished before empty coffers, while an aristocrat and a priest carry off sacks of money. (17, 18)

**Religious hatred** still contributed to unrest in almost every country of Europe. The Church, as we have seen in Chapter I, was inevitably interlocked with the State. Left: the centre of Catholic orthodoxy in France, the high altar of Notre-Dame in Paris. (19)

**Minorities suffered** in both Catholic and Protestant centres, despite much official toleration. In France the Calas case, exposed by Voltaire, drew attention to the persecution of Huguenots and resulted in more liberal laws; Calas was unjustly accused of murdering his son rather than see him turn Catholic. Right: the family of Calas after his rehabilitation. Below: anti-Catholic bigotry in England – the Gordon Riots of 1780, provoked by the Catholic Relief Bill, and (right) villagers burning an effigy of the Pope as late as 1793. Bottom: Spain remained almost medieval in its fanatical Catholicism – a procession of flagellants by Goya. (20–23)

'Enthusiasm', derided by the Enlightenment, was the life-blood of the dissenting Churches which sprang up in most Protestant countries as a reaction against the apathy and complacency of the establishment. John Wesley (right), founder of Methodism, preached a doctrine of individual conversion, a 'new birth' by which every soul finds God in its own experience. Below right: Methodist ministers went out to the people and became noted for their emotional oratory. The Quakers (below left, a meeting house in Amsterdam) placed similar emphasis on the individual conscience but practised inner contemplation and dispensed almost entirely with theology. (24, 25, 26)

The Jews in the West were still open to unfair discrimination. Right: German Jews forcibly conscripted into the army – an anti-Jewish cartoon. Above: 'Jew' Süss, the Duke of Württemberg's minister, hounded and killed after the death of his patron. (27, 28)

**The calender of revolution** in France began in May 1789 when, amidst mounting unrest, the States General were summoned. It consisted of three 'Estates' – clergy, nobility and people. The Third Estate, with some of the clergy, locked out of its meeting-room on 20th June, retired to a nearby tennis court and swore (above) never to separate until the Constitution had been established. (29)

**To avert catastrophe** in the face of anarchy and peasant risings throughout France, the liberal elements of the National Assembly suggested reforms which fired sudden general enthusiasm, and on the night of the 4th–5th of August (right) the privileges of nobles, tithe-holders, provincial estates, cities and corporations were voted away. (30)

**Popular ferment,** whipped up by demagogues forecasting a massacre of patriots, reached a climax on July 14th 1789, when the Bastille was stormed by the mob and the Governor, de Launay (seen above, on the right), murdered. The practical importance of the Bastille was small, its symbolic significance enormous. Royal authority had been defied – and not by the middle classes but by the urban masses. What had until then followed the pattern of other 18th-century revolutions now became something new, the unleashing of peasant and proletariat power, and a new type of leader arose to control a new situation. Right: Robespierre, the extremist deputy from Arras – uncompromising, incorruptible, implacable enemy of the monarchy. (31, 32)

**The power of the press,** inseparable from popular rule, was perhaps fully displayed for the first time in 1789. From before the meetings of the States General, a flood of newspapers and pamphlets was being sold in the streets (left), and the revolutionary leaders became known mainly through their journalism. Arthur Young noticed with surprise in June that while any number of inflammatory tracts were pouring out and being eagerly bought, there was no attempt on the part of the court to defend itself in the same way. (33)

**Freedom of trade,** the abolition of internal tariffs, had been demanded by Calonne in 1786 but was only achieved by the Revolution. This allegorical drawing (1, Liberty destroying the *barrière*, 2, Ceres and Bacchus entering Paris) shows Ledoux's building illustrated on p. 67. Below: pulling down the statue of Louis XIV in the Place des Victoires in 1792. (34, 35)

**The second stage** of the Revolution, bloodier and more radical than the first, overtook France in the summer of 1791, partly because of the threat of foreign intervention. Below left: the Jacobin Club decides in favour of war against Austria (a caricature showing Dumouriez, the leader of the war-party, as a goose). Hitherto the most that had been envisaged was a constitutional monarchy. Now in August 1792, the mob – acting without directive from the Legislative Assembly – attacked the Tuileries (above), where the King was living. The way was open for the Terror, from March 1793 to July 1794, when those suspected of treason, especially aristocrats, went to the scaffold. Below: a family arraigned before a revolutionary committee. (36, 37, 38)

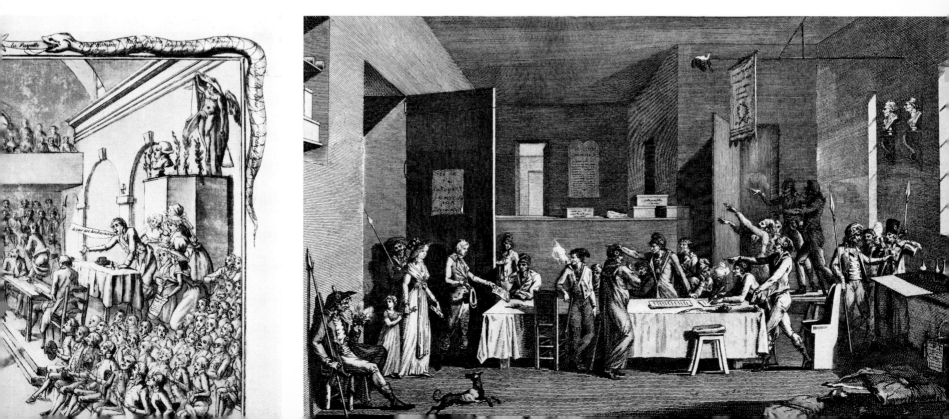

**Planting the tree of liberty:** the first two or three years of the Revolution were a period of idealism and hope. The State renounced aggression, practised the triad of virtues, Liberty, Equality and Fraternity, and confidently expected the rest of world to follow France's example. On the first anniversary of the fall of the Bastille 'trees of liberty' were planted all over the country – this at a time when the King was still officially the head of State. (39)

**The King's death** made retreat impossible. He was charged with treason, since he had been found to be in correspondence with Austria, but was condemned to death only by the narrowest majority. It was a victory for the radical faction; it committed France to republicanism and eventually to military dictatorship. After a reign notable chiefly for its failure to withstand pressure from his own aristocracy, Louis XVI died with dignity as its representative. (40)

# The End of the Ancien Régime

ALFRED COBBAN

GENERAL HISTORIES require titles and their chapters need headings. These are the signposts by which our route through history is charted. The names on them are of two different kinds. Sometimes they are contemporary terms which tell us what an age thought of itself, and sometimes they are the inventions of historians judging in retrospect. The Age of Enlightenment, the century of *lumières*, regarded itself as such in its own day. The description of its final years as the age of enlightened or benevolent despotism—though the term was not unknown to contemporaries—belongs to the second class. At the time it would have produced some ironic smiles, for despotism was not generally supposed to be enlightened, or even for that matter very benevolent, or assumed to be compatible with progress; and there was no doubt in the collective mind of Western civilization that enlightenment and progress were both characteristic of the age. It followed logically that despotism could not be.

## The rights of man

In the second half of the 18th century the optimism which was singled out in the Foreword as a mark of this age seemed to be increasingly justified. Trade, industry and agriculture, science and technology, exploration and conquest, population, the amenities of civilized life—in all these respects this volume has been a record of progress. That such an enlightened age should still have to suffer the devastation of war, spreading across the seas and to other continents, shocked its greater minds, evoking the satiric powers of Voltaire and the political genius of Rousseau. Even in this respect, however, there was hope. After the War of American Independence, at least Western Europe appeared to have settled its feuds and to be in the hands of statesmen who saw peace as the prime interest of their countries. And in domestic government and social habits, reforms which in the first half of the century had appeared in the books and the minds of men now moved into the field of law and action.

The development of the secular State and a corresponding decline of independent religious authority, which have already been referred to as major factors in the history of the century, facilitated the progress of one of the greatest reforms, the extension of the principle of toleration and the decline of religious persecution. Actual persecution, as distinct from civil and political discrimination, had already largely died out in Protestant countries, though even here we must distinguish between the tolerance of governments and enlightened society and the not always latent fanaticism of the masses. The Gordon Riots revealed something of the fires that smouldered beneath the surface in England, though more than religious passions were involved in them. In Roman Catholic countries the governing and educated élite had not yet abandoned the principle of persecution, but in the second half of the century we are faced rather with isolated episodes than a systematic policy of intolerance.

The best known case is that of Calas, a prosperous Huguenot citizen of Toulouse, whose son hanged himself in 1761. It was alleged that he had been murdered by his family because he had become a convert to Catholicism. The *Parlement* of Toulouse, which condemned Calas, tried the case in an atmosphere overheated by the defeats of the Seven Years' War and memories of the

struggle against the Huguenot Camisards under Louis XIV; it combined religious fanaticism and legal barbarity with judicial incompetence. An agitation taken up by Voltaire reversed their sentence, but by that time Calas had been tortured and broken on the wheel and his family pauperized and exiled. Such an episode did not stand alone. The new thing was not the fate of the Calas family but the indignation aroused by the conduct of the *Parlement* of Toulouse, reaching even as high as the Royal Council. The King was not deterred from rehabilitating the memory of Calas even by his coronation oath committing him to extirpate heresy; and opinion moved so rapidly from condemning persecution to granting privileges that in 1787 an edict of toleration of French Huguenots was passed. The new trend was not confined to France. Toleration was in the air. Austria passed an edict of toleration in 1781. Russia relaxed the official persecution of the Old Believers in 1785. In Spain the control of the Church by the Crown, particularly through the royal right of nominating bishops, which had always extended in principle to the Inquisition was now asserted in practice and used to moderate its rigours.

The acid test of religious tolerance was provided by the Jews. The Enlightenment was embarrassingly ambivalent in this respect, like its greatest figure Voltaire, who found the Mosaic law, the deeds of King David and the general history of an ancient middle eastern tribe distressingly unenlightened. However, it was in enlightened Europe of the West that Jews were most free from restrictions and penalties and that such as existed were gradually being relaxed. In Great Britain and Scandinavia Jews were already largely immune from civil disabilities, though they lacked political rights, as indeed did many others. The French poll tax on Jews was removed in 1784. In France, however, a distinction must be made between the former Portuguese Jews of Bordeaux, who had achieved positions of considerable equality, and the Jews of Alsace whose social position was much closer to that of the Jews of central and eastern Europe where ghettos kept them in isolation from the rest of the population, though still subject to financial exploitation by governments and murderous attacks by the people. A few central European Jews, like the famous Moses Mendelssohn, accepted the message of the Enlightenment, but most of his co-religionists were too deeply imbued with the ghetto mentality to think of breaking out; and even if they had done so the populations which surrounded them were still far closer to the Middle Ages than to the Enlightenment. In central and eastern Europe religious toleration stopped short at the limits of Christianity.

The treatment of Jews directly, as that of religious dissidents less directly, was bound up with ideas of human equality, which essentially all the reforms of the 18th century assumed in one way or another. The most flagrant breach of it was created by slavery and the slave trade which provided its raw material. Religious and democratic motivation combined in the agitation for their abolition. Quakers headed the committees which were founded in England about 1783 and which, in spite of the bitter opposition of mercantile interests, steadily won over public opinion. Fox, in one of the last and noblest of his acts, succeeded in carrying abolition of the slave trade in 1807. The motion was moved by one of his younger lieutenants, Grey, who was to carry parliamentary reform in 1832 and the abolition of slavery in British possessions in 1833.

329

The names of those who, in 1788, founded the *Société des Amis des Noirs* in France, including Condorcet, Lafayette, Sieyès, Brissot, Mirabeau, are sufficient to establish its connection with the revolutionary movement. In spite of the strong opposition of colonial interests, the progress of the slave population of the French colonies towards emancipation advanced along with the Revolution, burst into the bloodiest of race wars and then receded. Abolition of the slave trade was forced on Europe by Great Britain at the Congress of Vienna. It took a second revolution, in 1848, to abolish slavery in French possessions; and one of the bloodiest of civil wars to achieve the same in the great democracy of the West.

Religion and 'philosophy' also joined to promote the idea of equality in another field by extending the rudiments of education to all ranks of the community. With the rise of the modern bureaucratic State and the growth of trade and industry, there came the need for a larger section of the population to possess the elements of literacy. The extent of even a very elementary education varied greatly between countries and within them, but at least in western Europe there was more of it than used to be thought.

At the secondary and university level, education had practically reached its nadir in the 18th century. Exceptions should perhaps be made for some of the new universities in Germany, such as

*f 1*

*Education at elementary schools in the 18th century was generally more adequate than at secondary or university level. This German school of 1771 catered for gentlemen (in the background, practising sports) and house-servants (being taught useful skills). (1)*

Göttingen and Halle and for the Scottish and the New England universities; but the dead hand of religious orthodoxy lay heavy on most existing schools and colleges. Progress had to come from private or communal initiative, or where the State supplied some of the deficiencies of the Church. From Paris and London, Royal Academies for the advancement of the arts and sciences spread to every capital in Europe. Masonic lodges were centres for stimulating local intellectual activities and promoting new ideas in education, notably the famous Lodge of the Nine Sisters in Paris. In England education was saved by the exclusion of those who were not members of the Church of England from the moribund Anglican institutions of Oxford and Cambridge. This led to the foundation of the dissenting academies which, for a time, represented the high-water mark of educational progress.

*f 3*

The foundations were laid in this period for the great developments in depth and range of syllabus, and in social scope, of education in the 19th century; but it cannot be claimed that the revolutionary period in France built on these foundations. Beginning with high hopes for the progress of education, it put the clock back in respect of the education of the masses, which so far as it existed had been the work of the religious orders and so suffered from the hostility of the revolutionaries; while for counter-revolutionaries even a minimal education for the sons of the people now began to appear socially dangerous. On a higher educational level the dissolution of the Jesuit Order, controlling some five or six hundred schools throughout Europe, and the expulsion of thousands of experienced teachers, provided an opportunity for scholastic innovation. There is little evidence that it was taken. During the Revolution all education by the religious orders was temporarily ended in France, but despite the ideals represented by the new Central Schools there was no effective replacement and when the educational system was restored under Napoleon it was on the old lines.

p 32 (1)

*The Enlightenment made for the toleration of religious minorities, such as the Jews, and some Jews responded by adopting enlightened views. Moses Mendelssohn relinquished the claim of Judaism to possess the unique truth. (2)*

## Crime and punishment

Thus the achievements of the age of reform under the heading of equality were limited. Its key-word was rather humanity. Apart from war, the most notable example of inhumanity was in the criminal law. The ethical revolution implied in the term utilitarianism could not fail to be applied in this field. There is only space here to refer to one of the heroes of the struggle against the inhumanity of the law. The English reformer, John Howard, a country gentleman of independent means, was inevitably brought, when he became High Sheriff of Bedfordshire in 1773, into contact with prisons and prisoners. Horrified by what he saw, he began a tour of prisons, first in neighbouring counties, and then throughout England and Europe, where he died finally of jail fever at Cherson in the Ukraine in 1790. His reports to parliamentary committees and his *State of the Prisons*, published in 1777, made their mark on

p 285 (10)

*The 18th century was the great age of Freemasonry in its modern sense—i.e. not a professional guild but a secret society combining philanthropy and wealth. Masonic lodges, meeting-places of intellectual and socially-minded men, played a part in spreading liberal ideas. Here, at a meeting under the French Grand Master, one initiate (11) is received into the Lodge, while another (12) lies covered with a sheet waiting his turn. (3)*

public opinion, though actual reform of prisons was slow to follow. Even Howard accepted the need for many forms of physical penalties. Imprisonment, indeed, was commonly merely a means of keeping an accused person in security, not primarily regarded as a punishment for the crime. This may explain why the French *lettre de cachet* ordering the seizure of an individual, normally set no time limit to his detention, and why *habeas corpus* had no place in French law. What the Enlightenment thought of the criminal punishments of the age has already been explained. No order for judicial torture was issued in England after 1688, though physical punishments such as the pillory and flogging persisted.

p 291 (29)

The classic work on this subject, which deserves to be recalled again, is the Italian Beccaria's *Treatise of Crimes and Punishments*, published in 1764. There can hardly be any subject on which enlightened Europe was more of one mind than on the reform of the criminal laws, and perhaps no book which had such a rapid and unqualified effect. For once a great reforming treatise was not before its time, as a short list of dates will show. After the Union of the English and Scottish Parliaments the abolition of torture was extended to Scotland by an Act of 1708. Frederick II abolished it in Prussia, except in very grave cases such as treason, as soon as he came to the throne in 1740. Despite the writings of the *philosophes*, the French *Parlements* successfully resisted the abolition of legal torture until the eve of the Revolution; but it is remarkable that the Revolution, Terror and all, never reverted to the use of judicial torture once it had been abolished. In Russia inferior courts lost the power of ordering torture in 1762 and higher courts in 1801. The Spanish Inquisition ceased to use torture about 1816. Much more remained to be done to humanize the process of law and the minds of lawyers, but with humanitarianism a new principle had been introduced into the world. What it meant, and its capacity for extension, was put as clearly as by anyone by the greatest of its prophets, Jeremy Bentham. In his *Principles of Morals and Legislation*, printed in 1780 but first published in 1789, he wrote:

The day has been, I grieve to say in many places it is not yet past, in which the greater part of the species, under the denomination of slaves, have been treated by the law exactly upon the same footing as, in England for example, the inferior races of animals are still. The day *may* come when the rest of the animal creation may acquire those rights which never could have been withholden from them but by the hand of tyranny. The French have already discovered that the blackness of the skin is no reason why a human being should be abandoned without redress to the caprice of a tormentor [See Lewis XIVth's *Code Noir*]. It may come one day to be recognized, that the number of the legs, the villosity of the skin, or the termination of the *os sacrum*, are reasons equally insufficient for abandoning a sensitive being to the same fate. What else is it that should trace the insuperable line? Is it the faculty of reason, or, perhaps, the faculty of discourse? But a full-grown horse or dog is beyond comparison a more rational, as well as a more conversable animal, than an infant of a day, or a week, or even a month old. But suppose the case were otherwise, what would it avail? The question is not, Can they *reason*? nor, Can they *talk*? but, Can they *suffer*?

## 'Natural forces'

Along with the ethical revolution which produced this great wave of humanitarian reform, and not unconnected with it, were the beginnings of an administrative revolution. These need to be taken together because in causes and effects they frequently overlapped, and they were both part of the general movement that we call the Enlightenment. Scientific method in the discovery and analysis of facts, once it had entered the Western mind, could not be excluded from the field of social thought. The result was the birth of the social sciences, and with them of a new attitude towards government as subject to rational treatment and calculation. Public finance, trade, population were ceasing to be matters purely of guesswork.

For the first time government was beginning to possess a very rough approximation to accurate statistics to base its decisions on. Man was at last included in the natural order and therefore subject to the uniformities of nature.

The field in which social science found its amplest scope was that of economics. It developed in the form of two different and strongly opposed schools. In Great Britain and France social thought was essentially liberal and free from the belief of central and eastern Europe in the self-evident, self-sufficient strength and wisdom of government. The natural order in the West was one to which rulers and ruled were equally subject. It followed that the less government interfered with the natural course of economic life, the better for everybody. Trade, if left to itself, would find the natural channels determined by a beneficent Providence. The barriers imposed by external and internal tariffs, by prohibitions on new methods of manufacture and on entry into industry by closed guilds and corporations, by the survival of medieval restrictions on land usage, and by a host of other laws and customs, were denounced by Francis Hutcheson, Adam Smith and their disciples in Great Britain and by the Physiocrats in France. Italian reformers, most notably Beccaria, were subject to the same intellectual influences despite the absence of a free government as in England or a restless trend to political opposition as in France.

When we turn to the theorists of central Europe we discover that despotism was—naturally enough—no seed-bed for economic liberalism. The German Cameralists were the servants of the absolute State. Their aim was, by increasing the wealth of the State, to increase the power of the ruler. Individualism progressed in Great Britain and in New England, *étatisme* in central and eastern Europe. In France both trends can be detected simultaneously and in competition with one another. In all countries they extended over a broad field of government and are not to be regarded as confined purely to economic matters. They are more satisfactorily envisaged as aspects of a general movement in the direction of administrative rationalization. Where monarchy prevailed, as it did through most of Europe, this movement was bound to work to its advantage. Despotism might become a little more enlightened; it would certainly obtain the machinery for becoming more despotic. In so far as this could be brought about, it was bound to bring with it a change in the balance of power in a state to the disadvantage of the aristocracies, which everywhere limited the power of the monarchies. They would hardly welcome this and their reaction to it has left its mark on the declining 18th century.

## Background to revolution

The decades which preceded the French Revolution used to be called the Age of Enlightened Despotism. More recently they have been called the Age of the Democratic Revolution. There are good reasons for both these descriptions. So far as I know, a third description, which would be equally valid, has never been employed. I would be tempted to call it the Age of the Aristocratic Reaction. We owe to the French historian Georges Lefebvre our appreciation of the fact that the French Revolution began as an aristocratic movement, a revolt of the privileged orders against the monarchy. To a greater or less extent this was a challenge which many monarchies had to face at this time. As a general movement it has not been clearly brought into the light of history for two reasons. In the first place, the monarchical government usually withdrew the policies that provoked aristocratic opposition before the point of actual civil war had been reached; and secondly, where a struggle did break out, as in the Dutch Republic, the Austrian Netherlands and France, aristocratic and democratic movements were so interwoven in language and in personnel that only by a detailed study has it been possible to disentangle them. It might also be argued that from a broad historical point of view the aristocratic reaction demands less attention, since it was a defensive movement, the main object of which was to preserve the *status quo*.

*An English engraving of 1772 shows George III being driven headlong into a chasm by two horses, Pride and Obstinacy, who trample on the Constitution and Magna Charta, while America burns on the horizon. The King has shut his eyes and holds a paper inscribed 'I glory in the name of Englishman'. Lord Chatham, on crutches (he suffered from gout) runs after the coach trying to stop it, while a minister in the foreground offers the crowd money. (4)*

Since it was successful in doing this, over a large part of Europe the political structure continued to be monarchy tempered by aristocracy or vice versa.

However, this does not complete the picture of the historical significance of the aristocratic reaction. It could come to terms with the monarchies, but not so easily with the people. In general terms it may be said that monarchy bought off the aristocracies at the price of allowing them a freer hand to exploit the people. This in its turn produced, where the possibility existed, a reaction in the form of a democratic movement, directed not against the monarchy but against aristocracy.

Such a broad, general formula needs, of course, to be qualified in each particular case, but it helps us to understand even the most apparently anomalous of the 18th century revolutions and to justify the description of the American Revolution as democratic. There was a time when historical orthodoxy went in a different direction. For many years after Charles Beard wrote his *Economic Interpretation of the Constitution*, in 1913, the prevailing school of American historians saw the Revolution as a class movement, a revolt of the wealthy capitalist elements in the colonies against interference with trade by the royal government from abroad and against threats to the rights of property at home. If the American Revolution had really been only this it could count as one of the aristocratic revolts against monarchy. More recent research has shown the true complexity of the situation in the colonies and revealed Beard's thesis as an attempt by the careful selection of facts to support a preconceived theory. Certainly there was an aristocratic upper class in all the colonies and not only the plantation owners of the South. Some of the leaders of the revolution were unmistakably aristocratic. But there was also a middle and a labouring class, and at least in the New England colonies a good deal of social mobility between them. In these colonies, also, the political institutions contained strong democratic elements. A network of clubs and political associations of various kinds, as well as an extensive patriotic press, circulated democratic ideas. Different sectors of American society could support these ideas because of their obvious affiliation with constitutional ideas inherited from the struggles of 17th-century England.

In the light of this historic appeal it is all the more striking that republicanism did not appear before 1774, and even after the p 195<br/>(38) outbreak of actual war, with skirmishes at Lexington and Concord in 1775, battles for control of Boston and an American invasion of Canada, the Continental Congress still professed loyalty to the Crown. True, the struggle was presented by the parliamentary opposition in Great Britain as a revolt against the Crown, but Lord North, who was Prime Minister through all the crucial stages, was justified in denying this. 'The American War', he said of the opposition, 'was, as they suggest, the war of the Crown contrary to the wishes of the people. I deny it. It was the war of Parliament; there was not a step taken in it that had not the sanction of Parliament.' George III was certainly in agreement with his Parliament, f 4 but he was pushed into the role of a symbolic opponent to the Americans by the speeches put into his mouth in Parliament and the brilliant pamphleteering of such writers as Tom Paine. There can be little doubt, also, that forgetting the existence of slaves, as mostly they did, the revolutionaries effected a considerable political shift of power in the direction of democracy in the colonies themselves. There has been a tendency to ignore the large number of loyalists who fled the colonies. Their disappearance, it has been said, perhaps with some exaggeration, 'marked the disappearance of most of the colonial aristocracy'.

p 313–15 Whatever qualifications have to be made, the American Revolution was a new phenomenon. It created the first state in the modern world that might with some degree of plausibility be called democratic. Its ideals were even more important than its achievements. They were recorded for the contemporary world and for p 315<br/>(3) future generations in the Declaration of Independence voted on July 4, 1776. Admittedly, many of the Founding Fathers hardly realized the full significance of what they had done, and many of their successors would have undone it if they could. But there was no denying the meaning of their words or evading the ultimate implications of their ideals. The claim for all men of a right to life, liberty and the pursuit of happiness, was one that has the mark of

*John Wilkes, the witty, popular but unprincipled champion of the liberty of the individual, portrayed by Hogarth in 1763. The 'North Briton', visible on the left, was his newspaper. Hogarth had been attacked in No. 17—hence the malice of the drawing; No. 45 caused Wilkes to be arrested on a 'general warrant', later declared to be illegal. (5)*

genius on it. Once made it could only be forgotten by obliterating the civilization that had set it up. It would give the 18th century greatness if nothing else did.

The significance of the American Revolution would have been much less if it had stood alone. Instead, it was the spearhead of a widespread democratic movement in the West. It could plausibly, if with exaggeration, be described as a civil war in the English-speaking world. It coincided in time with the first struggle for parliamentary reform in Great Britain. With an electorate of a p 318–19<br/>(10–13) quarter of a million out of a population of some 7 or 8 million, Great Britain could claim a far wider representation of its people in the government than any other European country had, except momentarily, until well into the 19th century; but the trouble with representation is that having been given some, a nation always wants more. In addition, the distribution of seats was hopelessly erratic. This was its virtue, according to conservative thinkers like Burke, whose arguments were parodied a generation later by Thomas Love Peacock in the words of his fictional Commissioner of the Embankment, ironically made one of the seven great drunkards of Britain.

'Decay,' said Seithenyn, 'is one thing, and danger is another. Every thing that is old must decay. That the embankment is old, I am free to confess; that it is somewhat rotten in parts, I will not altogether deny; that it is any the worse for that, I do most sturdily gainsay. . . . The parts that are rotten give elasticity to those that are sound. . . . If it were all sound it would break by its own obstinate stiffness: the soundness is checked by the rottenness, and the stiffness is balanced by the elasticity. There is nothing so dangerous as innovation. . . . It was half rotten when I was born, and that is a conclusive reason why it should be three parts rotten when I die.'

Such was the British constitution. Rotten boroughs, with their voters (when there were any) in the pockets of the borough owners, provided a large part of the representation of the British people.

What did it matter, if the result was to ensure that control remained in the hands of the landed aristocracy who were the country's natural rulers?

On the other hand, well in advance of other countries, England had begun to experience an industrial revolution; its social effects were only in their beginnings, but a wealthy middle class with political aspirations was appearing in London and a few other large towns. Its resentment at aristocratic monopoly of power engendered real if sporadic class feeling, which was exploited by John Wilkes, who made a brilliant political success out of opposing the government. He was too much the self-seeking opportunist, devoid of principles, for the agitation he was connected with to have any deep or lasting political significance, but there were in action at the same time more sincere democrats upholding, as in America, the ideas of universal suffrage and natural rights. Such, for example, was John Cartwright, former naval officer from a county family, and Dr John Jebb, former lecturer at Cambridge, who adopted the cause of parliamentary reform as possibly an easier task than that which he had attempted in vain, the reform of the university. These, with others, formed in 1780 the Society for Promoting Constitutional Information, an appropriately unrevolutionary description for a very theoretical body of men.

More significant at the time than either the Wilkites or the Society was the movement for parliamentary reform associated with the name of Christopher Wyvill, a Yorkshire country gentleman. Though it had the support of some of the peers, in essence this was a movement directed against control of political life by the great aristocratic factions. It could therefore link country gentry with wealthy merchants of the cities, especially London, and the superior professional men. The American War gave the reformers their opportunity and for a brief period they seemed to be riding on the crest of the wave. In fact their appearance of strength was deceptive, as a comparison with the situation soon after in revolutionary France demonstrates. The social and economic discontent of the masses did not help them, for the very good reason that the masses were not discontented; the national economy remained generally flourishing until the last years of the century. Even if they could have done so, the men of property who were agitating for reform would not have dreamed of calling the mob to their aid, as the *Tiers Etat* did in Paris in 1789. When the mob came out in support of Wilkes it did a lot to alienate the reformers, and the Gordon Riots intensified the general alarm. Fox and the aristocratic Whigs proved more anxious to use the parliamentary reformers to secure power for their own faction than to put their votes at the service of reform: and the chief theoretician of the Rockinghams, Burke, was a bitter opponent of parliamentary reform. With the end of the American War the impetus went out of the English reform movement. The Younger Pitt had genuine sympathies with it, but after the defeat of his motions for reform of Parliament in 1783 and 1785 the whole movement disintegrated. When it revived, under the impulse given by the French Revolution, the pressure came much more from below, and events in Paris were not calculated to recommend the revived agitation to those above. With the aid of the reaction against the French Revolution the triumph of aristocracy in Great Britain was temporarily consolidated.

## Revolutions that failed

The troubles in Geneva, like those in Great Britain, represent primarily resentment at the monopoly of power by a narrow aristocracy. In this sense they can be regarded as an expression of democratic ideas and were to suffer a similar rebuff, though for different reasons. The adult male population of Geneva consisted approximately of 3,000 '*citoyens* and *bourgeois*', 4,000 *natifs* and 4,500 *habitants*. Political rights were confined to the first class, but though the '*citoyens* and *bourgeois*' theoretically had sovereign power it actually resided in the hands of a much narrower, closed oligarchy comprising a legislative Council of Two Hundred and an executive Small Council or Senate. Resentment at this monopoly of power produced occasional unrest in the course of the 18th century. Promises of reform had not been kept, partly because the influence of the three foreign powers which had the duty of guaranteeing the Genevan constitution—France, Berne and Zurich—was thrown

334

on the side of the *status quo*. When troubles broke out again, in 1780, and French intervention was criticized, Vergennes denounced the eight principal agitators and called for action to be taken against them. An involved struggle in Geneva was followed, in 1782, by the seizure of power by the *natifs* and the establishment of a *Commission de Sûreté*. Moderate as was the measure of democracy envisaged, it was more than enough for the guarantor powers. France and Berne, Zurich abstaining but Sardinia joining them, initiated a military blockade of Geneva. After about a month the city opened its gates and the leaders of the reform movement fled. Among them was Clavière, later finance minister of revolutionary France, and the little group of 'back-room boys' who supplied Mirabeau with his expertise on so many varied topics and wrote many of his speeches for him; for the link between the various revolutions before 1789 and the French Revolution was not only ideological but also personal.

The attempted—and nearly successful—Dutch revolution of 1787 reflected a much more complicated social and political situation. For the past two centuries power in most of the Dutch provinces had oscillated between the house of Orange, hereditary holders of the Stadtholderate, and the small urban patriciate of Regents. These represented the monarchical and aristocratic elements in the state respectively, which tends to be concealed by the fact that the landed nobles were often Orangist, as was the urban populace, while a wealthy bourgeoisie supported the aristocratic Regents. To add to the confusion, the lines of division were drawn in terms of foreign rather than domestic policy. The house of Orange being historically tied to the English connection, the Regents looked to France and brought the United Provinces into the American War of Independence on the French side. During the war ideas of liberty and patriotism spread and the Stadtholder was gradually stripped of the last relics of his constitutional powers and reduced to a nullity. Unkind critics might have said he was this already—'my booby of a nephew', Frederick II, whose niece the Stadtholder had married, called him. The process seemed on the point of completion when, in 1785, a formal defensive alliance was concluded between the United Provinces and France.

The pro-French faction now constituted a regular party, in which the bourgeois swamped the Regents, and developed a thorough-going democratic ideology. The French ambassador, concerned lest his government should take alarm at the constant appeals of the Patriots, as they called themselves, to the rights of the people, explained that these should not be misunderstood. 'By the *people*,' he wrote,

> 'is not meant the most wretched part of the nation, men deprived of the means of living in a condition of comfort. Only the class of bourgeois possessing a certain capital and contributing in a certain proportion to the expenses of the Republic is included in this term.'

Perhaps alone in Europe the Dutch Republic was a state in which such a bourgeoisie might aspire, by reason of its wealth and numbers, to rule. The only real forces on the other side were the army, still nominally under the command of the Stadtholder, and the 'people' in the different sense of the despised workers and peasants. To counteract the former, bourgeois Free Corps were formed, like the later French National Guard, and Holland, where the wealth was concentrated, withdrew the troops it paid to its own frontiers. By 1786 the Patriot Associations had gained control of most of the provinces. Under the protection of Louis XVI a democratic revolution, which was to be much more a foretaste of what was to come in France than the American Revolution had been, was taking place on the continent of Europe and on the very frontiers of France. This is why, although on such a small stage, the embryo revolution of the Dutch deserves greater attention than it has usually received.

There were major differences between the United Provinces and France, however, which ensured that the outcome would be very different in the two countries. The Dutch Republic was a federation, in which the other provinces, especially Zeeland, were jealous of the predominance of Holland and still retained their provincial autonomy. Even in Amsterdam, the stronghold of the popular societies, the dockyard workers could always be called out with

The Dutch Revolution of 1787 is one of the most interesting foreshadowings of the French Revolution two years later. A wealthy bourgeois class rebelled against the Stadtholder's party (which included not only the landed nobles but most of the urban populace) and raised an army, seen in an English satirical print (above) 'rehearsing' by firing at a Prussian hussar painted on a wall. When it came to real fighting, however, they were no match for the Prussians, who entered the country in support of the Stadtholder (Frederick William II's brother-in-law). Below: the Prussian attack on Weesp, September 30th, 1787. (6, 7)

cries of 'Up the Orange', and the large Jewish population traditionally looked to the Stadtholder for toleration against the more rigidly orthodox bourgeoisie. The urban patriciate was also now only a very half-hearted ally of the bourgeoisie; its traditional anti-Orangist sentiments were hardly enhanced when a Patriot mob sacked the house of its leading member in Amsterdam. A more important element in the situation was also now appearing. Foreign influence was capable of exercising a more decisive influence in little countries like Geneva or the United Provinces than it could later do in France. A new British ambassador was beginning to take steps to prevent the French from having it all their own way. With secret service funds he bought back to their Orangist allegiance some of the troops that had been taken into the pay of the States of Holland. The French, on their side, had to keep up the spirits of their supporters by providing funds for the payment of the Free Corps, whose local sources of supply were drying up.

p 14 (2)   The *dénouement* was to come about in a totally unexpected way. The Stadtholder, like Louis XVI, had a consort with considerably more character than he possessed himself. The Princess of Orange was a proud, commanding, high-spirited beauty and far more serious-minded than Marie-Antoinette. She was also, as has been said, the niece of Frederick the Great. She determined, in 1787, to go to the capital, The Hague, herself, since the Prince was obviously incapable of such a determined action, and there appeal for support, though this meant crossing hostile territory. She was intercepted, as was to be expected, by a detachment of Free Corps, and then—to the surprise of a generation that had not yet witnessed the October Days or Varennes—with her little party of three officers and one maid of honour, put under arrest in an inn. Neither side foresaw the consequences of this. The essential fact was that Frederick II, who was determined not to get involved in war with France, had died in 1786. His successor, Frederick William II, besides being the brother of the Princess of Orange which perhaps did not count for much with him, was anti-French and ready to emulate his predecessor's early glory. The arrest of the King of Prussia's sister was anyhow rather too much of an insult for him to swallow without at least a gesture of protest. In Great Britain meanwhile, faced with the prospect that the United Provinces would pass completely and finally into the French camp, the younger Pitt's government had determined that something more than secret service money was called for. The process of putting the Navy on a war footing was begun.

f 6, 7   Encouraged by this, Frederick William decided it was time to use the famous army he had inherited from Frederick II. Not for the last time, his commander, the Duke of Brunswick, marched west to put down a revolution; but, unlike the invasion which ended so shamefully at Valmy, this one proved little more than a military promenade. The regular troops of the Stadtholder stood aside. The largest concentration of the Patriot forces at Utrecht, under their commander, abandoned the city. A panic-stricken evacuation of Patriots followed and the town was surrendered by a servant girl at a window who saw a detachment of Prussian troops approaching. 'We are come to release your master,' they shouted. 'Is that so?' she replied, 'then up the Orange,' and hung out the Stadtholder's colours. A French army which was supposed to be approaching on the other side had vanished into thin air. Indeed, it had never existed, lacking funds to supply it with, for France was rapidly approaching its own revolution, in which all the scenes of the Dutch revolt were to be re-enacted on a larger scale, in a more terrible way and with very different results. Meanwhile the prematurely inflated democracy of the wealthy Dutch bourgeoisie had collapsed, its leaders had taken flight, and the United Provinces returned to the political mixture of aristocracy and monarchy, fortified with popular support, as before.

Another frustrated revolution has yet to be mentioned before we can discuss the French Revolution. The pattern varies greatly from one to another. Whereas in most cases the initiative came

f 8   from an urge to reform from below, in the Austrian Netherlands the trouble was sparked off by an attempt at reform from above by the Austrian imperial government. The revolt represented the reaction of the intensely provincial and Catholic Belgic provinces against Joseph II's centralizing and secularizing policy. In 1787,

336

under the leadership of the aristocratic lawyer, Van der Noot, the Estates of Brabant refused to vote taxes and Brussels was called to arms. The clergy played a large part in the public agitation. The Estates of other provinces joined in the resistance. Joseph dissolved them and abolished provincial rights. The aristocratic Van der Nootists were now joined by a democratic faction led by another lawyer, Vonck. In 1789 the Belgic towns all revolted and the Austrians had to evacuate the Netherlands. Similarly the Bishop of Liège was expelled from his independent principality. When Leopold II succeeded his brother in 1790, he rapidly reversed the measures that had aroused his subjects' antagonism. Meanwhile the inherent differences of opinion between aristocratic and democratic factions had come into the open and the conflict was once more a triangular one. Leopold was able to regain imperial authority without difficulty, at the same time restoring the rights of the Estates, when he sent in imperial troops in the autumn of 1790. Similarly he restored the authority of the Bishop of Liège. Once again aristocracy had won the day in alliance with a moderate monarchy.

**Unrest in France**

The last and greatest of the 18th-century revolutions embodied a   p 324–28
similar mixture of elements, though it also began as a purely aristocratic movement. In 1786 the French Controller General, Calonne, had come to the end of his credit; he had exhausted the policy of dealing with France's deficit by lavish expenditure, quenching fire by throwing oil on it, to quote Carlyle. He was an adventurous minister, a client of the King's younger brother, the Comte d'Artois, and perhaps already with the faith in aristocracy that he was to show as a leader of the Counter-Revolution later, for his solution now was to summon an Assembly of Notables, with the idea that they should vote the necessary new taxation. It opened in February 1787 in four bureaux, presided over by four princes of the blood and was a forlorn hope from the beginning. What Calonne was asking was for the privileged orders—nobles, clergy, members of the *Parlements*—voluntarily to sacrifice their fiscal privileges, and even more their positions of power, in the interests of a reforming bureaucratic monarchy. His central proposal was for a land tax, to be paid without exemption by all orders. The Provincial Estates, the bulwarks of privilege in the more favoured provinces, were to be replaced by a generalized system of Provincial Assemblies, which were to meet and vote without distinction of order. The network of internal customs dues by which internal French trade and industry were tied down and half strangled were to be replaced by a single customs duty at the frontiers.

Even without many other minor reforms this was a programme which would have meant a big step from the ancien régime into the modern world—far too big a step for the narrow-minded, egotistical prelates and *parlementaires* of the Assembly, though some of the more enlightened nobles might have been ready to take it. But reformers stand short shrift in a Court. The King would have supported Calonne, but the Queen was under the influence of his bitter enemies. After the death of Vergennes, early in 1787, he lacked support in the ministry. An attempted counter-attack in a pamphlet directed against his critics convinced them that he must be disposed of. Calonne was therefore dismissed, exiled and disgraced.

The obvious successor, Brienne, was his greatest rival, and pre-   p 321
decessor, Necker, whose own *Compte-Rendu*, disregarding the facts,   (17, 18)
had demonstrated the solvency of the State and therefore the lack of any need for fundamental reform. With the aid of skilful propaganda and an *à la mode* sentimental Rousseauism, Necker had won golden opinions—and loans—for the success with which, in charge of finances, he had ridden the storms of the American War. The King and Queen were among the few who appreciated that he had also sown the whirlwind, and they refused to have him in the ministry. The Queen's candidate, Loménie de Brienne, Archbishop of Toulouse, as president of the Estates of Languedoc had won a reputation as a reformer and he was appointed instead. He inherited as unfavourable a situation as could easily have been imagined. The Notables, having refused to agree to any new taxes, were dissolved, leaving the royal credit in an even more shaky position than before. Brienne's first positive action was an attempt to

'*Expeditious means of the French people for "unfurnishing" an aristocrat': the early stages of the Revolution saw the destruction of a great deal of property in the town and country houses of the gentry, but there was surprisingly little bloodshed. The 'Révolutions de France et de Brabant', from which this engraving of 1790 is taken, was a popular revolutionary journal.* (8)

introduce economy into the royal government. Pensions and places had proliferated to the Court nobles and their clients. To take only one example, France had 18 Marshals of France, and 1,261 Lieutenant-Generals, *Maréchaux de camp* and Brigadiers— more than in all the other armies of Europe put together. Guibert, a great war minister and a disciple of the King of Prussia, initiated a reform of the whole structure of the army. A pamphlet of 1789, addressed to the Nobles, showed how badly needed this was. 'Your sons,' it said, 'have scarcely attained the age of 21 and left the hands of their tutor, when you expect them to be put, in a superior rank, over Squadron-Leaders and Captains who have twice as many years length of service as they have years of age.' Unfortunately the reforms began with the provincial nobles and so antagonized them, leaving the great Court nobles still in possession of their privileged positions.

Brienne's ministry, however, went beyond Calonne in not merely proposing reforms but in putting them into operation. A number of *Caisses* which dealt with the royal income and expenditure were amalgamated in a single Treasury. A new *Compte-Rendu* was published in 1786, which was far more honest and accurate than any previous one. Brienne was blamed for the colossal deficit which he had merely revealed. An effective Bureau of Commerce was organized. A new Keeper of the Seals, Lamoignon, reformed some of the worst abuses of the criminal law, not uninfluenced by the public indignation aroused by the case of three men broken on the wheel for a murder. The victim of their crime unfortunately appeared subsequently alive and well, notwithstanding which the *Parlement* of Paris condemned a pamphlet rehabilitating the memory of the three supposed murderers. The *question préparatoire*—torture to secure a confession had already been abolished in 1780. Now

the *question préalable*—torture after conviction to secure a revelation of the names of any possible accomplices—was also abolished. The law courts were reformed. Protestants were conceded the right of civil registration of births, marriages and deaths, other projected concessions to them being barred by the clergy and *Parlements*. The reform of local government by the creation of Provincial Assemblies was continued. In fact, in happier circumstances this would have left its mark on history as a great reforming government. In the conditions of France in 1787 the attempt to reform old institutions before new ones had acquired the strength to take their place, the removal of some abuses leaving far more still intact, the weakening of the authority of royal *intendants* by turning them, in effect, into the servants of inexperienced Provincial Assemblies, could not but undermine royal authority and trouble men's minds with thoughts of further changes to come. These were being openly canvassed in the provincial reading-rooms, *sociétés de pensée* and new clubs that were springing up, and in a growing pamphlet literature.

Both the actions of the government and the reactions of the public were calculated to arouse the alarm of the privileged orders, and they had an instrument for the expression of their opposition in the venal, hereditary law-courts, possessing also executive powers, which constantly hampered the royal government even in peaceful times, claiming what was in effect a right of veto over royal legislation. The resistance came to a head in the meetings of the Court of Peers, including 144 *parlementaires*, 7 princes of the blood, 7 ecclesiastical peers and 27 lay peers. Behind them was a whole army of lawyers, *procureurs*, clerks, bailiffs, ushers, law students, capable by themselves of staging a formidable riot, and also capable of rallying, by bribery, displays of fireworks and vociferous appeals for the defence of the rights of the people, the law and the constitution, far larger crowds against alleged ministerial tyranny. The *Parlement* began their resistance—was it an accident?—by refusing to register a Stamp Act and other taxes. They were exiled, or more precisely sent into country retreat at Troyes, in August 1787. Rioting followed, which was suppressed by the troops, but the *Parlement* reluctantly gave way, registered the taxes and returned to Paris in September. It must not be forgotten that at the same time the provincial *Parlements* were engaged in a struggle with the local representatives of the King's authority in Rennes, Dijon, Bordeaux, Besançon, Grenoble. Their opposition held up the essential fiscal reforms.

France was back where she had been when Louis XV and Maupeou had dissolved the *Parlements* in 1771, faced with the alternative of bankruptcy or breaking the resistance of the *Parlements*. The same drastic remedy was attempted—abolition of the *Parlements* and their replacement with courts of royal nominees. This Brienne and Lamoignon did in May 1788. Paris remained peaceful but Rennes and Grenoble saw fighting in the streets. The officers of the army, with their own grievances, obeyed the government's commands laxly and reluctantly, thus cementing the alliance, which had been growing during the century, of robe and sword. The clergy gave their blessing to the rebels. And now a small party of Patriots, drawn from all the higher groups of society and imbued with a democratic ideology, or at least language, learnt from their American, Dutch and Genevan predecessors, began to appear on the scene and even more openly in print. They picked up a solution which the *Parlements* had rashly put forward to support their claim to represent the demands of the people, the appeal for a meeting of the States General. The diverse factions which were opposing Brienne's policy found a common bond of union in this demand. It rapidly became the universal panacea. The share of the Third Estate in this agitation must not be exaggerated. Only in Dauphiné did it really join in the struggle effectively, though there it took control and diverted it to its own ends. But the situation was at last developing into the triangular contest with which we are familiar. Brienne, in desperation, decided as his last throw on an alliance of the Crown with the Third Estate against the privileged orders—monarchy and democracy versus aristocracy. But aristocracy, already outraged by his campaign for economy, was not to be outmanoeuvred so easily. The Court brought all its pressure to bear on the King and Queen to secure his dismissal.

The former finance minister and chief author of the deficit, Necker, took his place, not because any of them really wanted him, but because he alone had the confidence of the people and was believed capable of working the miracle of saving French finances without anyone having to give up anything. The news of Necker's recall was announced on August 25, 1788—one of the forgotten great days of history. Paris was *en fête*, with processions, fireworks, houses illuminated, Brienne burnt in effigy, and a sprinkling of riots. Necker's solution was a simple one: abandon all the reforms of Brienne, let the opposition, *Parlements* and all, have everything their own way and deposit the whole problem on the lap of the States General, assumed to embody the will of the nation, like a whole orphanage of squalling brats entrusted to the all-wise and all-loving care of Mother Nature—a Rousseauist plan that the author of the *Social Contract* would have denounced for its irrational absurdity, the typical shrewd-silly scheme appropriate to the financier and born gambler (always from the highest motives) that Necker was.

The small groups of Patriots responded to the stimulus. A constitutional club formed in Paris in November 1788 provided a centre for the reformers. The names of leading members—La Fayette, the Marquis de Condorcet, the Vicomte de Noailles, La Rochefoucauld, Luynes, Aiguillon, Lauzun—are an indication of their social distinction. Even less elevated members—Mirabeau, the Conseillers Adrien Duport and Roederer, the famous lawyer Target—show that the Society of Thirty, as it came to be known to historians for no very obvious reason, was far from being the 'bourgeois' gathering it has been called. Nevertheless the Third Estate now had a programme, whether it was received from above or not. It was a simple one: double representation in the States

General so that it would equal in numbers the two privileged orders put together, the exclusion of members of the privileged orders from representation of the Third Estate, combined meetings of the three orders and vote by head. It seems that Necker favoured this programme but all he could get through the Royal Council on December 27, 1788, was a concession of double representation, which without voting by head was worthless.

## Mounting tension

The States General was summoned for May 1789. Apart from this decision, and making, rather inadequately, arrangements for the meeting, Necker's ministry put the government of France into cold storage until the burden could be passed on to the broader shoulders of the nation, and lived on the last scraps of credit that faith in his wonder-working powers had evoked. The nation had two traditional duties, to draw up *cahiers* of grievances and to elect representatives to the three orders. The first inaugurated a nation-wide debate, for everybody was agreed that there was an ample supply of grievances, but as to what these were they were not agreed, nor have historians been agreed since. Attempts have been made to generalize on a basis of the *cahiers* of nobles, clergy and Third Estate, but these large, simple divisions conceal too many differences, both social and regional, within them to provide a satisfactory basis of classification. In very general terms we may say that the nobles were prepared to make financial and some other concessions so long as their status was protected and an aristocratic constitution was set up, or as they claimed, restored. The clergy were primarily anxious that the toleration of non-Catholics should be kept within very strict limits and that the privileges, or as they said rights, of the Church remain intact. Differences of interest between the Court and country nobility and the higher clergy and parish *curés* and *vicaires* only came fully to the surface in the elections and later. It was in the Third Estate that the debate really raged. All over France the peasant communities produced their grievances against those who exploited them; and these exploiters were sometimes the nobles and clergy, through seigneurial dues and tithes, but also often the wealthier inhabitants of the neighbouring town who had acquired such dues and exploited them, sometimes mercilessly. The peasants complained of *banalités*, monopolies of mill, oven or wine-press, but who the culprit was, the remote owner or the miller or baker from the local town who took advantage of his monopoly, was not always evident. Tithes were a universal grievance of the peasants, but they did not blame the parish clergy, who got only a pittance out of them, but rather the great tithe-owners in abbeys and cathedral chapters or the lay seigneurs. The labour service of the *corvée* was sometimes complained of, but so was the tax which replaced it and fell on the richer peasants instead of—like the actual labour—on the poorer. The grievances of the poorer peasantry, alas, are only occasionally reflected in the rural *cahiers*. We get just enough to know that they existed. Similarly, in the urban *cahiers* the poorer population for the most part appears only as objects of pity or a source of social danger; while those claims of the peasantry which conflicted with the interests of the urban bourgeoisie were quietly dropped from the general bailliage *cahiers*.

There can be no reasonable doubt that in their specific and concrete clauses the *cahiers* reflected the actual grievances of the French population, at least above the level of the propertyless peasants, the urban unskilled workers and the poor. The more abstract and general clauses can obviously have meant little to the great mass of the people. These reflect the ideas and aspirations of the educated professional men and middle class property owners in the towns. In the country parishes, they doubtless expressed the views of the parish priest, or local lawyer, who acted as scribe for the villagers. On these, general statements may safely be made since they so frequently echo one another. From them can be extracted the social and political doctrines of the comparatively well-to-do Third Estate, who in their own opinion constituted the political nation of France. In the first place it is to be noted that there were no republicans. They all looked to the King to give France the reforms she so badly needed and to deal with the aristocracy that was their natural enemy. Secondly, they wanted a constitutional monarch, who would govern, but only in accord with laws made by the representatives of the nation, and whose ministers would in this respect be responsible to these representatives. Thirdly, they wanted a separation of powers, not on abstract grounds, but to prevent abuses such as executive interference with justice, or the obstacles that the *Parlements* had constantly placed in the way of legislative reforms. The idea of 'no taxation without representation' commonly appears, often in those precise words. A constitution, so that all should know the principles of government, and a declaration of rights, so that all should know their rights, were called for. Above all, the dominant idea was of the sovereignty of the people or nation. This was the fundamental principle and the most difficult to define. It was not sovereignty in the Rousseauist sense of the legislative sovereignty of the General Will of the whole people. It meant the transfer of the legislative powers of the King *in toto* to the representatives of the people; but the people did not mean everybody, or even all adult males, it stopped short at the propertied tax-paying classes.

The election of the Third Estate to the Constituent Assembly was on a surprisingly wide franchise but it inevitably produced a one-sided representation of the country. It was indirect, by the election of electors, and at the second stage practically the whole representation of the peasants was eliminated. The result was a generally wealthy, propertied and office-owning Assembly, with a large proportion of professional lawyers among them, determined to give France a constitution, to establish liberty and eliminate the fiscal and other advantages of the privileged orders, but not contemplating any other material social changes. The peasantry had different ideas. The general turmoil and the break-down of royal administration, the drawing up of the *cahiers*, aroused it not merely to a sense of its own grievances but to the attempt to remedy them. What now occurred over a large part of rural France was a mixture of *jacquerie* and panic. Peasant agitation against the traditional exploiters of town, château and abbey combined with the fear of an army of brigands hired by the aristocrats and let loose by them on the peaceful villages. The general result was attacks on a great many manor-houses and the destruction of a vast quantity of medieval manuscripts, in which were supposed to be recorded the dues and obligations of the peasants to their seigneurs. The nobles showed remarkably little disposition to defend themselves. The general lack of bloodshed in the whole prolonged episode has been attributed to the benevolent disposition of the peasantry. It was more probably due to the fact that many seigneurs were already absentee owners living in the towns, and any who did not and who knew that their unpopularity with the local peasantry had made them potential objects of attack fled to the protection of the nearest town as rapidly as they could. Sporadic outbreaks continued over a large part of the country for months, but it was in due course pacified after a fashion, either when the peasants had achieved their local objects or when punitive expeditions of bourgeois militia sent out from the towns had suppressed them with the sword and the gallows.

Despite these troubles the elections were able to take place in most of France peacefully. In May, the States General met at Versailles, with the traditional ceremony, now rather moth-eaten after nearly two centuries of disuse, and in the traditional three orders. The struggle that at once began was for the union of orders, without which the numerical preponderance of the Third Estate would have been valueless. Its weapon was the refusal to vote taxes until its demands had been granted. In their own interests the King and Queen should have sided with the Third Estate, but the influence of the Court was too strong and it was all for suppressing these troublesome reformers by force. Twice in the summer of 1789, in July and October, large reinforcements of royal troops were called to the neighbourhood of Paris for this purpose.

## The people in power

But now a new factor appeared in the situation, which neither the aristocrats who started the Revolution, nor the Third Estate who continued it, had reckoned on. After the general economic progress of the 18th century the reign of Louis XVI had been marked by a recession, intensified by a succession of disastrous harvests leading up to 1789. Coming on a population which had been expanding faster than food production, the result was a rise in prices, shortage

*The idea of liquidating the national deficit by confiscating Church property came from Talleyrand. In this satire, fat ecclesiastics are being squashed in a press to squeeze out their wealth, and emerge, noticeably thinner, on the left.* (9)

of supplies and widespread distress. An economic crisis was thus superimposed on the political crisis. The unemployed masters and journeymen of Paris provided the raw material for the crowds which thronged the streets in these days of political disturbance. The *Parlements* had stirred up mobs in their defence in the past. The Third Estate had not forgotten the lesson. The general uprising of the population of Paris, culminating in the attack on the Bastille on July 14 was its reply to the dismissal of Necker and the concentration of troops. The October Days, of October 5 and 6, when the royal family and the Assembly were brought back to Paris by the crowds triumphing, dealt the death blow to the aristocratic Counter-Revolution in France. Meanwhile the stubborn struggle of the Third Estate, aided by the sympathy of some nobles and many of the lesser clergy, had overcome the resistance of the first two orders. The three orders had been united in a single National or Constituent Assembly. The King's younger brother, Artois, and the extreme counter-revolutionaries, their attempted *coup* having failed, now began the first emigration. Everywhere a little sprinkling of the more hated of the privileged fled across the frontiers. Aristocracy had been taught that in a country like France it could only destroy the authority of the Crown at the price of undermining the defence of its own privileges. I say it had been taught this, but it did not learn the lesson, for it continued, in emigration and with the hope of foreign aid, its struggle to substitute what it believed was the old and genuine aristocratic constitution of France for the monarchical one. The struggle that Europe witnessed was once again a triangular one of monarchy, aristocracy and such democracy as the National Assembly could be supposed to embody.

The quality of the membership, and the ideals and achievements of the National Assembly, should not be underestimated. It did not have much difficulty in its first task, which was to decide on general abstract principles. They were embodied in the Declaration of Rights, which began by declaring men free and equal in rights. The object was not to abolish inequality, otherwise it could not have maintained that property was natural, inalienable, sacred and inviolable, but to abolish inequalities derived from privilege. Freedom was less qualified; it meant freedom from arbitrary arrest and freedom to express opinions in speech or writing. All the rights that were asserted were rights of individuals. The declaration was the climax of a great age of individualism.

Practical reforms accompanied general principles. The whole structure of French local government was reorganized, substituting for the thirty or so *généralités* 83 departments, with under them sub-divisions down to the commune, all controlled by committees elected from below instead of officials nominated from above. A long list of reforms bears witness to the good intentions and the practical achievements of the Constituent Assembly. Rights of citizenship were granted to Protestants and Jews. Civil registration

p 325 (31)

p 324 (29)

surprisingly little opposition, and it might have worked if other factors had not entered into the situation.

A very different reception was given to the law of July 1790 imposing a Civil Constitution on the Church, with all clerics chosen by the electorate on true democratic principles, extra-national authority such as that of the papacy excluded from the French Church, and the religious orders dissolved except provisionally those engaged in charitable work and teaching. Next to the declarations of war, this was the biggest mistake the Revolution made. Those who had learnt anti-clericalism at the feet of the *philosophes*, however rational their conclusions, could not appreciate the attachment of the ordinary Frenchman to the Catholic Church. The Civil Constitution and its consequences made a large part of the French people into enemies of the Revolution. It also made the more militant revolutionaries into bitter enemies of the Church. Especially when things began to go wrong and a scapegoat was looked for, the clergy, identifiable by their garb, were ideal victims. The militants of the Revolution had the oratory of the clubs and the venom of the journalists to arouse their passion for blood. The slaughter of occasional victims of mob violence during the early years of the Revolution, in an age accustomed to the bloodiest public executions, should not surprise us. The Terror proper only began when it was the other face of fear; and fear began when France believed, however mistakenly, that the mercenary armies of the despots of old Europe were gathering at her frontiers, prepared to bring rapine, ruin and the sword to her peaceful homes. The violent language of the *émigrés* was not calculated to make the average Frenchman doubt the fate in store for him; and when, in June 1791, the King and his family took flight for the frontier, only to be stopped, at the last moment, at Varennes, panic mingled with patriotic resolve to defend the Revolution and the *patrie* against all enemies, within and without.

f 10

The King had been brought back as a prisoner, but a prisoner whom the Constituent Assembly needed, for the Constitution it had made was essentially a monarchical one. The flight to Varennes was followed by the first serious public agitation for republicanism, but a great republican demonstration at the Champ de Mars on July 17 was repressed with heavy bloodshed by the National Guard. A secession threatened the dissolution of the Jacobin Club. Left-wing leaders were arrested or went into hiding. The constitution was voted and accepted, however much against his will, by the King. The crisis seemed to have been surmounted. The only cloud on the horizon was the passing, as almost the last act of the Constituent Assembly, by an alliance of extremists of the left and the right, of a self-denying ordinance, excluding from membership of the new Legislative Assembly all who had sat as members of the *Constituante* and so gained experience of the problem of government.

There was also another danger, though no one as yet imagined that it would come to dominate and dictate the whole future course of the Revolution. This was the shadow of war. The Constituent Assembly of 1789 was deeply imbued with an idealistic pacifism. It renounced all wars of conquest and pledged the French people never to employ its forces against the liberty of any other nation. The annexation of the papal enclaves of Avignon and the Venaissin, and of the possessions of the German princes on the left bank of the Rhine, could be considered as no infringement of this pledge. This peaceful stance was put to a considerable test by the violent denunciations that emerged from the *émigrés* and the Courts of old Europe, and reached a higher level in Burke's *Reflections*. From an early date the Queen was looking to the Powers for assistance and sending secret appeals, especially to her own country, Austria. She received such tepid answers that their unwillingness to intervene was only too apparent to her. They were secretly pleased to see France as a power eliminated from the map of Europe, so that her rivals — Russia, Prussia and Austria — could get on with the task of carving up Poland and Turkey between themselves; but the French people were impressed and alarmed by the bluster with which the Powers concealed their pacific intentions.

Moreover the Revolution had released a surge of national feeling in France, which was not to be contented simply with domestic reforms. At last France felt herself to be truly a nation, one and undivided. The symbol of this was the decree which

f 11

*In July 1740 all religious orders were dissolved in France. An illustration from a propaganda journal (above) shows an inventory being made of the monastery's wealth and the supposed joy of the monks and nuns at their release. In fact, it created more bitter enemies of the Revolution.* (10)

of birth, marriage and death was introduced. Heresy, *lèse-majesté* and magical practices ceased to be crimes punishable by law. Mutilation and forms of torture were no longer legal punishments, and death was only to be by means of the humanitarian instrument the invention of which is incorrectly attributed to Dr Guillotin. Privileged guilds and corporations were suppressed, as were all the innumerable internal customs duties which strangled French trade. After the famous night of the Fourth of August seigneurial dues, tithes, *corvées*, privileges of provinces, towns, abbeys, and a whole network of obligations which weighed so heavily on the peasants, were abolished or made purchasable. All these reforms were carried through with comparatively little opposition.

p 326
(34)
p 324
(30)

The curiously interdependent problems of the Church and finance aroused more serious difficulties. They became connected, as it were, by accident: the States General had been called to rescue the royal government from bankruptcy by voting new taxes. This was the thing which, concerned with the struggle over the union of orders, it had conspicuously failed to do. It took a cleric—not a very good one admittedly—to see the solution. Talleyrand proposed a bargain by which everyone would gain. The property of the French Church was to be nationalized and sold. Out of the proceeds the ecclesiastics would be paid a salary by the State, which would give the lower clergy a far better standard of living than they had had under the *ancien régime*. A surplus of some 50% would be left, which could be used as the backing for an issue of *assignats* to tide the State over the immediate financial crisis until the new taxes were voted and collected. The plan was accepted with

f 9

changed the King's title from 'King of France and Navarre' to *Roi des Français*—King of the French, head of a nation, not a mere territorial agglomeration like all the other rulers of Europe. The anti-Austrian sentiments which were so deeply rooted in French traditions found an outlet in the defence of the Revolution against the Queen and the supposed 'Austrian committee'. Democratic refugees from the other European revolutions agitated for French intervention in their countries. Royalists and republicans in France both saw war as their opportunity. Robespierre was one of the few who dared to oppose the flowing tide. On April 20, 1792, the motion declaring war on Austria was carried in the Assembly amid a transport of enthusiasm and with only seven opposing votes and the destiny of the Revolution was sealed. War meant inflation, economic dictatorship, conquest, empire, military rule, and Napoleon. The French armies that overran Europe took with them some of the gains of the Revolution but even these were not always well received. As Robespierre had wisely observed when war fever was sweeping the Legislative Assembly, nobody loves armed missionaries. Military conquest did not bring conversion. The Revolutionary and Napoleonic Wars brought with them reaction, even in France.

p 326
(36)

### Enlightenment and revolution

For the 18th century as the Age of Enlightenment the democratic revolutions were both triumph and disaster. They brought out many plans for reform, that had lain for long in the drawers of the bureaux and on the shelves of philosophical libraries, into practical politics. The examples of the revolt of the American colonies and of the French Revolution could not be forgotten or remain without influence; but war, religious revival, nationalism, and some would add an embryo totalitarianism, were not the fruits that the men of the Enlightenment expected from the seeds they had sown. Any

attempt at generalization, however, not only for the whole world but even for Europe, would be misleading. I began by saying that the 18th century would not be interpreted in this volume in strict chronological terms. Equally it has not been defined in geographical terms. Even in Europe, the Mediterranean, central and eastern countries had only been superficially touched by the influence of the Enlightenment. If reform was to come to them, it would be only in the form of the decrees of despots, and these strictly limited by what would be tolerated by their aristocracies. When the contagion of the French Revolution, carried by example or by arms, threatened to go beyond this, monarchy and aristocracy joined in repression at home and stubborn resistance abroad. To defeat the resistance it encountered, revolutionary France, as Sorel pointed out long ago, adopted the methods and principles of its enemies. It established an intensely conservative, centralized, nationalist state, which preserved its bonapartist foundations through a succession of political régimes.

Finally, whereas, again to quote Sorel, there had been in western Europe a political revolution, in eastern Europe it was a territorial one. The anarchic aristocracy of Poland was expurged from the map, and the anachronistic tyranny of Turkey driven back to the Balkans. The stronger despotisms of Russia, Prussia and Austria expanded to fill their vacant places. It should be added that a third revolution was also taking place. This was the Industrial Revolution, in which Great Britain led the world. All three revolutions were the children of the 18th century, and were inherited by the 19th, which through them made the world we inhabit. If so much that is evil today is, as always, the heritage of the past, much also is the invention of the present, and when we look back for the first appreciable signs of the spread of the ideals of humanity, it is also to what was called the Age of Enlightenment that we must look. This was the true greatness of the 18th century.

*The first anniversary of the Fall of the Bastille was marked by celebrations all over France. This engraving shows the 'fête vraiment nationale' held in the Champs de Mars; the numbers were estimated at 300,000. A wave of patriotism swept the whole country—a patriotism which was not, at this stage, anti-monarchist. The King's title was merely changed from 'Roi de France et de Navarre' to 'Roi des Français'. (11)*

341

# Postscript: on Music

ALFRED COBBAN

Clio is a serious-minded muse and more concerned with the working hours of all classes than with how they spent their leisure time. Yet in a general history, especially of the 18th century, entertainment cannot be wholly neglected, for it has necessary links with the progress of art and civilization. The brutal pleasures of cock-fighting, bear-baiting, bull-fighting, hunting, shooting and their like have no history except in the changing techniques of slaughter. The more civilized pastimes of painting, music and literature properly belong to the realm of history as well as of art. In the Middle Ages, with a few exceptions such as the ballads, they emerged from the Church. In the later Middle Ages and during the Renaissance we can follow their increasing secularization as an aristocracy grew up that required less crude pleasures than formerly. The pageant, the masque, the *fête galante* prepared the way for more sophisticated art forms. Moreover, in the 18th century a middle class possessed of wealth, leisure and culture had come into existence in Western Europe which wished to share in these.

The first secular art which was presented to a large audience was the art of the theatre. The more spectacular productions, with elaborate scenery, were invented for the delectation of the Courts, but then spread to public theatres, first perhaps in the wealthy republic of Venice. There, and elsewhere in Italy, opera became a craze in the 17th century. From Italy the cult spread to Austria and Germany, and thence to France and England.

The growth of a broader audience for the pleasures of the aristocracy was shown in other ways. In 1661, with the Commonwealth over, the New Spring Gardens were opened in London to such of the public as could afford the subscription. The name came, it is said, from the unsuspected *jets d'eau* that beset the path of the wanderer through the gardens. They were soon to be better known, and to pass through various vicissitudes of fashion and decay for nearly two centuries, as Vauxhall. One cannot see a perspective drawing of the Gardens without feeling that here is a petty Versailles of the middle classes. Similarly the châteaux in the country to which the French Court betook itself from the populous surroundings of the Louvre, and the country houses of the English aristocracy and gentry, set the fashion for a summer away from the capital in spas and—but not until the very end of the 18th century—seaside watering-places. Such entertainment as was needed in these and in the provincial towns of England was provided at the new Assembly Rooms. In its economic progress England was so far in advance of the rest of the world that the amenities of life, required by a well-to-do class of merchants and gentry, were naturally more marked there; but similar developments were not absent elsewhere.

Space is lacking here for a description of the lighter side of life in the 18th century, but two relevant developments cannot be passed over in silence. The theatre of the time falls properly under the head of entertainment; it is notable almost exclusively for its writers of comedy, the Restoration dramatists, with Congreve, Goldsmith and Sheridan in England; Molière, Marivaux, Beaumarchais in France; and in Italy, Goldoni.

Music, which may legitimately be considered among the greatest achievements of the 18th century, might also be reckoned among the entertainments of the leisure of aristocracy and middle class. Ballads and lyrics apart, its secularization came when it moved from the church to the theatre. After Monteverdi, in the first half of the 17th century, and, following on from him, Cavalli, Italian opera continued to be prolific but apart from Alessandro Scarlatti in Naples at the end of the century, did not remain on the same heights, though it flooded Austria and Germany. It created French opera through the Florentine Lully, who combined the Italian tradition of opera with the spectacular ballets that found so much favour in France. England had its own solitary and too short-lived genius in Purcell, whose *Dido and Aeneas* was performed in 1689, but he had no successor. The English operatic stage was to be dominated for the next generation by the great figure of Handel, while the Baroque tradition in opera continued to be represented in France well into the 18th century by Rameau.

The subjects of opera up to this point were predominantly tragic or heroic and the music essentially solemn and serious. A minor revolt came in England in 1728 when Gay's *Beggar's Opera* was put to the music of popular songs. Its phenomenal success began a pleasant but slight stream of ballad operas on the English stage. In Germany there was a not dissimilar development of *Singspiel*. In Italy the lighter passages, taken out of serious opera, had developed into the separate art form of *opera buffa*. This led to another revolt, marked by the joint appearance in Paris, in 1752, of the Italian *opera buffa* of Pergolesi, *La Serva Padrona*, produced first in Naples in 1731, and Jean-Jacques Rousseau's *Le Devin du Village*. The simple melody and spontaneity of the new style, compared with the heavy heroics of the old, opened an operatic war in Paris. The conflict of styles might not have had important musical consequences if the reform of opera had not been taken up by Gluck. His *Orpheus and Euridice*, of 1762, marks the beginning of a new phase in the history of opera, giving the first place to dramatic sincerity and intensity of feeling. A greater genius was to follow in the road pioneered by Gluck, when Mozart drew together the operatic threads of the whole century in a series of masterpieces.

But with Mozart we are reminded that opera is but one stream in the great musical outpouring of the age, running, if one may borrow terms from another art, from Baroque through Rococo to Classical. Compared with what followed, the 17th century had been a solemn and serious, even a tragic age. The genius of Johann Sebastian Bach carried the profundities of his music well into the 18th century, where they were lost in the lighter style of the new age. When he died, in 1750, his music was already out of fashion and the general public was to forget its greatness for almost a century. The more popular Italian style was cultivated and developed by Handel, whose operatic music following on Scarlatti and the Venetian tradition was written for the aristocracy, while his dramatic oratorios appealed to a wider public.

In a remarkable development of instrumental music these were only the greatest names among many. It might have seemed, in mid-18th century, that the lighter Rococo style was carrying the current of music into shallower waters, with the disappearance of composers on the level of Scarlatti, Vivaldi, Rameau, and the greater names of Bach and Handel. Gluck could not start a new age by himself. But now Haydn, who had been composing for many years, in the early 'seventies moved on from Rococo to

*An oratorio being rehearsed in 18th-century England: the director sits at the harpsichord in the centre, singers and chorus stand on the right, instrumentalists (mostly string players with one flute) to the left and in the foreground. The figure in the extreme right is thought possibly to be Handel.* (12)

what has been termed the Classical style. Even his vast outpouring of orchestral and chamber music might not have been sufficient if there had not been added to it the sublime genius of Mozart. In an eclectic but profoundly individual synthesis Mozart brings the music of the 18th century to a triumphant conclusion, summing up and transforming its achievements, and at the same time looking forward to the new age that was already waiting at the door with Beethoven.

To begin with entertainment and end with Mozart and Beethoven may seem more than inappropriate, but this indicates one way in which the better-off classes of the 18th century chose to spend their leisure and it would give a false impression of the age to refrain from saying so. It is necessary as a reminder that when

we have said the worst about Frederick the Great that we can, we should remember that he played the flute accompanied by his private orchestra. George II perhaps did not embody the height of contemporary civilization, but he and his consort deserve the credit of their cultivation of Handel. The colossal wealth and pride of the Hungarian magnates must be accepted as an historical fact whatever its social consequences, but among these was the thirty years' employment of Haydn by the Esterházys. And it must be remembered that in this brief section only a few of the highest peaks have been mentioned in what was an amazing Alpine range of musical attainment; the great geniuses rightly dominate the scene, but on the lower slopes a whole society of amateurs was making music or listening to it.

ATLANTIC OCEAN

NORTH SEA

MEDITER

SCOTLAND

IRELAND
Dublin

Glasgow • Edinburgh

Durham • Newcastle
Castle Howard
GREAT
Liverpool York
St Helens
WALES • Manchester
BRITAIN Nottingham
Blenheim Palace • Kings Lynn
• Birmingham Yarmouth
• Oxford Cambridge
Bristol • London
Exeter Bath Mereworth
Poole
Beachy Head

DENMARK-NORWAY
Copenhagen

Hamburg
HANOVER
BRAND
Berlin
Münster Potsdam
Göttingen Halle
Meissen SAXONY
Rossbach Dresde
HESSE
Düsseldorf
Amsterdam Cologne Aachen
The Hague • Utrecht
AUSTRIAN Tournai
Barfleur FLANDERS Brussels Liège
Le Havre Ramillies NETHERLANDS Namur Luxembourg Dettingen
Bayeux PICARDY Valenciennes Mainz Banz Vierzehnheiligen
Dieppe Fontenoy Trier Bamberg
St-Malo NORMANDY Rouen St-Gobain Speyer Würzburg Prague
BRITTANY Sèvres Versailles Valmy Neresheim BO
Rennes Port-Royal Paris LORRAINE Nancy Strasbourg Weltenburg
Quiberon Bay Meudon Seine Rhine Blenheim Rohr
Laval BAVARIA
Nantes Tours FRANCE Dijon Besançon Wies Munich
Loire NIVERNAIS Zurich
Ré La Rochelle Le Creusot SWITZERLAND TYROL CARINTH
Oléron Berne Yverdon
Geneva
Lyons Trent
Bordeaux SAVOY DOLOMITES
AUVERGNE Grenoble Bergamo Udine CARN
Rodez Turin Milan LOMBARDY Venice
Garonne MASSIF Parma PIEDMONT Genoa REPUBLIC OF
Toulouse CENTRAL LANGUEDOC Avignon Lucca Bologna
Tarn CEVENNES Marseilles Leghorn TUSCANY
Carcassonne Rhône Florence
PYRENEES ROUSSILLON COMTAT PAPAL STATES
VENAISSIN Rome

PORTUGAL
Lisbon

SPAIN
Madrid •
ARAGON
ANDALUSIA CATALONIA
Seville Barcelona
• Granada
Gibraltar

Ebro

SARDINIA

SICILY
Messina
Napl

SWEDEN

FINLAND

Helsinki

St Petersburg

Stockholm

ESTONIA

BALTIC SEA

Riga

LATVIA

Moscow

Königsberg

Danzig

PRUSSIA

Smolensk

RUSSIA

Minsk

Vistula

Warsaw

POLAND

Leuthen

SILESIA

Mollwitz

Lublin

Kiev

Kharkov

MORAVIA

Cracow

Dniepr

UKRAINE

AUSTRIA

Poltava

Vienna

Dniestr

Buda

Pest

HUNGARY

Temesvar

CRIMEA

Danube

Belgrade

Bucharest

Kutchuk Kainardji

BLACK SEA

OTTOMAN

Constantinople

EMPIRE

Salonika

ANEAN

Athens

Smyrna

# Select Bibliography

## I and X The pattern of government and Epilogue

ANDRÉ, L. *Louis XIV et l'Europe* (Paris, 1950)

CARSTEN, F. L. *The Origins of Prussia* (Oxford, 1954)

COBBAN, A. *Ambassadors and Secret Agents: the diplomacy of the First Earl of Malmesbury at the Hague, 1785–87* (London, 1954)

COBBAN, A. *A History of Modern France*, vol. i, *The Ancien Régime and the Revolution* (London, 1961)

FETJÖ, F. *Un Habsbourg Révolutionnaire: Joseph II* (Paris, 1953)

FLENLEY, R. *Modern German History* (rev. ed., London, 1959)

FORD, FRANKLIN F. *Robe and Sword: the regrouping of the French aristocracy after Louis XIV* (Harvard, 1953)

GERSHOY, L. *From Despotism to Revolution, 1763–1789* (New York, 1944)

GOOCH, G. P. *Louis XV* (London, 1956)

HUFTON, OLWEN H. *Bayeux in the late eighteenth century: a social study* (Oxford, 1967)

KLUYCHEVSKY, V. O. *Peter the Great* (London, 1959)

LEFEBVRE, G. *The Coming of the French Revolution* (Princeton, 1947)

NUSSBAUM, F. L. *The Triumph of Science and Reason, 1660–1685* (New York, 1953)

SAGNAC, P. *La formation de la société française moderne* (Paris, 1945–46)

SEE, H. *La vie économique et les classes sociales en France au XVIIIe siècle.* Also in translation (Paris, 1924)

SOREL, A. *L'Europe et la Révolution française*, vol. i, trans. and edited by A. Cobban and J. W. Hunt (London, 1969)

SUMNER, B. H. *Survey of Russian History* (London, 1944)

TOCQUEVILLE, A. DE *L'Ancien Régime.* Also in translation; many eds.

WANGERMANN, E. *From Joseph II to the Jacobin Trials* (Oxford, 1959)

ZELLER, G. 'De Louis XIV à 1789' in P. Renouvin (ed.), *Histoire des relations internationales* (Paris, 1955)

## II The architectural setting

HAMILTON, G. H. *The Art and Architecture of Russia* (London, 1954)

HAUTECOEUR, L. *Histoire de l'Architecture Classique en France*, vols. iii and iv (Paris, 1951–52)

HEMPEL, E. *Baroque Art and Architecture in Central Europe* (London, 1965)

KAUFMANN, E. *Architecture in the Age of Reason* (Harvard, 1955)

KUBLER, G. and SORIA, M. *Art and Architecture in Spain and Portugal and their American Dominions* (London, 1959)

LAVEDAN, P. *Histoire de l'Urbanisme (Renaissance et Temps Modernes)* (Paris, 1941)

MORRISON, H. *Early American Architecture* (Oxford, 1952)

PEVSNER, N. *An Outline of European Architecture*, 6th edition (London, 1960)

SUMMERSON, J. *Architecture in Britain, 1530–1830*, 4th edition (London, 1963)

WITTKOWER, R. *Art and Architecture in Italy, 1600–1750*, 2nd edition (London, 1965)

## III The technological imperative

BEER, SIR GAVIN DE *The Sciences were Never at War* (London, 1960)

BELL, E. T. *Men of Mathematics* (London, 1939)

CAMERON, H. C. *Sir Joseph Banks* (London, 1952)

ELLIS, AYTON *The Penny Universities: a History of the Coffee Houses* (London, 1956)

FAY, BERNARD 'Learned Societies in Europe and America in the Eighteenth Century', in *American Historical Review* (XXVII, 1931–32)

GAGER, C. STEWART 'Botanic Gardens of the World: models for a History', in *Botanic Garden Review*, Brooklyn (XXVII, 1938)

GREEN, J. REYNOLDS *History of Botany* (London, 1914)

HALL, A. R. *The Scientific Revolution 1500–1800. The formation of the Modern Scientific Attitude* (London, 1954)

HINDLE, BROOKE *The Pursuit of Science in Revolutionary America 1735–1789* (Chapel Hill, 1956)

KLEMM, F. *A History of Western Technology* (London, 1959)

McCLOY, SHELBY T. *French Inventions of the Eighteenth Century* (Kentucky, 1952)

PARTINGTON, J. R. *History of Chemistry* vol. iii (London, 1962)

*Philosophical Magazine*, 'Science in the Eighteenth Century', Special issue (London, 1948)

SCHOFIELD, ROBERT E. *The Lunar Society of Birmingham* (Oxford, 1963)

SMALLWOOD, W. M. and M. C. *Natural History and the American Mind* (New York, 1941)

STRUIK, D. *Yankee Science in the Making* (Boston, 1948)

TAYLOR, E. G. R. *The Mathematical Practitioners of Hanoverian England 1714–1840* (Cambridge, 1966)

WOLF, A. (with the co-operation of F. Dannemann and Angus Armitage), *A History of Science, Technology and Philosophy in the 16th and 17th Centuries.* Second edition prepared by Douglas McKie (London, 1950)

WOOLF, HENRY *The Transit of Venus: a Study of Eighteenth-Century Science* (Princeton, 1959)

## IV Countryside and industry

ASHTON, T. S. *An Economic History of England: the 18th century* (London, 1955)

*Cambridge Economic History of Europe*, vols. iv and vi (Cambridge, 1933). (Note: vol. v, which will specifically cover the 18th century, has not yet appeared. Vols. iv and vi, however, contain material relevant to this period)

GEORGE, D. *England in Transition* (London, 1953)

GLASS, D. V. and EVERSLEY, D. E. C. (eds.). *Population in History* (London, 1965)

GOODWIN, A. (ed.). *The European Nobility in the 18th century* (London, 1953)

HARTWELL, R. M. *The Causes of the Industrial Revolution in England* (London, 1965)

HEATON, H. *Economic History of Europe*, 2nd edition (New York, 1948)

JONES, E. L. *Agriculture and Economic Growth in England, 1650–1815* (London, 1967)

MANTOUX, P. *The Industrial Revolution in England in the 18th century*, revised edition, ed. T. S. Ashton (London, 1961)

MINGAY, G. E. *English Landed Society in the 18th century* (London, 1963)

*New Cambridge Modern History*, vol. vii, *The Old Regime, 1713–63* (Cambridge, 1957) and vol. viii, *The American and French Revolutions, 1763–93* (Cambridge, 1965)

SINGER, C. and others (eds.) *A History of Technology*, vols. iii and iv (London, 1957–58)

VAN BATH, B. H. SLICHER *Agrarian History of Western Europe* (London, 1963)

WILSON, C. *England's Apprenticeship, 1603–1763* (London, 1965)

## V Europe overseas

ANDREWS, C. M. *The Colonial Period in American History* (New Haven, 1934–38)

BEAGLEHOLE, J. C. *The Exploration of the Pacific* (London, 1934)

BEAGLEHOLE, J. C. (ed.) *The Journals of Captain James Cook on his Voyages of Discovery* (Cambridge, 1955–67)

BOXER, C. R. *The Dutch Seaborne Empire* (London, 1965)

BREBNER, J. B. *The Explorers of North America* (London, 1933)

*Cambridge History of the British Empire*, vol. iv, *British India* (Cambridge, 1929)

COUPLAND, R. *The British Anti-Slavery Movement* (London, 1964)

FAIRCHILD, H. N. *The Noble Savage* (New York, 1928)

GLAMANN, K. *Dutch-Asiatic Trade 1620–1740* (The Hague, 1958)

HARLOW, V. T. *The Founding of the Second British Empire 1763–1793* (London, 1952, 1964)

JAMES, C. L. R. *The Black Jacobins* (New York, 1963)

PARK, MUNGO *Travels of Mungo Park* (London, 1907)

PARRY, J. H. *The Spanish Seaborne Empire* (London, 1966)

PARRY, J. H., and SHERLOCK, P. M. *Short History of the West Indies* (London, 1956)

VLEKKE, B. H. M. *Nusantara, a History of Indonesia* (The Hague, 1959)

WILLIAMS, ERIC *Capitalism and Slavery* (Chapel Hill, 1944)

WRONG, G. M. *The Rise and Fall of New France*, 3 vols. (Toronto, 1928)

WYNDHAM, H. A. *Atlantic and Slavery* (London, 1935)

WYNDHAM, H. A. *Atlantic and Abolition* (London, 1937)

## VI War on a new scale

DELBRÜCK, H. *Geschichte der Kriegskunst im Rahmen der politischen Geschichte*, vol. iv, *Neuzeit* (Berlin, 1920)

DUFFY, C. *The Wild Goose and the Eagle. A Life of Marshal von Browne, 1705–1757* (London, 1964)

FULLER, J. F. C. *British Light Infantry in the Eighteenth Century* (London, 1925)

LAZARD, P. *Vauban* (Paris, 1934)

LÉONARD, E. G. *L'armée et ses problèmes au XVIIIe siècle* (Paris, 1958)

LEWIS, M. *The Navy of Britain* (London, 1948)

LUVAAS, J. (ed.) *Frederick the Great on the Art of War* (London, 1966)

MACKESY, P. *The War for America 1775–1783* (Harvard, 1964)

MAHAN, A. T. *The Influence of Sea Power upon History, 1660–1783* (London, 1890, reprint 1965)

PARES, R. *War and Trade in the West Indies, 1739–63* (London, 1963)

STOYE, J. *The Siege of Vienna* (London, 1965)

WILKINSON, S. *The French Army before Napoleon* (Oxford, 1915)

## VII Taste and patronage

ANTAL, F. 'The Moral Purpose of Hogarth's Art', in *Journal of Warburg and Courtauld Institutes*, XV (London, 1952)

BROOKNER, A. 'Aspects of Neoclassicism in French Painting', *Apollo* (London, 1957)

ETTLINGER, L. D. 'Jacques-Louis David and Roman Virtue', in *Journal of the Royal Society of Arts*, CXV (London, 1967)

HASKELL, F. *Patrons and Painters* (London, 1963)

HEMPEL, E. *Baroque Art and Architecture in Central Europe* (London, 1965)

LEVEY, M. *Painting in Eighteenth-Century Venice* (London, 1959)

LEVEY, M. *Rococo to Revolution* (London, 1966)

LOQUIN, J. *La peinture d'histoire en France de 1747 à 1785* (Paris, 1912)

MURZ, H. 'Italian Models of Hogarth's Picture Stories', in *Journal of Warburg and Courtauld Institutes*, XV (London, 1952)

PEVSNER, N. *Rococo Art from Bavaria* (London, 1956)

ROSENBLUM, R. *Transformations in late Eighteenth-Century Art* (Princeton, 1967)

SWEETMAN, J. E. 'Shaftesbury's Last Commission', in *Journal of the Warburg and Courtauld Institutes*, XIX (London, 1956)

WATERHOUSE, E. K. *Italian Baroque Painting* (London, 1963)

WATERHOUSE, E. K. *Painting in Britain 1530–1790* (London, 1953)

WIND, E. 'The Sources of David's Horaces', in *Journal of the Warburg and Courtauld Institutes*, IV (London, 1941)

WITTKOWER, R. *Art and Architecture in Italy 1600–1750*, 2nd edition (London, 1965)

## VIII The Enlightenment

BECKER, C. L. *The Heavenly City of the Eighteenth-Century Philosophers* (New Haven, 1932)

CASSIRER, E. *The Philosophy of the Enlightenment* (Princeton, 1951)

COBBAN, A. *In Search of Humanity: the Role of the Enlightenment in Modern History* (London, 1960)

DERATHÉ, R. *Jean-Jacques Rousseau et la science politique de son temps* (Paris, 1950)

DOBRÉE, B. *English Literature in the Early Eighteenth Century, 1700–1740* (Oxford, 1959)

EHRARD, J. *L'Idée de nature en France dans la première moitié du XVIIIe siècle* (Paris, 1963)

FABRE, J. *Stanislas-Auguste Poniatowski et l'Europe des lumières* (Paris, 1952)

FOLKIERSKI, W. *Entre le classicisme et le romantisme* (Cracow and Paris, 1925)

FRANCASTEL, P. (ed.) *Utopie et institutions au XVIIIe siècle* (Paris and The Hague, 1963)

FUBINI, M. (ed.) *La Cultura illuministica in Italia* (Rome, 1964)

GAY, P. *The Enlightenment: an Interpretation* (New York, 1966)

HAVENS, G. R. *The Age of Ideas* (New York, 1955)

HAZARD, P. *La Crise de la conscience européenne* (Paris, 1935)

HAZARD, P. *La Pensée européenne au XVIIIe siècle* (Paris, 1946)

HEER, R. *The Eighteenth-Century Revolution in Spain* (Princeton, 1958)

HETTNER, H. *Geschichte der deutschen Literatur im achtzehnten Jahrhundert* (Berlin, 1961)

KRAUSS, W. *Studien zur deutschen und französischen Aufkläfung* (Berlin, 1963)

MANUEL, F. *The Eighteenth Century confronts the Gods* (Cambridge, Mass., 1959)

MAUGAIN, G. *Étude sur l'évolution intellectuelle de l'Italie de 1657 à 1750 environ* (Paris, 1909)

MORNET, D. *Les origines intellectuelles de la Révolution française* (Paris, 1938)

NATALI, G. *Il Settecento*, 4th edition (Milan, 1955)

POMEAU, R. *La Religion de Voltaire* (Paris, 1956)

PROUST, J. *Diderot et l'Encyclopédie* (Paris, 1962)

SARRAILH, J. *L'Espagne éclairée de la seconde moitié du XVIIIe siècle* (Paris, 1954)

SHACKLETON, R. *Montesquieu: a critical biography* (Oxford, 1961)

STEPHEN, L. *History of English Thought in the Eighteenth Century*, 3rd edition (London, 1902)

VARTANIAN, A. *Diderot and Descartes* (Princeton, 1953)

WILSON, A. M. *Diderot, the Testing Years* (New York, 1957)

## IX The rise of the people

BLOCH, C. *L'assistance et l'état en France à la veille de la Révolution* (Paris, 1908)

BONENFANT, P. *Le problème du paupérisme en Belgique à la fin de l'ancien régime* (Brussels, 1932)

BUXHOEUDEN, O. DE *Les établissements de bienfaisance en Russie* (Colmar, 1887)

FUENTES MARTIÁÑEZ, M. *Despoblación y repoblación de España (1482–1920)* (Madrid, 1929)

GEORGE, M. D. *London Life in the Eighteenth Century* (London, 1965)

GILBOY, E. *Wages in Eighteenth-Century England* (Harvard, 1934)

GOUBERT, P. *Beauvais et le Beauvaisis de 1600 à 1730* (Paris, 1960)

HELLEINER, K. 'The Vital Revolution Reconsidered', in *Canadian Journal of Economics and Political Science*, XXIII (1957)

JUTIKKALA, E. 'The Great Finnish Famine in 1696–97', in *Scandinavian Economic History Review*, III (Copenhagen, 1955)

LE ROY LADURIE, E. 'Histoire et Climat', in *Annales, Économies, Sociétés et Civilisations* (1959)

MARSHALL, D. *The English Poor in the Eighteenth Century* (London, 1926)

MOLS, R. *Introduction à la démographie historique des villes d'Europe du XIVe au XVIIIe siècle* (Louvain, 1954–56)

NADAL, J. and GIRALT, E. *La population catalane de 1553 à 1717* (Paris, 1959)

OWEN, D. *English Philanthropy 1660–1960* (Harvard, 1964)

PINCHBECK, I. *Women Workers and the Industrial Revolution, 1750–1850* (London, 1930)

POINTRINEAU, A. *La vie rurale en Basse-Auvergne au XVIIIe siècle* (Paris, 1965)

SELLIN, J. T. *Pioneering in Penology* (Oxford, 1945)

SMITH, J. T. *Vagabondiana: Anecdotes of Mendicant Wanderers through the Streets of London* (London, 1817)

UTTERSTRÖM, G. 'Climatic Fluctuations and Population Problems in Early Modern History', in *Scandinavian Economic History Review*, III (Copenhagen, 1955)

VILAR, P. *La Catalogne dans l'Espagne Moderne* (Paris, 1962)

## X Epilogue: see Chapter I

# List and Sources of Illustrations

The page on which an illustration appears is shown by the first set of numerals, its plate or figure number by the second. Sources of photographs are given in italics.

## I The Pattern of Government

11 Reverse of a farthing issued at St Albans, England, 1796

13 1. Pierre Mignard I (1612–95): portrait of Louis XIV; c. 1658. Galleria Sabauda, Turin. Photo *Chomon-Perino*

14–15 2. Friedrich Tischbein (1750–1812): portrait of Frederica-Sophia-Wilhelmina of Prussia, Princess of Orange; c. 1789. Pastel. *Rijksmuseum, Amsterdam*
3. Franz Caspar Sambach (1715–95): *Archduke Leopold of Tuscany bestowing on his sons the Order of the Golden Fleece in 1772.* They later became Francis I of Austria and Ferdinand III of Tuscany. *Albertina, Vienna*
4. Bernardo Bellotto (1724–80): *Election of Polish King Augustus Stanislas Poniatowski in 1764* (detail); second version 1778. Painting based on eye-witness accounts and contemporary engravings. Mounted on right is Józef Sosnowski, Marshal of the Electoral Assembly, receiving the returns of the poll from Józef Podoski, Voivode of Płock. In background is *szopa*, temporary wooden shed for the Senate. *National Museum, Warsaw*
5. Coronation of Frederick I of Prussia in 1701, engraving from *Die Königlich Preussische Crönung, 1712*
6. Per Hilleström I (1732–1816): *Gustavus III mustering the citizens of Stockholm in 1790.* Stockholm Stadshus. Photo *Nationalmuseum, Stockholm*

16–17 7. Martin van Meytens II (1695–1770): *Maria Theresa and her family*; 1750. Kunsthistorisches Museum, Vienna. Photo *Meyer*
8. Francisco de Goya (1746–1828): *Charles III of Spain in hunting dress.* Prado, Madrid. Photo *Mas*
9. Louis Karavak (d. 1754): *Peter the Great of Russia in battle*; 1718. Hermitage, Leningrad. Photo *Novosti*
10. Edward Francis Cunningham (c. 1742–95): *Return of Frederick II of Prussia from a manoeuvre*; 1787. Staatliche Schlösser und Gärten, Potsdam-Sans Souci. In the caption 'son' should read 'nephew' and 'grandson' 'great-nephew'.
11. Johann Hieronymus Löschenkohl (d. 1807): *Catherine II of Russia meeting the Emperor Joseph II in 1787.* Historisches Museum der Stadt Wien. Photo *Meyer*

18–19 12. French school, second half 17th C: *Louis XIV at the Grotto of Thetis.* Versailles. Photo *Giraudon*
13. Jacques Gautier-Dagoty (1710–81): *Marie-Antoinette in her chamber at Versailles in 1775.* Versailles. Photo *Giraudon*
14. Pierre-Denis Martin (1663–1742): *Versailles in 1722, with Louis XV returning to take up residence.* Versailles. Photo *Giraudon*
15. François Marot (1666–1719): *Louis XIV instituting the Order of St Michael*; 1710. Versailles. Photo *Giraudon*

20–21 16. Nicholas Lancret (1690–1743): *'Lit de justice' held on the occasion of Louis XV's majority, 1723.* Louvre, Paris. Photo *Giraudon*
17. Karl Anton Hickel (1745–98): *The House of Commons in 1793.* National Portrait Gallery, London
18. Paul Carl Leygebe (1664–1730): *The 'Tabakscollegium' of Frederick I of Prussia in Berlin Palace*; 1710. Staatliche Schlösser und Gärten, Potsdam-Sans Souci
19. Conference room of the sovereign states of Holland and West Friesland, engraving by I. C. Philips; mid-18th C. British Museum, London. Photo *John Freeman*

22 20. Giovanni Paolo Pannini (1691/2–1765): *Pope Benedict XIV arriving at Sta Maria Maggiore* (detail); 1742. Palazzo Quirinale, Rome. Courtesy the Segretario Generale della Presidenza della Repubblica. Photo *Savio*

23–24 21. Pierre-Denis Martin (1663–1742): *Procession after Louis XV's coronation at Rheims, 26 Oct. 1722.* Versailles. Photo *Service de Documentation Photographique des Musées Nationaux*

25 22. Carl Gustav Pilo (1712–92): *Coronation of Gustavus III of Sweden in 1773* (detail). *Nationalmuseum, Stockholm*

26–27 23. Michel Barthélémy Ollivier (1712–84): *Mozart playing at the Princesse de Conti's tea party 1763/4* (detail); Louvre, Paris. Photo *Scala*
24. Johann Franz Greippel (1720–98): *Performance of Gluck's 'Il Parnasso Confuso' in Schönbrunn in 1765.* Hofburg, Vienna. Photo *Georg Westermann Verlag*
25. Pietro Domenico Olivero (1679–1755) and collaborators: *Interior of the Teatro Regio in Turin.* Probably represents the opening evening of the theatre on 26 Dec 1740, with a performance of *Arsace* by Feo and decor by Giuseppe Bibiena. *Museo Civico, Turin*

28–29 26. *Interior of the Pantheon, Oxford Street in 1772.* Mezzotint by Richard Earlom after drawing by Charles Brandoin (1733–1807). British Museum, London
27. Luis Paret y Alcázar (1746–99): *The antique shop.* Collection Lázaro, Madrid. Photo *Mas*
28. Joseph van Aken (1709–49): *Saying Grace.* Courtesy of the Ashmolean Museum, Oxford
29. Jan Joseph Horemans II (1714–c. 1790): *Landlord and tenant*; 1764. Metropolitan Museum of Art, New York, (purchase 1871)
30. Philibert-Louis Debucourt (1755–1832): *Promenade in the Galerie du Palais Royal*; 1787. Photo *Bulloz*

30 31. John Wootton (1686–1765): *John Warde and his family outside Squerryes Court, Kent*; 1735. By kind permission of Major and Mrs J. B. Warde. Photo *John Webb (Brompton Studio)*

32. Jean-François de Troy (1679–1752): *A reading from Molière*; 1740. By kind permission of the Marchioness of Cholmondeley. Photo *John Webb (Brompton Studio)*

32 1. Satire on the 'death' of the Society of Jesus, 1773 (*Ultima funeris pompa extinctu Ordinis Iesuitarum*). British Museum, London

35 2. Diet of the Empire. Vignette on map of the empire by Herman Moll, dedicated to the Duke of Marlborough, 1712. British Museum, London

37 3. Execution of the Strieltzy in 1699 (detail), from *Diarium itineris in Moscoviam, ?*1700 by Johann Georg Korb

38 4. Satire on the first partition of Poland, 1772 ('The Polish plum-cake'). Engraving from Westminster Magazine, 1774

39 5. Dutch broadside on English Revolution 1688 ('The wounded French bear') 3 Jan. 1689. British Museum, London

## II The Architectural Setting

41 Trade token depicting the Crescent, issued at Buxton, Derbyshire; 1796

43 1. Würzburg: staircase of the Residenz by Johann Balthasar Neumann; designed 1735. Fresco by Giovanni Battista Tiepolo; 1752–3. Photo *Gundermann*

44–5 2. Rome: façade of Sta Maria delle Pace by Pietro da Cortona; 1656–7. Photo *Mansell Collection*
3. Rome: Palazzo Odescalchi by Gianlorenzo Bernini; begun 1664. Photo *Mansell Collection*
4. Rome: S. Carlo alle Quattro Fontane by Francesco Borromini; 1638–46. Photo *Mansell Collection*
5. Turin: S. Lorenzo by Guarino Guarini; 1668–87. Photo *Edwin Smith*
6. Paris: Third project for the east front of the Louvre by Gianlorenzo Bernini; 1665. Engraving by Jean Marot; c. 1660–70. Photo *Courtauld Institute of Art, London*
7. Paris: East front of the Louvre by Claude Perrault; begun 1667. Photo *A. F. Kersting*
8. Paris: Dome of the Invalides by Jules-Hardouin Mansart; 1680–91. Photo *Martin Hürlimann*
9. Versailles by Louis Le Vau and Jules-Hardouin Mansart; 1661–1756. Photo *French Government Tourist Office, London*

46–7 10. Vienna: Schönbrunn by Johann Bernhard Fischer von Erlach; begun 1696. Painting of the garden façade by Bernardo Bellotto; 1759. Kunsthistorisches Museum, Vienna. Photo *Georg Westermann Verlag*
11. Vienna: The Great Gallery of Schönbrunn by Johann Bernard Fischer von Erlach; interior decoration finished 1780. Photo *Toni Schneiders*
12. Vienna: The Upper Belvedere by Johann Lukas von Hildebrandt; 1721–2. Photo *Toni Schneiders*

48–9 13. London: Elevation of river front of Whitehall Palace. First scheme for William III by Sir Christopher Wren; 1698. Ink and wash drawing. *All Souls' College Library, Oxford*
14. Stockholm: Royal Palace by Nicodemus Tessin I; begun 1698. Painting by Johan Sefreuborn; 1776. Rådhus, Stockholm. Photo *City Museum, Stockholm*
15. Berlin: Royal Palace by Andreas Schlüter; begun c. 1698 (now destroyed). Photo *Bildarchiv Foto Marburg*
16. Caserta: Garden façade of the Palazzo Reale by Luigi Vanvitelli; 1751–74. Photo *Georgina Masson*
17. Woodstock, Oxfordshire: Portico of Blenheim Palace by Sir John Vanbrugh, 1705–24. Photo *Edwin Smith*
18. Pommersfelden: portico of Schloss Weissenstein by Johann Dientzenhofer; 1711–18. Photo *Edwin Smith*
19. Yorkshire: the Great Hall of Castle Howard by Sir John Vanbrugh; 1699–1712. Photo *J. F. Kersting*
20. Caserta: staircase of the Palazzo Reale by Luigi Vanvitelli; 1751–74. Photo *Georgina Masson*
21. Pommersfelden: the staircase of Schloss Weissenstein, by Johann Dientzenhofer; 1711–18. Photo *Toni Schneiders*
22. Vienna: Lower hall of the Upper Belvedere by Johann Lukas von Hildenbrandt; 1721–22. Photo *Toni Schneiders*

50–1 23. Peterhof by Jean-Baptiste Alexandre Le Blond; 1716–17. Remodelled by Bartolommeo Francesco Rastrelli; 1747–53. Photo *J. E. Dayton*
24. Leningrad: Winter Palace, by Bartolommeo Francesco Rastrelli; 1754–62. Photo *J. E. Dayton*
25. Tsarskoe Selo: Great Palace by Bartolommeo Francesco Rastrelli; 1749–56. Photo *J. Massey Stewart*
26. Turin: ballroom of Stupinigi by Filippo Juvarra, 1729–33. Photo *Scala*

52–3 27. Dresden: The Zwinger by Mathäus Daniel Pöppelmann; plans 1694, built 1709–18. Painting by Bernardo Bellotto; 1758. Staatliche Kunstsammlungen Dresden. Photo *Reinhold*
28. Würzburg: garden front of the Residenz by Johann Balthasar Neu-

mann; begun 1719 in consultation with Hildebrandt, de Cotte and Boffrand, structurally complete 1744. Photo *A. F. Kersting*

29. Potsdam: garden front of Sans Souci by Georg Wenceslaus von Knöbelsdorff; 1745–47. Photo *Edwin Smith*

54–5 30. Rome: façade of S. Giovanni in Laterano by Alessandro Galilei; 1733–36. Photo *Mansell Collection*

31. Paris: façade of St Sulpice by Giovanni Niccolo Servandoni; 1737. (North tower by J. F. T. Chalgrin 1777–88.) Photo *Bulloz*

32. Besançon: the Madeleine by Nicholas Nicole; 1749. Photo *Archives Photographiques*

33. Salzburg: the Kollegienkirche by Johann Bernhard Fischer von Erlach; 1694–1707. Photo *Toni Schneiders*

34. Vienna: the Karlskirche by Johann Bernhard Fischer von Erlach; begun 1716. Photo *Toni Schneiders*

35. London: St Mary-le-Strand by James Gibbs; 1714–17. Photo *National Monuments Record (Crown Copyright)*

36. London: St Martin-in-the-Fields by James Gibbs; 1721–26. Photo *A. F. Kersting*

37 London: Christ Church, Spitalfields by Nicholas Hawksmoor; 1714–29. Photo *A. F. Kersting*

38. London: St Anne's, Limehouse by Nicholas Hawksmoor; 1714–30. Photo *A. F. Kersting*

39. London: St John's, Smith Square, Westminster by Thomas Archer; 1714–28. Photo *A. F. Kersting*

40. Dresden: exterior of the Frauenkirche by Georg Bähr; 1725–43, (now destroyed). Photo *Deutsche Fotothek Dresden*

41. Dresden: interior of the Frauenkirche by Georg Bähr; 1725–43, (now destroyed). Photo *Deutsche Fotothek Dresden*

56–7 42. Turin: the Superga by Filippo Juvarra; 1717–31. Photo *A. F. Kersting*

43. Turin: Chiesa del Carmine by Filippo Juvarra; 1732–35. Photo *G. Rampazzi*

44. Granada: Sacristy of the Charterhouse by Luis de Arevalo; 1727–64. Photo *Mas*

45. Toledo: the *Transparente* in the cathedral by Narciso Tomé; 1721–32. Photo *Mas*

58–9 46. Banz: Benedictine abbey church by Johann Dientzenhofer; 1710–18. Photo *Toni Schneiders*

47. Vierzehnheiligen pilgrimage church by Johann Balthasar Neumann, exterior; 1743–72. Photo *Hirmer Fotoarchiv Munich*

48. Brunau: Church of St Margeretha by Christoph Dientzenhofer; 1708–15. Photo *Státní Ustav Památkové Péce a Ochrany Prirody v Praze*

49. Gabel: Church of St Laurence by Johann Lukas von Hildebrandt; begun 1699. Photo *Státní Ustav Památkové Péce a Ochrany Prirody v Praze*

50. Melk: the monastery by Jakob Prandtauer; 1702–14. Photo *Toni Schneiders*

51. Munich: interior of St John Nepomuk by Cosmas Damian and Egid Quirin Asam; 1733–46. Photo *Helga Schmidt-Glassner*

52. Munich: exterior of St John Nepomuk by Cosmas Damian and Egid Quirin Asam; 1733–46. Photo *Hirmer Fotoarchiv Munich*

60 53. Weltenburg: Altar figure of St George in the Benedictine abbey church by Egid Quirin Asam; 1721–24. Church built 1716–23. Photo *P. Cannon-Brookes*

61–2 54. Die Wies: interior of the pilgrimage church by Dominikus Zimmermann; 1746–54. Photo *Toni Schneiders*

63 55. Rohr: Assumption group in the monastery church by Egid Quirin Asam; 1723. Church built 1717–25. Photo *Hirmer Fotoarchiv Munich*

64–5 56. Kutna Hora: vault of the cathedral of Sta Barbara; 1515. Photo *Peter Cannon-Brookes*

57. Kladruby: vault of the Benedictine abbey by Johann Santini Aichel; 1712–26. Photo *Peter Cannon-Brookes*

58. Banz: vault of the Benedictine abbey church; 1710–18. Photo *A. F. Kersting*

59. Vierzehnheiligen pilgrimage church by Johann Balthasar Neumann, interior; 1743–72. Photo *A. F. Kersting*

60. Munich: *Spiegelsaal* of the Amalienburg, Schloss Nymphenburg by François de Cuvilliès; 1734–39. Photo *Michael Holford*

61. Munich: *Reiche Zimmer* of the Residenz by François de Cuvilliès; 1730–37. Photo *Bayer. Verwaltung der Staatl. Schlösser, Gärten und Seen*

66–7 62. Rome: the Arch of Constantine from *Antiquita Romane de' tempi della Repubblica* by Giovanni Battista Piranesi; 1748. Photo *J. R. Freeman*

63. Baalbec: General view of the temples from *The Ruins of Balbec otherwise Heliopolis, in Coelosyria* by Robert Wood; 1757. Photo *J. R. Freeman*

64. Athens: elevation of the Tower of the Winds, from *The Antiquities of Athens and other monuments of Greece*, 1762–1816, by James Stuart and Nicholas Revett. Photo *J. R. Freeman*

65. Athens: The Propylaea, from *Les Ruines des plus beaux monuments de la Grèce*, 1758 by J. D. Le Roy. Photo *John Freeman*

66. Split (Spalato): Elevation of the portico to the Vestibulum, from *The Ruins of the Palace of the Emperor Diocletian at Spalato, in Dalmatia*, 1764, by Robert Adam. Photo *R. B. Fleming*

67. London: view of the Stock Office in the Bank of England by Sir John Soane; 1792. Courtesy the Trustees of Sir John Soane's Museum, London. Photo *R. B. Fleming*

68. Design for a cenotaph to Newton by Etienne Louis Boullée; 1784. (Fol. Ha. 57 f. 126 v). *Bibliothèque Nationale, Paris*

69. Paris: *Barrière de la Villette* by Claude Nicolas Ledoux; 1785–89. Photo *Giraudon*

70. London: west towers of Westminster Abbey by Nicholas Hawksmoor; 1734–45. Photo *Edwin Smith*

71. Twickenham, Middlesex: Long Gallery at Strawberry Hill by Horace Walpole; 1748–77. Photo *Edwin Smith*

72. Wiltshire: north-west view of Fonthill Abbey by James Wyatt; 1796–1807 (now demolished). From *Illustrations of Fonthill Abbey*, 1823, by John Britton. Photo *R. B. Fleming*

68–9 73. Tsarskoe Selo: Pavillion by Charles Cameron; c. 1780. Photo *Catherine Cruft*

74. Middlesex: east ante-room of Syon House by Robert and James Adam; 1762–63. Photo *John Webb (Brompton Studio)*

75. Chiswick House by Lord Burlington; begun 1725. Photo *A. F. Kersting*

76. Paris: École Militaire by Jacques-Ange Gabriel; 1751–58. Photo *Marianne Adelmann*

77. Paris: The Panthéon from designs by Jacques Germain Soufflot and others; begun 1757. Photo *Giraudon*

78. Paris: Bagatelle in the Bois de Boulogne by François-Joseph Bélanger; 1777. Photo *Giraudon*

79. Versailles: the Petit Trianon by Jacques-Ange Gabriel; 1762–68. Photo *Giraudon*

70–1 80. Essex: Wanstead House by Colen Campbell; 1715–20 (demolished 1822). Engraving by J. Fittler after G. Robertson. British Museum, London. Photo *R. B. Fleming*

81. London: courtyard of Somerset House by Sir William Chambers; 1776–80. Photo *A. F. Kersting*

82. London: front drawing of No. 20 Portman Square by Robert Adam; 1775–77. Photo *Copyright Country Life*

83. York: The Assembly Rooms by Lord Burlington; 1730. Photo *Copyright Country Life*

84. Berlin: the Brandenburg Gate by C. G. Langhans; 1789–93. Photo *Martin Hürlimann*

85. Paris: École de Médecine by Jacques Gondoin; 1769–76. Photo *Bildarchiv Foto Marburg*

86. Richmond, Virginia: The State Capitol by Thomas Jefferson; 1785–96. Photo *Ewing Galloway*

87. Versailles: *Ailes Gabriel* by Jacques-Ange Gabriel; 1756. Photo *A. F. Kersting*

88. Paris: Hôtel de Salm by Jacques-Ange Gabriel; 1782–86. Photo *Archives Photographiques*

89. Bordeaux: staircase in the Grand Theatre by Victor Louis; 1777–80. Photo *Helga Schmidt-Glassner*

90. Bordeaux: auditorium of the Grand Theatre by Victor Louis; 1777–80. Photo *Helga Schmidt-Glassner*

72–3 91. Bath: civic schemes by John Wood I and II; 1704–54. British Museum, London. Photo *R. B. Fleming*

92. London: Hanover Square, promoted by Richard Lumley, Earl of Scarborough, c. 1717. Engraving by Pollard and Jukes after Edward Dayes; 1787. British Museum, London. Photo *R. B. Fleming*

93. Nancy: Place Stanislas by Emmanuel Héré de Corny; 1750–57. Gouache. Musée Historique Lorrain, Nancy. Photo *G. Mangin*

94. Copenhagen: the Amalienborg by Nicolas Eigtved; begun 1749. Photo *The Danish Tourist Office, London*

74–5 95. Paris: general plan of the city from *Monuments érigés en France à la gloire de Louis XV*, 1765, by Pierre Patte. Photo *John Freeman*

96. London: plan of Hyde Park with the city and liberties of Westminster from *London and Westminster Improved* 1766 by John Gwynne. Photo *John Freeman*

97. Paris: Place Louis XV (now Place de la Concorde) by Jacques-Ange Gabriel; 1753–70. Engraving by Taraval. British Museum, London. Photo *R. B. Fleming*

98. Aranjuez: plan of the city; civic scheme 1748–78. Engraving after Domingo de Aguirie. Photo *Mas*

99. Karlsruhe: civic scheme by Jakob Friedrich von Betzendorf; 1715–19. Photo *Bildstelle der Stadt Karlsruhe*

100. Lisbon: Commercial Square (Praca do Comércio); civic scheme by Manuel da Maia, 1756–59. Photo *Portuguese Information, Tourist and Trade Office, London*

101. Bordeaux: Place de la Bourse by Jacques Jules Gabriel; designed 1733. Photo *Boudot-Lamotte*

102. Washington: plan of the city from *An historical, geographical, commercial and philosophical view of the American United States* 1795 by W. Winterbotham. Photo *John Freeman*

103. Chaux: perspective view of the town from *L'Architecture considérée*, 1804–46 by Claude Nicolas Ledoux. Photo *John Freeman*

76 104. Wiltshire: view of the gardens at Stourhead by Sir Henry Hoare and 'Capability' Brown; begun 1740s. Photo *Edwin Smith*

105. Kew: view of the Pagoda by

Sir William Chambers; 1757–63. Photo *Colour Library International*

78 1. Frontispiece (detail), from *Essai sur l'Architecture*, 1755, by Abbé Laugier

79 2. Golden House of Nero. Engraving from *Entwurf einer historischen Architektur*, 1721, by Johann Bernhard Fischer von Erlach

80 3. Vienna: ground-plan of Schönbrunn, after drawing by Johann Bernhard Fischer von Erlach in University Library, Zagreb

81 4. Caserta: ground-plan of Palazzo Reale

82 5. Rome: ground-plan of S. Andrea al Quirinale

6. Rome: ground-plan of S. Carlo alle Quattro Fontane

7. Vienna: ground-plan of the Karlskirche. After engraving in *Entwurf einer historischen Architektur*, 1721, by Johann Bernhard Fischer von Erlach

8. Gabel: ground-plan of church of St Laurence. (After B. Grimschitz, *Johann Lucas von Hildebrandt*, 1932)

83 9. Banz: ground-plan of Benedictine abbey church. (After Dr Hans Reuther, Hanover)

10. Munich: ground-plan of St John Nepomuk. (After N. Lieb and M. Hirmer, *Barockkirchen zwischen Donau und Alpen*, 1953)

11. Steinhausen: ground-plan of the church. (After N. Lieb and M. Hirmer, *Barockkirchen zwischen Donau und Alpen*, 1953)

12. Die Wies: ground-plan of the pilgrimage church

13. Vierzehnheiligen: ground-plan of the pilgrimage church. After Gurlitt, *Geschichte des Barockstiles*, 1887

84 14. Paris: ground-plan of the Panthéon

85 15. London: ground-plan of St Martin-in-the-Fields. After Gibbs, *A Book of Architecture*, 1728

86 16. Dresden: ground-plan of the Frauenkirche

87 17. Kent: elevation of Mereworth. Engraving from *Vitruvius Britannicus or the British Architect*, 1717–25, by Colen Campbell

88 18. Buckinghamshire: view of the Queen's Theatre from the Rotunda, Stowe. Engraving by Rigaud after Baron; 1739. British Museum, London. Photo *R. B. Fleming*

89 19. Buckinghamshire: view of the Queen's Theatre from the Rotunda, Stowe. Engraving by G. Bickham after Chatelain; 1753. British Museum, London. Photo *R. B. Fleming*

20. Paris: ground-plan of Place Louis XV (now Place de la Concorde) from: *Monuments érigés en France à la gloire de Louis XV*, Paris 1765, by Pierre Patte

21. Nancy: plan of the Place Royale. Engraving from *Plans et élévations de la Place Royale de Nancy*, 1753, by Emmanuel Héré de Corny

92–3 22. Edinburgh: plan for new part of the city by James Craig (begun 1767). Engraving; 1768. British Museum, London. Photo *R. B. Fleming*

## III The Technological Imperative

95 Trade token depicting iron bridge at Coalbrookdale, issued in Shropshire by Reynolds & Co.

97 1. Jacques de Lajoue (1686–1761): *Le Cabinet Physique de M. Bonnier de la Mosson* (detail). By kind permission of Sir Alfred Beit, Bart. Photo *John Webb (Brompton Studio)*

98–99 2. British school: *Scene in a coffee-house*; c. 1700. British Museum, London. Photo *R. B. Fleming*

3. Louis XIV and Colbert visiting the Académie des Sciences. From *Mémoires pour servir à l'histoire naturelle des animaux*, 1671, by C. Per-

rault. Bibliothèque Nationale, Paris

4. John Zoffany (1733–1810): *William Hunter lecturing to the Royal Academy as Professor of Anatomy*; c. 1775. By courtesy Royal College of Physicians of London

5. University Library of Göttingen. Engraving by Georg-Daniel Heumann (1691–1759). *Germanisches Nationalmuseum, Nuremberg*

6. Laboratory at Altdorf University. Engraving by I. G. Puschner from *Amoenitates Altdorfinae*, c. 1720. British Museum, London. Photo *R. B. Fleming*

7. *Ideal Conception of a Natural History Cabinet*. Engraving by Vincent from *Elenchus tabularum*, 1719

100–1 8. *Banksia serrata (Proteaceae)*. Watercolour after preliminary sketch by Sydney Parkinson, made at Botany Bay in 1770. This plant is native to New South Wales and Victoria, and was completely unknown to the Old World before being discovered by Banks and Solander. British Museum (Natural History). Photo *R. B. Fleming*

9. *Aechmea nudicaulis (Bromeliaceae)*. Watercolour by Sydney Parkinson from specimen collected by Banks and Solander in Rio de Janeiro in 1768. It was called 'Bromelia bracteata' by Banks, but not published by him and now known by the above title. This epiphyte grows perched on the branches of trees, and the rosette of leaves forms a tank collecting water in which mosquitoes breed. British Museum (Natural History). Photo *R. B. Fleming*

10. Jean-Baptiste Hilair (1753–1822): *Le Jardin des Plantes*; 1794. One of a series of watercolours of different parts of the *jardin*. This shows the 'seedling garden', the building on the left to house delicate plants and experiments; the frames on either side of it for seedlings of tropical plants, and those in front for the culture of bulbs and tubers from the Cape of Good Hope. Bibliothèque Nationale, Paris. Photo *Françoise Foliot*

11. James Gillray (1757–1815): *The Great South Sea Caterpillar transformed into a Bath Butterfly*. British Museum, London. Photo *R. B. Fleming*

12. South American vulture, from *Histoire Naturelle*, 1770–83, by Georges-Louis Leclerc, Comte de Buffon

102–3 13. William Herschel's forty-foot telescope. Engraving from the *Philosophical Transactions*, 1795. *Science Museum, London*

14. The Octagon Room in the Royal Observatory in Flamsteed's time, showing observers with quadrant and telescope. *Science Museum, London*

15. Nuremberg Observatory in 1716. Engraving by Christoph Weigel after Adam Delsenbach (1687–1765). *Kunstsammlung der Veste Coburg*

16. Joseph Wright of Derby (1734–97): *The Orrery*; 1766. Derby Art Gallery. Photo *Courtauld Institute of Art*

17. Map of the moon. Engraving from *Opera Inedita*, Göttingen, 1775, by Johann Tobias Mayer

104–5 18. Antonio Joli de Dipi (c. 1700–77): *View of Thames with unfinished Westminster Bridge* (detail); c. 1745. *Courtesy the Leonard Koetser Gallery, London*

19. Joseph Vernet (1714–89): *Construction of a major road*; 1775. Louvre, Paris. Photo *Giraudon*

20. Pierre-Denis Martin (1663–1742): *Waterworks and aquaduct at Marly*. Versailles. Photo *Service de Documentation Photographique des Musées Nationaux*

21. The cast-iron bridge near Coalbrookdale, erected in 1779. Engraving by William Ellis after Michael Angelo Rooker (1743–1801). One of the earliest views of this bridge, 1782. Courtesy *Allied Ironfounders Ltd*

106–7 22. Jacques-Louis David (1748–1825): *Lavoisier and his wife*. Private Collection. Photo *Bulloz*

23. Gun-towing vehicle, originated by Nicolas Joseph Cugnot and developed by the Paris arsenal. *Musée des Techniques–CNAM Paris*

23. Experiment to prove oxygen necessary to respiration. Drawing by Mme Lavoisier from *Traité élémentaire de chimie*, 1789 by Antoine Lavoisier

25. Thomas Rowlandson (1756–1827): *Gas light in Pall Mall* (detail); 1809. *Science Museum, London*

26. Cure for paralytic and rheumatic conditions. Engraving from *Electrical Medicine*, 1766, by J. G. Schaeffer

27. Electrical experiment on weight gain and loss. Engraving from *Recherches sur les causes particulières des phénomènes électriques*, 1749, by Jean Antoine Nollet

28. Electrical experiment on muscular movement. Engraving after J. Zambelli from *De viribus electricitatis in motu musculari*, second edition Bologna 1792, by Luigi Galvani

29. Alexandre-Evariste Fragonard (1780–1850): *Volta presenting his pile battery to Napoleon* (detail). Wildenstein Collection. Photo *Bulloz*

108 30. Observation balloon at the Battle of Fleurus, 1794. Painting on lid of snuff-box. *Science Museum, London*

31. *Poisson Aérostatique enlevé à Plazentia Ville d'Espagne et dirigé par Dom Joseph Patinho jusqu'à la Ville de Coria . . . le 20 mars 1784*. Coloured engraving. By kind permission of Lord Kings Norton. Photo *John Webb (Brompton Studio)*

110 *1*. Atlas of blood vessels in human body from *Icones Anatomicae*, 1743–56, by Albrecht von Haller

*2*. Canals and locks from section on hydraulics in Diderot and d'Alembert's *Encyclopédie* (Recueil des Planches), 1762–72 (Long bars Ab and Ca are for opening and closing lock gates)

111 *3*. Experiment with phlogiston from *Opuscoli scelti* of the Italian Academy of Sciences, 1778

*4*. *Le bain de propreté* from *Dictionnaire des Arts et Métiers*, 1761 onwards, ed. Réaumur (Key: A. bath tub; B. waste pipe and tap with C. drain; D. bucket for mixing hot and cold water in bath; E. funnel to take hot water direct from tap to bottom of bath; F. slipper; G. depilatory mitt; H. hot and cold water taps connecting to cisterns behind wall; I. and K. brazier for heating water in bath if cistern not available)

112 *5*. New engine for driving piles. Engraving from *Course of Experimental Philosophy*, 1745, by J. T. Desaguliers

*6*. Old Newgate Prison, showing ventilators devised by Stephen Hales. British Museum, London

113 *7*. Transit of Venus across the solar disc in 1769, observed by Chappe from San Joseph, California. From *Observations Astronomiques*, 1772, by Comte Giovanni Domenico Cassini

114 *8*. Medical garden at Altdorf University. Engraving by I. G. Puschner from *Amoenitates Altdorfinae*, c. 1720. British Museum, London

115 *9*. Chelsea Physic Garden, engraving by John Haynes, 1753. By permission of the Committee of Management of Chelsea Physic Garden. Photo *John Freeman*

116 *10*. Handwritten titlepage of *Preliminaries to the Nuptials of Plants (Praeludia sponsaliarum plantarum)*, 1729, by Linnaeus. Courtesy Upsala University Library

117 *11*. Classification of plants, from *Genera Plantarum*, Leiden 1737, by Linnaeus

*12*. Illustration to experiment 'Whereby to find out the force with which Trees imbibe moisture' from *Vegetable Staticks*, 1727, by Stephen Hales

*13*. *Observations sur les pucerons*. Engraving by Haussard from *Traité d'insectologie*, 1745, by Charles Bonnet

118 *14*. Illustrations from *Observations upon the generation, composition and decomposition of animal and vegetable substances*, 1749, by J. T. Needham (Fig. 1 'represents the origin of spermatic animals'; Fig. A represents one of the first Zoophites discovered by Needham, showing 'the plant throwing out its animals')

119 *15*. Watchmaker's screw-cutting lathe, from *L'art du tourneur*, 1701 by Charles Plumier

120 *16*. Pont Sainte Maxence on the Oise from *Description . . . des Ponts*, 1782, by Jean Perronet

*17*. Four-armed bridge over the navigation canals of Ardres and Calais, from *Architecture Hydraulique*, 1737–53, by Forest de Belidor

121 *18*. Methods of filling a *montgolfière* and a *charlière*, from *History and Practice of Aerostation*, 1785, by Tiberius Cavallo (Key: Fig. 1. Scaffold 6–8 feet from ground with well in centre connecting to fire below, providing hot air to fill *montgolfière*; Fig. 3. Barrels of hydrogen to fill *charlière*)

## IV Countryside and Industry

123 Trade token depicting the interior of a smithy, issued by John Wilkinson at Willey, Warwickshire; 1787

125 1. Jean-Baptiste Oudry (1686–1755): *The Farm* (detail); 1750. Louvre, Paris. Photo *Giraudon*

126–27 2. Surveyors at work. Watercolour drawing on Henlow Enclosure. Award Map by John Goodman Maxwell, a surveyor of Spalding; 1798. *County Record Office, Bedford*

3. Frontispiece from *The Country Gentleman and Farmer's Monthly Directory*, 1727, by Richard Bradley

4. George Stubbs (1724–1806): *Haymakers*; 1785. Private Collection. Photo *L. and M. Taylor*

5, 6, and 7. A dairy, flax-making and shepherds. Engravings from *Oeconomus prudens et legalis*, Nuremberg, 1705, by Franz Philipp Florin

8. Foresters at work, frontispiece from *Manner of Raising, Ordering and Improving Forest Trees*, 1724 by M. Cook

9. George Dance (1741–1825): portrait of Arthur Young; 1794. *National Portrait Gallery, London*

10. Surveyors at work. Watercolour drawing on Henlow Enclosure. Award Map by John Goodman Maxwell, a surveyor of Spalding; 1798. *County Record Office, Bedford*

11. Agriculture plate, from the *Encyclopédie, (Recueil des Planches)*, 1762–72, by Diderot and d'Alembert.

12. Four-wheeled drill-plough with a seed and manure hopper, invented 1745, from *The Farmer's Instructor*, 1750. Photo *Museum of English Rural Life, University of Reading*

13. Rotherham Plough. *Science Museum, London (Crown Copyright)*

128–29 14. Thomas Weaver (1774–1843): Thomas Coke, first Earl of Norfolk and his sheep; c. 1800. Holkham Hall. By kind permission of the Earl of Leicester. Photo *John Webb (Brompton Studios)*

15. Hog at Tidmarsh Farm. Hand-coloured etching and aquatint, published by E. Walker; c. 1798. Photo *Museum of English Rural Life, University of Reading*

16. J. Digby Curtis: *Robert Bakewell's 'Two-Pounder'*; 1790. Agricultural Economics Research Institute Library, University of Oxford. Photo *M. R. Dudley*

17. George Stubbs (1724–1806): *Lincolnshire Ox*; exhibited at the Royal Academy of Arts 1790. *Walker Art Gallery, Liverpool*

18. John Boultbee (1753–1812): *Robert Bakewell on a bay cob*; last quarter of the 18th century. *Leicester City Art Gallery*

130–31 19. Nymphenburg: porcelain figure of Columbine from a model by F. A. Bustelli; c. 1755–60. *Victoria and Albert Museum, London (Crown Copyright)*

20. Meissen: painted porcelain figure of a lady in a hooped skirt; c. 1745. *Victoria and Albert Museum, London (Crown Copyright)*

21. Chelsea: porcelain figure of an actor in pseudo-Turkish costume, painted in enamel colours and gilt; c. 1765. *Victoria and Albert Museum, London (Crown Copyright)*

22. French commode with a serpentine marble top by Gandreau and gilt bronze mounts by Caffieri; c. 1739. *By permission of the Trustees of the Wallace Collection, London (Crown Copyright)*

23. English silver sauce-boat made by Samuel Courtauld. London, 1751–52

24. English silver coffee-pot made by Samuel Courtauld. London, 1730–31

25. French 'fauteuil à la Reine' with floral Beauvais tapestry, fluted tapering legs, arm-rest terminations in the form of Ionic capitols; c. 1780. *By permission of the Trustees of the Wallace Collection, London (Crown Copyright)*

26. Wedgwood coffee-pot in lilac jasperware; late 18th C. *Victoria and Albert Museum, London (Crown Copyright)*

27. English side-chair in Cuban or Honduran mahogany, the back with strap-work splat, seat covered in green damask. *Irwin Untermyer Collection, New York*

132–33 28. Per Hilleström I (1732–1816): *In the Foundry*; 1781. *Nationalmuseum, Stockholm*

29. Leonard Defrance (1735–1805): *The Colliery*; 1778. Musée de l'Art Wallon, Liège. Photo *Service T.I.P.*

30. Per Hilleström I (1732–1816): *Interior of Prins Gustav Mine, Falun*; 1784. *Stora Kopparbergs Berglags AB, Falun*

134–35 31. Atmospheric steam engine invented by Thomas Newcomen c. 1705. Engraving by Henry Beighton F.R.S.; 1717. *Science Museum, London*

32. Rotative steam-engine made by James Watt and Matthew Boulton; 1784. *Science Museum, London (Crown Copyright)*

33. F. von C. Breda: portrait of James Watt (detail); 1792. *National Portrait Gallery, London*

34. Joseph Wright of Derby (1734–97): portrait of Sir Richard Arkwright (detail); 1789–90. By kind permission of Colonel Peter Arkwright. Photo *Courtauld Institute of Art, London*

35. Improved water-frame spinning-machine; c. 1775. *Science Museum, London (Crown Copyright)*

36. British School: *Backbarrow Furnace, North Lancashire*; c. 1730–40. By kind permission of Major J. U. Machell. Photo *Manchester City Art Gallery*

136 37. Attrib. to George Robertson (1742–88): *Nant-y-Glo Iron-works*; c. 1788. Watercolour. *National Museum of Wales, Cardiff*

38. Joseph Wright of Derby (1734–97): *Joseph Arkwright's Cotton Mills, Cromford, near Matlock*; c. 1782–83.

Malcolm McPherson; 3, Farquhar Shaw; 4, Twelve of the Scots Guards to shoot them; 5, Six more ready to dispatch them; 6, Two reverends praying with them; 7, Sergeant-major Ellison giving the signal with his handkerchief; 8, Three hundred of the Scots Guards in 3 lines; 9, One hundred Highland prisoners to see the execution; 10, The coffins). British Museum, London

190–91 26. William Hogarth (1697–1764): *March to Finchley in 1745* (detail); 1746. The Thomas Coram Foundation for Children, London. Photo *John Webb (Brompton Studio)*
27. John Wootton (1686–1765): *General Richard Onslow inspecting the Horse Grenadier Guards* (detail); 1756. *Beaverbrook Art Gallery, Fredericton*
28. Encampment of the Austrian army. Engraving by Georg Balthasar Probst; c. 1760. *Anne S.K. Brown Military Collection, Providence, R.I.*
29. Adam Frans van der Meulen (1632–90): *Camp of Louis XIV before Tournai* (detail). *Musée des Beaux-Arts, Nancy*

192–93 30. Infantry and field artillery, detail from drawing of Battle of Gadebusch 1712. Krigsarkivet, Stockholm. Photo *Kungl. Armémuseum, Stockholm*
31. Prussian infantry advancing in oblique formation. Engraving by Georg Stettner of the Battle of Liegnitz in Silesia; 1760. *Anne S.K. Brown Military Collection, Providence, R.I.*
32. Winter battle. Engraving by J.C. Czerny of the Austrian attack on the Prussian position near Görlitz on New Year's Day 1757. British Museum, London
33. Dan Andersson Stawert: *Battle of Düna 1701*. Drottningholm Palace. Photo *Nationalmuseum, Stockholm*
34. Infantry in square formation. Engraving from *Der Vollkommene teutsche Soldat*, Leipzig, 1726, by Hans Friedrich von Fleming
35. Siege of Gibraltar, attack of the combined Spanish forces by land and sea, 13 September 1782. Wash drawing by Thomas Malton I (1726–1801) after G. F. Koehler, aide-de-camp of General Eliott. *National Maritime Museum, Greenwich*
36. Victory of the Prussian army over combined Austrian and Saxon forces near Wilsdorf on 15 December 1745. Engraving c. 1745. *Anne S.K. Brown Military Collection, Providence, R.I.*

194–95 37. Louis-Nicolas van Blarenberghe (1716–94): *Battle of Fontenoy 1745*. Versailles. Photo *Giraudon*
38. Lexington militia disperses after volley from Pitcairn's advance guard; 1775. Coloured engraving by Amos Doolittle (1745–1832). *New York Public Library*

196–97 39. *Diagram of all the items comprised in military architecture, or the art of fortification*, Amsterdam c. 1700 (An English version also published). *National Maritime Museum, Greenwich*
40. Diagrammatic illustration of siege operations. Engraving from *Der Vollkommene teutsche Soldat*, Leipzig 1726, by Hans Friedrich von Fleming
41. Dominic Serres (1722–93): *Storming of Moro Castle, Havana 1762* (detail). Storming party composed of 9th Foot supported by 35th. The Earl of Albermarle, on loan to the National Maritime Museum, Greenwich. Photo *John Webb (Brompton Studio)*
42. Saps. Engraving from *De l'attaque et de la défense des places*, The Hague 1737, by Vauban
43. Dominic Serres (1722–93): *Battery before Moro Castle, Havana*

*1762* (detail). The Earl of Albermarle, on loan to the National Maritime Museum. *National Maritime Museum, Greenwich*
44. *Opening of the trench*. From series of engravings by Martin Engelbrecht after Jacques Rigaud illustrating various methods of siege and attack, probably based on Siege of Barcelona 1714; c. 1750. *Anne S.K. Brown Military Collection, Providence, R.I.*

198–99 45. Nikolaj-Abraham Abildgaard (1743–1809): *Opening of the docks at Copenhagen by Christian VI*. Statens Museum for Kunst, Copenhagen. Photo *Ole Woldbye*
46. Joseph Vernet (1714–89): *Port of Toulon* (detail): 1755. Musée de la Marine, Paris
47. John Cleveley II (1747–86): *George III reviewing the fleet at Spithead* (detail). Private Collection. Photo *John Webb (Brompton Studio)*
48. Nicholas Pocock (1740–1821): *His Majesty's Docks at Chatham* (detail); late 18th C. National Maritime Museum, Greenwich Hospital Collection. Photo *John Webb (Brompton Studio)*

200–1 49. Attrib. to Isaac Sailmaker (c. 1633–1721): *The Britannia* (detail). First rate of 100 guns built by Sir Phineas Pett; in service 1682–1715. *National Maritime Museum, Greenwich*
50. Section through a warship. Engraving from *L'art de bâtir les vaisseaux*, 1719, by Cornelis van Eyk
51. Attrib. to Willem van de Velde I (1611–93): *Battle of the Texel 1673* (detail). Last action of the third Dutch War. *National Maritime Museum, Greenwich*
52. Dominic Serres (1722–93): *Battle of Negapatam 6 July 1782, (beginning of action)*; 1786. English squadrons on left, French on right. Third action of English East Indies fleet under Sir Edward Hughes against the famous Bailli de Suffren. *Greenwich Hospital Collection*
53. *Battle of Hangöudd, 1714*. Engraving by Maurice Bagouy. Royal Library, Stockholm
54. Nicholas Pocock (1740–1821): *The Bellerophon passing through the French line*, (detail); 1794. By kind permission of Major Hope Johnstone. Photo *National Gallery of Scotland*
55. Dominic Serres (1722–93): *Frigate off the coast* (detail). By kind permission of W. J. Miller and Son, Wooler, Northumberland. Photo *Sotheby and Co.*
56. *Admiral Rodney breaking the line at the Battle of the Saints, 1782*. Engraving by J. Wells after Thomas Walker. *National Maritime Museum, Greenwich*

202 57. Abraham Storck (1635–c. 1710): *The Four Days' Fight, 1–4 June 1666* (detail). *National Maritime Museum, Greenwich*

205 1. Russian navy at end of 17th C. Engraving to illustrate 'Catalogus navium Tzarea classis' from *Diarium itineris in Moscoviam*, ?1700, by Johann Georg Korb

206 2 *and* 3. Diagrams to illustrate mechanism of matchlock and flintlock. *Drawings by Trevor Hodgson*
4. Drill exercises, from *Der Vollkommene teutsche Soldat*, Leipzig 1726 by Hans Friedrich von Fleming
5. Swiss field artillery, 1717. Engraving by Melchior Füeslin. *Germanisches Nationalmuseum, Nuremberg*

207 6. Gun foundry, from *Mémoires d'artillerie*, 1697 by Surirey de Saint-Rémy

208 7 *and* 9. Midship frame and deck plan, from *Universal Dictionary of the Marine*, 1769, by William Falconer
8. Frederick II of Prussia taking a review. Engraving by Daniel

Chodowiecki from J. B. Basedow's *Elementarwerk*, 1774

210 10. Royal bodyguard swearing loyalty to Frederick William I of Prussia in 1713. Engraving by Pieter Schenk I (1660–1718/9). British Museum, London
11. Naval architects. Engraving by Nicolas Ozanne (1728–1811) from *Elémens de l'architecture Navale*, 1758 by M. Duhamel du Monceau

211 12. Ships under construction and being launched, from *L'art de bâtir les vaisseaux*, 1719, by Cornelis van Eyk

212 13. Billeting. Engraving by E. Bück. *Germanisches Nationalmuseum, Nuremberg*

213 14. Military punishments. Engraving by Daniel Chodowiecki from J. B. Basedow's *Elementarwerk*, 1774
15. A German village being plundered, 1771. British Museum, London

214 16. Sketch by Frederick the Great of the German position at Battle of Mollwitz, 1741. *Staatsbibliothek Berlin Bildarchiv*

215 17. Plan of order of attack from *De l'attaque et de la défense des places*, The Hague 1737, by Vauban

## VII Taste and Patronage

217 Trade token issued in London by P. Ratley, 'Dealer in drawgs pictes & curiosoties'

219 1. François Boucher (1703–70): *Portrait of Madame de Pompadour*; 1758. *Victoria and Albert Museum, London (Crown Copyright)*

220–21 2. *Exhibition of the Royal Academy of Painting in 1771*. Mezzotint after Charles Brandoin. British Museum, London
3. Giovanni Paolo Pannini (1691/2–1765): *Cardinal Valentini-Gonzaga in his imaginary picture gallery* (detail); 1749. Wadsworth Atheneum, Hartford, Conn. Photo *Gabinetto Fotografico Nazionale, Rome*
4. Michel-Ange Houasse (1680–1730): *Drawing academy*. La Granja, Segovia. Photo *Mas*
5. John Zoffany (1733–1810): '*Cognoscenti' in the Uffizi* (detail); 1780. *Reproduced by gracious permission of Her Majesty the Queen*
6. John Zoffany (1733–1810): *Charles Townley in his Antique Gallery*; c. 1805. Burnley Art Gallery. Photo *Fotografico Nazionale*

222–23 7. Luca Giordano (1632–1705): *Triumph of Judith*; 1704. Fresco on ceiling of Treasury Chapel in Certosa di S. Martino, Naples. Photo *Pedicini*
8. Cosmas Damian Asam (1686–1739): *Ascension of St George into Heaven*; 1721. Fresco on dome of Weltenburg abbey church, with stucco by Egid Quirin Asam. Photo *A. F. Kersting*

224–25 9. Paul Troger (1698–1762): *Glorification of the Trinity by the Virgin and saints*; 1752. Fresco on dome of Dreieichen church. Photo *Kindler*
10. Johann Michael Rottmayr (1654–1730): *S. Carlo Borromeo interceding for plague victims*; 1727–30. Fresco on dome of Karlskirche, Vienna
11. Franz Anton Maulpertsch (1724–96): *Baptism of Christ* (detail); c. 1766. Fresco on ceiling of Divinity School in Old University, Vienna. Photo *Bildarchiv d. Öst. Nationalbibliothek*
12. Giambattista Tiepolo (1696–1770): interior of Kaisersaal, Würzburg Residenz showing (centre back) Emperor Frederick Barbarossa giving the Dukedom of Franconia to Bishop Herold of Würz-

burg; 1750–53. Architecture by Johann Balthasar Neumann. Photo *A. F. Kersting*
13. Vienna: interior of the Hofbibliothek, by Johann Bernhard Fischer von Erlach; 1722. Photo *Bildarchiv d. Öst. Nationalbibliothek*
14. Daniel Gran (1694–1757): *Apotheosis of the Emperor Charles VI and the Humanities*; 1726–30. Ceiling fresco in the Hofbibliothek, Vienna. Photo *Bundesdenkmalamt, Vienna*
15. Anton Raphael Mengs (1728–79): *Parnassus*; 1761. Mural decoration in Villa Albani, Rome. Photo *Mansell Collection*

226–27 16. Luca Carlevaris (1665–1731): *Arrival of the Earl (later Duke) of Manchester in Venice in 1707, to take up his position as British Ambassador*. Birmingham City Art Gallery. Photo *Lewis Brown Associates*
17. Antonio Canale (Canaletto) (1697–1768): *Sta Maria della Salute, Venice*. Staatliche Museen, Berlin Dahlem. Photo *Steinkopf*
18. Francesco Guardi (1712–93): *Torre di Mestre (Tower of Malghera)*; c. 1770–80. National Gallery, London. Photo *John Webb*

228–29 19. Sebastiano Ricci (1659–1734): *The Resurrection* (detail); c. 1712. Ceiling fresco in the Chapel. Courtesy the Commissioners of the Royal Hospital, Chelsea. Photo *John Webb (Brompton Studio)*
20. Gian Antonio Pellegrini (1675–1741): *Kimbolton Castle staircase decoration*; c. 1711. Oil on plaster. Photo *Eileen Tweedy*
21. Giambattista Tiepolo (1696–1770): *Cleopatra's Banquet*, detail of fresco in Palazzo Labia, Venice; c. 1745. *ERI-Edizioni RAI, Radiotelevisione Italiana*

230–31 22. Ignaz Günther (1725–75): *The Annunciation*; 1764. Weyarn, Bavaria. Photo *Hirmer Fotoarchiv, Munich*
23. Etienne Falconet (1716–91): *Peter the Great*; 1782. Leningrad. Photo *Courtauld Institute of Art*
24. Josef Thaddäus Stammel (1699–1765): *Death*; c. 1760. Abbey Library, Admont. Photo *Bildarchiv d. Öst. Nationalbibliothek*
25. Louis François Roubiliac (1702/5–62): *The Nightingale Tomb*; 1761. Westminster Abbey, London. Photo *Radio Times Hulton Picture Library*
26. Antonio Canova (1757–1822): *Charles III of Naples*; 1820. Piazza del Plebiscito, Naples. Photo *Mansell Collection*
27. Ferdinand Dietz (died c. 1780): *Pegasus Fountain* at Veitshöchheim; 1765–8. Photo *Gundermann*
28. Georg Raphael Donner (1692–1741): *Providence from Fountain of the Mehlmarkt, Vienna*; 1738. Austrian Baroque Museum, Vienna. Photo *Reclam Jun. Verlag, Stuttgart*
29. Carlo Vanvitelli (1739–1821): *Acteon torn to death by dogs*, from the *Fountain of Diana*; last quarter of 18th C. Fountain designed by Vanvitelli, executed by Neapolitan sculptors. Photo *Mansell Collection*

232 30. Antoine Watteau (1684–1721): *Embarkation from Cythera*; 1717. Second version, painted for the collector Jean de Jullienne. *Verwaltung der Staatlichen Schlösser und Gärten, Berlin*
31. Thomas Gainsborough (1727–88): *The Morning Walk*; c. 1785. Portrait of William Hallett and his wife shortly after their marriage. National Gallery, London. Photo *John Webb (Brompton Studio)*

233–34 32. Antoine Watteau (1684–1721): *L'Enseigne de Gersaint*; 1720. *Verwaltung der Staatlichen Schlösser und Gärten, Berlin*
33. Nicholas Lancret (1690–1743): *Youth*; shortly before 1735. National Gallery, London
34. Jean-Baptiste Pater (1695–1736): *Fête Galante*. Kenwood.